W9-AOA-716

BEGINNING HTML & CSS

BEGINNING

HTML & CSS

BEGINNING

HTML & CSS

Rob Larsen

WILEY

Wiley Publishing, Inc.

Beginning HTML & CSS

Published by
John Wiley & Sons, Inc.
10475 Crosspoint Boulevard
Indianapolis, IN 46256
www.wiley.com

ISBN: 978-1-118-34018-9
ISBN: 978-1-118-34028-8 (ebk)
ISBN: 978-1-118-41651-8 (ebk)
ISBN: 978-1-118-65351-7 (ebk)

Manufactured in the United States of America

10 9 8 7 6 5 4 3 2 1

For general information on our other products and services please contact our Customer Care Department within the United States at (877) 762-2974, outside the United States at (317) 572-3993 or fax (317) 572-4002.

Wiley publishes in a variety of print and electronic formats and by print-on-demand. Some material included with standard print versions of this book may not be included in e-books or in print-on-demand. If this book refers to media such as a CD or DVD that is not included in the version you purchased, you may download this material at http://booksupport .wiley.com. For more information about Wiley products, visit www.wiley.com.

Library of Congress Control Number: 2012954405

For Jo & Ingmar. I'll take good care of Jude.

ABOUT THE AUTHOR

ROB LARSEN has more than 13 years of experience as a front-end engineer and team lead, building websites and applications for some of the world's biggest brands.

He is an active writer and speaker on web technology with a special focus on emerging standards like HTML5, CSS3, and the ongoing evolution of the JavaScript programming language. He is co-author of *Professional jQuery* (Wrox). He's also active in the open source community, helping to bridge the gap between the front lines of web development and the people actively working on the tools that drive the web.

In his career Rob has spent time at Sapient Global Markets, Isobar, The Brand Experience, and Cramer and as an independent consultant. Over the years, he has solved unique problems for clients such as Samsung, Adidas, Motorola, Philips, Reebok, Gillette, Boston's Museum of Science, and Harvard Kennedy School.

(PHOTO BY RICARDO SALEMA: www.ricardosalema.com)

CREDITS

Executive Editor
Carol Long

Project Editor
Katherine Burt

Technical Editor
Dan Maharry

Production Editor
Daniel Scribner

Copy Editor
San Dee Phillips

Editorial Manager
Mary Beth Wakefield

Freelancer Editorial Manager
Rosemarie Graham

Associate Director of Marketing
David Mayhew

Marketing Manager
Ashley Zurcher

Business Manager
Amy Knies

Production Manager
Tim Tate

Vice President and Executive Group Publisher
Richard Swadley

Vice President and Executive Publisher
Neil Edde

Associate Publisher
Jim Minatel

Project Coordinator, Cover
Katie Crocker

Compositor
Craig Woods, Happenstance Type-O-Rama

Proofreader
Nicole Hirschman

Indexer
Robert Swanson

Cover Designer
Elizabeth Brooks

Cover Image
©Aliaksandr Zabudzko/iStockphoto

ACKNOWLEDGMENTS

I'D LIKE TO THANK CAROL LONG and the rest of the folks at Wiley for giving me this opportunity. Without it, I probably would have spent half the summer playing video games.

I have to thank Katherine Burt a million times over for her patience and assistance in getting this slow-to-start monster up to speed.

Dan Maharry's technical insight has been invaluable—teaching me a thing or two every chapter and asking the right questions throughout the process. It's a much better book for his involvement.

At the pace I wrote some of this I'd be nuts not to thank our copy editor, San Dee Phillips. I should have apologized in advance.

I'd also like to thank Lynn Haller from Studio B for her ongoing help in navigating the business side of book writing.

I've got to give a big shout-out to John Duckett—standing on the shoulders of giants and all that.

As always, I want to thank all the great front-end engineers I've worked with at Cramer, Isobar, and Sapient for pushing me to be a better programmer, manager, and colleague.

Finally, I'd like to thank my wife for her support and understanding throughout this process. I couldn't have done it without her.

CONTENTS

INTRODUCTION

THERE ARE A LOT OF BOOKS about building web pages, so thank you for picking up this one. I've spent the last 13 years building websites, so hopefully I've picked up a thing or two that I can share with you to make your purchase worthwhile.

If you're just starting out with building web pages, you've picked a great time to get started. The way web pages are built is changing right now in a big way. While the same basic technologies we've used for the last 15–20 years are still in place, there are new versions available that have people like me very excited for the future of the web.

This book presents a practical introduction to the process of making websites using a blend of the latest and greatest techniques, as well as a healthy understanding of some older technologies that have been around for a while. The techniques described in this book are informed by having solved real-world problems; so, although it has an eye toward the future it's grounded in the act of making websites today.

You will learn a few different languages to create effective and attractive web pages:

➤ HTML is needed to explain the *structure* of a web page. This page is made up of a lot of words. On web pages, it is the job of HTML to explain the structure of the words—which words form a heading, where paragraphs start and end, and which text should have bullet points. This language also specifies things such as the links between different web pages, where images should appear, where videos should appear, and forms for entering text.

➤ CSS is used to control how your pages look. For example, you can use CSS to specify that a typeface should be a large, bold Arial typeface or that the background of a page should be a light green. You can also use CSS to control where different items appear on a page, such as placing three columns of text next to each other.

➤ JavaScript can add interactivity to your web pages. JavaScript is a huge topic in itself, so it is not covered in the same depth as HTML and CSS, but I teach you just enough JavaScript to write your own basic scripts and to be able to effectively use jQuery, the most popular JavaScript library in the world.

ABOUT THE BOOK

As you have already seen, you'll learn how to control the structure of a web page using HTML, how to style it using CSS, and how to add interactivity using JavaScript and jQuery. Learning *how* this code works will give you a solid foundation for building websites, and alongside this you will see plenty of practical advice that helps you learn about issues you are likely to meet when you start building sites.

While learning how to code, you will see lots of advice on *usability*—how to build websites that are easy to use and enable visitors to achieve what they came for. In several parts of the book, I also discuss issues regarding accessibility—making a site available to as many users as possible (in particular, people with disabilities, who may have impaired vision or difficulty using a mouse). In the same way that many countries have laws requiring architects to design buildings that are accessible, there are strict accessibility guidelines for building websites to ensure they do not exclude visitors. A little careful thought before you build your website means that people with vision impairments can either view your site with larger text or have it read to them by a piece of software called a *screen reader*. Whole books are dedicated to the topics of usability and accessibility and are aimed at web developers who need to learn how to make their code more accessible and usable. My aim is to teach you to code with these principles in mind from the start.

Although it is important to learn the latest practices for creating web pages using these languages, if you intend to create websites that anyone can access, you will also have to learn some older aspects of the languages you meet. This is important because not everyone has the latest web browser installed on his or her computer; as a result, the latest features may not work for everyone, and in such cases you need to learn techniques that will work in some older browsers that are still popular today.

By the end of this book, you will be writing web pages that not only use the latest technologies but also are still viewable by older browsers—pages that look great and can also be accessed by those with visual and physical impairments. These are pages that not only address the needs of today's audiences but can also work on emerging technologies—and therefore the skills you will learn should be relevant longer.

WHO THIS BOOK IS FOR

This book is written for anyone who wants to learn how to create web pages, and for people who may have dabbled in writing web pages (perhaps using some kind of web page authoring tool), but who want to really understand the languages of the web, to give them more control over the pages they create.

More experienced web developers can also benefit from this book because it teaches some of the latest technologies and encourages them to embrace web standards that not only meet the needs of the new devices that access the web but also help make their sites available to more visitors.

You don't need any previous programming experience to work with this book. This is one of the first steps on the programming ladder. Whether you are just a hobbyist or want to make a career of web programming, this book will teach you the basics of programming for the web.

WHAT THIS BOOK COVERS

By the end of this book, you will be able to create professional-looking and well-coded web pages.

Not only will you learn the code that makes up HTML, but you will also see how to apply this code so you can create sophisticated layouts for your pages, positioning text and images where you would like them to appear and getting the colors and fonts you want. Along the way, you will see how to make your pages easy to use and available to the biggest audience possible.

The main technologies covered in this book are HTML and CSS. You will also learn the basics of JavaScript—enough to work on some examples that add interactivity to your pages and enable you to work with jQuery.

The code I encourage you to write is based on what are known as web standards; HTML and CSS are all created and maintained by the World Wide Web Consortium, or W3C (www.w3.org/), an organization dedicated to the development of the web. You will also learn about some features that are not in these standards; it is helpful to know about some of these in case you come across such markup and need to know what it does. Where these are introduced, I make it clear they are not part of the standard.

WHAT YOU NEED TO USE THIS BOOK

All you need to work through this book is a computer with a web browser (preferably the latest version of Firefox, Chrome, or Internet Explorer 9 or higher), and a simple text editor such as Notepad or Sublime Text on Windows or TextEdit or Sublime Text on Mac.

HOW THIS BOOK IS ORGANIZED

The first chapter of this book will show you that the main task in creating a website is *marking up* the text you want to appear on your site, using *elements* and *attributes*. As you will see, these elements and attributes describe the structure of a document (what is a heading, what is a paragraph of text, what is a link, and so on).

The first six chapters of the book describe the different elements and attributes that make up HTML and how you can use them to write web pages. These chapters are organized into task-related areas, such as structuring a document into headings and paragraphs; creating links between pages; adding images, audio, and video; and displaying tables. With each task or topic that is introduced, you will see an example first to give you an idea of what is possible; then you can look at the elements and attributes used in detail.

When you first read this book, you do not need to closely read the detailed explanations of every single element. As long as you understand the gist of the markup, feel free to move on, and then come back and look at the finer detail when you need it.

Each chapter ends with exercises designed to get you working with the concepts you've just learned. Don't worry if you have to go back and review the content of the chapter in order to complete the exercises; this book has been created with the intention that it should be a helpful reference for years to come, so don't feel that you need to learn everything by heart. Along the way, you'll see which browsers support each element and you'll learn plenty of handy tips, tricks, and techniques for creating professional web pages.

Once you have seen how to create and structure a document using HTML, Chapters 7, 8, and 9 will show you how to make your pages look more attractive using CSS. For example, you'll learn how to change the typefaces and size of fonts, color of text, backgrounds, and borders that go around items. In addition, you'll learn how to control where items appear on the page, which will enable you to create attractive layouts.

Having worked through the three chapters on CSS, and using the examples in the book, you should be able to write quite complex web pages. The chapters up to that point can then act as a helpful reference you can keep coming back to, and the examples will act as a toolkit for building your own sites.

Chapter 10 introduces you to JavaScript, a programming language that enables you to add interactivity to your pages. While the entire JavaScript language is too large to teach you in one chapter, you will learn how to create your own basic scripts and also how to integrate scripts other people have written into your pages.

Chapters 11 and 12 introduce you to jQuery, a library that helps you code JavaScript more easily. jQuery is by far the most popular library for working with JavaScript. It's easy to use and fun, and it lies at the center of a vast ecosystem of scripts that you can use to enhance your own site.

The final chapter, Chapter 13, includes some checklists. These bring together some topics that are dotted throughout the book.

I have also included several helpful appendices, including a reference to HTML elements and CSS properties. There is an appendix that explains how HTML and CSS specify colors. Other appendices show you available character encodings, language codes, and escape characters that can be used with HTML, XHTML, CSS, and JavaScript. Finally, there is an appendix that outlines the major differences between the last two major versions of HTML.

CONVENTIONS

To help you get the most from the text and keep track of what's happening, I've used a number of conventions throughout the book.

TRY IT OUT

The *Try It Out* is an exercise you should work through, following the text in the book.

1. They usually consist of a set of steps.
2. Each step has a number.
3. Follow the steps through with your copy of the database.

> **WARNING** *Boxes like this one hold important, not-to-be-forgotten information that is directly relevant to the surrounding text.*

> **NOTE** *Notes, tips, hints, tricks, and asides to the current discussion are offset and placed in italics like this.*

As for styles in the text:

➤ I *italicize* new terms and important words when I introduce them.

➤ I show keyboard strokes like this: Ctrl+A.

➤ I show filenames, URLs, and code within the text like so: `persistence.properties`.

➤ Code appears like this:

```
We use a monofont type with no highlighting for most code examples.
We use bolding to emphasize code that's particularly important in the present context.
```

SOURCE CODE

As you work through the examples in this book, you may choose either to type in all the code manually or to use the source code files that accompany the book. All of the source code used in this book is available for download at `www.wrox.com`. Specifically for this book, the code download is on the Download Code tab at `www.wrox.com/remtitle.cgi?isbn=9781118340189`. You can also search for the book at `www.wrox.com` by ISBN (the ISBN for this book is to find the code.

> **NOTE** *Because many books have similar titles, you may find it easiest to search by ISBN; this book's ISBN is 978-1-118-34018-9.*

Once you download the code, just decompress it with your favorite compression tool. Alternately, you can go to the main Wrox code download page at `www.wrox.com/dynamic/books/download.aspx` to see the code available for this book and all other Wrox books.

ERRATA

I've made every effort to ensure that there are no errors in the text or in the code. However, no one is perfect, and mistakes do occur. If you find an error in this book, such as a spelling mistake or faulty piece of code, I would be very grateful for your feedback. By sending in errata you may save another reader hours of frustration, and at the same time you will be helping to provide even higher quality information.

To find the errata page for this book, go to www.wrox.com and locate the title using the Search box or one of the title lists. Then, on the book details page, click the Book Errata link. On this page you can view all errata that have been submitted for this book and posted by Wrox editors.

> **NOTE** *A complete book list including links to errata is also available at* www.wrox.com/misc-pages/booklist.shtml.

If you don't spot "your" error on the Errata page, click the Errata Form link and complete the form to send us the error you have found. We'll check the information and, if appropriate, post a message to the book's errata page and fix the problem in subsequent editions of the book.

P2P.WROX.COM

For author and peer discussion, join the P2P forums at p2p.wrox.com. The forums are a web-based system for you to post messages relating to Wrox books and related technologies and interact with other readers and technology users. The forums offer a subscription feature to e-mail you topics of interest of your choosing when new posts are made to the forums. Wrox authors, editors, other industry experts, and your fellow readers are present on these forums.

At http://p2p.wrox.com you will find a number of different forums that will help you not only as you read this book but also as you develop your own applications. To join the forums, just follow these steps:

1. Go to p2p.wrox.com and click the Register link.
2. Read the terms of use and click Agree.
3. Complete the required information to join, as well as any optional information you wish to provide, and click Submit.
4. You will receive an e-mail with information describing how to verify your account and complete the joining process.

> **NOTE** *You can read messages in the forums without joining P2P, but in order to post your own messages, you must join.*

Once you join, you can post new messages and respond to messages other users post. You can read messages at any time on the web. If you would like to have new messages from a particular forum e-mailed to you, click the Subscribe to this Forum icon by the forum name in the forum listing.

For more information about how to use the Wrox P2P, be sure to read the P2P FAQs for answers to questions about how the forum software works, as well as many common questions specific to P2P and Wrox books. To read the FAQs, click the FAQ link on any P2P page.

Structuring Documents for the Web

In this chapter, you learn the key concept to create any web page: how to give it *structure*. You need to add structure to a document so that web browsers can present the page to people who visit your site in a way they can understand. For example, imagine a news article that contains a headline (or title) and several paragraphs of text; if you want to put this article on the web, you would need to add structure to the words in the document so that the browser knows which words are the headline, and where each paragraph starts and ends. To give a document structure, you need to learn how to create web pages using HTML.

A WEB OF STRUCTURED DOCUMENTS

Every day, you come across all kinds of printed documents—newspapers, train timetables, and insurance forms. You can think of the web as being a sea of documents that all link together and bear a strong similarity to the printed documents that you meet in everyday life.

Take the example of a newspaper. A newspaper consists of several stories or articles (and probably a fair smattering of advertisements, too). Each story has a headline and then some paragraphs, perhaps a subheading, and then some more paragraphs; it may also include a picture or two.

The structure of articles on news websites is similar to the structure of articles in newspapers. Each article consists of headings, paragraphs of text, and some pictures. (Sometimes the pictures might be replaced by a video.) The parallel is quite clear; the only difference is that in a newspaper you may have several stories on a single page, whereas on the web each story tends to get its own page. The news websites also often use homepages that display the headline and a brief summary of the stories.

Consider another example: You're catching a train to see a friend, so you check the schedule or timetable to see what time the train leaves. The main part of the schedule is a *table* telling you what times trains arrive and when they depart from different stations. You can probably think of several types of documents that use tables. From the listings in the financial supplement of your paper to the TV schedule, you come across tables of information every day—and often when this information is put on the web, these tables are re-created.

Another common type of printed document is a *form*. For example, think about a common form from an insurance company. Such a form contains fields to write your name, address, and the amount of coverage, along with check boxes to indicate the number of rooms in the house and what type of lock is on the front door. There are lots of forms on the web, from simple search boxes that ask what you are looking for to the registration forms you are required to fill out before you can place an online order for books or CDs.

As you can see, there are many parallels between the structure of printed documents you come across every day and pages you see on the web. When you are writing web pages, it is the HTML code you start learning in this chapter that tells the web browser how the information you want to display is structured—what text to put in a heading, paragraph, or table, and so on so that the browser can present it properly to the user.

INTRODUCING HTML5

Even if you have never seen any HyperText Markup Language (HTML) code, you may know that it is used to create web pages. There have been five versions of HTML since the web began, and the development of the language is overseen by an organization called the World Wide Web Consortium (W3C).

This book focuses on the latest version of the language, popularly referred to as HTML5. There are two other versions you might encounter. These are HTML 4.01, the last major version of the language from December 1999, and a stricter version from 2000 called Extensible HyperText Markup Language (XHTML). XHTML is still popular in some applications, so important differences between it and HTML5 will be called out in the text.

> **NOTE** *Generally, you see just the term HTML used in the rest of this book. The one exception is when there is a feature or convention related to a single version.*

As its name suggests, HTML is a *markup language*, which may sound complicated until you realize that you come across markup every day. When creating a document in a word processor, you can add styles to the text to explain the document's structure. For example, you can distinguish headings from the main body of the text using a heading style (usually with a larger font). You can use the Return (or Enter) key to start a new paragraph. You can insert tables into your document to hold data or create bulleted lists for a series of related points, and so on. Although this does affect the presentation of the document, the key purpose of this kind of markup is to provide a structure that makes the document easier to understand.

When marking up documents for the web, you perform a similar process, except you do it by adding things called *tags* to the text. With HTML, the key thing to remember is that you must add the tags to indicate the structure of the document (not how you want it to be presented); for example, which part of the document is a heading, which parts are paragraphs, what belongs in a table, and so on. Browsers such as Internet Explorer, Firefox, and Google Chrome all use this markup to help present the text in a familiar fashion, similar to that of a word processor—main headings are bigger than the text in paragraphs, there is space above and below each paragraph, and lists of bullet points have a circle in front of them.

> **NOTE** *Although earlier versions of HTML enabled you to control the presentation of a document—such as which typefaces and colors a document should use—HTML markup is not supposed to be used to style the document; that is the job of Cascading Style Sheets (CSS), which you meet in Chapter 7, "Cascading Style Sheets."*

Now have a look at a simple web page (ch01_eg01.html). You don't need any special programs to write web pages; you can simply use a text editor such as Notepad on Windows or TextEdit on a Mac and save your files with the .html or .htm file extension.

```
<html>
  <head>
    <title>Popular Websites: Google</title>
  </head>
  <body>
    <h1>About Google</h1>
    <p>Google is best known for its search engine, although
       Google now offers a number of other services.</p>
    <p>Google's mission is to organize the world's
       information and make it universally accessible and
       useful.</p>
    <p>Its founders Larry Page and Sergey Brin started
       Google at Stanford University.</p>
  </body>
</html>
```

This may look a bit confusing at first, but it will all make sense soon. As you can see, there are several sets of angle brackets with words or letters between them, such as `<html>`, `<head>`, `</title>`, and `</body>`. These angle brackets and the words inside them are known as *tags*, and these are the markup previously mentioned. Figure 1-1 illustrates what this page would look like in a web browser.

As you can see, this document contains the heading "About Google" and a paragraph of text to introduce the company. Note also that it says "Popular Websites: Google" in the top-left corner of the browser window; this is known as the *title* of the page (to the right it says Mozilla Firefox, which is the browser this page was opened in).

To understand the markup in this first example, you need to look at what is written between the angle brackets and compare that with what you see in the figure, which is what you do next.

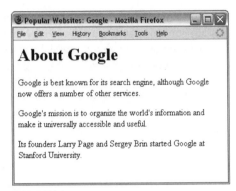

FIGURE 1-1

Tags and Elements

If you look at the first and last lines of the code for the previous example, you see pairs of angle brackets containing the letters "html". Starting on the first line, the first angled bracket looks like a less-than sign (<); then there are the letters "html," followed by a second angled bracket, which looks like a greater-than sign (>). The two brackets and all the characters between them are known as a *tag*.

In this example, there are lots of tags, and they are all in pairs; there are *opening tags* and *closing tags*. The closing tag is always slightly different from the opening tag in that it has a forward slash (/) after the first angled bracket: `</html>`.

A pair of tags and the content these include are known as an *element*. In Figure 1-2, you see the heading for the page of the previous example.

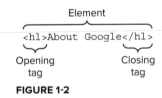

FIGURE 1-2

The opening tag says, "This is the beginning of a heading" and the closing tag says, "This is the end of a heading." Like most tags in HTML, the text inside the angled brackets explains the purpose of the tag—here `h1` indicates that it is a level 1 heading (or top-level heading). As you will see shortly, there are also tags for subheadings (`<h2>`, `<h3>`, `<h4>`, `<h5>`, and `<h6>`). If you don't put tags around the words "About Google," it is just another bit of text; it would not be clear that these words formed the heading.

Now look at the three paragraphs of text about the company; each one is placed between an opening `<p>` tag and a closing `</p>` tag. And you guessed it, the p stands for paragraph.

> **WARNING** *You must understand the basic distinction between tags and elements: A tag usually consists of left-angle and right-angle brackets and letters and numbers between those brackets, whereas elements are the opening and closing tags plus anything between the two tags.*

> **WARNING** To be precise, there are also tags that consist of just one left-angle bracket and one right-angle bracket, with no content and no closing tag. These are also elements.

As you can see, the tags throughout this example actually describe what you will find between them, creating the structure of the document. The text between the `<h1>` and `</h1>` tags is a heading, and the text between the opening `<p>` and closing `</p>` tags makes up paragraphs. Indeed, the whole document is contained between opening `<html>` and closing `</html>` tags.

You often find that terms from a family tree are used to describe the relationships between elements. For example, an element that contains another element is known as the *parent*, whereas the element that's between the parent element's opening and closing tags is called a *child* of that element. So, the `<title>` element is a child of the `<head>` element, the `<head>` element is the parent of the `<title>` element, and so on. Furthermore, the `<title>` element can be thought of as a grandchild of the `<html>` element.

Additionally, if two elements are children of the same parent, they are referred to as *siblings*.

It is worth noting that the tags in this example are all in lowercase characters; you sometimes see web pages written in HTML where tags are uppercase (or a mix of uppercase and lowercase letters). When XHTML was introduced, with its stricter rules, it stated that all tags were written in lowercase. Technically, HTML5 loosens these restrictions to enable mixed case. In practice you generally see lowercase even in HTML5 documents.

> **NOTE** Even though HTML5 enables mixed case tags, lowercase should be used for consistency with XHTML documents, which require lowercase tags.

Separating Heads from Bodies

Whenever you write a web page in HTML, the whole of the page is contained between the opening `<html>` and closing `</html>` tags, just as it was in the previous example. Inside the `<html>` element, there are two main parts to the page:

➤ **The `<head>` element:** Often referred to as the head of the page, this contains information *about* the page. (This is not the main content of the page.) For example, it might contain a title and a description of the page or instructions on where a browser can find CSS rules that explain how the document should look. It consists of the opening `<head>` tag, the closing `</head>` tag, and everything in between.

➤ **The `<body>` element:** Often referred to as the body of the page, this contains the information you actually see in the main browser window. It consists of the opening `<body>` tag, the closing `</body>` tag, and everything in between.

Together, the <html>, <head>, and <body> elements make up the skeleton of an HTML document—they are the foundation upon which every web page is built.

Inside the <head> element of the first example page, you see a <title> element:

```
<head>
  <title>Popular Websites: Google</title>
</head>
```

Between the opening <title> tag and the closing </title> tag are the words "Popular Websites: Google," or the title of this web page. Figure 1-1 shows the words at the top of the browser window, which is where browsers such as Internet Explorer, Firefox, and Chrome display the title of a document. It is also the name they use when you save a page in your Favorites List, and it helps search engines understand what your page is about. The <title> element is mandatory for all web pages.

The real content of your page is held in the <body> element, which is what you want users to read, and this is shown in the main browser window.

> **WARNING** The <head> element contains information about the document, which is not displayed within the main page. The <body> element holds the actual content of the page viewed in your browser.

You may have noticed that the tags in this example appear in a symmetrical order. If you want to have one element inside another, both the element's opening and closing tags must be inside the containing element. For example, the following is allowed:

```
<p> This paragraph contains some <em>emphasized text.</em></p>
```

whereas the following is wrong because the closing </em> tag is not inside the paragraph element:

```
<p> This paragraph contains some <em>emphasized text. </p></em>
```

In other words, if an element is to contain another element, it must wholly contain that element. This is referred to as *nesting* your elements correctly.

Attributes Tell You about Elements

Attributes in HTML are much like the attributes you experience every day. They are the qualities that describe a person or thing, such as a *tall* man or a *brown* dog. Similarly, HTML elements can be described in ways that web browsers can understand. This section looks at attributes, starting with the most important one that beats at the heart of the web.

What differentiates web documents from standard documents are the *links* (or *hyperlinks*) that take you from one web page to another. Look at a link by adding one to the example you just looked at. Links are created using an <a> element. (The a stands for anchor.)

You can add a link from this page to Google in a new paragraph at the end of the document. There is just one new line in this example (ch01_eg02.html) and that line is highlighted:

```
<html>
  <head>
    <title>Popular Websites: Google</title>
  </head>
  <body>
    <h1>About Google</h1>
    <p>Google is best known for its search engine, although Google now offers a
        number of other services.</p>
    <p>Google's mission is to organize the world's information and make it
        universally accessible and useful.</p>
    <p>Its founders Larry Page and Sergey Brin started Google at Stanford
University.</p>
    <p><a href="http://www.Google.com/">Click here to visit Google's Web
    site.</a></p>
  </body>
</html>
```

Inside this new paragraph is the `<a>` element that creates the link. Between the opening `<a>` tag and the closing `</a>` tag is the text that you can click, which says, "Click here to visit Google's Web site." Figure 1-3 shows you what this page looks like in a browser.

If you look closely at the opening tag of the link, it carries something called an *attribute*. In this case, it's the `href` attribute; this is followed by an equal sign and then a pair of quotation marks, which contain the URL for Google's website. In this case, the `href` attribute tells you where the link should take you. You look at links in greater detail in the Chapter 3, "Links and Navigation," but for the moment this illustrates the purpose of attributes.

FIGURE 1-3

> ➤ Attributes are used to say something about the element that carries them, and they always appear on the opening tag of the element that carries them. Almost all attributes consist of two parts: a name and a value. The *name* is the property of the element that you want to set. In this example, the `<a>` element carries an attribute whose name is `href`, which you can use to indicate where the link should take you.

> ➤ The *value* is what you want the value of the property to be. In this example, the value was the URL of the site that the link should take you to, so the value of the `href` attribute is `http://www.google.com`.

The value of the attribute should always be put in double quotation marks and separated from the name with the equal sign.

There are several attributes in HTML5 that do not consist of a name/value pair but consist of just a name. These are called boolean attributes and you will learn more about those in the section "Attribute Groups."

Another common attribute on anchors is the `title` attribute, which gives a plain language description of the target of the link. You could add one to the example to inform people that Google is a popular search engine.

```
<a href="http://www.Google.com"
    title="Google.com is the world's most popular search engine">
```

This illustrates that elements can carry several attributes; although, an element should never have two attributes of the same name.

Learning from Others by Viewing Their Source Code

When HTML first came out, a lot of people learned how to create pages by using a handy feature that you can find in most common browsers: the ability to look at the source code that made the page.

If you go to the View menu in your browser and then look for an option that says View Source or Page Source, you should see the code that created the page.

If you want to see how the author of a page achieved something on a page, this can be a handy technique. Figure 1-4 shows how to look at the source of the author's homepage. (The window on the right contains the source for the page.)

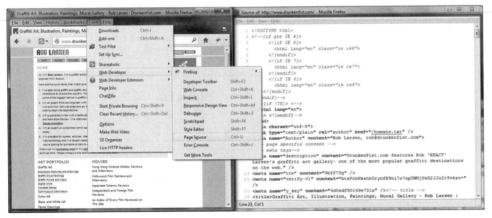

FIGURE 1-4

Elements for Marking Up Text

You now know that an HTML page (also sometimes referred to as an HTML document) consists of elements that describe how its content is structured. Each element describes what you will find between its opening and closing tags. The opening tags can also carry attributes that tell you more about that particular element.

Equipped with this knowledge, you can find that much of learning HTML is a matter of learning what elements you can use, what each of these elements does, and what attributes each can carry.

ATTRIBUTE GROUPS

As you have seen, attributes live on the opening tag of an element and provide extra information about the element that carries them. Many attributes consist of a *name* and a *value*; the name reflects a property of the element the attribute describes, and the value is a value for that property. For example, the `lang` attribute describes the language used within that element; a value such as EN-US would indicate that the language used inside the element is U.S. English.

Some attributes consist of only a name, such as `required` or `checked`. These are called boolean attributes. To say something is a boolean (which you learn more about in Chapter 10, "Learning JavaScript") is to indicate that it can be in one of two states: true or false. For HTML attributes the presence of one of the boolean attributes in a tag indicates that the value is true. So, the following are equivalent:

```
<input type="text" required >
<input type="text" required="true">
```

Many of the elements in HTML can carry some or all the attributes you will meet in this section. At first some of them may sound a little abstract; although, they will make more sense as you see them used throughout the book. So don't worry if they do not make much sense at first.

In this section, you look at three groups of attributes common to many HTML elements:

➤ **Core attributes:** Including the `class`, `id`, `style`, and `title` attributes

➤ **Internationalization attributes:** For example, the `dir` and `lang` attributes

➤ **Accessibility attributes:** For example, `accesskey` and `tabindex`

> **WARNING** *Together, the core attributes and the internationalization attributes are known as universal attributes.*

Core Attributes

The four core attributes that you can use on the majority of HTML elements (although not all) are:

```
id title class style
```

Throughout the rest of the book, these attributes are revisited when they have special meaning for an element that differs from the description given here; otherwise their use can generally be described as you see in the subsections that follow.

The id Attribute

You can use the id attribute to uniquely identify any element within a page. You might want to uniquely identify an element so that you can link to that specific part in the document or to specify that a CSS style or piece of JavaScript should apply to the content of just that one element within the document.

The syntax for the id attribute is as follows (where *string* is your chosen value for the attribute):

```
id="string"
```

For example, you can use the id attribute to distinguish between two paragraph elements, like so:

```
<p id="accounts">This paragraph explains the role of the accounts department.</p>
<p id="sales">This paragraph explains the role of the sales department.</p>
```

Following are some special rules for the value of the id attribute:

➤ Must begin with a letter (A–Z or a–z) and can then be followed by any number of letters, digits (0–9), hyphens, underscores, colons, and periods. (You may not start the value with a digit, hyphen, underscore, colon, or period.)

➤ Must remain unique within that document; no two id attributes may have the same value within one HTML page. This case should be handled by the class attribute.

The class Attribute

You can use the class attribute to specify that an element belongs to a *class* of elements. For example, you might have a document that contains many paragraphs, and a few of those paragraphs might contain a summary of key points, in which case you could add a class attribute whose value is summary to the relevant <p> elements to differentiate those paragraphs from the rest in the document.

```
<p class="summary">Summary goes here</p>
```

It is commonly used with CSS, so you learn more about the use of the class attribute in Chapter 7, which introduces CSS. The syntax of the class attribute is as follows:

```
class="className"
```

The value of the attribute may also be a space-separated list of class names, for example:

```
class="className1 className2 className3"
```

The title Attribute

The title attribute gives a suggested title for the element. The syntax for the title attribute is as follows:

```
title="string"
```

The behavior of this attribute depends upon the element that carries it; although, it is often displayed as a tooltip or while the element loads. Not every element that *can* carry a title attribute actually needs one, so when you meet an element that particularly benefits from use of this attribute, you will see the behavior it has when used with that element.

The style Attribute

The style attribute enables you to specify CSS rules within the element. You meet CSS in Chapter 7, but for now, here is an example of how it might be used:

```
<p style="font-family:arial; color:#FF0000;">Some text.</p>
```

As a general rule, however, it is best to avoid the use of this attribute. If you want to use CSS rules to govern how an element appears, it is better to use a separate style sheet instead. The only place where this attribute is still commonly used is when it is set with JavaScript. You learn more about that in Chapter 11, "Working with jQuery," when you're introduced to jQuery's powerful tools for manipulating HTML elements.

Internationalization

The web is a worldwide phenomenon. Because of this, there are mechanisms built into the tools that drive the web that allow authors to create documents in different languages. This process is called *internationalization.*

Two common internationalization attributes help users write pages for different languages and character sets:

```
dir lang
```

You look at each next, but it is worth noting that even in current browsers, support for these attributes is still patchy. Therefore where possible you should specify a character set that creates text in the direction you require.

The website of a helpful W3C document that describes internationalization issues in greater detail is found at www.w3.org/TR/i18n-html-tech-char/; although, you briefly look at each of these attributes next.

> **NOTE** *The internationalization attributes are sometimes referred to as the i18n attributes, an odd name that comes from the draft-ietf-html-i18n specification in which they were first defined.*

The dir Attribute

The dir attribute enables you to indicate to the browser the direction in which the text should flow: left to right or right to left. When you want to indicate the directionality of a whole document (or the majority of the document), use it with the `<html>` element rather than the `<body>` element for two reasons: Its use on the `<html>` element has better support in browsers, and it can apply to the header elements as well as those in the body. You can also use the `dir` attribute on elements within the body of the document if you want to change the direction of a small portion of the document.

The `dir` attribute can take one of two values, as you can see in Table 1-1.

TABLE 1-1: dir Attribute Values

VALUE	MEANING
ltr	Left to right (the default value)
rtl	Right to left (for languages such as Hebrew or Arabic that are read right to left)

The lang Attribute

The `lang` attribute enables you to indicate the main language used in a document.

The `lang` attribute was designed to offer language-specific display to users; although, it has little effect in the main browsers. The benefits of using the `lang` attribute are for search engines (which can tell the user which language the document is authored in), screen readers (which might need to pronounce different languages in different ways), and applications (which can alert users when either they do not support that language or it is a different language than their default language). When used with the `<html>` element, the attribute applies to the whole document; although, you can use it on other elements, in which case it just applies to the content of those elements.

The values of the `lang` attribute are ISO-639-1 standard two-character language codes. If you want to specify a dialect of the language, you can follow the language code with a dash and a subcode name. Table 1-2 offers some examples.

TABLE 1-2: lang Attribute Values

VALUE	MEANING
ar	Arabic
en	English
en-us	U.S. English
zh	Chinese

You can find a list of language codes for most of the main languages in use today in Appendix G, "Language Codes."

CORE ELEMENTS

Now take a closer look at the four main elements that form the basic structure of every document: `<html>`, `<head>`, `<title>`, and `<body>`. These four elements should appear in every HTML document that you write, and you will see them referred to throughout this book as the *skeleton* of the document.

About DOCTYPEs

Although the four main elements describe the skeleton of a document, one final piece qualifies the document as a whole. The DOCTYPE (for DOCument TYPE) tells the browser what rules to follow when showing the document to the user. These rules are called *modes*. This book focuses on the HTML5 DOCTYPE that puts the browser into *strict mode*. You can think of strict mode as the browser acknowledging the author wanting to play by the rules. The other common mode, *quirks mode*, tells the browser you will use some funky rules, which have their origins in the late 1990s. You don't want to have anything to do with quirks mode.

So what does the HTML5 DOCTYPE look like?

```
<!doctype html>
```

Start all your documents with that DOCTYPE, and your pages will always render in the correct mode.

The basic skeleton of an HTML5 page therefore looks like this:

```
<!doctype html>
<html>
  <head>
    <title>The Skeleton of an HTML5 Document</title>
  </head>
  <body>
  </body>
</html>
```

The <html> Element

The `<html>` element is the containing element for the whole HTML document. After the DOCTYPE declaration, each HTML document should have an opening `<html>` tag, and each document should end with a closing `</html>` tag.

The `<html>` element can also carry the following attributes, which you learned about in the "Attribute Groups" section:

```
id dir lang
```

The <head> Element

The `<head>` element is just a container for all other header elements. It is the first thing to appear after the opening `<html>` tag.

Each `<head>` element should contain a `<title>` element indicating the title of the document; although, it may also contain any combination of the following elements, in any order:

➤ `<base>`, which you will meet in Chapter 3, "Links and Navigation"

➤ `<link>` to link to an external file, such as a style sheet, which you see in Chapter 7

➤ `<style>` to include CSS rules inside the document, covered in Chapter 7

➤ `<script>` for including script in the document, which you see in more detail in Chapter 10

➤ `<meta>`, which includes information about the document such as a description or the name of the author

The opening `<head>` tag can carry the following attributes:

```
id dir lang
```

> **NOTE** One meta tag you should be aware of is `<meta charset=utf-8>`. This tag and attribute combination tells the browser which character set to use. Character sets are collections of characters used to render written language. For the most part, using utf-8 is going to be the best bet on the web. Utf-8 contains every character in the Unicode character set (over one million characters), which means it can render text in everything from English to Chinese to Russian.
>
> For an in-depth discussion of character encoding, see Joel Sposky's article, "The Absolute Minimum Every Software Developer Absolutely, Positively Must Know about Unicode and Character Sets (No Excuses!)," found at www.joelonsoftware .com/articles/Unicode.html.

The `<title>` Element

You should specify a title for every page that you write using the `<title>` element (which, as you saw earlier in the chapter, is a child of the `<head>` element). It is presented and used in several ways:

➤ At the top of a browser window (as you saw in the first example and Figure 1-1)

➤ As the default name for a bookmark in browsers such as IE, Firefox, and Chrome

➤ By search engines that use its content to help index pages

Therefore, you must use a title that describes the content of your site. For example, the homepage of this book should not just say "Homepage"; rather it should describe what your site is about. Rather than just saying "Wrox Homepage," it is more helpful to write:

```
<title>Wrox: Programming Books, Learn HTML, CSS, ASP.Net, PHP</title>
```

The test for a good title is whether visitors can tell what they will find on that page just by reading the title, without looking at the actual content of the page, and whether it uses words that people would use if they were going to search for this kind of information.

The `<title>` element should contain only the text for the title; it may not contain any other elements. The `<title>` element can carry the following attributes:

```
id dir lang
```

Links and Style Sheets

Although you'll learn more about CSS and JavaScript later in the book, they are going to be a common element on every page you look at and build, so it's important that we quickly cover how to include them in your web pages.

Adding a style sheet relies on the `<link>` element. The `<link>` element also uses the `href` attribute, which you learned about already, to point to a resource on the web. In this case, instead of pointing to a new page or website to visit when a link is clicked, it points to the location of a file containing style information for the current page. The `rel` (for relation) attribute indicates that the linked document is a style sheet and should be handled accordingly.

```
<link rel="stylesheet" href="css/main.css">
```

Adding a script to the page is even easier. You add a `<script>` element to the page and add a `src` attribute pointing to the location of the JavaScript file you want to use.

```
<script src="js/main.js"></script>
```

> **WARNING** *Always include the closing* `</script>` *tag when inserting a script element, even if, as in this case, there's no content between the opening and closing tags. If you don't, strange things can happen.*

You need to start using one piece of JavaScript. Now that you know how to add a script to the page, you're ready to learn about the HTML5 Shiv and Modernizr.

Ensuring Backward Compatibility for HTML5 Tags

There's one final element you see in many HTML5 documents. Because of a wrinkle in the way that Internet Explorer deals with unknown HTML elements, you need to include a small piece of JavaScript in the head of your document. If you don't, things look wrong when you view your pages in Internet Explorer 8 or less. It's called the HTML5 Shiv, and including it in your pages looks something like this:

```
<script src="http://cdnjs.cloudflare.com/ajax/libs/html5shiv/3.6/html5shiv.min.js">
</script>
```

As for what it does, for the time being, just know that it needs to be there, or you'll get unpredictable results in IE8 and older.

If you're interested in the history of this small but vitally important script, see Paul Irish's article, "The History of the HTML5 Shiv," at http://paulirish.com/2011/the-history-of-the-html5-shiv/.

Building on the HTML5 Shiv, there's another library you'll encounter in this book. It's called Modernizr and at its core includes the HTML5 Shiv for backward compatibility; in addition, it adds in tests for emerging web features that you can use when building sites. That way you can ensure that you're not trying to serve something to a browser that can't actually handle it. You'll learn about Modernizr throughout the book, but for now the following code sample shows how to include Modernizr:

```
<script
src="http://cdnjs.cloudflare.com/ajax/libs/modernizr/2.6.1/modernizr.min.js">
</script>
```

The power of Modernizr will become more apparent throughout the book. For now the examples in the book use the simpler HTML5 Shiv to ensure compatibility with Internet Explorer 8 and below.

And now, with that trip through the head, you're ready to start adding in the star of the show, the content of your page.

The <body> Element

The <body> element appears after the <head> element, and as you have already seen, it contains the part of the web page that you actually see in the main browser window, which is sometimes referred to as *body content*. The <body> element can carry all the attributes from the *attribute groups*.

Common Content Elements

You spend most of the remaining part of this chapter learning the different elements you can use to describe the structure of text. These include:

➤ The six levels of headings: <h1>, <h2>, <h3>, <h4>, <h5>, and <h6>

➤ Paragraphs <p>, preformatted sections <pre>, line breaks <br />, and addresses <address>

➤ Grouping elements: <div>, <header>, <hgroup>, <nav>, <section>, <article>, and <hr>

➤ Presentational elements: <b>, <i>, <sup>, and <sub>

➤ Phrase elements: <em>, <strong>, <abbr>, <dfn>, <blockquote>, <q>, <cite>, <code>, <kbd>, <var>, and <samp>

➤ Lists such as unordered lists using <ul> and <li>; ordered lists using <ol> and <li>; and definition lists using <dl>, <dt>, and <dd>

➤ Editing elements: <ins> and <del>

That may sound like a lot of elements, but you might be surprised at how quickly you can move through them.

BASIC TEXT FORMATTING

Because almost every document you create contains some form of text, the elements you are about to meet are likely to feature in most pages that you will build. In this section, you learn how to use *basic text formatting elements*:

➤ `<h1>`, `<h2>`, `<h3>`, `<h4>`, `<h5>`, and `<h6>`

➤ `<p>`, `<br>`, and `<pre>`

As you read through this section, one browser might display each of these elements in a certain way, and another browser might display the same page in a slightly different way. For example, the typefaces used, the font sizes, and the spaces around these elements may differ between browsers. (And therefore the amount of space a section of text takes up can vary, too.)

Before you look at the elements, it helps to know how text displays by default without any elements. This helps demonstrate the importance to use markup to tell the browser if you want it to treat text differently.

White Space and Flow

Before you start to mark up your text, it's best to understand what HTML does when it comes across spaces and how browsers treat long sentences and paragraphs of text.

You might think that if you put several consecutive spaces between two words, the spaces would appear between those words onscreen, but this is not the case; by default, only one space displays. This is known as *white space collapsing*. Similarly, if you start a new line in your source document, or you have consecutive empty lines, these will be ignored and simply treated as one space, as will tab characters. For example, consider the following paragraph (taken from `ch01_eg03.html` in the code samples):

```
<p>This    paragraph shows how    multiple spaces      between      words are
treated as a single space. This is known as white space collapsing, and
the big spaces between    some of the    words will not appear   in the
browser.

It also demonstrates how the browser will treat multiple carriage returns
(new lines) as a single space, too.</p>
```

In Figure 1-5 the browser treats the multiple spaces and several carriage returns (where text appears on a new line) as if there were only one single space. It also enables the line to take up the full width of the browser window.

Now look at the code for this example again, and compare where each new line starts in the code with where each new line starts onscreen. Unless told otherwise, when a browser displays text, it automatically takes up the full width of the screen and *wraps* the text onto new lines when it runs out of space (refer to Figure 1-5). You can see the effect of this better if you open this example in a browser and try resizing the browser window (making it smaller and larger) and notice how the text wraps at new places on the screen. (This example is available with the rest of the download code for this book at `www.wrox.com`.)

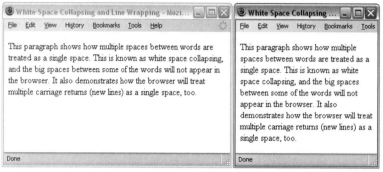

FIGURE 1-5

White space collapsing can be particularly helpful because it enables you to add extra spaces into your HTML that do not show up when viewed in a browser. You can use these spaces to indent your code, which makes it easier to read. The first two examples in this chapter demonstrated indented code, where child elements are indented from the left to distinguish them from their parent elements, which is used this throughout this book to make the code more readable. (If you want to preserve the spaces in a document, you need to use either the `<pre>` element, which you learn about later in the chapter, or an entity reference such as ` `, a nonbreaking space, which you learn about in Appendix F, "Special Characters.")

Now that you know how multiple spaces and line breaks are collapsed, you can see why you must learn how to use the elements in the rest of this chapter to break up and control the presentation of your text.

Creating Headings Using `<hn>` Elements

No matter what sort of document you create, most documents have headings in one form or another. Newspapers use headlines; a heading on a form tells you the purpose of the form; the title of a table of sports results tells you the league or division the teams play in; and so on.

In longer pieces of text, headings can also help structure a document. If you look at the table of contents for this book, you can see how different levels of headings have been arranged to add structure to the book, with subheadings under the main headings.

HTML offers six levels of headings, which use the elements `<h1>`, `<h2>`, `<h3>`, `<h4>`, `<h5>`, and `<h6>`. Browsers display the `<h1>` element as the largest of the six and `<h6>` as the smallest. (Although you can see in Chapter 7 that you can use CSS to override the size and style of any of the elements.) The levels of headings would look something like those in Figure 1-6 (`ch01_eg04.html`).

> **WARNING** *Most browsers display the contents of the `<h1>`, `<h2>`, and `<h3>` elements larger than the default size of text in the document. The content of the `<h4>` element would be the same size as the default text, and the content of the `<h5>` and `<h6>` elements would be smaller unless you instruct them otherwise using CSS.*

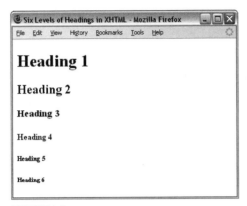

FIGURE 1-6

Here is another example of how you might use headings to structure a document (ch01_eg05.html), where the <h2> elements are subheadings of the <h1> element. (This actually models the structure of this section of the chapter.)

```
<h1>Basic Text Formatting</h1>
<p> This section is going to address the way in which you mark up text.
Almost every document you create will contain some form of text, so this
will be a very important section. </p>
<h2>White Space and Flow</h2>
<p> Before you start to mark up your text, it is best to understand what HTML does
when it comes across spaces and how browsers treat long sentences and
paragraphs of text.</p>
<h2>Creating Headings</h2>
<p> No matter what sort of document you are creating, most documents have
 headings in some form or other...</p>
```

Figure 1-7 shows how this will look.

Basic Text Formatting

This section is going to address the way in which you mark up text. Almost every document you create will contain some form of text, so this will be a very important section.

White Space and Flow

Before you start to mark up your text, it is best to understand what HTML does when it comes across spaces and how browsers treat long sentences and paragraphs of text.

Creating Headings

No matter what sort of document you are creating, most documents have headings in some form or other...

FIGURE 1-7

The six heading elements can all carry the universal attributes:

```
class id style title dir lang
```

Creating Paragraphs Using the <p> Element

The <p> element offers another way to structure your text. Each paragraph of text should go in between an opening <p> and closing </p> tag, as in this example (ch01_eg06.html):

```
<p>Here is a paragraph of text.</p>
<p>Here is a second paragraph of text.</p>
<p>Here is a third paragraph of text.</p>
```

When a browser displays a paragraph, it usually inserts a new line before the next paragraph and adds a little bit of extra vertical space, as shown in Figure 1-8.

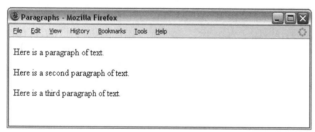

FIGURE 1-8

The <p> element can carry all the universal attributes:

```
class id style title dir lang
```

Creating Line Breaks Using the
 Element

Whenever you use the <br> element, anything following it starts on the next line. The <br> element is an example of an *empty element*; you don't need opening *and* closing tags, because there is nothing to go in between them.

You can use multiple <br> elements to push text down several lines, and many designers use two line breaks between paragraphs of text rather than using the <p> element to structure text, as follows:

```
Paragraph one<br><br>
Paragraph two<br><br>
Paragraph three<br><br>
```

Although two <br> elements look similar to using a <p> element, remember that HTML markup is supposed to describe the structure of the content. So if you use two <br> elements between paragraphs, you are not describing the document structure.

> **NOTE** *Strictly speaking, do not use <br> elements to position text; use them only within a block-level element. The <p> element is a block-level element; you learn more about these in the "Understanding Block and Inline Elements" section.*

Here you can see an example of the <br> element in use within a paragraph (ch01_eg07.html):

```
<p>When you want to start a new line you can use the line break element.
So, the next<br />word will appear on a new line.</p>
```

Figure 1-9 shows you how the line breaks look after the words "next" and "do."

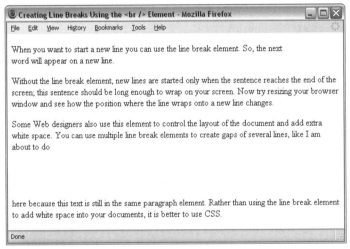

FIGURE 1-9

The <br> element can carry the following attributes:

```
class id style title
```

Creating Preformatted Text Using the <pre> Element

Sometimes you want your text to follow the exact format of how it is written in the HTML document; you don't want the text to wrap onto a new line when it reaches the edge of the browser. You also don't want it to ignore multiple spaces, and you want the line breaks where you put them.

Any text between the opening <pre> tag and the closing </pre> tag preserves the formatting of the source document. You should be aware, however, that most browsers display this text in a monospaced font by default. (Courier is an example of a monospaced font because each letter of the alphabet takes up the same width. Compare this to a nonmonospaced font, where an *i* is usually narrower than an *m*.)

The most common uses of the `<pre>` element are to represent computer source code. For example, the following shows some JavaScript inside a `<pre>` element (`ch01_eg08.html`):

```
<pre>
function testFunction( strText ){
    console.log( strText )
}
</pre>
```

Figure 1-10 shows how the content of the `<pre>` element displays in the monospaced font. More important, you can see how it follows the formatting shown inside the `<pre>` element—the white space is preserved.

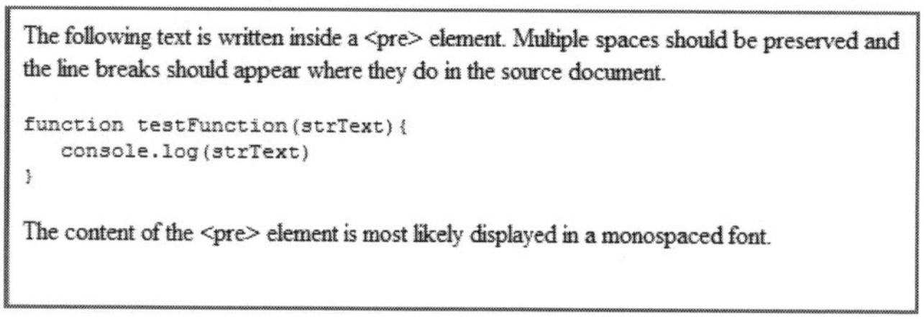

The following text is written inside a `<pre>` element. Multiple spaces should be preserved and the line breaks should appear where they do in the source document.

```
function testFunction(strText){
    console.log(strText)
}
```

The content of the `<pre>` element is most likely displayed in a monospaced font.

FIGURE 1-10

Although tab characters can have an effect inside a `<pre>` element, and a tab is supposed to represent eight spaces, the implementation of tabs varies across browsers, so it is advisable to use spaces instead.

You will come across more elements that you can use to represent code in the next chapter, "Fine-tuning Your Text," which covers the `<code>`, `<kbd>`, and `<var>` elements.

TRY IT OUT   Basic Text Formatting

Now that you've seen the basic elements that you can use to format your text—headings and paragraphs—it's time to put that information to work.

In this example, you create a page for a fictional company called Example Café. You will work on this example throughout the book to build up an entire site. This page is going to be the homepage for the site, introducing people to the café:

1. Add the skeleton of the document: the DOCtype declaration and the `<html>`, `<head>`, `<title>`, and `<body>` elements.

```
<!doctype html>
<html>
  <head>
    <title>Example Cafe - community cafe in Newquay, Cornwall, UK </title>
  </head>
  <body>
  </body>
</html>
```

The entire page is contained in the `<html>` element. The `<html>` element can contain only two child elements: the `<head>` element and `<body>` element. The `<head>` element contains the title for the page, and you can tell from the title of the page the type of information the page contains.

Meanwhile, the `<body>` element contains the main part of the web page, the part that viewers actually see in the main part of the web browser.

2. Add to your page a main heading and some level 2 headings to add structure to the information on the page:

```
<body>
  <h1>EXAMPLE CAFE</h1>
  <h2>A community cafe serving home cooked, locally sourced, organic food</h2>
  <h2>This weekend's special brunch</h2>
</body>
```

3. Fill out the page with some paragraphs that follow the headings:

```
<body>
  <h1>EXAMPLE CAFE</h1>
    <p>Welcome to example cafe. We will be developing this site throughout
    the book.</p>
  <h2>A community cafe serving home cooked, locally sourced, organic food</h2>
    <p>With stunning views of the ocean, Example Cafe offers the perfect
environment to unwind and recharge the batteries.</p>
    <p>Our menu offers a wide range of breakfasts, brunches and lunches,
    including a range of vegetarian options.</p>
    <p>Whether you sip on a fresh, hot coffee or a cooling smoothie, you never
    need to feel rushed - relax with friends or just watch the world go by.</p>
  <h2>This weekend's special brunch</h2>
    <p>This weekend, our season of special brunches continues with scrambled egg
    on an English muffin. Not for the faint-hearted, the secret to these eggs is
    that they are made with half cream and cooked in butter, with no more than
    four eggs in the pan at a time.</p>
</body>
```

4. Save the file as `index.html` and then open it in a web browser. The result should look something like Figure 1-11. The name `index.html` is often given to the homepage of sites built in HTML.

How It Works

The basic skeleton, the `<head>` and `<body>` elements, combined with a mix of `<p>` elements and headings might be simple, but it represents a complete web page. The default rendering of a `<p>` element and the `<h1>` and `<h2>` elements give this page solid structure even without any style information.

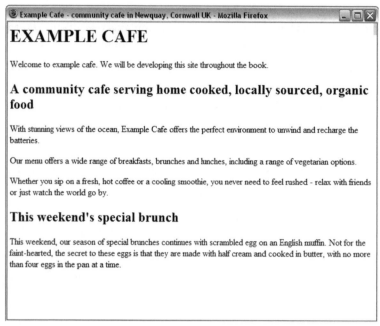

FIGURE 1-11

UNDERSTANDING BLOCK AND INLINE ELEMENTS

Now that you have seen many of the elements that you can use to mark up text, you must consider all the elements that live inside the `<body>` element because each can fall into one of two categories:

➤ Block-level elements

➤ Inline elements

This is quite a conceptual distinction, but it has important ramifications for other features of HTML.

Block-level elements appear on the screen as if they have a carriage return or line break before and after them. For example, the `<p>`, `<h1>`, `<h2>`, `<h3>`, `<h4>`, `<h5>`, `<h6>`, `<ul>`, `<ol>`, `<dl>`, `<pre>`, `<hr />`, `<blockquote>`, and `<address>` elements are all block-level elements. They all start on their own new lines, and anything that follows them appears on its own new line, too.

Inline elements, on the other hand, can appear within sentences and do not need to appear on new lines of their own. The `<b>`, `<i>`, `<u>`, `<em>`, `<strong>`, `<sup>`, `<sub>`, `<small>`, `<ins>`, `<del>`, `<code>`, `<cite>`, `<dfn>`, `<kbd>`, and `<var>` elements are all inline elements.

For example, look at the following heading and paragraph; both of these elements start on new lines, and anything that follows them goes on a new line, too. Meanwhile, the inline elements in the paragraph are not placed on their own new lines. Here is the code (ch01_eg09.html):

```
<h1>Block-Level Elements</h1>
  <p><strong>Block-level elements</strong> always start on a new line. The
  <code>&lt;h1&gt;</code> and <code>&lt;p&gt;</code> elements will not sit
  on the same line, whereas the inline elements flow with the rest of the
  text.</p>
```

You can see what this looks like in Figure 1-12.

FIGURE 1-12

Strictly speaking, inline elements may not contain block-level elements and can appear only within block-level elements. (So you should not have a <b> element outside a block-level element.) Block-level elements, meanwhile, can contain other block-level elements and inline elements.

GROUPING CONTENT

You can find one of the most interesting new additions to the HTML5 specification in a number of new elements added to aid in grouping content. As you just learned, elements represent the different parts of an article with different levels of headings and paragraphs. As you'll learn throughout the chapter, there are many other elements left to mark up to describe text.

One thing that was lacking was the ability to group all that well-described content into meaningful ways. So, although you could write an article and mark up each paragraph meaningfully, it wasn't possible to indicate that the entire block of text was an article. HTML5 changes that with the addition of several new elements designed to enable you to more accurately group content.

This section introduces the various ways to group content in HTML.

The New Outline Algorithm in HTML5

In adding these new grouping elements, the authors of the specification made a change to the way headings are used in HTML. Before HTML5, the general standard was to have one <h1> element per page. The basic idea was that the entire HTML document was by itself a standalone element and should therefore have just one overall outline with a single <h1> at the top of the tree.

As the web evolved to contain more complicated, compound documents, this concept no longer held true for many of the documents on the web. With a blog, you can easily have several separate articles all contained in a single HTML document. Each of those articles could contain a logical outline of its own, independent of the rest of the page. Because of this, the ability to add more than one <h1> to the page inside different sectioning elements was added.

As you'll learn throughout this section and as you continue to work with HTML5, there's much greater flexibility in the ways you can structure pages using the new markup.

As an aid to work with HTML5 documents, there's a handy bookmarklet and Google Chrome extension called the HTML5 Outliner (h5o) that can help to analyze the structure of your pages. Even experienced authors find it useful, so it's definitely good to have on hand to make sure your pages make sense at the outline level. You can download it from Google code: http://code.google.com/p/h5o/.

The <div> Element

Before the extension of the grouping elements in HTML5, the most common container for groups of HTML elements was the <div>. It represents a generic block of content and is designed to be used with classes and ids to give structure to documents. Taking the markup from Example Café, you could mark it up with <div> elements representing different content sections.

For example, if you want to set the header apart in some way, you can mark it up like the following example. Using a <div> with a class of header you can encapsulate the site title and tagline into a single structure:

```
<div class="header">
  <h1>EXAMPLE CAFE</h1>
  <p>Welcome to example cafe. We will be developing this site throughout
the book.</p>
</div>
```

Although this is actually quite useful for styling and scripting, there's no semantic meaning behind the <div>, no matter how well chosen the classes or ids are. As you see throughout this section, the new sectioning elements in HTML5 enhance the utility of the <div> with (mostly) straightforward semantic meaning.

The <header> Element

As part of the development of the new specification, the editor of the HTML standard, Ian Hickson, did a survey of the web and identified common markup patterns. Some of these he captured as new HTML elements. This is one such element.

As you saw in the previous example, the concept of a "header" for common introductory or navigation content is a useful one and was repeated over and over on the web. Marking up the previous example with a <header> simplifies the markup and imparts more semantic meaning to the page.

```
<header>
  <h1>EXAMPLE CAFE</h1>
  <p>Welcome to example cafe. We will be developing this site throughout
the book.</p>
</header>
```

Although this example shows a header generated at the page level, you can also use headers within other grouping elements. For example, an `<article>` element, which you'll learn about shortly, can have its own header containing information about the author, the data published, and the title of the article.

The <hgroup> Element

The `<hgroup>` element is designed to group together multiple levels of headings that have some logical connection, for example, subheadings, alternative titles, or taglines.

Adding an `<hgroup>` element, and a silly tagline, to the previous example illustrates how to use the `<hgroup>` element:

```
<header>
  <hgroup>
    <h1>EXAMPLE CAFE</h1>
    <h2>Serving Home Style Example Markup since 2012</h2>
  </hgroup>
</header>
```

The <nav> Element

The `<nav>` element represents a navigation section of the page, containing a list of links to other pages or site sections within the site or application. Because the Example Café site is going to have more than one page, look at one way to mark up a simple menu linking to other pages on the site. In this example you can see a series of `<p>` tags, containing links to the site's other pages. Later you learn about working with lists and learn a more common pattern for marking up navigational elements. For now, just focus on the use of the `<nav>` element.

```
<nav>
  <p><a href="recipes.html">Recipes</p>
  <p><a href="menu.html">Menu</a></p>
  <p><a href="opening_times.html">Opening Times</a></p>
  <p><a href-"contact.html">contact</a></p>
</nav>
```

The <section> Element

The `<section>` element is used to represent a section of a document or application. A `<section>` differs from a `<div>`, the most generic content grouping element, by the idea that content contained in a `<section>` is designed to be part of the document's outline.

Although the Example Café site is going to have separate pages, it can conceivably be one page broken into several sections. A simplified example, just using the headings for each section and no content, would look something like this:

```
<section>
  <h1>Introduction</h1>
</section>
<section>
```

```
    <h1>Recipes</h1>
  </section>
  <section>
    <h1>Menu</h1>
  </section>
  <section>
    <h1>Opening Times</h1>
  </section>
  <section>
    <h1>Contact</h1>
  </section>
```

The \<article\> Element

In the words of the specification, you can use an `<article>` element to mark up "independent content." That's not the friendliest description, so it's useful to think of common examples such as a blog post, a forum post, a movie review, a news article, or an interactive widget. The basic rule of thumb is that if the content can be syndicated or shared without the rest of the site context, it should be marked up as an article. For example, a short, glowing review of the Example Café might be marked up like the following example:

```
<article>
  <h1>Example Cafe, Great Food Delivered with Superior Markup and Style</h1>
  <p>It's rare to find a restaurant that combines as many exemplary elements as
the example café. From the superior markup of the café's website to the
delicious dishes served with care nothing about the Example Café is
left to chance.</p>
</article>
```

The \<hr\> Element

The `<hr>` element creates a horizontal rule across the page. It is an empty element, rather like the `<br>` element.

```
<hr>
```

This is frequently used to separate distinct sections of a page where a new heading is not appropriate.

The \<blockquote\> Element

When you want to quote a passage from another source, you should use the `<blockquote>` element. Note that there is a separate `<q>` element for use with smaller quotations, as discussed in the next section. Here's `ch01_eg10.html`:

```
<p>The following description of the blockquote element is taken from
the WHATWG site:</p>
<blockquote> The blockquote element represents a section that is quoted from
another source. Content inside a blockquote must be quoted from another
source, whose address, if it has one, may be cited in the
cite attribute.</blockquote>
```

Text inside a `<blockquote>` element is usually indented from the left and right edges of the surrounding text, and some browsers use an italicized font. (Use it only for quotes—if you simply want an indented paragraph of text, use CSS.) You can see what this looks like in Figure 1-13.

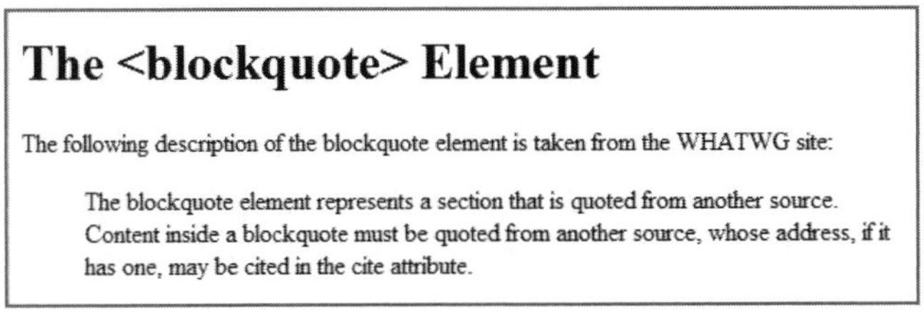

The \<blockquote> Element

The following description of the blockquote element is taken from the WHATWG site:

> The blockquote element represents a section that is quoted from another source. Content inside a blockquote must be quoted from another source, whose address, if it has one, may be cited in the cite attribute.

FIGURE 1-13

Using the cite Attribute with the \<blockquote> Element

You can use the `cite` attribute on the `<blockquote>` element to indicate the source of the quote. The value of this attribute should be a URL pointing to an online document; if possible, the exact place in that document. Browsers do not currently do anything with this attribute, but it means the source of the quote is there should you need it in the future (`ch01_eg11.html`).

```
<blockquote cite=
"http://developers.whatwg.org/grouping-content.html#the-blockquote-element">
The blockquote element represents a section that is quoted from another source.
Content inside a blockquote must be quoted from another source, whose address,
if it has one, may be cited in the cite attribute.</blockquote>
```

The \<aside> Element

The `<aside>` element is used to mark up related content such as pull quotes, sidebars, and ads. The content in the aside should be related to the surrounding content.

Pulling the first glowing sentence of the previous review illustrates a simple usage of the `<aside>` element.

```
<article>
  <h1>Example Cafe, Great Food Delivered with Superior Markup and Style</h1>
  <p>It's rare to find a restaurant that combines as many exemplary elements as
the example café. From the superior markup of the café's website to the
delicious dishes served with care nothing about the Example Café is left
to chance.</p>
  <aside> It's rare to find a restaurant that combines as many exemplary
elements as the example café.</aside>
</article>
```

The \<footer> Element

Like the `<header>`, the `<footer>` was an extremely common `class` and `id` name found during Ian Hickson's survey of the web. A common usage of the footer is for legal copy. On some sites, such as those of pharmaceutical companies or financial services firms, this can be quite a large block of text, sometimes stretching to several screen's worth of text. Thankfully Example Café doesn't have quite the same legal and regulatory overhead, so you can just add a simple copyright notice into your `<footer>`.

```
<footer>
  <p>All content copyright Example Café 2012</p>
</footer>
```

The <address> Element

The `<address>` element is used to mark up contact information for an article element or for the document as a whole. In this example you add it as contact information in the footer.

```
<footer>
  <address>For more information contact <a href="mailto:examplecafe@example.com">
Example Café via email</address>
  <p>All content copyright Example Café 2012</p>
</footer>
```

WORKING WITH LISTS

There are many reasons you might want to add a list to your pages, from putting your five favorite albums on your homepage to including a numbered set of instructions for visitors to follow (such as the steps you follow in the Try It Out examples in this book).

You can create three types of lists in HTML:

➤ **Unordered:** Like lists of bullet points

➤ **Ordered:** Use a sequence of numbers or letters instead of bullet points

➤ **Definition:** Enable you to specify a term and its definition

You can think of more uses for the lists as you meet them and start using them.

Using the <ul> Element to Create Unordered Lists

If you want to make a list of bullet points, write the list within the `<ul>` element (which stands for *unordered list*). Each bullet point or line you want to write should then be contained between opening `<li>` tags and closing `</li>` tags. (The li stands for *list item*.)

You should always close the `<li>` element. Even though you might see some HTML pages that leave off the closing tag, this is a bad habit you should avoid.

If you want to create a bulleted list, you can do so like this (ch01_eg12.html):

```
<ul>
  <li>Bullet point number one</li>
  <li>Bullet point number two</li>
  <li>Bullet point number three</li>
</ul>
```

In a browser, this list would look something like Figure 1-14.

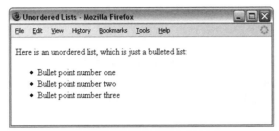

FIGURE 1-14

As promised, the following shows the list of links from the illustration of the `<nav>` element reworked to use an unordered list. Navigation elements on the web are commonly marked up using lists, so it's useful to get used to that pattern as soon as possible.

```
<nav>
  <ul>
    <li><a href="recipes.html">Recipes</li>
    <li><a href="menu.html">Menu</a></li>
    <li><a href="opening_times.html">Opening Times</a></li>
    <li><a href-"contact.html">contact</a></li>
  </ul>
</nav>
```

The `<ul>` and `<li>` elements can carry all the universal attributes and UI event attributes.

Ordered Lists

Sometimes, you want your lists to be ordered. In an ordered list, rather than prefixing each point with a bullet point, you can use either numbers (1, 2, 3), letters (A, B, C), or Roman numerals (i, ii, iii) to prefix the list item.

An ordered list is contained inside the `<ol>` element. Each item in the list should then be nested inside the `<ol>` element and contained between opening `<li>` and closing `</li>` tags (ch01_eg13.html).

```
<ol>
  <li>Point number one</li>
  <li>Point number two</li>
  <li>Point number three</li>
</ol>
```

The result should be similar to what you see in Figure 1-15.

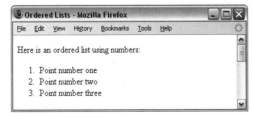

FIGURE 1-15

In Chapter 7, in the section on styling lists with CSS, you learn about customizing the type of glyph used for your ordered lists.

Using the start Attribute to Change the Starting Number in Ordered Lists

If you want to specify the number that a numbered list should start at, you can use the start attribute on the <ol> element. The value of this attribute should be the numeric representation of that point in the list (ch01_eg14.html).

```
<ol start="4">
  <li>Point number one</li>
  <li>Point number two</li>
  <li>Point number three</li>
</ol>
```

You can see the result in Figure 1-16.

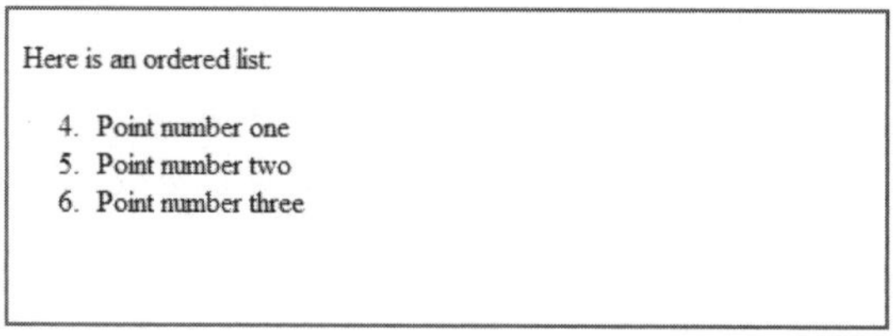

Here is an ordered list:

4. Point number one
5. Point number two
6. Point number three

FIGURE 1-16

Count Down in Your Ordered Lists with the reversed Attribute

The boolean reversed attribute allows you to reverse the order of ordered lists, counting down from the highest number (supported only in Chrome). The following code sample shows this in action (ch01_eg15.html).

```
<ol reversed>
  <li>Point number one</li>
  <li>Point number two</li>
  <li>Point number three</li>
</ol>
```

You can see the count begin with "3" in Figure 1-17.

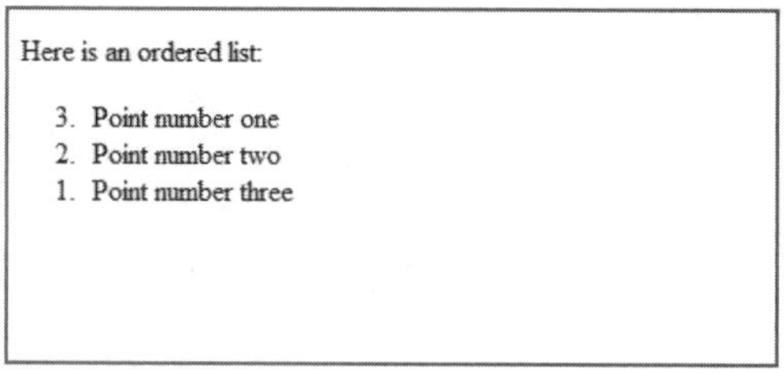

Here is an ordered list:

3. Point number one
2. Point number two
1. Point number three

FIGURE 1-17

Specify a Marker with the type Attribute

The `type` attribute allows you to specify the class of markers to use with ordered lists. Table 1-3 shows the available options. If you use this attribute, keep in mind that the values are case-sensitive.

TABLE 1-3: type Attribute Values

KEYWORD	STATE	DESCRIPTION
1	decimal	Decimal number (default)
a	lower-alpha	Lowercase Latin alphabet
A	upper-alpha	Uppercase Latin alphabet
i	lower-roman	Lowercase Roman numerals
I	upper-roman	Uppercase Roman numerals

The following code sample (`ch01_eg16.html`) shows a list using the lowercase Latin alphabet.

```
<ol type="a">
  <li>Point number one</li>
  <li>Point number two</li>
  <li>Point number three</li>
</ol>
```

You can see the count begin with "a" in Figure 1-18.

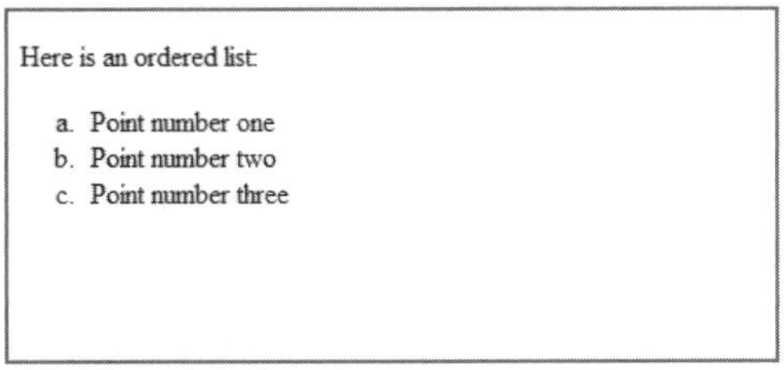

Here is an ordered list:

    a. Point number one
    b. Point number two
    c. Point number three

FIGURE 1-18

Definition Lists

The HTML5 spec states `<dl>` is for description lists, which have a slightly wider remit than term and definition. "The `<dl>` element represents a description list, which consists of zero or more term-description (name/value) groupings; each grouping associates one or more terms/names (the contents of `<dt>` elements) with one or more descriptions/values (the contents of `<dd>` elements)."

The definition list is a special kind of list for providing terms followed by a short text definition or description for them. Definition lists are contained inside the `<dl>` element. The `<dl>` element then contains alternating `<dt>` and `<dd>` elements. The content of the `<dt>` element is the term you define. The `<dd>` element contains the definition of the previous `<dt>` element. For example, here is a definition list that describes the different types of lists in HTML (ch01_eg17.html):

```
<dl>
   <dt>Unordered List</dt>
   <dd>A list of bullet points.</dd>
   <dt>Ordered List</dt>
   <dd>An ordered list of points, such as a numbered set of steps.</dd>
   <dt>Definition List</dt>
   <dd>A list of terms and definitions.</dd>
</dl>
```

In a browser, this looks something like Figure 1-19.

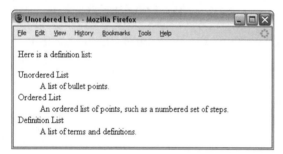

FIGURE 1-19

Each of these elements can carry the universal attributes and UI event attributes.

Nesting Lists

You can nest lists inside other lists. For example, you might want a numbered list with separate points corresponding to one of the list items. Number each nested list separately, unless you specify otherwise using the start attribute. And you should place each new list inside a `<li>` element (ch01_eg18.html):

```
<ol type="I">
   <li>Item one</li>
   <li>Item two</li>
   <li>Item three</li>
   <li>Item four
      <ol type="i">
         <li>Item 4.1</li>
         <li>Item 4.2</li>
```

```
      <li>Item 4.3</li>
    </ol>
  </li>
  <li>Item Five</li>
</ol>
```

In a browser, this looks something like Figure 1-20.

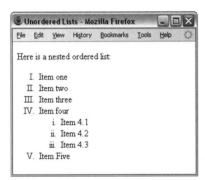

FIGURE 1-20

SUMMARY

In this chapter, you learned about the similarities between web pages and print documents; for example, a news story in print or on the web consists of a headline, some paragraphs of text, maybe some subheadings, and one or more pictures. On the web you need to explain the structure of these documents, and you can do that using HTML.

You know that HTML5 is the latest version of the HTML5 specification, and you know the special DOCTYPE used to put HTML documents into standards mode.

You have learned that the content of a web page is marked up using elements that describe the structure of the document. These elements consist of an opening tag, a closing tag, and some content between the opening and closing tags. To alter some properties of elements, the opening tag may carry attributes, and attributes are commonly written as name/value pairs. They can also be empty elements.

You also learned a lot of new elements and the attributes they can carry. You've seen how every HTML document should contain at least the `<html>`, `<head>`, `<title>`, and `<body>` elements. In the next chapter you learn about fine-tuning your text by adding meaning for both humans and computers, more specific structure and other features that will greatly enrich your web pages.

EXERCISES

1. Mark up the following list, with inserted and deleted content:

Ricotta pancake ingredients:

- ➤ 1 ~~1/2~~ <u>3/4</u> cups ricotta
- ➤ 3/4 cup milk
- ➤ 4 eggs
- ➤ 1 cup plain <u>white</u> flour
- ➤ 1 teaspoon baking powder
- ➤ ~~75g~~ <u>50g</u> butter
- ➤ pinch of salt

The answers to all the exercises are in Appendix A, "Answers to Exercises."

▶ **WHAT YOU LEARNED IN THIS CHAPTER**

TOPIC	KEY TAKEAWAY
HTML	HTML is the foundation that the World Wide Web is built upon.
Tags, elements, and attributes	Tags, elements, and attributes combine to describe content for the web.
Paragraphs and headers	HTML offers tools to create basic document outlines, including different levels of headers and plain paragraphs.
Grouping content	Starting with HTML5, there are several ways to group content in HTML, including elements that describe quotes, headers, footers, and articles.
Lists	HTML has several tools for marking up lists.

Fine-tuning Your Text

WHAT YOU WILL LEARN IN THIS CHAPTER

➤ Fine-tuning your text with markup that defines importance and emphasis

➤ Marking up text that describes the time, abbreviations, code, and more

WROX.COM CODE DOWNLOADS FOR THIS CHAPTER

You can find the wrox.com code downloads for this chapter at `www.wrox.com/remtitle .cgi?isbn=9781118340189` on the Download Code tab. The code is in the Chapter 2 download and individually named according to the names throughout the chapter.

Beyond the basic structural elements outlined so far, you can use a wide range of elements to mark up your text. The following chapter introduces these elements. After working through it, you'll have all the elements you might need to mark up almost any kind of content you can dream up.

ELEMENTS THAT DESCRIBE TEXT-LEVEL SEMANTICS

This section introduces a number of elements, which will help you more precisely describe text. Starting with elements that help you describe the importance or emphasis of text and working through elements that describe structured data such as time or represent programmatic code, this chapter adds a much richer set of tools to mark up your web pages.

The <span> Element

The `<span>` element is a close cousin to the `<div>`. It's a generic element with no semantic value that you can use to group inline elements. So, if you have a part of a sentence or paragraph you want to group, you can use the `<span>` element. Here you can see a `<span>` element added to indicate which content refers to an inventor. It contains both a strong element and some text.

```
<div class="footnotes">
  <h2>Footnotes</h2>
  <p><span class="inventor"><strong>1</strong> The World Wide Web was
    invented by Tim Berners-Lee</span></p>
  <p><strong>2</strong> The W3C is the World Wide Web Consortium
    which maintains many Web standards</p>
</div>
```

On its own, this would have no effect on how the document looks visually, but it does add extra meaning to the markup, which now groups the related elements. It's particularly helpful to attach special styles to these elements using CSS rules.

The `<em>` Element

The content of an `<em>` element is intended to be a point of emphasis in your document, and it usually displays in italicized text. The kind of emphasis intended is on words such as "must" in the following sentence:

```
<p>You <em>must</em> remember to close elements in HTML.</p>
```

You should use this element only when you want to add emphasis to a word, not just because you want to make the text appear italicized. If you just want italic text for stylistic reasons—without adding emphasis—you can either use the `<i>` element or preferably use CSS.

The `<strong>` Element

The `<strong>` element is intended to show strong emphasis for its content—stronger emphasis than the `<em>` element. As with the `<em>` element, you should use the `<strong>` element only when you want to add strong emphasis to part of a document. Most visual browsers display the strong emphasis in a bold font.

```
<p><em>Always</em> look at burning magnesium through protective colored
glass as it <strong>can cause blindness</strong>.</p>
```

Figure 2-1 shows how the `<em>` and `<strong>` elements are rendered in Firefox (`ch02_eg01.html`).

You need to remember that how the elements are presented (italics or bold) is largely irrelevant. You should use these elements to add emphasis to phrases and therefore give your documents greater meaning, rather than to control how they appear visually. As you can see in Chapter 7, it is quite simple with CSS to change the visual presentation of these elements—for example, to highlight any words inside an `<em>` element with a yellow background and make them bold rather than italic.

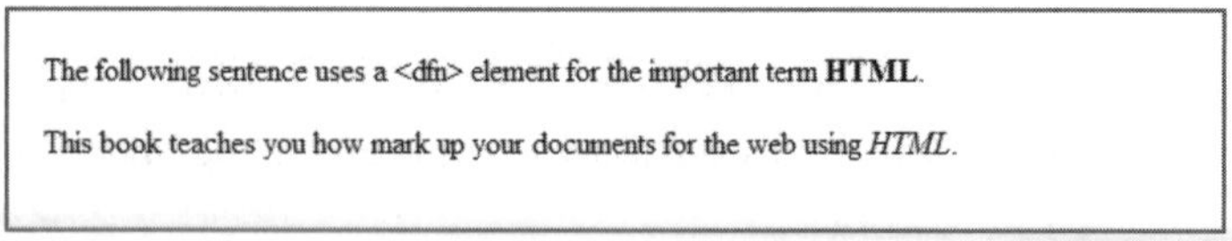

The following sentence uses a `<dfn>` element for the important term **HTML**.

This book teaches you how mark up your documents for the web using *HTML*.

FIGURE 2-1

The <b> Element

Anything that appears in a <b> element displays in bold, like the word "bold" here:

```
The following word uses a <b>bold</b> typeface.
```

For those interested in typography, it is worth noting that this does not necessarily mean the browser will use a boldface version of a font. Some browsers use an algorithm to take a normal version of a font and make the lines thicker (giving it the appearance of being bold).

The <i> Element

The content of an <i> element displays in italicized text, like the word "italic" here:

```
The following word uses an <i>italic</i> typeface.
```

This does not necessarily mean the browser looks for an oblique or italicized version of the font. Most browsers use an algorithm to put the lines on a slant to simulate an italic font.

<strong> versus <b> and <em> versus <i>

You probably wonder why elements present the same way when shown in a browser and which one you should use. <strong> and <em> are generally recommended over <b> and <i> because the strength and emphasis aren't necessarily tied to typographic conventions. This means they can more sensibly be used in a screen reader or other implementation not dependent on a certain type style.

The <small> Element

The <small> element is used for "fine print." Disclaimers, caveats, and copyrights are typical usages of the <small> element.

```
<small id="copyright">© Rob Larsen 2012</small>
```

The <cite> Element

If you quote a text, you can indicate the source by placing it between an opening <cite> tag and a closing </cite> tag. As you would expect in a print publication, the content of the <cite> element renders in italicized text by default (ch02_eg02.html).

```
This chapter is taken from <cite>Beginning Web Development</cite>.
```

If you reference an online resource, you should place your <cite> element inside an <a> element, which, as you see in Chapter 3, creates a link to the relevant document.

There are several applications that potentially could make use of the <cite> element. For example, a search application could use <cite> tags to find documents that reference certain works. Or a browser could collect the content of <cite> elements to generate a bibliography for any given document; although, at the moment it is not widely enough used for either feature to exist.

The <q> Element

Use the <q> element when you want to add a quote within a sentence, rather than as an indented block on its own (ch02_eg03.html):

```
<p>As Dylan Thomas said, <q>Somebody's boring me. I think it's me</q>.</p>
```

The HTML recommendation says that the text enclosed in a <q> element should begin and end in double quotes. Firefox inserts these quotation marks for you, but IE8 was the first version of Internet Explorer to support the <q> element. So, if you want your quote to be surrounded by quotation marks, be warned that IE7 and earlier versions of IE do not display them. If you still need to support IE7 and older, you *can* use CSS to fix this issue, so all is not lost.

The <q> element can also carry the cite attribute. The value should be a URL pointing to the source of the quote.

The <dfn> Element

The <dfn> element enables you to specify that you are introducing a special term. Its use is similar to the italicized notes in this book used to introduce important new concepts.

Typically, use the <dfn> element the first time you introduce a key term and only in that instance. Most recent browsers render the content of a <dfn> element in an italic font.

For example, you can indicate that the term "HTML" in the following sentence is important and should be marked as such:

```
This book teaches you how to mark up your documents for the Web using
<dfn>HTML</dfn>.
```

Figure 2-2 shows the use of the <dfn> element (ch02_eg04.html).

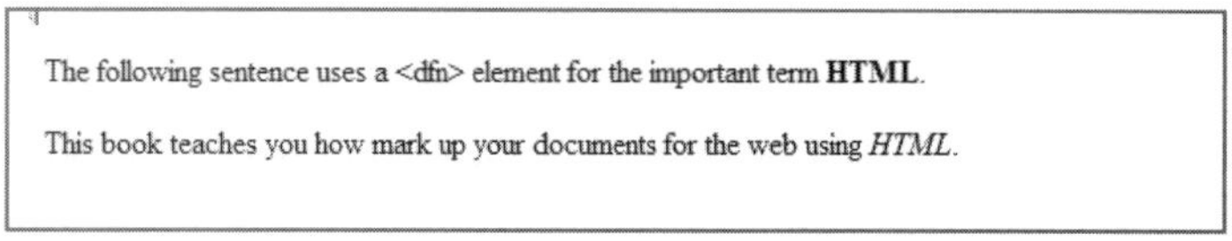

The following sentence uses a <dfn> element for the important term **HTML**.

This book teaches you how mark up your documents for the web using *HTML*.

FIGURE 2-2

The <abbr> Element

You can indicate when you use an abbreviated form or acronym by placing the abbreviation between opening <abbr> and closing </abbr> tags.

When possible, consider using a title attribute whose value is the full version of the abbreviations. For example, if you want to indicate that HTML is an acronym for HyperText Markup Language, you can use the <abbr> element like so:

```
This book teaches you how to mark up your documents for the Web using <dfn>
<abbr title="HyperText Markup Language">HTML</abbr></dfn>
```

If you abbreviate a foreign word, you can also use the `lang` attribute to indicate the language used.

The <time> Element

You can use the `<time>` element alongside the associated `datetime` attribute to mark up text representing time in various forms. It consists of a `<time>` element along with an optional `datetime` attribute. The contents of the `<time>` element display in the browser, and the contents of the `datetime` attribute are designed to be a computer-readable representation of the same information. If you neglect to include a `datetime` attribute, the contents of the `<time>` element must be in one of the formats shown in Table 2-1.

TABLE 2-1: Options for the datetime Attribute

FORMAT	EXAMPLE
Valid month string	`<time>2013-1</time>`
Valid date string	`<time>2013-1-1</time>`
Valid year-less date string	`<time>1-1</time>`
Valid time string	`<time>11:11</time>`
Valid local date and time string	`<time>2013-1-1T11:11</time>`
Valid time zone offset string	`<time>+0000</time>` `<time>-0800</time>`

Valid global date and time string	`<time>2013-1-1T14:54+0000</time>`
	`<time>2013-1-1T06:54-0800</time>`
	`<time>2013-1-1T06:54:39-0800</time>`

Valid week string	`<time>2013-W1</time>`
Valid non-negative integer representing a year	`<time>2013</time>`
Valid duration string	`<time>2h 3m 38s</time>`

Using a `datetime` attribute enables you to present a friendly date for your users and still leverage one of the more computer-useful representations (refer to Table 2-1). Marking up a valid date string with a more human-readable name might look like the following examples:

```
<time datetime="2013-1-1">New Year's Day 2013</time>

<time datetime="2004-10-27T20:25">On a late October night</time>, the Boston
Red Sox played in the decisive game four of the 2004 World Series

The world marathon record now sits at <time datetime="2h 3m 38s">
just over two hours</time>
```

The <code> Element

If your pages include any programming code (which is not uncommon on the web), the following four elements will be of particular use to you. You must place any code that you want to appear on a web page inside a <code> element. Usually the content of the <code> element is presented in a monospaced font, just like the code in most programming books (including this one).

> **WARNING** When you are trying to display code on a web page (for example, if you were creating a page about web programming), and you want to include angled brackets, you cannot just use the opening and closing angle brackets inside these elements because the browser could mistake these characters for actual markup. Use < instead of the left-angle bracket (<), and use > instead of the right-angle bracket (>). These replacement sets of characters are known as escape codes or character entities, and a full list of them appears in Appendix F.

Here is an example of the <code> element used to represent an <h1> element and its content in HTML (ch02_eg05.html):

```
<p><code>&lt;h1&gt;This is a primary heading&lt;/h1&gt;</code></p>
```

Figure 2-3 shows how this would look in a browser.

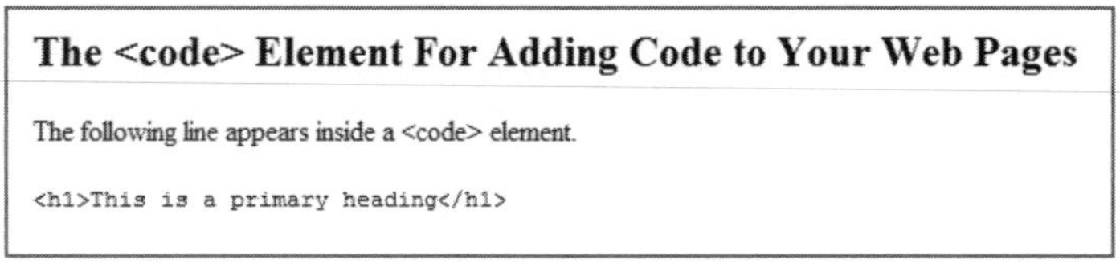

The <code> Element For Adding Code to Your Web Pages

The following line appears inside a <code> element.

```
<h1>This is a primary heading</h1>
```

FIGURE 2-3

The <code> element is often used with the <pre> element so that the formatting of the code is retained.

<figure> and <figcaption> Elements

You can use the <figure> element and the associated <figcaption> element to mark up and annotate figures or illustrations that might be referenced in text but aren't part of the main flow of the document. Using a small <code> element illustrates how you might use <figure> to illustrate some of the code from this book.

```
<figure id="14">
  <figcaption> using the code element to represent an h1 element and its
content in HTML</figcaption>
    <code>&lt;h1&gt;This is a primary heading&lt;/h1&gt;</code>
</figure>
```

The <var> Element

The <var> element is another of the elements added to help programmers. You usually use it with the <pre> and <code> elements to indicate that the content of that element is a variable that can be supplied by a user (ch02_eg06.html).

```
<p><code>console.log( "<var>user-name</var>" )</code></p>
```

Typically, the content of a <var> element is italicized (refer to Figure 2-4). Chapter 10, "Learning JavaScript," covers the concept of variables.

The <samp> Element

The <samp> element indicates sample output from a program, script, or the like. Again, it is mainly used when documenting programming concepts, for example (ch02_eg07.html):

```
<p>The following line uses the &lt;samp&gt; element to indicate the output from
a script or program.</p>
<p><samp>This is the output from our test script.</samp></p>
```

This tends to display in a monospaced font, as you can see in Figure 2-4.

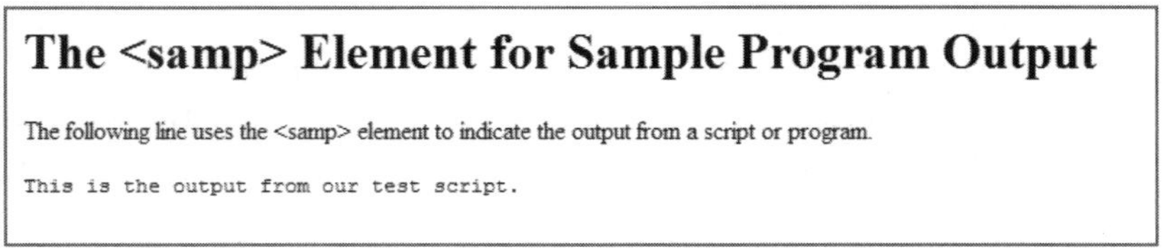

The <samp> Element for Sample Program Output

The following line uses the <samp> element to indicate the output from a script or program.

`This is the output from our test script.`

FIGURE 2-4

The <kbd> Element

If, when talking about computers, you want to tell a reader to enter some text, you can use the <kbd> element to indicate what should be typed in, as in this example (ch02_eg08.html):

```
<p>To force quit an application in Windows, hold down the <kbd>ctrl</kbd>,
<kbd>alt</kbd> and <kbd>delete</kbd> keys together.</p>
```

The content of a <kbd> element is usually represented in a monospaced font, rather like the content of the <code> element. Figure 2-5 shows you what this would look like in a browser.

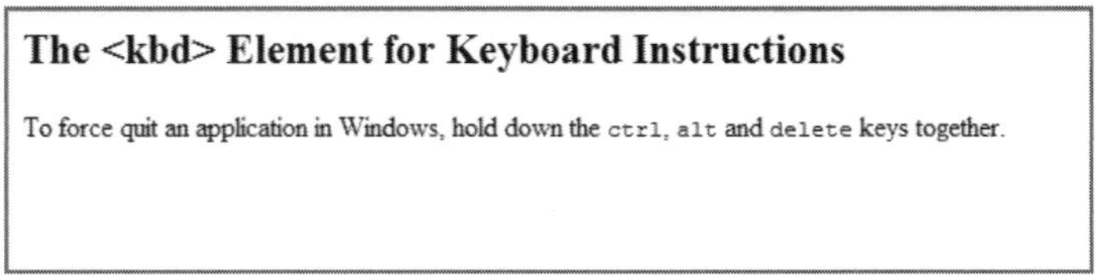

The <kbd> Element for Keyboard Instructions

To force quit an application in Windows, hold down the `ctrl`, `alt` and `delete` keys together.

FIGURE 2-5

The <sup> Element

The content of a <sup> element is written in superscript; it displays one-half a character's height above the other characters and is also often slightly smaller than the text surrounding it.

```
Written on the 31<sup>st</sup> February.
```

The <sup> element is especially helpful to add exponential values to equations, and add the *st*, *nd*, *rd*, and *th* suffixes to numbers such as dates. However, in some browsers, you should be aware that it can create a taller gap between the line with the superscript text and the line above it.

The <sub> Element

The content of a <sub> element is written in subscript; it displays one-half a character's height beneath the other characters and is also often slightly smaller than the text surrounding it.

```
The EPR paradox<sub>2</sub> was devised by Einstein, Podolsky, and Rosen.
```

The <sub> element is particularly helpful to create footnotes.

The <mark> Element

You can use the <mark> element to highlight text in a document. The goal of <mark> is to draw attention to content in a document outside of any emphasis the original author intended. Use this the same way you use a highlighter in a paper book, or as is common on some sites, use <mark> to indicate the presence of a particular search term in a block of text. The following code shows the word "HTML5" highlighted using <mark> in a block of text.

```
<p> This book focuses on the latest version of the language, popularly referred
to as <mark>HTML5</mark>. There are two other versions you might encounter.
These are HTML 4.01, the last major versions of the language from December 1999
and a stricter version from 2000 called XHTML (Extensible Hypertext Markup
Language). XHTML is still very popular in some applications so important
differences between it and <mark>HTML5</mark> will be called out in
the text. </p>
```

TRY IT OUT | **Using Text Markup**

Now that you've looked at the different elements and attributes you can use to mark up text, it is time to put them into practice. In this example, you use a selection of markup to create a page for your café site that displays a recipe for the world's best scrambled eggs. So open up your text editor or web page authoring tool and follow these steps:

1. Add the skeleton elements for the document: <html>, <head>, <title>, and <body>:

```
<!doctype html>
<html>
  <head>
    <title>Wrox Recipes - World's Best Scrambled Eggs</title>
  </head>
  <body>
  </body>
</html>
```

You have seen the skeleton several times now, so move on to add some content.

2. Add some appropriate heading elements into the body of the document; these help add structure to the page:

```
<body>
  <h1>Wrox Recipes - World's Best Scrambled Eggs</h1>
  <h2>Ingredients</h2>
  <h2>Instructions</h2>
</body>
```

3. After you add the `<h1>` element that tells you the recipe is for scrambled eggs, add a bit of an explanation about the recipe (and why it is the World's Best). Use several of the elements you have previously met in these two paragraphs.

```
<h1>Wrox Recipes - World's Best Scrambled Eggs</h1>
  <p>I adapted this recipe from a book called
<a href="http://www.amazon.com/exec/obidos/tg/detail/-/0864119917/">
      <cite>Sydney Food</cite>
    </a> by Bill Grainger. Ever since tasting
   these eggs on my 1<sup>st</sup> visit to Bill's restaurant in Kings
   Cross, Sydney, I have been after the recipe. I have since transformed
   it into what I really believe are the <em>best</em> scrambled eggs
   I have ever tasted.</p>
  <p>This recipe is what I call a <q>very special breakfast</q>; just look at
   the ingredients to see why. It has to be tasted to be believed.</p>
```

In the first sentence, the `<cite>` element indicates a reference to the book this recipe is adapted from. The next sentence makes use of the `<sup>` element, so you can write "1st" and use superscript text. This makes the gap between the first line and the second line of text larger than the gap between the second and third lines of text because the superscript letters poke above the line. In the final sentence of the first paragraph, there is emphasis on the word "best" because these actually are the *best* scrambled eggs you'll ever taste.

In the second paragraph, another of the elements is at work; you use the `<q>` element for a quote.

4. After the first `<h2>` element, list the ingredients in an unordered list:

```
<h2>Ingredients</h2>
  <p>The following ingredients make one serving:</p>
    <ul>
      <li>2 eggs</li>
      <li>1 tablespoon of butter (10g)</li>
      <li>1/3 cup of cream <i>(2 3/4 fl ounces)</i></li>
      <li>A pinch of salt</li>
      <li>Freshly milled black pepper</li>
      <li>3 fresh chives (chopped)</li>
    </ul>
```

In the line that describes how much cream you need, provide an alternative measure in italics.

5. Add the instructions after the second `<h2>` element in a numbered list:

```
<h2>Instructions</h2>
  <ol>
    <li>Whisk eggs, cream, and salt in a bowl.</li>
```

```
<li>Melt the butter in a non-stick pan over a high heat <i>(taking care
    not to burn the butter)</i></li>
<li>Pour egg mixture into pan and wait until it starts setting around
    the  edge of the pan (around 20 seconds).</li>
<li>Using a wooden spatula, bring the mixture into the center as if it
    were an omelet, and let it cook for another 20 seconds.</li>
<li>Fold contents in again, leave for 20 seconds, and repeat until
  the eggs are only just done.</li>
<li>Grind a light sprinkling of freshly milled pepper over the eggs
  and blend in some chopped fresh chives.</li>
</ol>
<p>You should only make a <strong>maximum</strong> of two servings per
  frying pan.</p>
```

The numbered list contains an italicized comment about not burning the butter, and the final paragraph contains a strong emphasis that you should cook no more than two batches of these eggs in a pan.

6. Save this example as `recipes.html`. When you open it in a browser you should see something like Figure 2-6.

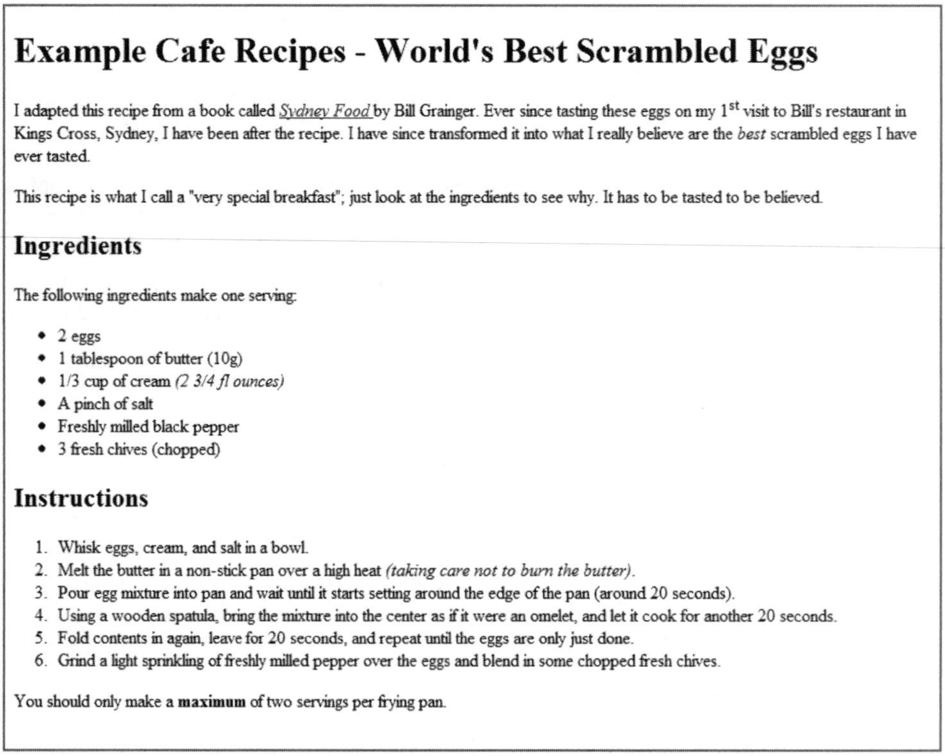

Example Cafe Recipes - World's Best Scrambled Eggs

I adapted this recipe from a book called <u>_Sydney Food_</u> by Bill Grainger. Ever since tasting these eggs on my 1st visit to Bill's restaurant in Kings Cross, Sydney, I have been after the recipe. I have since transformed it into what I really believe are the _best_ scrambled eggs I have ever tasted.

This recipe is what I call a "very special breakfast"; just look at the ingredients to see why. It has to be tasted to be believed.

Ingredients

The following ingredients make one serving:

- 2 eggs
- 1 tablespoon of butter (10g)
- 1/3 cup of cream _(2 3/4 fl ounces)_
- A pinch of salt
- Freshly milled black pepper
- 3 fresh chives (chopped)

Instructions

1. Whisk eggs, cream, and salt in a bowl.
2. Melt the butter in a non-stick pan over a high heat _(taking care not to burn the butter)_.
3. Pour egg mixture into pan and wait until it starts setting around the edge of the pan (around 20 seconds).
4. Using a wooden spatula, bring the mixture into the center as if it were an omelet, and let it cook for another 20 seconds.
5. Fold contents in again, leave for 20 seconds, and repeat until the eggs are only just done.
6. Grind a light sprinkling of freshly milled pepper over the eggs and blend in some chopped fresh chives.

You should only make a **maximum** of two servings per frying pan.

FIGURE 2-6

I hope you will enjoy the eggs—go on; you know you want to try them now.

How It Works

Adding elements that describe content at a more granular level allows you to craft content that has greater meaning for both humans and computers. Through the proper use of these elements you can emphasize the importance of certain instructions; you can indicate that the source of a phrase is a quotation or change the voice to indicate an aside.

EDITING TEXT

When working on a document with others, it helps if you can see changes that another person has made. Even when working on your own documents, it can be helpful to keep track of changes you make. Two elements are specifically designed for revising and editing text:

➤ The `<ins>` element for when you want to add text (usually shown underlined in a browser)

➤ The `<del>` element for when you want to delete some text (usually shown crossed out in a browser)

Here you can see some changes made to the following HTML (`ch02_eg09.html`):

```
<h1>How to Spot a Wrox Book</h1>
<p>Wrox-spotting is a popular pastime in bookshops. Programmers like to find
the distinctive <del>blue</del><ins>red</ins> spines because they know that
Wrox books are written by <del>1000 monkeys</del><ins>Programmers</ins> for
Programmers.</p>
<ins><p>Both readers and authors, however, have reservations about the use
of photos on the covers.</p></ins>
```

This example would look something like Figure 2-7 in a browser.

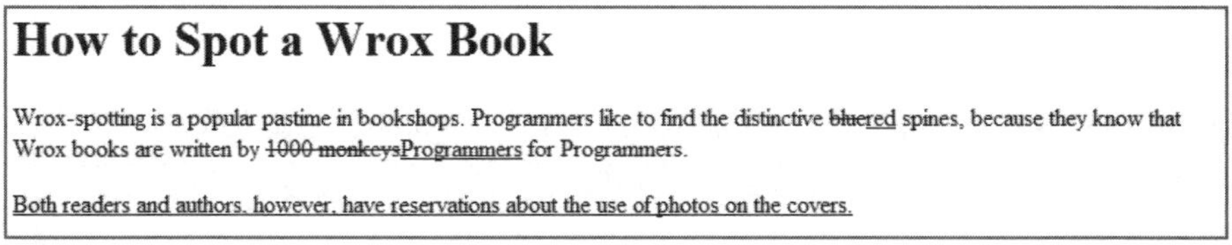

How to Spot a Wrox Book

Wrox-spotting is a popular pastime in bookshops. Programmers like to find the distinctive ~~blue~~red spines, because they know that Wrox books are written by ~~1000 monkeys~~Programmers for Programmers.

Both readers and authors, however, have reservations about the use of photos on the covers.

FIGURE 2-7

These features would also be particularly helpful as editing tools to note changes and modifications made by different authors.

> **NOTE** *If you are familiar with Microsoft Word, you'll see the* `<ins>` *and* `<del>` *elements are similar to a feature called Track Changes (which you can find under the Tools menu). The Track Changes feature underlines new text additions and crosses through deleted text.*

> **NOTE** *You must be careful when using* `<ins>` *and* `<del>` *to ensure that you do not end up with a block-level element (such as a* `<p>` *or an* `<h2>` *element) inside an inline element (such as a* `<ins>` *or* `<del>` *element).*

You can use the `title` attribute to provide information as to who added the `<ins>` or `<del>` element and why it was added or deleted. This information is offered to users as a tooltip in the major browsers.

You might also use the `cite` attribute on the `<ins>` and `<del>` element to indicate the source or reason for a change; although, this attribute is quite limiting because the value must be a URI.

The `<ins>` and `<del>` elements can also carry a `datetime` attribute whose value is a date and time in the following format:

```
YYYY-MM-DDThh:mm:ssTZD
```

This formula breaks down as follows:

➤   YYYY represents the year.

➤   MM represents the month.

➤   DD represents the day of the month.

➤   T is a separator between the date and time.

➤   hh is the hour.

➤   mm is the number of minutes.

➤   ss is the number of seconds.

➤   TZD is the time zone designator.

For example, `2013-04-16T20:30-05:00` represents 8:30 p.m. on April 16, 2013, according to U.S. Eastern Standard Time.

> **NOTE** *As you can see, the* `datetime` *attribute is rather long to be entered by hand and is more likely to be entered by a program that enables users to edit web pages.*

> **REFERENCE** *When you learn how to use CSS in Chapter 7, you can see how to show and hide the inserted and deleted content as required.*

USING CHARACTER ENTITIES FOR SPECIAL CHARACTERS

You can use most alphanumeric characters in your document, and they will display without a problem. However, some characters have special meaning in HTML, and for some characters you cannot enter a keyboard equivalent. For example, you cannot use the angle brackets that start and end tags because the browser can mistake them for markup. You can, however, use a set of different characters known as *character entities* to represent these special characters. Sometimes you also see character entities referred to as *escape characters*.

You can add all special characters into a document using the numeric entity for that character, and some also have named entities, as shown in Table 2-2.

TABLE 2-2: Numeric and Named Entities for Common Characters

CHARACTER	NUMERIC ENTITY	NAMED ENTITY
"	&#034;	&quot;
&	&#038;	&amp;
<	&#060;	&lt;
>	&#062;	&gt;

A full list of character entities (or special characters) appears in Appendix F.

COMMENTS

You can put comments between any tags in your HTML documents. Comments use the following syntax:

```
<!-- comment goes here -->
```

Anything after `<!--` until the closing `-->` does not display. It can still be seen in the source code for the document but is not shown onscreen.

It is good practice to comment your code, especially in complex documents, to indicate sections of a document and any other notes to anyone looking at the code.

You can even comment out whole sections of code. In the following snippet of code, you would not see the content of the `<h2>` element. You can also see comments indicating the section of the document, who added it, and when it was added.

```
<!-- Start of Footnotes Section added 04-24-04 by Bob Stewart -->
  <!-- <h2>Character Entities</h2> -->
  <p><strong>Character entities</strong> can be used to escape special
  characters that the browser might otherwise think have special meaning.</p>
<!-- End of Footnotes section -->
```

SUMMARY

In this chapter, you learned a lot of new elements and the attributes they can carry to describe the structure of text:

➤ Presentational elements: `<b>`, `<i>`, `<sup>`, and `<sub>`

➤ Phrase elements: `<em>`, `<strong>`, `<abbr>`, `<dfn>`, `<blockquote>`, `<q>`, `<cite>`, `<code>`, `<kbd>`, `<var>`, and `<samp>`

➤ Editing elements: `<ins>` and `<del>`

You will obviously use some of these elements more than others, but where an element fits the content you want to mark up, from paragraphs to addresses, you should try to use these because structuring your text properly helps it last longer than if you just format it using line breaks. As browsers and search engines support more and more of these elements, you will gain additional benefit.

EXERCISES

1. Mark up the following sentence with the relevant presentational elements.

```
The 1st time the bold man wrote in italics, he emphasized several key words.
```

2. You have already created the homepage for the Example Café site that you will build throughout the book. You also created a recipes page. Now you need to create three more pages so that you can continue to build the site in upcoming chapters. Each page should start like the homepage, with a level 1 heading titled **Example Café**, followed by this paragraph: **Welcome to Example Café. We will be developing this site throughout the book.** After this:

a. For a menu page, add a level 2 heading titled **Menu**. This should be followed by a paragraph saying, **The menu will go here.** Update the content of the `<title>` element to reflect that this page will feature the menus at the café. Save the file with the name `menu.html`.

b. For an opening times page, add a level 2 heading saying **Opening hours**. This should be followed by a paragraph saying, **Details of opening hours and how to find us will go here.** Update the `<title>` element to reflect that the page tells visitors opening hours and where to find the café. Save the file with the name `opening.html`.

c. For the contact page, add a level 2 heading titled **Contact**. This page should contain the address: **12 Sea View, Newquay, Cornwall, UK**. Update the `<title>` element to reflect that the page tells visitors how to contact the café.

The answers to all the exercises are in Appendix A, "Answers to Exercises."

▶ **WHAT YOU LEARNED IN THIS CHAPTER**

TOPIC	KEY TAKEAWAY
Elements for text-level-semantics	HTML provides a broad range of elements and attributes to better describe the content of your web pages. Using them helps both humans and computers better understand your text.

3

Links and Navigation

WHAT YOU WILL LEARN IN THIS CHAPTER

- ➤ How to link between pages of your site
- ➤ How to link to other sites
- ➤ How to structure the folders on your website
- ➤ How to link to specific parts of a page in your site

WROX.COM CODE DOWNLOADS FOR THIS CHAPTER

You can find the wrox.com code downloads for this chapter at `www.wrox.com/remtitle` `.cgi?isbn=9781118340189` on the Download Code tab. The code is in the Chapter 3 download and individually named according to the names throughout the chapter.

What distinguishes the web from other mediums is the way in which a web page can contain links (or *hyperlinks*) that you can click to be taken from one page to another page. The link can be a word, phrase, or image.

When you link to another page in your own website, the link is an *internal link*. When you link to a different site, it is an *external link* and uses what's known as an *absolute URL*—a URL that includes the full web address (like `http://www.google.com/`). In this chapter you learn how to create both types of links. You also see how you can link to a specific point within a page.

Although you can learn the basics of linking from one web page to another fairly quickly, you also must learn some other concepts, such as how to structure your site well by storing different files in separate folders or *directories*. When you understand directory structure, you can link between pages of your own site using shorter links called *relative URLs*.

BASIC LINKS

You can specify a link using the `<a>` element. Anything between the opening `<a>` tag and the closing `</a>` tag becomes part of the link that users can click in a browser.

Linking to Other Web Pages

To link to another web page, the opening `<a>` tag must carry an attribute called `href`; the value of the `href` attribute is the name of the file you are linking to.

For example, here is the `<body>` of the page `ch03_eg01.html`. This page contains a link to a second page called `index.html`:

```
<body>
    <p>Return to the <a href="index.html">home page</a>.</p>
</body>
```

As long as `index.html` is in the same folder as `ch03_eg01.html`, when you click the words "home page," the `index.html` page loads into the same window, replacing the current `ch03_eg01.html` page. As you can see from Figure 3-1, the content of the `<a>` element forms the link.

FIGURE 3-1

This is how the links for the download code for this chapter work. Remember that you can view the source of a page at any time to see what is going on in an HTML page. Why not try it on the download code now?

If you want to link to a different site, you can use the `<a>` element again, but this time you specify the full web address for the page you want to link to rather than just the filename. Here is an example of a link that takes you to an external site, in this case the Wrox website (`ch03_eg02.html`):

```
<body>
    <p>Why not visit the <a href="http://www.wrox.com/">Wrox Web site</a>?</p>
</body>
```

As you can see, the value of the `href` attribute is what you would type into a browser if you want to visit the Wrox website; the full web address is often referred to as a Uniform Resource Locator (URL). Since it includes the full web address, it's referred to as an Absolute URL.

When creating any link, you should try to make it concise and use words that let people know what they will see if they click the link. One reason for this is that links are usually presented in a different color than the surrounding text, which makes them stick out more than the text around them. As a result, many people scan pages for links when they want to go to the next page without reading the entire page. Therefore, people are more likely to keep exploring your website if the links are easy to read and have a better explanation than just Click Here.

Many web designers also use images inside the `<a>` element, which is something you see in the next chapter. When you use an image, you should make sure that the image gives a clear indication of where the link takes you.

You can also use the `title` attribute on a link; the value of the `title` attribute should be a description of what the link takes you to, which displays in a tooltip when you hover over the link. This can be helpful if you do use an image for a link.

Following is a link to the Google homepage (ch03_eg03.html):

```
<p><a href="http://www.Google.com/" title="Search the Web with Google">Google</a>
is a very popular search engine.</p>
```

Figure 3-2 shows the `title` attribute, which gives further information about the link to the user, when the cursor is held over the link.

You should be aware that everything inside the `<a>` element renders as a link, including white space around the text or images. Therefore, avoid spaces directly after an opening `<a>` tag or before the closing `</a>` tag. For example, consider the following link with spaces just inside the `<a>` element (ch03_eg04.html):

FIGURE 3-2

```
Why not visit the<a href="http://www.wrox.com/"> Wrox Web site </a>?
```

As you can see in Figure 3-3, these spaces in the link are underlined.

FIGURE 3-3

It is far better to use white space outside of these tags, like so:

```
Why not visit the <a href="http://www.wrox.com/">Wrox Web site</a>?
```

Of course, you should still have spaces between words inside the `<a>` element; it's just best if they are not inside the beginning or end of the link.

Linking to E-mail Addresses

You've probably seen a web page with an e-mail address that, when clicked, opens a new e-mail in your e-mail program, with the To field pre-populated with the e-mail address.

To create a link to an e-mail address, you need to use the following syntax with the `<a>` element (ch03_eg05.html):

```
<a href="mailto:name@example.com">name@example.com</a>
```

Here, the value of the `href` attribute starts with the keyword `mailto`, followed by a colon, and then the e-mail address you want the mail sent to. As with any other link, the content of the `<a>` element is the visible part of the link shown in the browser, so this would also work:

```
<a href="mailto:name@example.com">E-mail us</a>.
```

There is one drawback to putting your e-mail address on a web page: Some less scrupulous inhabitants of the web use little programs to automatically search websites for e-mail addresses. After they find e-mail addresses on websites, they start sending spam to those addresses.

Following are alternatives to creating a link to an e-mail address:

➤ Use an e-mail form that visitors fill out instead because automated programs cannot use contact forms to collect e-mail addresses. The drawback is that an e-mail form requires a script to run on the web server (written in a language such as ASP.NET or PHP). Chapter 6, "Forms," provides an example of an e-mail form.

➤ Write your e-mail address into the page using JavaScript (covered in Chapter 11, "Working with jQuery"). The idea behind this technique is that the programs that scour the web for e-mail addresses cannot read the JavaScript version of an address.

Now that you've gotten a glimpse at how links are created, it's time to put what you've learned into practice with a small coding exercise.

TRY IT OUT   **Creating Simple Links**

Now it's your turn to create a page that has three types of links: an internal link, an external link, and an e-mail link. You develop the Example Café site you started in the previous chapter, so open the `contact.html` page in the sample application folder from Chapter 1, "Structuring Documents for the Web":

1. Check that the page looks like this:

```
<!doctype html>
<html>
<head>
  <meta charset="utf-8">
  <title>Example Cafe - community cafe in Newquay, Cornwall, UK</title>
  </head>

<body>

  <h1>EXAMPLE CAFE</h1>
  <p>Welcome to Example Cafe. We will be developing this site throughout
     the book.</p>

  <h2>Contact</h2>
  <address>12 Sea View, Newquay, Cornwall, UK</address>

</body>
</html>
```

2. Add navigation between the pages of the site. You saw what this looks like when you learned about the `<nav>` element in the first chapter. This section looks at this in detail. Replace the first paragraph (after the `<h1>` element) with links to the three other pages of the site. Each `<a>` element should contain the name of the page it links to, as shown here. Group these links inside a `<nav>` element:

```
<h1>EXAMPLE CAFE</h1>
  <nav>
    <a href="">HOME</a>
    <a href="">MENU</a>
    <a href="">RECIPES</a>

  </nav>
```

3. Add the name of the contact page, but do not make it a link because this is the page that the user is already on; they do not need a link to it:

```
<h1>EXAMPLE CAFE</h1>
  <nav>
    <a href="">HOME</a>
    <a href="">MENU</a>
    <a href="">RECIPES</a>
    CONTACT
  </nav>
```

4. Add the filename of each of these pages as the value of the `href` attribute:

```
<h1>EXAMPLE CAFE</h1>
  <div>
    <a href="index.html">HOME</a>
    <a href="menu.html">MENU</a>
    <a href="recipes.html">RECIPES</a>
    CONTACT
</div>
```

Because these pages are all in the same folder, you need to specify only the filename; you do not need a full URL.

5. Under the paragraph containing the address, add a link to the following page on Google Maps, like so: info@examplecafe.com:

```
<p><a href="http://maps.google.com/maps?q=newquay">Find us on Google Maps</a></p>
```

This time the value of the `href` attribute is the web address you would type into your browser to find a map of Newquay in Google Maps.

6. Under the Google Maps link, add a link to send an e-mail to info@examplecafe.com:

```
<p><a href="mailto:info@examplecafe.com">Mail Example Cafe</a></p>
```

This time the value of the `href` attribute begins with `mailto:` and is followed by the e-mail address.

7. Save this file as `contact.html` in the same folder as the sample application for this chapter. Then open it up and take a look at it in your browser. You should end up with something that looks like Figure 3-4.

FIGURE 3-4

How It Works

This example uses three separate styles of URL to create links. The relative URLs used for site navigation are resolved based on the location of the page; the absolute URL pointing to Google Maps represents the full address of that resource, and the e-mail links will open the user's e-mail client in order to send you an e-mail.

You have now seen how to create basic types of links, and you are ready to delve into the more in-depth topics. But first you need to read through a few pages that explain more about how you should organize the files in your website into folders, and also understand the anatomy of a URL (the address that identifies pages and other resources on your website).

UNDERSTANDING DIRECTORIES AND DIRECTORY STRUCTURES

A *directory* is simply another name for a folder on a website; in the same way that your hard drive contains different folders, a website can be said to contain directories. Usually you find that a website contains several directories and that each directory contains different parts of a website. For example, a big site with several subsections will have a separate directory for each section of that site and also different directories for different types of files. (For example, images may live in one directory and style sheets in another.)

In the same way that you probably organize the files on your hard drive into separate folders, you must organize the files on your website into directories so that you can find what you are looking for more easily and keep control of all the files. As you can imagine, if all the files used in a website resided in the same directory, that directory would quickly get large and complicated.

Figure 3-5 shows an example directory structure for a news site with separate folders for each section. The Music section has its own folders for subsections about Features, MP3s, and Reviews. In addition, the main folder has separate folders for different types of files used in the site: images, scripts, and style sheets.

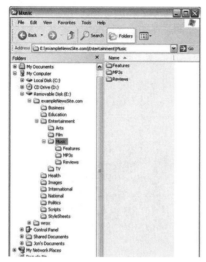

FIGURE 3-5

When you start to build any website, you should create a good directory structure that can withstand growth. It's surprising how a small website can quickly grow and contain many more files than you initially imagined.

As you learn about linking, it's helpful to learn some of the terms used in describing directory structures and the relationships between directories, so refer to Figure 3-5 to see an example directory structure:

➤ The *root directory* (or root folder) is the main directory that holds the whole of your website; in this case, it is called exampleNewsSite.com.

➤ A *subdirectory* is a directory that is within another directory. Here, Film is a subdirectory of Entertainment.

➤ A *parent directory* is one that contains another directory. Here, Entertainment is the parent directory of Arts, Film, Music, and TV.

UNDERSTANDING URLS

A *Uniform Resource Locator*, or *URL*, specifies where you can find a resource on the web; you are probably most used to thinking of them as web addresses. As you move around the web, you see the URL of each web page in the address bar of your browser.

If you look at the example URL in Figure 3-6, there are three key parts to the URL: the scheme, the host address, and the filepath.

Now look at each of these in turn.

FIGURE 3-6

The *scheme* identifies the way a file transmits. Most web pages use something called the *HyperText Transfer Protocol* (*HTTP*) to pass information to you, which is why most web pages start with `http://`. Although you might have noticed other prefixes such as `https://` when doing banking online (which is a more secure form of http) or `ftp://` when downloading large files.

The *host address* is usually the domain name for the site, for example, `wrox.com`. Often you see www before the domain name; although, it is not actually part of the domain name. The host address can also be a number called an IP address.

> **NOTE** *All computers connected to the Internet use an IP address. An IP address is a set of up to 12 digits separated by a period (full stop) symbol. When you enter a domain name into a browser, behind the scenes the name converts into the IP address for the computer(s) that stores the website. This is done by consulting a domain name server (DNS), which keeps a directory of domain names and the corresponding IP addresses.*
>
> *Interestingly, at one point, the Internet was running out of IP addresses, so the Internet Engineering Task Force (IETF) introduced Internet Protocol version 6 (IPv6), which is a new system of IP addressing that allows for many more available addresses.*

The *filepath* always begins with a forward slash character and may consist of one or more directory names. (Remember, a directory is just another name for a folder on the web server.) The filepath may end with a filename at the end. Here, `BeginningHTML.html` is the filename:

```
/books/BeginningHTML.html
```

The filepath usually corresponds to the directory structure of the website, so in this case you could find the `BeginningHTML.html` page in a directory called `books`.

It is not just web pages that have their own URLs; every file on the web, including each image, has its own URL. So the filename could be an image rather than an HTML page.

If a filename is not given, the web server usually does one of three things (depending upon how it is configured):

➤ Looks for a default file and returns that. For websites written in HTML, the default file is usually `index.html`. If no filepath is specified, the server looks for a file called `index.html` in the root folder, or if a directory is specified, it looks for an `index.html` file in that directory.

➤ Offers a list of files in that directory.

➤ Shows a message saying that the page cannot be found or that you cannot browse the files in a folder.

When linking to pages on your website, you do not need to use all three parts of the URL. You can just use the filepath and filename, as you see in the next section.

Absolute and Relative URLs

An *absolute URL* contains everything you need to uniquely identify a particular file on the Internet. This is what you would type into the address bar of your browser to find a page. For example, to get the page about film on the fictional news site you met earlier in the chapter, you might type in the following URL. You may find it helpful to refer to Figure 3-5 to see how the filepath corresponds to the directory structure:

```
http://www.exampleNewsSite.com/Entertainment/Film/index.html
```

As you can see, absolute URLs can quickly get quite long, and every page of a website can contain many links. When linking to a page on your own site, however, you can use a shorthand form: relative URLs.

A *relative URL* indicates where the resource is in relation to the current page. The examples earlier in this chapter, which link to another page in the same directory, are relative URLs. You can also use relative URLs to specify files in different directories. For example, imagine you are looking at the homepage for the entertainment section of the following fictional news site:

```
http://www.exampleNewsSite.com/Entertainment/index.html
```

You want to add a link to the index pages for each of the subsections: Film, TV, Arts, and Music. Rather than including the full URL for each page, you can use a relative URL, for example:

```
Film/index.html
TV/index.html
Arts/index.html
Music/index.html
```

This is a lot quicker than having to write out the following:

```
http://www.exampleNewsSite.com/Entertainment/Film/index.html
http://www.exampleNewsSite.com/Entertainment/TV/index.html
http://www.exampleNewsSite.com/Entertainment/Arts/index.html
http://www.exampleNewsSite.com/Entertainment/Music/index.html
```

> **NOTE** Web servers usually have the concept idea of a default document. This means that any request for a directory is passed along to a default document. On many servers, this tends to be `index.html`, which would make the list of long articles easier to use.

You might be interested to know that your web browser still requests the full URL, not the shortened relative URL, but it is the browser that is actually doing the work of turning the relative URLs into full absolute URLs.

Another benefit to using relative URLs within your site is that you can develop the site on your desktop or laptop without having bought a domain name. You can also change your domain name or copy a subsection of one site over to a new domain name without having to change all the links because each link is relative to other pages within the same site.

> **NOTE** *Relative URLs work only on links within the same website; you cannot use them to link to pages on other domain names.*

The subsections that follow provide a summary of the different types of relative URLs you can use.

Same Directory

When you want to link to, or include, a resource from the same directory, you can just use the name of that file. For example, to link from the homepage (`index.html`) to the Contact Us page (`contactUs.html`), you can use the following:

```
contactUs.html
```

Because the file lives in the same folder, you do not need to specify anything else.

Subdirectory

The Film, TV, Arts, and Music directories from Figure 3-5 were all subdirectories of the Entertainment directory. If you write a page in the Entertainment directory, you can create a link to the index page of the subdirectories like so:

```
Film/index.html
TV/index.html
Arts/index.html
Music/index.html
```

You must include the name of the subdirectory, followed by a forward slash character, and the name of the page you want to link to.

For each additional subdirectory, just add the name of the directory followed by a forward slash character. So, if you create a link from a page in the root folder of the site (such as the site's main homepage), use a relative URL such as the following to reach the same pages:

```
Entertainment/Film/index.html
Entertainment/TV/index.html
Entertainment/Arts/index.html
Entertainment/Music/index.html
```

Parent Directory

If you want to create a link from one directory to its parent directory (the directory that it is in), use the `../` notation of two periods or dots followed by a forward slash character. For example, from a page in the Music directory to a page in the Entertainment directory, your relative URL looks like this:

```
../index.html
```

If you want to link from the Music directory to the root directory, you repeat the notation:

```
../../index.html
```

Each time you repeat the `../` notation, you go up another directory.

From the Root

You can indicate a file relative to the root folder of the site. So, if you want to link to the `contactUs.html` page from any page within the site, use its path preceded by a forward slash. For example, if the Contact Us page is in the root folder, you just need to enter

```
/contactUs.html
```

Alternatively, you can link to the Music section's index page from anywhere within that site using the following:

```
/Entertainment/Music/index.html
```

The forward slash at the start indicates the root directory, and then the path from there is specified.

The <base> Element

As mentioned earlier, when a browser comes across a relative URL, it actually transforms the relative URL into a full absolute URL. The <base> element enables you to specify a base URL for a page that all relative URLs will be added to when the browser comes across a relative URL.

You specify the base URL as the value of the `href` attribute on the <base> element. For example, you might indicate a base URL for `http://www.exampleSite2.com/` as follows:

```
<base href="http://www.exampleSite2.com/" />
```

In this case, a relative URL like this one

```
Entertainment/Arts/index.html
```

ends up with the browser requesting this page:

```
http://www.exampleSite2.com/Entertainment/Arts/index.html
```

Apart from the `href` attribute, the only other attribute a <base> element can carry is the `id` attribute.

CREATING IN-PAGE LINKS WITH THE <A> ELEMENT

You have already seen examples of using the <a> element to create links. The rest of the chapter looks more closely at the <a> element, and you can see how to use it to link to a specific part of a page.

As with all journeys, links have a starting point known as the *source* and a finishing point known as the *destination*. In HTML both points are called *anchors*. Each link that you see on a page that you can click is a *source anchor*, created using the <a> element. You can also use the <a> element to create markers in parts of your pages that enable you to link directly to that part of the page. These markers are called *destination anchors*.

Creating a Source Anchor with the href Attribute

The source anchor is what most people think of when talking about links on the web—whether the link contains text or an image. It is something you can click expecting to be taken somewhere else.

As you have already seen, any text contained between the opening <a> tag and closing </a> tag forms part of the link that a user can click. The URL the user should be taken to is specified as the value of the href attribute.

For example, when you click the words Wrox Website (which you can see are inside the <a> element), the link takes you to http://www.wrox.com/:

```
Why not visit the <a href="http://www.wrox.com/">Wrox Website</a> to
find out about some of our other books?
```

If the following link were placed on the homepage of the fictional news site you have been looking at, it would take you to the main Film page of that site:

```
You can see more films in the <a href="Entertainment/Film/index.html">film
section</a>.
```

By default, the link looks something like the one shown in Figure 3-7, underlined and in blue text.

You need to specify a destination anchor only if you want to link to a specific part of a page, as described in the next section.

FIGURE 3-7

Creating a Destination Anchor Using the name and id Attributes (Linking to a Specific Part of a Page)

If you have a long web page, you might want to link to a specific part of that page to save the user from having to scroll up and down the page to find the relevant part. The *destination anchor* enables the page author to mark specific points in a page that a source anchor can point to.

Common examples of linking to a specific part of a page that you might have seen used on web pages include:

➤ Back to Top links at the bottom of a long page

➤ A list of contents on a page that takes the user to the relevant section of that page

➤ Links within text to footnotes or definitions

You create a destination anchor using the <a> element again, but when it acts as a destination anchor rather than using an href attribute, you use the id attribute.

If you look at the source code of some older web pages, you may see a name attribute used as well, or even instead of the id attribute. You may remember from Chapter 1 that the name and id attributes were two of the universal attributes that most elements can carry. The id attribute is now the preferred way to create a destination anchor, but it was introduced only in version 4 of HTML, and the name attribute was used to perform the same function in previous versions.

By way of example, imagine that you have a long page with a main heading and several subheadings. The whole page does not fit on the screen at once, forcing the user to scroll, so you want to add links at the top of the page that take readers directly to each of the section headings on that page.

Before you can create links to each section of the page (using the source anchors), you must add the destination anchors. Here you can see that inside the \<h2\> subheading elements, there is an `id` attribute whose value identifies each section. Remember that a page should not contain two `id` attributes that have the same value.

```
<h1>Linking and Navigation</h1>
<h2 id="URL">URLs</h2>
<h2>id="SourceAnchors">Source Anchors</h2>
<h2id="DestinationAnchors">Destination Anchors</h2>
<h2id="Examples">Examples</h2>
```

With destination anchors in place, you can now add source anchors to link to these sections. To link to a particular section, the value of the `href` attribute in the source anchor should be the same as the value of the `id` attribute on the corresponding destination element, preceded by a pound or hash sign (#).

```
<nav>
  <p>This page covers the following topics:</p>
  <ul>
   <li><a href="#URL">URLs</a></li>
   <li><a href="#SourceAnchors">Source Anchors</a></li>
   <li><a href="#DestinationAnchors">Destination Anchors</a></li>
   <li><a href="#Examples">Examples</a></li>
  </ul>
</nav>
```

If you look at Figure 3-8, you can see how the page has several links to the sections of the page, and in Figure 3-9, you can see what happens when the user clicks the second link and is taken directly to that section of the page. You can see the full code for this example in the download code for this chapter (`ch03_eg06.html`).

FIGURE 3-8

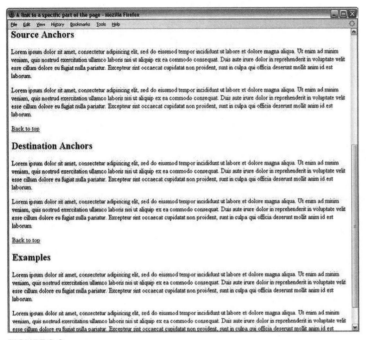

FIGURE 3-9

If people want to link to a specific part of this web page from a different website (such as the section on Source Anchors), they would add the full URL for the page, followed by the pound or hash sign and then the value of the `id` attribute, as follows:

```
http://www.example.com/HTML/links.html#SourceAnchors
```

> **WARNING** *The value of a* `name` *or* `id` *attribute should be unique within the page, and source anchors should use the same combination of uppercase and lowercase characters as used in the destination anchors.*

The <a> Element's Other Attributes

The <a> element can carry several attributes that you have not yet met. Although these attributes are not used as much as those covered up to this point, for completeness it is worth quickly looking at them.

The <a> element supports all the universal attributes and the following attributes:

```
accesskey href hreflang rel style tabindex target type
```

The accesskey Attribute

The `accesskey` attribute creates a keyboard shortcut that you can use to activate a link. For example, if you gave the `accesskey` attribute a value of `t`, when the user presses the T key along with either the Alt key or the Ctrl key (depending on the operating system), the link activates.

In some browsers, when a link activates, the browser immediately follows the link. In some other browsers, the link is just highlighted, and the user must press the Enter (or Return) key for the link to be followed.

The `accesskey` attribute should be specified on the source anchor. For example, if you want to follow a link to the top of the page when the user presses the T key on his keyboard (with either Alt or Ctrl), you use the `accesskey` attribute like so:

```
<a id="bottom" accesskey="t">Back to top</a>
```

The key is case-insensitive. You see more about the `accesskey` attribute (and some examples) when you look at forms in Chapter 6.

The hreflang Attribute

The `hreflang` attribute indicates which language the page you are linking to is written in. It's designed to be used when linking to a page in a different language from the current document, and the value of this attribute is a two-letter language code, for example:

```
<a href="http://www.amazon.co.jp/" hreflang="JA">Amazon Japan</a>
```

Appendix G, "Language Codes," lists the language codes that are possible values for this attribute.

The rel Attribute

Use the `rel` attribute on the source anchor to indicate the relationship between the current document and the resource specified by the `href` attribute. The major browsers do not currently make any use of this attribute; although, automated applications could be written to use this information. For example, the following link uses the `rel` attribute to indicate that its destination is a glossary of terms used in the document:

```
For more information, please read the  <a href="#glossary"
rel="glossary">glossary</a>.
```

Table 3-1 shows possible values of the `rel` attribute.

TABLE 3-1: Possible Values of the rel Attribute

VALUE	DESCRIPTION
toc (or contents)	A document that is a table of contents for the current document
Index	A document that is an index for the current document

continues

TABLE 3-1 *(continued)*

VALUE	DESCRIPTION
Glossary	A document containing a glossary of terms that relate to the current document
Copyright	A document containing the copyright statement for the current document
Start	A document that is the first in a series of ordered documents, of which this is one document
Next	A document that is next in a series of ordered documents, of which this is one document
prev (or previous)	A document that is previous in a series of ordered documents, of which this is one document
Help	A document that helps users understand or navigate the page and/or site
Chapter	A document that acts as a chapter within a collection of documents
Section	A document that acts as a section in a collection of documents
Subsection	A document that acts as a subsection in a collection of documents
Appendix	A document that acts as an appendix in a collection of documents
Author	Identifies a URL that serves as the homepage of the author of an article
Me	Indicates the author of the current document is also the owner of the associated URL

The tabindex Attribute

To understand the tabindex attribute, you need to know what it means for an element to gain *focus*. Any element that a user can interact with can gain focus. If users click the Tab key on their keyboard when a page loads, the browser moves focus between the parts of the page that users can interact with. The parts of the page that can gain focus include links and some parts of forms (such as the boxes that enable you to enter text). When a link receives focus, and the users press Enter on the keyboard, the link activates.

You can see focus working on the Google website; if you repeatedly press the Tab key, you should see focus pass between links on the page. After it has passed across each link in turn, it goes to the box where you enter search terms, across the site's buttons, and usually ends up back where you typed in the URL. Then it cycles around the same elements again as you keep pressing Tab.

The tabindex attribute enables you to specify the order in which, when the Tab key is pressed, the links (or form controls) obtain focus. So, when the user clicks the Tab key, you may want the focus to land on the key items on the page that the user might want to interact with (skipping some of the less-used features).

The value of the `tabindex` attribute is a number between 0 and 32767. A link whose `tabindex` attribute has a value of 1 receives focus before a link with a `tabindex` value of 20. (And if a value of 0 is used, the links appear in the order in which they appear in the document.) Chapter 6 shows some examples of the `tabindex` being used with forms.

Elements without a `tabindex` receive focus *after* an element with a `tabindex` set in the order they appear in the document.

The target Attribute

By default, when you use the `<a>` element to create a link, the document you are linking to opens in the same browser window. If you want the link to open in a new browser window, you can use the `target` attribute with a value of `_blank`.

```
<a href="Page2.html" target="_blank">Page 2</a>
```

The title Attribute

As mentioned at the start of the chapter, you should use a `title` attribute on any links that contain images. It can also help provide additional information to visitors in the form of a visual text tooltip in most browsers or an auditory clue in voice browsers for the visually impaired. Figure 3-2 near the beginning of this chapter showed you what the `title` attribute looks like in Firefox when a user hovers over the link.

The type Attribute

The `type` attribute specifies the MIME type of the link. MIME types can be compared to file extensions but are more universally accepted across different operating systems. For example, an HTML page would have the MIME type `text/html`, whereas a JPEG image would have the MIME type `img/jpeg`. (Appendix H, "MIME Media Types," includes a list of common MIME types.)

Following is an example of the type attribute used to indicate that the document the link points to is an HTML document:

```
<a href="index.html" type="text/html">Index</a>
```

Theoretically, the browser could use the information in the type attribute to either display it differently or indicate to the user what the format of the destination is; although none use it at present.

TRY IT OUT   **Creating Links within Pages**

Now it's your turn to try making a long page with links between different parts of the page. In this example, you create the menu for your Example Café. So open the `menu.html` page from the sample application in your text editor or authoring tool:

1. The page should look like this when you begin:

```
<!doctype html>
<html>

<head>
```

```
      <title>Example Cafe - community cafe in Newquay, Cornwall, UK</title>
   </head>
   <body>
      <h1>EXAMPLE CAFE</h1>
      <p>Welcome to Example cafe. We will be developing this site throughout
         the book.</p>

      <h2>Menu</h2>
      <p>The menu will go here.</p>
   </body>
   </html>
```

2. After the <h1> element, replace the first paragraph with a <nav> element containing the links for the navigation, just like the ones you created in the previous Try It Out for the contact.html page. The only difference this time is that the CONTACT option is a link, but the MENU option is not a link.

```
   <nav>
     <a href="index.html">HOME</a>
     MENU
     <a href="recipes.html">RECIPES</a>
     <a href="opening.html">OPENING</a>
     <a href="contact.html">CONTACT</a>
   </nav>
```

3. Below this, add the headings for the different courses on offer.

4. Each heading should have a destination anchor so that you can link directly to that part of the page, and the value of the id attribute describes that section. The main heading also needs a destination anchor because it will be used for Back to Top links. Remember that destination anchors require some content, so these anchors contain the text for the heading:

```
<h1 id="top">Example Cafe Menu</h1>
<h2 id="starters">Starters</h2>
<h2 id="mains">Main Courses</h2>
<h2 id="desserts">Desserts</h2>
```

5. Under the heading for the Example Café Menu, add links to the destination anchors for each course. These should go inside a <p> element:

```
<p><a href="#starters">Starters</a> | <a href="#mains">Main Courses</a> | <a
href="#desserts">Desserts</a></p>
```

6. At the bottom of the page, you have a note that states any items marked with a letter v are suitable for vegetarians. Links next to vegetarian items point to this note, so it needs to have a destination anchor:

```
<p><small><a id="vegetarian">Items marked with a (v) are suitable
for vegetarians.</a></small></p>
```

7. You can just add in the items on the menu in a bulleted list. The vegetarian items have a link down to the description of vegetarian dishes. Don't forget to add the Back to Top links under each list.

```
<h2><a id="starters">Starters</a></h2>
<ul>
  <li>Chestnut and Mushroom Goujons (<a href="#vegetarian">v</a>)</li>
```

```
    <li>Goat Cheese Salad  (<a href="#vegetarian">v</a>)</li>
    <li>Honey Soy Chicken Kebabs</li>
    <li>Seafood Salad</li>
</ul>
<p><small><a href="#top">Back to top</a></small></p>

<h2><a id="mains">Main courses</a></h2>
<ul>
    <li>Spinach and Ricotta Roulade (<a href="#vegetarian">v</a>)</li>
    <li>Beef Tournados with Mustard and Dill Sauce</li>
    <li>Roast Chicken Salad</li>
    <li>Icelandic Cod with Parsley Sauce</li>
    <li>Mushroom Wellington (<a href="#vegetarian">v</a>)</li>
</ul>
<p><small><a href="#top">Back to top</a></small></p>

<h2><a id="desserts">Desserts</a></h2>
<ul>
    <li>Lemon Sorbet (<a href="#vegetarian">v</a>)</li>
    <li>Chocolate Mud Pie (<a href="#vegetarian">v</a>)</li>
    <li>Pecan Pie (<a href="#vegetarian">v</a>)</li>
    <li>Selection of Fine Cheeses from Around the World</li>
</ul>
<p><small><a href="#top">Back to top</a></small></p>
```

8. Save your example as `menu.html` and take a look at it in your browser. You should end up with something that looks like Figure 3-10.

FIGURE 3-10

How It Works

The `id` attributes act as a signpost, denoting specific areas on the page. Web browsers will scroll the page to those specific areas as needed in the act of either clicking an in-page link or navigating to a page that includes a hash value in the url (like `menu.html#starters`.)

ADVANCED E-MAIL LINKS

As you saw at the beginning of the chapter, you can make a link open up the user's default e-mail editor and automatically address an e-mail to you—or any other e-mail address you give. This is done like so:

```
<a href="mailto:info@example.org">info@example.org</a>
```

You can also specify some other parts of the message, such as the subject, body, and e-mail addresses that should be *cc*'d or *bcc*'d on the message.

To control other properties of the e-mail, place a question mark after the e-mail address and then use name/value pairs to specify the additional properties. The name and the value are separated by an equal sign.

For example, to make the subject line of the e-mail "Inquiry," you would add the `subject` property name followed by an equals sign (`=`), and then the term `Inquiry`, like so:

```
<a href="mailto:info@example.org?subject=Inquiry">
```

You can specify more than one property by separating the name/value pairs with an ampersand (`&`). Here you can see that the subject and a CC address have been added in:

```
<a href="mailto:info@example.org?subject=HTML&cc=sales@example.org"></a>
```

Table 3-2 includes a full list of properties you can add.

TABLE 3-2: Available E-mail Link Properties

PROPERTY	PURPOSE
Subject	Adds a subject line to the e-mail; you can add this to encourage the user to use a subject line that makes it easier to recognize where the mail has come from.
Body	Adds a message into the body of the e-mail; although you should be aware that users could alter this message.

cc	Sends a carbon copy of the mail to the *cc*'d address; the value must be a valid e-mail address. If you want to provide multiple addresses, you simply repeat the property, separating it from the previous one with an ampersand.
bcc	Secretly sends a carbon copy of the mail to the *bcc*'d address without any recipient seeing any other recipients; the value must be a valid e-mail address. If you want to provide multiple addresses, simply repeat the property, separating it from the previous one with an ampersand.

If you want to add a space between any of the words in the subject line, you should add `%20` between the words instead of the space. If you want to create a line break in the body of the message, you should add `%0D%0A` (where 0 is a zero, not a capital O).

While an e-mail link can create an e-mail with all these properties set, it does not stop users from editing the values in their e-mail program.

It is common practice to add only the e-mail address in e-mail links. If you want to add subject lines or message bodies, you may decide to use an e-mail form instead, like the one you see in Chapter 6. (Although these do require a script on the server that can process the form and send the e-mail.)

SUMMARY

In this chapter you learned about links. Links enable users to jump between pages and even between parts of an individual page (so that they don't have to scroll to find the place they need).

You have seen that you can use the `<a>` element to create source anchors, which are what most people think of when you mention links on the web. The content of the source anchor is what users can click—and this should usually be an informative, concise description of what users see when they click the link (rather than text such as "click here"), or it can be an image (as you see in Chapter 4, "Images, Audio, and Video").

You also learned how to link to specific parts of a page using the `id` attribute.

Along the way, you learned more about URLs, in particular the difference between an absolute URL, as with those that appear in the address bar of your browser, and relative URLs, which describe where a resource is in relation to the document containing it. Learning the different ways in which relative URLs can be used can also be helpful as you head to the next chapter and learn about adding images and other objects into your documents.

EXERCISES

1. Look at the Try It Out example where you created a menu, and create a new page that links directly to each course on the menu. Then add a link to the main Wrox website (www.wrox.com). The page should look something like Figure 3-11.

FIGURE 3-11

2. Go back to the pages in the sample application to ensure that you have updated the navigation for each page.

The answers to all the exercises are in Appendix A, "Answers to Exercises."

▶ **WHAT YOU LEARNED IN THIS CHAPTER**

TOPIC	KEY TAKEAWAY
Links	Links are the connective tissue of the web and are the single defining feature that originally sets the web apart from other media.
URLs	URLs are the addressing system of the web. In the context of building web pages there are two kinds of links: absolute URLs and relative URLs. Absolute URLs represent the complete web address. Relative URLs are pieced together using the existing site context as a starting point.
In-page links	Using the `id` attribute and the URL hash you can link to specific points on a web page.

Images, Audio, and Video

WHAT YOU WILL LEARN IN THIS CHAPTER

➤ How to add images to a web page

➤ What the different types of image formats are and where to use each

➤ How to add audio and video to your web pages

➤ All about the `<video>`, `<audio>`, and `<object>` elements

WROX.COM CODE DOWNLOADS FOR THIS CHAPTER

The wrox.com code downloads for this chapter are found at www.wrox.com/remtitle .cgi?isbn=9781118340189 on the Download Code tab. The code is in the Chapter 4 download and individually named according to the names throughout the chapter.

In this chapter, you learn how to add images, animations, audio, and video to your site. This should start to breathe some life into the pages you've been creating so far.

You start by learning how to add images to your documents using the `<img>` element. You also learn how to make an image a link, and even how to divide an image into sections so that different parts of the image link to different pages, which is known as an *image map*. Then you look at some of the main image formats used on the web (JPEG, GIF, and PNG) and learn which image format to use for different types of images. This is important because it can greatly affect the speed with which your web pages load. (And as you know, slow websites frustrate users.)

After you finish with images, you look at how to add some more multimedia content to your site in the form of Flash and the new HTML5 `<video>` and `<audio>` elements. In doing so, you also meet the `<object>`, `<param>`, and `<embed>` elements. By the end of the chapter, your pages should look more exciting.

ADDING IMAGES USING THE <IMG> ELEMENT

Images are added to a site using the <img> element, which must carry at least two attributes: the src attribute, indicating the source of the image, and an alt attribute, which provides a description of the image.

For example, the following line would add the image called logo.gif into the page (in this case, the image lives in a directory called images). You can find this code at ch04_eg01.html.

```
<img src="logo.gif" alt="Wrox logo" >
```

Figure 4-1 shows what this image looks like in a browser.

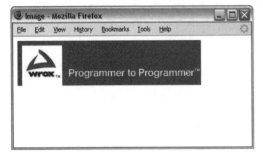

FIGURE 4-1

In addition to carrying all the universal attributes, the <img> element can carry the following attributes:

```
src alt height width ismap usemap
```

The src Attribute

The src attribute tells the browser where to find the image. The value is a URL and, just like the links you met in the previous chapter, the URL can be an absolute URL or a relative URL.

```
<img src="logo.gif" >
```

Generally speaking, images for your site should always reside on your server or on another server you control. It is not good practice to link to images on other sites because if the owner of the other site decides to move that image, your users will no longer see the image.

Because the images are on your server, rather than being an absolute URL, the value is more likely to be a relative URL that uses the same shorthand notations you met in the previous chapter when relative URLs were introduced.

Most web page authors create a separate directory (or folder) in the website for images. If you have a large site, you might even create different folders for different types of images. For example, you might keep any images used in the design of the interface (such as logos or buttons) separate from images used in the content of the site.

The alt Attribute

The `alt` attribute should appear on every `<img>` element and its value should be a text description of the image.

```
<img src="logo.gif" alt="Wrox logo" >
```

Often referred to as *alt text*, the value of this attribute should describe the image because of the following:

➤ If the browser cannot display the image, this text alternative is shown instead.

➤ Web users with visual impairments often use software called a *screen reader* to read a page to them, in which case the alt text describes the image they cannot see.

➤ Although search engines are clever, they cannot yet describe or index the contents of an image; therefore, providing a text alternative helps search engines index your pages and helps visitors find your site.

Sometimes images do not convey any information and are used only to enhance the layout of the page. (For example, you might have an image that is just a decorative element and does not add any information to the page.) In such a case, the `alt` attribute should still be used but given no value, as follows:

```
<img src="stripy_page_divider.gif" alt="" >
```

As you'll see in Chapter 7, "Cascading Style Sheets," decorative elements are usually best handled with CSS. Still, there are situations in which decorative images are unavoidable. In those exceptions this is the correct pattern.

The height and width Attributes

The `height` and `width` attributes specify the height and width of the image, and the values for these attributes are almost always shown in pixels. (If you are not familiar with the concept of pixels, look at this in the section "Choosing the Right Image Format.")

```
<img src="logo.gif" alt="Wrox Logo" height="120" width="180" >
```

Technically, the values of these attributes can be a percentage of the browser screen. Or if the image is inside an element that takes up only part of the page, known as a *containing element*, it would be a percentage of the containing element. If you do use a percentage, the number will be followed by a percent sign, but for most web pages this is rare, and showing an image at any size other than the size at which it was created can result in a distorted or fuzzy image.

Specifying the size of the image is considered good practice, so you should try to use these attributes on any image that you put on your pages.

It also helps a page to load faster and more smoothly because the browser knows how much space to allocate to the image, and it can correctly render the rest of the page while the image is still loading.

Also, if for some reason the image doesn't load, you'll also have the browser draw an empty box of the given height and width with the alt text within it.

Although you can tell the browser to display images smaller or larger than they actually are (by telling the browser that the width and height are different from what they actually are), you should avoid doing this because your image will not be as clear. Rather, you should aim to create versions of images at the same size that you will use them on your web pages. Programs such as Photoshop, Photoshop Elements, Paint Shop Pro, or GIMP can help you do this.

It is also important not to use images bigger than they are shown on screen (for example, you should not use an image 800 pixels by 800 pixels if you will show it only at 100 pixels by 100 pixels on the screen) because the smaller an image, the smaller the size of the file (in terms of kilobytes). And the smaller the file size, the quicker the image loads in the browser. Also, for putting your site on the web for others to see, it might save you money because you are often charged in relation to the total size of all the files you send to the people who visit your site.

Likewise, it is important not to show images larger than they actually are. If you have a small image (say, 100 pixels by 100 pixels) and try to display it much larger (say, 300 pixels by 300 pixels) it will appear grainy (as shown in Figure 4-2).

Although it is not a good idea to do so, if you just specify the height or width attribute and leave out the other one, your browser will show the image to scale. Assume for a moment that you have an image that is 200 pixels wide by 100 pixels tall. If you just specify the width of the image as 200 pixels, it would try to show the image at its correct size: 200 pixels wide by 100 pixels tall. However, if you said that the image was 100 pixels wide and did not specify the height, the browser would try to make the image 50 pixels tall. Because it is 50 percent the width of the original image, it would display the image at 50 percent of its height. In other words, it maintains the *aspect ratio* of an image (its width divided by its height).

You could even distort images by providing a different width in relation to height.

Figure 4-2 shows an image at its actual size (top: 130 pixels by 130 pixels); the image magnified (middle: the width attribute is given a value of 160 pixels); and the image distorted (bottom: the width attribute is given a value of 80 pixels and the height attribute a value of 150 pixels).

Here is the code for this example (ch04_eg02.html):

```
<p>Fixed size: width 130 height 130</p>
<img src="images/apple.jpg" alt="Photo of red apple" width="130"
    height="130" >
<p>Enlarged: width 160 (no height specified)</p>
<img src="images/apple.jpg" alt="Photo of red apple" width="160" >
<p>Stretched: width 80 height 150</p>
<img src="images/apple.jpg" alt="Photo of red apple" width="80" height="150" >
```

Adding Images to a Web Page

Now that you've learned the basics of how images work, it's time to roll up your sleeves and use one in a web page.

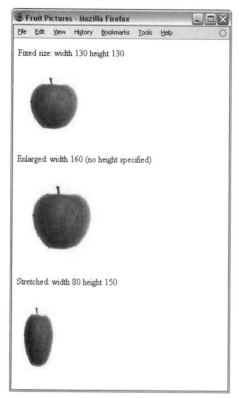

FIGURE 4-2

Adding Images to a Document

In this example, you add some images to the café example. You add a logo for the café and also a picture of the special brunch offer. So, open the homepage in a text editor or web page authoring tool and follow these steps:

1. Replace the <h1> heading with the logo.gif in the images folder of the sample application.

```
<img src="images/logo.gif" alt="example café logo" width="194" height="80" >
```

2. The src attribute indicates the URL for the image. The URLs in this example are all relative URLs pointing to an images directory inside the folder that the example page is in.

3. Add the following after the navigation and before the <h2> element:

```
<img src="images/scrambled_eggs.jpg" width="622" height="370" alt="Photo of
    scrambled eggs on an English muffin" >
```

4. The width and height attributes tell the browser how big the image should be displayed.

5. Save the file and open it in your browser. You should end up with something that resembles Figure 4-3.

FIGURE 4-3

How It Works

The image element is referred to as a *replaced element*. Replaced elements are HTML elements whose content is provided by another resource, in this case the `scrambled_eggs.jpg` referenced in the `src` attribute. This image has intrinsic properties including height, width, and aspect ratio. This is why you can supply only one or none of the dimensions, and the browser can figure out the rest by itself, according the image the proper space within the layout. Here you provide those dimensions to help the browser render more efficiently, but it's not necessary because of the nature of replaced elements. You'll learn about three more replaced elements throughout this chapter: `<video>`, `<audio>`, and `<object>`.

USING IMAGES AS LINKS

It's easy to turn an image into a link. Rather than putting text between the opening `<a>` tag and the closing `</a>` tag (as you saw in the previous chapter), you simply place an image inside these tags. Images are often used to create graphical buttons or links to other pages, as follows (`ch04_eg03.html`):

```
<a href="http://www.wrox.com">
  <img src="images/wrox_logo.gif" alt="Wrox logo"
    width="338" height ="79" >
</a>
```

You can see what this looks like in Figure 4-4. This screenshot was purposely taken in IE to show you how IE draws a blue (appears grey in the black-and-white image) border around any image inside an `<a>` element. There is nothing in the HTML specification that says a border should be drawn around images that are links, and none of the other browsers do this.

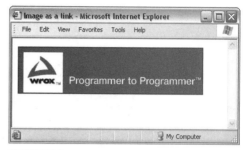

This border doesn't look nice, so you could use CSS to indicate that any `<img>` elements inside an `<a>` element should have no border. (You learn how to do this in Chapter 7.)

FIGURE 4-4

CHOOSING THE RIGHT IMAGE FORMAT

Images and graphics can bring your site to life, but you must learn how to prepare images for the web. Otherwise, they can significantly increase the time it takes for a page to load.

When writing sites on your desktop or laptop computer, you may not realize how long a page will take to load; files that are sitting on your computer will load a lot faster than they would if they were on the Internet. Therefore, choosing the right image format and saving your images correctly can ensure that your site will not load unnecessarily slow—and this should result in happier visitors.

> **NOTE** *For practice purposes, you can download images from other sites by right-clicking the image (or Ctrl+Clicking) and selecting either the* download image to disk *or* save image as *options. Remember, however, that images are subject to copyright, and you could land yourself in legal trouble if you use other people's images on your site.*

Most static images on the web are classified as *bitmapped images*. Bitmapped images divide a picture into a grid of *pixels* and specify the color of each pixel individually. If you look closely at your computer screen, you might see the pixels that make up the screen. There are several different bitmap formats; common ones include JPEG, GIF, TIFF, PNG, and the rather confusingly named bitmap or BMP.

Figure 4-5 shows a bitmap image with one section modified so that you can see how pixels make up the image.

The number of pixels in every square inch of the image is referred to as the *resolution* of the image. It is normal to save images that will be used on the web at a resolution of 72 pixels per inch because this corresponds with the number of pixels in a square inch on your computer screen. By contrast, images used in print are usually supplied to printers at 300 dots per inch.

The more pixels or dots per inch an image contains, the larger the size (in KB) of the file, and the larger the file, the longer it takes to transfer over the web. Therefore, any images that you use on the web should be saved at a resolution of 72 dots per inch.

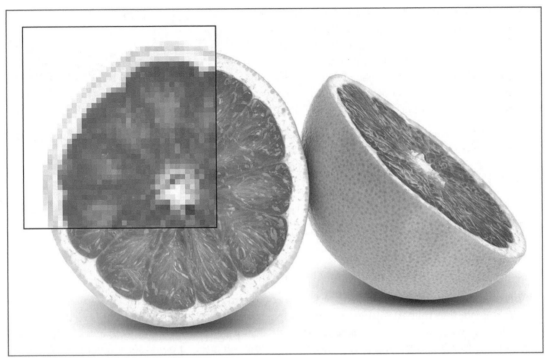

FIGURE 4-5

> **NOTE** *Although you can easily save an image that is 300 dots per inch at 72 pixels per inch for the web, you cannot simply increase an image from 72 pixels per inch to 300 dots per inch because you do not know what color the 228 missing pixels should be. If you just try to increase the resolution of the image, it often looks grainy. Therefore, when you have a high-resolution 300-dots-per-inch picture, you should make a copy of it for use on the web and keep the original version separately.*

Browsers tend to support three common bitmap graphics formats, and most graphics programs save images in these formats:

➤ **GIF:** Graphics Interchange Format (pronounced either "gif" or "jif")

➤ **JPEG:** Joint Photographic Experts Group (pronounced "jay-peg")

➤ **PNG:** Portable Network Graphics (pronounced "pee-en-gee" or "ping")

Now take a quick look at each of these because understanding how the format works helps you choose how to save an image.

GIF Images

Graphics Interchange Format (GIF) images are created using a palette of up to 256 colors, and each pixel of the image is one of these 256 colors. Every different GIF image can have a different palette of 256 colors selected from a range of more than 16 million colors. The program that saves the image also selects the palette that best represents the images.

The GIF file stores the palette of colors in a *lookup table*, and each pixel references the color information in the lookup table rather than each pixel specifying its own color information. The advantage of this technique is that if many pixels use the same colors, the image does not repeat the same color information, and the result is a smaller file size. This makes GIF images more suited to graphics (where there are often areas of the same color—known as a *flat color*) and less suited to photographs (where there are often many more different colors).

This way to store images is an *indexed color format*. Figure 4-6 shows a GIF file created in Adobe Photoshop. You can see the color palette for this image represented in the set of squares halfway down the image on the right.

FIGURE 4-6

If a GIF contains fewer than 16 colors (in which case it can be referred to as a 4-bit GIF), the image will be less than one-half the file size of a GIF using 256 colors (an 8-bit GIF). Therefore, if you create an image that uses fewer than 16 colors, it is worth checking whether your program automatically saves your image as a 4-bit GIF because this results in a smaller file that's quicker to download than an 8-bit GIF.

> **NOTE** *Even if your image looks as though it features just two colors, say a black-and-white line drawing, it may use many more colors. For example, if you have a line drawing where the edges have been smoothed out by the graphics program (a process known as anti-aliasing), your image contains more than two colors because the edges use a variety of other colors to make them look smooth.*

If the GIF needs to use more than 256 colors, most graphics programs, when saving GIFs, use a technique called *dithering* to better represent the extra colors. This means that they use two or more colors in adjacent pixels to create an effect of a third color. Dithering has the following two drawbacks:

➤ If you place a flat color next to a dithered color, you see where the change occurs (because the dithered color consists of more than one color).

➤ It can result in some *banding* in colors. For example, when there is a smooth transition between one color and another color (referred to as a *gradient*), many more than 256 shades may be required to show the gradient. Therefore, dithering would be used, but the result might be that the smooth gradient now looks like a series of stripes.

Figure 4-7 illustrates how even a simple gradient, when saved as a GIF, can result in banding because the image contains more than 256 colors. The bottom part of this image zooms into an area of the gradient where you can see that the gradient has vertical lines rather than a smooth transition from black to white.

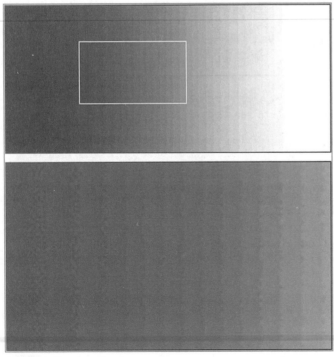

FIGURE 4-7

Because GIFs support only 256 colors and must use dithering to achieve any further colors, they are not suitable for detailed photographs, which tend to contain many more than 256 colors. If you have a photograph, gradient, or any image with similar shades of the same color next to each other, you are often better off using a JPEG, which can support unlimited colors, or sometimes a PNG—both of which you'll learn about shortly.

GIFs do have another handy feature: You can specify one or more colors in a GIF to represent a *transparent background*—in parts of the image that are the specified colors, the background will be allowed to show through.

This technique works best with images that have perfectly straight edges because when you have a curved edge, an image editing program often anti-aliases the edge (use several shades) to make the image look smooth, as shown in Figure 4-8.

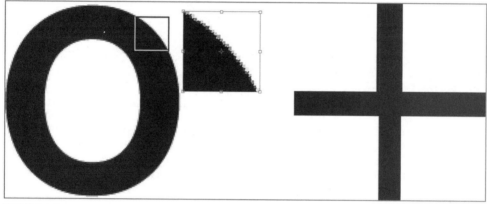

FIGURE 4-8

However, in a transparent GIF each pixel is either on or off, opaque or transparent—there are no degrees of transparency. As a result, if you try to use it with curved corners, the corners may appear pixelated. To help overcome this problem, you should try to make the transparency color as close to the background color as possible. (Or if you use Photoshop, you can use the matte feature.)

Figure 4-9 shows how a pixelated effect is created when a GIF is not created on a suitable background. Notice the lighter pixels around the corners in particular.

To make GIF files smaller, you can compress them using a technique called *LZW compression*, which scans rows of the image looking for consecutive pixels that share the same color. When it comes across pixels that are the same color, it indicates that from this point, *x* number of pixels should be written using the same color.

FIGURE 4-9

LZW compression is known as a *lossless compression* technique because no data is lost; therefore, there is no loss of quality. This is contrasted with *lossy compression* techniques where some of the data is discarded during compression and therefore cannot be recovered from the compressed file.

Animated GIFs

GIF images can store more than one frame (or copy of the image) within a file, allowing the GIF to rotate between the versions/frames and create a simple animation. It works in a similar way to a flip-book animation, where the drawing on each page of the book changes slightly from the previous one so that when a user flips the pages it looks as if the images are moving.

This works well if your animated image contains large areas of flat color because when the image is compressed after the initial frame has been recorded, only the pixels that have changed need to be stored with each subsequent frame. It is far less suitable, however, for photographic images because many more of the pixels change, resulting in a large image.

> **NOTE** *It is also worth mentioning that attention-grabbing animated GIFs are often frowned upon by professional web designers, who tend to use them only sparingly.*

Figure 4-10 shows you an animated GIF created in Adobe Image Ready. The window on the right shows you that there are three dots on separate layers of the image. The window at the bottom shows you that in frame 1 of the animation, only the bottom dot shows; in frame two, the bottom and middle dots show; and in the third frame, all three dots show. Under each frame of the animation you can see how long each frame should appear. (In each case it is 1 second.)

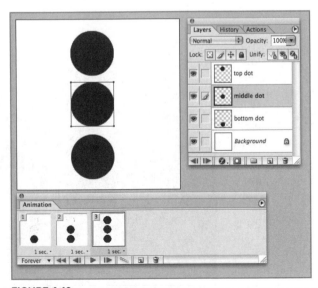

FIGURE 4-10

JPEG Images

The JPEG image format was developed as a standard for storing and compressing images such as photographs that use a wide range of colors. When you save a JPEG, you can usually specify by how much, if at all, you want to compress the image—which depends upon the image quality you want. The process to compress a JPEG involves discarding color data that people would not normally perceive, such as small color changes. However, because the image format discards this data when the image is compressed, some of the data is lost, and the original cannot be re-created from a compressed version—hence it is known as *lossy compression*.

The amount of compression you apply will change from image to image, and you can judge how much to compress a JPEG only by looking at it. Hence the size of the file varies depending upon how much you compress the image. When you save the image, you are often asked for a percentage of quality to be used; 100 percent does not compress the picture at all, and for a photo you can often get down to approximately 60–70 percent (but not usually much lower). Some programs use words such as excellent, very good, good, and so on instead of percentages to describe the image quality.

A good image-editing program enables you to compare the original image side by side with the compressed version as you choose how much compression to add. Figure 4-11 shows you how Adobe Photoshop enables you to compare two versions of the image next to each other as you prepare to save the JPEG for the web. On the left, you have the original image, and on the right is the version that it saves for use on the web. Photoshop also provides an estimated download time for the graphic at that size, which can help you estimate how well it will work when it's on the web.

FIGURE 4-11

Because the JPEG format was designed to work with photo-realistic images, it does not work so well with images that have large amounts of flat color or high-contrast hard edges (such as lettering and line drawings). As you increase compression in a JPEG, you may also see banding start to show in colors that are similar.

PNG Images

The Portable Network Graphics format is the most recent format on the block. It was developed in the late 1990s because the company that owns the patent for GIFs (Unisys) decided to charge companies that developed software for creating and viewing GIFs a license fee to use the technology. Although web designers and web surfers are not directly affected by this charge, the companies that make the software they use are.

The PNG format was designed for the same uses as GIF images, but while it was created, the designers decided to solve what they thought were some of the disadvantages with the GIF format. The result is two types of PNG. The 8-bit PNG has the same limitations as an 8-bit GIF—only 256 colors, and when transparency is used each pixel is either on or off. Then there is the enhanced PNG-24, a 24-bit version, which has two major advantages:

➤ The number of colors available for use in an image is not restricted, so any color can be included without losing any data.

➤ A map (like the lookup table that indicates the color of each pixel in GIFs) provides different levels of transparency for every pixel, which allows for softer, anti-aliased edges.

Furthermore, all PNGs tend to compress better than a GIF equivalent. The PNG format was adopted slowly because some older browsers did not fully support the format. Although basic support was offered in early versions of browsers, some of the more advanced features took longer to be implemented. For example, Internet Explorer was unable to deal with transparency correctly until version 7. The story now is much different, with excellent support for PNGs across all the major browsers.

> **NOTE** *Unless you need to support those older browsers (and sometimes even if you do because there are ways to mitigate the issues), PNG is the suggested format for any of the uses described for both the PNG and GIF formats.*

> **NOTE** *There are two PNG-based alternatives to animated gifs: Multiple-image Network Graphics (MNG), (*`http://www.libpng.org/pub/mng/`*) and Animated PNGs (APNG) (*`https://wiki.mozilla.org/APNG_Specification`*). Unfortunately there is almost no support for MNGs, and only Opera 9+ and Firefox 3+ support APNGs.*

Keeping File Sizes Small

You usually want to save the images for your site in the format that best compresses the image and therefore results in a smaller file size. Not only can your pages load faster, but also you can save on the charges to host your site.

Usually one or another format will be the obvious choice for you. The rule of thumb is as follows:

➤ Use JPEGs for photo-realistic pictures with a lot of detail or subtle shade differences you want to preserve.

➤ Use PNGs for images with flat color (rather than textured colors) and hard edges, such as diagrams, text, or logos.

Look at the following images (see Figure 4-12)—one is a photograph of a cat, and the other is a black-and-white cartoon.

FIGURE 4-12

Table 4-1 shows you the file size of each of these saved as an 8-bit PNG and as a JPEG (where the JPEG is saved at 60 percent quality).

TABLE 4-1: Size Comparison across Different Image Formats

IMAGE	JPEG	PNG
Cat	72.1 k	210 k
Cartoon	39.3 k	22.5 k

As you can see, the cartoon has areas of flat, plain color, whereas the photo of the cat uses lots of different shades. Therefore, the cartoon is better suited to the GIF or PNG formats, whereas the photo of the cat with all its shadows is suited better to the JPEG format.

> **NOTE** *Good image editing software is helpful if you use a lot of images on your site. Adobe Photoshop is the most popular software used by professionals; although, it is expensive. There is, however, a limited functionality version called Photoshop Elements that includes many of the common features—including the Save for Web options. Three other popular image-editing programs are Paint Shop Pro (available from Corel at* www.corel.com*) and two free image-editing programs: One is called Gimp (which you can download from* www.gimp.org*); the other is called Paint.net. It's unfortunate that it's available only for Windows, but it offers a good alternative if you're on that platform.*

If you need to include many large, complex photographic images on your site, it's good practice to offer users smaller versions of the images when the pages first load and then add a link to the larger version. These smaller images are often referred to as *thumbnails*, and you usually see them in image galleries or on pages that contain summaries of information (such as the homepages of news sites and pages that list several products, from which you link to a page with more detail and larger images). Figure 4-13 shows you an example of using thumbnails in an image gallery. (The small images at the bottom are smaller in physical size and file size than the counterparts that show at the top.)

FIGURE 4-13

When creating the smaller version, scale the image down in an image-editing program. Do not simply alter the `width` and `height` attributes of the `<img>` element because users still must download the full-sized image even though they see only a smaller version of it. (The full-sized image takes longer to download.) By creating a special thumbnail of any smaller images you use, your pages can load a lot quicker.

> **NOTE** *You may hear of a format called Vector format, which is more popular in illustration and animation software. Flash and SVG employ vector graphics. Vector formats store information in terms of coordinates, between which lines are drawn. Inside these lines a colored fill may be specified. Because they are based on coordinates, it is easy to increase the physical size of the image by increasing the gap between each point that the coordinates are plotted against. SVG has long suffered from issues with browser support, but with support in all major browsers including Internet Explorer 9 and the demands of high-resolution monitors, SVG's time might finally be here. SVG isn't covered in this book, but if you want to know more about it, the WebPlatform SVG topic (*`http://docs.webplatform.org/wiki/svg`*) is a good place to start.*

ADDING FLASH, VIDEO, AND AUDIO TO YOUR WEB PAGES

You spent the first half of the chapter looking at adding images to your web pages, and in the second half of the chapter you look at adding video and audio to your pages. At one point this was relatively straightforward. If you learned just a *little* bit about Adobe Flash, you could easily embed audio and video on your pages, and that media would be available to the vast majority of Internet users.

Unfortunately, for people who make websites, this is no longer the case. With the explosive growth of mobile devices and the lack of support for Flash on iOS (the operating system for Apple products) adding audio and video to pages is a lot more complicated than it used to be.

The following section simplifies the issues as much as possible. The hope is that you can handle the most common scenarios you'll encounter. Reading this chapter won't make you an expert on the different ways video and audio on the Internet work, but you will have the foundation needed to get up and running.

The basic approach these days is to serve video and audio to all modern browsers (the latest versions of Chrome, Firefox, Internet Explorer, and Safari) using the new HTML5 `<video>` element and then use Adobe Flash to serve video to users of Internet Explorer 8 or below. You'll learn how to do this later in this chapter. First, you learn about the most common example of embedding rich media on the web today, using a third-party service such as YouTube. These companies take the business of putting video on the web and make it as simple as possible, providing a simple interface to upload video, hosting services for video content, and easy-to-use embed code. Under the hood, they use the same techniques you'll learn about later in the chapter; they just hide all the complexity from their end users.

Adding YouTube Movies to Your Web Pages

By far, the most common way to host and share video is with Google's YouTube service. Whether you upload your own content or want to share content from another YouTube user, the method to embed the video is the same.

YouTube has made it easy for users to embed the YouTube Player on their pages. This is done simply by copying and pasting a line of code from the YouTube site into any web page; Figure 4-14 shows you where to find this line of code.

FIGURE 4-14

Looking at it you see that it introduces a new element, the `<iframe>`. The `<iframe>` element doesn't, by itself, have anything to do with video. The `<iframe>`, or *inline frame*, is a special element that enables you to embed another web page within a web page using the familiar `src` attribute. By embedding the `<iframe>` from YouTube in a small corner of your site, you can always be sure to get the latest content and code that YouTube offers. All it takes is to paste that small `<iframe>` code snippet anywhere within the body of your page, and you have a world-class video solution.

Here's the code for this example (ch04_eg04.html):

```
<iframe width="420" height="315"
    src="http://www.youtube.com/embed/J---aiyznGQ"
    frameborder="0" allowfullscreen></iframe>
```

If you decide to take advantage of YouTube or another similar service, this simple example is all you need to build off to handle serving video to the widest possible audience with the minimum amount of fuss.

That said, it's not always possible or preferable to host video with a service such as YouTube. In a situation like that it helps to understand how to embed video intelligently. To do this you must learn about two new elements: `<object>` and `<video>`. In addition, to share audio files in the same way you would share `<video>`, you must learn about the `<audio>` element.

Adding Rich Media with the `<audio>` and `<video>` Elements

Any rich media solution for the modern web starts with the new `<audio>` and `<video>` elements, which work similarly, so many of the lessons you learn about one applies to the other. You focus mostly on `<video>` in this section, but you see an example of `<audio>` in action as well.

`<video>` is designed to work just like the `<img>` element you learned about earlier in this chapter. The most basic usage is a `<video>` element with `src`, `height`, and `width` attributes (ch04_eg05.html). As a note, this and the following examples in this section work only in Internet Explorer 9, Chrome, and Safari. You learn why that is in the upcoming section on containers and codecs.

```
<video width="720" height="480" src="central.mp4">
```

In addition to the global attributes, `<video>` supports the following attributes:

```
poster preload autoplay mediagroup loop muted
controls crossorigin
```

With the exception of the `crossorigin` attribute that you learn about when you explore JavaScript and Ajax in Chapter 12, "jQuery: Beyond the Basics," the following section introduces these attributes with simple examples.

Controlling Playback with the preload, autoplay, loop, and muted Attributes

These four attributes set parameters for how the video should behave without user interaction. All these are boolean attributes.

The `preload` attribute indicates that the browser should begin to download the video referenced in the `src` attribute even before the user presses Play. The `preload` attribute is defined in the specification as a "hint." This means browser vendors can decide in certain situations, for example, on a mobile device, to ignore this attribute (ch04_eg06.html).

```
<video width="720" height="480" src="video/central.mp4" preload>
```

The `autoplay` attribute indicates whether the video should automatically play when the page is loaded. Unless you have an extremely well-thought-out reason for doing this, don't. Let your site visitors choose when to play your video (ch04_eg07.html).

```
<video width="720" height="480" src=" video/central.mp4" autoplay>
```

`loop`, as the name implies, indicates that the browser should start the video over when playback is complete (ch04_eg08.html).

```
<video width="720" height="480" src=" video/central.mp4" loop>
```

`muted` indicates whether the video player should play the associated audio track (ch04_eg09.html).

```
<video width="720" height="480" src=" video/central.mp4" muted>
```

Using the poster Attribute to Customize the Initial Frame

The `poster` attribute defines an image used as a placeholder until the video plays. If there is no `poster` attribute defined, the first frame of the video is used as the poster (ch04_eg10.html).

```
<video width="720" height="480" src=" video/central.mp4" poster="central.jpg">
```

Adding Video Playback Controls with the controls Attribute

If you've ever used a stereo with physical knobs and buttons, an MP3 player, the music player on your smartphone, or a video player on your desktop, you're familiar with playback controls. The boolean `controls` attribute indicates whether the browser should include playback controls. Figure 4-15 illustrates two `<video>` elements, one with the `controls` attribute and the other without (ch04_eg11.html).

```
<video width="720" height="480" src=" video/central.mp4" controls>
```

FIGURE 4-15

Adding Audio to Your Web Pages Using the <audio> Element

As you learned, the `<audio>` element works the same way as the `<video>` element. As the following code sample (`ch04_eg12.html`) shows, an `<audio>` element and an `src` attribute are enough to get audio onto your pages.

```
<audio src="audio/pink_noise.mp3">
```

`<audio>` also supports the following attributes that you learned about earlier in the chapter:

```
crossorigin preload autoplay loop muted controls
```

On Containers and Codecs

There are actually two reasons video on the web is complicated these days. The first is limited Flash support on mobile devices. The other is because of the tricky case of containers and codecs. Disputes about containers and codecs are why the examples in this section work only in a subset of modern browsers.

Without going into too much detail, containers can be thought of as file formats designed to hold other stuff (in this case video or audio). Codecs are coding/decoding systems that translate the 1s and 0s of binary data into something you can hear and see. The combination of a container such as MPEG Layer 4 (the `.mp4` files you've seen in the video examples so far in this chapter) and a codec such as h.264 defines the kind of rich media files you see on the web.

This isn't the sort of thing the average web author should worry about. You should just create a great video and share it with the world. Unfortunately, for political, sociological, and business reasons, this isn't the case. It's getting better, and perhaps at some point in the future (maybe by the time you read this) it will be solved. The issue is that, for a long time, there was a divide between two different camps about which container/codec combination would be best for the future of the web. The divide was between Apple and Microsoft standing firmly behind the patent-encumbered h.264 and MPEG4, and Google, Opera, and Mozilla backing free, open, and royalty-free video formats such as WebM or OGG/Theora.

On the audio front, the story was similar with Microsoft and Apple standing behind the ubiquitous MP3 format and Firefox and Opera backing OGG/Vorbis.

In March 2012, after a long stalemate Mozilla backed down and decided to support h.264, but as of this writing that support is still unscheduled.

So, for now, Mozilla's Firefox does support the `<video>` and `<audio>` elements, just not with the most common formats.

The next section shows you how to embed Flash movies. Although Flash isn't nearly as important as it once was, it still comes up and is a key component to cross-browser web video, so you must have a basic understanding of how it works.

Adding Flash Movies to Your Web Pages

Flash started as a way to add animations into web pages but quickly evolved to offer a high level of interactivity and the capability to deal with images, audio, and video. The momentum that Flash enjoyed for many years may have been dulled by Apple's refusal to add support for Flash to iOS, but it still remains a popular way to add audio and video to web pages and is a required technology to provide the broadest possible support for video in all browsers.

Most Flash files are created using the Flash authoring environment, which Adobe charges for. A lot of sites offer tools such as MP3 players, video players, slideshows, and more, all written in Flash, which you can use on your site without purchasing a copy of Flash authoring program. Although creating your own Flash files from scratch is beyond the scope of this book, you see how to include in your HTML pages Flash files that have already been written.

If you work on a project using the Flash authoring tool, your projects will be saved with the .fla file extension. (And they are commonly referred to as FLA files.) But before you can use such a file on the web, you must *export* it in the .swf format. When files have been exported into the .swf format, they go by one of two names, either SWF (sometimes pronounced "swiff") files or *Flash movies*. (Rather confusingly, they can be called Flash movies even if they do not contain any video.)

With the exception of Chrome, which ships with Flash built directly into the browser, the major browsers don't play SWF files by themselves; rather, they rely on a free plug-in called the *Flash Player*. The Flash Player is often pre-installed on computers, but it can also be downloaded from the Adobe.com website.

Now briefly recap what you have learned about Flash because there was quite a lot to take in:

- ➤ You pay for the Flash authoring environment that enables you to create and edit FLA files. These files are saved with the .fla file extension.

- ➤ When you want to use Flash files on the web, you export them to SWF files or Flash movies. These files have the .swf file extension.

- ➤ Except for Chrome, the free Flash Player plug-in needs to be installed for the browser to play the SWF files.

Now look at the code used to add Flash to a page. It uses the `<object>` element and several child `<param>` elements to indicate different characteristics of the movie to the browser (ch04_eg13.html).

```
<object width="550" height="400">
<param name="allowScriptAccess" value="always" />
<param name="allowFullScreen" value="false" />
<param name="movie" value="flash/this-changes-everything.swf" />
<param name="loop" value="false" />
  <embed src="flash/this-changes-everything.swf" loop="false"
  allowScriptAccess="sameDomain"
  allowFullScreen="false" width="550" height="400" />
</object>
```

On the opening `<object>` tag, you can see that the `width` and `height` attributes specify the size of the Flash movie. These behave just like the `width` and `height` attributes on the `<img>` element, indicating how much space this item needs.

Inside the `<object>` element, you can see four `<param>` elements, each of which has a `name` and `value` attribute:

➤ The first indicates that a movie is to be loaded, along with the URL for the movie.

➤ The second indicates whether the player should allow the user to view the movie in full-screen mode.

➤ The third is a special property, which, in this case, is used to ensure that the Flash movie can be played from different websites.

➤ The fourth indicates whether the movie should return to the beginning and start over when playback is completed.

These parameters are specific to this example and do not necessarily apply to all Flash movies. Other parameters may be specific to a version of Flash; for example, the ability to show full-screen Flash movies was introduced in Flash 9, which was released in 2006.

For compatibility reasons, an `<object>` element often contains an `<embed>` element, and this is no exception. You may have noticed that the `<embed>` element does not contain any `<param>` elements; rather, it uses attributes on the opening tag to provide the same information. The first attribute is an `src` attribute—just like the one used on the `<img>` element indicating where to find the Flash file. This is followed by a `type` attribute indicating that the file is a Flash movie. The next three attributes match the `<param>` elements you just met. The last two, `width` and `height`, specify the size of the Flash movie.

For several years, the standard is to use JavaScript to include Flash movies in pages, rather than the `<object>` and `<embed>` elements. This is true of both the web development community and the Adobe authoring environment.

When adopting this technique, you create the page using a `<div>` element to hold the Flash movie, and you should use CSS to make sure that the `<div>` element is the same width and height as the SWF file you want to include. (You learn how to set the size of a `<div>` element in Chapter 7.) This `<div>` element should also have an `id` attribute to uniquely identify that element.

Inside that `<div>` element you can use text and images that will be shown to users who do not have Flash installed.

A JavaScript is then added to the page; this script checks whether the browser has Flash Player installed. If it is installed, the JavaScript replaces the content of the specified element `<div>` with the SWF file.

The JavaScript checks not only that the user has Flash Player installed but also that it is the required version. As you might have guessed, over the years there have been several versions of Flash, and the latest versions have new and improved features. But not everyone has the latest version of the plug-in, and if a browser does not have the minimum version required to play the SWF file, the JavaScript will not attempt to load the Flash, leaving behind the content of the `<div>` element.

The most popular script for this is called SWFObject, which you can download from `http://code.google.com/p/swfobject/`. You do not need any experience with JavaScript to use this technique.

Now look at an example; load exactly the same Flash movie that you saw in the previous example, but this time use SWFObject (version 2.2) to include it in the page (ch04_eg14.html):

```
<!DOCTYPE html>
<html >
  <head>
  <meta charset="utf-8">
    <title>Adding a flash movie with SWF Object</title>
  </head>
  <body>

    <div id="flash_movie">This element can contain content
    that search engines can index, and which is helpful to
    those who do not have Flash installed.</div>
    <script type="text/javascript" src="swfobject.js"></script>
    <script type="text/javascript">
        swfobject.embedSWF("flash/this-changes-everything.swf",
          "flash_movie", "550", "400", "8.0.0");
    </script>
  </body>
</html>
```

Although the code is quite different, in the browser this example looks just like the previous one. The only difference is the title of the page indicates that it has been written using SWFObject.

In this example, the <div> element carries an id attribute with a value of "flash_movie". (The id attribute is used to uniquely identify an element within a web page.) It is this element that will be replaced with the Flash movie if the user has the appropriate version of Flash Player installed.

At the bottom of the page, you can see two <script> elements. The first includes a separate JavaScript file whose location is specified using the src attribute (just as the src attribute on an image specifies where the image can be found):

```
<script type="text/javascript" src="swfobject.js"></script>
```

As you can see, it loads a file called swfobject.js, and it is this file that does most of the work. You do not need to understand the content of this file or how it works, but if you are curious, you can have a look at it in a text editor or any HTML editing tool. The second <script> element calls the script included in the previous line and tells it five things so that it can do its job:

```
<script type="text/javascript">
    swfobject.embedSWF("flash/this-changes-everything.swf", "flash_movie",
      "550", "400", "8.0.0");
  </script>
```

The five parameters passed in are shown in bold:

➤ "flash/this-changes-everything.swf" is the location of the Flash movie to be played.

➤ "flash_movie" is the value of the id attribute of the element that is to be replaced.

➤ "550" indicates the width of the movie in pixels.

➤ "400" indicates the height of the movie in pixels.

➤ "8.0.0" is the minimum version of Flash Player required to play the movie.

This approach has two additional advantages not mentioned yet:

➤ It is considered to be better for search engines. Because search engines cannot index Flash content well, they see the HTML content that would have been replaced.

➤ It is also considered good for accessibility purposes, because if users have disabled Flash, there is alternative content for them.

As already mentioned, there are several places where you can download Flash movies that you can use on your own sites (without necessarily using the Flash authoring tool). A good starting place is http://ActiveDen.net/, which features works by many authors.

Now that you know about both the <video> element and Flash, it's time to put them together to create your own cross-browser video solution.

Cross-Browser Video—Using Video for Everybody

Although you should definitely look to leverage third-party services if you're interested in serving video to the largest possible audience with the smallest amount of effort, there are times when you want to serve video on your own terms.

The simplest approach to this is with a clever markup pattern called Video for Everybody (http://camendesign.com/code/video_for_everybody). Video for Everybody defines a pattern that uses the HTML5 <video> element wrapped around a Flash movie in a way that automatically chooses the appropriate method to play the video. The basic pattern is a <video> element with one or more <source> child elements. <source> elements work like the src attribute you're familiar with—directing the browser to a video resource. The only difference is that they can be combined with other <source> elements to give the browser multiple options for playback content. After the <source> elements, a Flash video player or Flash movie is included to handle the fallback for older versions of Internet Explorer.

An example would look like the following code (ch04_eg15.html). This version has three <source> elements, one containing an MP4 (for Internet Explorer 9+, Safari, Chrome, and Mobile Safari), webm (a higher quality option available to Firefox and Opera), and ogv (an option available for older versions of Firefox). It then falls back to a Flash movie for older versions of Internet Explorer.

```
<video width="720" height="480" controls>
  <source src="video/central.mp4"  type="video/mp4" />
  <source src="video/central.webm"  type="video/webm" />
  <source src="video/central.ogv"  type="video/ogg" />
  <object width="720" height="480"
    type="application/x-shockwave-flash"
    data="video/central.swf">
    <param name="movie" value="video/central.swf" />
  </object>
</video>
<p> <strong>Download Video:</strong>
 <a href="video/central.mp4">"MP4"</a>
<a href="video/central.ogv">"Ogg"</a>
</p>
```

It takes some effort to encode video in more than one format, and having four copies of a video adds significantly to the amount of storage needed for a site's video assets. For these reasons and the simplicity of the code needed, it's much easier at this time to use a third-party service. These services will take care of the different browsers and encoding and hosting the various formats. That said, if you need to host you own video, this is the pattern to use.

Cross-browser audio can be handled in a similar manner to the Video for Everybody pattern. The following code sample (ch04_eg16.html) shows an <audio> element with two separate child <source> elements pointing to an MP3 (Chrome, Internet Explorer 9+, Safari) and an OGG/Vorbis file (Firefox, Opera). In addition, a simple Flash-based MP3 player called Dewplayer is used to provide a fallback for Internet Explorer 8 and below. To use Dewplayer, you need to pass the MP3 filename as a query parameter and Dewplayer takes care of the rest, serving audio in pretty much any browser that matters.

```
<audio controls>
  <source src="audio/pink_noise.mp3"  type="audio/mp3" >
  <source src="audio/pink_noise.ogg"  type="audio/ogg" >
    <object data="flash/dewplayer.swf?mp3=audio/pink_noise.mp3"
      width="200" height="20" id="dewplayer">
      <param name="wmode" value="transparent">
      <param name="movie"
        value="flash/dewplayer.swf?mp3=audio/pink_noise.mp3">
    </object>
</audio>
```

Video Size

When showing any video, you need to be aware of the physical size at which you are showing the video. It might be nice to show the video as large as possible, but the larger the video, the larger the file size, and big files can be an issue for a couple of reasons:

➤ The smaller the file, the faster it downloads. Users are less likely to watch videos that take a long time to download, or keep pausing when the viewer tries to watch them.

➤ The bigger the file, the more bandwidth you use. (*Bandwidth* is the total size of files sent to visitors to your site.) Because companies that host websites often charge for bandwidth, you could end up with large bills if your video is popular. This is another reason why many people host their videos on sites such as YouTube—not only is it easy to upload video content and put it on your page, but it is also cheaper.

So there is always a balancing act between having a video big enough to show people what you want them to see and having one not so big that it will not play smoothly on the average broadband connection.

If you have a long video, you might also want to consider splitting it into sections. By doing this you are less likely to pay for viewers to download an entire video that they may not watch to the end.

A Closer Look at the <object> and <param> Elements

Now that you have seen several examples of how to add rich media to your web pages, this chapter finishes with a closer look at the <object> and <param> elements in the same way previous chapters covered the syntax of other elements.

The `<object>` element can carry all the universal attributes and the following attributes:

```
data height width
tabindex usemap
```

Take a look at each of these, although the ones you most commonly use are the `classid` attribute, the `type` attribute, and the `id` attributes (discussed in Chapter 1, "Structuring Documents for the Web").

The data Attribute

If the object has a file to process or play, the `data` attribute specifies the URL for that file. For example, here is a URL to an MP3:

```
data="http://www.example.com/mp3s/newsong.mp3"
```

This is similar to the `src` attribute used on the `<img>` element, and the value can be a relative URL.

The height and width Attributes

The `height` and `width` attributes specify the height and width of an object. The values should be in pixels or a percentage of the containing element. They are treated just like `height` and `width` attributes of the `<img>` element. The use of these attributes should make the page load faster because the browser can lay out the rest of the page without completely loading the object.

The tabindex Attribute

The `tabindex` attribute indicates the tab index of the object within a page. Tabbing order is discussed in Chapter 5, "Tables."

The usemap Attribute

The `usemap` attribute indicates that the object is an image map containing defined areas that are hyperlinks. Its value is the map file used with the object. It can be a complete URL to an external file or a reference to the value of an inline `<map>` element's `name` attribute.

The <param> Element

The `<param>` element is used to pass parameters to an object. The kinds of parameters an object requires depend upon what the object does; for example, if an object has to load a Flash MP3 player into the page, you will probably need to specify where the MP3 file can be found. Alternatively, if you add a video to a page, your object might allow you to tell it whether to automatically play the video when the page loads or whether to wait for the user to press a Play button for it to start.

In addition to the universal attributes and basic events, the `<param>` element can carry the following attributes:

```
name  value
```

The `name` and `value` attributes act as a name/value pair (rather like attributes themselves). The `name` attribute provides a name for the parameter you pass to the application, whereas `value` gives the value of the parameter.

Here are a couple of examples taken from a QuickTime movie. The first parameter indicates the source of the file loaded to play, whereas the second indicates that the movie should start playing automatically as it loads (without the user having to start it):

```
<param name="src" value="movieTrailer.mov" >
<param name="autoplay" value="true" >
```

If you work with a Java applet, you could use the `name` and `value` attributes to pass values into a method.

SUMMARY

In this chapter, you learned how to make your pages look more exciting by adding images and other multimedia objects.

Images can add life to a page, but they can also increase the time it takes to load a page. Therefore, it pays to save any images you want to show on the web in JPEG, GIF, or PNG formats, which compress well (creating smaller files) while retaining quality.

The GIF and PNG formats are the formats of choice for images with flat colors, whereas JPEGs are better for photographic images and graphics with gradients of the same color.

When looking at images, you also learned how to make image links, and how to create an image map, which divides an image into separate parts that you can click.

Then, you saw how to add video and audio to your site. You learned that the easiest way to do this is to leverage a third-party service such as YouTube.

You also learned about Flash and how to combine `<video>` with Flash to serve video to a wide audience using the Video for Everybody pattern.

Now you should be well equipped to add images and rich media to your pages to make them look appealing and attract more visitors.

EXERCISES

1. Add the images of icons that represent a diary, a camera, and a newspaper to the following example. All the images are provided in the `images` folder in the download code for Chapter 4.

```
<h1>Icons</h1>
<p>Here is an icon used to represent a diary.</p>
<img src="images/diary.gif" alt="Diary" width="150" height="120" >

<p>Here is an icon used to represent a picture.</p>
Camera image goes here
```

```
<p>Here is an icon used to represent a news item.</p>
Newspaper image goes here
```

Your finished page should resemble Figure 4-16.

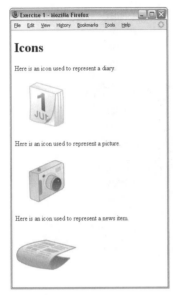

FIGURE 4-16

2. Look at the images shown in Figures 4-17 and 4-18 to decide whether you are more likely to get smaller file sizes and better quality images if you save them as PNGs or JPEGs.

FIGURE 4-17

FIGURE 4-18

3. Go through the files for the sample application and replace the main heading with the logo on each page. On every page except for the homepage, make sure that the image links back to the `index.html` page.

The answers to all the exercises are in Appendix A, "Answers to Exercises."

▶ **WHAT YOU LEARNED IN THIS CHAPTER**

TOPIC	KEY TAKEAWAY
The `<img>` element	The `img` element is a replaced element that enables you to insert image files directly into your pages.
File formats	Use JPGs for photographs and PNGs for images with a limited number of colors.
The `<audio>` and `<video>` elements	Insert audio and video files into your pages with these replaced elements.
Flash	Flash is a proprietary technology from Adobe that enables you to embed animations and rich media in older browsers.

5

Tables

WHAT YOU WILL LEARN IN THIS CHAPTER

➤ What are tables and how are they used in HTML

➤ Basic table elements and attributes

➤ How to create accessible tables

WROX.COM CODE DOWNLOADS FOR THIS CHAPTER

You can find the wrox.com code downloads for this chapter at `www.wrox.com/remtitle .cgi?isbn=9781118340189` on the Download Code tab. The code is in the Chapter 5 download and individually named according to the names throughout the chapter.

Tables display information in rows and columns; they are commonly used to display all manner of data that fits in a grid such as train schedules, television listings, financial reports, and sports results. In this chapter, you learn when to use tables and the markup that you need to create them.

To begin this chapter, you look at some examples of tables and then quickly move to the basic elements used to create them. Having learned the basics, you can then learn some of the more advanced features of tables such as adding captions and headings and achieving more complicated table layouts. The chapter ends with a discussion of accessibility issues that relate to tables, because you must understand how a screen reader would read the contents of a table for users with visual impairments.

INTRODUCING TABLES

To work with tables, you need to start thinking in *grids*, so start by looking at some examples of how popular websites use tables.

Figure 5-1 shows the NFL website, which has the standings for each team in a table. You can see a list of teams on the left, and for each team there are columns providing different stats, including number of games won, lost, or tied.

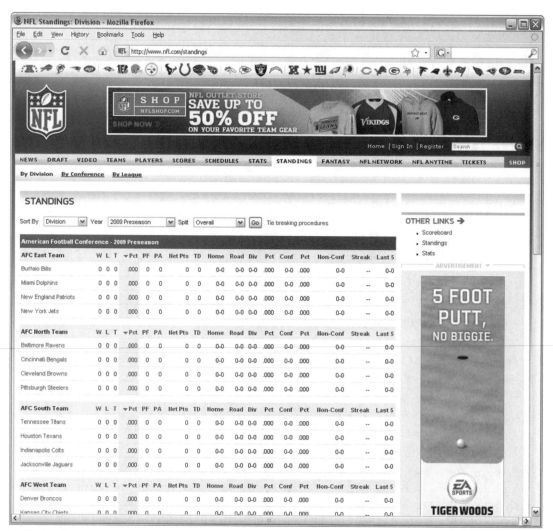

FIGURE 5-1

Figure 5-2 shows the Bloomberg website, which displays major stock markets. In this case, there are tables for different regions around the world. (You can see North and Latin America as the first region, followed by Europe, Africa, and the Middle East.) Each table contains the major indexes trading in that region down the left side, followed by columns that show the current value, fluctuations in values, and date/time of the stats.

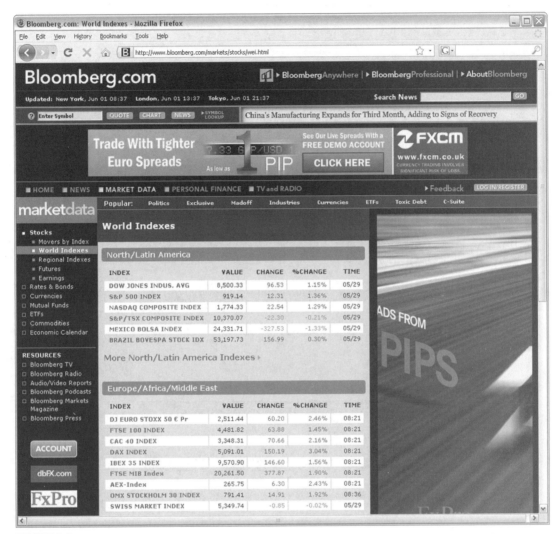

FIGURE 5-2

Figure 5-3 shows the website for the Heathrow Express, a train between Central London and London's Heathrow Airport. The tables on this page show the times that the trains run.

In Figure 5-4, you can see *The New York Times* website. On this page, the tables provide television listings.

These examples give you a better idea of what a table is and when you might want to use one. Not every website that displays stock market data or television listings should use a table—rather you consider using a table when you need to display information that sits well in a grid of rows and columns. If you look at a web page and want to know whether that page uses a table to control how the data is laid out, you can always look at the source for that page and look for the elements you read about in this chapter.

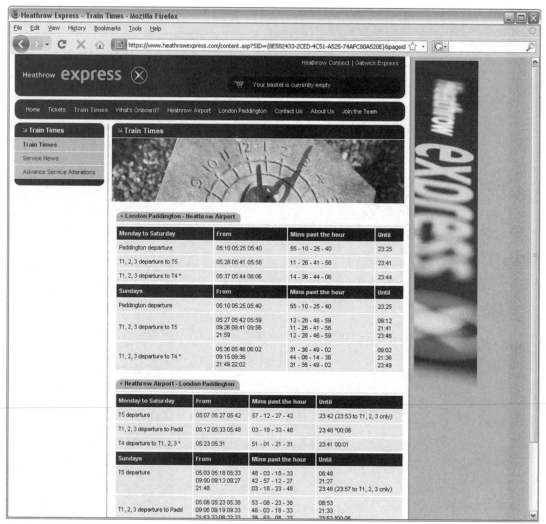

FIGURE 5-3

You can think of a table as being similar to a spreadsheet because it is made up of rows and columns, as shown in Figure 5-5.

Here you can see a grid of rectangles. Each rectangle is known as a *cell*. A *row* consists of a set of cells on the same line from left to right, and a *column* consists of a line of cells going from top to bottom.

Now look at an example of a basic HTML table so that you can see how it is created (see Figure 5-6).

FIGURE 5-4

You create a table in HTML using the `<table>` element. Inside the `<table>` element, the table is written out row by row. A row is contained inside a `<tr>` element, which stands for *table row*. Each cell is then written inside the row element using a `<td>` element, which stands for *table data*.

Following is the code used to create this basic table (`ch05_eg01.html`):

```
<table border="1">
  <tr>
    <td>Row 1, Column 1</td>
    <td>Row 1, Column 2</td>
  </tr>
  <tr>
    <td>Row 2, Column 1</td>
```

```
      <td>Row 2, Column 2</td>
    </tr>
  </table>
```

ROWS

↓ COLUMN 1	↓ COLUMN 2	↓ COLUMN 3	↓ COLUMN 4
ROW 1➡	ROW 1➡	ROW 1➡	ROW 1➡
↓ COLUMN 1	↓ COLUMN 2	↓ COLUMN 3	↓ COLUMN 4
ROW 2➡	ROW 2➡	ROW 2➡	ROW 2➡
↓ COLUMN 1	↓ COLUMN 2	↓ COLUMN 3	↓ COLUMN 4
ROW 3➡	ROW 3➡	ROW 3➡	ROW 3➡
↓ COLUMN 1	↓ COLUMN 2	↓ COLUMN 3	↓ COLUMN 4
ROW 4➡	ROW 4➡	ROW 4➡	ROW 4➡
↓ COLUMN 1	↓ COLUMN 2	↓ COLUMN 3	↓ COLUMN 4
ROW 5➡	ROW 5➡	ROW 5➡	ROW 5➡

COLUMNS

FIGURE 5-5

When writing code for a table in a text editor, you should start each row and cell on a new line and indent table cells inside table rows as shown. If you use a web page authoring tool such as Dreamweaver, it probably automatically indents the code for you.

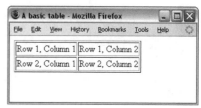

FIGURE 5-6

Many web page authors find it particularly helpful to indent the code for a table because leaving off just one tag in a table can prevent the entire table from displaying properly. Indenting the code makes it easier to keep track of the opening and closing of each element.

Take a look at the same code again. This time, it has not been split onto separate lines or indented, which is much harder to read.

```
<table border="1"><tr><td>Row 1, Column 1</td><td>Row 1, Column 2</td></tr><tr>
<td>Row 2, Column 1</td><td>Row 2, Column 2</td></tr></table>
```

All tables follow this basic structure; although additional elements and attributes enable you to control the presentation of tables. If a row or column should contain a heading, use a `<th>` element in place of the `<td>` element for the cells that contain a heading. By default, most browsers render the content of a `<th>` element in bold text.

> **WARNING** Each cell must be represented by either a `<td>` or a `<th>` element for the table to display correctly, even if there is no data in that cell.

Now take a look at a slightly more complicated table (see Figure 5-7). This time the table includes headings. In this example, the table shows a financial summary for a small company.

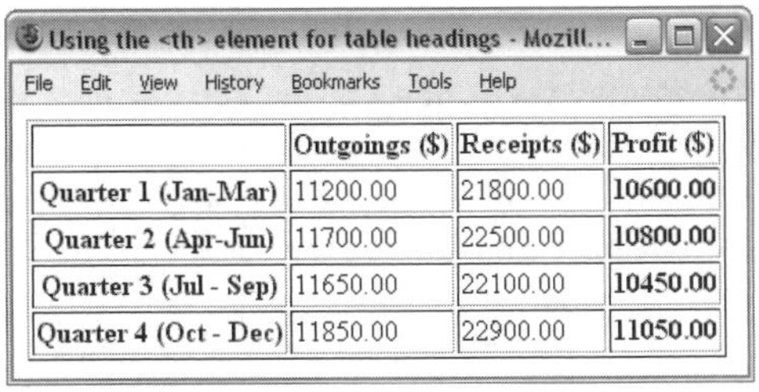

	Outgoings ($)	Receipts ($)	Profit ($)
Quarter 1 (Jan-Mar)	11200.00	21800.00	10600.00
Quarter 2 (Apr-Jun)	11700.00	22500.00	10800.00
Quarter 3 (Jul - Sep)	11650.00	22100.00	10450.00
Quarter 4 (Oct - Dec)	11850.00	22900.00	11050.00

FIGURE 5-7

Here is the code used to create this table (`ch05_eg02.html`):

```
<table border="1">
  <tr>
    <th></th>
    <th>Outgoings ($)</th>
   <th>Receipts ($)</th>
    <th>Profit ($)</th>
  </tr>
  <tr>
    <th>Quarter 1 (Jan-Mar)</th>
    <td>11200.00</td>
    <td>21800.00</td>
    <td><b>10600.00</b></td>
  </tr>
  <tr>
    <th>Quarter 2 (Apr-Jun)</th>
    <td>11700.00</td>
    <td>22500.00</td>
    <td><b>10800.00</b></td>
  </tr>
  <tr>
    <th>Quarter 3 (Jul - Sep)</th>
    <td>11650.00</td>
    <td>22100.00</td>
    <td><b>10450.00</b></td>
  </tr>
```

```
<tr>
  <th>Quarter 4 (Oct - Dec)</th>
  <td>11850.00</td>
  <td>22900.00</td>
  <td><b>11050.00</b></td>
</tr>
</table>
```

The first row is made entirely of headings for outgoings, receipts, and profit. The top-left cell in Figure 5-7 is empty; in the code for the table; you still need an empty <td> element to tell the browser that this cell is empty. (Otherwise it has no way to know that there is an empty cell.)

In each row, the first cell is also a table heading cell (indicated using a <th>), which states which quarter the results are for. Then the remaining three cells of each row contain table data contained inside the <td> elements.

The figures showing the profit (in the right column) are contained within a <b> element, which shows the profit figures in a bold typeface. This demonstrates how any cell can contain all manner of markup. The only constraint on placing markup inside a table is that it must nest within the table cell element (whether a <td> or a <th> element). You cannot have an opening tag for an element inside a table cell and a closing tag outside that cell—or vice versa.

When creating tables, many people do not actually bother with the <th> element and instead use the <td> element for every cell—including headers. You should, however, aim to use the <th> element whenever you have a table heading. This is especially true when you use the scope attribute (which you learn about in the next section, "Basic Table Elements and Attributes"), as it is valid only for <th> elements.

> **NOTE** As you can see from the examples so far in this chapter, tables can take up a lot of space and make a document longer, but clear formatting of tables makes it much easier to see what is going on in your code. No matter how familiar the code looks when you write it, you will be glad that you made good use of structure if you have to come back to it a year later. Most good code editors have the option to format HTML automatically. No matter what code editor you use, you should familiarize yourself with the tools available to automatically format code for you.

BASIC TABLE ELEMENTS AND ATTRIBUTES

Now that you've seen how basic tables work, this section describes the elements in a little more detail, introducing the attributes they can carry. Some of the attributes enable you to create more sophisticated table layouts. Skim through this section quickly; when you know what you can do with the markup, you can always come back again and study the markup closely to see how to achieve what you want.

The <table> Element Creates a Table

The <table> element is the containing element for all tables. It can carry the following attributes:

➤ All the universal attributes

➤ Basic event attributes for scripting

The dir Attribute

The dir attribute is supposed to indicate the direction of text used in the table. Possible values are ltr for left to right text and rtl for right to left (for languages such as Hebrew and Arabic):

```
dir="rtl"
```

If you use the dir attribute with a value of rtl on the <table> element, the cells appear from the right first, and each consecutive cell is placed to the left of that one.

The <tr> Element Contains Table Rows

The <tr> element contains each row in a table. Anything appearing within a <tr> element should appear on the same row.

The <td> and <th> Elements Represent Table Cells

Every cell in a table is represented by either a <td> element for cells containing table data or a <th> element for cells containing table headings.

By default, the contents of a <th> element usually display in a bold font, horizontally aligned in the center of the cell. The content of a <td> element, meanwhile, usually displays left-aligned and not in bold (unless otherwise indicated by CSS or another element).

The <td> and <th> elements can both carry the same set of attributes, and the attribute applies only to that one cell carrying it. Any effects these attributes have override settings for the table as a whole or any containing element (such as a row).

In addition to the universal attributes and the basic event attributes, the <td> and <th> elements can also carry the following attributes:

```
colspan headers
  rowspan
```

<th> elements can also carry the scope attribute.

The colspan Attribute

Use the colspan attribute when a cell should span across more than one column. The value of the attribute specifies how many columns of the table a cell spans across. (See the section "Spanning Columns Using the colspan Attribute.")

```
colspan="2"
```

The headers Attribute

The `headers` attribute indicates which headers correspond to that cell. The value of the attribute is a space-separated list of the header cells' `id` attribute values:

```
headers="income q1"
```

The main purpose of this attribute is to support voice browsers. When a table is read to you, it can be hard to keep track of which row and column you are on; therefore, the `header` attribute reminds users which row and column the current cell's data belongs to.

The rowspan Attribute

The `rowspan` attribute specifies the number of rows of the table a cell spans across, the value of the attribute being the number of rows the cell stretches across. (See the example in the section "Spanning Rows Using the rowspan Attribute.")

```
rowspan="2"
```

The scope Attribute

You can use the `scope` attribute to indicate which cells the current header provides a label or header information for. You can use it instead of the `headers` attribute in basic tables, but it does not have much support.

```
scope="range"
```

Table 5-1 shows the possible values of the attribute.

TABLE 5-1: Possible Values for the scope Attribute

VALUE	PURPOSE
row	Cell contains header information for that row.
col	Cell contains header information for that column.
rowgroup	Cell contains header information for that rowgroup (a group of cells in a row created using the `<thead>`, `<tbody>`, or `<tfoot>` elements).
colgroup	Cell contains header information for that colgroup (a group of columns created using the `<col>` or `<colgroup>` element, both of which are discussed in the section "Grouping Sections of a Table").

Creating a Basic Table

Now that you've learned the basic elements and attributes of tables, you can create a table displaying information concerning the hours of operation of the Example Café.

An Opening Hours Table

In this example, you create a table that shows the opening hours of the Example Café website you have been working on throughout the book. The table looks like the one shown in Figure 5-8.

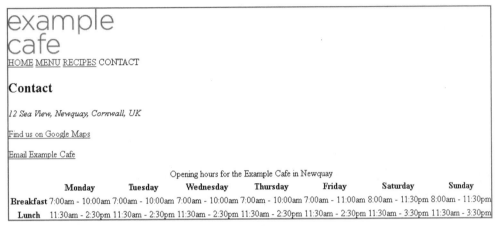

FIGURE 5-8

1. Open the `contact.html` file in your text or HTML editor and add a table to show serving hours beneath the e-mail link.

2. The table is contained within the `<table>` element, and its content is then written out a row at a time. The table has three rows and eight columns.

Starting with the top row, you have eight table heading elements. The first `<th>` element is empty because the top-left corner cell of the table is empty. The next seven elements contain the days of the week.

In the second row of the table, the first cell acts as a heading for that row, indicating the meal (breakfast). The remaining cells show what times these meals are served. The third row follows the same format as the second row but shows times for lunch.

```
<table>
  <tr>
    <th></th>
    <th>Monday</th>
    <th>Tuesday</th>
    <th>Wednesday</th>
    <th>Thursday</th>
    <th>Friday</th>
    <th>Saturday</th>
    <th>Sunday</th>
  </tr>
  <tr>
    <th>Breakfast</th>
    <td>7:00am - 10:00am</td>
    <td>7:00am - 10:00am</td>
```

```
      <td>7:00am - 10:00am</td>
      <td>7:00am - 10:00am</td>
      <td>7:00am - 11:00am</td>
      <td>8:00am - 11:30pm</td>
      <td>8:00am - 11:30pm</td>
    </tr>
    <tr>
      <th>Lunch</th>
      <td>11:30am - 2:30pm</td>
      <td>11:30am - 2:30pm</td>
      <td>11:30am - 2:30pm</td>
      <td>11:30am - 2:30pm</td>
      <td>11:30am - 2:30pm</td>
      <td>11:30am - 3:30pm</td>
      <td>11:30am - 3:30pm</td>
    </tr>
</table>
```

As long as you accept that each row is written out in turn, you should have no problem creating quite complex tables.

3. Save your file as `contact.html`.

How It Works

As you learned, the `<table>` element represents a grid of information. The `<table>` element serves as a container for the rows of data, represented by the `<tr>` elements. The `<tr>` elements, in turn, contain the tabular data contained in the `<td>` elements. Following this simple pattern you can build out large grids of data or information easily.

ADDING A CAPTION TO A TABLE

Whether your table shows results for a scientific experiment, values of stocks in a particular market, or what is on television tonight, each table should have a caption so that visitors to your site know what the table is for.

Even if the surrounding text describes the content of the table, it is good practice to give the table a formal caption using the `<caption>` element. By default, most browsers display the contents of this element centered above the table, as shown in Figure 5-10 in the next section.

The `<caption>` element appears directly after the opening `<table>` tag; it should come before the first row:

```
<table>
  <caption> Opening hours for the Example Cafe</caption>
  <tr>
```

By using a `<caption>` element, rather than just describing the purpose of the table in a previ-ous or subsequent paragraph, you are directly associating the content of the table with this description—and this association can be used by screen readers and by applications that process web pages (such as search engines).

GROUPING SECTIONS OF A TABLE

In this section, you look at some techniques that enable you to group together cells, rows, and columns of a table, and learn the advantages that doing this can bring. In particular, you see how to do the following:

➤ Use the `rowspan` and `colspan` attributes to make cells stretch over more than one row or column.

➤ Split a table into three sections: a head, body, and foot.

➤ Group columns using the `<colgroup>` element.

➤ Share attributes between unrelated columns using the `<col>` element.

Spanning Columns Using the colspan Attribute

As you saw when looking at the `<td>` and `<th>` elements, both can carry an attribute called `colspan` that enables the table cell to span (or stretch) across more than one column.

Figure 5-9 shows a table that has three rows; the cells of the table are shaded to illustrate the `colspan` attribute in action:

➤ The first row has three columns of equal width, and there is one cell for each column.

➤ In the second row, the first cell is the width of one column, but the second cell spans the width of two columns.

➤ The third row has just one cell that spans all three columns.

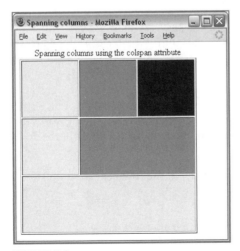

FIGURE 5-9

Now take a look at the code for this example to see how the `colspan` attribute is used. This example also uses CSS classes (which you'll learn how to define in Chapter 7, "Cascading Style Sheets") to illustrate a point visually (`ch05_eg03.html`):

```
<table>
<caption>Spanning columns using the colspan attribute</caption>
  <tr>
    <td class="one"> </td>
    <td class="two"> </td>
    <td class="three"> </td>
  </tr>
  <tr>
    <td class="one"> </td>
    <td colspan="2" class="two"> </td>
  </tr>
  <tr>
    <td colspan="3" class="one"> </td>
  </tr>
</table>
```

In the first row, you can see that there are three `<td>` elements, one for each cell.

In the second row, there are only two `<td>` elements, and the second of these elements carries a `colspan` attribute. The value of the `colspan` attribute indicates how many columns the cell should stretch across. In this case, the second cell spans two columns; therefore, it has a value of 2.

In the final row, there is just one `<td>` element, and this time the `colspan` attribute has a value of 3, which indicates that it should take up three columns.

As mentioned at the start of this chapter, when dealing with tables you must think in terms of grids. This grid is three cells wide and three rows tall, so the middle row could not have two equal-sized cells. (Because they would not fit in the grid—you cannot have a cell spanning 1.5 columns.)

An example of where the `colspan` attribute might be useful is in creating a timetable or schedule where the day is divided into hours—some slots lasting 1 hour, others lasting 2 to 3 hours.

You might also have noticed the use of the nonbreaking space character (` `) in the cells, which is included so that the cell has some content; without content for a table cell, some browsers cannot display the background color.

Spanning Rows Using the rowspan Attribute

The `rowspan` attribute does much the same thing as the `colspan` attribute, but it works in the opposite direction: It enables cells to stretch vertically across cells. You can see the effect of the `rowspan` attribute in Figure 5-10.

When you use a `rowspan` attribute, the corresponding cell in the row beneath it must be left out (`ch05_eg04.html`):

```
<table>
<caption>Spanning rows using the rowspan attribute</caption>
  <tr>
    <td class="one"> </td>
    <td class="two"> </td>
```

```
        <td rowspan="3" class="three"> </td>
      </tr>
      <tr>
        <td class="one"> </td>
        <td rowspan="2" class="two"> </td>
      </tr>
      <tr>
        <td class="one"> </td>
      </tr></table>
```

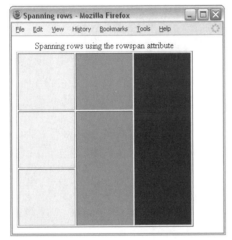

FIGURE 5-10

Splitting Up Tables Using a Head, Body, and Foot

There are occasions in which you may want to distinguish between the body of a table (where most of the data is held) and the headings or maybe even the footers. For example, think of a bank statement: You may have a table where the header contains column headings, the body contains a list of transactions, and the footer contains the balance in the account.

If the table is too long to show on a screen, the header and footer might remain in view all the time, whereas the body of the table gains a scrollbar. Similarly, when printing a long table that spreads over more than one page, you might want the browser to print the head and foot of a table on each page. Unfortunately, the main browsers do not yet support these ideas, although there are options to implement this using CSS or JavaScript. However, if you add these elements to your tables, you can use CSS to attach different styles to the contents of the `<thead>`, `<tbody>`, and `<tfoot>` elements. It can also help those who use aural browsers, which read pages to users.

The three elements for separating the head, body, and foot of a table follow:

➤ `<thead>` to create a separate table header

➤ `<tbody>` to indicate the main body of the table

➤ `<tfoot>` to create a separate table footer

A table may also contain several <table> elements to indicate different "pages," or groups of data.

Here you can see an example of a table that makes use of these elements (ch05_eg05.html):

```
<table>
  <thead>
    <tr>
      <th>Transaction date</th>
      <th>Payment type and details</th>
      <th>Paid out</th>
      <th>Paid in</th>
      <th>Balance</th>
    </tr>
  </thead>
  <tfoot>
    <tr>
      <td></td>
      <td></td>
      <td>$1970.27</td>
      <td>$2450.00</td>
      <td>$8940.88</td>
    </tr>
  </tfoot>
  <tbody>
    <tr>
      <td>12 Jun 12</td>
      <td>Amazon.com</td>
      <td>$49.99</td>
      <td></td>
      <td>$8411.16</td>
    </tr>
    <tr>
      <td>13 Jun 12</td>
      <td>Total</td>
      <td>$60.00</td>
      <td></td>
      <td>$8351.16</td>
    </tr>
    <tr>
      <td>14 Jun 12</td>
      <td>Whole Foods</td>
      <td>$75.28</td>
      <td></td>
      <td>$8275.88</td>
    </tr>
    <tr>
      <td>14 Jun 12</td>
      <td>Visa Payment</td>
      <td>$350.00</td>
      <td></td>
      <td>$7925.88</td>
    </tr>
    <tr>
      <td>15 Jun 12</td>
      <td>Cheque 122501</td>
      <td></td>
```

```
          <td>$1450.00</td>
          <td>$9375.88</td>
        </tr>
      </tbody>
      <tbody>
        <tr>
          <td>17 Jun 12</td>
          <td>Murco</td>
          <td>$60.00</td>
          <td></td>
          <td>$9315.88</td>
        </tr>
        <tr>
          <td>18 Jun 12</td>
          <td>Wrox Press</td>
          <td></td>
          <td>$1000.00</td>
          <td>$10315.88</td>
        </tr>
        <tr>
          <td>18 Jun 12</td>
          <td>McLellans Bakery</td>
          <td>$25.00</td>
          <td></td>
          <td>$10290.88</td>
        </tr>
        <tr>
          <td>18 Jun 12</td>
          <td>Apple Store</td>
          <td>$1350.00</td>
          <td></td>
          <td>$8940.88</td>
        </tr>
      </tbody>
    </table>
```

Figure 5-11 shows what this example looks like in Firefox, which supports the thead, tbody, and tfoot elements. This example uses CSS to give the header and footer of the table a background shade.

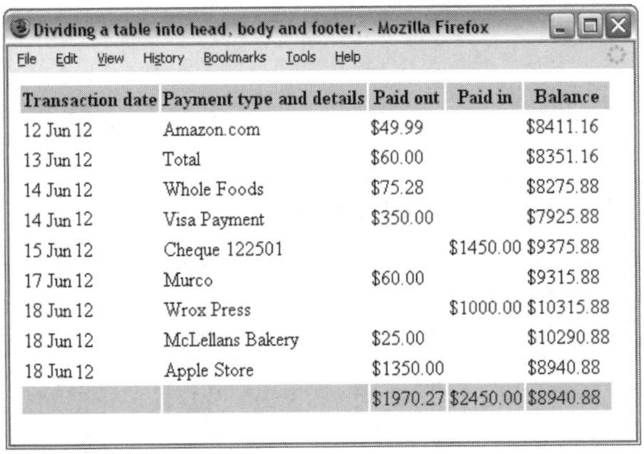

FIGURE 5-11

Grouping Columns Using the `<colgroup>` Element

If two or more columns are related, you can use the `<colgroup>` element to explain that those columns are grouped together.

For example, in the following table, there would be six columns. The first four columns are in the first column group, and the next two columns are in the second column group (ch05_eg06.html):

```
<table>
  <colgroup span="4" class="mainColumns" />
  <colgroup span="2" class="subTotalColumns" />
  <tr>
    <td>1</td>
    <td>2</td>
    <td>3</td>
    <td>4</td>
    <td>5</td>
    <td>6</td>
  </tr>
</table>
```

When the `<colgroup>` element is used, it comes directly after the opening `<table>` tag and carries a span attribute, which indicates how many columns the group contains.

In this example, the class attribute is used to attach CSS rules that tell the browser the width of each column in the group and the background color for each cell. You learn more about CSS in Chapter 7, but it is worth noting that some browsers support only a subset of the CSS rules for this element.

You can see what this example looks like in Figure 5-12. 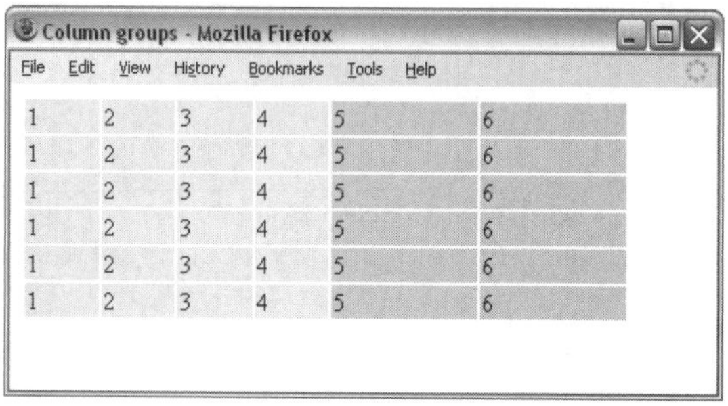

FIGURE 5-12

Columns Sharing Styles Using the `<col>` Element

The `<col>` element was introduced to specify attributes of the columns in a `<colgroup>` (such as width or alignment of cells within that column). Unlike the `<colgroup>` element, the `<col>` element does not imply structural grouping and is therefore more commonly used for presentational purposes.

The `<col>` elements are always empty elements; they do not have any content, although they do carry attributes.

For example, the following table would have six columns, and the first five, although not a group in their own right, could be formatted differently than the last column because it belongs to a separate set (ch05_eg07.html):

```
<table>
  <colgroup span="6">
    <col span="5" class="mainColumns" />
    <col span="1" class="totalColumn" />
  </colgroup>
  <tr>
    <td></td>
    ...
    <td></td>
  </tr>
</table>
```

You can see what this looks like in Figure 5-13.

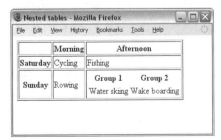

FIGURE 5-13

The attributes that the `<col>` element can carry are the same as for the `<colgroup>` element.

NESTED TABLES

As mentioned earlier in the chapter, you can include markup inside a table cell, as long as the whole element is contained within that cell. This means you can even place another entire table inside a table cell, creating what's referred to as a *nested table*. Figure 5-14 shows you an example of a table that shows a schedule for a weekend of activities.

FIGURE 5-14

In the bottom-right cell of this table is a second table that divides up the attendees into two groups. (ch05_eg08.html):

```
<table>
  <tr>
    <th></th>
    <th>Morning</th>
    <th>Afternoon</th>
  </tr>
  <tr>
    <th>Saturday</th>
    <td>Cycling</td>
    <td>Fishing</td>
  </tr>
  <tr>
    <th>Sunday</th>
    <td>Rowing</td>
    <td>
        <table>
          <tr>
              <th>Group 1</th>
              <th>Group 2</th>
            </tr>
          <tr>
            <td>Water skiing</td>
            <td>Wake boarding</td>
            </tr>
        </table>
      </td>
  </tr>
</table>
```

Now that you've seen how to create a nested table, it is worth noting that they should be used sparingly because they are quite hard for those who rely upon screen readers to follow. You see this in the next section.

ACCESSIBLE TABLES

By their nature, tables can contain a lot of data and provide a helpful visual representation of this information. When looking at a table, it is easy to scan across rows and up and down columns to find a particular value or compare a range of values. If you think back to the examples you saw at the start of the chapter (the NFL sports results or the train timetable), you would not need to read all the content of the table just to find out how your team is doing this season or when a train is leaving.

However, for those who listen to pages on a voice browser or a screen reader, tables can be much harder to understand. For example, if you imagine having a table read to you, it would be much more difficult to compare entries across a row or column because you have to remember what you have heard so far. (It is not as easy to scan back and forth.)

Yet with a little thought or planning, you can make tables a lot easier for all to understand. Here are some things you can do to ensure your tables are easy to understand:

- ➤ Add captions to your tables. The `<caption>` element clearly associates a caption with a table, and the screen reader can read the caption to users before they see the table so that they know what to expect. If the listener knows what to expect, it is easier to understand the information.

- ➤ Always try to use the `<th>` element to indicate a table heading.

- ➤ Always put headings in the first row and the first column.

- ➤ Avoid using nested tables (like the one you saw in the previous section) because this can make it harder for the user of a screen reader to follow.

- ➤ Avoid using `rowspan` and `colspan` attributes, which again make it harder for the user with a screen reader to follow. If you do use them, make sure that you use the `scope` and `headers` attributes, which are discussed shortly.

- ➤ Learn how a voice browser or screen reader would read a table and the order in which the cells are read out; this can help you to understand how to structure your tables for maximum ease of use. (You see examples of this in the following section.)

- ➤ If you use the `scope` and `headers` attributes to clearly indicate which headings apply to which rows and columns, screen readers can help users retrieve headings for a particular cell. If you imagine someone having a table read to him, the screen reader often gives the user an option to hear the headers that are relevant to that cell again (without having to go up to the first row or back to the first cell in the column to hear the heading that corresponds with that cell).

You already saw how to add a caption to a table, so move on to see how tables are read to a user, or how they are *linearized*.

How to Linearize Tables

When a screen reader is used to read a table, it tends to perform *linearization*, which means that the reader starts at the first row and reads the cells in that row from left to right, one by one, before moving on to the next row, and so on until the reader has read each row in the table. Consider the following simple table (ch05_eg09.html):

```
<table border="1">
  <tr>
    <td>Column 1, Row 1</td>
    <td>Column 2 Row 1</td>
  </tr>
  <tr>
    <td>Column 1, Row 2</td>
    <td>Column 2, Row 2</td>
  </tr>
</table>
```

Figure 5-15 shows what this simple table would look like in a browser.

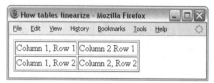

FIGURE 5-15

The order in which the cells in Figure 5-16 would be read is therefore

➤ Column 1 Row 1

➤ Column 2 Row 1

➤ Column 1 Row 2

➤ Column 2 Row 2

This small example is fairly easy to follow. But imagine a larger table: The headings will be read first, followed by a row of data. If the table had several more columns, it would be hard to remember which column you were in. (Even worse, if you use nested tables, it becomes far harder for users to follow where they are because one table cell can contain an entirely new table that often has different numbers of rows or columns.)

Luckily, most screen readers can remind users of the column and row they are currently in, but this works better when the table uses `<th>` elements for headers. And if you build a complex table, you can also enhance this information using the `id`, `scope`, and `headers` attributes, covered in the following section.

Using the id, scope, and headers Attributes

The `id`, `scope`, and `headers` attributes have already been mentioned in this chapter, when you looked at the attributes that the `<td>` and `<th>` elements can carry. Here you look at how they can be used to record the structure of a table better and make it more accessible.

When you make a cell a heading, adding the `scope` attribute to the `<th>` element helps you indicate which cells that element is the heading for. If you give it a value of `row`, you indicate that this element is the header for that row; given the value of `column`, it indicates that it is the header for that column. You can also have values for a `rowgroup` or `columngroup`, as shown in Table 5-2.

TABLE 5-2: Possible Values for the scope Attribute

VALUE	PURPOSE
row	Cell contains header information for that row.
col	Cell contains header information for that column.

VALUE	PURPOSE
rowgroup	Cell contains header information for that rowgroup—a group of cells in a row created using the `<thead>`, `<tbody>`, or `<tfoot>` elements. (There is no corresponding element for columns like the `<colgroup>` element.)
colgroup	Cell contains header information for that colgroup (a group of columns created using the `<col>` or `<colgroup>` element).

The `headers` attribute performs the opposite role to the `scope` attribute because it is used on `<td>` elements to indicate which headers correspond to that cell. The value of the attribute is a space-separated list of the header cells' `id` attribute values, so here you can tell that the headers for this cell would have `id` attributes whose values are `income` and `q1`.

```
headers="income q1"
```

The main purpose of this attribute is to support voice browsers. When a table is read to you, it can be hard to keep track of which row and column you are on; therefore, the `header` attribute reminds users which row and column the current cell's data belongs to.

Creating an Accessible Table

You now have the tools needed to create an accessible table.

TRY IT OUT An Accessible Timetable

In this Try It Out, you create a new page for the Example Café website featuring a timetable for a weekend cookery course, with morning and afternoon sessions over 2 days, as shown in Figure 5-16.

FIGURE 5-16

Although you cannot see it from this screenshot, the table is specifically designed to be accessible for those with visual impairments.

1. Set up the skeleton:

```
<!DOCTYPE html>
<html>
<head>
  <meta charset="utf-8" />
  <title>Ultimate brunch Course</title>
</head>
<body>
</body>
</html>
```

2. The table has three rows and three columns; the first row and the left column contain headings and therefore use `<th>` elements. The remaining table cells use a `<td>` element. While you are adding these elements, add in some content for the table, too:

```
<body>
<table>
  <tr>
    <th></th>
    <th>Saturday</th>
    <th>Sunday</th>
  </tr>
  <tr>
    <th>Morning</th>
    <td>Baking bread: loaves, croissants and muffins.</td>
    <td>Sweet treats: pancakes and waffles.</td>
  </tr>
  <tr>
    <th>Afternoon</th>
    <td>Eggs 4 ways: boiled, scrambled, poached, fried.</td>
    <td>Fry pan specials: Fritters and hash browns.</td>
  </tr>
</table>
</body>
```

3. The next stage is to add `id` attributes to the `<th>` elements that have content, and header attributes to the `<td>` elements to indicate which headers apply to those elements; this approach improves accessibility for visitors who use screen readers. The value of the `header` attributes should correspond to the values of the `id` attributes indicating which headings correspond to each cell:

```
<table>
  <tr>
    <th></th>
    <th id="Saturday" scope="col">Saturday</th>
    <th id="Sunday" scope="col">Sunday</th>
  </tr>
  <tr>
    <th id="Morning scope="row">Morning</th>
    <td headers="Saturday Morning" Baking bread: loaves,
croissants and muffins.</td>
```

```
        <td headers="Sunday Morning" >Eggs 4 ways: boiled,
    scrambled, poached, fried </td>
      </tr>
      <tr>
        <th id="Afternoon" scope="row">Afternoon</th>
        <td headers="Saturday Afternoon">Sweet treats:
    pancakes and waffles.</td>
        <td headers="Sunday Afternoon">Fry pan specials:
    Fritters and hash browns.</td>
      </tr>
    </table>
```

4. Save your file as `course.html`. This example is quite a bit more complex than most tables you will come across. Not many people have gotten into the practice of using the `id` and `header` attributes on `<table>` elements, but it makes tables a lot easier to use for those with visual impairments, in particular on larger tables that have a lot of columns and rows. You won't usually see the `abbr` attribute used on table cells. If you look at the code for other people's websites, you are still more likely to see the use of lots of deprecated attributes rather than these attributes.

How It Works

The combination of the `id` attribute and the headers attribute enables screen readers to associate headers with table data cells. By matching the values of the header attributes with the corresponding values of the associated `id` attributes, there's an explicit connection between the `<td>` and `<th>` elements.

> **NOTE** *Including attributes like these can help set you apart from other coders who have not yet learned to make their tables more accessible. Furthermore, awareness of accessibility issues is required in an increasing number of jobs, so you should learn how to use such attributes.*

SUMMARY

In this chapter, you have seen how tables can be a powerful tool when creating pages. You have seen how all tables are based on a grid pattern and use the four basic elements: `<table>`, which contains each table; `<tr>`, which contains the rows of a table; `<td>`, which contains a cell of table data; and `<th>`, which represents a cell that contains a heading.

You have also seen how you can add headers, footers, and captions to tables. It is particularly helpful to add a `<thead>` and `<tfoot>` element to any table that may be longer than a browser window or sheet of printed paper because these could help a reader relate between the content and the information in headers or footers.

You can now make cells span both columns and rows; although, you should avoid doing this in tables that contain data because it makes them harder for aural browsers to read to a user. You have also seen how to group columns so that you can preserve structure, and so they can share styles and attributes.

Finally, you saw some of the accessibility issues for the use of tables. You must be aware of the process of linearization, which a screen reader performs before reading a table to a user, so that your sites are accessible to users with visual impairments. You also need to know how to provide extra information that indicates the headers for each cell.

In the next chapter, you learn about using forms to collect information from visitors.

EXERCISES

1. Where should the `<caption>` element for a table be placed in the document and, by default, where is it displayed?

2. In what order would the cells in Figure 5-17 be read aloud by a screen reader?

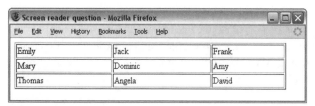

FIGURE 5-17

The answers to all the exercises are in Appendix A, "Answers to Exercises."

▶ **WHAT YOU LEARNED IN THIS CHAPTER**

TOPIC	KEY TAKEAWAY
Tables	Tables allow you to preset structured content in an easy to digest format.
Grouping table section	You should use all the tools available to you to properly group content in tables.
Accessibility	Tables are difficult for screen readers to manage, so using the tools available to enhance table accessibility is the key to ensuring the widest possible audience has access to your content.

Forms

WHAT YOU WILL LEARN IN THIS CHAPTER

- ➤ How to create a form
- ➤ How to use different types of form controls
- ➤ What happens to the data a user enters
- ➤ How to make forms accessible
- ➤ How to structure the content of forms

WROX.COM CODE DOWNLOADS FOR THIS CHAPTER

The wrox.com code downloads for this chapter are found at www.wrox.com/remtitle
.cgi?isbn=9781118340189 on the Download Code tab. The code is in the Chapter 6
download and individually named according to the names throughout the chapter.

Almost every time you want to collect information from a visitor to your site, you need to use
a *form*. Some forms are quite complex, such as those that enable you to book plane tickets or
purchase insurance online. Others are quite simple, such as the search box on the homepage
of Google.

Many online forms bear a strong resemblance to paper forms. On paper, forms are made up of
areas to enter text, boxes to check, options to choose from, and so on. Similarly, on the web you
can create a form by combining *form controls*, such as textboxes (to enter text into), check boxes
(to place a cross in), select boxes and radio buttons (to choose from different options), and so on.
In this chapter, you learn how each of these different types of controls can be combined into a
form to collect all kinds of information from visitors to your site.

> **NOTE** *HTML is used only to present the form to the user; it does not enable you to say what happens with that data after it is collected. To get a better idea of what happens to the data after it is collected from a form, you must look at a book on a server-side language, such as ASP.NET or PHP. (You can find a range of books on these topics at* www.wrox.com.*)*

INTRODUCING FORMS

Start by looking at a couple examples of forms. Figure 6-1 shows the Google homepage, which contains two kinds of form controls:

➤   **Text input:** Where you enter your search term.

➤   **Submit buttons:** Send the form to the server. There are two on this form: You can see the words Google Search written on the first one and I'm Feeling Lucky on the second.

FIGURE 6-1

Now look at a more complicated example. Figure 6-2 shows part of an insurance form, which actually spreads over several pages. This form has many more types of controls:

➤   **Select boxes:** Sometimes referred to as drop-down lists (refer to the top-left of Figure 6-2), to choose from a list of provided answers.

➤   **Radio buttons:** Such as the ones in the top-right corner with Yes or No options. When you have a group of radio buttons, you can pick only one response.

➤ **Check boxes:** Such as the ones at the bottom of the screenshot indicating how you can be contacted (by e-mail, post, or phone). When you have a group of check boxes, you can pick more than one response.

➤ **Text inputs:** To enter a variety of information, or in this case a date of birth and registration number.

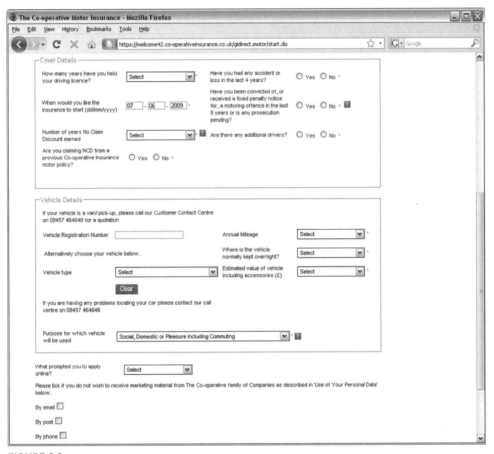

FIGURE 6-2

Several other form controls are not shown in these examples. You'll learn about all these throughout the chapter.

Any form that you create lives inside a `<form>` element, and the form controls (the text input boxes, drop-down boxes, check boxes, a submit button, and so on) live between the opening `<form>` and closing `</form>` tags. A `<form>` element can also contain other HTML markup as you would find in the rest of a page.

After users enter information into a form, they usually must click a *submit button*. (Although the actual text on the button may say something different such as Search, Send, or Proceed—and often pressing the Return key on the keyboard has the same effect as clicking this button.) This indicates that the user has filled out the form, and this usually sends the form data to a web server.

On a traditional web page, after form data arrives at the server, a script or other program processes the data and sends a new web page back to you. The returned page responds to a request you have made or acknowledges an action you have taken. There's a variation on this called Ajax that you'll learn about in Chapter 13, "Checklists," where all these actions take place on the same page. The rest of this chapter focuses on the traditional pattern.

For example, you might want to add the search form shown in Figure 6-3 to your page (ch06_eg01.html).

You can see that this form contains a textbox for users to enter the keywords of what they are searching for, and a submit button with the word Search on it. When users click the Search button, the information is sent to the server, which then processes the data and generates a new page for users telling what pages meet the search criteria (Figure 6-4).

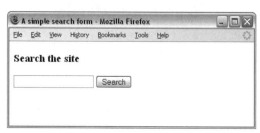

FIGURE 6-3

When a browser sends data to the server, it is transmitted in *name/value* pairs. The *name* corresponds to the name of the form control, and the *value* is what the user has entered (if the user can type an answer) or the value of the option selected (if there is a list of options to choose from).

Each item needs both a name and a value because if you have five textboxes on a form, you need to know which data corresponds to which textbox. The processing application can then process the information from each form control individually.

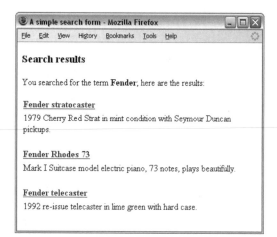

FIGURE 6-4

Here is the code for the simple search form shown in Figure 6-3:

```
<form action=" http://www.example.org/search.aspx " method="get">
   <h3>Search the site</h3>
   <input type="text" name="txtSearchItem">
   <input type="submit" value="Search">
</form>
```

The <form> element carries an attribute called action whose value is the URL of the page on the web server that handles search requests. Meanwhile, the method attribute indicates which of two HTTP methods—get and post—are used in getting the form data to the server. (You learn the difference between these methods in the section "Sending Form Data to the Server.")

To create forms, you first need to look at the <form> element in a little more detail and then go through the different types of form controls to see how they sit inside the <form> element.

CREATING A FORM WITH THE <FORM> ELEMENT

As you have already seen, forms live inside an element called `<form>`. The `<form>` element can also contain other markup, such as paragraphs, headings, and so on; although, it may not contain another `<form>` element.

Providing you keep your `<form>` elements separate from each other (and no `<form>` element contains another `<form>` element), your page may contain as many forms as you like. For example, you might have a login form, a search form, and a form to subscribe to a newsletter, all on the same page. If you do have more than one form on a page, users can send the data from only one form at a time to the server.

In a traditional web page, every `<form>` element should carry at least two attributes:

```
action method
```

A `<form>` element may also carry all the universal attributes and the following attributes:

```
enctype novalidate target autocomplete accept-charset
```

The action Attribute

The `action` attribute indicates what happens to the data when the form is submitted. Usually, the value of the `action` attribute is a page or program on a web server that receives the information.

For example, if you have a login form consisting of a username and password, the details the user enters may get passed to a page written in ASP.NET on the web server called `login.aspx`, in which case the `action` attribute could read as follows:

```
<form action="http://www.example.org/membership/login.aspx">
```

The method Attribute

Form data can be sent to the server in two ways, each corresponding to an *HTTP method*:

➤   The `get` method, which sends data as part of the URL. This is the default.

➤   The `post` method, which hides data in the HTTP headers.

You learn more about these two methods in the section "Sending Form Data to the Server," where you learn what they mean and when you should use each one.

The id Attribute

The `id` attribute enables you to uniquely identify the `<form>` element within a page, just as you can use it to uniquely identify any element on a page.

It is good practice to give every `<form>` element an `id` attribute because many forms make use of style sheets and scripts, which may require the use of the `id` attribute to identify the form.

The value of the `id` attribute should be unique within the document and should also follow the other rules for values of the `id` attribute mentioned in Chapter 1, "Structuring Documents for the Web." Some people start the value of id and name attributes for forms with the characters frm and then use the rest of the value to describe the kind of data the form collects—for example, frmLogin or frmSearch.

The name Attribute

As you have already seen through its use on other elements, the name attribute is the predecessor to the id attribute, and as with the id attribute, the value should be unique to the document.

Generally, you do not need to use this attribute, but when you do use it, you can give it the same value as the id attribute. You often see the value of this attribute begin with the characters frm followed by the purpose of the form (such as frmLogin or frmSearch).

The enctype Attribute

If you use the HTTP post method to send data to the server, you can use the enctype attribute to specify how the browser encodes the data before it sends it to the server. Browsers tend to support three types of encoding:

➤ application/x-www-form-urlencoded, which is the standard method most forms use. Browsers use this because some characters, such as spaces, the plus sign, and some other nonalphanumeric characters, cannot be sent to the web server. Instead, they are replaced by other characters that are used to represent them.

➤ multipart/form-data, which enables the data to be sent in parts, where each consecutive part corresponds to a form control, in the order it appears in the form. It is commonly used when visitors need to upload files (such as photos) to a server. Each part can have an optional content-type header of its own indicating the type of data for that form control.

➤ text/plain, which sends the data to the server as unmodified, plain text.

If this attribute is not used, browsers use the first value. As a result, you are likely to use this attribute only if your form allows users to upload a file (such as an image) to the server, or if they are going to use non-ASCII characters, in which case the enctype attribute should be given the second value:

```
enctype="multipart/form-data"
```

The accept-charset Attribute

Different languages are written in different *character sets* or groups of characters. However, when creating websites, developers do not always build them to understand all different languages. The idea behind the accept-charset attribute is that it specifies a list of character encodings that a user may enter and that the server can then process. Values should be a space-separated or comma-delimited list of character sets (as shown in Appendix E, "Character Encodings").

For example, the following indicates that a server accepts UTF-8 encodings:

```
accept-charset="utf-8"
```

If no accept-charset attribute is set, any character set is valid.

The novalidate Attribute

The `novalidate` attribute is a boolean attribute that indicates whether the form should be validated when submitted. If present, the browser should *not* validate the form prior to submission.

```
<form
  action="http://www.example.org/membership/login.aspx"
  novalidate >
```

This attribute is currently supported in Chrome 6+, Firefox 4+, Opera 10.6+, and Internet Explorer 10+.

The target Attribute

The `target` attribute specifies a named window or keyword for the processing of the form submission.

To process a form in a new window, for example, you could set the `target` of a `<form>` element to `"_blank"`.

```
<form
  action="http://www.example.org/membership/login.aspx"
  target="_blank" >
```

The autocomplete Attribute

This attribute indicates whether or not the browser should auto-fill form values. Setting it to `off` indicates that the browser should not auto-fill any values. The default value is `on`.

```
<form
  action="http://www.example.org/membership/login.aspx"
  autocomplete="off" >
```

This attribute is currently supported in Chrome 17+, Firefox 4+, Safari 5.2+, and Opera 10.6+.

FORM CONTROLS

This section covers the different types of form controls that live inside the `<form>` element to collect data from a visitor to your site, including:

➤ Text input controls, including many new HTML5 inputs

➤ Buttons

➤ Check boxes and radio buttons

➤ Select boxes (sometimes referred to as drop-down menus and list boxes)

➤ File select boxes

➤ New HTML5 form elements such as progress bars and meters

➤ Hidden controls

Text Inputs

Text input boxes are used on many web pages. Possibly the most famous text input box is the one in the middle of the Google homepage that enables you to enter what you want to search for.

On a printed form, the equivalent of a text input is a box or line on which you write a response.

For a long time there were only three types of text input used on forms:

➤ **Single-line text input controls:** Used for items that require only one line of user input. They are created using the `<input>` element and sometimes referred to simply as *textboxes*.

➤ **Password input controls:** These are just like the single-line text input, except they mask the characters a user enters so that the characters cannot be seen on the screen. They tend to show either an asterisk or a dot instead of each character the user types so that someone cannot simply look at the screen to see what a user types in. Password input controls are mainly used for entering passwords on login forms or sensitive details such as credit card numbers. They are also created using the `<input>` element.

➤ **Multiline text input controls:** Used when the user is required to give details that may be longer than a single sentence. Multiline input controls are created with the `<textarea>` element.

This simple view has changed with HTML5. The HTML5 specification added many new types of `<input>` elements that correspond to common types of data on the web. The list of new `<input>` elements follows:

➤ **color:** For choosing a color by using a color wheel.

➤ **date:** For entering a calendar date.

➤ **datetime:** For entering a date and time with the time zone set to Greenwich/Universal Time.

➤ **datetime-local:** For entering a local date and time.

➤ **email:** For entering either a single e-mail address or a list of e-mail addresses. Multiple addresses can be entered in a comma-separated list.

➤ **month:** For entering a year and month.

➤ **number:** For numerical input.

➤ **range:** Unlike the normal text inputs in this list, this input type is generally represented as a slider that enables the user to choose a value from a range of numerical values.

➤ **search:** For entering search terms.

➤ **tel:** For entering telephone numbers.

➤ **time:** For entering a time consisting of hours, minutes, seconds, and fractional seconds.

➤ **url:** For entering website URLs.

➤ **week:** For entering a date that is made up of a year and week number. An example of this format is 2013-W01 for the first week of 2013.

Now take a look at each of these types of input in turn.

Single-Line Text Input Controls

The most basic single-line text input controls are created using an `<input>` element whose `type` attribute has a value of `text`. Here is a basic example of a single-line text input used for a search box (ch06_eg02.html):

```
<form action="http://www.example.org/search.aspx" method="get" name="frmSearch">
  <p>Search:<br>
    <input type="text" name="txtSearch" value="Search for" size="20"
maxlength="64"></p>
    <p><input type="submit" value="Submit"></p>
  </form>
```

Figure 6-5 shows what this form looks like in a browser.

FIGURE 6-5

> **NOTE** Just as some people try to start form names with the characters `frm`, it is also common to start text input names with the characters `txt` to indicate that the form control is a textbox. This can be particularly handy when working with the data on the server to remind you what sort of form control sent that data. However, some programmers prefer not to use this notation, so if you work with someone else on a project, it is worth discussing that person's preference at the start of the work.

Table 6-1 lists the attributes the `<input>` element can carry when its `type` attribute is set to `text` for a text input control. The purpose of the `name` attribute is quite specific on this element and different from its use on other elements you have met already.

TABLE 6-1: Attributes for a Standard Text Input

ATTRIBUTE	PURPOSE
name	This attribute is also required and gives the name part of the name/value pair sent to the server. (Remember: Each control on a form is represented as a name/value pair where the name identifies the form control, and the value is what the user entered.)
value	Provides an initial value for the text input control that the user sees when the form loads. You would use this attribute only if you want something to be written in the text input when the page loads (such as a cue to tell users what they should enter). The new placeholder attribute does a better job at this hinting task. The value attribute is also used for scripting, as you'll learn in Chapter 10, "Learning JavaScript."
size	Enables you to specify the width of the text input control in terms of characters; the search box in the earlier example is 20 characters wide. The size property does not affect how many characters users can enter (in this case they could enter 40 characters even when the size property has a value of 20); it just indicates how many characters wide the input will be. If users enter more characters than the size of the input, they can scroll right and left using the arrow keys to see what they have entered.
maxlength	Enables you to specify the maximum number of characters a user can enter into the textbox. Usually after the maximum number of characters has been entered, even if the user keeps pressing more keys, no new characters will be added.
placeholder	Represents a short hint that displays as the initial value in the input field.

When an <input> element's type attribute has a value of text, it can also carry the following attributes:

➤ All the universal attributes

➤ disabled, readonly, form, autocomplete, autofocus, list, pattern, required, and dirname

Password Input Controls

If you want to collect sensitive data such as passwords and credit card information, you can use the password input. The password input masks the characters the user types on the screen by replacing them with either a dot or an asterisk, so that they would not be visible to someone looking over the user's shoulder.

Password input controls are created almost identically to the single-line text input controls, except that the type attribute on the <input> element is given a value of password.

Here you can see an example of a login form that combines a single-line text input control and a password input control (ch06_eg03.html):

```
<form action="http://www.example.com/login.asp" method="post">
  <p>Username:<br>
```

```
      <input type="text" name="txtUsername" value="" size="20" maxlength="20"></p>
    <p>Password:
      <input type="password" name="pwdPassword" value="" size="20"
maxlength="20"></p>
    <p><input type="submit" value="Log in"></p>
  </form>
```

> **NOTE** As you can see, it is common to start the name of any password with the characters pwd so that when you come to deal with the data on the server, you know the associated value came from a password input box.

Figure 6-6 shows you how this login form might look in a browser when the user starts entering details.

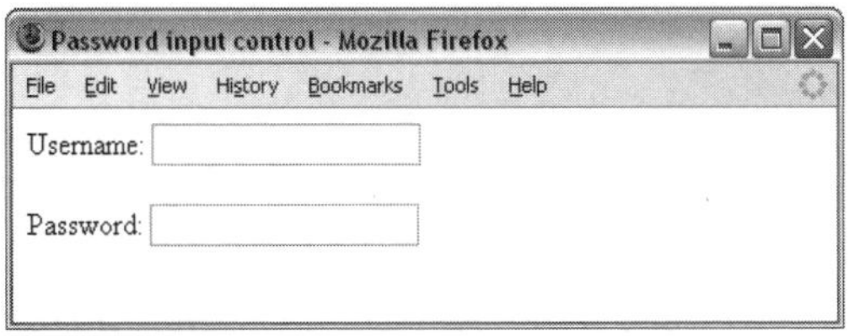

FIGURE 6-6

Password inputs accept the same attributes as plain text inputs.

> **NOTE** Although passwords are hidden on the screen, they are still sent across the Internet as clear text, which is not considered secure. To make them secure you must use an SSL connection between the client and server and encrypt any sensitive data (such as passwords and credit card details). SSL connections and encryption should be covered in a book about server-side languages such as ASP.NET and PHP.

Multiple-Line Text Input Controls

If you want to allow a visitor to your site to enter more than one line of text, you must create a multiple-line text input control using the `<textarea>` element.

Here is an example of a multiple-line text input used to collect feedback from visitors to a site (ch06_eg04.html):

```
<form action="http://www.example.org/feedback.asp" method="post">
  <p>Please tell us what you think of the site and then click submit:</p>
  <textarea name="txtFeedback" rows="20" cols="50">
  Enter your feedback here.
  </textarea>
  <p><input type="submit" value="Submit"></p>
</form>
```

The text inside the `<textarea>` element is not indented (in the same way that other code in this book is indented). Anything written between the opening and closing `<textarea>` tags is treated as if it were written inside a `<pre>` element, and formatting·of the source document is preserved. If the words "Enter your feedback here" were indented in the code, they would also be indented in the resulting multiline text input on the browser.

Figure 6-7 shows what this form might look like.

In the figure, you can see the writing between the opening `<textarea>` and closing `</textarea>` tags, which is shown in the text area when the page loads. Users can delete this text before adding their own text, and if they do not delete the text from the textbox, it will be sent to the server when the form is submitted. Users often type after any text written in a `<textarea>` element, so you may choose to avoid adding anything in between the elements, but you should still use both opening and closing `<textarea>` tags. Otherwise, older browsers may not render the element correctly.

The `<textarea>` element can take the attributes shown in Table 6-2.

FIGURE 6-7

TABLE 6-2: Common Attributes for the <textarea> Element

ATTRIBUTE	PURPOSE
name	The name of the control. This is used in the name/value pair that is sent to the server.
rows	Used to specify the size of a `<textarea>`; it indicates the number of rows of text a `<textarea>` element should have and therefore corresponds to the height of the text area.
cols	Used to specify the size of a `<textarea>`; it specifies the number of columns of text and therefore corresponds to the width of the box. One column is the average width of a character.

The attributes shown in Table 6-3 are newly added to the `<textarea>` element. Since they're new, some of them have limited support across browsers. Generally, they're supported in Firefox 4+, Safari 5.2+, Chrome 10+, Opera 10.6+, and IE10+. For specifics on any attribute and up-to-date information on this and other questions about what form elements and attributes are supported, keep your eye on "The Current State of HTML5 Forms" found at `http://www.wufoo.com/html5/`.

TABLE 6-3: New Attributes for the <textarea> Element

ATTRIBUTE	PURPOSE
maxlength	Maximum number of characters the user can enter.
autofocus	Boolean attribute that indicates that the element should have focus when the page loads.
required	Boolean attribute that indicates whether the input is a required element.
placeholder	Specifies a sample value to show users as a hint.
dirname	Provides a name for a text directional hint.
wrap	Specifies whether the text in a text area should be forced to wrap at the value of the cols attribute.
disabled	Boolean attribute that disables the select box, preventing user intervention.
form	Indicates the association <form> element for the <textarea> element. Value represents the id of the associated <form>.
readonly	Boolean attribute that indicates whether the user can edit the form field.

The <textarea> element can also take all the universal attributes.

By default, when a user runs out of columns in a <textarea>, the text is wrapped onto the next line (which means it just flows onto the next line as text in a word processor does), but the server receives it as if it were all on one line. Because some users expect the sentences to break where they see them break on the screen, the wrap attribute enables you to indicate how the text should be wrapped. Possible values are as follows:

➤ soft (the default), which means wherever the text wraps, users see it on the new line, but it is transmitted to the server as if it were all on the same line, unless users press the Enter key, in which case it is treated as a line break.

➤ hard, which means wherever the text wraps, it is transmitted to the server as a new line.

New HTML5 Input Types and Attributes

This section introduces you to the new HTML5 <input> types and to several new attributes that significantly enhance the power of the once lowly <input>. These take the <input> element beyond simple text and into much more specific options that better map to real-world use cases.

Support for these elements and attributes is interesting. For details or to test your own browser, go to Mike Taylor's site: http://miketaylr.com/code/input-type-attr.html, browse the table at http://wufoo.com/html5/, or check out the latest at http://caniuse.com/#feat=forms. Generally, support is available in the latest versions of all the major browsers, including Internet Explorer 10. Thankfully, because of the way browsers treat unknown input types, all is not lost if your target audience includes older versions of Internet Explorer or other browsers. Basically, browsers treat any `<input>` with an unknown type as type `text`, which means that you can still collect the data, even if the specific UI enhancements provided by the new inputs aren't available. Similarly, browsers ignore any attributes they don't understand, so although the features might not be supported, it's safe to include them even when a visitor uses an older browser such as Internet Explorer 6.

You must think about the experience for users with older browsers. In some cases it might be enough to simply present the form element as a simple text `<input>`. Other times it might be worth looking into a *polyfill* solution. Polyfills are small libraries, usually written in JavaScript that provide support for new features in older browsers. You look at one of these in the section on the `placeholder` attribute, but there are many available polyfills for a variety of HTML5 features. The Modernizr project keeps a list at its project site: `https://github.com/Modernizr/Modernizr/wiki/HTML5-Cross-Browser-Polyfills`. This is an important concept to grasp as you work with more advanced technologies.

Now look at some of these new elements in action. The following form presents a website registration form marked up using the following new `<input>` types: `tel`, `url`, `email`, `date`, and `color` (ch06_eg05.html).

```
<form action="http://www.example.org/feedback.asp" method="post">
  <p>Name:<br>
    <input type="text" name="txtName" value="" size="20" maxlength="20"></p>
  <p>Telephone Number:<br>
    <input type="tel" name="txtTel" value="" size="20" maxlength="20"></p>
  <p>Email:<br>
     <input type="email" name="txtEmail" value="" size="20" maxlength="20"></p>
  <p>Favorite Color:<br>
    <input type="color" name="txtColor" value="" size="20" maxlength="20"></p>
  <p>Date of Birth:<br>
     <input type="date" name="txtDate" value="" size="20" maxlength="20"></p>
    <p><input type="submit" value="Submit"></p>
</form>
```

Figure 6-8 shows how this page looks in Google Chrome 21. This version of Chrome supports both date and color. In this illustration the calendar control of the date input is expanded to show just how much power is packed into these new text inputs. Before these new inputs were introduced, creating a similar datepicker control would take dozens of kilobytes of JavaScript and CSS, complicated markup, and multiple images. Using a control provided by the browser is less complicated for authors and is much faster because all the various files needed for a JavaScript datepicker add overhead to the page.

Figure 6-9 illustrates how these new inputs look in Firefox 15, which doesn't support either input type. As you can see, they look exactly like a standard text input and work exactly the same as well, which means that even if users don't have the best available browser, they can still enter the information needed to fill out the form.

Now that you've seen some of the new input types in action, it's time to look at some of the other new attributes for input controls in HTML5. Like the new input types, these new attributes replace common interaction or programming patterns found on the web with controls provided by the browser. In some cases, using these new attributes is trickier than using the new input types. With the new input types, all you have to do is assume that users with older browsers will just enter their answers with text and be prepared to handle that kind of input on the server side. In the case of some of these new attributes, the functionality they provide, such as form validation, might need to be provided using JavaScript and other technologies, for users of older browsers. As you've read, these technology fallbacks are called polyfills.

FIGURE 6-8

FIGURE 6-9

The next section shows how to use the new `placeholder` attribute and shows how to supply a simple, third-party polyfill for the functionality in older browsers. Following that, you learn about some of the other important new attributes.

Using the placeholder Attribute to Illustrate Example Input

As you saw in the section on basic inputs, the value attribute is often used to provide a sample input. The downside to this technique is that users don't always clear the input so that example text is often included as part of the data sent to the server. To fix this, people script the input to show a default value until the input is given focus. *Focus* indicates that the form element is the current one being interacted with by the user. After a form element has focus, the JavaScript can clear out the input value and ready the form field for user input. The placeholder attribute replicates this behavior without the need for scripting. The following code sample (ch06_eg06.html) shows what this looks like.

```
<form action="http://www.example.org/feedback.asp" method="post">
  <p>Name:<br>
     <input type="text" name="txtName" value="" size="20" maxlength="20"
placeholder="Rob Larsen"></p>
   <p><input type="submit" value="Submit"></p>
</form>
```

To add support for a placeholder in older browsers, you need to add a JavaScript file from the Placeholder.js project https://github.com/jamesallardice/Placeholders.js and then run a small piece of JavaScript to initialize support (ch06_eg06.html).

```
<script src="Placeholders.js"></script>
<script>
Placeholders.init();
</script>
```

Hopefully, you won't need to do much of this, but if you need to use a new feature, this is the best way to add support for older browsers. Now that you've seen a simple example of how to handle polyfill solutions, it's time to look at the rest of the important new attributes.

> **NOTE** *Not every polyfill solution is as easy or as foolproof as the* placeholder. *In addition, some new HTML5 features are impossible to polyfill. You must do a little research before you decide to use one of the newest features. As the web evolves, the question of how to support older browsers evolves with it, so having awareness of the basic pattern for support can serve you well for a long time to come.*

Ensuring User Privacy and Security with the autocomplete Attribute

Web browsers typically offer the ability to save form entries to save time when filling out forms with similar information. This is a convenient feature, but there are times where this is dangerous behavior. For example, saving and redisplaying a credit card number, bank account number, or Social Security code could be catastrophic if you entered that information on a public computer. Similarly, login and password information can be convenient to have prepopulated, but it's a serious security hole.

Setting the autocomplete attribute allows web authors to control whether form entries should be cached. autocomplete takes two different values: on and off. on indicates that the values are safe to save and prepopulate. `off` indicates that they should not be saved. The following example shows a simple login and password form with `autocomplete` set to `off` (ch06_eg07.html).

```
<form action="http://www.example.com/login.asp" method="post">
  <p>Username:<br>
    <input type="text" name="txtUsername" value="" size="20"
      maxlength="20" autocomplete="off"></p>
  <p>Password:
    <input type="password" name="pwdPassword" value="" size="20"
      maxlength="20" autocomplete="off"></p>
  <p><input type="submit" value="Log in"></p>
</form>
```

Ensuring Information Is Provided with the required Attribute

Often information in a form is required. For example, if you request an insurance quote for your car, the make and model of the car and the address where it's parked at night would be information needed to provide a reasonable quote. In those cases you can use the `required` attribute to ensure that the form will be submitted only if there's content in the required fields. The following text sample shows `required` attributes in use on a simple form (ch06_eg08.html), and Figure 6-10 shows the result of an attempted form submission with the `required` input left empty.

```
<form action="http://www.example.org/feedback.asp" method="post">
  <p>Name:<br>
    <input type="text" name="txtName" value="" size="20" maxlength="20"
placeholder="Rob Larsen" required></p>
  <p><input type="submit" value="Submit"></p>
</form>
```

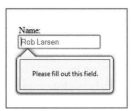

FIGURE 6-10

Buttons

Buttons are most commonly used to submit a form; although, they are sometimes used to clear or reset a form and even to trigger client-side scripts. (For example, on a basic loan calculator form within the page, a button might be used to trigger the script that calculates repayments without sending the data to the server.) You can create a button in three ways:

➤ Using an `<input>` element with a `type` attribute whose value is `submit`, `reset`, or `button`

➤ Using an `<input>` element with a `type` attribute whose value is `image`

➤ Using a `<button>` element

With each different method, the button appears slightly different.

Creating Buttons Using the <input> Element

When you use the <input> element to create a button, the type of button you create is specified using the type attribute. The type attribute can take the following values to create a button:

➤   submit, which creates a button that submits a form when pressed

➤   reset, which creates a button that automatically resets form controls to their initial values as they were when the page loaded

➤   button, which creates a button that is used to trigger a client-side script when the user clicks that button

Here you can see examples of all three types of buttons (ch06_eg09.html):

```
<form action="http://www.example.org/feedback.aspx" method="post">
  <p>
    <input type="submit" name="btnVoteRed" value="Vote for reds">
  </p>
  <p>
    <input type="submit" name="btnVoteBlue" value="Vote for blues">
  </p>
  <p>
    <input type="reset" value="Clear form">
  </p>
  <p>
    <input type="button" value="Calculate" onclick="calculate()">
  </p></form>
```

Figure 6-11 shows what these buttons might look like in Firefox on a PC. (A Mac displays them in the standard Mac style for buttons.)

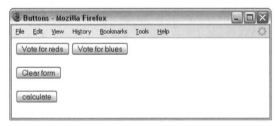

FIGURE 6-11

Table 6-4 shows the attributes used by the buttons.

TABLE 6-4: Common Attributes for Buttons

ATTRIBUTE	PURPOSE
type	Specifies the type of button you want and takes one of the following values: submit, reset, or button.
name	Provides a name for the button. You need to add only a name attribute to a button if there is more than one button on the same form. (In which case it helps to indicate which of the buttons was clicked.) It is considered good practice, however, to give the button a name anyway to provide an indication of what the button does.
value	Enables you to specify what the text on the button should read. If a name attribute is given, the value of the value attribute is sent to the server as part of the name/value pair for this form control. If no value is given, then no name/value pair is sent for this button.

The attributes in Table 6-5 are newly added to <input> elements of type submit, reset, or button.

TABLE 6-5: New Attributes for <input> Elements of Type submit, reset, or button

ATTRIBUTE	PURPOSE
autofocus	Boolean attribute that indicates the element should have focus when the page loads.
disabled	Boolean attribute that disables the select box, preventing user intervention.
form	Indicates the association <form> element for the <textarea> element. value should represent the id of the associated <form>.

An <input> of type submit, reset, or button can also take all the universal attributes.

If you do not use the value attribute on the submit button, you may find that a browser displays text that is inappropriate to the purpose of the form—for example, IE displays the text Send Query, which is not ideal for a login button form.

Using Images for Buttons

You can use an image for a button rather than use the standard button that a browser renders for you. Creating an image button is similar to creating any other button, but the type attribute has a value of image:

```
<input type="image" src="submit.jpg" alt="Submit" name="btnImage">
```

> **NOTE** *You can start the value of a* name *attribute for a button with the characters* btn, *in keeping with the naming convention mentioned earlier. (When you refer to the name of the form control in other code, the use of this prefix helps remind you what type of form control the information came from.)*

Because you are creating a button that has an image, you need to have two additional attributes, which are listed in Table 6-6.

TABLE 6-6: Important Attributes for <input> Type image

ATTRIBUTE	PURPOSE
src	Specifies the source of the image file.
alt	Provides alternative text for the image. This displays when the image cannot be found and also read to people using voice browsers.
height	Specifies the height of the image.
width	Specifies the width of the image.

In addition to the attributes mentioned in Table 6-6 and the global attributes, this input type also supports the following attributes: `disabled`, `form`, `formaction`, `autofocus`, `formenctype`, `formmethod`, `formtarget`, and `formnovalidate`.

If the image button has a `name` attribute, when you click it, the browser sends a name/value pair to the server. The name will be what you provide for the `name` attribute, and the value will be a pair of x and y coordinates for where on the button the user clicked.

In Figure 6-12, you can see a graphical submit button. Both Firefox and IE change the cursor when the user hovers over one of these buttons to help users know that they can click it.

FIGURE 6-12

Creating Buttons Using the <button> Element

The <button> element is a more recent introduction that enables you to specify what appears on a button between an opening <button> tag and a closing </button> tag so you can include textual markup or image elements between these tags.

Browsers offer a relief (or 3-D) effect on the button, which resembles an up or down motion when the button is clicked.

Here are some examples of using the `<button>` element (ch06_eg10.html):

```
<form action="http://www.example.org/feedback.aspx" method="post">
<p>
<button type="submit">Submit</button>
</p>
<p>
  <button type="reset"><b>Clear this form</b> I want to start again</button>
</p>
<p>
<button type="button"><img src="submit.gif" alt="submit"></button>
</p></form>
```

As you can see, the first submit button just contains text, the second reset button contains text and other markup (in the form of the `<b>` element), and the third button contains an `<img>` element.

Figure 6-13 shows what these buttons would look like.

FIGURE 6-13

In addition to the attributes mentioned above and the global attributes, this `<button>` element also supports the following attributes: `disabled`, `name`, `autofocus`, and `value`.

Check Boxes

Check boxes are like light switches; they can be either on or off. When they are checked, they are on—the user can simply toggle between on and off positions by clicking the check box.

Check boxes can appear individually, with each having its own name, or they can appear as a group of check boxes that share a control name and allow users to select several values for the same property.

Check boxes are ideal form controls when you need to allow a user to

➤ Provide a simple yes or no response with one control (such as accepting terms and conditions)

➤ Select several items from a list of possible options (such as when you want users to indicate all the skills they have from a given list)

A check box is created using the `<input>` element whose `type` attribute has a value of `checkbox`. Following is an example of some check boxes that use the same control name (`ch06_eg11.html`):

```
<form action="http://www.example.com/cv.aspx" method="get" name="frmCV">
Which of the following skills do you possess? Select all that apply.<br>
   <input type="checkbox" name="chkSkills" value="html">HTML <br>
   <input type="checkbox" name="chkSkills" value="CSS">CSS<br>
   <input type="checkbox" name="chkSkills" value="JavaScript">JavaScript<br>
   <input type="checkbox" name="chkSkills" value="aspnet">ASP.Net<br>
   <input type="checkbox" name="chkSkills" value="php">PHP
</form>
```

> **NOTE** For consistency with the naming convention you have used for form elements throughout the chapter, you can start the name of check boxes with the letters `chk`.

Figure 6-14 shows how this form might look in a browser. Note how there is a line break after each check box, so that each clearly appears on its own line. (If you have check boxes side by side, users are likely to get confused about which label applies to which check box.)

Because all the selected skills will be sent to the processing application in the form of name/value pairs, if someone selects more than one skill, there will be several name/value pairs sent to the server that all share the same name.

FIGURE 6-14

In contrast, here is a single check box, acting like a simple yes or no option:

```
<form action="http://www.example.org/accept.aspx" name="frmTandC" method="get">
  <input type="checkbox" name="chkAcceptTerms" checked>
  I accept the <a href="terms.htm">terms and conditions</a>.<br>
  <input type="submit">
</form>
```

The `<input>` element that creates this check box does not carry a `value` attribute. In the absence of a `value` attribute, the value is `on`. In this example, you can also see a boolean attribute called `checked`, which indicates that when the page loads, the check box is selected.

Table 6-7 shows common attributes that an `<input>` element whose `type` attribute has a value of `checkbox` can carry.

TABLE 6-7: Important Attributes for <input> Type checkbox

ATTRIBUTE	PURPOSE
type	Indicates that you want to create a check box.
name	Gives the name of the control. Several check boxes may share the same name, but this should happen only if you want users to have the option to select several items from the same list—in which case, they should be placed next to each other on the form.
value	The value that will be sent to the server if the check box is selected.
checked	Indicates that when the page loads the check box should be selected.

Check boxes can also carry the following attributes:

➤ All universal attributes

➤ disabled, form, autofocus, and required

Radio Buttons

Radio buttons are similar to check boxes in that they can be either on or off, but there are two key differences:

➤ When you have a group of radio buttons that share the same name, only one of them can be selected. After one radio button has been selected, if the user clicks another option, the new option is selected and the old one is deselected.

➤ You should not use radio buttons for a single form control where the control indicates on or off because after a lone radio button has been selected, it cannot be deselected again (without writing a script to do that).

Therefore, a group of radio buttons is ideal if you want to provide users with a number of options from which they must pick only one. In such situations, an alternative is to use a drop-down select box that allows users to select only one option from several. Your decision between whether to use a select box or a group of radio buttons depends on three things:

➤ **Users' expectations:** If your form models a paper form where users would be presented with several check boxes, from which they can pick only one, then you should use a group of radio buttons.

➤ **Seeing all the options:** If users would benefit from having all the options in front of them before they pick one, you should use a group of radio buttons.

➤ **Space:** If you are concerned about space, for example, on a mobile device, a drop-down select box takes up far less space than a set of radio buttons.

> **NOTE** *The term "radio buttons" comes from old radios. On some old radios, you could press only one button at a time to select the radio station you wanted to listen to from the ones that had been set. You could not press two of these buttons at the same time on your radio, and pressing one would pop the other out.*

The `<input>` element is again called upon to create radio buttons, and this time the `type` attribute should be given a value of `radio`. For example, here radio buttons are used to allow users to select which class of travel they want to take (ch06_eg12.html):

```
<form action="http://www.example.com/flights.aspx" name="frmFlightBooking"
      method="get">
  Please select which class of travel you wish to fly: <br>
  <input type="radio" name="radClass" value="First">First class <br>
  <input type="radio" name="radClass" value="Business">Business class <br>
  <input type="radio" name="radClass" value="Economy">Economy class <br>
</form>
```

As you can see, the user should be allowed to select only one of the three options, so radio buttons are ideal. You can also start the name of a radio button with the letters `rad`. Figure 6-15 shows you what this might look like in a browser.

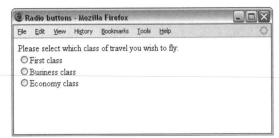

FIGURE 6-15

Table 6-8 lists common attributes for an `<input>` element whose `type` attribute has a value of `radio`.

TABLE 6-8: Common Attributes for Radio Buttons

ATTRIBUTE	PURPOSE
type	To indicate that you want a radio button form control.
name	The name of the form control.
value	Used to indicate the value that will be sent to the server if this option is selected.
checked	Indicates that this option should be selected by default when the page loads. Remember that there is no point using this with a single radio button because a user can't deselect the option.

Radio buttons can also take the following attributes:

➤ All the universal attributes

➤ `disabled`, `form`, `autofocus`, and `required`

> **NOTE** *When you have a group of radio buttons that share the same name, some browsers automatically select the first option as the page loads, even though they are not required to do so in the HTML specification. Therefore, if your radio buttons represent a set of values—say for a voting application—you might want to set a medium option to be selected by default so that should some users forget to select one of the options, the results are not overly biased by the browser's selection. To do this, you should use the checked attribute.*

Select Boxes

A drop-down select box enables users to select one item from a drop-down menu. Drop-down select boxes can take up far less space than a group of radio buttons.

Drop-down select boxes can also provide an alternative to single-line text input controls where you want to limit the options that a user can enter. For example, imagine that you were asking which country someone was from. If you had a textbox, visitors from the United States could enter different options such as U.S.A., U.S., United States, America, or North America, whereas with a select box you could control the options they could enter.

A drop-down select box is contained by a `<select>` element, whereas each individual option within that list is contained within an `<option>` element. For example, the following form creates a drop-down select box for the user to select a color (`ch06_eg13.html`):

```
<select name="selColor">
  <option selected="selected" value="">Select color</option>
  <option value="red">Red</option>
  <option value="green">Green</option>
  <option value="blue">Blue</option>
</select>
```

As you can see here, the text between the opening `<option>` tags and the closing `</option>` tags is used to display options to the user, whereas the value that would be sent to the server if that option were selected is given in the `value` attribute. You can also see that the first `<option>` element does not have a value and that its content is `Select color`; this is to indicate to users that they must pick one of the color choices. Finally, notice again the use of the letters `sel` at the start of the name of a select box.

Figure 6-16 shows what this would look like in a browser.

The width of the select box will be the width of the longest option displayed to the user; in this case, it will be the width of the text `Select color`. You can update the width of the box using CSS, which you learn about in Chapter 7.

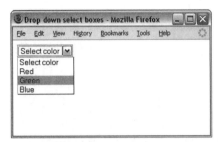

FIGURE 6-16

The <select> Element

The <select> element is the containing element for a drop-down list box; it can take the attributes shown in Table 6-9.

TABLE 6-9: Common Attributes for <select> Elements

ATTRIBUTE	PURPOSE
name	The name for the control.
size	Can be used to present a scrolling list box, as you will see shortly. Its value would be the number of rows in the list that should be visible at the same time.
multiple	This boolean attribute enables a user to select multiple items from the menu. If the attribute is not present, the user may select only one item. The use of this attribute changes the presentation of the select box, as you see in the section "Selecting Multiple Options with the Multiple Attribute."

According to the HTML specification, a <select> element *must* contain at least one <option> element; although, in practice it should contain more than one <option> element. After all, a drop-down list box with just one option might confuse a user.

Check boxes can also carry the following attributes:

➤ All universal attributes

➤ disabled, form, autofocus, and required

The <option> Element

Inside any <select> element, you can find at least one <option> element. The text between the opening <option> and closing </option> tags displays to the user as the label for that option. The <option> element can take the attributes shown in Table 6-10.

TABLE 6-10: Attributes of the <option> Element

ATTRIBUTE	PURPOSE
value	The value sent to the server if this option is selected.
selected	This boolean attribute specifies that this option should be the initially selected value when the page loads. This attribute may be used on several <option> elements even if the <select> element does not carry the multiple attribute.
label	An alternative way of labeling options, which uses an attribute rather than element content. This attribute is particularly useful when using the <optgroup> element, which is covered in the section "Grouping Options with the <optgroup> Element."
disabled	Boolean attribute that disables the select box, preventing user intervention.

Creating Scrolling Select Boxes

As mentioned earlier, you can create scrolling menus where users can see a few of the options in a select box at a time. To do this, you just add the size attribute to the <select> element. The value of the size attribute is the number of options you want to be visible at any one time.

Although scrolling select box menus are rarely used, they can give users an indication that several possible options are open to them and enable them to see a few of the options at the same time. Following is the code for a scrolling select box that enables the user to select a day of the week (ch06_eg14.html):

```
<form action="http://www.example.org/days.aspx" name="frmDays" method="get">
  <select size="4" name="selDay">
    <option value="Mon">Monday</option>
    <option value="Tue">Tuesday</option>
    <option value="Wed">Wednesday</option>
    <option value="Thu">Thursday</option>
    <option value="Fri">Friday</option>
    <option value="Sat">Saturday</option>
    <option value="Sun">Sunday</option>
  </select>
<br><br><input type="submit" value="Submit">
</form>
```

As Figure 6-17 shows, users can clearly see that they have several options; to save space only a few of the available options are shown.

The multiple attribute, which you meet in the next section, is not used on this element.

FIGURE 6-17

Selecting Multiple Options with the multiple Attribute

The `multiple` attribute enables users to select more than one item from a select box. When you use this attribute, it is always a good idea to tell people how to select multiple items: by holding down the Control key and clicking the items they want to select.

The addition of this attribute automatically makes the select box look like a scrolling select box. Here you can see an example of a multiple-item select box that enables users to select more than one day of the week (`ch06_eg15.html`):

```
<form action="http://www.example.org/days.aspx" method="get" name="frmDays">
  Please select more than one day of the week (to select multiple days
    hold down the control key and click on your chosen days):<br>
  <select name="selDays" multiple>
    <option value="Mon">Monday</option>
    <option value="Tue">Tuesday</option>
    <option value="Wed">Wednesday</option>
    <option value="Thu">Thursday</option>
    <option value="Fri">Friday</option>
    <option value="Sat">Saturday</option>
    <option value="Sun">Sunday</option>
  </select>
  <br><br><input type="submit" value="Submit">
</form>
```

The result is shown in Figure 6-18, where you can see that even without the addition of the `size` attribute, the select box is still represented in the same way as a scrolling one.

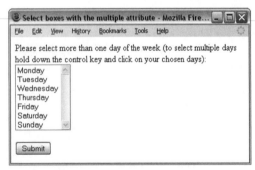

FIGURE 6-18

Grouping Options with the <optgroup> Element

If you have a long list of items in a select box, you can group them together using the `<optgroup>` element, which acts just like a container element for all the elements you want within a group.

The <optgroup> element must carry a label attribute whose value is a label for that group of options. In the following example, you can see how the options are grouped in terms of type of equipment (ch06_eg16.html):

```
<form action="http://www.example.org/info.aspx" method="get" name="frmInfo">
  Please select the product you are interested in:<br>
  <select name="selInformation">
    <optgroup label="Hardware">
      <option value="Desktop">Desktop computers</option>
      <option value="Laptop">Laptop computers</option>
    </optgroup>
    <optgroup label="Software">
      <option value="OfficeSoftware">Office software</option>
      <option value="Games">Games</option>
    </optgroup>
    <optgroup label="Peripherals">
      <option value="Monitors">Monitors</option>
      <option value="InputDevices">Input Devices</option>
      <option value="Storage">Storage</option>
    </optgroup>
  </select>
  <p><input type="submit" value="Submit"></p>
</form>
```

Different browsers display <optgroup> elements in different ways. Figure 6-19 shows how Safari on a Mac displays options held by <optgroup> elements, whereas Figure 6-20 shows the result in Firefox on a PC.

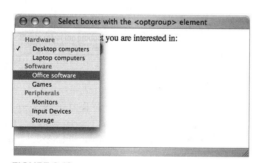

FIGURE 6-19

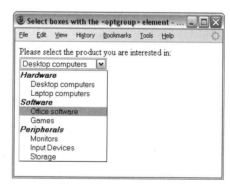

FIGURE 6-20

Attributes for Select Boxes

For completeness, the following is the full list of attributes that the <select> element can carry:

➤ disabled, form, size, multiple, required, and autofocus

➤ All universal attributes

Meanwhile, the `<option>` element can carry the following attributes:

➤ `label`, `selected`, `value`, and `disabled`

➤ All universal attributes

File Select Boxes

If you want to allow users to upload a file to your website from their computers, you must use a *file upload box*, also known as a *file select box*. This is created using the `<input>` element (again), but this time you give the `type` attribute a value of `file` (ch06_eg17.html):

```
<form action="http://www.example.com/imageUpload.aspx" method="post"
      name="fromImageUpload" enctype="multipart/form-data">
  <input type="file" name="fileUpload" accept="image/*">
<p><input type="submit" value="Submit"><p>
</form>
```

> **NOTE** *When you use a file upload box, the* `method` *attribute of the* `<form>` *element must be* `post`.

At the beginning of the chapter, you learned about some attributes in this example:

➤ The `enctype` attribute has been added to the `<form>` element with a value of `multipart/form-data` so that each form control is sent separately to the server. This is required on a form that uses a file upload box.

➤ The `accept` attribute has been added to the `<input>` element to indicate the MIME types of the files that can be selected for upload. In this example, the `accept` attribute is indicating that any image format can be uploaded because the wildcard character (the asterisk) has been used after the `image/` portion of the MIME type. This attribute is currently supported only by Opera 11+, Chrome 16+, Firefox 9+, and Internet Explorer 10+.

In Figure 6-21 you can see that when you click the Browse button in Firefox, a file dialog box opens up enabling you to browse to a file and select which one you want to upload. It is worth noting that different browsers sometimes show this control in slightly different ways. (For example, Safari has a button saying Choose File instead of Browse.)

An `<input>` element whose `type` attribute has a value of `file` can take the following attributes:

➤ `name`, `disabled`, `form`, `accept`, `autofocus`, `required`, and `multiple`

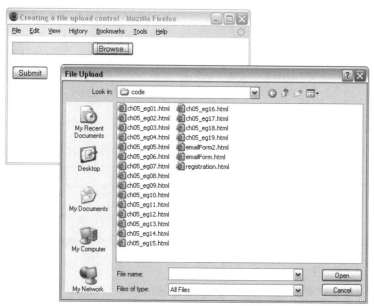

FIGURE 6-21

Hidden Controls

Sometimes you want to pass information between pages without users seeing it; to do this, you can use *hidden form controls*. Although users cannot see them in the web page, if they were to look at the source code for the page, they would see the values in the code. Therefore, hidden controls should not be used for any sensitive information that you do not want the user to see.

> **NOTE** You may have come across forms on the web that span more than one page. Long forms can be confusing, and splitting them up can help a user. In such cases, it is often necessary to pass values that a user has entered into the first form (on one page) onto the form in the second page, and then onto another page. Hidden elements are one way in which programmers can pass values between pages.

You create a hidden control using the `<input>` element whose `type` attribute has a value of `hidden`. For example, the following form contains a hidden form control indicating which section of the site users were on when they filled in the form (ch06_eg18.html):

```
<form action="http://www.example.com/vote.aspx" method="get" name="fromVote">
  <input type="hidden" name="hidPageSentFrom" value="home page">
  <input type="submit" value="Click if this is your favorite page of our
  site. ">
</form>
```

Hidden form controls need both the name and value attributes to be sent with the rest of a form.

> **NOTE** Chapter 8, "More Cascading Style Sheets," discusses how you can also hide form controls using the CSS display and visibility properties.

New HTML5 Form Elements

In addition to the new <input> types, the new HTML specification added several completely new form elements. As was the case with many of the new form types, several of these new form elements replace common patterns on the web that were previously created using copious amounts of JavaScript, CSS, and markup.

This section introduces three of the most useful: <progress>, <meter>, and <datalist>. The others are <output> for the output of mathematical exercises or other calculations and <keygen>, which is used with cryptography.

Track Completion of a Task with the New <progress> Element

The <progress> element is designed to represent the progress through a task. For example, you could use <progress> to track the amount of a file downloaded or the percentage of a survey completed. In addition to the global attributes you've already learned about, <progress> also makes specific use of two attributes to craft the display.

➤ max, indicates the maximum value of the <progress> element.

➤ value, indicates the amount completed.

If you include both, the progress bar will be colored proportionately to the amount completed. The following code sample shows this usage of <progress> (ch06_eg19.html):

```
Your progress through this book<br>
<progress value="6" max="13">
```

Figure 6-22 shows the rendering of this variation.

If you fail to indicate a value, the rendering of the element changes from a *determinate* <progress> element to one that's *indeterminate*. The rendering of an indeterminate <progress> is different in that it doesn't show a specific percentage of completion and instead cycles through the possible values in an

FIGURE 6-22

animation oddly reminiscent of the sweeping eye effect seen in the Cylons from the *Battlestar Galactica* television show. To see it properly, test the following code (ch06_eg20.html) in a supporting browser (as of this writing Internet Explorer 10, Firefox, Chrome, Safari, and Opera):

```
Your progress through this book<br>
<progress max="13">
```

Represent Scalar Measurement within a Range with the \<meter> Element

Similar to the \<progress> element, the \<meter> element enables you to display a gauge. A good example of this might be disk usage. The following example shows the current usage of the author's e-mail inbox (ch06_eg21.html). \<meter> uses a min attribute to add a lower (potentially nonzero) bound to the \<meter>. You can see an illustration of the \<meter> element rendered by Google Chrome in Figure 6-23:

```
<p>You are currently using 510MB out of 950MB available. </p>
<meter min="0" value="510" max="950">
```

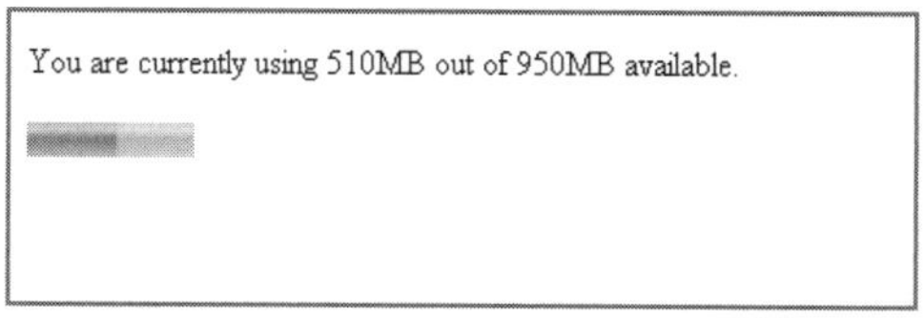

FIGURE 6-23

\<meter> accepts the following attributes:

- ➤ high specifies the low end of the "high" range.

- ➤ low specifies the high end of the "low" range.

- ➤ max sets the maximum range for the progress element.

- ➤ min sets the minimum range for the progress element.

- ➤ optimum represents the optimal numeric value.

- ➤ value specifies how much of the task has been completed.

Create an Autocomplete List with an \<input> and the New \<datalist> Element

Using a \<datalist> enables you to pair the flexibility to have a plain text entry field with a list of prepopulated options available for the user to choose from. You're probably familiar with this functionality from sites, such as Google, that offer suggestions as you type.

Normally, this is accomplished with JavaScript. Doing it with just HTML elements is accomplished with one new \<input> attribute, list, and the \<datalist> element. You pair the \<datalist> element with a series of nested \<option> elements. These options directly populate a list of options that narrow down as the user types (ch06_eg22.html).

```
<form action="http://www.example.org/info.asp" method="get" name="frmInfo">
  Please indicate your area of interest:<br>
  <input type="text" name="txtName" value="" size="20" maxlength="20"
list="tech">
  <datalist id="tech">
    <option value="CSS">
    <option value="HTML">
    <option value="JavaScript">
  </datalist>
</form>
```

Figure 6-24 shows how this combination looks in Google Chrome.

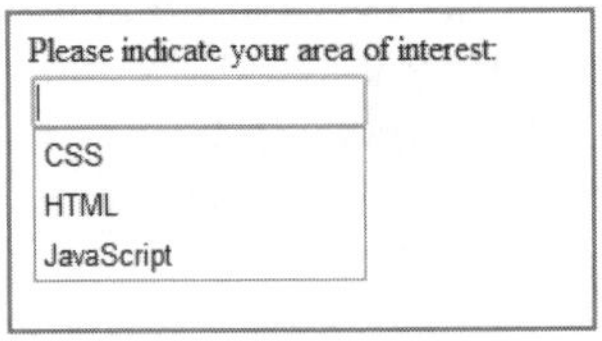

Please indicate your area of interest:

CSS
HTML
JavaScript

FIGURE 6-24

CREATING A CONTACT FORM

Now that you've learned about the basics of HTML forms, it's time to try out what you've learned with a very common example, a contact form.

TRY IT OUT Creating a Contact Form

In this example, you combine several of the form controls to make up a contact form for the Example Café.

1. Create a new HTML document with the skeleton in place. Then add a heading:

```
<!DOCTYPE html>
<html>
<head>
  <title>Contact Us</title>
</head>
<body>

<h1>Contact Us</h1>
<p>Use the following form to send a message to Example Cafe</p>

</body>
</html>
```

2. The form is going to be placed in a table with two columns so that the instructions are in the left column, and the form controls are aligned in the right column. (Without this, the form controls would look uneven across the page.) As you'll learn as you go through Chapter 7, "Cascading Style Sheets" and Chapter 8, "More Cascading Style Sheets," it's preferable to create effects like this using CSS. For now, stick to using tables.

3. In the first two rows, add a text input for the visitor's e-mail address using an `<input>` element whose `type` attribute has a value of `email`. Set the size of the form control and the maximum number of characters a user can enter.

4. Add the following table under the paragraph that tells people to use the form to send a message:

```
<table>
    <tr>
        <td>Your email</td>
```

```
    <td><input type="email" name="txtFrom" id="emailFrom"
      size="20" maxlength="250"></td>
  </tr>
```

5. This first row of the table is followed by a second row containing a text area for their message. The size of the text area is specified using the `rows` and `cols` attributes:

```
<tr>
  <td>Message</td>
  <td><textarea name="txtBody" id="emailBody" cols="50"
  rows="10"></textarea></td>
</tr>
```

6. In the next row, add a select box so that users can tell you how they heard of the café:

```
<tr>
  <td>How did you hear of us?</td>
  <td>
    <select name="selReferrer">
      <option value="google">Google</option>
      <option value="ad">Local newspaper ad</option>
      <option value="friend">Friend</option>
      <option value="other">Other</option>
    </select>
  </td>
</tr>
```

7. In the final row, add a check box to indicate whether visitors want to sign up for e-mail updates. This is created with the `<input>` element, whose `type` attribute has a value of `checkbox`. The check box should be selected by default, and this is indicated using the `checked` attribute:

```
<tr>
  <td>Newsletter</td>
  <td><input type="checkbox" name="chkBody" id="newsletterSignup"
    checked>
    Ensure this box is checked if you would like to
    receive email updates</td>
</tr>
</table>
```

8. Add a submit button, again using the `<input>` element so that the visitor can send the message to the café:

```
<input type="submit" value="Send message">
```

9. Save the file as `emailForm.html` and open it in your browser; it should look something like Figure 6-25.

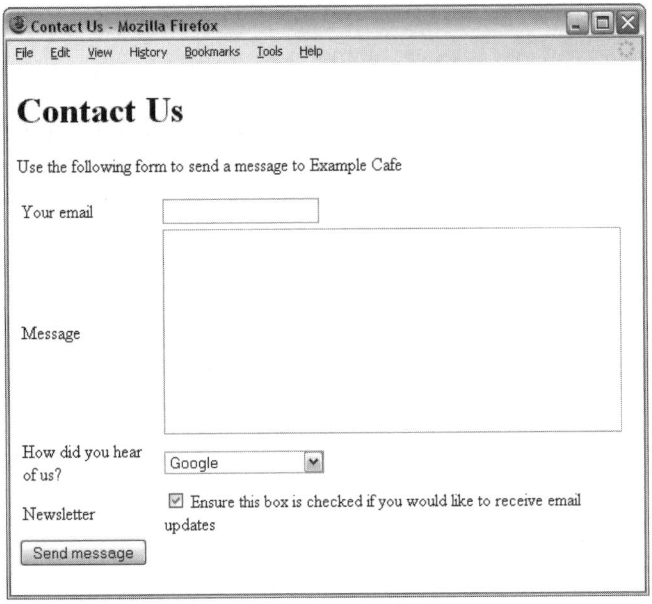

FIGURE 6-25

How It Works

Forms provide an interface for your users to enter text. The action indicates the server resource that will handle the data, and the type indicates how the data will be sent—either as a series of query paramaters appended to the URL (get) or as part of the HTTP headers (post). When the form is submitted, the data is sent to the server as a series of name/value pairs. For example, the selReferrer <select> box could be sent to the server with a value of google or friend.

Now that you've seen the basics of forms, it is time to look at more advanced features that you can use to enhance your forms.

CREATING LABELS FOR CONTROLS AND THE <LABEL> ELEMENT

Forms can be confusing enough at the best of times. You have probably received many insurance and tax forms that left you scratching your head.

If you create a form for your site, it is worth spending time to provide good labeling so that users know what data they should enter and where. If visitors have difficulty understanding your form, they will be less likely to complete the form (in particular if they purchase something), or they are more likely to make a mistake when filling it in.

Some form controls, such as buttons, already have labels. For the majority of form controls, however, you must provide the label.

For controls that do not have a label, you should use the `<label>` element. This element does not affect the form in any way other than telling users what information they should be entering (ch06_eg23.html).

```html
<form action="http://www.example.org/login.aspx" method="post" name="frmLogin">
  <table>
    <tr>
      <td><label for="Uname">User name</label></td>
      <td><input type="text" id="Uname" name="txtUserName"></td>
    </tr>
    <tr>
      <td><label for="Pwd">Password</label></td>
      <td><input type="password" id="Pwd" name="pwdPassword"></td>
    </tr>
  </table>
</form>
```

> **NOTE** You can see that this form has been placed inside a table; this ensures that even if the labels are of different lengths, the text inputs are aligned in their own column. If a list of text inputs is not aligned, it can be harder to use. In the chapters on CSS, you learn how you can implement this same layout without using a table.

As you can see here, the `<label>` element carries an attribute called `for`, which indicates the form control associated with the label. The value of the `for` attribute should be the same as the value of the `id` attribute on the corresponding form control. For example, the textbox form control, where users enter their username, has an `id` attribute whose value is `Uname`, and the label for this textbox has a `for` attribute whose value is also `Uname`.

Figure 6-26 shows what this login screen looks like.

The label may be positioned before or after the control. For textboxes and drop-down select boxes, it is generally good practice to have the label on the left or above the form control, whereas for check boxes and radio buttons, it is often easier to associate the label with the correct form control if they are on the right.

FIGURE 6-26

> **NOTE** You should have a new `<label>` element for each form control.

Another way to use the `<label>` element is as a containing element. When you use the `<label>` element this way, you do not need to use the `for` attribute because it applies to the form element that is inside it. This kind of label is sometimes known as an *implicit label*, for example:

```html
<form action="http://www.example.org/login.aspx" method="post" name="frmLogin">
  <label>Username <input type="text" id="Uname" name="txtUserName"></label>
  <label>Password <input type="password" id="Pwd" name="pwdPassword">
  </label>
</form>
```

The drawback to this approach is that you cannot control where the label appears in relation to the form control.

STRUCTURING YOUR FORMS WITH <FIELDSET> AND <LEGEND> ELEMENTS

Large forms can be confusing for users, so it's good practice to group together related form controls. The `<fieldset>` and `<legend>` elements do exactly this—help you group controls.

➤ The `<fieldset>` element creates a border around the group of form controls to show that they are related.

➤ The `<legend>` element enables you to specify a caption for the `<fieldset>` element, which acts as a title for the group of form controls. When used, the `<legend>` element should always be the first child of the `<fieldset>` element.

Figure 6-27 shows these elements in action. You can see that the form has been divided into four sections: Contact Information, Competition Question, Tiebreaker Question, and Enter Competition.

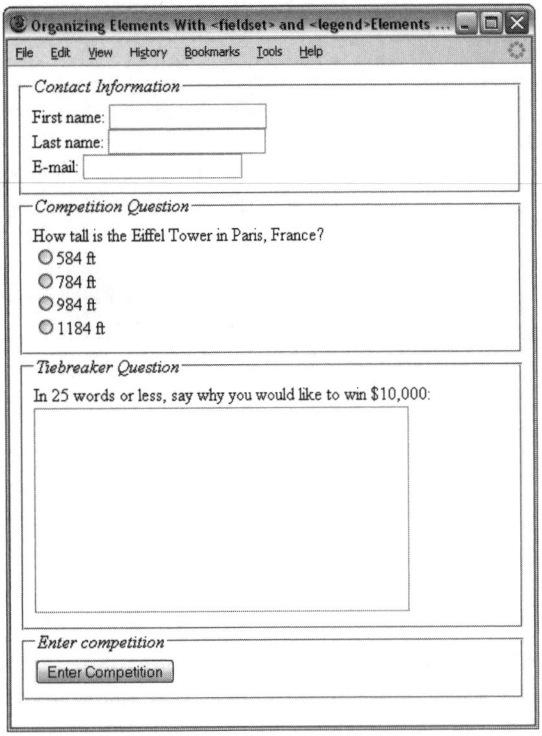

FIGURE 6-27

Now take a look at the code for this example. You can see how the <fieldset> elements create borders around the groups of form controls, and how the <legend> elements are used to title the groups of controls. Remember, when you use the <legend> element, it must be the first child of the <fieldset> element (ch06_eg24.html).

```
<form action="http://www.example.org/competition.aspx" method="post"
name="frmComp">
 <fieldset>
  <legend><em>Contact Information</em></legend>
   <label>First name: <input type="text" name="txtFName" size="20">  </label><br>
   <label>Last name: <input type="text" name="txtLName" size="20"></label>
   <br>
   <label>E-mail: <input type="text" name="txtEmail" size="20"></label>
   <br>
 </fieldset>
 <fieldset>
 <legend><em>Competition Question</em></legend>
  How tall is the Eiffel Tower in Paris, France? <br>
  <label><input type="radio" name="radAnswer" value="584">
     584ft</label><br>
  <label><input type="radio" name="radAnswer" value="784">
     784ft</label><br>
  <label><input type="radio" name="radAnswer" value="984">
     984ft</label><br>
  <label><input type="radio" name="radAnswer" value="1184">
      1184ft</label><br>
 </fieldset>
 <fieldset>
   <legend><em>Tiebreaker Question</em></legend>
     <label>In 25 words or less, say why you would like to win $10,000:
       <textarea name="txtTiebreaker" rows="10" cols="40"></textarea>
     </label>
 </fieldset>
 <fieldset>
   <legend><em>Enter competition</em></legend>
     <input type="submit" value="Enter Competition">
 </fieldset>
</form>
```

The <fieldset> element can take the following attributes:

➤ All the universal attributes.

➤ name, disabled, and form

The <legend> element can take all the universal attributes.

FOCUS

When a web page featuring several links or several form controls loads, you may have noticed that you can use your Tab key to move between those elements (or Shift+Tab to move backward through elements). As you move between them, the web browser tends to add some type of border or highlighting to that element (be it a link or a form control). This is known as *focus*.

Only elements that a user can interact with, such as links and form controls, can receive focus. Indeed, if a user is expected to interact with an element, that element must receive focus.

An element can gain focus in four ways:

> ➤ An element can be selected using a pointing device such as a mouse or trackball.

> ➤ Elements that can gain focus can be navigated between using the keyboard—often using the Tab key (or Shift+Tab to move backward through elements). As you are about to see, the elements in some documents can be given a fixed *tabbing order*, indicating the order in which elements gain focus when the user presses the Tab key.

> ➤ A web page author can indicate that an element should receive focus when a user presses a keyboard shortcut known as an *access key*. For example, if the page author set the access key on a search box to be the key for the letter *s*, on a PC you would likely press the Alt key plus the access key (Alt+S), whereas on a Mac you would press the Control key with an access key (Control+S), and the corresponding form control would gain focus.

> ➤ If the autofocus attribute is set on an element, the element gains focus once the document is loaded. Only one element in a form should have the autofocus attribute set.

Tabbing Order

If you want to control the order in which elements can gain focus, you can use the tabindex attribute to give that element a number between 0 and 32767, which becomes part of the tabbing order. Every time the user presses the Tab key, the focus moves to the element with the next highest tabbing order. (And again, Shift+Tab moves focus in reverse order.)

After a user tabs through all elements in a document that can gain focus, then focus may be given to other browser features (most commonly the address bar).

To demonstrate how tabbing order works, the following example gives focus to the check boxes in a different order than you might expect (ch06_eg25.html):

```
<form action="http://www.example.com/tabbing.aspx" method="get"
  name="frmTabExample">
  <input type="checkbox" name="chkNumber" value="1" tabindex="3"> One<br>
  <input type="checkbox" name="chkNumber" value="2" tabindex="7"> Two<br>
  <input type="checkbox" name="chkNumber" value="3" tabindex="4"> Three<br>
  <input type="checkbox" name="chkNumber" value="4" tabindex="1"> Four<br>
  <input type="checkbox" name="chkNumber" value="5" tabindex="9"> Five<br>
  <input type="checkbox" name="chkNumber" value="6" tabindex="6"> Six<br>
  <input type="checkbox" name="chkNumber" value="7" tabindex="10"> Seven<br>
  <input type="checkbox" name="chkNumber" value="8" tabindex="2"> Eight<br>
  <input type="checkbox" name="chkNumber" value="9" tabindex="8"> Nine<br>
  <input type="checkbox" name="chkNumber" value="10" tabindex="5"> Ten<br>
  <input type="submit" value="Submit">
</form>
```

In this example, the check boxes receive focus in the following order:

```
4,  8,  1,  3,  10,  6,  2,  9,  5,  7
```

Figure 6-28 shows how Firefox for PC by default gives a yellow outline to form elements as they gain focus. (Other browsers give a different outline. Internet Explorer uses blue lines.) The item is zoomed in on focus so that you can see it in closer detail.

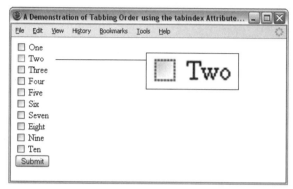

FIGURE 6-28

Elements that could gain focus but do not have a `tabindex` attribute are automatically given a value of 0. Therefore, when you specify a `tabindex` value, it should be 1 or higher, rather than 0.

If two elements have the same value for a `tabindex` attribute, they will be navigated in the order in which they appear in the document. So, after the elements that have a `tabindex` of 1 or more have been cycled through, the browser cycles through the remaining elements (which have a value of 0) in the order in which they appear in the page.

> **NOTE** *If an element is disabled, it cannot gain focus and does not participate in the tabbing order. Also, if you use a Mac, you may need to check your Keyboard Shortcuts settings in system preferences. At the bottom of the window where it says Full Keyboard Access, this needs to have the All Controls option selected.*

Access Keys

Access keys act just like keyboard shortcuts. The access key is a single character from the document's character set expected to appear on the user's keyboard. When this key is used with another key or keys (such as Alt with IE on Windows, Alt and Shift with Firefox on Windows, and Control on an Apple), the browser automatically goes to that section. (Exactly which key must be used with the access key depends upon the operating system and browser.)

The access key is defined using the `accesskey` attribute. The value of this attribute is the character (and key on the keyboard) you want the user to press (with the other key/keys dependent upon the operating system and browser).

To see how access keys work, you can revisit the example of a competition form (ch06_eg24.html), which was covered in the section "Structuring Your Forms with <fieldset> and <legend> Elements" earlier in this chapter. Now the accesskey attributes can be added to the <legend> elements:

```
<legend accesskey="c"><u>C</u>ontact Information</legend>
<legend>Competition Question</legend>
<legend accesskey="t"><u>T</u>iebreaker Question</legend>
<legend>Enter competition</legend>
```

The new version of this file is ch06_eg26.html in the download code. (Extra <br> elements have been added to show how the screen scrolls to the appropriate section when an access key is used.) As a hint to users that they can use the access keys as shortcuts, information has also been added to the information in the <legend> element by underlining the access key. Figure 6-29 shows how this updated example looks in a browser.

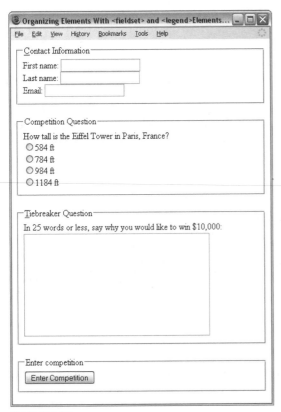

FIGURE 6-29

The effect of an access key being used depends upon the element that it is used with. With <legend> elements, such as those shown previously, if the page is longer than the viewport, the browser scrolls to that part of the page automatically and gives focus to the first form control in the section. When used with form controls, those elements gain focus. As soon as the element gains focus, the user should interact with it (by either typing in text controls or pressing the Enter or Return key with other form controls).

When you are using letters a–z, it does not matter whether you specify an uppercase or lowercase access key; although, strictly speaking, it should be lowercase.

DISABLED AND READ-ONLY CONTROLS

Throughout the chapter, you have seen that several of the elements can carry attributes called `disabled` and `readonly`:

➤ The `readonly` attribute prevents users from changing the value of the form controls themselves; although, it may be modified by a script. The name and value of any `readonly` control will be sent to the server.

➤ The `disabled` attribute disables the form control, or set of form controls in a `<fieldset>` element, so that users cannot alter it. A script can be used to re-enable the control, but unless a control is re-enabled, the name and value will not be sent to the server.

The `readonly` attribute is particularly helpful when you want to stop visitors from changing a part of the form, perhaps because it must not change (for example, if you put terms and conditions inside a text area).

The `disabled` attribute is particularly helpful when preventing users from interacting with a control until they have done something else. For example, you might use a script to disable a submit button until all the form fields contain a value.

Table 6-11 shows which form controls work with the `readonly` and `disabled` attributes.

TABLE 6-11: Elements That Support the readonly and disabled Attributes

ELEMENT	READONLY	DISABLED
`<textarea>`	Yes	Yes
`<input type="text">`	Yes	Yes
`<input type="checkbox">`	No	Yes
`<input type="radio">`	No	Yes
`<input type="submit">`	No	Yes
`<input type="reset">`	No	Yes
`<input type="button">`	No	Yes
`<input type="color">`	No	Yes
`<input type="date">`	Yes	Yes

continues

TABLE 6-11 *(continued)*

ELEMENT	READONLY	DISABLED
`<input type="datetime">`	Yes	Yes
`<input type="datetime-local">`	Yes	Yes
`<input type="email">`	Yes	Yes
`<input type="file">`	No	Yes
`<input type="month">`	Yes	Yes
`<input type="number">`	Yes	Yes
`<input type="range">`	No	Yes
`<input type="search">`	Yes	Yes
`<input type="tel">`	Yes	Yes
`<input type="url">`	Yes	Yes
`<input type="week">`	Yes	Yes
`<input type="time">`	Yes	Yes
`<select>`	No	Yes
`<option>`	No	Yes
`<optgroup>`	No	Yes
`<keygen>`	No	Yes
`<fieldset>`	No	Yes
`<button>`	No	Yes

Table 6-12 indicates the main differences between the `readonly` and `disabled` attributes.

TABLE 6-12: Differences between readonly and disabled Attributes

ATTRIBUTE	READONLY	DISABLED
Can be modified	Yes by script, not by user	Not while disabled
Will be sent to server	Yes	Not while disabled
Will receive focus	Yes	No
Included in tabbing order	Yes	No

SENDING FORM DATA TO THE SERVER

When your browser requests a web page and when the server sends a page back to the browser, you use the HyperText Transfer Protocol (HTTP).

There are two methods that a browser can use to send form data to the server—HTTP get and HTTP post—and you specify which should be used by adding the method attribute on the <form> element.

If the <form> element does not carry a method attribute, then by default the get method will be used. If you use a file upload form control, you must choose the post method. (And you must set the enctype attribute to have a value of multipart/form-data.) Now take a closer look at each of these methods.

HTTP get

When you send form data to the server using the HTTP get method, the form data is appended to the URL specified in the action attribute of the <form> element.

The form data is separated from the URL using a question mark. Following the question mark, you get the name/value pairs for each form control. Each name/value pair is separated by an ampersand (&).

For example, take the following login form, which you saw when the password form control was introduced:

```
<form action="http://www.example.com/login.aspx" method="get">
Username:
<input type="text" name="txtUsername" value="" size="20" maxlength="20"><br>
Password:
<input type="password" name="pwdPassword" value="" size="20" maxlength="20">
<input type="submit">
</form>
```

When you click the submit button, your username and password are appended to the URL http://www.example.com/login.aspx in the *query string*. It should look like this:

```
http://www.example.com/login.aspx?txtUsername=Bob&pwdPassword=LetMeIn
```

When a browser requests a URL with any spaces or unsafe characters such as /, \ , =, &, and + (which have special meanings in URLs), they are replaced with a hex code to represent that character. This is done automatically by the browser and is known as *URL encoding*. When the data reaches the server, the server usually un-encodes the special characters automatically.

One of the advantages of passing form data in a URL is that it can be bookmarked. If you look at searches performed on major search engines such as Google, they tend to use the get method so that the page can be bookmarked.

The get method, however, has some disadvantages. Indeed, when sending sensitive data such as the password shown here, or credit card details, you should not use the get method because the sensitive data becomes part of the URL and is in full view to everyone (and could be bookmarked).

You should not use the HTTP `get` method when

➤ You deal with sensitive information, such as passwords or credit card details (because the sensitive form data would be visible as part of a URL).

➤ You update a data source such as a database or spreadsheet (because someone could make up URLs that would alter your data source).

➤ Your form contains a file upload control (because uploaded files cannot be passed in the URL).

In these circumstances, you should use the HTTP `post` method.

HTTP post

When you send data from a form to the server using the HTTP `post` method, the form data is sent transparently in the *HTTP headers*. Although you do not see these headers, they are not, strictly speaking, secure on their own. If you send sensitive information such as credit card details, the data should be sent under a *Secure Sockets Layer* (*SSL*) and should be encrypted. For more information about SSL, there's a gentle introduction available at `https://computing.ece.vt.edu/~jkh/ Understanding_SSL_TLS.pdf`.

If the login form you just saw was sent using the `post` method, it could be represented like this in the HTTP headers:

```
User-agent: MSIE 10
Content-Type: application/x-www-form-urlencoded
Content-length: 35
...other headers go here...
txtUserName=Bob&pwdPassword=LetMeIn
```

The last line is the form data, which is in exactly the same format as the data after the question mark in the `get` method—it would also be URL-encoded, so any spaces or unsafe characters such as /, \, =, &, and + (which have special meanings in URLs) are replaced with a hex code to represent that character as they were in HTTP `get` requests.

There is nothing to stop you from using the `post` method to send form data to a page that also contains a query string. For example, you might have one page to handle users who want to subscribe to or unsubscribe from a newsletter, and you might choose to indicate whether users want to subscribe or unsubscribe in the query string. Meanwhile, you might want to send their actual contact details in a form that uses the `post` method because you are updating a data source. In this case, you could use the following `<form>` element:

```
<form action="http://www.example.com/newsletter.asp?action=subscribe"
    method="post">
```

The only issue with using the HTTP `post` method is that the information the user entered on the form cannot be bookmarked in the same way it can when it is contained in the URL. So you cannot use it to retrieve a page that was generated using specific form data as you can when you bookmark a page generated by most search engines, but it is good for security reasons.

CREATING MORE USABLE FORM FIELDS

Now it's time to enhance the form you created earlier using the usability tools you've picked up in the past few sections.

TRY IT OUT Contact Form Revisited

It is time to revisit the contact form from the earlier "Try It Out" section in this chapter. This time, you use techniques learned in the latter part of the chapter to add a new field and to make it more usable.

1. Open the file `emailForm.html` that you made earlier in the chapter, and save it as `emailForm2.html` so that you have a different copy to work with.

2. You should place `<label>` elements around the instructions that described the purpose of the form control. This `<label>` element should carry the `for` attribute, whose value is the value of the `id` attribute on the corresponding form control, like this one:

```
<tr>
  <td><label for="emailFrom">Your email</label></td>
  <td><input type="email" name="txtFrom" id="emailFrom"
    size="20" tabindex="1" maxlength="250"></td>
</tr>
```

3. Add in a new single-line text input to the beginning of the form, indicating to whom the message is sent. This input should be read-only:

```
<tr>
  <td><label for="emailTo">To</label></td>
  <td><input type="text" name="txtTo" readonly="readonly"
    id="emailTo" size="20" value="Example Cafe"></td>
</tr>
```

4. Set the tab index so that the input that allows visitors to enter their e-mail addresses receives focus first, followed by the text area where the visitors enter their messages:

```
<tr>
  <td><label for="emailFrom">Your email</label></td>
  <td><input type="email" name="txtFrom" id="emailFrom" size="20"
    tabindex="1" maxlength="250"></td>
</tr>

<tr>
  <td><label for="emailBody">Message</label></td>
  <td><textarea name="txtBody" id="emailBody" cols="50" rows="10"
tabindex="2"></textarea></td>
</tr>
```

5. Now split the form into two sections using the `<fieldset>` element. To make sure that the elements nest correctly, each fieldset needs its own table. The first section indicates that it is for information about the visitor's message.

```
<fieldset>
    <legend>Your message:</legend>
    <table>
      <tr>
        <td><label for="emailTo">To</label></td>
        <td><input type="email" name="txtTo" readonly="readonly" id="emailTo"
          size="20" value="Example Cafe"></td>
      </tr>

      <tr>
        <td><label for="emailFrom">Your email</label></td>
        <td><input type="text" name="txtFrom" id="emailFrom" size="20"
          tabindex="1" maxlength="250"></td>
      </tr>

      <tr>
        <td><label for="emailBody">Message</label></td>
        <td><textarea name="txtBody" id="emailBody" cols="50" rows="10"
          tabindex="2"></textarea></td>
      </tr>

    </table>
  </fieldset>
```

6. The second section is for information about the company (how the user found the site and if the user wants to be on the mailing list):

```
<fieldset>
    <legend>How you found us:</legend>
    <table>
      <tr>
        <td><label for="emailBody">How did you hear of us</label></td>
        <td>
        <select name="selReferrer">
          <option value="google">Google</option>
          <option value="ad">Local newspaper ad</option>
          <option value="friend">Friend</option>
          <option value="other">Other</option>
        </select>
          </td>
      </tr>

      <tr>
        <td><label for="newsletterSignup">Newsletter</label></td>
        <td><input type="checkbox" name="chkBody" id="newsletterSignup"

      checked="checked"> Ensure this box is checked if you would like
        to receive email updates</td>
      </tr>
    </table>
  </fieldset>
```

This extended registration form is now a lot more usable. If you save the file again and open it in your browser, you should find something that resembles Figure 6-30.

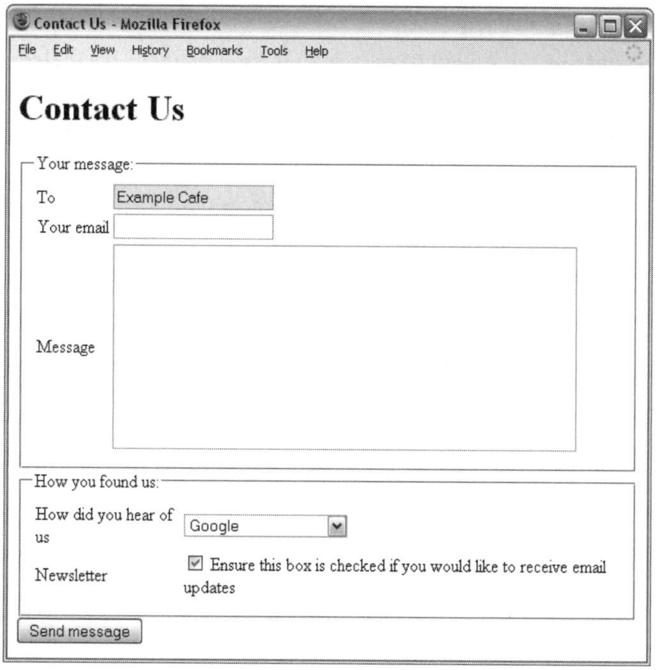

FIGURE 6-30

How It Works

Ensuring forms are easy to use is a vital piece of any successful site. In this Try It Out, you added labels to your form using the `<label>` element, then you utilized the `readonly` attribute to add the e-mail address to which you want the form sent, preventing the visitor from making changes. Finally, you added some organization using the `tabindex` attribute to create a tabbing order and the `<fieldset>` element to define sections of the form. These enhancements go a long way toward increasing the usability of your forms.

SUMMARY

This chapter introduced you to the world of creating online forms, which are a vital part of many sites. In most cases, when you want or need to directly collect information from a visitor to your site, you will use a form, and you have seen several examples of forms.

You learned how a form lives inside a `<form>` element, and that inside a form there are one or more form controls. You know how to use the `<input>` element to create several kinds of form controls, including many different types of single-line text input controls, as well as check boxes, radio buttons, file upload boxes, buttons, and hidden form controls. You can also use the `<textarea>` elements to create multiple line text inputs and the `<select>` and `<option>` elements to create select boxes. You also learned about new HTML5 elements such as `<progress>` and `<meter>` used for marking up complicated UI components simply.

After you create a form with its form controls, you need to ensure that each element is labeled properly so that users know what information they should enter or which selection to make. You can also organize larger forms using the `<fieldset>` and `<label>` elements and aid navigation with `tabindex` and `accesskey` attributes.

Finally, you learned when you should use the HTTP `get` or `post` methods to send form data to the server.

Next you'll learn about how to add style with CSS to the content you've learned to mark up in these chapters on HTML.

EXERCISES

1. Create an e-mail feedback form that looks like the one shown in Figure 6-31.

Reply to ad

Use the following form to respond to the ad:

To
[Star Seller]

To
[   ]

Subject
[   ]

Body
[   ]

[Send email]

FIGURE 6-31

The first textbox is a `readonly` textbox so that the user cannot alter the name of the person the e-mail is sent to.

2. Create a voting or ranking form that looks like the one shown in Figure 6-32.

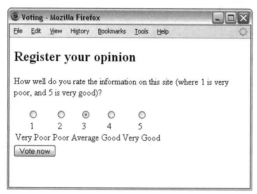

FIGURE 6-32

The following `<style>` element was added to the `<head>` of the document to make each column of the table the same fixed width with text aligned in the center. (You'll see more about this in Chapter 7, "Cascading Style Sheets.")

```
<head>
  <title>Voting</title>
  <style type="text/css">
    td {
      width:100px;
      text-align:center;
    }
  </style>
</head>
```

The answers to all the exercises are in Appendix A, "Answers to Exercises."

► **WHAT YOU LEARNED IN THIS CHAPTER**

TOPIC	KEY TAKEAWAY
The `<form>` element	The basic building block for all data collection on the web.
The `<input>` element	Various flavors of input designed to handle different kinds of data such as e-mail addresses, URLs, or just plain text.
Buttons	There are multiple ways to insert buttons into your page including a separate `<input>` type and the `<button>` element.
`<select>` boxes	`<select>` boxes enable you to provide a predefined set of choices for your users to choose from when inputting data.
New HTML5 form elements	Form elements such as `<meter>` and `<progress>` replace common JavaScript components with easy-to-use native implementations.

Cascading Style Sheets

WHAT YOU WILL LEARN IN THIS CHAPTER

➤ What makes up a CSS rule

➤ How properties and values control the presentation of different elements within your document

➤ How to control the presentation of text using CSS

➤ How CSS is based on a box model, and how you set different properties for these boxes (such as width and styles of borders)

WROX.COM CODE DOWNLOADS FOR THIS CHAPTER

The wrox.com code downloads for this chapter are found at www.wrox.com/remtitle .cgi?isbn=9781118340189 on the Download Code tab. The code is in the Chapter 7 download and individually named according to the names throughout the chapter.

Having learned how to structure the content of your documents using HTML's wide variety of elements and attributes, you can now start making your pages look a lot more exciting.

In this chapter, you learn how to use *cascading style sheets* (CSS) to take control of the style of your pages, including the color and size of fonts, the width and color of lines, and the amount of space between items on the page. The cascading style sheets specification works by enabling you to specify *rules* that say how the content of elements within your document should appear. For example, you can specify that the background of the page is a cream color, the contents of all <p> elements should display in gray using the Arial typeface, and all <h1> elements should be in red using the Times New Roman typeface.

By the end of the chapter, you should be confidently writing CSS style sheets and should have learned many of the properties you can use to affect the presentation of any document using CSS.

INTRODUCING CSS

CSS works by enabling you to associate *rules* with the elements that appear in a web page. These rules govern how the content of those elements should be rendered. Figure 7-1 shows an example of a CSS rule, which is made up of two parts:

➤ The *selector* indicates which element or elements the declaration applies to. (If it applies to more than one element, you can have a comma-separated list of several elements.)

➤ The *declaration* sets out how the elements referred to in the selector should be styled.

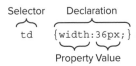

FIGURE 7-1

The rule in Figure 7-1 applies to all `<td>` elements and indicates that they should be 36 pixels wide.

The declaration is also split into two parts, separated by a colon:

➤ A *property* is the property of the selected element(s) that you want to affect, in this case the `width` property.

➤ A *value* is a specification for this property; in this case it is that table cells should be 36 pixels wide.

This is similar to the way that HTML elements can carry attributes and how the attribute controls a property of the element; the attributes' value would be the setting for that property. For example, a `<td>` element could have a `width` attribute whose value is the width you want the table to be:

```
<td width="36"></td>
```

With CSS, however, rather than specifying the attribute on each instance of the `<td>` element, the selector indicates that this one rule applies to all `<td>` elements in the document.

Here is an example of a CSS rule that applies to several different elements (the `<h1>`, `<h2>`, and `<h3>` elements). A comma separates the name of each element that this rule applies to. The rule also specifies several properties for these elements with each property-value pair separated by a semicolon. Note how all the properties are kept inside the curly braces:

```
h1, h2, h3 {
   font-weight : bold;
   font-family : arial;
   color : #000000;
   background-color : #FFFFFF;
}
```

Even if you have never seen a CSS rule before, you should now have a good idea of what this rule does. There are three heading elements named in the selector (<h1>, <h2>, and <h3>), and this rule says that where these headings are used they will be written in a bold Arial font in black with a white background.

> **NOTE** *If there is only one property-value pair in the declaration, you do not need to end it with a semicolon. However, because a declaration can consist of several property-value pairs, and each property-value pair within a rule must be separated by a semicolon, it is good practice to start adding semicolons every time you write a rule in case you want to add another rule later. If you forget to add the semicolon, any further property-value pairs will be ignored.*

A Basic Example

Now look at an example that shows how a set of CSS rules can transform the look of an HTML page. CSS rules can live inside the HTML document. Although, this example makes a separate file to hold the CSS rules, and the HTML page contains a link to this file, which is known as a *style sheet*.

Before you meet the style sheet, look at Figure 7-2, which shows the HTML page you will be styling on its own before the CSS rules have been attached.

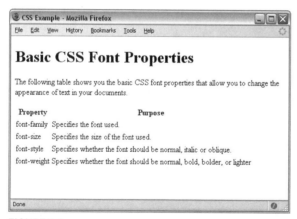

FIGURE 7-2

The code for the page you saw in Figure 7-2 (ch07_eg01.html) contains a heading, a paragraph, and a table. Inside the <head> element is a <link> element that tells the browser where to find the style sheet that will style this page; the location of the style sheet is given as the value of the href attribute. Also look at how some of the <td> elements carry a class attribute whose value is code. This distinguishes the table cells that contain code from other <td> elements in the document.

```
<!DOCTYPE html>
<html>
<head>
  <title>CSS Example</title>
```

```
    <link rel="stylesheet" href="ch07_eg01.css">
</head>

<body>

<h1>Basic CSS Font Properties</h1>
<p>The following table shows you the basic CSS font properties that allow
you to change the appearance of text in your documents.</p>

<table>
  <tr>
    <th>Property</th>
    <th>Purpose</th>
  </tr>
  <tr>
    <td class="code">font-family</td>
    <td>Specifies the font used.</td>
  </tr>
  <tr>
    <td class="code">font-size</td>
    <td>Specifies the size of the font used.</td>
  </tr>
  <tr>
    <td class="code">font-style</td>
    <td>Specifies whether the font should be normal, italic or oblique.</td>
  </tr>
  <tr>
    <td class="code">font-weight</td>
    <td>Specifies whether the font should be normal, bold, bolder, or lighter</td>
  </tr>
</table>

</body>
</html>
```

Now look at how to style this page. Figure 7-3 shows how the page looks with the style sheet attached.

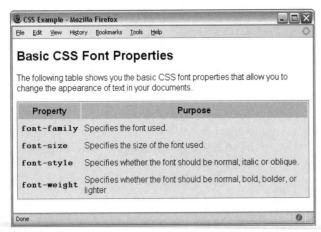

FIGURE 7-3

You can create a style sheet in the same editor you use to create your HTML pages. After you create a CSS file, it is saved with the file extension .css.

The style sheet for this example (ch07_eg01.css) uses several CSS rules. Now go through them one at a time so that you can see what each one does.

Before the first rule, however, there is a comment to tell you which file this style sheet was written for. Anything between the opening /* and closing */ is ignored by the browser and therefore does not have an effect on the appearance of the page:

```
/* Style sheet for ch07_eg01.html */
```

After the comment, the first rule applies to the <body> element. It specifies that the default color of any text and lines used on the page will be black and that the background of the page should be white. The colors here are represented using a hex code. (Appendix D, "Color Names and Values," covers the different ways to specify colors.) It also states that the typeface used throughout the document should be Arial. If Arial is not available, Verdana will be used instead; failing that, it will use its default font group that corresponds to that generic font group.

```
body {
  color:#000000;
  background-color : #ffffff;
  font-family : arial, verdana, sans-serif;
}
```

> **NOTE** *I always specify a* background-color *property for the body of a document because some people change the default background color of the windows on their computers (so that it is not a glaring white). If you do not set this property, the background color of those users' browsers will be whatever color they selected.*

The next two rules simply specify the size of the contents of the <h1> and <p> elements, respectively. (As you will see in the section "Lengths," px stands for pixels.)

```
h1 {
  font-size : 18px;
}
p {
  font-size : 12px;
}
```

Next, it is time to add a few settings to control the appearance of the table. First, give it a light gray background. Then, draw a border around the edge. Three properties are used to describe the border: The first says it is a solid line (rather than a dashed or dotted line), the second says it should be 1 pixel thick, and the third specifies that it should be light gray:

```
table {
  background-color : #efefef;
  border-style : solid;
  border-width : 1px;
  border-color : #999999;
}
```

Within the table, the table headings should have a medium gray background color (slightly darker than the main body of the table); the text should appear in a bold font; and between the edge of the cell and the text, there should be 5 pixels of padding. (As you will see in more detail in the section "The padding Property," *padding* is the term used for the space between the edge of a box and the content inside it.)

```
th {
   background-color : #cccccc;
   font-weight : bold;
   padding : 5px;
}
```

The individual table data cells also have 5 pixels of padding (like the headings). Adding this space makes the text much easier to read, and without it the text in one column might run up right next to the text in the neighboring column:

```
td {
   padding : 5px;
}
```

Finally, you may have noticed in Figure 7-3 that the cells of the table that contained the names of CSS properties were in a Courier font. If you look at the corresponding table cells in the HTML document, they carried a class attribute whose value was code. On its own, the class attribute does not change the display of the document (refer to Figure 7-2), but the class attribute does enable you to associate CSS rules with elements whose class attribute has a specific value. Therefore, the following rule applies only to <td> elements that carry a class attribute whose value is code, not to all <td> elements:

```
td.code {
   font-family : courier, courier-new, serif;
   font-weight : bold;
}
```

When you want to specify an element whose class attribute has a specific value, you put the value of that class attribute preceded by a period (or full stop) symbol.

There you have the first example; you can find the code for this example (ch07_eg01.html) with the download code for the rest of the book. This example provides you with an overview of how CSS works. Therefore, for the rest of this chapter and the following chapter you need to look at

➤ The properties you can use to control the appearance of various elements, and the values they can take. The different properties are grouped throughout this chapter and the next. For example, the properties that affect the appearance of fonts are together, those that affect borders are together, and so on.

➤ Different selectors that enable you to specify which elements these properties apply to. The basic example featured just a few of the many methods you can use to indicate which elements are controlled by which style rules.

➤ How CSS treats each element in a web page as if it were in its own box and how this affects the way in which you lay out web pages.

Along the way you also see where you can use CSS rules in your documents, the units of measurements used in CSS (such as pixels and percentages), and a powerful concept called *inheritance*.

Inheritance

One of the powerful features of CSS is that when a property has been applied to one element, it will often be *inherited* by child elements (elements contained within the element that the rules were declared upon). For example, after the `font-family` property had been declared for the `<body>` element in the previous example, it applied to all the elements inside the `<body>` element. This saves you from repeating the same rules for every element that makes up a web page.

If another rule is more specific about which elements it applies to, then it overrides any properties associated with the `<body>` element or any other containing element. In the preceding example, most of the text was in an Arial typeface, as specified in the rule associated with the `<body>` element; although, there were a few table cells that used a Courier typeface. The table cells that were different had a `class` attribute whose value was `code`:

```
<td class="code">font-size</td>
```

Here you can see the rule associated with these elements:

```
td.code {
  font-family : courier, courier-new, serif;
  font-weight : bold;
}
```

This rule takes precedence over the one associated with the `<body>` element because the selector is more specific about which element it applies to. The W3C site (`http://www.w3.org/TR/CSS21/cascade.html#specificity`) offers a set of rules for determining how specific a rule is. Warning, it's not for the faint of heart.

The way in which some properties inherit saves you from writing out rules and all the property-value pairs for each element and makes for a more compact style sheet. Appendix C, "CSS Properties," is a handy reference and tells you which ones do and do not inherit.

WHERE YOU CAN ADD CSS RULES

The example that you saw at the beginning of the chapter placed the CSS rules in a separate file known as an *external style sheet*. CSS rules can also appear in two places inside the HTML document:

➤ Inside a `<style>` element, which sits inside the `<head>` element of a document

➤ As a value of a `style` attribute on any element that can carry the `style` attribute

When the style sheet rules are held inside a `<style>` element in the head of the document, they are referred to as an *internal style sheet*.

```
<head>
  <title>Internal Style sheet</title>
  <style type="text/css">
  body {
    color : #000000;
    background-color : #ffffff;
    font-family : arial, verdana, sans-serif;
  }
```

```
  h1 {
    font-size : 18pt;
  }
  p {
    font-size : 12pt;
  }
</style>
</head>
```

When `style` attributes are used on HTML elements, they are known as *inline style rules*, for example:

```
<td style="font-family:courier; padding:5px; border-style:solid;
border-width:1px; border-color:#000000; ">
```

Here you can see that the properties are added as the value of the `style` attribute. You still need to separate each property from its value with a colon and each of the property-value pairs from each other with a semicolon. However, there is no need for a selector here (because the style is automatically applied to the element that carries the `style` attribute), and there are no curly braces.

You should generally avoid using both inline style rules and internal style sheets in favor of using external style sheets. There are some cases in which both are useful, but external sheets are much easier to maintain. You learn more about this in the "Advantages of External Style Sheets" section.

As you've already learned, external style sheets are loaded using the `<link>` element. Before moving on, take a slightly more in-depth look at the `<link>` element and associated attributes.

The <link> Element

The `<link>` element is used in web pages to describe the relationship between two documents; for example, it can be used in an HTML page to specify a style sheet that should be used to style a page. You may also see the `<link>` element used in HTML pages for other purposes, for example, to specify an RSS feed that corresponds with a page.

It is a different kind of link than the `<a>` element because the two documents are automatically associated—the user does not need to click anything to activate the link.

The `<link>` element is always an empty element, and when used with style sheets, it must carry two attributes: `rel` and `href`. Here is an example of the `<link>` element used in an HTML page indicating that it should be styled by a CSS file called `interface.css`, which lives in a subdirectory called CSS:

```
<link rel="stylesheet"  href="../CSS/interface.css">
```

In addition to the core attributes, the `<link>` element can also take the following attributes:

```
charset href hreflang media rel type sizes target
```

You have met many of these already, so the more important ones are discussed in the following sections.

The rel Attribute

The `rel` attribute is required and specifies the relationship between the document containing the link and the document being linked to. The key value for working with style sheets is `stylesheet`:

```
rel="stylesheet"
```

The other possible values for this element are discussed in Chapter 3, "Links and Navigation."

The href Attribute

The `href` attribute specifies the URL for the document being linked to:

```
href="../stylesheets/interface.css"
```

The value of this attribute can be an absolute or relative URL (which were covered in Chapter 3, "Links and Navigation"), but it is usually a relative URL because the style sheet is part of the site.

The media Attribute

The `media` attribute specifies the output device that is intended for use with the document:

```
media="screen"
```

Although this attribute is not always used, it is important because people access the Internet in different ways using different devices. Table 7-1 shows the possible values.

TABLE 7-1: Values of the media Attribute

VALUE	USES
screen	Nonpaged computer screens (such as desktop computers and laptops)
tty	Media with a fixed-pitch character grid, such as teletypes, terminals, or portable devices with limited display capabilities
Tv	TV devices with low-resolution, color screens, and limited ability to scroll down pages
print	Printed documents, which are sometimes referred to as *paged media* (and documents shown onscreen in print preview mode)
projection	Projectors
handheld	Handheld devices, which often have small screens, rely upon bitmapped graphics, and have limited bandwidth
braille	Braille tactile feedback devices
embossed	Braille paged printers
speech	Speech synthesizers
all	Suitable for all devices

The <style> Element

The <style> element is used inside the <head> element to contain style sheet rules within a web page, rather than linking to an external document. It is also sometimes used when a single page needs to contain just a few extra rules that do not apply to the other pages of the site that all share the same style sheet.

For example, here is a style sheet attached to the HTML document using the <link> element you just learned about, as well as a <style> element containing an additional rule for <h1> elements:

```
<head>
  <title>
  <link rel="stylesheet" href="../styles/mySite.css">
  <style type="text/css">
    h1 {
      color:#FF0000;
    }
  </style>
</head>
```

When you use the <style> element it should always carry the type attribute although it's not mandatory. In addition to all the global attributes, it can carry:

```
type media scoped
```

Advantages of External Style Sheets

If two or more documents are going to use a style sheet, you should use an external style sheet. There are several reasons for this, including the following:

➤ It saves you repeating the same style rules in each page.

➤ You can change the appearance of several pages by altering just the style sheet rather than each individual page. This means it is easier to update your site if you want to, for example, change the style of font used in all headings or alter the color of all links.

➤ After a visitor to your site has downloaded the CSS with the first page of your site that uses it, subsequent pages will be quicker to load (because the browser retains a copy of the style sheet and the rules do not need to be downloaded for every page). This also puts less strain on the server (the computer that sends the web pages to the people viewing the site) because the pages it sends out are smaller.

➤ The style sheet can act as a style template to help different authors achieve the same style of document without learning all the individual style settings.

➤ Because the web pages do not contain the style rules, different style sheets can be attached to the same document. So you can use the same HTML document with one style sheet when the viewer is on a desktop computer, another style sheet when the user has a handheld device, another style sheet when the page is being printed, another style sheet when the page is being viewed on a TV, and so on. You can reuse the same document with different style sheets for different visitors' needs.

➤ A style sheet can import and use styles from other style sheets, allowing for modular development and good reuse.

➤ If you remove the style sheet, you can make the site more accessible for those with visual impairments because you are no longer controlling the fonts and color schemes.

It is fair to say, therefore, that whenever you write a whole site, you should use an external style sheet to control the presentation of it (rather than putting CSS rules in the individual web pages). Although, as you see in the next chapter, you might use several external style sheets for different aspects of the site.

CSS PROPERTIES

You now know that styling a web page using CSS involves creating rules, and these rules contain two parts: a selector to indicate which elements the rule applies to and one or more properties that control the presentation of these elements. So, if there is a part of the page that you want to make a certain color or size, then you need to use the correct selector to target that part of the page and the correct properties to change their appearance accordingly.

The properties are grouped together into related functionality; for example, there are properties that enable you to control the presentation of tables, lists, and backgrounds. The following list shows the main properties available to you, all of which you meet in this chapter or Chapter 8, "More Cascading Style Sheets."

FONT

font

font-family

font-size

font-style

font-variant

font-weight

TEXT

color

direction

letter-spacing

text-align

text-decoration

text-indent

text-shadow

text-transform

unicode-bidi

white-space

word-spacing

BACKGROUND

background

background-attachment

background-color

background-image

background-position

background-repeat

BORDER

border

border-color

border-style

border-width

border-bottom

border-bottom-color

border-bottom-style

border-bottom-width

border-left

border-left-color

border-left-style

border-left-width

border-right

border-right-color

border-right-style

border-right-width

border-top

border-top-color

border-top-style

border-top-width

MARGIN

margin

margin-bottom

margin-left

margin-right

margin-top

PADDING

padding

padding-bottom

padding-left

padding-right

padding-top

DIMENSIONS

height

line-height

max-height

max-width

min-height

min-width

width

POSITIONING

bottom

clip

left

overflow

right

top

vertical-align

z-index

OUTLINES

outline

outline-color

outline-style

outline-width

TABLE

border-collapse

border-spacing

caption-side

empty-cells

table-layout

LIST and MARKER

list-style

list-style-image

list-style-position

list-style-type

marker-offset

GENERATED CONTENT

content

counter-increment

counter-reset

quotes

CLASSIFICATION

clear

cursor

display

float

position

visibility

In addition there is a new version of CSS, CSS3, which focuses on *modules*. These modules are broken into separate areas of focus. The following modules are the focus of Chapter 9, "Rounded Corners, Animations, Custom Fonts, and More with CSS3":

➤ Selectors

➤ Color

➤ Backgrounds and Borders

➤ Multicolumn Layout

➤ Media Queries

➤ Fonts

➤ 2D Transforms

➤ 3D Transforms

➤ Animations and Transitions

There are also some properties that are not covered in this book, either because they are rarely used or because there is little support for them. (For example, aural style sheets because there are not many aural browsers that support them.) You can find out more about these properties on the following websites, or you can read a book dedicated to CSS:

➤ `www.w3.org/style/css/`

➤ `www.devguru.com/Technologies/css/quickref/css_index.html`

CONTROLLING TEXT

Several properties enable you to control the appearance of text in your documents. These can be split into two groups:

➤ Those that directly affect the *font* and its appearance. (These include the typeface used, whether it is regular, bold, or italic, and the size of the text.)

➤ Those that would have the same effect on the text irrespective of the font used. (These include the color of the text and the spacing between words or letters.)

Table 7-2 lists the properties that directly affect the font (the first of these two groups):

TABLE 7-2: Font Properties

PROPERTY	PURPOSE
font	Enables you to combine several of the following properties into one.
font-family	Specifies the typeface or family of the font that should be used.
font-size	Specifies the size of the font.
font-weight	Specifies whether the font should be normal or bold.
font-style	Specifies whether the font should be normal, italic, or oblique.
font-variant	Specifies whether the font should be normal or small caps.

Before looking at these properties in detail, it helps to understand some key terms used in typography. Perhaps most important, a font is not the same thing as a typeface:

➤ A *typeface* is a family of fonts, such as the Arial family.

➤ A *font* is a specific member of that family, such as Arial 12-point bold.

You often see the terms used interchangeably, but it is helpful to be aware of the distinction.

Typefaces tend to belong to one of two groups: serif and sans-serif fonts. Serif fonts have extra curls on letters. For example, in Figure 7-4, the first *l* contains a *serif* on the top of the letter and at the bottom of the letter, whereas sans-serif fonts have straight ends to the letters, such as in the second example.

The third common style of a typeface is a monospaced serif font. Every letter in a monospaced font is the same width, whereas nonmonospaced fonts have different widths for different letters. (For example, in serif and sans-serif fonts, the *l* tends to be narrower than the *m*.)

serif font   sans-serif font   monospace font

FIGURE 7-4

Serif fonts are generally assumed to be easier to read for large amounts of printed text. But on the Internet many people find serif fonts harder to read for long stretches, largely because the resolution of a computer screen is not as good as printed documents, which makes the less detailed sans-serif fonts easier to read.

So that you can study the properties that affect fonts, most of the examples in the following section use a similar structure. Paragraphs of text will be repeated, and each <p> element carries a class attribute with a different value, for example:

```
<p class="sans-serif">Here is some text in a sans-serif font.</p>
<p class="serif">Here is some text in a serif font.</p>
<p class="monospace">Here is some text in a monospaced font.</p>
```

You can then see how different properties affect each <p> element by writing a separate rule for each paragraph. You can use the value of the class attributes in the CSS selectors to create rules that apply just to one <p> element at a time.

The font-family Property

The font-family property enables you to specify the typeface that should be used for any text inside the element(s) that a CSS rule applies to.

When choosing typefaces you must know that without using the @font-face directive, covered in Chapter 9, browsers can display only HTML text in the font you have specified if that typeface is installed on that computer. So, if you specify a font such as Futura or Garamond, and I do not have it on my computer, I would see the text in a different font—not the one you specified.

This is why, if you look at a selection of websites, most rely heavily on a small selection of typefaces installed on most computers that access the web, in particular Arial, Courier/Courier New, Georgia, Times/Times New Roman, and Verdana. (From this list, Arial and Verdana are particularly popular because they are considered easy to read online.)

To help matters, you can specify a list of typefaces so that if users do not have your first choice of typeface installed on their computer, the browser can try to show the text in your second or third choice. Each typeface in the list is separated by a comma, and if the name contains spaces (such as `times new roman` or `courier new`) you should place the name of the typeface in double quotation marks (`ch07_eg02.css`), like so:

```
p.sans-serif {
  font-family : arial, verdana, sans-serif;
}
p.serif {
  font-family : times, "times new roman", serif;
}
p.monospace {
  font-family : courier, "courier new", monospace;
}
```

Figure 7-5 shows what this example would look like in a browser; you can see the different types of fonts used for each paragraph (`ch07_eg02.html`).

FIGURE 7-5

You may notice that each list of typefaces in the previous example ends with so-called *generic font names* (sans-serif, serif, and monospace). The idea behind these is that each computer will have a font that corresponds to one of five generic font groups (sans-serif, serif, monospace, cursive, and fantasy), and if it cannot find the typefaces you have specified, it can use its choice of font that corresponds to that generic font group, as shown in Table 7-3.

TABLE 7-3: Generic Font Names

GENERIC FONT NAME	TYPE OF FONT	EXAMPLE
serif	Fonts with serifs	Times
sans-serif	Fonts without serifs	Arial
monospace	Fixed-width fonts	Courier
cursive	Fonts that emulate handwriting	Comic Sans
fantasy	Decorative fonts for titles and so on	Impact

One thing to consider when choosing a list of fonts is that each font can be of different heights or widths, so you probably want to choose a list of fonts that are of a similar size. (Otherwise, the layout could look different to what you expect.) For example, Courier New is quite short and wide, so if this were your first choice, it would not be good to have Impact as a second choice because Impact is quite tall and narrow.

If you want to use a specific typeface, you must wade into the slightly scary waters of web fonts. Chapter 9 covers the benefits and shortcomings of this new technology.

The font-size Property

The `font-size` property enables you to specify a size for the font. You often see the value for this property specified in pixels, like so:

```
p.twelve {
   font-size : 12px;
}
```

However, you can provide a value in many ways:

➤ **Length:** (Along with pixels, there are several other units of length that you will learn about in the section "Lengths" later in this chapter.)

```
px em ex pt in cm pc mm rem vw vh
```

➤ **Absolute size:** Each of these values corresponds to a fixed size:

```
xx-small x-small small medium large x-large xx-large
```

➤ **Relative size:** This value is relative to the surrounding text:

```
smaller larger
```

➤ **Percentage:** A percentage is calculated as a proportion of the parent element:

```
2% 10% 25% 50% 100%
```

Here is an example of each of these ways to specify a value for the `font-size` property:

```
p.one {
   font-size : xx-small;
}
p.twelve {
   font-size : 12px;
}
p.thirteen {
   font-size : 3pc;
}
p.fourteen {
   font-size : 10%;
}
```

Figure 7-6 shows how a selection of these font sizes works in the browser. (`ch07_eg03.html` and `ch07_eg03.css` contain several examples of different ways to specify size and compare how they look.)

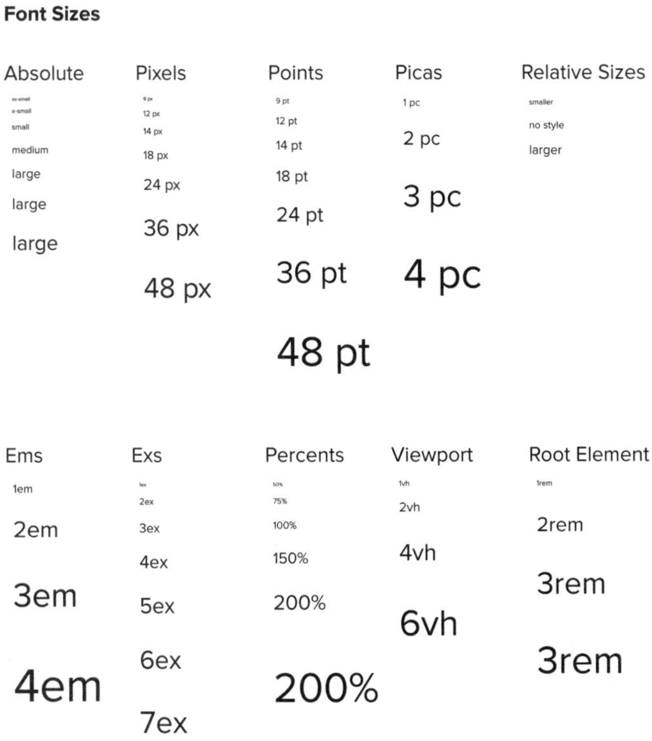

Font Sizes

Absolute	Pixels	Points	Picas	Relative Sizes
xx-small	9 px	9 pt	1 pc	smaller
x-small	12 px	12 pt		no style
small	14 px	14 pt	2 pc	larger
medium	18 px	18 pt		
large	24 px	24 pt	3 pc	
large	36 px			
large	48 px	36 pt	4 pc	
		48 pt		

Ems	Exs	Percents	Viewport	Root Element
1em	1ex	50%	1vh	1rem
2em	2ex	75%	2vh	2rem
	3ex	100%		
3em	4ex	150%	4vh	3rem
	5ex	200%	6vh	
4em	6ex	200%		3rem
	7ex			

FIGURE 7-6

The font-weight Property

Most fonts have different variations, such as bold and italic. When typographers create a new font, it is not unusual for them to individually craft a separate, thicker version of each character for the bold variation.

Despite all this careful work, rather than finding the bold version of a typeface, browsers tend to use an algorithm that takes the normal version of the font and makes it thicker. Because it uses an algorithm, it means you can also create a lighter version of fonts. This is what the `font-weight` property is for.

The possible values for `font-weight` are:

```
normal bold bolder lighter 100 200 300 400 500 600 700 800 900
```

The following example uses several of these values (`ch07_eg04.css`):

```css
p.one {
   font-weight : normal;
}
p.two {
   font-weight : bold;
}
p.three {
   font-weight : normal;
}
p.three span {
   font-weight : bolder;
}
p.four {
   font-weight : bold;
}
p.four span {
   font-weight : lighter;
}
p.five {
   font-weight : 100;
}
p.six {
   font-weight : 200;
}
```

Figure 7-7 shows you how these values appear in the browser (`ch07_eg04.html`).

Of these values, `bold` is most commonly used. Although, you might see the use of `normal`. (Especially if a large section of text is already bold and an exception must be created in which just a few words are not in bold.)

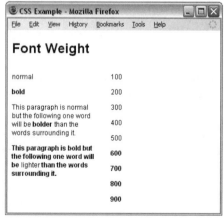

FIGURE 7-7

The font-style Property

The font-style property enables you to specify that a font should be normal, italic, or oblique, and these are the values of the font-style property, for example (ch07_eg05.css):

```
p.one {
   font-style : normal;
}
p.two {
   font-style : italic;
}
p.three {
   font-style : oblique;
}
```

Figure 7-8 shows you how these values appear in the browser (from ch07_eg05.html).

In typography, an italic version of a font would normally be a specifically stylized version of the font based on calligraphy, whereas an oblique version of the font would take the normal version of the font and place it at an angle. In CSS, when you specify a font-style property should be italic, browsers usually take the normal version of the font and simply render it at an angle (as you would expect with an oblique version of a font).

FIGURE 7-8

The font-variant Property

There are two possible values for the font-variant property: normal and small-caps. A small caps font looks like a smaller version of the uppercase letterset.

For example, look at the following paragraph, which contains a <span> with a class attribute (ch07_eg06.html):

```
<p>This is a normal font, but then <span class="smallcaps">there
are some small caps</span> in the middle.</p>
```

Now look at the style sheet (ch07_eg06.css):

```
p {
   font-variant : normal;
}
span.smallcaps {
   font-variant : small-caps;
}
```

As you can see from Figure 7-9, the rule associated with the <span> element indicates that its content should be shown in small caps.

FIGURE 7-9

TEXT FORMATTING

In addition to the properties that affect the font, several properties affect the appearance or formatting of your text (independently from the font it is shown in), as shown in Table 7-4.

TABLE 7-4: Text Formatting Properties

PROPERTY	PURPOSE
color	Specifies the color of the text.
text-align	Specifies the horizontal alignment of the text within its containing element.
vertical-align	Specifies the vertical alignment of text within its containing element.
text-decoration	Specifies whether the text should be underlined, overlined, or strikethrough.
text-indent	Specifies an indent from the left border for the text.
text-transform	Specifies that the content of the element should all be uppercase, lowercase, or capitalized.
text-shadow	Specifies that the text should have a drop shadow.
letter-spacing	Controls the width between letters (known to print designers as *tracking*).
word-spacing	Controls the amount of space between each word.
white-space	Specifies whether the white space should be collapsed, preserved, or prevented from wrapping.
direction	Specifies the direction of text (similar to the dir attribute).

The color Property

The `color` property enables you to specify the color of the text. The value of this property is most commonly a hex code for a color or a color name. (Both Chapter 9 and Appendix D further discuss the way in which colors are specified for the web.)

For example, the following rule (`ch07_eg07.css`) would make the content of paragraph elements red, as shown in `ch07_eg07.html`:

```
p {
   color : #ff0000;
}
```

The text-align Property

The `text-align` property works like the deprecated `align` attribute would with text. It aligns the text within its containing element or the browser window. Table 7-5 displays possible values.

TABLE 7-5: Possible Values for the text-align Property

VALUE	PURPOSE
left	Aligns the text with the left border of the containing element.
right	Aligns the text with the right border of the containing element.
center	Centers the content in the middle of the containing element.
justify	Spreads the width across the whole width of the containing element.
start	Added in CSS3, aligns inline contents to the start of the line box.
end	Added in CSS3, aligns inline contents to the end of the line box.

Figure 7-10 shows you how these would work in a table that is 500 pixels wide.

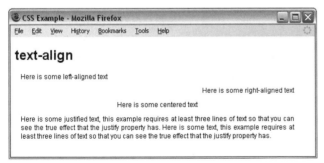

FIGURE 7-10

Here are the rules for each row of this example (`ch07_eg08.css`):

```
.leftAlign {
  text-align : left;
}
.rightAlign {
  text-align : right;
}
.center {
  text-align : center;
}
.justify {
  text-align : justify;
}
```

The effects of these rules are shown in `ch07_08.html`.

The vertical-align Property

The `vertical-align` property is useful when working with inline elements, in particular images and portions of text. It enables you to control their vertical positioning within the containing element, for example:

```
span.footnote {
  vertical-align : sub;
}
```

It can take several values, as shown in Table 7-6.

TABLE 7-6: Values for the vertical-align Property

VALUE	PURPOSE
baseline	Aligns to the baseline of the parent element. (This is the default setting.)
sub	Makes the element subscript. With images, the top of the image should be on the baseline. With text, the top of the font body should be on the baseline.
super	Makes the element superscript. With images, the bottom of the image should be level with the top of the font. With text, the bottom of the descender (the parts of letters such as *g* and *p* that go beneath the line of text) should align with the top of the font body.
top	Aligns the top of the text and the top of the image with the top of the tallest element on the line.
text-top	Aligns the top of the text and the top of the image with the top of the tallest text on the line.

middle	Aligns the vertical midpoint of the element with the vertical midpoint of the parent.
bottom	Aligns the bottom of the text and the bottom of the image with the bottom of the lowest element on the line.
text-bottom	Aligns the bottom of the text and the bottom of the image with the bottom of the lowest text on the line.

This property may also accept inherit, a length and a percentage value.

You can try out all these in your browser using ch07_eg09.html.

Figure 7-11 shows some of these values.

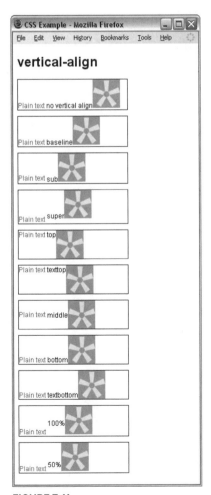

FIGURE 7-11

The text-decoration Property

The text-decoration property enables you to specify the values, as shown in Table 7-7.

TABLE 7-7: Values for the text-decoration Property

VALUE	PURPOSE
underline	Adds a line under the content.
overline	Adds a line over the top of the content.
line-through	Adds a line through the middle of the content, such as strikethrough text. In general, this should be used only to indicate text marked for deletion.
none	Removes any text-decoration on an element.

Here are these properties used on separate paragraphs (ch07_eg10.css):

```
p.underline {
  text-decoration : underline;
}
p.overline {
  text-decoration : overline;
}
p.line-through {
  text-decoration : line-through;
}
```

Figure 7-12 shows you what they look like in Firefox (ch07_eg10.html).

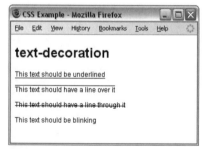

FIGURE 7-12

The text-indent Property

The text-indent property enables you to indent the first line of text within an element. In the following example it has been applied to the second paragraph (ch07_eg11.html):

```
<p>This paragraph should be aligned with the left-hand side of the browser. </p>
<p class="indent">Just the first line of this paragraph should be indented by
3 em, this should not apply to any subsequent lines in the same paragraph. </p>
```

Now, here is the rule that indents the second paragraph (ch07_eg11.css):

```css
.indent {
  text-indent : 3em;
}
```

You can see what this looks like in Figure 7-13.

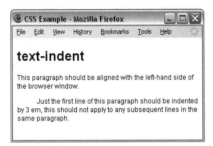

FIGURE 7-13

The text-shadow Property

The text-shadow property is supposed to create a *drop shadow*, which is a dark version of the word just behind it and slightly offset. This has often been used in print media, and its popularity has meant that is has gained its own CSS property. The value for this property is quite complicated because it can take a color followed by three lengths (ch07_eg12.css):

```css
.dropShadow {
  text-shadow : #999999 10px 10px 3px;
}
```

After the color has been specified, the first two lengths specify how far from the original text the drop shadow should fall (using X and Y coordinates), whereas the third specifies how blurred the drop shadow should be.

This property is supported in all the major browsers, including Internet Explorer 10 or later. Figure 7-14 shows what this example (ch07_eg12.html) looks like in Safari on a Mac.

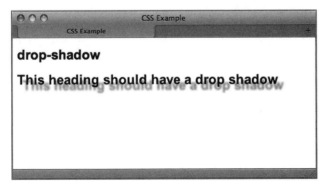

FIGURE 7-14

The text-transform Property

The `text-transform` property enables you to specify the case for the content of an element. The possible values are shown in Table 7-8.

TABLE 7-8: Values for the text-transform Property

VALUE	PURPOSE
none	No change takes place.
capitalize	Capitalizes the first letter of every word.
uppercase	Makes the entire content of the element uppercase.
lowercase	Makes the entire content of the element lowercase.

To demonstrate this property, in the following example there are four paragraphs (ch07_eg13.html):

```
<p class="none">This text has not been transformed</p>
<p class="capitalize">The first letter of each word will be capitalized</p>
<p class="uppercase">All of this text will be uppercase</p>
<p class="lowercase">ALL OF THIS TEXT WILL BE LOWERCASE</p>
```

Here you can see the four different values for the `text-transform` property in use (ch07_eg13.css):

```
p.none {
  text-transform : none;
}
p.capitalize {
  text-transform : capitalize;
}
p.uppercase {
  text-transform : uppercase;
}
p.lowercase {
  text-transform : lowercase;
}
```

Figure 7-15 shows you how the paragraphs would appear in a browser with these styles applied.

FIGURE 7-15

The letter-spacing Property

The `letter-spacing` property controls something that print designers refer to as *tracking*: the gap between letters. Loose tracking indicates that there is a lot of space between letters, whereas tight tracking refers to letters squeezed together. No tracking refers to the normal gap between letters for that font.

If you want to increase or decrease the spacing between letters, you most likely specify this in pixels or something known as an *em*. (Although, it can be any unit of length that CSS supports—you look at the CSS units of length in the "Length" section in this chapter.)

If you have a section of text where letter spacing has been altered, you can specify that an element should have no tracking using the keyword `normal`.

The first paragraph of the following example shows normal tracking. The second paragraph shows a gap of 3 pixels used between each letter. The third paragraph shows a gap between each letter of 0.5 em. The final paragraph shows spacing cut by 1 pixel from what it would have been in normal tracking (`ch07_eg14.css`):

```
.two {
  letter-spacing : 3px;
}
.three {
  letter-spacing : 0.5em;
}
.four {
  letter-spacing : -1px;
}
```

Figure 7-16 gives you an indication of what this looks like in a browser (`ch07_eg14.html`).

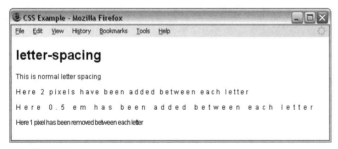

FIGURE 7-16

The word-spacing Property

The `word-spacing` property sets the gap between words, and its value should be a unit of length. In the following example (`ch07_eg15.css`), in the first paragraph there is a standard gap between each of the words. In the second paragraph the gap is 10 pixels between each of the words. In the final paragraph the gap has been cut to 1 pixel less than normal spacing:

```
.two {
  word-spacing : 20px;
}
.three {
  word-spacing : -1px;
}
```

Figure 7-17 gives you an indication of what this looks like (ch07_eg15.html).

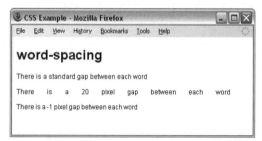

FIGURE 7-17

The white-space Property

As you saw in Chapter 1, browsers change any two or more spaces next to each other into a single space and make any carriage returns a single space. The white-space property controls whether white space is preserved, offering the same results as the HTML <pre> element where white space is preserved and the nowrap attribute where text is broken only onto a new line if explicitly told to. Table 7-9 shows the possible values for this property.

TABLE 7-9: Values for the white-space Property

VALUE	PURPOSE
normal	Follows normal white space collapsing rules.
pre	Preserves white space just as in the <pre> element of HTML, but the formatting is whatever is indicated for that element. (It is not a monospaced font by default like the <pre> element.)
nowrap	Breaks text onto a new line only if explicitly told to with a element; otherwise text does not wrap.

For example, you can use the white-space property like so (ch07_eg16.css):

```
.pre {
  white-space : pre;
```

```
    }
    .nowrap {
        white-space : nowrap;
    }
```

You can see both of these properties working in Figure 7-18 (ch07_eg16.html).

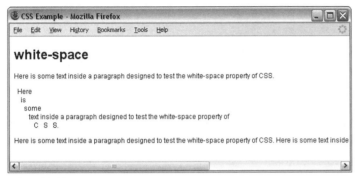

FIGURE 7-18

The direction Property

The direction property is rather like the dir attribute and specifies the direction in which the text should flow. Table 7-10 shows the possible values.

TABLE 7-10: Values for the direction Property

VALUE	PURPOSE
ltr	The text flows from left to right.
rtl	The text flows from right to left.
inherit	The text flows in the same direction as its parent element.

For example, here are rules for two paragraphs indicating different directions for the text (ch07_eg17.css used with ch07_eg17.html):

```
    p.ltr {
        direction : ltr;
    }
    p.rtl {
        direction : rtl;
    }
```

In practice, both IE and Firefox use this property much as the align attribute is used. The value rtl simply right-aligns text, as shown in Figure 7-19. Note, however, that the period (or full stop) is to the left of the sentence in the paragraph that is supposed to be running right to left.

FIGURE 7-19

TEXT PSEUDO-CLASSES

While you are learning about text, there are two pseudo-classes that can help you work with text. These pseudo-classes enable you to render either the first letter or the first line of an element in a different way than the rest of that element.

The first-letter Pseudo-Class

The `first-letter` pseudo-class enables you to specify a rule just for the first letter of an element. This is most commonly used on the first character of a new page, either in some magazine articles or in books.

Here is an example of the `first-letter` pseudo-class applied to a `<p>` element that has a `class` attribute whose value is `introduction`. Note how the selector for the element and the `first-letter` pseudo-class are separated by a colon (`ch07_eg18.css` used with `ch07_eg18.html`):

```
p.introduction:first-letter {
   font-size : 42px;
}
```

Figure 7-20 shows the effect of this `first-letter` pseudo-class (and also shows the next pseudo-class you look at).

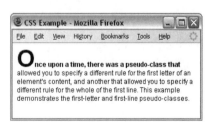

FIGURE 7-20

The first-line Pseudo-Class

The `first-line` pseudo-class enables you to render the first line of any paragraph differently from the rest of the paragraph. Commonly, this is a bold font so that the reader can clearly see an introduction (for articles) or the first line (for poems).

The name of the pseudo-class is separated from the selector for the element by a colon:

```
p.introduction:first-line {
   font-weight : bold;
}
```

It is worth trying this example out in a browser because if you resize the window so that there is less text on the first line, you can see how only the first line of text in the browser is given this new style. Refer to Figure 7-20 to see the `first-line` pseudo-class in action, which also demonstrates the `first-letter` pseudo-class.

STYLING TEXT

The single most common task with CSS on the web is styling text. In this next Try It Out, you style text on the sample website.

TRY IT OUT Styling the Example Café Text

Now that you've learned about using CSS to format text, it is time to put what you have learned into practice by adding styles to the Example Café website.

1. To create an external style sheet, start your text editor and create a file called `interface.css`. Save it in a folder called `css` with the rest of the Example Café files. At the beginning of the style sheet, add a comment to explain what the style sheet is for:

```
/* style sheet for Example Cafe */
```

2. The default font family should be Arial. If the user does not have Arial installed, suggest Verdana, failing which the computer's default is sans-serif font.

```
body {
   font-family : arial, verdana, sans-serif;
}
```

3. To have the headings stand out in a different font, have Georgia as the first choice for headings, then Times, and finally the default serif font. To have them appear in gray rather than black, specify a color for the headings using the `color` property (which is discussed in more detail in the following chapter). Because you want to make all headings the same, specify the styles in a single rule like so:

```
h2 {
  font-family : georgia, times, serif;
  color : #666666;
}
```

4. The paragraphs of text might look a little better slightly smaller than the default size of text, so make them 90 percent of the default size. Also make the text dark gray rather than black.

```
p {
  font-size:90%;
  color:#333333;
}
```

5. Now look at the navigation. In particular, you want to control the appearance of the links in the navigation. To do this, open the HTML pages and add an `id` attribute to the `<nav>` element that contains the navigation.

```
<nav id="navigation">
  HOME
  <a href="menu.html">MENU</a>
  <a href="recipes.html">RECIPES</a>
  <a href="opening.html">OPENING</a>
  <a href="contact.html">CONTACT</a>
</nav>
```

6. To add a selector (which specifies that you want to select only `<a>` elements that live inside an element that has an `id` attribute whose value is `navigation`), use the hash or pound symbol followed by the value of the `id` attribute. Specify that these links should be a light blue to match the logo:

```
#navigation a {
  color:#3399cc;
}
```

7. By default, links appear with underlines; you can remove these by using the `text-decoration` property with a value of `none`:

```
#navigation a {
  color : #3399cc;
  text-decoration : none;
}
```

8. In the HTML pages, you need to add the `<link>` element, which associates the style sheet with the pages. Add this to every page:

```
<link rel="stylesheet" href="css/interface.css">
```

Now all the pages in the example use this same style sheet, and your homepage should look a little more like the example in Figure 7-21.

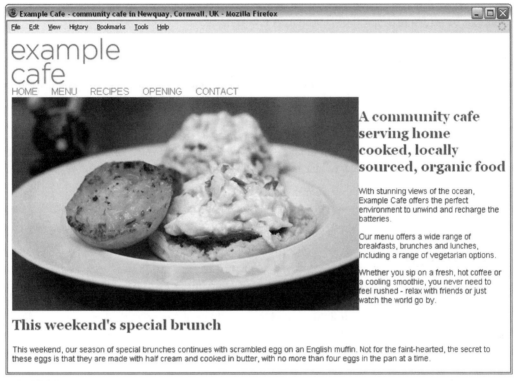

FIGURE 7-21

How It Works

CSS rules are applied to elements using a system that uses specificity to calculate which properties should be applied to which elements. In this case there are only two sources for properties: the style sheet you created and the default styling present in every browser. In this case the rules you've written override the default browser styling. You'll learn more about how specificity works as you continue to learn about CSS, beginning with an in-depth look at selectors in the next section.

SELECTORS

So far, you have seen lots of examples of properties that affect the presentation of text, and you have seen how you can apply these properties to elements using style rules. Before continuing to look at more properties, you need to look at some more fundamental issues. Start by looking at how you can use a different type of a *selector* to specify which elements a style sheet rule can apply to. There are actually several ways to do this, not just by using the names of the elements as you have seen so far in this chapter (which is, incidentally, known as a *simple selector*) or using the value of the `class` attribute or `id` attribute. Learn how in the next few sections.

Universal Selector

The *universal selector* is an asterisk; it is like a wildcard and matches all element types in the document.

```
*{}
```

If you want a rule to apply to all elements, you can use this selector. Sometimes it is used for default values that apply to the whole of the document (such as a `font-family` and `font-size`) unless another more specific selector indicates that an element should use different values for these same properties.

It is slightly different from applying default styles to the `<body>` element because the universal selector applies to every element and does not rely on the property inherited from the rules that apply to the `<body>` element.

The Type Selector

The *type selector* matches all the elements specified in the comma-delimited list. It enables you to apply the same rules to several elements. For example, if you want to apply the same rules to different sized heading elements, the following would match all `h1`, `h2`, and `h3` elements:

```
h1, h2, h3 {}
```

The Class Selector

The *class selector* enables you to match a rule with an element (or elements) carrying a `class` attribute whose value matches the one you specify in the class selector. For example, imagine you have an `<aside>` element with a `class` attribute whose value is `BackgroundNote`, like so:

```
<aside class="BackgroundNote">This paragraph contains an aside.</aside>
```

You can use a class selector in one of two ways here. One way is to simply assign a rule that applies to any element that has a `class` attribute whose value is `BackgroundNote`, like so, preceding the value of the `class` attribute with a period or full stop:

```
.BackgroundNote {}
```

Or you can create a selector that selects only the `<aside>` elements that carry a `class` attribute with a value of `BackgroundNote` (not other elements) like so:

```
aside.BackgroundNote {}
```

If you have several elements that can all carry a `class` attribute with the same value (for example, an `<aside>` element and a `<div>` element could both use the `class` attribute with the same value) *and* you want the content of these elements to display in the same manner, use the former notation. If the styles you define are specific to just the `<aside>` element whose `class` attribute has a value of `BackgroundNote`, use the latter notation.

A `class` attribute can also contain several values separated by a space, for example:

```
<p class="important code">
```

You can use the following syntax to indicate an element that has a `class` attribute whose value contains both `important` and `code`. (Although, IE7 was the first version of Internet Explorer to support this syntax.)

```
p.important.code {}
```

The ID Selector

The *id selector* works just like a class selector but works on the value of `id` attributes. Rather than using a period or full stop before the value of the `id` attribute, you use a hash or pound sign (#). So an element with an `id` attribute whose value is `abstract` can be identified with this selector.

```
#abstract
```

Because the value of an `id` attribute should be unique within a document, this selector should apply only to the content of one element. (And you should not need to specify the element name.)

> **NOTE** *Because of the way browsers calculate which styles to apply to an element, supplying an element name with your selector actually slows down your page slightly. The browser must parse all elements of that type and check to see if they have the matching `id` attribute instead of simply targeting the unique element specific in your selector.*

The Child Selector

The *child selector* matches an element that is a direct child of another. In this case it matches any `<b>` elements that are direct children of `<td>` elements. The names of the two elements are separated by a greater-than symbol (>) to indicate that `b` is a child of `td`, which is referred to as a *combinator*:

```
td>b {}
```

This would enable you to specify a different style for `<b>` elements that are direct children of the `<td>` element compared with `<b>` elements that appear elsewhere in the document.

As a direct child of the `<td>` element, no other tags would sit between the opening `<td>` tag and the `<b>` element. For example, the following selector does not make sense because the `<b>` element should not be a direct child of a `<table>` element. (Instead, a `<tr>` element is more likely to be the direct child of a `<table>` element.)

```
table>b {}
```

IE7 was the first version of Internet Explorer to support the child selector.

The Descendant Selector

The *descendant selector* matches an element type that is a descendant of another specified element (or nested inside another specified element), not just a direct child. Although the greater-than symbol is the combinator for the child selector, for the descendent selector the combinator is the space. Look at this example:

```
table b {}
```

In this case, the selector matches any `<b>` element that is a child of the `<table>` element, which means it would apply to `<b>` elements both in `<td>` and `<th>` elements.

This is a contrast to the child selector because it applies to all the children of the `<table>` element, rather than just the direct children.

The Adjacent Sibling Selector

An *adjacent sibling selector* matches an element type that is the next sibling of another. For example, if you want to make the first paragraph after any level 1 heading a different style from other `<p>` elements, you can use the adjacent sibling selector like so to specify rules for just the first `<p>` element to come after any `<h1>` element:

```
h1+p {}
```

IE7 was the first version of Internet Explorer to support the adjacent sibling selector.

The General Sibling Selector

The *general sibling selector* matches an element type that is a sibling of another; although, it does not need to be the directly preceding element. So, if you have two `<p>` elements that are siblings of an `<h1>` element, they would both use the rules of this selector.

```
h1~p {}
```

The general sibling selector is part of CSS3, which you'll learn more about in Chapter 9. IE7 was the first version of Internet Explorer to support the general sibling selector, and Firefox 2 was the first version of Firefox to support it.

Using Child and Sibling Selectors to Reduce Dependence on Classes in Markup

The child and adjacent sibling selectors are both important because they can reduce the number of class attributes you need to add into an HTML document.

It is easy to add classes for all kinds of eventualities. For example, if you want the first paragraph after an <h1> element to show in bold, you might be tempted to add a class attribute to the first <p> element after every <h1> element. Although this works, your markup can be littered with all kinds of classes that are only there to make it easier to control the presentation of the pages.

If you then decide you wanted the first two <p> elements after every <h1> element to be bold, you might go back and add in new class attributes for the second <p> elements after every <h1> element. So the child and adjacent sibling selectors add a lot of flexibility to how you style documents and can make for much cleaner markup.

Look at the following HTML content (ch07_eg19.html):

```
<p>Paragraph One: not inside a div element.</p>
<div>
  <p>Paragraph One: inside a div element</p>
  <p>Paragraph Two: inside a div element </p>
  <p>Paragraph Three: inside a div element </p>
  <p>Paragraph Four: inside a div element </p>
  <p>Paragraph Five: inside a div element </p>
</div>
```

Using the child and adjacent sibling selectors only, you can create a page that looks like the one shown in Figure 7-22.

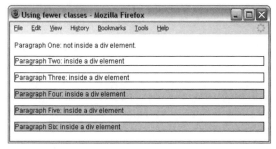

FIGURE 7-22

The three different paragraph styles are:

➤ The first paragraph has no border or background color.

➤ The paragraphs inside the <div> element all have borders.

➤ The last three paragraphs have a gray background and border.

The different paragraph styles are not specified with three different classes, but rather one rule controls the font used for all paragraphs (ch07_eg19.css):

```
p {
  font-family : arial, verdana, sans-serif;
}
```

The following is the second rule for any paragraph that is a child of a <div> element. (Because the first paragraph is not inside a <div> element, the rule does not apply to the first paragraph.)

```
div>p {
  border : 1px solid #000000;
}
```

The third rule matches any paragraph that is also a third consecutive <p> element. (Because the fourth and fifth <p> elements have two previous <p> elements, this rule applies to them and the third <p> element inside the <div>.)

```
p+p+p {
  background-color : #999999;
}
```

Remember that this example cannot work in IE6 or earlier versions of Internet Explorer because these selectors were first introduced in IE7.

> **NOTE** *While it doesn't always make a perceptible difference, it's useful to note that CSS selectors using classes and* ids *are faster than other selectors like child and sibling selectors.* Ids *are especially fast. This is usually only important when you have very complex web pages. For more information, read the article "Writing Efficient CSS" found at* https://developer.mozilla.org/en-US/docs/CSS/ Writing_Efficient_CSS.

Attribute Selectors

Attribute selectors enable you to use the attributes that an element carries, and their values, in the selector. There are several types of attribute selectors, and they enable complex ways to select elements in a document.

The use of attribute selectors is fairly limited because they have been supported only in the latest versions of browsers. Some of the attribute selectors in Table 7-11 are from CSS3, which you'll learn more about in Chapter 9.

TABLE 7-11: CSS Attribute Selectors

NAME	EXAMPLE	MATCHES
Existence selector	`p[id]`	Any `<p>` element carrying an attribute called `id`.
Equality selector	`p[id="summary"]`	Any `<p>` element carrying an attribute called `id` whose value is `summary`.
Space selector	`p[class~="HTML"]`	Any `<p>` element carrying an attribute called `class`, whose value is a list of space-separated words, one of which is exactly the same as `HTML`.
Hyphen selector	`p[language|="en"]`	Any `<p>` element carrying an attribute called `language` whose value begins with `en` and is followed with a hyphen. (This particular selector is designed for use with language attributes.)
Prefix selector (CSS3)	`p[attr^"b"]`	Any `<p>` element carrying any attribute whose value begins with `b` (CSS3).
Substring selector (CSS3)	`p[attr*"on"]`	Any `<p>` element carrying any attribute whose value contains the letters `on` (CSS3).
Suffix selector (CSS3)	`p[attr$"x"]`	Any `<p>` element carrying any attribute whose value ends in the letter `x` (CSS3).

Internet Explorer implemented these attribute selectors in IE7. Firefox started to support them in Firefox 2.

Now look at an example of using these attribute selectors. Here are seven different paragraph elements, each carrying different attributes/attribute values (ch07_eg20.html):

```
<p id="introduction">Here's paragraph one; each paragraph has different
attributes.</p>
<p id="summary">Here's paragraph two; each paragraph has different attributes.</p>
<p class="important HTML">Here's paragraph three; each paragraph has different
attributes.</p>
<p language="en-us">Here's paragraph four; each paragraph has different
attributes.</p>
<p class="begins">Here's paragraph five; each paragraph has different
attributes.</p>
<p class="contains">Here's paragraph six; each paragraph has different
attributes.</p>
<p class="suffix">Here's paragraph seven; each paragraph has different
attributes.</p>
```

Now look at a CSS style sheet that uses attribute selectors to associate different style rules with each of these elements (`ch07_eg20.css`):

```css
p[id] {
   border : 1px solid #000000;
}
p[id="summary"] {
   background-color : #999999;
}
p[class~="HTML"] {
   border : 3px solid #000000;
}
p[language|="en"] {
   color : #ffffff;
   background-color : #000000;
}
p[class^="b"]{
   border : 3px solid #333333;
}
p[class*="on"] {
   color : #ffffff; background-color:#333333;
}
p[class$="x"] {
   border : 1px solid #333333;
}
```

You can see the result in Firefox 3.0 in Figure 7-23.

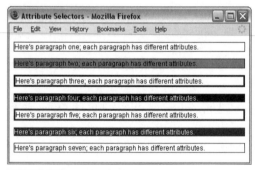

FIGURE 7-23

All selectors should match the case of the element name that they are supposed to match.

As a general rule, the latest versions of Chrome, Safari, Firefox, and Internet Explorer 9+ support all the CSS selectors you will encounter in this book. IE8 was the first version of Internet Explorer to support the CSS2 selectors. Older versions of Internet Explorer are problematic except for the most basic selectors. For a complete list, check the support table from Browse Em All found at `http://www.browseemall.com/Blog/post/2012/03/16/The-cross-browser-compatibility-guide-CSS-selectors-browser-support.aspx`.

LENGTHS

You have already seen that the values of some CSS properties are given as *lengths* (such as the size of fonts, height of lines of text, and gaps between words and letters), and you will come across more properties whose values are expressed as lengths throughout the chapters on CSS. So, now take a moment to look at the three ways lengths can be specified in CSS:

➤ Relative units

➤ Absolute units

➤ Percentages

Relative Units

There are three types of relative units: the pixel (px), which relates to the resolution of the screen, and the em and ex, both of which relate to the size of fonts.

px

The *pixel*, referred to in code as px, is by far the most commonly used unit of length in CSS. A pixel is the smallest unit of resolution on a screen, and if you look closely at your screen, you might just see the square dots that are the pixels.

Technically, the size of a layout that uses pixels as a unit of measurement *can* depend upon the viewing medium, which is why it is counted as a relative unit.

Most computer screens have a resolution of 72 dots per inch (dpi), but laser and bubble jet printers are usually set with a higher resolution—for example, 300 dpi. In contrast, mobile devices can have a lower resolution than computer screens or (for some smartphones such as the iPhone) a higher resolution.

So, a table that is 500 pixels wide could be 9.9444 inches wide on a 72 dpi screen, 1.666 inches wide at 300 dpi, or 13.888 inches wide on a 32 dpi screen. (And a screen that is only 32 dpi is unlikely to be that much more than 13 inches wide.)

In reality, when you print a web page from your browser, it adjusts the pixels to present a readable version of the document. CSS recommends that in such cases user agents rescale pixel units so that when a document is read at arm's length 1 pixel would correspond to approximately 0.28 mm or $1/90$ of an inch.

em

An *em* is equivalent to the height of the current font, and because the size of fonts can vary throughout a document, the height of the em unit can be different in different parts of the document. Furthermore, because users can change the size of text in their browser, the em unit can vary in relation to the size of the text that the user has selected.

This means that the em unit is most commonly used for measurements of elements that contain text and for controlling spacing between text. (For example, you can use it in the line-height property to set the gaps between lines of text in relation to their height.)

Although the `em` unit is equivalent to the height of a font, it is often thought to have derived from the width of a lowercase *m*; you may also hear the term *en*, which equates to half an *em*.

ex

The *ex* should be the height of a lowercase *x*. Because different fonts have different proportions, the ex is related to the font size and the type of font. In Figure 7-24, you can see the *x* in the Courier typeface is smaller than the *x* in the Impact typeface.

FIGURE 7-24

New Relative Units: rem, vh, and vw

You may encounter three new relative units introduced in the CSS Values and Units Candidate Recommendation (`http://www.w3.org/TR/css3-values/`): rem, vh, and vw.

➤ rem units are equal to the font size of the root element—a "root em." This allows you to use font-relative sizing with less complexity than with the traditional path of `em` units and percentage-based heights/widths.

➤ vh units are equal to 1 percent of the viewport height. vw units are equal to 1 percent of the viewport width. This allows for viewport-relative layouts. If the viewport changes (for example, in the change from portrait to landscape on a tablet), these units scale proportionally.

rem units are supported in IE9+ and the latest versions of the other major desktop browsers. As of this writing vh and vw support is only in IE10+, Chrome 20+, Firefox 19+, Safari 6+, and with partial support in Opera 12.5.

Absolute Units

Generally speaking, *absolute units* are used far less than relative units. (And you rarely come across designs that use these units of measurement.) Table 7-12 shows the absolute units used in some CSS properties.

TABLE 7-12: Absolute Units in CSS

UNIT	FULL NAME
pt	Point
pc	Pica
in	Inch

cm	Centimeter
mm	Millimeter

You shouldn't need clarification for inches, millimeters, or centimeters, but the other two are more interesting. A point is $1/72$ of an inch (the same as a pixel in most computer screen resolutions), and a pica is $1/12$ of an inch (12 points). Typographers tend to use points to measure font sizes and leading (the gaps between lines), whereas picas measure line lengths.

Percentages

Percentages give a value in relation to another value. For example, if your page contains only two paragraphs, and you want each to take up one-half of the width of the browser, you might give the paragraphs a width property with a value of 50%. However, if the <p> element were inside another element that you knew was 500 pixels wide, they would take up 50 percent of the width of that containing element (or 250 pixels) each.

INTRODUCING THE BOX MODEL

The *box model* is an important concept in CSS because it determines how elements are positioned within the browser window. It gets its name because CSS treats every element as if it were in a *box*.

As you can see in Table 7-13, every box has three properties you must be aware of.

TABLE 7-13: Important Box Model Properties

PROPERTY	DESCRIPTION
border	Even if you cannot see it, every box has a border. This separates the edge of one box from other surrounding boxes.
margin	The margin is the distance between the border of a box and the box next to it.
padding	This padding is the space between the content of the box and its border.

You can get a better idea of these properties in Figure 7-25, which shows the various parts of the box. (The black line is the border.)

You can use CSS to individually control the border, margin, and padding on each side of a box; you can specify a different width, line-style, and color for each side of the box's border.

The padding and margin properties are especially important in creating what designers refer to as *white space*; this is the space between the various parts of the page. For example, if you have a box with a black border and the box contains black text, you would not want the text to touch the border because it would make the text harder to read. Giving the box *padding* helps separate the text from the line around the edge.

FIGURE 7-25

Meanwhile, suppose you have two boxes next to each other, both with borders. If there is not a margin between them, the boxes will run into each other, and the line where the boxes meet could look thicker than the other lines.

There is, however, an interesting issue with margins: When a bottom margin of one element meets the top margin of another, only the larger of the two shows. (If they are the same size, the margin is equivalent to the size of the larger of the two margins.) Figure 7-26 shows the vertical margins of two adjacent boxes collapsing. (This applies only to vertical margins; the same is not true for left and right margins.)

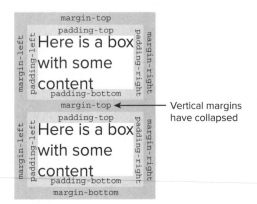

FIGURE 7-26

To understand how the box model works with elements, look at the example in the next section.

An Example Illustrating the Box Model

To illustrate the box model, you can add a border to each of the elements in a web page. The `<body>` element creates one box that contains the whole page, and inside that box each heading, paragraph, image, or link creates another box. First, here is the HTML for the page (ch07_eg21.html):

```
<h1>Thinking Inside the Box</h1>
<p class="description">When you are styling a web page with CSS you
must start to think in terms of <b>boxes</b>.</p>
<p>Each element is treated as if it generates a new box. Each box can have
new rules associated with it.</p>
<img src="images/boxmodel.gif" alt="How CSS treats a box">
<p>As you can see from the diagram above, each box has a <b>border</b>.
Between the content and the border you can have <b>padding</b>, and
outside of the border you can have a <b>margin</b> to separate this box
from any neighboring boxes.</p>
```

Using just one CSS rule, you can see how each element involved with the body of the document—<body>, <h2>, <p>, <img>, and <b>—is treated as if it were in a separate box. You can do this by adding a CSS rule that adds a border around each of these elements. You learn more about these properties shortly (ch07_eg21.css).

```
body, h1, p, img, b {
    border-style : solid;
    border-width : 2px;
    border-color : #000000;
    padding:2px;
}
```

Each box can be presented differently. For example, you can give the <h1> and <bold> elements a gray background to help distinguish them from other elements.

```
h1, b {
    background-color : #cccccc;
}
```

Figure 7-27 shows you what this page looks like in a browser. Although it is not too attractive, the lines show you the borders of the boxes (and demonstrate how boxes are created for each element).

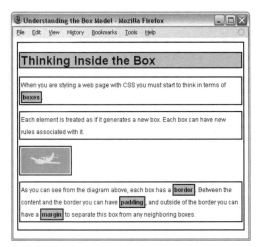

FIGURE 7-27

You may remember from Chapter 1 that there is a difference between *block-level elements* and *inline elements*. The difference becomes quite important when working with CSS because it determines how each box displays.

➤   The <h1> and <p> elements are examples of block-level elements. Each block-level element starts on a new line, and the box around a block-level element takes up the full width of the browser (or the full width of the element it sits inside).

➤   The <b> element is an example of an inline element. Its box sits in the middle of the paragraph and it does not take up the width of a whole line. (It *flows* within its containing element.)

The <img> element may look like it is a block-level element because it starts on its own line, but it is actually an inline element. You can tell this because the border around it takes up only the width of the image; if it were a block-level element, the border would reach across the full width of the browser. The image is on its own line only because the elements on either side of it *are* block-level elements. (And therefore the surrounding elements appear on their own lines.)

Now that you know how each element is treated as if it were in its own box, look at the properties that control the borders, padding, and margins for each box.

The border Properties

The border properties enable you to specify how the border of the box representing an element should look. There are three properties of a border you can change:

➤ border-color to indicate the color a border should be

➤ border-style to indicate whether a border should be a solid, dashed, or double line, or one of the other possible values

➤ border-width to indicate the width a border should be

The border-color Property

The border-color property enables you to change the color of the border surrounding a box, for example:

```
p {
  border-color : #ff0000;
}
```

The value can be any valid color value. (Colors are discussed in greater detail in Appendix D.)

You can individually change the color of the bottom, left, top, and right sides of a box's border using the following properties:

➤ border-bottom-color

➤ border-right-color

➤ border-top-color

➤ border-left-color

The border-style Property

The border-style property enables you to specify the line style of the border:

```
p {
  border-style : solid;
}
```

The default value for this property is none, so no border would be shown automatically. Table 7-14 shows the possible values.

TABLE 7-14: Values for the border-style Property

VALUE	DESCRIPTION
none	There is no border. (Equivalent of `border-width:0;`)
solid	The border is a single solid line.
dotted	The border is a series of dots.
dashed	The border is a series of short lines.
double	The border is two solid lines; the value of the `border-width` property creates the sum of the two lines and the space between them.
groove	The border looks as though it is carved into the page.
ridge	The border looks the opposite of `groove`.
inset	The border makes the box look like it is embedded in the page.
outset	The border makes the box look like it is coming out of the canvas.
hidden	Same as `none`, except in terms of border-conflict resolution for table elements.

Figure 7-28 shows an example of what each of these would look like (taken from `ch07_eg22.html`). Note that even though the last four examples in Figure 7-27 look similar, they are different, and you can try them for yourself with the download code for this example.

You can individually change the style of the bottom, right, top, and left borders of a box using the following properties:

➤ `border-bottom-style`

➤ `border-right-style`

➤ `border-top-style`

➤ `border-left-style`

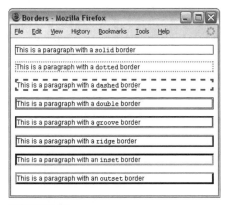

FIGURE 7-28

The border-width Property

The `border-width` property enables you to set the width of your borders; usually the width is specified in pixels.

```
p {
  border-style : solid;
  border-width : 4px;
}
```

The value of the `border-width` property cannot be given as a percentage; although, you could use any absolute unit or relative unit, or one of the following values:

➤ `thin`

➤ `medium`

➤ `thick`

The actual width of the `thin`, `medium`, and `thick` values are not specified in the CSS recommendation in terms of pixels, so the actual width that corresponds to these keywords is dependent on the browser.

You can individually change the width of the bottom, right, top, and left borders of a box using the following properties:

➤ `border-bottom-width`

➤ `border-right-width`

➤ `border-top-width`

➤ `border-left-width`

Expressing border Properties Using Shorthand

The `border` property enables you to specify color, style, and width of lines in one property:

```
p {
  border : 4px solid red;
}
```

If you use this shorthand, the values should not have anything (other than a space) between them. You can also specify the color, style, and width of lines individually for each side of the box in the same way using these properties:

➤ `border-bottom`

➤ `border-top`

➤ `border-left`

➤ `border-right`

The padding Property

The `padding` property enables you to specify how much space should appear between the content of an element and its border:

```
td {
   padding : 5px;
}
```

The value of this property is most often specified in pixels. Although, it can use any of the units of length you met earlier, a percentage, or the word `inherit`.

The padding of an element does not inherit by default, so if the `<body>` element has a padding property with a value of 50 pixels, this does not automatically apply to all other elements inside it. If the value `inherit` is applied to any elements, only then can they have the same padding as their parent elements.

If a percentage is used, the percentage is of the containing box, and if the value of 10 percent is specified, there would be 5 percent of each side of the box as padding.

You can specify different amounts of padding inside each side of a box using the following properties:

- ➤ `padding-bottom`
- ➤ `padding-top`
- ➤ `padding-left`
- ➤ `padding-right`

The `padding` attribute is especially helpful to create white space between the content of an element and any border it has. Look at the following two paragraphs in Figure 7-29.

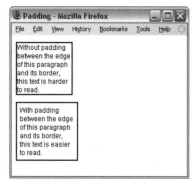

FIGURE 7-29

If you look at the CSS rules for these two paragraph elements, you can see that by default the first paragraph has no padding. It must be specified if you want a gap like the one shown in the second paragraph (ch07_eg23.css).

```
.a, .b {
  border-style : solid;
  border-color : #000000;
  border-width : 2px;
  width : 100px;
}
.b {
  Padding : 5px;
}
```

Sometimes, an element might not have a visible border, but it has a background color or pattern. In such cases giving the box some padding can help make your design more attractive.

The margin Property

The margin property controls the gap between boxes, and its value is either a length, a percentage, or inherit, each of which has exactly the same meaning as it did for the padding property you just saw.

```
p {
  margin:20px;
}
```

As with the padding property, the values of the margin property are not inherited by child elements unless you use the value inherit.

Also, remember that when one box sits on top of another box, only the larger of the two margins shows (or if both are equal, the size of one margin).

You can also set different values for the margin on each side of the box using the following properties:

➤ margin-bottom

➤ margin-top

➤ margin-left

➤ margin-right

If you look at the following example (see Figure 7-30, which shows ch07_eg24.html), you can see three paragraphs, which look as if they are spaced equally. However, they have taller margins on the top than the bottom, and therefore where two boxes meet, the bottom margin is ignored—the margins are *collapsed*. (This happens only to the vertical margins, not the left and right margins.)

The example also shows how to set the left and right margins on the side of inline elements—where you see the highlighted words. Again, this is not the most attractive example, but it illustrates how both block and inline boxes use margins.

The words in the paragraphs that are emphasized using the <em> element have `margin-left` and `margin-right` properties set. Because these <em> elements also have a background color set, you can actually see how the margins to the left and the right separate the words from the surrounding words (refer to Figure 7-30).

Here are the rules from `ch07_eg24.css`:

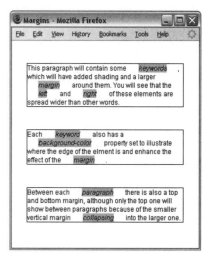

FIGURE 7-30

```
body {
  color : #000000;
  background-color : #ffffff;
  font-family : arial, verdana, sans-serif;
  font-size : 12px;
}
p {
  margin-top : 40px;
  margin-bottom : 30px;
  margin-left : 20px;
  margin-right : 20px;
  border-style : solid;
  border-width : 1px;
  border-color : #000000;}
em {
  background-color : #cccccc;
  margin-left : 20px;
  margin-right : 20px;
}
```

Dimensions of a Content Box

Now that you've seen the border that surrounds every content box, the padding that can appear inside the border of each content box, and the margin that can go outside the border, it is time to look at the properties that enable you to control the dimensions of content boxes, shown in Table 7-15.

TABLE 7-15: Content Box Properties

PROPERTY	PURPOSE
height	Sets the height of a box.
width	Sets the width of a box.
line-height	Sets the height of a line of text (such as leading in a layout program).

continues

TABLE 7-15 *(continued)*

PROPERTY	PURPOSE
max-height	Sets the maximum height for a box.
min-height	Sets the minimum height for a box.
max-width	Sets the maximum width for a box.
min-width	Sets the minimum width for a box.

The height and width Properties

The height and width properties enable you to set the height and width for content boxes. They can take values of a length, a percentage, or the keyword auto. (The default value is auto, which means the content box is just large enough to house its contents.)

Here you can see the CSS rules for two paragraph elements, the first with a class attribute whose value is one and the second whose class attribute has a value of two (ch07_eg25.css):

```
p.one {
    width : 200px;
    height : 100px;
    padding : 5px;
    margin : 10px;
    border-style : solid;
    border-color : #000000;
    border-width : 2px;}
p.two {
    width : 300px;
    height : 100px;
    padding : 5px;
    margin : 10px;
    border-style : solid;
    border-color : #000000;
    border-width : 2px;
}
```

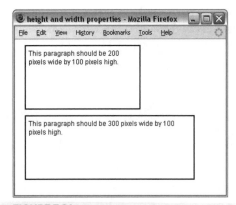

FIGURE 7-31

As you can see in Figure 7-31, the first paragraph is 200 pixels wide and 100 pixels high, whereas the second paragraph is 300 pixels wide and 100 pixels high.

The most common unit of measurement for boxes is pixels. Although, percentages and ems are often used in layouts that stretch and contract to fit the size of the browser window.

The line-height Property

The line-height property is one of the most important properties when laying out text. It enables you to increase the space between lines of text (known to print designers as *leading*).

The value of the line-height property can be a length or a percentage. It is a good idea to specify this property in the same measurement in which you specify the size of your text.

Here you can see two rules setting different line-height properties (ch07_eg26.css):

```
p.two {
  line-height : 16px;
}
p.three {
  line-height : 28px;
}
```

As you can see in Figure 7-32, the first paragraph does not have a line-height attribute, whereas the second and third paragraphs correspond to the preceding rules. Adding some extra height between each line of text can often make it more readable, especially in longer articles.

In long paragraphs try to use leading of approximately 1.5 times the height of the font. This property can also be helpful when you need to add spacing around single lines of text.

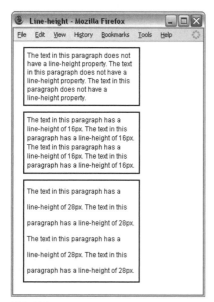

FIGURE 7-32

The max-width and min-width Properties

The `max-width` and `min-width` properties enable you to specify a maximum and a minimum width for a content box. This should be particularly useful if you want to create parts of pages that stretch and shrink to fit the size of users' screens. The `max-width` property can stop a box from being so wide that it is hard to read (lines that are too long are harder to read on screens), and `min-width` can help prevent boxes from being so narrow that they are unreadable. IE7 and Firefox 2 were the first of the major browsers to support these properties.

The value of these properties can be a number, a length, or a percentage, and negative values are not allowed. For example, look at the following rule, which specifies that a `<div>` element may not be less than 200 pixels wide and no wider than 500 pixels wide (`ch07_eg27.css`):

```
div {
  min-width : 200px;
  max-width : 500px;
  padding : 5px;
  border : 1px solid #000000;
}
```

You can see what this looks like in Figure 7-33, which shows two browser windows, and you can try it for yourself using `ch07_eg27.html` in the code download. The first window is opened to more than 500 pixels wide, and the box does not stretch wider than 500 pixels. The second window is closed to less than 200 pixels, at which point the browser starts to show a horizontal scrollbar because you cannot see the full width of the box.

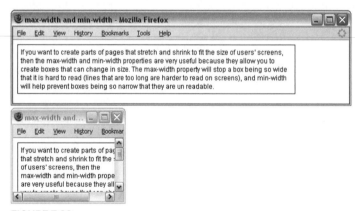

FIGURE 7-33

The min-height and max-height Properties

The `min-height` and `max-height` properties correspond with the `min-width` and `max-width` properties, but specify a minimum height and maximum height for the content box. Again, IE7 and Firefox 2 were the first major browsers to support these properties.

The value of these properties can be a number, a length, or a percentage, and negative values are not allowed. Look at the following example (ch07_eg28.css):

```
div {
  min-height : 150px;
  max-height : 200px;
  padding : 5px;
  border : 1px solid #000000;
}
```

Again, these properties are useful to create layouts that can be resized depending upon the size of the user's browser window. However, you can see an interesting phenomenon in Figure 7-34: If the content of the box takes up more space than the box is allowed because of these rules, the content can overflow out of the box. (You learn how to deal with this in the next section.)

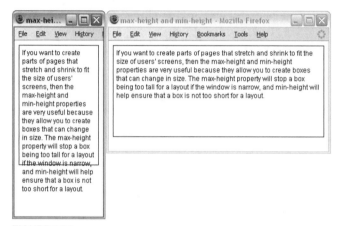

FIGURE 7-34

The overflow Property

As you just saw in Figure 7-34, when you control the size of a box, the content you want to fit in the box might require more space than you have allowed for it. This happens not only with the min-height and max-height or min-width and max-width properties but also for a number of other reasons.

The overflow property was designed to deal with these situations and can take one of the values shown Table 7-16.

TABLE 7-16: overflow Property Values

VALUE	PURPOSE
hidden	The overflowing content is hidden.
visible	The overflowing content is visible outside of the box.

continues

TABLE 7-16 *(continued)*

VALUE	PURPOSE
scroll	The box is given scrollbars to allow users to scroll to see the content.
auto	The box is given scrollbars when necessary.
inherit	The box inherits its overflow properties from its parent.

Now look at the following example, where the width of two <div> elements has been controlled by the max-height and max-width properties so that the content of the <div> elements does not fit in the box. For the first element, the overflow property is set to have a value of hidden and the second to have a value of scroll (ch07_eg29.css).

```
div {
   max-height : 75px;
   max-width : 250px;
   padding : 5px;
   margin : 10px;
   border : 1px solid #000000;
}
div.one {
   overflow : hidden;
}
div.two {
   overflow : scroll;
}
```

Now take a look at Figure 7-35, which shows ch07_eg29.html. You can see the effect of these two properties—in the first box the text is simply cut off when it runs out of space, and in the second box a scrollbar is created allowing users to scroll to the appropriate content.

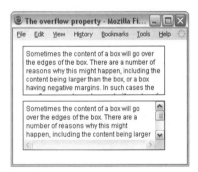

FIGURE 7-35

The Internet Explorer Box Model and box-sizing: border-box

In the early days of CSS development, two competing box models were introduced. You've met one already: The one that's been the CSS standard for many years. The other one was introduced by early versions of Internet Explorer. Those early versions of IE treated the width of a box as though it included the width of any border it had been given *and* the width of the padding in the size of the box. The CSS specification says that the width of a box should only be the width of the content (not including the border or padding). You can see this in Figure 7-36.

W3C Box Model

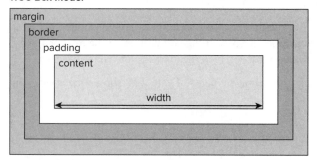

IE Box Model

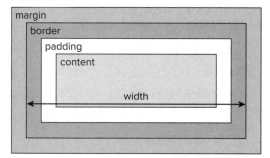

FIGURE 7-36

This divergent set of rules was a problem. IE6 resolved this problem because it could run in the two "modes" you learned about in Chapter 1:

➤ The standards-compliant mode follows the CSS specification.

➤ The Quirks mode retains the alternative box mode. IE6 or above can run in Quirks mode when there is no !DOCTYPE declaration.

A funny thing happened after this "IE box model bug" was fixed. People took a sober look at the Internet Explorer box model and recognized that it made more sense than the standard box model. Translating a design that featured a box measured at 500 pixels with 20 pixels of padding meant doing a bit of math. Although the common sense "width" was 500 pixels, the width *property* would have to be set to 460px to account for the padding. This is counterintuitive, and forcing humans to do math when inputting display rules into a *computer* isn't the most efficient distribution of resources.

Enter the new CSS box-sizing property. box-sizing enables you to choose between the CSS standard and the border-box box model. border-box maps to the Internet Explorer box model. This property is supported in Internet Explorer 8 and above, as well as all other major browsers, so if you don't have to support IE7, border-box can make your work with CSS much easier.

Let computers *compute*.

CREATING A STYLE SHEET FOR CODE

In the following Try It Out, you practice formatting text for use as computer code.

TRY IT OUT A Style Sheet for Code

I often find the need to display code online. So I wrote the following style sheet to enable me to define styles similar to those you see in this book, for showing code on the web. As you will see in the next chapter, this code can then be included in other style sheets when needed, which means it is a reusable style sheet.

The style sheet features several styles for block and inline elements. Table 7-17 shows the styles you will create.

TABLE 7-17: Styles for Code Samples

STYLE NAME	INLINE OR BLOCK	USE
codeInText	Inline	For a bit of code written in the middle of a sentence, shown in a monospace font.
codeForeground	Block	Highlighted code in a monospace font for showing examples.
codeBackground	Block	Like codeForeground, but not highlighted because it has been seen before or is not the key point of the example.
keystroke	Inline	Keys a user should enter on the keyboard, distinguishable because it is italic.
importantWords	Inline	The first use of a key term; helps users scan the document because it appears in a bold font.
boxText	Block	Creates a block of important or key notes that is in a box and has background shading.
background	Block	Creates a block of italic text that has an aside or interesting note.

1. Create class selectors for each of these styles. Element names are not used for several of the styles here because the styles could apply to different elements. (For example, box text could be in a `<p>` element or a `<div>` grouping other elements.) The selectors that do use elements are the ones representing code.

```
code.codeInText{}
code.codeForeground {}
code.codeBackground {}
.keystroke {}
.importantWords {}
.boxText {}
.background {}
```

2. Start adding declarations to each selector inside the curly brackets. First is the `codeInText` style for words that appear in the middle of a sentence or paragraph that represent code. In the same tradition as most written matter on programming, the code displays in a monospaced font. The first choice of typeface—specified using the `font-family` property—is Courier, failing which the browser should try to find Courier New. If it cannot find that typeface, it uses its default mono-spaced font. (Although most computers do have Courier or Courier New installed.)

3. To make the code easier to read, this font appears in bold text, as indicated using the `font-weight` property.

```
.codeInText {
  font-family : courier, "courier new", monospace;
  font-weight : bold;
}
```

4. The second style is the `codeForeground` style. This style uses the same type of font as the `codeInText` style. Fill out the style as follows:

```
.codeForeground {
  font-family : courier, "courier new", monospace; font-weight:bold;
  letter-spacing : -0.1em;
  display : block;
  background-color : #cccccc;
  padding : 0.5em;
  margin-bottom : 1em;
  margin-top : 1.5em;
}
```

Here are a few things to take note of:

➤ The `codeForeground` style should always be displayed as a block-level element, but just in case the class is incorrectly used with an inline element, the `display` property is used with a value of `block` to ensure that it is displayed as a block. (You see more of this property in Chapter 8.)

➤ You also see that the `letter-spacing` property has been used with a negative value because monospace fonts tend to take up quite a bit of width on the page. So, to help get as many characters as possible on the same line, it is given a value of –0.1 of an em (or 10 percent of a font's height).

➤ All lengths in the style sheet are specified in ems so that they relate to the default size of the text in the document. If some of these elements were given in absolute sizes, they might have suddenly appeared a lot smaller or larger than the surrounding text.

➤ The background color of the `codeForeground` style is gray. This helps the code stand out and makes it more readable. A one and one-half em-sized padding has been added inside the box so that the text does not go right to the edge of the background color—this also makes the code easier to read.

➤ The margin ensures that the box does not touch any other boxes or paragraphs. It has a smaller margin on the bottom than the top, as do all the styles in this style sheet that use the margin property.

5. The `codeBackground` style is identical to the `codeForeground` style except that the `background-color` is white. Add the following code to the empty rule:

```
.codeBackground {
    font-family : courier, "courier new", monospace; font-weight:bold;
    letter-spacing : -0.1em;
    display : block;
    background-color : #ffffff;
    padding : 0.5em;
    margin-bottom : 1em;
    margin-top : 1em;}
```

6. The `keyStroke` style is in a Times typeface, or Times New Roman if Times is not available; otherwise, the default serif typeface for the browser is used. The `keyStroke` style should look like the following:

```
.keyStroke {
    font-family : times, "Times New Roman", serif;
    font-style : italic;
}
```

7. The `importantWords` style is simply bold, so add the single property-value pair shown here:

```
.importantWords {
    font-weight : bold;
}
```

8. The `boxText` style has a bold font with a light gray background; what differentiates it is that it has a border. The class definition should look like this when all is said and done:

```
.boxText {
    font-weight : bold;
    background-color : #efefef;
    width : 90%;
    padding : 1em;
    margin-left : 3em;
    margin-right : 3em;
    margin-bottom : 1em;
    margin-top : 1.5em;
    border-style : solid;
    border-width : 1px;
    border-color : #000000;
}
```

9. As with the `codeForeground` style, `boxText` has some padding so that the text does not reach the border—making it easier to read—and it has a margin to inset it from the left and right as well as vertically to separate it from other elements. Note that the bottom margin is slightly smaller than the top margin.

10. The final style is the `background` style. This style is italic and has the same amount of padding and margins as the `boxText` style. Build out the definition so that it looks like this:

```
.background {
    font-style : italic;
    width : 90%;
    padding : 1em;
```

```
    margin-left : 3em;
    margin-right : 3em;
    margin-bottom : 1em;
    margin-top : 1em;
}
```

11. For this example, a rule is included for the `<p>` element and a rule for the `<body>` element. (Although they are not part of the standard CSS used for code styles.) Make sure you define both of those elements as follows:

```
body {
    color : #000000;
    background-color : #ffffff;
    font-family : arial, verdana, sans-serif;
    font-size : 12px;
}
p {
    margin-bottom : 1em;
    margin-top : 1.5em;
}
```

12. Save this file as `codeStyles.css`. Then take a look at the following HTML, which makes use of this style sheet. As you can see, the `<link>` element indicates that this is the style sheet to be used for this example. You can then see the elements with the `class` attributes that relate to these styles:

```
<!DOCTYPE html>
<html>
<head>
  <title>CSS Example</title>
  <link rel="stylesheet" href="codeStyles.css">
</head>

<body>
<p>You are about to see some <code class="codeInText">codeInText</code>
  followed by some <span class="importantWords">importantWords</span>,
  and the font for a <span class="keystroke">keystroke</span>.</p>

<p>Next you will see some foreground code:</p>
<code class="codeForeground">p {
  font-family : arial, sans-serif;
  font-weight : bold;
}</code>

<p>Next you will see some background code:</p>
<code class="codeBackground">p {
  font-family : arial, sans-serif;
  font-weight : bold;
}</code>

<p class="boxText">This is some boxed text for important statements.</p>

<p class="background">Here is a background comment or aside.</p>
</body>
</html>
```

If you look at this example in the browser, it should look like Figure 7-37.

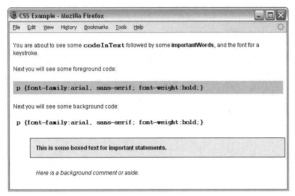

FIGURE 7-37

How It Works

This simple combination of a "code" font, font weights, letter spacing, and background colors produces a flexible system to display code on the web. The CSS rules replace the default rendering for several elements with ones better suited to code rendering.

Courier and other monospaced fonts are used for programming (and programming examples) for several reasons, including:

➤ Common programming punctuation is easier to read in a monospaced font ! () {} : versus ! () {} :.

➤ Line lengths are always the same. Eighty characters are always the same length on screen. This enables strings of the same character length to line up, no matter what characters the string consists of.

➤ Lookalikes are easier to spot: ll (lowercase L/uppercase i) versus lI.

SUMMARY

In this chapter, you learned how to write CSS. You have seen that a style sheet is made up of rules that first select the element or elements to which the rules apply and then contain property-value pairs that specify how the element's content should appear.

You have learned how you can change the appearance of fonts and text.

You now know that CSS manages to render a document by treating each element as if it were a separate box and then using the properties to control how each box should appear. You also learned how to set the dimensions and borders, padding, and margins for each box.

In the next chapter, you not only learn some more properties but also see how you can use CSS to position elements on a page, which enable you to create attractive layouts for pages. You even see how you can insert content from a style sheet into a document, deal with bulleted lists, create counters, and more.

EXERCISES

1. In this exercise (and the next), you continue to work on the Example Café website. Open the index. html page, and add a `<div>` element just inside the opening `<body>` tag and the closing `</body>` tag. Then give the element an `id` attribute whose value is `page`. Repeat this for each page of the site.

  a. In the style sheet add a rule that gives this element a margin, border, and padding so that it looks like the border in Figure 7-38.

FIGURE 7-38

  b. Create a CSS rule that can make the following changes to the navigation:

  i. Add a single-pixel gray border on the top and bottom.

  ii. Give it 20 pixels of margin above and below the gray lines.

  iii. Give it 10 pixels of padding on the top and bottom in the box.

  iv. Add a margin to the right of each link in the navigation.

  c. Give the main image on the homepage a `class` attribute whose value is `main_image`. Then create a rule that gives the image a single-pixel black border, and also give the image a 10-pixel margin on the right and bottom sides of the image.

  d. Increase the gaps between each line of text within paragraphs to 1.3 em.

2. For this exercise, take a look at the following HTML:

```
<!DOCTYPE html>
<html>
<head>
  <title>Font test</title>
  <link rel="stylesheet" href="tableStyles.css" />
</head>
<body>
<table>
  <tr>
    <th>Quantity</th>
    <th>Ingredient</th>
  </tr>
  <tr class="odd">
    <td>3</td>
    <td>Eggs</td>
  </tr>
  <tr>
    <td>100ml</td>
    <td>Milk</td>
  </tr>
  <tr class="odd">
    <td>200g</td>
    <td>Spinach</td>
   </tr>
    <tr>
      <td>1 pinch</td>
      <td>Cinnamon</td>
    </tr>
  </table>
 </body>
 </html>
```

Now create the `tableStyles.css` style sheet, which makes this example look like it does in Figure 7-39.

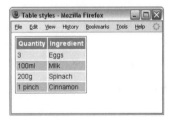

FIGURE 7-39

Don't worry about getting the sizes exactly the same as the screenshot, but do make sure you have padding in the cells and a border around the outside. The white border is created by default in IE; you will find out how to remove this in Chapter 8.

The answers to all the exercises are in Appendix A, "Answers to Exercises."

▶ WHAT YOU LEARNED IN THIS CHAPTER

TOPIC	KEY TAKEAWAY
CSS	The technology that enables you to adjust the look and feel of web pages.
CSS text	Using fonts, font size, font weight, color, and other properties, you can adjust the appearance of web text.
Selectors	Selectors enable you to target specific HTML elements for styling.
The box model	Elements in HTML are treated like boxes by CSS. The system of laying out boxes with heights, widths, padding, borders, and margins is called the box model. In modern browsers there are two options, the CSS standard and border-box, which maps to the old Internet Explorer "IE box model bug."

More Cascading Style Sheets

➤ Styling links

➤ Setting document backgrounds

➤ Styling bullet points and numbered lists

➤ Changing the appearance of tables

➤ Adjusting the outlines around boxes

➤ Adding content to the HTML document before or after an element

➤ Understanding three positioning schemes that enable you to determine where on a page a box appears

WROX.COM CODE DOWNLOADS FOR THIS CHAPTER

The wrox.com code downloads for this chapter are found at www.wrox.com/remtitle .cgi?isbn=9781118340189 on the Download Code tab. The code is in the Chapter 8 download and individually named according to the names throughout the chapter.

In this chapter, you continue to learn how to use CSS to control the presentation of HTML web pages, starting with CSS properties that enable you to control the presentation of links, backgrounds, list styles, table styles, and outlines around boxes. You then learn a technique to add content to a page (even if it were not in the HTML document) using the :before and :after pseudo-classes. Finally, you see how to use CSS to position boxes on the page, which enables you to create attractive layouts for your pages.

LINKS

By default, most browsers show links in blue with an underline and change the color of links you have already visited, unless you tell them to do otherwise. The following are properties often used with links:

➤   `color`: Changes the colors of the links

➤   `background-color`: Highlights the link, as if it had been highlighted with a highlighter pen

➤   `text-decoration`: Commonly used to control whether the link is underlined; although, it can also specify that text should have a strikethrough, blink, or be overlined

Although you can just create rules that apply to the `<a>` element to set properties such as `color` and `text-decoration`, there are also four *pseudo-classes* that can give you greater control over the presentation of links, as shown in Table 8-1.

TABLE 8-1: Link Pseudo-Classes

PSEUDO-CLASS	PURPOSE
link	Styles for links in general
visited	Styles for links that have already been visited
hover	Styles for when someone is hovering over a link
active	Styles for links that are currently active (being clicked)

Using these pseudo-classes enables you to change properties of links when the user hovers over them (making them a slightly different color, maybe adding a highlight and underlining them) and also the properties of links that have been visited (for example, making them a slightly different color—which helps users know where they have been).

When used, these properties should be specified in the order listed in the previous table. Here is an example that can change the styles of links as users interact with them (`ch08_eg01.css`):

```
body {
  background-color : #ffffff;
}
a {
  font-family : arial, verdana, sans-serif;
  font-size : 12px;
  font-weight : bold;
}
a:link {
  color : #0000ff;
  text-decoration : none;
}
a:visited {
  color : #333399;
```

```
    text-decoration : none;
}
a:link:hover {
  background-color : #e9e9e9;
  text-decoration : underline;
}
a:active {
  color : #0033ff;
  text-decoration : underline;
}
```

Figure 8-1 gives you an idea of how links will look with this style sheet. Although, it is rather hard to see the full effect of this in print, with the links changing as the user rolls the mouse over links and visits the sites, so try out the example (ch08_eg01.html) with the downloaded code for this chapter.

FIGURE 8-1

BACKGROUNDS

As you saw in the last chapter, CSS treats each element as if it were its own box. You can control the background of these boxes using the properties shown in Table 8-2 (when used on the <body> element they affect the entire browser window).

TABLE 8-2: Background Properties

PROPERTY	PURPOSE
background-color	Specifies a background color.
background-image	Specifies an image to use as the background.
background-repeat	Indicates whether the background image should be repeated.

continues

TABLE 8-2 *(continued)*

PROPERTY	PURPOSE
background-attachment	Indicates a background image should be fixed in one position on the page, and whether it should stay in that position when the user scrolls down the page.
background-position	Indicates where an image should be positioned.
background	A shorthand form that enables you to specify all of these properties.

The background-color Property

The background-color property enables you to specify a single solid color for the background of any element.

When the background-color property is set for the <body> element, it affects the whole document, and when it is used on any other element, it uses the specified color inside the border of the box created for that element.

The value of this property can be any valid color value. (Colors are covered in greater depth in Appendix D, "Color Names and Values.") For example (ch08_eg02.css):

```
body {
  background-color : #cccccc;
  color : #000000;
}
b {
  background-color : #FF0000;
  color : #FFFFFF;}
p {
  background-color : rgb(255,255,255);
}
```

ch08_eg02.html (shown in Figure 8-2) used the previous styles from ch08_eg02.css.

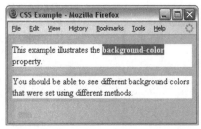

FIGURE 8-2

> **NOTE** *I add a rule for the* `<body>` *element to set the* `background-color` *property for every style sheet I write because some people set their computers to have a background other than plain white (often because it causes less strain on their eyes). When the background color of an operating system is changed, browsers usually use that color, too (along with applications such as word processors). If you do not specify this property, you cannot guarantee that the visitors to the site have the same background color as you want them to have.*

The background-image Property

As its name suggests, the `background-image` property enables you to add an image to the background of any box in CSS. This can be useful in many situations, from adding a subtle texture or shading to adding a distinctive design to the back of elements or entire pages.

The value for this property should start with the letters `url`, followed by the URL for the image in brackets and quotes like so:

```
body {
   background-image : url("images/background.gif");
}
```

If both a `background-image` property and the `background-color` property are used, then the `background-image` property takes precedence. It is good practice to supply a `background-color` property with a background image and give it a value similar to the main color in the background image because the page uses this color while the background image loads or if it cannot display the image for any reason.

Here is an example of using a single background image, which is 200 pixels wide and 150 pixels high. By default, this image is repeated across the page (`ch08_eg03.css`). The `background-color` property is set to be the same color as the background of the image (just in case the image cannot be loaded):

```
body {
   background-image : url("images/background.gif");
   background-color : #cccccc;
}
```

Figure 8-3 shows what this looks like in a browser (`ch08_eg03.html`).

This is not a great example of how to use a background image because there is not enough contrast between the colors used in the background image and the text that appears on top of it, which makes the text harder to read. But it does illustrate the point that you must make sure that there is sufficient contrast between any background image and the writing that appears on top of it; otherwise, users will have trouble reading the text.

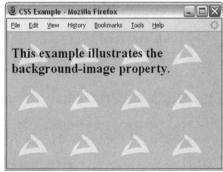

FIGURE 8-3

If you do use an image behind text, it is worth remembering that low-contrast images (images made up of similar colors) often make better backgrounds because it is harder to find a color that will be readable on top of a high-contrast image.

Figure 8-4 shows an improved example of the background image, where the text is on a solid color, which makes it easier to read. This time a larger image is also used (ch08_eg04.html).

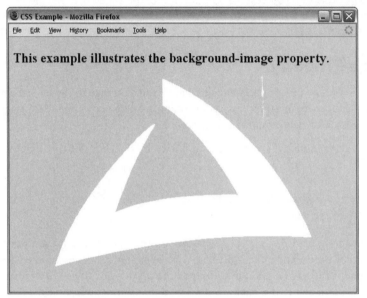

FIGURE 8-4

There are a few points to note about how background images work:

➤ There is no way to express the intended width and height of a background image, so you need to save it at the size you want it to appear.

➤ There is no equivalent to the alt attribute (alternative text for those who cannot see the image for any reason); therefore, a background image should not be used to convey any important information that is not described on the page in text as well.

➤ Background images are often shown on the page after other items have been rendered, so it can look as if they take a long time to load.

The background-repeat Property

When you specify a background-image, and the box is bigger than the image, then the image is repeated to fill up the whole box, creating what is known as *wallpaper*.

If you do not want your image to repeat all over the background of the box, you should use the background-repeat property, which has four helpful values, as you can see in Table 8-3.

TABLE 8-3: Values of the background-repeat Property

VALUE	PURPOSE
repeat	This causes the image to repeat to cover the whole page. (It is the default and rarely used.)
repeat-x	The image will be repeated horizontally across the page (not down the whole page vertically).
repeat-y	The image will be repeated vertically down the page (not across horizontally).
no-repeat	The image displays only once.

These different properties can have interesting effects. It is worth looking at each in turn. You have already seen the effect of the repeat value. (This is the default behavior when the property is not used.) The value repeat-x creates a horizontal bar following the browser's x-axis (ch08_eg05.css):

```
body {
    background-image : url("images/background_small.gif");
    background-repeat : repeat-x;
}
```

You can see the result of using this property in Figure 8-5.

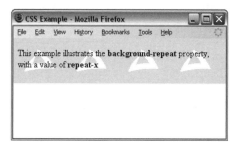

FIGURE 8-5

The repeat-y value works just like repeat-x but in the other direction, vertically following the browser's y-axis (ch08_eg06.css):

```
body {
    background-image : url("images/background_small.gif");
    background-repeat : repeat-y;
}
```

In Figure 8-6, you can see the result with the sidebar coming down the left.

The final value was no-repeat, leaving one instance of the image that by default will be in the top-left corner of the browser window (ch08_eg07.css):

```
body {
    background-image : url("images/background_small.gif");
```

```
    background-repeat : no-repeat;
    background-color : #eaeaea;
}
```

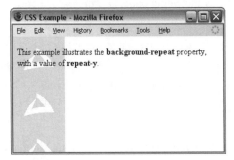

FIGURE 8-6

You can see the result in Figure 8-7; note how the background color of the page has been set to the same color as the image you have been using—this makes the image blend in with the page better.

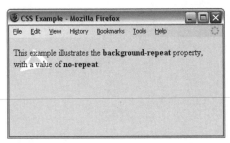

FIGURE 8-7

The background-position Property (for Fixing Position of Backgrounds)

You may want to alter the position of this image, and you can do this using the `background-position` property, which takes the values shown in Table 8-4.

TABLE 8-4: Values of the background-position Property

VALUE	MEANING
x% y%	Percentages along the x (horizontal) and y (vertical) axis
x y	Absolute lengths along the x (horizontal) and y (vertical) axis in pixels
left	Shown to the left of the page or containing element

center	Shown to the center of the page or containing element
right	Shown to the right of the page or containing element
top	Shown at the top of the page or containing element
center	Shown at the center of the page or containing element
bottom	Shown at the bottom of the page or containing element

Here is an example of fixing the position of the image, as shown in Figure 8-8 (ch08_eg08.css):

```
body {
   background-image : url("images/background_small.gif");
   background-position : 50% 20%;
   background-repeat : no-repeat;
   background-color : #eaeaea;
}
```

This image is horizontally centered (because it should be 50 percent of the screen's width from the left side of the page) and one-fifth of the way down from the top of the screen (because it is positioned 20 percent of the window height from the top of the screen). It is worth trying this example in the code download (ch08_eg08 .html) and changing the size of the browser window to see how the background image remains in the center of the browser window horizontally and one-fifth of the way down the window vertically when you change the size of the window.

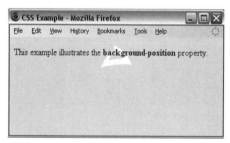

FIGURE 8-8

The background-attachment Property (for Watermarks)

When you specify a background image, you can use the background-attachment property (values shown in Table 8-5) to specify whether the image is fixed in its position, or whether it moves as the user scrolls up and down the page.

TABLE 8-5: Values for the background-attachment Property

VALUE	PURPOSE
fixed	The image does not move if the user scrolls up and down the page.
scroll	The image stays in the same place on the background of the page. If the user scrolls up or down the page, the image moves, too.

Here is an example where the image stays in the middle of the page even when the user scrolls further down (ch08_eg09.css):

```
body {
   background-image : url("images/background_small.gif");
   background-attachment : fixed;
   background-position : center;
   background-repeat : no-repeat;
   background-color : #eaeaea;
}
```

Figure 8-9 shows that the user has scrolled halfway down the page and the image is in the center of the browser window. (The background looks exactly the same as it would have when the user was at the top of the page.)

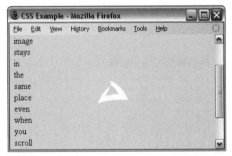

FIGURE 8-9

The background Property (the Shorthand)

The `background` property enables you to specify several of the background properties at once. The values can be given in any order, and if you do not supply one of the values, the default value will be used.

➤ background-color

➤ background-image

➤ background-repeat

➤ background-attachment

➤ background-position

For example, you can just write

```
body {
    background: #cc66ff url("images/background_small.gif")
 fixed no-repeat center;
}
```

This creates exactly the same effect as the example shown in Figure 8-9.

LISTS

In Chapter 1, "Structuring Documents for the Web," you learned how to use the `<ul>` and `<li>` elements to create lists with bullet points (also known as unordered lists) and the `<ol>` and `<li>` elements to create numbered (or ordered) lists. In this section you learn about the CSS properties you can use to control lists (shown in Table 8-6).

TABLE 8-6: List Properties

PROPERTY	PURPOSE
list-style-type	Enables you to control the shape or appearance of the marker. (The marker is another name for the bullet point or number.)
list-style-position	When a list item takes up more than one line, this property specifies where the marker should appear in relation to the text.
list-style-image	Specifies an image for the marker rather than a bullet point or number.
list-style	Serves as shorthand for the preceding properties.
marker-offset	Specifies the distance between a marker and the text in the list.

The list-style-type Property

The `list-style-type` property enables you to control the shape or style of a bullet point (also known as a *marker*) for unordered lists and the style of numbering characters in ordered lists.

Table 8-7 shows the values for an unordered list.

TABLE 8-7: list-style-type Values for Unordered Lists

VALUE	MARKER
none	None
disc	Filled-in circle (default)
circle	Empty circle
square	Filled-in square

Table 8-8 shows the values for ordered lists.

TABLE 8-8: list-style-type Values for Ordered Lists

VALUE	MEANING	EXAMPLE
decimal	Number	1, 2, 3, 4, 5
decimal-leading-zero	0 before the number	01, 02, 03, 04, 05
lower-alpha | lower-latin	Lowercase alphanumeric characters	a, b, c, d, e
upper-alpha | upper-latin	Uppercase alphanumeric characters	A, B, C, D, E
lower-roman	Lowercase Roman numerals	i, ii, iii, iv, v
upper-roman	Uppercase Roman numerals	I, II, III, IV, V
lower-greek	Lowercase classical Greek	α, β, δ, ε, θ
armenian	Armenian numbering	ա, բ, գ, դ, ե
georgian	Georgian numbering	ა, ბ, გ, დ, ე

The list-style-type property can be used either on the `<ul>` and `<ol>` elements (in which case it applies to the entire list) or on the individual `<li>` elements. The following example demonstrates all these styles (ch08_eg10.html):

```
li.a {
  list-style-type : none;
}
li.b {
  list-style-type : disc;
}
li.c {
  list-style-type : circle;
}
li.d {
  list-style-type : square;
}
li.e {
  list-style-type : decimal;
}
li.f {
  list-style-type : lower-alpha;
}
li.g {
  list-style-type : upper-alpha;
}
li.h {
  list-style-type : lower-roman;
```

```
  }
  li.i {
    list-style-type : upper-roman;
  }
  li.j {
    list-style : georgian;
  }
  li.k {
    list-style : armenian;
  }
  li.l {
    list-style : lower-greek;
  }
```

You can see the result with examples of each kind of bullet in Figure 8-10.

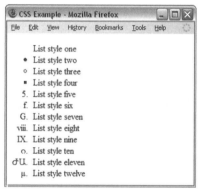

FIGURE 8-10

The list-style-position Property

Lists are indented into the page, and the `list-style-position` property indicates whether the marker should appear inside or outside of the box containing the main points. There are two values for this property, as shown in Table 8-9.

TABLE 8-9: Values for the list-style-position Property

VALUE	PURPOSE
inside	The marker is inside the block of text (which is indented).
outside	The marker sits to the left of the block of text. (This is the default value if this is not specified.)

Here you can see how this property is written; in this case it is given on the `<ul>` or `<ol>` elements (`ch08_eg11.css`):

```
ul {
  list-style-position : outside;
}
ol {
  list-style-position : inside;
}
```

Figure 8-11 shows what this would look like in a browser.

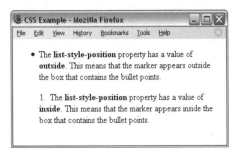

FIGURE 8-11

As you can see, the text is indented in both cases, and the value of this property indicates whether the marker is inside the box or outside of the box.

The list-style-image Property

The `list-style-image` property enables you to specify an image so that you can use your own bullet style. The syntax is similar to the `background-image` property; the value starts with the letters `url` and is followed by the URL for the image in brackets and quotation marks (`ch08_eg12.css`):

```
li {
  list-style-image: url("images/bulletpoint.gif");
}
```

Figure 8-12 shows some triangular bullet points.

If the image cannot display, the browser displays a dot rather than a broken image symbol.

FIGURE 8-12

NOTE *If you use nested lists, this value inherits from its parent element. To prevent this from happening, you can use the* list-style-image *property on the nested list and give it a value of* none.

The list-style Property (the Shorthand)

The list-style property is a way to express more than one of these properties at once. They should appear in the order: type, position, image—for example:

```
ul {
   list-style : circle inside;
}
```

Remember that you can also set the border, padding, and margin properties for `<ul>`, `<ol>`, `<li>`, `<dl>`, `<dt>`, and `<dd>` elements because each element has its own box in CSS.

TABLES

In the last chapter, you saw a couple examples that use CSS with tables. Properties commonly used with the `<table>`, `<td>`, and `<th>` elements include the following:

➤ border to set the properties of the border of a table.

➤ padding to set the amount of space between the border of a table cell and its content—this property is important to make tables easier to read.

➤ Properties to change text and fonts.

➤ text-align to align writing to the left, right, or center of a cell.

➤ vertical-align to align writing to the top, middle, or bottom of a cell.

➤ width to set the width of a table or cell.

➤ height to set the height of a cell (often used on a row as well).

➤ background-color to change the background color of a table or cell.

➤ background-image to add an image to the background of a table or cell.

You should be aware that, apart from the background-color and height properties, it is best to avoid using these properties with `<tr>` elements because browser support for these properties on rows is not as good as it is for individual cells.

To demonstrate how some of these properties are used with a table, take a look at the one shown in Figure 8-13. It might look familiar because you saw it at the beginning of the last chapter, but this time it has an added `<caption>` element (ch08_13.html).

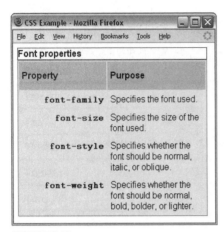

FIGURE 8-13

Now look at the style sheet for this table (ch08_eg13.css):

```css
body {
  color : #000000;
  background-color : #ffffff;
}
h1 {
  font-size : 18pt;
}
p {
  font-size : 12pt;
}
table {
  background-color : #efefef;
  width : 350px;
  border-style : solid;
  border-width : 1px;
  border-color : #999999;
  font-family : arial, verdana, sans-serif;}
caption {
  font-weight : bold;
  text-align : left;
  border-style : solid;
  border-width : 1px;
  border-color : #666666;
  color : #666666;
}
th {
  height : 50px;
  font-weight : bold;
  text-align : left;
  background-color : #cccccc;
}
```

```
td, th {
  padding : 5px;
}
td.code {
  width : 150px;
  font-family : courier, courier-new, serif;
  font-weight : bold;
  text-align : right;
  vertical-align : top;
}
```

Here are some key points to note about this example. You will be altering settings of some of these properties using new properties that you will meet throughout this section.

➤ The rule for the <table> element uses a width property to fix the width of the table to 350 pixels; otherwise, it would take up as much of the screen as needed to show as much text as possible on one line.

➤ The rule for the <table> element also has a border property set, which creates a single-pixel border all around the table. Note, however, that none of the other cells in the table inherits this property.

➤ The rule that applies to the <caption> element has its font-weight, border, and text-align properties set. By default the text is normal (not bold), aligned in the center, and without a border.

➤ The rule that applies to the <th> element sets the height of the headings to 50 pixels, and the text is aligned left (rather than centered, which is the default).

➤ There is a rule that applies to both the <th> and <td> elements, and this indicates that both should have a padding property set to 5px so that the content of the cells does not touch the border of those cells. Creating space around the cells is important and makes the table more readable.

➤ The final rule states that the <td> elements whose class attribute has a value of code are given a width property whose value is 150px (150 pixels). This ensures that the content of this whole column remains on one line. Unfortunately, there is no way to assign a style to a column, but in the case of the width property, after it has been set on one element, it does not need to be set on all the others in the column.

You might also have noticed in Figure 8-13 that there is a white line around the two columns (which is particularly noticeable around table header cells). Browsers automatically add this to separate each cell from its neighbor. You can, however, remove this gap using a property called border-spacing, which you learn about in the next section.

Table-Specific Properties

In the following section you meet five properties that can be used only with tables, and also some values for the border-style property that apply only to tables (shown in Table 8-10).

TABLE 8-10: Table-Specific Properties

PROPERTY	PURPOSE
border-collapse	Where the borders of two table cells touch, this property indicates whether *both* borders should be visible, or whether the browser should pick just one of the borders to show.
border-spacing	Specifies the width of the space that should appear between table cells.
caption-side	Specifies which side of a table the caption should appear on.
empty-cells	Specifies whether the border should be shown if a cell is empty.
table-layout	If the space you have allocated for a table is not enough to fit the contents, browsers often increase the size of the table to fit the content in—this property can force a table to use the dimensions you specify.

The border-collapse Property

Where two table cells meet, you can tell the browser to show just one of the borders (rather than both—which is the default behavior). You can do this using the border-collapse property, which can take two values, as shown in Table 8-11.

TABLE 8-11: Values of the border-collapse Property

VALUE	PURPOSE
collapse	Horizontal borders collapse and vertical borders abut one another.
separate	Separate rules are observed. This value opens up additional properties to give you further control.

If two adjacent table cells have different border styles, and you have specified that borders should be collapsed, there is a complex set of rules to specify which border should be shown—rather than try to learn these rules, it is quicker to simply try your table out in a browser.

To illustrate how the border-collapse property works, the following style rules apply to two tables: The first has a border-collapse property with a value of collapse; the second has a value of separate; and both tables contain adjacent cells with dotted and solid lines (ch08_eg14.css):

```
table.one {
  border-collapse : collapse;
}
table.two {
  border-collapse : separate;
}
td.a {
  border-style : dotted;
  border-width : 3px;
```

```
    border-color : #000000;
    padding : 10px;
  }
  td.b {
    border-style : solid;
    border-width : 3px;
    border-color : #333333;
    padding : 10px;
  }
```

Figure 8-14 shows how, with a value of `collapse`, the browser collapses borders into each other so that the solid border takes precedence over the dotted border. This wouldn't look as odd if the borders were both solid, but it does illustrate the point well.

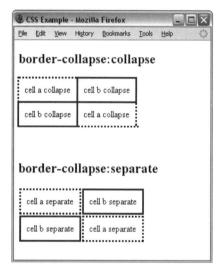

FIGURE 8-14

If you do not specify that the borders should be collapsed, then two further properties control border presentation:

➤   `border-spacing`

➤   `empty-cells`

The following sections discuss these properties.

The border-spacing Property

The `border-spacing` property specifies the distance that separates adjacent cells' borders. If you provide one value, it applies to both vertical and horizontal borders:

```
table.one {
  border-spacing : 15px;
}
```

Or you can specify two values, in which case the first refers to the horizontal spacing and the second to the vertical spacing:

```
table.two {
  border-spacing : 2px 8px;
}
```

You can see what this looks like in Figure 8-15 (ch08_eg15.html styled with ch08_eg15.css).

FIGURE 8-15

The empty-cells Property

The empty-cells property indicates whether a cell without any content should have a border displayed. It can take one of three values, as you can see in Table 8-12.

TABLE 8-12: Values of the empty-cells Property

VALUE	PURPOSE
show	Borders show even if the cell is empty. (This is the default value.)
hide	Borders are hidden if a cell is empty.
inherit	Borders obey the rules of the containing table (only of use in nested tables).

> **NOTE** *If you want to explicitly hide or show borders of empty cells, you should use the* empty-cells *property because some versions of IE and Firefox treat empty cells differently.*

Here you can see a table with two empty cells: an empty `<th>` element and an empty `<td>` element (ch08_eg16.html):

```
<table>
  <tr>
    <th></th>
    <th>Title one</th>
    <th>Title two</th>
  </tr>
  <tr>
    <th>Row Title</th>
    <td>value</td>
    <td>value</td>
  </tr>
  <tr>
    <th>Row Title</th>
    <td>value</td>
    <td></td>
  </tr>
</table>
```

The following code shows the `empty-cells` property used to hide borders of empty cells in the `<table>` element (ch08_eg16.css):

```
table {
  width : 350px;
  border-collapse : separate;
  empty-cells : hide;}
td {
  padding : 5px;
  border-style : solid;
  border-width : 1px;
  border-color : #999999;
}
```

Figure 8-16 shows what the table looks like without borders for empty cells.

FIGURE 8-16

The caption-side Property

The `caption-side` property is for use with the `<caption>` element to indicate on which side of the table the caption should go. Table 8-13 lists the possible values.

TABLE 8-13: Values of the caption-side Property

VALUE	PURPOSE
top	The caption appears above the table (the default).
right	The caption appears to the right of the table.
bottom	The caption appears below the table.
left	The caption appears to the left of the table.

For example, here you can see the caption is set to the bottom of the table (ch08_eg17.css):

```
caption {
  caption-side : bottom
}
```

Figure 8-17 shows you the caption-side property at work; you can see that the caption for this table has moved to the bottom of the table (rather than the top).

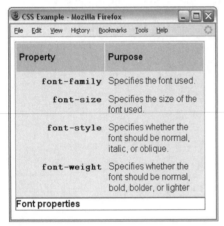

FIGURE 8-17

The table-layout Property

When you specify a width for a table or table cell, but the content does not fit into the space you have allowed, a browser can give the table more space to fit the content. The table-layout property enables you to force the browser to stick to the widths you specify, even if this makes the content unreadable.

Table 8-14 shows the three possible values this property can take.

TABLE 8-14: Values of the table-layout Property

VALUE	PURPOSE
auto	The browser looks through the entire table for the widest unbreakable content in the cells. This is slower at rendering but more useful if you do not know the exact size of each column. This is the default value.
fixed	The width of a table cell depends only on the widths you specified for the table and its cells. This speeds up rendering.
inherit	Obeys the rules of the containing table (only of use in nested tables).

In the following example there are two tables, each with just one cell. The cells contain the letters of the alphabet, and there is a space before the last three letters. Normally, each table cell will be as wide as the longest unbroken set of characters in a cell—in this case, the letters *A* through *W* (ch08_eg18.html).

```
<table class="one">
  <tr>
    <td>ABCDEFGHIJKLMNOPQRSTUVW XYZ</td>
  </tr>
</table>

<table class="two">
  <tr>
    <td>ABCDEFGHIJKLMNOPQRSTUVW XYZ</td>
  </tr>
</table>
```

Now, if you look at the CSS for this example, you can see that the width of the table is set to 75 pixels—not enough for the letters *A* through *W*. One table has the table-layout property set to auto, the other to fixed (ch08_eg18.css).

```
table {
  width : 75px;
}
table.one {
  table-layout : auto;
}
table.two {
  table-layout : fixed;
}
td {
  padding : 5px;
  border-style : solid;
  border-width : 1px;
  border-color : #999999;
}
```

You can see the results of this example in Figure 8-18; by default the table makes enough space for the letters *A* through *W*. However, when the second table is forced to stick to the width specified in the CSS, the letters spill over the edge of the table.

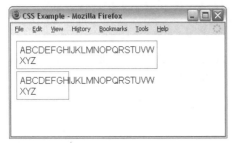

FIGURE 8-18

To prevent the letters spilling over the edge, you could use the `overflow` property.

OUTLINES

Outlines are similar to the borders that you met in the last chapter, but there are two crucial differences:

➤ An outline does not take up space.

➤ Outlines do not need to be rectangular.

The idea behind the outline properties is that you might want to highlight some aspect of a page for the user; this property enables you to do that without affecting the flow of the page (where elements are positioned) in the way that a physical border would take up space. It's almost as if the outline style sits on top of the page.

> **NOTE** *Unfortunately, the outline properties are not supported by Internet Explorer 7 (or earlier versions). They do work in other major browsers; although, there can be some slight variations in appearance in different browsers.*

Table 8-15 lists the four outline properties.

TABLE 8-15: Outline Properties

PROPERTY	PURPOSE
outline-width	Specifies the width of the outline.
outline-style	Specifies the line style for the outline.

outline-color	Specifies the color of the outline.
outline	Shorthand for above properties in the pattern: width, style, color.

Note that the outline is always the same on all sides; you cannot specify different values for different sides of the element.

The outline-width Property

The outline-width property specifies the width of the outline to be added to the box. Its value should be a length or one of the values thin, medium, or thick—just like the border-width attribute.

```
input {
  border-width : 2px;
}
```

The outline-style Property

The outline-style property specifies the style for the line (solid, dotted, or dashed) that goes around the box. Its value should be one of the values used with the border-style property you learned about in Chapter 7, "Cascading Style Sheets," for example:

```
input {
  outline-style : solid;
}
```

The outline-color Property

The outline-color property enables you to specify the color of the outline. Its value can be any valid color value, for example:

```
input {
  outline-color : #ff0000;
}
```

The outline Property (the Shorthand)

The outline property is the shorthand that enables you to specify values for any of the three properties discussed previously in any order you like. The following example features a paragraph of text:

```
<p>Inside this paragraph the word in <b>bold</b> is going to have an outline.</p>
```

There is a rule that says the contents of the <b> element should have an 8-pixel dashed red border around the edge (ch08_eg19.css):

```
b {
  outline : #ff0000 8px dashed;
}
```

Figure 8-19 shows what this example looks like; although the border is gray here, not red. Note how the outline does not affect the position of other items on the page (in the same way that the border properties would); it just sits on top of the rest of the page.

FIGURE 8-19

THE :FOCUS AND :ACTIVE PSEUDO-CLASSES

You may remember in Chapter 6, "Forms," the topic of focus. An element needs to gain focus if a user interacts with it; for example, focus can be given to links and form controls.

When an element gains focus, browsers tend to give it a slightly different appearance. The :focus pseudo-class enables you to associate extra rules with an element when it gains focus to make it more pronounced. Meanwhile the :active pseudo-class enables you to associate further styles with elements when they are activated—such as when a user clicks a link.

Here is an example of a rule that can change the background-color property of an <input> element when it gains focus (ch08_eg20.css):

```
input {
  border : none;
  background-color : #dddddd;
}
input:focus {
  background-color : #c4c4c4;
}
```

As you can probably imagine, this could offer users help to know which item they should currently be filling in as they work their way through a form. Figure 8-20 shows the form input has focus with a darker background than other input elements.

IE8 was the first version of IE to support the :focus pseudo-class. It's long been supported in all other major browsers.

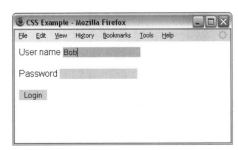

FIGURE 8-20

GENERATED CONTENT

CSS2 introduced a powerful way to add content before or after a specified element, even if it were not in the HTML document. To do this, the `:before` and `:after` pseudo-elements are added to the selector, and then the `content` property is used to specify what should be inserted into the document.

The `:before` and `:after` pseudo-elements work to a limited degree in IE7 or higher and have good support in the other major browsers.

> **NOTE** In CSS3, pseudo-elements are specified with a double colon to differentiate them from pseudo-classes—`::before`, `::after`, `::first-letter`, and `::first-line`. Most browsers will accept them with a single colon as well. Internet Explorer 8 only supports the single-colon version. If you need to support that browser, you should use the single-colon version. Otherwise, the double-colon version is the pattern to use.

The :before and :after Pseudo-Elements

The `:before` and `:after` pseudo-elements enable you to add text before or after each instance of an element defined in a selector. For example, the following CSS rule adds the words "You need to register to read the full article" after each instance of a `<p>` element that carries the `class` attribute whose value is `abstract` (ch08_eg21.css):

```
p.abstract:after {
   content : "You need to register to read the full
   article.";
   color:#ff0000;
}
```

Here you can see that the pseudo-element `:after` is used at the end of the selector. Then, inside the declaration, you can see the `content` property; the text in quotes will be added to the end of the element. The `content` property can add a number of types of content to the document, not just text, and you see these in the next section.

The default styles for the parent element will be adopted if no other declarations are added to the rule. Although, in this example a property was added to indicate that the content should be written in red. You can see this pseudo-element in use in Figure 8-21.

FIGURE 8-21

> **NOTE** *By default, the element created using these pseudo-classes will be inline unless you use the* display *property with a value of* block. *If the element identified in the selector is an inline element, you should not use the* display *property to turn it into a block-level element.*

The content Property

The content property is used with the :before and :after pseudo-elements to indicate what content should be added to the document. Table 8-16 lists the values it can take; each value inserts different types of content into the HTML document it is supposed to be styling.

TABLE 8-16: Values of the content Property

VALUE	PURPOSE
A string	Inserts plain text. (The term *string* is a programming term for a set of alphanumeric characters, not a CSS property.) The text may not include quotes (which in turn means that it cannot include HTML markup that carries attributes).
A URL	The URL can point to an image, a text file, or an HTML file to be included at this point.
A counter	A counter for numbering elements on the page (discussed in the next section).
attr(x)	The value of an attribute named *x* that is carried on that element. (This is of more use to languages other than HTML.)
open-quote	Inserts the appropriate opening quote symbol (see the "Quotation Marks" section).
close-quote	Inserts the appropriate closing quote symbol (see the "Quotation Marks" section).
no-open-quote	Do not use any opening quotes.
no-close-quote	Do not use a closing quote (of particular use in prose where one person speaks for a long time and style dictates the quote is closed only on the last paragraph).

Counters

You have already seen how you can create a numbered list using the <ol> element, so the concept of automatic numbering is not new. The counter() function is different from numbered lists because you can create a counter that increments each time a browser comes across any specified element—not just an <li> element.

The idea is particularly helpful if you want to automatically number sections of a document without them being a list. It also means that items will automatically be renumbered if extra elements are added or removed (without having to go into the document and manually renumber each item).

To see how it works, create an example in which the sections of a document are numbered using the `counter()` function. Here is the HTML (`ch08_eg22.html`):

```
<body>
<h1> Introducing Web Technologies</h1>
  <h2>Introducing HTML</h2>
  <h2>Introducing CSS</h2>
  <h2>Introducing XHTML</h2>
<h1> Structure of Documents</h1>
  <h2>Text</h2>
  <h2>Lists</h2>
  <h2>Tables</h2>
  <h2>Forms</h2>
</body>
```

The example contains two counters, one called `chapter` and the other called `section`. Each time an `<h1>` element comes up, the `chapter` counter is incremented by 1, and each time the `<h2>` element comes up, the `section` counter is incremented by 1.

Furthermore, each time the browser comes across an `<h1>` element, it inserts the word "Chapter" and the number in the counter before the content of the `<h1>` element. Meanwhile, each time the browser comes across an `<h2>` element, it displays the number of the `chapter` counter, then a period or full stop, and then the value of the `section` counter.

The result should look like Figure 8-22.

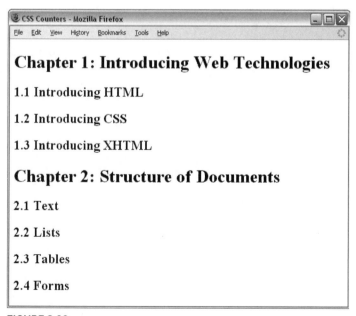

FIGURE 8-22

Now look at how this works. First, it is worth noting that you use the `counter-reset` property on the `<body>` element to create the `chapter` and `section` counters and set them to zero.

```
body {
   counter-reset : chapter;
   counter-reset : section;
}
```

Then there are the CSS rules using the `:before` pseudo-class to insert the automatic numbering of sections. First, look at the rule that adds the word "Chapter" and the chapter number before every `<h1>` element. If you look at the `content` property, the value has a set of quotes containing the word "Chapter," followed by the `counter()` function. (Inside the brackets you see the name of the counter.) After this, you see another set of quotes containing the colon symbol followed by a space:

```
h1:before {
   content : "Chapter " counter(chapter) ": ";
}
```

The `content` property that adds the section numbering before the `<h2>` elements starts with the `counter()` function calling the `chapter` counter, follows that with a period (or full stop) in quotes, and then calls the `counter()` function again, this time with the section number:

```
h2:before {
   content: counter(chapter) "." Counter (section) " ";
}
```

Each time the browser comes across an `<h2>` element, it should increment the `section` counter using the `counter-increment` property:

```
h2 {
   counter-increment : section;
}
```

Each time the browser comes across an `<h1>` element, it should increment the `chapter` counter using the `counter-increment` property and reset the `section` counter:

```
h1 {
   counter-increment : chapter;
   counter-reset : section;
}
```

When you put these rules together, they should look like this (`ch08_eg22.css`):

```
body {
   counter-reset : chapter;
   counter-reset : section;
}
h1:before {
   content : "Chapter " counter(chapter) ": ";
}
h2:before {
   content : counter(chapter) "." Counter (section) " ";
}
```

```
h1 {
  counter-increment : chapter;
  counter-reset : section;
}
h2 {
  counter-increment : section;
}
```

The first version of IE to support the counter functions was IE8. They are supported in all other major browsers.

Quotation Marks

The `content` property can use the values `open-quote` and `close-quote` to add quotation marks before and after occurrences of specified elements.

IE8 was the first version of Internet Explorer to support these properties. They're supported in all other major browsers. Here is the HTML for this example: (ch08_eg23.html):

```
<h1>Generated quotes</h1>
<p>Here are some quotes from Oscar Wilde:</p>
<blockquote>Consistency is the last refuge of the unimaginative.</blockquote>
<blockquote>If you want to tell people the truth, make them laugh,
otherwise they'll kill you.</blockquote>
<blockquote>It is a very sad thing that nowadays there is so little useless
information.</blockquote>
```

And now to add the quotes before and after the <blockquote> element, use the following CSS (ch08_eg23.css):

```
blockquote:before {
  content: open-quote;
}
blockquote:after {
  content: close-quote;
}
```

You can see the result in Figure 8-23.

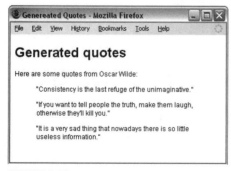

FIGURE 8-23

MISCELLANEOUS PROPERTIES

There are a few helpful properties that have not yet been covered, which you look at next:

➤   The `cursor` property

➤   The `display` property

➤   The `visibility` property

The cursor Property

The `cursor` property enables you to specify the type of mouse cursor that should be displayed to the user. For example, when an image is used for a submit button on a form, this property is often used to change the cursor from an arrow to a hand, providing a visual clue to users that they can click it. Figure 8-24 shows some of the cursor types available for you to use—although, you see only one at a time if you try the example (`ch08_eg24.html`).

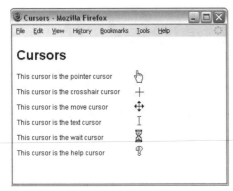

FIGURE 8-24

As a general rule, you should use these values to add only helpful information for users in places they would expect to see that cursor—for example, using a crosshair on a link may confuse users.

Table 8-17 shows possible values for the `cursor` property.

TABLE 8-17: Values for the cursor Property

VALUE	DESCRIPTION
auto	The shape of the cursor depends on the context area it is over (a text cursor over text, a hand over a link, and so on).
crosshair	A crosshair or plus sign.
default	Usually an arrow.

pointer	A pointing hand.
move	A grasping hand (ideal if you are doing drag-and-drop script).
e-resize ne-resize nw-resize n-resize se-resize sw-resize s-resize w-resize	Indicate that an edge can be moved. For example, if you were stretching a box with the mouse, the se-resize cursor is used to indicate a movement starting from the southeast corner of the box.
text	Similar to the vertical bar I.
wait	An hourglass.
help	A question mark or balloon, ideal for use over help buttons.
<url>	The source of a cursor image file.
progress	A progress indicator. Differs from wait in that the user can interact with the application.

The display Property

The display property can be used to force an element to be either a block-level or an inline box. For example, to make an inline element such as a link into a block-level box, you would use the following:

```
a {
  display : block;
}
```

Or you could make a block-level box such as a paragraph into an inline box like so:

```
p {
  display : inline;
}
```

You may also want to use the value none to indicate that the box should not be displayed. When this value is used, it does not take up any space on the page—it is treated as if it were not in the markup at all.

```
p {
  display : none;
}
```

There's a useful combination of both inline and block-level characteristics called inline-block, which lets an element flow inline like a <b> or <span> but still allows it to accept some block-like attributes such as width and height.

```
p {
  display : inline-block;
}
```

This property can take other values, but they're rarely used in practice.

The visibility Property

The visibility property enables you to hide a box from view. When you give the visibility property a value of hidden, you do not see the content of the element, but it still affects the layout of the page. (It takes up the same amount of space that it would if you could see the element on the page—if you want to make something disappear without taking up space, you should use the display property that you just met in the previous section.) A common use of the visibility property would be to hide error messages that display only if the user needs to see them. The visibility property can also take a value of visible to show the element (which is the default state for all elements), as shown in Table 8-18.

TABLE 8-18: Values for the visibility Property

VALUE	PURPOSE
visible	The box and its contents are shown to the user (the default state for all elements).
hidden	The box and its contents are made invisible; although, they still affect the layout of the page.

For example, here are four paragraphs of text (ch08_eg25.html):

```
<body>
  <p>Here is a paragraph of text.</p>
  <p>Here is a paragraph of text.</p>
  <p class="invisible">This paragraph of text should be invisible.</p>
  <p>Here is a paragraph of text.</p>
</body>
```

Note that the third paragraph has a class attribute whose value indicates that it's part of the invisible class. Now look at the rule for this class (ch08_eg25.css):

```
p.invisible {
  visibility : hidden;
}
```

You can see from Figure 8-25 that the invisible paragraph still takes up space, but it is not visible to the user.

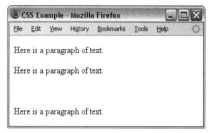

FIGURE 8-25

Remember that the source code still contains whatever is in the invisible paragraph, so you should not use this to hide sensitive information such as credit card details or passwords.

ADDITIONAL RULES

Before you move on to look at how you can use CSS to position elements on a page, take a look at two rules:

➤ @import imports another style sheet into the current style sheet.

➤ !important indicates that some rules should take precedence over others.

The @import Rule: Modularized Style Sheets

The @import rule enables you to import styles from another style sheet. It must appear right at the start of the style sheet before any of the rules, and its value is a URL. It can be written in one of two ways:

```
@import "mystyle.css";
@import url("mystyle.css");
```

Either works fine. The significance of the @import rule is that it enables you to develop your style sheets with a modular approach. You can create separate style sheets for different aspects of your site. This concept was introduced in the last chapter when you created a style sheet for code styles. Now if you want to include those styles in any other style sheet you write, rather than repeat them, you just use the @import rule to bring those rules into the style sheet you are writing.

Here is an example of a style sheet that imports the codeStyles.css style sheet from the last chapter. (For convenience, this file has been copied into the folder for the code download for this chapter.) This example is ch08_eg26.css:

```
@import "codeStyles.css"
body {
  background-color : #ffffff;
  font-family : arial, verdana, helvetica, sans-serif;}
h1 {
  font-size : 24pt;
}
```

As you can see, it does not contain many rules; the code styles have all been taken from the imported style sheet. Figure 8-26 shows a page that uses this style sheet that has imported the styles for the code (ch08_eg26.html).

FIGURE 8-26

You might also consider developing modular style sheets that control appearance of forms, different layouts, and so on. If a style sheet contains a rule for one element (say the <body> element was given a black background color), this rule would take precedence over any conflicting rules that applied to imported style sheets (for example, if there were a rule in the imported style sheet indicating that the <body> element should be given a red background color).

> **WARNING** *While using* @import *can help you organize your style sheets, it does come with a performance penalty because it blocks parallel downloads. (For more information, refer to* www.stevesouders.com/blog/2009/04/09/dont-use-import/*.) For optimal performance, you want as many resources to be downloaded at one time as possible. CSS files attached to a page using* <link> *will download in parallel. Using* @import *causes them to download sequentially.*

The !important Rule

When there is a chance that two style sheet rules might conflict with each other, you can use the !important rule to indicate that this particular rule should take precedence over others. This can be helpful if you develop modular style sheets and you want to ensure that a rule in the included style sheets takes precedence over any conflicting rules in the style sheet containing the @import rule (which would otherwise have taken precedence).

> **WARNING** *If you want to play nice with other code authors, you should use* !important *only as a last resort. It can cause confusion when another author is trying to override a style using specificity and fails, only to discover an* !important *rule lurking in another style sheet.*

It can also be helpful when users have set their own style sheets. Part of the aim of separating style from content, using CSS to style web pages, was to make them more accessible to those with visual impairments. So after you have spent your valuable time learning about CSS and how to write your style sheets to make your sites attractive, users can create their own style sheets that can override your settings!

In reality, few people do create their own CSS style sheets to view pages the way they want, but the ability is there and was designed for those with disabilities. By default, your style sheet rather than theirs should be viewed; however, the users' style sheet can contain the `!important` rule, which says "override the site's style sheet for this property." For example, a user might use the rule like so:

```
p {
  font-size : 18pt !important;
  font-weight : bold !important;
}
```

There is nothing you can do to force users to use your style sheet, but in practice, a small percentage (if any) of your visitors will create their own style sheets, so you should not worry about it—it's covered here only so that you understand what the rule is and why you may come across it.

> **NOTE** In CSS1, the `!important` rule allowed authors to overrule users' style sheets, but this was switched over in the second version.

POSITIONING AND LAYOUT WITH CSS

Up to this point, you have learned how the content of each element is represented in CSS using a box, and you've seen many of the properties you can use to affect the appearance of the box and its content. Now it's time to look at how to control where the boxes should be positioned within a page.

In CSS, there are three common *positioning schemes* that enable you to control layout of a page: *normal*, *float*, and *absolute* positioning. In the following sections, you see how you can use each of these to indicate where the content of an element should appear on the page.

Although the CSS positioning schemes were not intended to be a mechanism to control the layout of pages, they have become the standard way to lay out pages on the web. For the rest of the chapter, you look at how you can control where boxes appear on the page using CSS.

> **NOTE** Before CSS, web designers commonly used tables to control the layout of web pages. Although you still occasionally see tables used for this purpose, they were designed to contain tabular data, and you should aim to control layout of new pages using CSS instead. If you use CSS to control layout rather than tables, your pages will be smaller (in terms of lines of code), easier to adapt to different devices, easier to redesign, faster to load, and more visible to search engines.

Normal Flow

By default, elements are laid out on the page using *normal* or *static flow*. In normal flow, the block-level elements within a page flow from top to bottom (remember that each block-level element appears as if it is on a new line), and inline elements flow from left to right (because they do not start on a new line).

For example, each heading and paragraph should appear on a different line, whereas the contents of elements such as <b>, <em>, and <span> sit within a paragraph or other block-level element. They do not start on new lines.

Figure 8-27 illustrates this with three paragraphs, each of which is a block-level element sitting on top of the other. Inside each paragraph is an example of an inline element, in this case the <b> element (ch08_eg27.html).

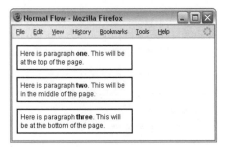

FIGURE 8-27

If you want the content of elements to appear in other places than where they would in normal flow, you have two properties to help you: position and float.

The position Property

The position property enables you to specify how you want to control the position for a box (and is generally used to take items out of normal flow). It can take the four values listed in Table 8-19.

TABLE 8-19: Values of the position Property

VALUE	MEANING
static	This is the same as normal flow and is the default, so you rarely (if ever) see it specified.
relative	The position of the box can be offset from where it would be if it were left in normal flow.

absolute	The box is positioned exactly using *x* and *y* coordinates from the top-left corner of the containing element.
fixed	The position is calculated from the top-left corner of a browser window and does not change position if the user scrolls the window.

You see how these are used in the coming sections.

Box Offset Properties

As you see in the coming sections, when boxes have a position property whose value is relative, absolute, or fixed, they also use *box offset* properties to indicate where these boxes should be positioned. Table 8-20 lists the box offset properties.

TABLE 8-20: Values for the Box Offset Properties

PROPERTY	MEANING
top	Offset position from the top of the containing element
left	Offset position from the left of the containing element
bottom	Offset position from the bottom of the containing element
right	Offset position from the right of the containing element

Each can take a value of a length, a percentage, or auto. Relative units, including percentages, are calculated for the containing boxes' dimensions or properties.

Relative Positioning

Relative positioning enables you to move a box in relation to where it would appear in normal flow. For example, you might move a box 30 pixels down from where it would appear in normal flow, or 100 pixels to the right. It is displaced from where it would be in normal flow using the box offset properties.

Now go back to the last example you met in the previous section when looking at normal flow and move the second paragraph using relative positioning, as shown in Figure 8-28.

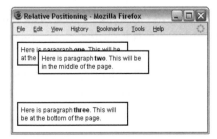

FIGURE 8-28

The second paragraph in this example is offset from where it would be in normal flow (where it was in the last example) by 40 pixels from the left and 40 pixels from the top—note the minus sign, which raises it above its position in normal flow (ch08_eg28.css).

```
p {
  border-style : solid;
  border-color : #000000;
  border-width : 2px;
  padding : 5px;
  background-color : #FFFFFF;
}
p.two {
  position : relative;
  left : 40px;
  top : -40px;
}
```

The value of the box offsets is most commonly given in pixels or a percentage.

> **NOTE** *You should specify only a left or right offset and a top or bottom offset. If you specify both left and right or both top and bottom, the right or bottom offset will be ignored.*

When you use relative positioning, some boxes can overlap others, as in the previous example. Because you offset a box relative to normal flow, if the offset is large enough, one box ends up on top of another. This might create an effect you are looking for; however, there are a couple pitfalls you must be aware of:

➤ Unless you set a background for a box (either a background color or image) the box will be transparent by default, making any overlapping text an unreadable mess. In the preceding example, the background-color property was used to make the background of the paragraphs white and thereby prevent this from happening.

➤ The CSS specification does not say which element should appear on top when relatively positioned elements overlap each other, so there can be differences between browsers. (Although, you can control this using the z-index property, which you meet shortly.)

Absolute Positioning

Absolute positioning takes an element out of normal flow, allowing you to fix its position. You can specify that an element's content should be absolutely positioned by giving it the position property with a value of absolute. Then you use the box offset properties to position it where you want.

The box offsets fix the position of a box relative to the *containing block*—which is slightly different from a containing element because it is a containing element whose position property is set to relative, absolute, or fixed.

Now look at the following style sheet. This style sheet is for use with three paragraphs again, but this time the paragraphs are held within a `<div>` element that also uses absolute positioning (ch08_eg29.css):

```
div.page {
   position : absolute;
   left : 50px;
   top :  100px;
   border-style : solid;
   border-width : 2px;
   border-color : #000000;
}
p {
   background-color : #FFFFFF;
   width : 200px;
   padding : 5px;
   border-style : solid;
   border-color : #000000;
   border-width : 2px;
}
p.two {
   position : absolute;
   left : 50px;
   top :  -25px;}
```

Figure 8-29 shows what this would look like in a browser; as you can clearly see, the second paragraph is no longer in the middle of the page. The second paragraph element has been taken out of normal flow because the third paragraph is now in the place where the second paragraph would have been if it participated in normal flow. Furthermore, it even appears before the first paragraph and over to the right!

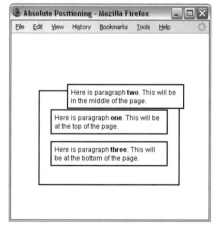

FIGURE 8-29

The presence of the <div class="page"> element here is to show that the paragraph is being positioned according to the containing block—the absolutely positioned <div> element.

Absolutely positioned elements always come out above relatively positioned elements, as you see here, unless you use the z-index property (which you'll learn about later in this chapter).

It is also worth noting that because absolutely positioned boxes are taken out of normal flow, even if two vertical margins meet, their margins do not collapse.

Fixed Positioning

The final value you need to be aware of for the position property is the value fixed. This value specifies not only that the content of the element should be completely removed from normal flow, but also that the box should not move when users scroll up or down a page.

Although Firefox, Safari, and Chrome have offered support for fixed positioning for a while, IE7 was the first version of Internet Explorer to support it.

You can use the following sample of HTML from ch08_eg30.html to demonstrate fixed positioning. This example continues with several more paragraphs so that you can see the page scrolling while the content of the <div> element remains fixed at the top of the page:

```
<div class="header">Beginning Web Development</div>
<p class="one">This page has to contain several paragraphs so you can see
the effect of fixed positioning. Fixed positioning has been used on the
header so it does not move even when the rest of the page scrolls.</p>
```

Here you can see the style sheet for this example (ch08_eg30.css). The header has the position property with the value fixed and is positioned to the top left of the browser window:

```
div.header {
  position : fixed;
  top :  0px;
  left : 0px;
  width : 100%;
  padding : 20px;
  font-size : 28px;
  color : #ffffff;
  background-color : #666666;
  border-style : solid;
  border-width : 2px;
  border-color : #000000;
}
p {
  width : 300px;
  padding : 5px;
  color : #000000;
  background-color : #FFFFFF;
  border-style : solid;
  border-color : #000000;
  border-width : 2px;
}
p.one {
  margin-top : 100px;
}
```

Figure 8-30 shows you what this fixed header element looks like even though the user has scrolled halfway down the page.

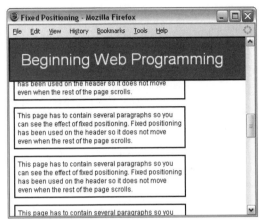

FIGURE 8-30

The z-index Property

Elements positioned using absolute and relative positioning often overlap other elements. When this happens the default behavior is to have the first elements underneath later ones. This is known as *stacking context*. You can specify which of the boxes appears on top using the z-index property. If you are familiar with graphic design packages, the stacking context is similar to using the "bring to top" and "send to back" features.

The value of the z-index property is a number, and the higher the number the nearer the top that element should display. (For example, an item with a z-index of 10 appears on top of an item with a z-index of 5.)

To better understand z-index, look at another example of absolute positioning—this time there are just three paragraphs (ch08_eg31.html):

```
<p class="one">Here is paragraph <b>one</b>.
  This will be at the top of the page.</p>
<p class="two">Here is paragraph <b>two</b>.
  This will be underneath the other elements.</p>
<p class="three">Here is paragraph <b>three</b>.
  This will be at the bottom of the page.</p>
```

Each of these paragraphs shares common width, background-color, padding, and border properties, which are specified in the first rule. (This saves you from repeating the same properties for each individual <p> element.) Then each paragraph is positioned separately using absolute positioning. Because these paragraphs now all overlap, the z-index property is added to control which one appears on top; the higher the value, the nearer the top it ends up (ch08_eg31.css):

```
p {
  width : 200px;
  background-color : #ffffff;
```

```
      padding : 5px;
      margin : 10px;
      border-style : solid;
      border-color : #000000;
      border-width : 2px;
    }
    p.one {
      z-index : 3;
      position : absolute;
      left : 0px;
      top : 0px;
    }
    p.two {
      z-index : 1;
      position : absolute;
      left : 150px;
      top : 25px;}
    p.three {
      z-index : 2;
      position : absolute;
      left : 40px;
      top : 35px;
    }
```

Figure 8-31 shows how the second paragraph now appears to be underneath the first and third paragraphs, and the first one remains on top.

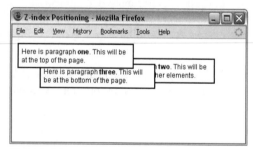

FIGURE 8-31

Floating Using the float Property

The `float` property enables you to take an element out of normal flow and place it as far to the left or right of a containing box as possible.

Anything else that lives in the containing element will flow around the element associated with the `float` property (just like text and other elements can flow around an image).

Whenever you specify a `float` property on an element, you must also set a `width` property indicating the width that the box should take up. Otherwise, it automatically takes up 100 percent of the width of the containing box, leaving no space for things to flow around it and therefore making it appear like a plain block-level element.

To indicate that you want a box floated to either the left or the right of the containing box, you set the `float` property, which can take one of the values listed in Table 8-21.

TABLE 8-21: Values of the float Property

VALUE	PURPOSE
left	The box is floated to the left of the containing element, and the content of the containing element flows to the right of it.
right	The box is floated to the right of the containing element, and the content of the containing element flows to the left of it.
none	The box is not floated and remains where it would have been positioned in normal flow.
inherit	The box takes the same property as its containing element.

When a box uses the `float` property, vertical margins will not be collapsed above or below it like block boxes in normal flow can be (because it has been taken out of normal flow). The floated box will be aligned with the top of the containing box.

Look at the following HTML (ch08_eg32.html) to see how the first `<aside>` element has a `class` attribute whose value is `pullQuote`:

```
<body>
  <h1>Heading</h1>
    <aside class="pullQuote">Here is the pullquote. It will be removed from
    normal flow and appear on the right of the page.</aside>
    <p>This is where the story starts and it will appear at the top of the
    page under the heading. You can think of it as the first paragraph of an
    article or story. In this example, the pull quote gets moved across to the
    right of the page. There will be another paragraph underneath.</p>
    <p>Here is another paragraph. This one will be at the bottom of the page.</p>
  </body>
```

As this example shows, the first `<p>` element is taken out of the normal flow and placed to the right of the containing `<body>` element using the `float` property with a value of `right` (ch08_eg32.css):

```
body {
  color : #000000;
  background-color : #ffffff;
  font-size : 12px;
  margin : 10px;
  width : 514px;
  border :  1px solid #000000;
}
p {
  background-color : #FFFFFF;
  border : 2px solid #000000;
  padding : 5px;
  margin : 5px;
```

```
    width : 500px;
}
.pullQuote {
  float : right;
  width : 150px;
}
```

You can see how the content of the `<aside>` element with the `class` attribute whose value is `pullQuote` ends up to the right of the page, with the content of the paragraph flowing to the left and then underneath it, as shown in Figure 8-32.

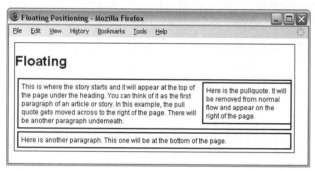

FIGURE 8-32

The clear Property

The `clear` property is especially helpful when you are working with boxes that are floated. Content can flow around a floated element (refer to Figure 8-32); however, you might not want this to happen. You might prefer that nothing sits next to the floated element, and that surrounding content be pushed underneath the floated element. This is what the `clear` property is for, and Table 8-22 shows you the values that this property can take.

TABLE 8-22: Values of the clear Property

VALUE	PURPOSE
left	The element with the `clear` property cannot have content on the left-hand side of it.
right	The element with the `clear` property cannot have content on the right-hand side of it.
both	The element with the `clear` property cannot have content to the left or right of it.
none	Allows floating on either side.

Now look at an example. The HTML page uses exactly the same structure as the last example, but this time the style sheet ensures that nothing sits next to the pull quote.

To ensure that the second paragraph does not wrap around the pull quote, use the `clear` property on the rule for the `<aside>` elements indicating that nothing should appear to the left of it; you can see this new property is highlighted in the following code (ch08_eg33.css):

```
p {
    background-color : #FFFFFF;
    border : 2px solid #000000;
    padding : 5px;
    margin : 5px;
    width : 500px;
    clear : right
}
```

Figure 8-33 shows you how the `clear` property works in this example, ensuring that the second and third paragraphs sit below the pull quote.

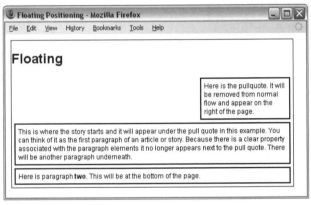

FIGURE 8-33

Building a Sample Layout

Now it's time to put the positioning and layout lessons you've just learned into practice in the following Try It Out.

TRY IT OUT **A Sample Layout**

In this Try It Out, you create a sample page layout that uses a combination of the techniques you learned in this chapter to control the layout of the page using CSS.

The page you work with is shown in Figure 8-34 without the style sheet attached.

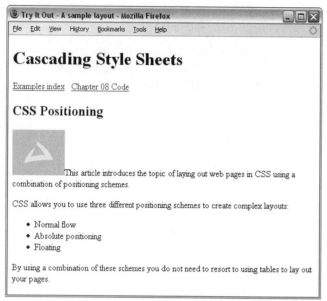

FIGURE 8-34

Here is the body of the HTML code for this example (`samplePage.html`):

```
<body>
<h1>Cascading Style Sheets</h1>
  <div class="nav"><a href="../index.htm">Examples index</a>
      <a href="download.html">Chapter 8 Code</a></div>
<h2>CSS Positioning</h2>
  <p class="abstract"><img class="floatLeft" src="images/background.gif"
      alt="wrox logo">This article introduces the topic of laying out
      web pages in CSS using a combination of positioning schemes.</p>
  <p>CSS allows you to use three different positioning schemes to create
      complex layouts:</p>
  <ul>
    <li>Normal flow</li>
    <li>Absolute positioning</li>
    <li>Floating</li>
  </ul>
  <p>By using a combination of these schemes you do not need to resort to
      using tables to lay out your pages.</p>
</body>
```

This example illustrates some of the issues that you need to be aware of with CSS—in particular, it is important to demonstrate that while you have seen some helpful properties, some of them are supported only in the latest browsers. Although you can design your site in such a way that it works with most browsers, you might not get some techniques to work in all the browsers you want them to, so you need to test your site thoroughly.

In Firefox, this Try It Out example looks like Figure 8-35, and you would get a similar result in IE7+.

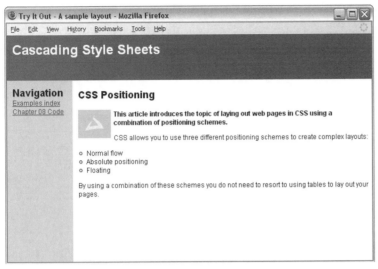

FIGURE 8-35

However, Figure 8-36 shows you what this page would look like in IE6. In particular note how there is no longer the word Navigation before the links in the left, and how the heading CSS Positioning sits further down the page. So if you still have visitors coming to your site who use IE6, you need to consider which features will and won't work and check your page in IE6 before publishing the site. Less and less people are using IE6, but it still is popular in some areas (China, for example) so it's good to be aware that there are some limitations with that browser.

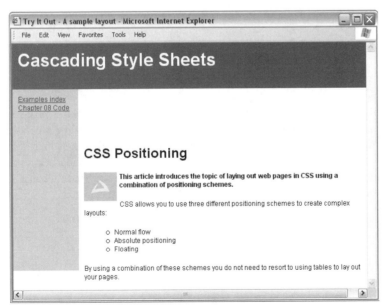

FIGURE 8-36

To start working on the CSS file for this page, start your web page editor and follow these steps:

1. Create a file called `samplePage.css`, add the elements from the HTML page, and use class selectors where appropriate to identify each type of element. You should end up with a list like the one that follows; then you can look at the rule for each element in turn.

```
body {}
h1 {}
div.nav {}
h2 {}
p {}
p.abstract {}
img {}
ul {}
```

2. The rule for the `<body>` element sets up some defaults for the page.

```
body {
  color : #000000;
  background-color : #ffffff;
  font-family : arial, verdana, sans-serif;
  font-size : 12px;
}
```

3. The header for the site uses fixed positioning to take it out of normal flow and anchor it to the top of the page even if the user scrolls. It also has a `z-index` property to ensure that this heading remains on top of the navigation.

```
h1 {
  position : fixed;
  top : 0px;
  left : 0px;
  width : 100%;
  color : #ffffff;
  background-color : #666666;
  padding : 10px;
  height : 60px;
  z-index : 2;
}
```

4. The navigation is also removed from normal flow because it is absolutely positioned. It is positioned 80 pixels from the top so that the links will not disappear underneath the page's heading when the page first loads. The navigation is placed in a box that is 100 pixels wide and 300 pixels high with a light gray background. As a visitor scrolls down the page, the navigation will go underneath the heading for the page because you have not specified a `z-index` property, and the heading has a `z-index` property with a value of 2.

```
div.nav {
  position : absolute;
  top : 80px;
  left : 0px;
  width : 100px;
```

```
    height : 300px;
    padding : 10px;
    background-color : #efefef;
}
```

5. You may have noticed that the navigation bar contains the word Navigation, which was not in the original HTML file. This style sheet uses the CSS `:before` pseudo-class to add this word in. You can see here that it also has other styles associated with it.

```
div.nav:before {
    content : "Navigation ";
    font-size : 18px;
    font-weight : bold;
}
```

6. The rule for the `<h2>` element needs to be indented from the left because the navigation takes up the first 120 pixels to the left of it. It also has padding at the top to bring the text underneath the heading.

```
h2 {
    padding : 80px 0px 0px 130px;
}
```

7. There are two rules for paragraphs. The first rule is for all paragraphs, and the second one ensures that the abstract of the article is in bold. As with the `<h2>` element, all paragraphs need to be indented from the left.

```
p {
    padding-left : 115px;
}
p.abstract{
    font-weight : bold;
}
```

8. The image that sits in the first paragraph is floated to the left of the text. As you can see, the text in the paragraph flows around the image. It also has a 5-pixel margin to the right.

```
img {
    float : left;
    width : 60px;
    margin-right : 5px;
}
```

9. The rule for the unordered list element needs to be indented further than the paragraphs or level 2 heading. It also specifies the style of bullet to be used with the `list-style` property.

```
ul {
    clear : left;
    list-style : circle;
    padding-left : 145px;
}
```

10. Save your style sheet as `samplePage.css` and try loading the `samplePage.html` file that is going to use it.

How It Works

Laying out web pages using CSS is as much art as it is a technical exercise. Knowing when to use floats, when to use absolute positioning, and when to just let the document flow is something you'll never stop learning about no matter how long you build sites. As this example illustrates, successful layouts are often a combination of two or more of these layouts and positioning techniques.

For example, a layout that features floated columns might set one of the columns to be `position:relative` without associated offset properties to absolutely position child elements within the column. Or a simple, single column layout might leverage floated elements to break up the monotony of stacked block-level elements. Experimenting with these techniques and examining layouts you encounter on the web can help you solve most of the layout issues you will encounter.

SUMMARY

In this chapter you learned the CSS properties that enable you to control lists, links, tables, outlines, and backgrounds with CSS. You then saw how CSS enables you to add content from the style sheet into the document. The `:before` and `:after` pseudo-classes enable you to add content before or after an element specified in the selector. This includes text, an image, or content from a file. You can even add automatic numbering or counting of any element using the `counter()` function and can manage complex sets of quotation marks. (Although not all browsers support all these functions yet.)

You also learned how to use the `@import` rule to include rules from other style sheets into the current one and create modularized style sheets that enable you to reuse the same rules on different sites, whereas the `@charset` rule indicates which character set is used in the style sheet.

Finally, this chapter looked at the three main positioning schemes in CSS: normal flow (and its offshoot relative positioning); absolute positioning (and its offshoot fixed positioning); and floating. These are powerful tools for controlling where the content of a document should appear; they complete the picture of separating style from content.

EXERCISES

1. In this exercise, you create a linked table of contents that sits at the top of a long document in an ordered list and links to the headings in the main part of the document.

The HTML file `exercise1.html` is provided with the download code for this book, ready for you to create the style sheet. Your style sheet should do the following:

➤ Set the styles of all links including active and visited links.

➤ Make the contents of the list bold.

➤ Make the background of the list light gray and use padding to ensure the bullet points show.

➤ Make the width of the links box 250 pixels wide.

➤ Change the styles of heading bullet points to empty circles.

➤ Change the style of link bullet points to squares.

Your page should look something like Figure 8-37.

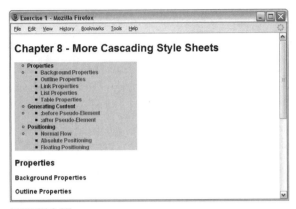

FIGURE 8-37

2. In this exercise, you test your CSS positioning skills. You should create a page that represents the links to the different sections of the chapter in a different way. Each of the sections must be shown in a different block, and each block must be absolutely positioned in a diagonal top-left to bottom-right direction. The middle box should appear on top, as shown in Figure 8-38.

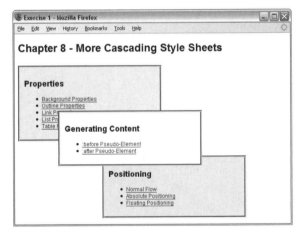

FIGURE 8-38

You can find the source HTML file (`exercise2.html`) with the download code for this chapter.

The answers to all the exercises are in Appendix A, "Answers to Exercises."

▶ **WHAT YOU LEARNED IN THIS CHAPTER**

TOPIC	KEY TAKEAWAY
Styling backgrounds	You can use solid colors and images. Images can be tiled in different ways, can be attached to certain areas, or can fill the entire element.
Styling lists	You can change the appearance of lists by customizing the size, shape, and position of the bullet.
Outlines	CSS outlines are similar to CSS borders, with the key difference that they don't figure into the calculation of the box offset.
Positioning and layout	Layouts on the web are accomplished using a combination of the three available layout schemes: normal, absolute positioning, and floats. Learning the strengths and weaknesses of each and how they support each other is an important piece of the web development toolkit.

Rounded Corners, Animations, Custom Fonts, and More with CSS3

WHAT YOU WILL LEARN IN THIS CHAPTER

➤   How to use new CSS3 selectors

➤   How to set variable opacity elements with the new CSS3 Color module

➤   New options for multi-column layouts

➤   How to create drop shadows and rounded corners without using any images

➤   How to apply custom fonts to the web using the @font-face directive

➤   How to add animations, transitions, and transformations without using any JavaScript

WROX.COM CODE DOWNLOADS FOR THIS CHAPTER

The wrox.com code downloads for this chapter are found at www.wrox.com/remtitle .cgi?isbn=9781118340189 on the Download Code tab. The code is in the Chapter 9 download and individually named according to the names throughout the chapter.

In this chapter, you learn about the latest version of the CSS specification, CSS3. Unlike previous versions of the specification, CSS3 consists of smaller specifications that focus on particular areas of interest. These are called *modules*. CSS3 significantly increases the power of CSS.

First, you focus on more mature modules—ones that have been in development for the longest time and are furthest along the road to standardization. These include new options for selecting elements and adjusting the color of elements, new border and background options, and new functionality that enables you to specify CSS styles based on attributes of your visitors' browsers and devices.

Then you learn about newer modules that might not be completely finalized but are still available in some browsers. This section includes CSS features that enable you to lay out pages using a grid system, options for animation, and transitions between element states, and the ability to transform HTML elements in two and three dimensions.

After reading this chapter you'll be prepared to start using the latest tools available for styling elements.

THE MODULAR APPROACH OF CSS3

Unlike the previous incarnations of the specification, which were large documents that covered the entirety of each generation of CSS, the latest version of CSS takes a modular approach to specification design. CSS3 modules enhance functionality introduced in previous versions of the specification.

This approach means that the folks writing specifications and implementing them in browsers can focus on different parts of the emerging CSS landscape at different times. It also means that some modules are much further along than others for both the specification process and browser implementation.

This chapter focuses on two classes of CSS3 modules—ones that are further along the specification path and those that are newer.

Although there's mixed support in browsers for both types, the ones that are more mature are less likely to change in any appreciable way in the future and somewhat safer to start using now.

MATURE CSS3 MODULES

The modules in this section are all mature, having been in development for five or more years, and all are *proposed recommendations*, *candidate recommendations*, or *recommendations in the W3C's completeness hierarchy*. Defined simply, a proposed recommendation is the second-to-last step, and a candidate recommendation is the last step before a specification reaches the recommendation stage. A recommendation is an official standard. That means these modules are done or are close to done.

More Powerful CSS Selectors

The CSS3 Selector module expands on the CSS selectors you met in Chapter 7, "Cascading Style Sheets," with a number of new options. These options enable a precise selection of elements based on the position in the document, the value of attributes, the UI state, and even whether the element has any children.

Table 9-1 lists these new selectors.

TABLE 9-1: New CSS3 Selectors

NAME	EXAMPLE	MATCHES
Attribute Starts with Selector	`p[name^="value"]`	Any `<p>` element carrying an attribute called `name` whose value begins with the string `value`.
Attribute Ends with Selector	`p[name$="value"]`	Any `<p>` element carrying an attribute called `name` whose value ends with the string `value`.
Attribute Contains Selector	`p[name*="value"]`	Any `<p>` element carrying an attribute called `name` whose value contains the string `value`.
Root Selector	`:root`	The root of the document. In HTML documents this is always the HTML element.
Nth Child Selector	`p:nth-child(n)`	Any `<p>` element, the nth child of its parent.
Nth Last Child Selector	`p:nth-last-child(n)`	Any `<p>` element, the nth child of its parent, counting from the last one.
Nth of Type Selector	`p:nth-of-type(n)`	Any `<p>` element, the nth sibling of its type.
Nth Last of Type Selector	`p:nth-last-of-type(n)`	Any `<p>` element, the nth sibling of its type, counting from the last one.
Last Child Selector	`p:last-child`	Any `<p>` element, last child of its parent.
First of Type Selector	`p:first-of-type`	Any `<p>` element, first sibling of its type under its parent.
Last of Type Selector	`p:last-of-type`	Any `<p>` element, last sibling of its type under its parent.
Only Child Selector	`p:only-child`	Any `<p>` element, only child of its parent.
Only of Type Selector	`p:only-of-type`	Any `<p>` element, only sibling of its type.
Empty Selector	`p:empty`	Any `<p>` element that has no children (including text nodes).

continues

TABLE 9-1 *(continued)*

NAME	EXAMPLE	MATCHES
Target Selector	`p:target`	Any `<p>` element being the target of the referring URL.
Enabled/Disabled Selectors	`input:enabled` `input:disabled`	An `<input>` element that is either enabled or disabled.
Checked Selector	`input:checked`	An `<input>` element of type check box which is checked.
Not Selector	`p:not(".special")`	A `<p>` element not of class `.special`.
Next Siblings Selector	`div ~ p`	Any `<p>` element preceded by a `<div>` element.

These selectors are supported by Internet Explorer 9+ and all the other major browsers. The following HTML file illustrates several of these selectors (ch09_eg01.html):

```
<p>This is the first child of the body.</p>
<p>This is the second child of the body.
  This input is disabled <input type="text" disabled></p>
<p>This is the third paragraph. The text here is blue.</p>
<p>This paragraph includes two links, one is
  <a href="https://www.example.com">secure, starting with 'http://'</a>
  the other is to a <a href="http://ww.example.org/">.org</a></p>
<div></div>
<p>This element is preceded by an empty &lt;div&gt;</p>
<p>This is the last child</p>
```

The associated CSS file (ch09_eg01.css) uses the first child selector to increase the size of the first paragraph. Following are two examples of the nth-child selector, changing the font-family and color of the second and third paragraphs. In the next section, the attribute starts with and ends with selectors that match `<a>` elements containing two different URL values. One matches against links beginning with https: indicating that they are secure, and the other matches against .org/ at the end of the link to target nonprofit organizations. The disabled selector is used after that to give a slightly thicker, gray border to the disabled `<input>` element. You then see the empty selector used to give a background color, height, and width to the empty `<div>` element. Finally, the previous sibling's selector is used to change the font-size, color, and font-family of any `<p>` elements that follow any `<div>` elements in the document.

```
a[ href^="https" ] {
  color : red;
}
a[ href$="org/" ] {
  color : purple;
}
```

```
input:disabled{
  border : 2px solid #000000;
};
p:nth-child(2) {
  font-family : arial, helvetica, sans-serif;
}
p:first-child {
  font-size : 125%;
}
p:nth-child(3) {
  color : #006699;
}
div:empty {
  height : 100px;
  width : 200px;
  background : #666666;
}
div~p {
  font-size : 200%;
  color : #666666;
  font-family : consolas, courier, "courier new", monospace;
}
```

Figure 9-1 shows this style sheet rendered in Firefox 15.

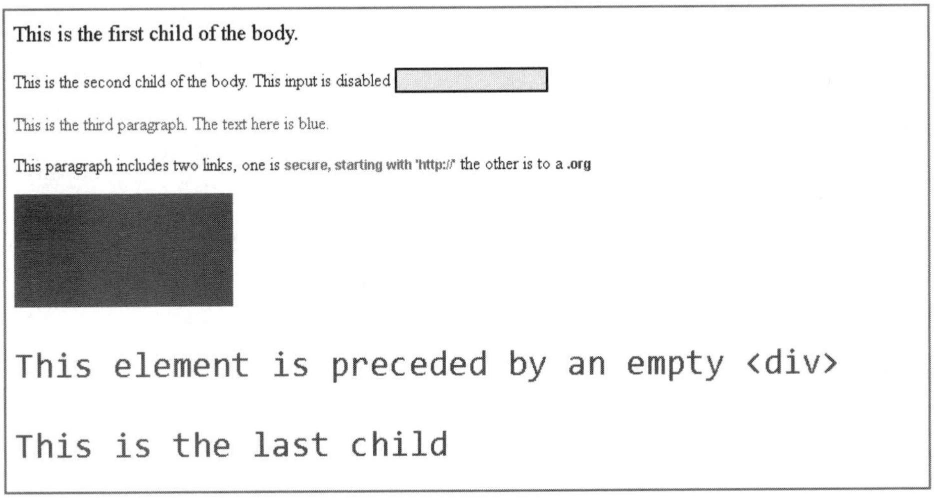

This is the first child of the body.

This is the second child of the body. This input is disabled

This is the third paragraph. The text here is blue.

This paragraph includes two links, one is secure, starting with 'http://' the other is to a .org

This element is preceded by an empty <div>

This is the last child

FIGURE 9-1

Advanced Color Options

The CSS3 Color module expands on the color options that you already learned about in Chapter 7. These additions include a new method for defining colors and ways to specify the translucency of an element by defining its *opacity* or *alpha*.

Use New, Easier-to-Understand, Numerical Color Values with HSL

You've seen one example of a numerical color value with RGB color values. CSS3 adds one new option based on hue, saturation, and lightness (HSL). HSL is an alternative to RGB, which more closely mirrors the way that people actually *think* about color. Instead of mixing three RGB values together to create the target color, HSL enables you to set the hue with one number between 0 and 360 (for example, 0 = red, 120 = green, and 240 = blue) and then adjust the richness or saturation (0 percent is gray; 100 percent is full saturation) of the color and the amount of lightness/darkness (0 percent lightness is black, 100 percent lightness is white, and 50 percent lightness is normal) as needed. The hue and saturation values are expressed as percentages.

The following example (`ch09_eg02.html`) shows how easy it is to tweak colors using HSL notation. The nine `<div>` elements in the following example are grouped in three sections.

```
<section>
  <h1>Changing Just the Hue</h1>
  <div class="one"></div>
  <div class="two"></div>
  <div class="three"></div>
</section>
<section>
  <h1>Changing just the Saturation</h1>
  <div class="four"></div>
  <div class="five"></div>
  <div class="six"></div>
</section>
<section>
  <h1>Changing Just the Lightness</h1>
  <div class="seven"></div>
  <div class="eight"></div>
  <div class="nine"></div>
</section>
```

In the attached CSS (`ch09_eg02.css`) classes are used for the three `<div>` elements in each section. One section focuses on changing just the hue, one section focuses on the saturation, and the other section focuses on just the lightness.

```
div {
  height:25px;
  width:300px;
}
.one {
  background-color : hsl( 111,50%,50% );
}
.two {
  background-color : hsl( 222,50%,50% );
}
.three {
  background-color : hsl( 333,50%,50% );
}
.four {
  background-color : hsl( 333,10%,67% );
}
.five {
  background-color : hsl( 333,50%,67% );
```

```
    }
    .six {
      background-color : hsl( 333,90%,67% );
    }
    .seven {
      background-color : hsl( 333,65%,67% );
    }
    .eight {
      background-color : hsl( 333,65%,44% );
    }
    .nine {
      background-color : hsl( 333,65%,22% );
    }
```

As Figure 9-2 illustrates, there's a clear, common sense connection between the component values and the final color. By changing just one human-friendly (as opposed to computer-friendly) value, you can easily adjust colors. (The subtle nuances of hue, saturation and lightness are lost to some degree in grey-scale. The full-color version of Figure 9-2 is available for download with the code for this chapter, at www.wrox.com/remtitle.cgi?isbn=9781118340189 on the Download Code tab.)

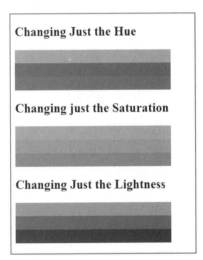

FIGURE 9-2

Control Transparency with RGBA, HSLA, and the opacity Property

The CSS3 Color module also adds the ability to set the level of transparency on elements. It does this in two ways: as a fourth *alpha value* added to RGB and *HSL color values* and with the stand-alone opacity property.

Adding transparency to both HSL and RGB colors is handled the same way. You simply add a fourth alpha value between 0 (completely transparent) and 1 (completely opaque):

```
    h1 {
      background-color : hsla( 0, 100%, 50%, 0.5 );
    }
```

```
h2 {
  background-color : rgba( 255, 0, 0, 0.5);
}
```

Setting opacity is similar in that it takes an argument representing the level of opacity between 0 and 1. The difference is that, although HSLA or RGBA enables you to target transparency to one specific component of the element, using the `opacity` property sets the entire element's transparency, including all child elements. The two `<div>` elements in the following code sample (`ch09_eg03.html`) illustrate this difference.

```
<div class="opacity">
  <p>This element has a 50% opacity</p>
</div>
<div class="hsla">
  <p>This element has 50% alpha</p>
</div>
```

The CSS (`ch09_eg03.css`) defines the two classes to have the equivalent background color (pure red) and equivalent transparency. The difference, as shown in Figure 9-3, is that the example using HSLA leaves the foreground text untouched and completely opaque. Compare that to the example using the `opacity` property where the text is also set to 50 percent transparency.

```
.opacity {
  opacity : .5;
  background-color : #ff0000;
}
.hsla {
  background-color : hsla( 0,100%,50%,.5 )
}
```

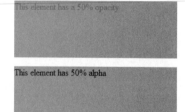

FIGURE 9-3

Table 9-2 shows browser support for these new color values.

TABLE 9-2: Browser Support for New Color Values

VALUE	IE	FF	SAFARI	CHROME	OPERA
hsl	9	1	3.1	1	9.5
hsla	9	3	3.1	1	10
rgba	9	3	3.1	1	10

Backgrounds and Borders Module

It would be hard to definitively prove, but based on the sites the author has seen and built over the years, rendering elements with rounded corners and drop shadows has wasted more developer time and more kilobytes downloaded than any other design motif over the past 10–15 years. Traditionally done using a combination of extra elements, images, and copious amounts of CSS, these design elements were common on designer wish lists for CSS features. Thankfully, with the Backgrounds and Borders module, these two features are now available directly in the browser; no extra images or markup needed.

As with many things on the web, there is one small catch. Browsers are taking the standards process much more seriously these days. Part of that new dedication is the desire to implement new and proposed features as soon as possible to allow web developers to test them and produce valuable feedback. Because these features might end up changing, the idea of using browser prefixes was struck upon to indicate that the feature being used is experimental. Using those rounded corners as an example, note that the default property name is `border-radius`. In older browsers based on the WebKit open source project (most notably Chrome and Safari), this property was exposed as `-webkit-border-radius`. So, for maximum support you would write your CSS rule like this:

```
-webkit-border-radius: 12px; /* Safari 3-4, iOS 1-3.2, Android ≤1.6 */
border-radius: 12px; /* Opera 10.5, IE9+, Safari 5 */
/* Chrome, Firefox 4+, iOS 4, Android 2.1+ */
```

As you go through the samples in this chapter, any rules where vendor prefixes matter are pointed out. If you're going to use any of these rules that rely on vendor prefixes, using a site such as http://css3please.com/ that allows you to edit CSS3 rules right in your web browser might make things a little easier. Figure 9-4 shows CSS3, Please! in action.

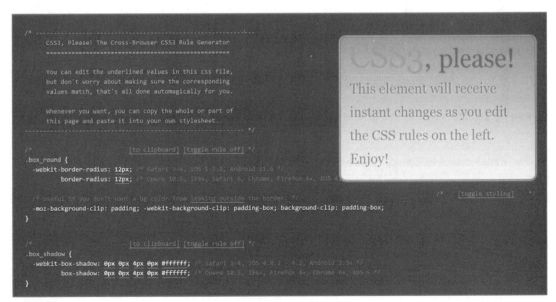

FIGURE 9-4

There are other tools available to help you with vendor prefixes. If you're a user of Microsoft's Visual Studio, for example, there are tools in the Web Essentials add-in that take care of them for you. There's also a JavaScript library called "-prefix-free" (http://leaverou.github.com/prefixfree/) that can make working with them during development very easy. If you get serious about using these new features, you'll find a system that works with your development style.

Now that you've learned about vendor prefixes and had a sneak peek at the syntax for `border-radius` in the previous example, it's time to look at a full example of rounded corners and drop shadows in action.

The markup (`ch09_eg04.html`) is simple—just a single `<div>` element with an `<h1>` and `<h2>` inside to spice things up.

```
<div>
  <h1>Rounded Corners!</h1>
  <h2>Drop Shadow!</h2>
</div>
```

The CSS (`ch09_eg04.css`) shows the two new properties in action. The `border-radius` is set to 12 pixels, which is measured like the radius you might remember from geometry class—from the center to the edge of the circle. Figure 9-5 illustrates this measurement.

FIGURE 9-5

The `drop-shadow` property takes five values.

➤ The horizontal offset of the shadow.

➤ The vertical offset of the shadow.

➤ The third value is the blur radius; the larger the value, the more the shadow's edge is blurred.

➤ The spread distance; how much the shadow "bleeds."

➤ The color of the shadow.

```
div {
  padding : 10px;
  width : 400px;
```

```
    -webkit-border-radius : 12px;
    border-radius : 12px;
    -webkit-box-shadow : 0px 0px 4px 0px #000000;
    box-shadow : 0px 0px 4px 0px #000000;
}
```

It helps to experiment with `drop-shadow` to get a sense of how the different values interact to create different effects. This is one of the great benefits of a site such as CSS3, Please because it enables you to see the changes in real time.

Table 9-3 shows browser support for `border-radius` and `box-shadow`.

TABLE 9-3: Browser Support for Borders and Backgrounds

FEATURE	INTERNET EXPLORER	GOOGLE CHROME	FIREFOX	SAFARI	OPERA
box-shadow	9.0+	4.0+	3.5+	3.1+	10.5+
border-radius	9.0+	4.0+	3.0+	3.1+	10.5+

Multi-column Layout Module

Multiple-column layouts, where text is flowed across several separate blocks of text, are a common design element in the world of print. It has never been possible on the web. Although you've already seen ways to separate out content into different columns, laying out a single block of text across two or three columns while keeping all the text within the same element is impossible.

The Multi-column Layout module changes this, enabling you to set multiple columns for a single element. There are two ways to set the number of columns for an element. The first is with the `column-count` property, which simply enables you to set the number of columns for the element. The other way is to use the `column-width` property, which enables you to set a specific width for each column. This is useful for variable width elements where you want to control the width of the columns for better readability.

The markup in the example is simple (`ch09_eg05.html`), featuring one `<div>` element with a class of `fixed-width` and another `<div>` element with a class of `percentage-width`. Both contain a paragraph or two of nonsense text.

```
<div class="fixed-width">
<p>Proident accusamus readymade, exercitation wolf ullamco quinoa
chambray. Tattooed est gluten-free, tumblr ethical sartorial pickled.
…</p>
</div>
<div class="percentage-width">
<p>Proident accusamus readymade, exercitation wolf ullamco quinoa
flexitarian chambray. Tattooed est gluten-free, tumblr ethical sartorial
 pickled … keffiyeh nesciunt american apparel.</p>
<p>Proident accusamus readymade, exercitation wolf ullamco quinoa
flexitarian chambray. Tattooed est gluten-free, tumblr ethical
sartorial pickled…
</p>
</div>
```

The CSS (ch09_eg05.css) sets up columns using both techniques. The class .fixed-width sets the width of the element to 500px. Three columns are defined with 15 pixels of gap between each of them. The class .percentage-width uses column-width to create 100-pixel columns that number as many as the 100 percent <div> requires.

Notice the use of the -webkit- and -moz- browser prefixes here because both Firefox and Chrome/Safari require the prefixed version.

Figure 9-6 shows this layout in Firefox:

```
.fixed-width {
  width:500px;
  height:200px;
  -webkit-column-count: 3;
  -webkit-column-gap: 15px;
  -moz-column-count: 3;
  -moz-column-gap: 15px;
  column-count: 3;
  column-gap: 15px;
}
.percentage-width {
  width:100%;
  height:200px;
  -webkit-column-width: 100px;
  -webkit-column-gap: 15px;
  -moz-column-width: 100px;
  -moz-column-gap: 15px;
  column-width: 100px;
  column-gap: 15px;
}
```

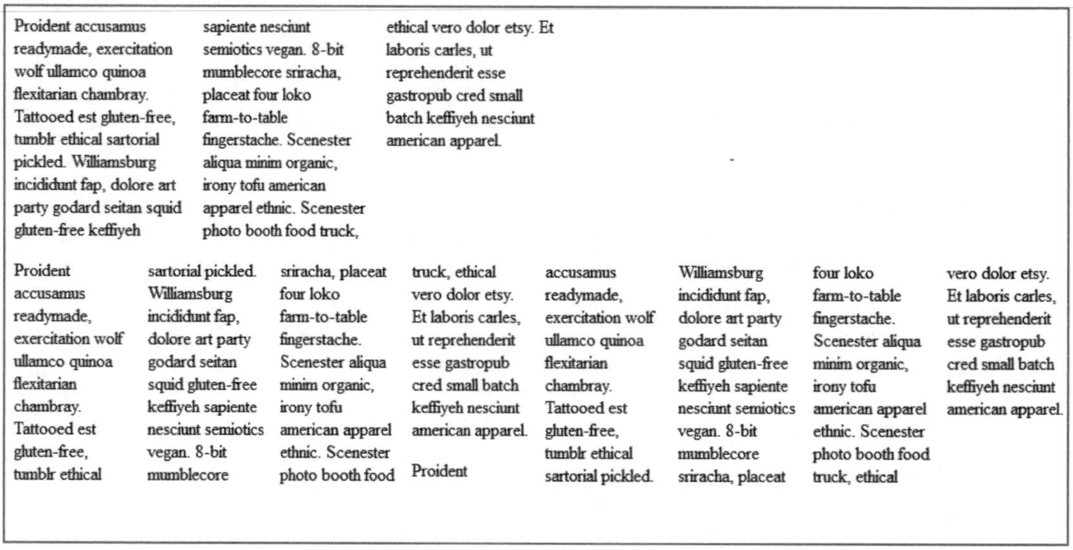

FIGURE 9-6

> **NOTE** *Using multi-column layouts changes the way that content flows, so pay attention to the* overflow *property when creating multi-column layouts in CSS. If the* overflow *property is set to* auto *or* overflow *and the text is larger than the containing element, you see more columns than you've defined. The text over-flows horizontally and not vertically as it normally does. In this case, the browser calculates the width of each column as if it were going to fit as defined by the* column-count *property and then continues to add new columns outside of the containing box. Figure 9-7 illustrates what this looks like in a* <div> *element set to 300 pixels with a* column-count *of 2. An entire column appears outside the box.*

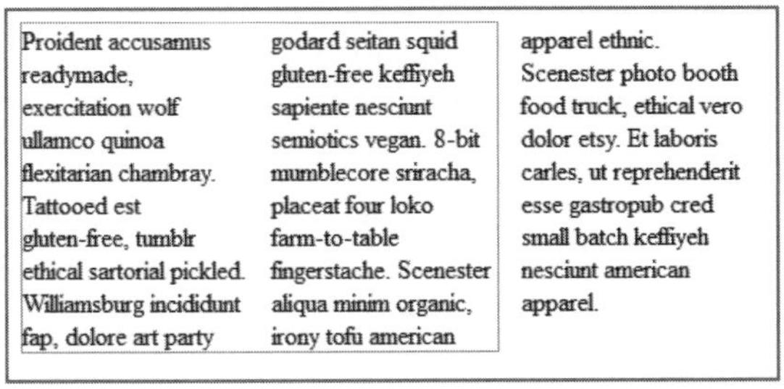

Proident accusamus readymade, exercitation wolf ullamco quinoa flexitarian chambray. Tattooed est gluten-free, tumblr ethical sartorial pickled. Williamsburg incididunt fap, dolore art party godard seitan squid gluten-free keffiyeh sapiente nesciunt semiotics vegan. 8-bit mumblecore sriracha, placeat four loko farm-to-table fingerstache. Scenester aliqua minim organic, irony tofu american apparel ethnic. Scenester photo booth food truck, ethical vero dolor etsy. Et laboris carles, ut reprehenderit esse gastropub cred small batch keffiyeh nesciunt american apparel.

FIGURE 9-7

Table 9-4 illustrates browser support for Multi-column Layouts.

TABLE 9-4: Browser Support for Multi-column Layouts

INTERNET EXPLORER	GOOGLE CHROME	FIREFOX	SAFARI	OPERA
10.0+	4.0+	2.0+	3.1+	11.2+

Media Queries

Media Queries extend the @media rules of CSS (commonly used to provide a style sheet for printing or for voice browsers) and the media attribute in HTML, adding parameters such as display size, color depth, and aspect ratio that you can test against. This allows you to adjust your designs based on device or browser characteristics.

Media Queries play a major part in *Responsive Web Design*, a new technique for designing and developing websites that allows them to display in a wide variety of devices. A good introduction to Responsive Web Design is the article that introduced the technique to the wider web audience, Ethan Marcotte's *A List Apart* article "Responsive Web Design" at http://www.alistapart.com/articles/responsive-web-design/.

The following code sample (ch09_eg06.html) shows Media Queries in action. The markup is simple: a <div> element with an id of "container" containing two paragraphs.

```
<div id="container">
  <p>Proident accusamus readymade, exercitation wolf ullamco quinoa
flexitarian chambray. Tattooed est gluten-free, tumblr ethical...</p>
  <p>Proident accusamus readymade, exercitation wolf ullamco quinoa
flexitarian chambray. Tattooed est gluten-free, tumblr ethical ...</p>
</div>
```

The CSS (ch09_eg06.css) defines the #container element with a width of 940 pixels, a height of 200 pixels, and 450-pixel columns. Following that, you see the first of your Media Queries. The @ media section initializes the Media Query, and the screen keyword indicates that this rule is for use in a screen display (as opposed to a printer or with a voice browser). The and keyword then ties the screen display to another rule, the actual query. This is max-width with a value of 999 pixels. Reading this in plain English, this rule means, "If this is a screen display and the screen is no wider than 999 pixels, apply the following CSS rules."

The rules for this query change the width to better fit in an 800-pixel display, change the background-color, and change the column-width to better fit in the new layout.

The third rule uses the same pattern (with a different value) and reads, in plain English, "If this is a screen display and the screen is no wider than 480 pixels, apply the following CSS rules." Those rules change the width to fit the new screen resolution, and the height to accommodate stacking columns and the background-color.

```
#container {
  background-color : #fe57a1;
  height : 200px;
  width : 940px;
  padding : 10px;
  -webkit-column-width: 450px;
  -webkit-column-gap: 15px;
  -moz-column-width: 450px;
  -moz-column-gap: 15px;
  column-width: 450px;
  column-gap: 15px;
}
@media screen and (max-width:999px) {
  #container {
    width: 740px;
    background-color : #b3d4fc;
    -webkit-column-width: 350px;
    -webkit-column-gap: 15px;
    -moz-column-width: 350px;
    -moz-column-gap: 15px;
    column-width: 350px;
    column-gap: 15px;
  }
}

@media screen and (max-width:480px)
```

```
{
  #container {
    width : 400px;
    background-color : #ffcc00;
    height : 400px;


  }
}
```

Figure 9-8 shows the three states of this style sheet in Google Chrome.

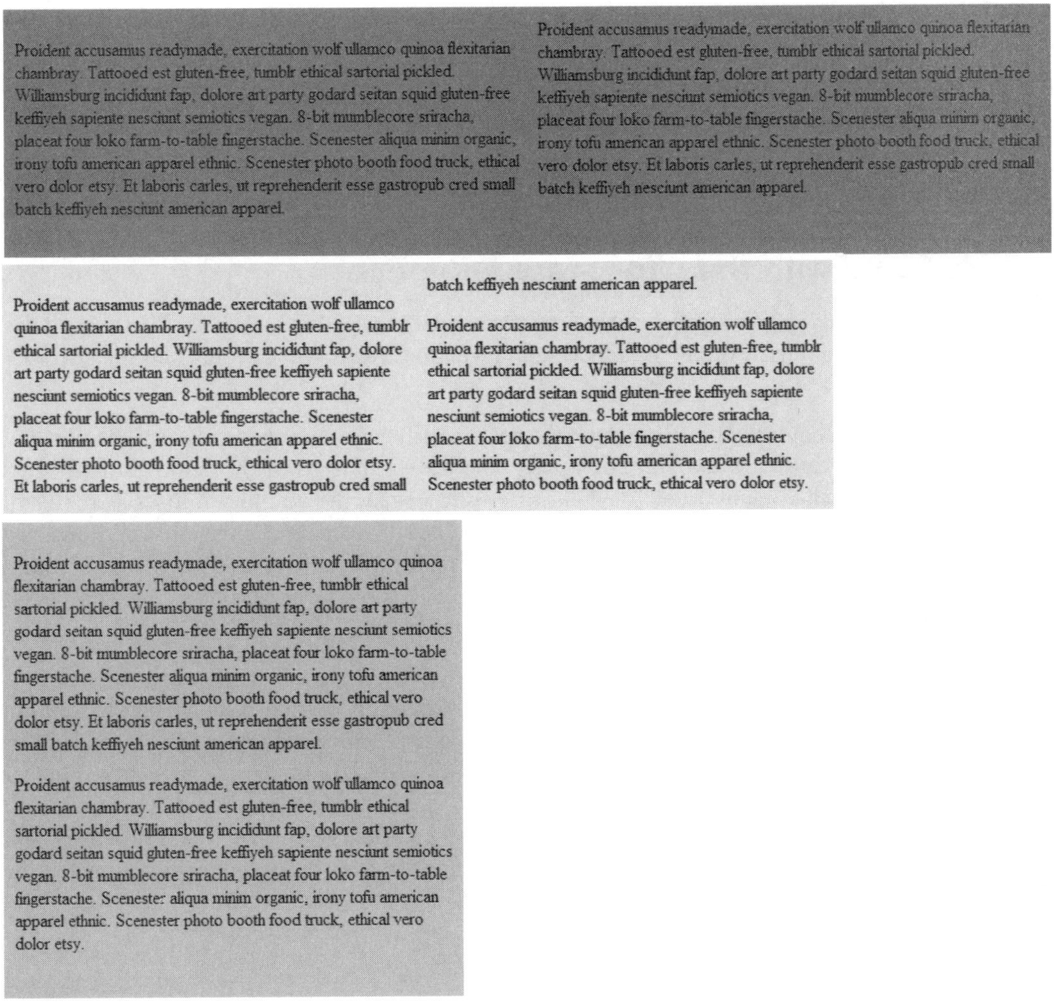

FIGURE 9-8

Table 9-5 indicates support for Media Queries in the major desktop browsers.

TABLE 9-5: Browser Support for Media Queries

INTERNET EXPLORER	GOOGLE CHROME	FIREFOX	SAFARI	OPERA
9.0+	4.0+	3.5+	4.0+	9.5+

NEW AND IN-DEVELOPMENT MODULES

With the exception of the Fonts module, this section serves as a quick introduction to some of the new CSS3 modules. Although these modules are extremely exciting, the support landscape is relatively thin, and the opportunity for polyfills or designing around the lack of certain features is more difficult. If you have a specific target audience, you might use these today, but for most people these aren't going to be ready for production use. Still, they show the powerful new direction CSS is taking.

Start with one that you can, with some attention to detail, use today with wide browser support—the CSS3 Fonts module.

Custom Fonts with the @font-face Directive

The most important component of the new Fonts module is the `@font-face` rule. This rule allows for much greater control of type on the web by enabling you to directly embed fonts into the document using CSS rules.

As you learned in Chapter 7, fonts on the web are normally based on the fonts available on a user's computer. Because few users are designers who have hundreds or thousands of fonts on their machines, this has meant that, for the history of the web, the number of fonts available to web designers and developers has been limited. The `@font-face` rule changes this. As long as the font license allows for embedding on the web, you can use the `@font-face` rule to allow your users to download and use that font for your web page. This opens up a wide range of possibilities for type on the web.

The basic format of an `@font-face` rule looks like the following snippet. It opens with the `@font-face` directive, which basically tells the browser "This style sheet is going to define a font." After that the `font-family` is defined. This property allows you to define a keyword to use as a reference to the new font. Just like you could type **Arial** or **Helvetica** in a `font` declaration to reference those fonts on a user's computer, you can now use *FontName* to reference your newly defined `font-family` in your CSS rules. The `src` property works just like every other `src` attribute or property you've learned about in the book; it identifies a web resource to download the font face. This can be a resource on your own web server or a third-party service.

```
@font-face {
  font-family: FontName;
  src: url(http://example.com/fonts/FontName.ttf);
}
```

On Font Formats, Compatibility, and the Evolution of the Bulletproof @font-face Syntax

The previous syntax tells only part of the story. Although many browsers support the `@font-face` directive, different browsers support different font *formats*.

Thankfully, like the `<video>` element you learned about in Chapter 5, "Tables," there are ways to layer different formats to provide the broadest possible support. This pattern has been the subject of much community discussion. To read about *why* this pattern works, keep an eye on Paul Irish's post at `http://paulirish.com/2009/bulletproof-font-face-implementation-syntax/`. Paul regularly updates this post with new information as it becomes available.

Paul's version has been improved upon by the community, culminating with the current champion, the "Fontspring @Font-Face Syntax." This syntax is illustrated in the following code snippet. In this example you create a new `font-family` called *InconsolataMedium*. The two separate `src` properties and multiple `url` values combine to provide support for a wide range of devices.

```
@font-face {
  font-family: 'InconsolataMedium';
  src: url('Inconsolata-webfont.eot');
  src: url('Inconsolata-webfont.eot?#iefix') format('embedded-opentype'),
   url('Inconsolata-webfont.woff') format('woff'),
   url('Inconsolata-webfont.ttf') format('truetype'),
   url('Inconsolata-webfont.svg#InconsolataMedium') format('svg');
  font-weight: normal;
  font-style: normal;
}
```

If this looks slightly complicated (and it is) and you're not familiar with the ways to create the different font formats (not many people are), you can use the FontSquirrel font generator, which creates the different font formats and creates the proper CSS snippet for you. You can access the font generator at `http://www.fontsquirrel.com/fontface/generator`.

Adding Custom Fonts to Example Café

The best way to learn this somewhat complicated process for adding custom fonts is to practice in the following Try It Out.

TRY IT OUT Adding a Custom Font

Adding custom fonts is an advanced CSS feature that will add some pizzazz to the Example Café website.

1. Start your text editor and open `interface.css`, the CSS file for your site.

2. You want to change the default font for the header elements on the site to be Droid Serif, a font provided free by the Google Android team. To download it in every version needed and generate the `@font-face` code needed to embed the font, go to `http://www.fontsquirrel.com/fonts/Droid-Serif` and click the @font-face Kit button (see Figure 9-9).

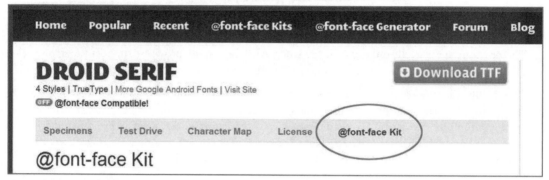

FIGURE 9-9

3. Choose the default options and then hit the large Download @font-face Kit button. This download will be a zip file containing each of the different font formats, an HTML file, and a CSS file. Extract the zip file and then move the font files to a new folder in your example site called `fonts`.

4. Open the example `stylesheet.css` file in your @font-face kit. The code in it will look like the following:

```css
@font-face {
  font-family: 'DroidSerifRegular';
  src: url('DroidSerif-Regular-webfont.eot');
  src: url('DroidSerif-Regular-webfont.eot?#iefix')
       format('embedded-opentype'),
    url('DroidSerif-Regular-webfont.woff') format('woff'),
    url('DroidSerif-Regular-webfont.ttf') format('truetype'),
    url('DroidSerif-Regular-webfont.svg#DroidSerifRegular')
       format('svg');
  font-weight: normal;
  font-style: normal;
}
@font-face {
  font-family: 'DroidSerifItalic';
  src: url('DroidSerif-Italic-webfont.eot');
  src: url('DroidSerif-Italic-webfont.eot?#iefix')
       format('embedded-opentype'),
    url('DroidSerif-Italic-webfont.woff') format('woff'),
    url('DroidSerif-Italic-webfont.ttf') format('truetype'),
    url('DroidSerif-Italic-webfont.svg#DroidSerifItalic')
       format('svg');
  font-weight: normal;
  font-style: normal;
}
@font-face {
  font-family: 'DroidSerifBold';
  src: url('DroidSerif-Bold-webfont.eot');
```

```
      src: url('DroidSerif-Bold-webfont.eot?#iefix')
           format('embedded-opentype'),
        url('DroidSerif-Bold-webfont.woff') format('woff'),
        url('DroidSerif-Bold-webfont.ttf') format('truetype'),
        url('DroidSerif-Bold-webfont.svg#DroidSerifBold')
        format('svg');
      font-weight: normal;
      font-style: normal;
    }
    @font-face {
      font-family: 'DroidSerifBoldItalic';
      src: url('DroidSerif-BoldItalic-webfont.eot');
      src: url('DroidSerif-BoldItalic-webfont.eot?#iefix')
           format('embedded-opentype'),
        url('DroidSerif-BoldItalic-webfont.woff') format('woff'),
        url('DroidSerif-BoldItalic-webfont.ttf') format('truetype'),
        url('DroidSerif-BoldItalic-webfont.svg#DroidSerifBoldItalic') format('svg');
      font-weight: normal;
      font-style: normal;
    }
```

5. You need to adjust all the URLs to match the new `fonts` subfolder you've created. Taking the example of the DroidSerifRegular definition, your new definition will look like the following:

```
    @font-face {
      font-family: 'DroidSerifRegular';
      src: url('../fonts/DroidSerif-Regular-webfont.eot');
      src: url('../fonts/DroidSerif-Regular-webfont.eot?#iefix')
           format('embedded-opentype'),
        url('../fonts/DroidSerif-Regular-webfont.woff') format('woff'),
        url('../fonts/DroidSerif-Regular-webfont.ttf') format('truetype'),
        url('../fonts/DroidSerif-Regular-webfont.svg#DroidSerifRegular')
        format('svg');
      font-weight: normal;
      font-style: normal;
    }
```

6. Now focus on the header elements. Instead of using Georgia, the header elements use DroidSerifRegular. You still use Georgia as a backup in case something goes wrong with the custom font or a user visits the site with a much older browser. The new header definitions will look like this:

```
    h1, h2, h3, h4 {
      font-family : DroidSerifRegular, georgia, times, serif;
      color : #666666;
    }
```

7. Now all the pages in the example should be using this same style sheet, and your homepage should look like the example in Figure 9-10.

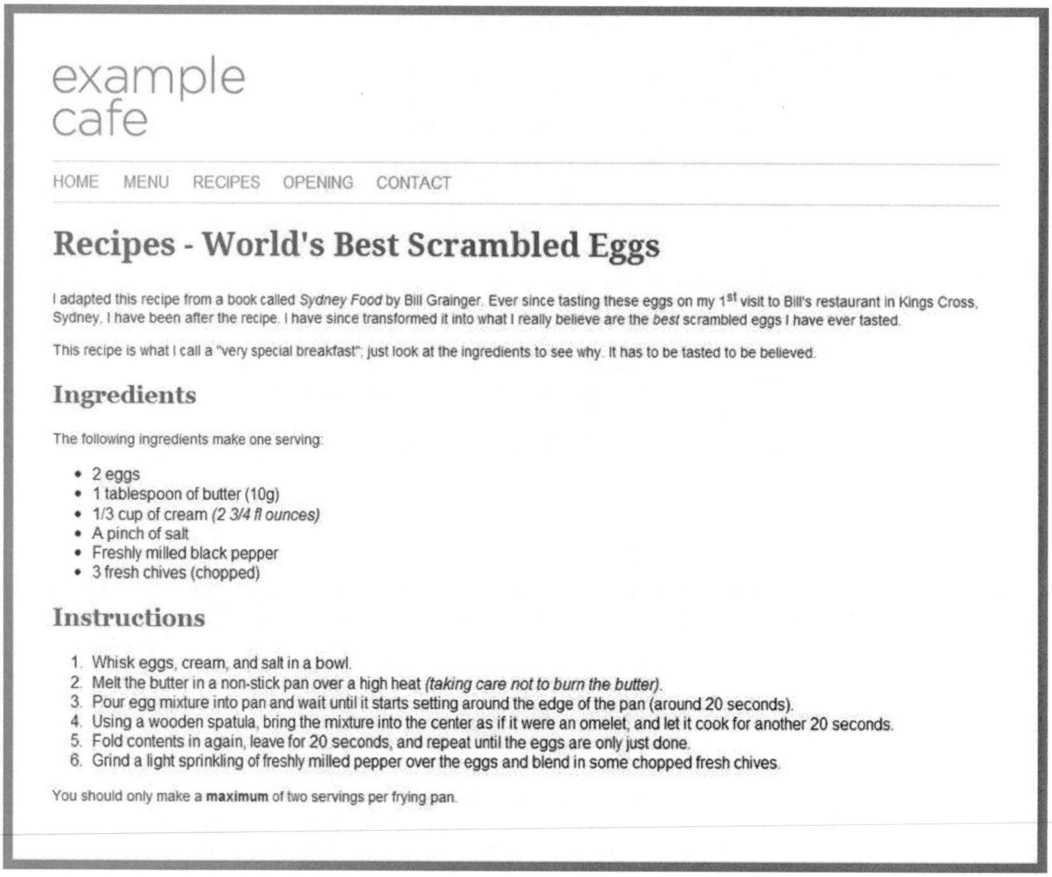

example cafe

HOME   MENU   RECIPES   OPENING   CONTACT

Recipes - World's Best Scrambled Eggs

I adapted this recipe from a book called *Sydney Food* by Bill Grainger. Ever since tasting these eggs on my 1st visit to Bill's restaurant in Kings Cross, Sydney, I have been after the recipe. I have since transformed it into what I really believe are the *best* scrambled eggs I have ever tasted.

This recipe is what I call a "very special breakfast"; just look at the ingredients to see why. It has to be tasted to be believed.

Ingredients

The following ingredients make one serving:

- 2 eggs
- 1 tablespoon of butter (10g)
- 1/3 cup of cream *(2 3/4 fl ounces)*
- A pinch of salt
- Freshly milled black pepper
- 3 fresh chives (chopped)

Instructions

1. Whisk eggs, cream, and salt in a bowl.
2. Melt the butter in a non-stick pan over a high heat *(taking care not to burn the butter)*.
3. Pour egg mixture into pan and wait until it starts setting around the edge of the pan (around 20 seconds).
4. Using a wooden spatula, bring the mixture into the center as if it were an omelet, and let it cook for another 20 seconds.
5. Fold contents in again, leave for 20 seconds, and repeat until the eggs are only just done.
6. Grind a light sprinkling of freshly milled pepper over the eggs and blend in some chopped fresh chives.

You should only make a **maximum** of two servings per frying pan.

FIGURE 9-10

How It Works

The `@font-face` rule creates a new font-family entry that represents the downloaded file. Whenever you want to reference it, you simply need to reference the short name you've given the file. Technically, you could name the new font-family almost anything that strikes your fancy; it simply makes more sense to choose a name that precisely describes the font in question. The next developer who has to edit your CSS might not appreciate you calling a particular font BibFortuna, no matter how much of a Star Wars fan you are.

This combination of font formats and `@font-face` declaration provides support for Safari 5.03+, IE 6+, Firefox 3.6+, Chrome 8+, iOS 3.2+, Android 2.2+, and Opera 11+.

Advanced CSS Manipulations with Transforms, Animations, and Transitions

The modules in this section can get quite advanced, and support for them is still a bit spotty. Still, they're exciting, so it's worthwhile to take a quick tour through them. This section briefly introduces each feature and provides a simple demo to show the basic technique and format.

2D Transforms

The 2D Transforms module introduces a new property that allows for the rotation, translation, and scaling of a box, without changing its place in the flow of the document. Table 9-6 lists the common values of the `transform` property and gives a small example of each.

TABLE 9-6: Potential CSS 2D Transform Values

VALUE	DESCRIPTION	EXAMPLE
translate	Moves an element up/down, left/right without changing the element's place in the flow of the document.	`transform : translate( 10px, 10px );`
translateX	Moves an element left or right without changing the element's place in the flow of the document.	`transform : translateX( 10px);`
translateY	Moves an element up or down without changing the element's place in the flow of the document.	`transform : translateY( 10px);`
rotate	Rotates an element around an axis. The rotation can be specified in degrees or using other values like the `turn` keyword.	`transform : rotate(180deg)`
scale	Scales an element without changing the element's place in the document. `scale` is set as a multiple of 1, so `scale(2)` tells the browser to make the element twice as big.	`transform : scale( 2 )`
scaleX	Scales an element on its x-axis without changing the element's place in the document.	`transform : scaleX( 2 )`
scaleY	Scales an element on its y-axis without changing the element's place in the document.	`transform : scaleY( 2 )`

The following code sample (`ch09_eg07.html`) shows both `scale` and `rotate` in action. The first `<div>` is rotated 20 degrees. The second `<div>` is scaled down by 1/2. For reference, the background image of the page shows the position of each `<div>` in the flow of the document.

```
<div id="rotate">
  <p>The background image of the page shows the original orientation of
  this element</p>
```

```
</div>
<div id="scale">
  <p>Scaled. This div is defined as 500px x 200px, but is scaled to be much
    smaller as the background image of the page shows.</p>
</div>
```

As you can see, the CSS (ch09_eg07.css) needs to leverage browser prefixes for several different browsers.

```
div {
  position : absolute;
  width : 500px;
  height : 200px;
 }
#rotate {
  -webkit-transform : rotate(20deg);
  -moz-transform : rotate(20deg);
  -ms-transform : rotate(20deg);
  -o-transform : rotate(20deg);
  transform : rotate(20deg);
  background : #00ffcc;
  top : 100px;
  left : 50px;
}
#scale {
  -webkit-transform : scale(0.5);
  -moz-transform : scale(0.5);
  -ms-transform : scale(0.5);
  -o-transform : scale(0.5);
  transform : scale(0.5);
  background : #ccff00;
  top : 400px;
  left : 50px;
}
```

Figure 9-11 shows the result of the transformations in Google Chrome.

There's an additional transform function, matrix, which is easiest to understand mathematically. If you're interested in learning more about matrix, look at the article "The CSS3 matrix() Transform for the Mathematically Challenged" at http://www.useragentman.com/blog/2011/01/07/css3-matrix-transform-for-the-mathematically-challenged/, which does an admirable job of explaining it without resorting to purely mathematical terms.

3D Transforms

Developed with the SVG specification, the 3D Transforms module extends 2D Transforms with a perspective transform function and 3D variations on some 2D transformation functions you've already seen: matrix3d, translate3d, translateZ, scale3d, scaleZ, rotate3d, rotateY, rotateX, and rotateZ.

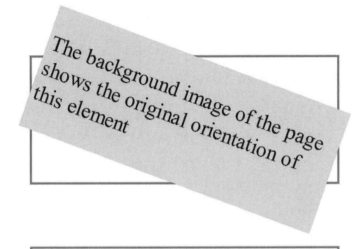

Scaled. This div is defined as 500px x 200px, but is scaled to be much smaller as the background image of the page shows.

FIGURE 9-11

The following code snippet (ch09_eg08.css) illustrates the use of perspective on a single <div> (ch09_eg08.html). The perspective transform function takes a value in pixels, which defines how deep the perspective "box" should be. It's then rotated on its *y* axis using rotateY.

```
#perspective {
  top : 100px;
  left : 50px;
  position : absolute;
  -webkit-transform : perspective(500px) rotateY(75deg);
  -moz-transform : perspective(500px) rotateY(75deg);
  -ie-transform : perspective(500px) rotateY(75deg);
  transform : perspective(500px) rotateY(75deg);
  width : 500px;
  height : 200px;
  background : #ccff00;
}
```

Figure 9-12 shows this rendered in Google Chrome.

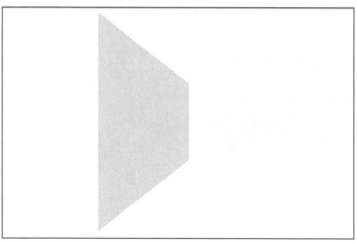

FIGURE 9-12

CSS Animations and CSS Transitions

The Animations module enables you to assign an animation to an element. You do this by specifying the properties to animate, the timing, and the units to change during the animation.

The Transitions module defines a property to animate the transitions between pseudo-classes, for example, when an element enters or leaves the :hover state.

After developers have relied entirely on JavaScript for these kinds of effects for many years, it's nice to rely on standardized, browser-optimized functionality for these interface enhancements. Defining a specific mechanism for animations also enables browsers to optimize the visual display of animations. Up until the introduction of CSS animations, there was no way to indicate to the browser that the set of JavaScript instructions it was running should be optimized to look like a smooth animation in the eyes of a human being. With CSS animations that mechanism now exists.

The following code sample (ch09_eg09.html) shows a simple animation of a single <div> element. The CSS source code (ch09_eg09.css) here is simplified, using only the unprefixed properties. In practice, prefixes for Safari and Chrome (-webkit-), Firefox (-moz-), and Opera (-o-) should be used. They're in place in the downloaded CSS file.

The <div> is initially set as a 100-pixel square pinned to the left edge of the browser. You should be familiar with all these rules now. The new pieces are in the @keyframes directive and in the new CSS animation- properties. The @keyframes directive creates a reference to a new animation named scroll, which instructs the browser to animate the <div> to the far left edge of the page and rotate the element 180 degrees. The animation-name property references that same named animation. The animation-duration property indicates that the animation should take 5 seconds. The animation-iteration-count property indicates that the animation should run infinitely.

Finally, the `animation-direction` property indicates that the animation should reverse directions each time it runs.

```
#animated {
  position : absolute;
  width : 100px;
  height : 100px;
  left:0px;
  top:100px;
  background: #ffcc00;
  animation-name: scroll;
  animation-duration: 5s;
  animation-iteration-count: infinite;
  animation-timing-function: ease-in-out;
  animation-direction: alternate;

}
@keyframes scroll {
  to {
    left:100%;
    transform: rotate(180deg);
  }
}
```

CSS Transitions are similar to animations in that they put the onus of creating smooth animations onto the browser. Although JavaScript developers are a smart crowd, they don't have the same access to the inner workings of the computer that the browser vendors do, including access to the Graphics Processing Unit (GPU.)

The following code sample (`ch09_eg10.css`) shows a simple transition in action. In it a simple menu, created using `<li>` elements, transitions, on hover, between two shades of blue. It's also made slightly larger.

In the standard state, the `transition-property` is set to `background-color,width,height`. This defines the properties to animate. In addition, the `transition-duration` property is set to `1s`. In the `li:hover` definition `background-color,width,height` are defined and `transition-duration` is also set to `1s`. This ensures that the properties are animated both in and out of the hover event.

```
#transition li{
  font:16px arial, helvetica, sans-serif;
  color:#fff;
  padding:2px 10px;
  width :  200px;
  list-style-type : none;
  height : 50px;
  background-color : #06F;
  -webkit-transition-property: background-color,width,height;
  -moz-transition-property: background-color,width,height;
  -o-transition-property:  background-color,width,height;
  transition-property:  background-color,width,height;

  -webkit-transition-duration: 1s;
  -moz-transition-duration: 1s;
  -o-transition-duration: background-color 1s;
  transition-duration: background-color 1s;
```

```
}
#transition li:hover {
  background-color: #036;
  width:225px;
  height:60px;
  -webkit-transition-duration: 1s;
  -moz-transition-duration: 1s;
  -o-transition-duration: 1s;
  transition-duration: 1s;

}
```

Table 9-7 shows browser support for transforms and animations.

TABLE 9-7: Browser Support for Advanced CSS3 Features

FEATURE	INTERNET EXPLORER	GOOGLE CHROME	FIREFOX	SAFARI	OPERA
2D Transforms	9.0+	4.0+	3.5+	3.1+	10.5+
3D Transforms	10.0+	12.0+	10.0+	4.0+	None
Animations	10.0+	4.0+	5.0+	4.0+	12.0+
Transitions	10.0+	4.0+	4.0+	3.1+	10.5+

SUMMARY

In this chapter you learned about several new CSS3 features. You first learned about the new modular design of CSS3 and how this new approach means there are some modules that are nearly complete in development and others are much newer and not quite finished.

You then learned about new, powerful ways to select elements for styling. Then you were introduced to advanced color options, including ones using hue, saturation, and lightness, as well as options for creating elements with variable opacity using the opacity property or by defining an alpha channel on RGB or HSL colors.

You learned how to simply implement some common design motifs including rounded corners, drop shadows, and multi-column test displays. You also learned about Media Queries, which enable you to specify style rules for specific device or browser characteristics. Finally you learned about new CSS3 features including animations and transitions.

EXERCISES

1. In this exercise, you create a linked table of contents that sits at the top of a long document in an ordered list and links to the headings in the main part of the document.

The HTML file `exercise1.html` is provided with the download code for this book, ready for you to create the style sheet. Your style sheet should do the following:

➤ Round the corners of the `#contents <div>` element with a 12-pixel corner radius.

➤ Make the background color of the `#contents` element 70 percent opaque, leaving the text black.

➤ Change the font to be Inconsolata using `http://www.fontsquirrel.com/fonts/ Inconsolata`.

Your page should look something like Figure 9-13.

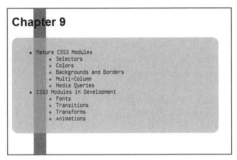

FIGURE 9-13

2. In this exercise, you test your understanding of `border-radius` and the Transitions module to make a neat hover effect. Your style sheet should do the following:

➤ Set 1 second transitions for both the `:hover` and standard state. Transition the `border-radius` and `background-color` properties.

➤ In the `#hover:hover` definition, change the background color to `#00ccff` and change the `border-radius` to be 100 pixels, which makes the box a circle.

The hover state of your page should look like Figure 9-14.

FIGURE 9-14

You can find the source HTML file (`exercise2.html`) with the download code for this chapter.

The answers to all the exercises are in Appendix A, "Answers to Exercises."

▶ WHAT YOU LEARNED IN THIS CHAPTER

TOPIC	KEY TAKEAWAY
New CSS selectors	Learning about new, more precise selectors enables you to easily select HTML elements for custom styles.
Alpha versus opacity	Adding an alpha channel to an RGB or HSL color value makes a semi-transparent *background*. Using the `opacity` property makes the entire element (including children) semi-transparent.
Browser prefixes	Certain, new CSS properties require browser prefixes. You can use an online tool such as CSS3, Please to create rules that rely on browser prefixes.
Fonts	CSS fonts can be used today, as long as you use the latest version of the bulletproof `@font-face` syntax.
Transitions and animations	Used with care, owing to compatibility issues, Transitions and Animations can add smooth animations and effects to your web pages.

10

Learning JavaScript

WHAT YOU WILL LEARN IN THIS CHAPTER

➤ How to start with programming JavaScript

➤ How the Document Object Model enables you to access and manipulate HTML elements

➤ How to apply logic to your JavaScript programs

➤ How to loop through collections of information with JavaScript

➤ How to work with dates, math, and other built-in JavaScript features

WROX.COM CODE DOWNLOADS FOR THIS CHAPTER

You can find the wrox.com code downloads for this chapter at `www.wrox.com/remtitle .cgi?isbn=9781118340189` on the Download Code tab. The code is in the Chapter 10 download and individually named according to the names throughout the chapter.

Many programming languages exist today, and in this chapter, you begin learning the basics of a programming language called *JavaScript*. JavaScript is by far the most common programming language used on web pages. *jQuery*, a framework created to make working with JavaScript easier and more fun, is the most popular way to work with JavaScript on the web.

Although you can't learn everything there is to learn about jQuery and JavaScript in this book, many free jQuery resources are on the web that you can use today to enhance your pages. Therefore, the aim of this chapter is to teach you enough to start using these scripts in your web pages and to understand how they work. You can customize these scripts and write some basic scripts of your own based upon what you learn in this chapter. In addition, this is a good introduction to general programming concepts.

JavaScript gives web developers a programming language to use in web pages that enables them to perform tasks such as the following:

➤ Read elements from documents and write new elements and text into documents.

➤ Manipulate or move text.

➤ Perform mathematical calculations on data.

➤ React to events, such as a user clicking a button.

➤ Retrieve the current date and time from a user's computer or the last time a document was modified.

➤ Determine the user's screen size, browser version, or screen resolution.

➤ Perform actions based on conditions such as alerting users if they enter the wrong information into a form.

You might need to read through this chapter more than once to get a good grasp of what you can do with JavaScript. Then, after you see the examples in the next three chapters, you should have a better idea of its power. There is a lot to learn, but these three chapters should get you well on your way.

> **WARNING** *JavaScript is not the same as Java, which is a different programming language.*

WHAT IS PROGRAMMING ABOUT?

As you see in this chapter, programming is largely about performing different types of calculations upon various types of data (including numbers, text, and graphics). In all programming languages you can perform tasks such as

➤ Performing mathematical calculations on numbers such as addition, subtraction, multiplication, and division.

➤ Working with text to find out how long a sentence is, or where the first occurrence of a specified letter is within a section of text.

➤ Checking if one value (a number or letter) matches another.

➤ Checking if one value is shorter or longer, lower or higher than another.

➤ Performing different actions based on whether a condition (or one of several conditions) is met. For example, if a user enters a number less than 10, a script or program can perform one action; otherwise it performs a different action.

➤ Repeating an action a certain number of times or until a condition is met (such as a user pressing a button).

These actions might sound rather simple, but they can be combined so that they become complicated and powerful. As you will see, different sets of actions can be performed in different situations a numbers of times to create a huge variety of results.

But before you can learn how to perform these kinds of calculations, first, you need some data for the programming language to work with, and you need to know how the language can work with this data. For your purpose, the data with which you work is the web page loaded in the browser at the time. When the browser loads a page, it stores it in an electronic form that programmers can then access through an *interface*. The interface is a little like a predefined set of questions and commands. For example, you can ask questions such as

➤ What is the title of the page?

➤ What is the third item in the bulleted list whose `id` attribute has a value of `ToDoList`?

➤ What is the URL of the page in the first link on the page?

You can also use commands to tell the browser to change some of these values, or even add new elements into the page. The interface that works with web pages is the *Document Object Model (DOM)*.

In *object-oriented* programming languages, real-life objects are represented (or modeled) using a set of *objects*, which form an *object model*. For example, a car object might represent a car, a `basket` object might represent a shopping basket, and a `document` object could represent a document such as a web page.

Each object can have a set of *properties* that describes aspects of the object. A `car` object might have properties that describe its color or engine size. A `basket` object might have properties that describe the number of items it contains or the value of those items. A `document` object has properties that describe the background color of the web page or the title of the page.

Then there are *methods*; each method describes an action that can be done to (or with) the object. For example, a method of an object representing a car might be to accelerate or to change gear. A method of a shopping basket might be to add an item or to recalculate the value of items in the basket. A method on a document could be to write a new line of text into the web page.

Finally, there are *events*. In a programming language, an event is the object putting up its hand and saying, "*x* just happened," usually because a program might want to do something as a result of the event. For example, a `car` object might raise an event to say the ignition started or that it is out of fuel. A `basket` might raise an event when an item is added to it or when it is full. A document might raise an event when the user presses Submit on a form or clicks a link. Furthermore, an event can also trigger actions; for example, if a car is out of fuel, the car will stop.

An object model is therefore a description of how a program can represent real-life entities using a set of objects, and it also specifies a set of methods, properties, and events an object may have.

All the main browsers implement an object model called the DOM that was devised to represent web pages. In this DOM, the page as a whole is represented using a `document` object.

The DOM describes how you can

➤ Get and set properties of a web page such as the background color.

➤ Call methods that perform actions such as writing a new line into a page.

➤ React to events such as a user pressing a Submit button on a form.

Web browsers implement the DOM as a way for programming languages to access (and work with) the content of web pages. When you have learned how the DOM enables you to access and change web pages, you can then see how the programming language can ask the DOM about the web page, perform calculations with the data it receives back, and then tell the browser to change something based upon these calculations.

If you think of the DOM as an interface between the browser and the programming language, you can compare it to a remote control that acts as the interface between your TV and you. You know that pressing 1 on your remote control turns your TV to channel 1, or that the volume-up button increases the volume. If you call up the TV schedule, you can see what is on next, and you might choose to change the channel (or turn the TV off) as a result. Similarly, the DOM is like the remote control that enables a programming language (such as JavaScript) to work with the browser (and the web page in that browser).

To take the remote control analogy a little further, it doesn't matter what language you speak; as long as someone presses the right button on the remote, the TV behaves in the same way. If you get a new TV, the core functions of the remote will be similar. When you are working with the DOM, it does not matter what language you program with. As long as you use the right properties and methods, the effect will be the same.

Also, under the covers, it does not matter how your remote tells the TV to turn up the volume, as long as the effect is the same. (The volume goes up.) Likewise, it doesn't matter how the browser retrieves the title of the page when you ask for it, or the background color of the page when you ask for that, as long as it returns it to you in the way you expect (which is specified in the DOM).

The point of this analogy is that your script can achieve the same goal in any browser that implements the DOM. It does not matter how a browser implements the DOM, as long as you can ask it for properties, or to perform methods in the standard way set out in the DOM, and you then get the results in an expected format. How the browser actually does the work under the hood does not matter.

In the rest of this chapter, you look at how the DOM enables you to work with a web page; then you look at JavaScript to see what you can do with this data and how you can use it to get and set values of the document, call methods, and respond to events.

> **NOTE** *Just like there are new versions of CSS and HTML, there's a new version of the DOM in the works: DOM Level 4 (*`http://www.w3.org/TR/domcore/`*). It ties in directly with the work that's going on with HTML5 and will also be a core improvement to the tools used to build the web.*

HOW TO ADD A SCRIPT TO YOUR PAGES

JavaScript can be either embedded in a page or placed in an external script file (rather like CSS). But to work in the browser, the browser must have JavaScript enabled. (The major browsers enable users to disable JavaScript; although, few people do.)

You add scripts to your page inside the `<script>` element.

> **NOTE** *You often see a* `type="text/javascript"` *attribute on script tags. Because JavaScript is the primary programming language of the web, this* `type` *attribute is unnecessary.*

Here you see a simple script that writes the words "My first JavaScript" into the page (`ch10_eg01.html`):

```
<html>
<body>
  <script>
    document.write("My first JavaScript")
  </script>
</body>
</html>
```

In this case, you use the `write()` method to add a new line of text into the web page. (And the web page is represented using the `document` object.) The text is added into the page where the script is written in the page. Figure 10-1 shows what this simple page would look like.

FIGURE 10-1

Where you put your JavaScript within a page is important. If you put it in the body of a page—as in this example—it runs (or executes) in-place as the page loads. Whenever the browser encounters a script block it executes it before going on to read the rest of the HTML. You rarely do this. This is bad for both page performance and maintenance.

Instead you should write your JavaScript in external documents that have the file extension `.js` (in the same way that you write external style sheets) and link to them in the `<head>` or the bottom of your `<body>` element. Using external JavaScript files is a particularly good option because

➤ If your script is used by more than one page, you do not need to repeat the script in each page that uses it.

➤ If you want to update your script, you need to change it only in one place.

➤ It makes the HTML page cleaner and easier to read.

When you place your JavaScript in an external file, you need to use the `src` attribute on the `<script>` element; the value of the `src` attribute should be an absolute or relative URL pointing to the file containing the JavaScript, for example:

```
<script src="scripts/validation.js"></script>
```

> **NOTE** *Generally, it's good practice to place your external JavaScript at the bottom of your* `<body>` *element. Doing this makes your page appear faster to your users. Because JavaScript can change the contents of the page (like with the* `document` `.write` *you've already seen), browsers can block other downloads and rendering whenever it encounters JavaScript. When this blocking occurs nothing else happens on the page. You want to avoid this, and the easiest way to do that is by putting your scripts at the bottom of the* `<body>` *element.*

Comments in JavaScript

You can add comments to your JavaScript code in two ways. The first way is illustrated in the following code snippet; anything on the same line after the two forward slash characters is treated as a comment:

```
<script
  document.write("My first JavaScript") // comment goes here
</script>
```

You can also comment out multiple lines using the following syntax, holding the comment between the opening characters /* and closing characters */ like so:

```
/* This whole section is commented
out so it is not treated as a part of
the script. */
```

This is similar to comments in CSS.

> **NOTE** *As with all code, it's good practice to comment your code clearly, even if you are the only person likely to be using it because what might have seemed clear when you wrote a script might not be so obvious when you come back to it later.*

The <noscript> Element

The `<noscript>` element offers alternative content for users who have disabled JavaScript. It can contain any HTML content that the author wants to be seen in the browser if the user does not have JavaScript enabled.

> **NOTE** *Strictly speaking, the W3C's recommendation is that the content of this element should be displayed only when the browser does not support the scripting language required; however, the browser manufacturers have decided that it should also work when scripting is disabled.*

CREATE AN EXTERNAL JAVASCRIPT

Since it's a best practice to use external scripts, it's time to learn how to create one.

TRY IT OUT   Creating an External JavaScript

You have already seen a basic example of a JavaScript that writes to a page. In this example, you move that code to an external file. The external file can write some text to the page.

1. Open your editor and type the following code:

```
document.write("Here is some text from an external file.");
```

2. Save this file as `external.js`.

3. Open a new page in your editor and add the following. The `<script>` element is empty this time but carries the `src` attribute whose value is the JavaScript file (just as it does on the `<img>` element). This may be a relative or full URL.

```
<!DOCTYPE html>
<html>
<head><title>External script</title></head>
<body>
  <script src="external.js"></script>
  <noscript>This only shows if the browser has JavaScript turned off.
  </noscript>
</body>
</html>
```

4. Save this example as `ch10_eg02.html` and open it in your browser. You should see something like Figure 10-2.

FIGURE 10-2

How It Works

The external JavaScript file is read by the browser and executed directly in the place it was inserted into the document. This is exactly equivalent to embedding the script directly in the page.

This `document.write` technique is used by many third-party scripts to add advanced functionality to your web pages.

THE DOCUMENT OBJECT MODEL

As mentioned at the start of the chapter, in the context of a web page, JavaScript doesn't do much more than enable you to perform calculations or work with basic strings. To make a document more interactive, the script needs to access the contents of the document and know when the user is interacting with it. The script does this by interacting with the browser by using the properties, methods, and events set out in the DOM interface.

The DOM represents the web page loaded into the browser using a series of objects. The main object is the `document` object, which in turn contains several other child objects.

The DOM explains what properties of a document a script can retrieve and which ones it can alter; it also defines some methods that can be called to perform an action on the document.

Accessing Values Using Dot Notation

To access the properties and methods of the different objects you encounter in JavaScript, you list the objects, methods, or properties in order. Each object, property, or method is separated by a period or full-stop character; hence, this is a *dot notation*.

For example, to access any CSS class names on the `<body>` element, you would type the following:

```
document.body.className
```

This statement has three parts separated by periods, to get to the CSS class name:

➤ The word `document` indicates you are accessing the `document` object.

➤ The word `body` corresponds to the `<body>` element.

➤ The `className` indicates that you want to access any CSS classes attached to the body.

Each object has different properties, objects, and methods that you can access. You continue to see this dot notation used to access them throughout the next three chapters.

Different Types of Objects

You will come across several types of objects in JavaScript, each of which is responsible for a related set of functionalities. For example, the `document` object has methods and properties that relate to the document; the `forms` collection, which is part of the `document` object, deals with information regarding forms; and so on. As you are about to see, there can be lots of different objects, each of which deals with a different set of functionalities and properties.

Here are some of the types of objects you are likely to come across:

➤ **W3C DOM objects:** These are like those already covered in this chapter; although, in more recent browsers several more objects are made available to enable you more control over a document.

➤ **Built-in objects:** Several objects are part of the JavaScript language. These include the `Date` object, which deals with dates and times, and the `Math` object, which provides mathematical functions. You learn more about these built-in objects later in the chapter.

➤ **Custom objects:** If you start to write advanced JavaScript, you might even start creating your own JavaScript objects that contain related functionality; for example, you might have a `validation` object that you have written just to use to validate your forms.

Although the creation of custom objects isn't covered in this chapter, you learn about the built-in objects later in this chapter.

STARTING TO PROGRAM WITH JAVASCRIPT

Now that you have seen how JavaScript can access a document in the web browser using the DOM, it is time to look at how you use these properties and methods in scripts.

The JavaScript Console

While you are learning about JavaScript to add interactivity to your web pages, you must know that JavaScript can run in different environments. It can run on a web server or as a separate program on your computer. It can also run in a browser outside of the context of a web page. All the major web browsers now come with a special interface for running JavaScript, called the *console*. The console is used by JavaScript programmers to log messages about the state of their application. It also enables you to run JavaScript commands outside the context of a web page. This is great because it enables you to experiment with the fundamentals of the JavaScript programming language interactively. You can type a command or a series of commands and then see the results immediately. You can try this with some of the examples in this book.

For example, to launch the console in Google Chrome, press Control+Shift+J (Windows) or Command+Option+J (Mac). To try out the most common console command, type the following and press Return:

```
console.log( "this is the console" );
```

Your message displays as shown in Figure 10-3.

FIGURE 10-3

This works because the console makes use of a `console` object that has methods, such as `log()`, which enables you to write messages to the console.

Table 10-1 lists the shortcuts needed to open the console in all the major browsers.

TABLE 10-1: Opening the JavaScript Console

BROWSER	MAC SHORTCUT	PC SHORTCUT
Google Chrome	`Command+Option+J`	`Control+Shift+J`
Safari[1]	`Command+Option+C`	`Control+Alt+C`
Internet Explorer		Press `F12`; open the Console tab.
Firefox	`Command+Option+K`	`Control+Shift+K`
Firefox (with Firebug installed)[2]	Press `F12`; open the Console tab.	Press `F12`; open the Console tab.
Opera	`Command+Option+I` to open Dragonfly, and then open the Console tab.	`Control+Shift+I` to open Dragonfly, and then open the Console tab.

[1] The Develop tab needs to be enabled. See `www.mac-geeks.de/2008/03/20/safari-developer-mode/`.
[2] A handy set of developer tools is available from `http://getfirebug.com/`.

You'll see more examples of the console in use in the next three chapters.

General Programming Concepts

As mentioned earlier, a programming language mainly performs calculations. So here are the key concepts you need to learn to perform different types of calculations:

➤ A *variable* is used to store some information; it's like a little bit of the computer's memory where you can store numbers, *strings* (which are a series of characters), or references to objects. You can then perform calculations to alter the data held in variables within your code.

➤ *Operators* perform functions on variables. There are different types of operators, for example:

➤ *Arithmetic operators* enable you to do things such as add (+) numbers together, or subtract (–) one from another (providing they are numbers).

➤ *Comparison operators* enable you to compare two strings and see if one is the same as the other, or different (for example, whether x is equal to y or whether a is greater than b).

➤ *Functions* are parts of a script grouped together to perform a specific task. For example, you could have a function that calculates loan repayments, and when you tell the loan calculator function the information it needs (the amount of money to be borrowed, the number of years the loan will last, and the interest rate) the function can return the monthly payment. Functions are objects in their own right and are similar to things called methods; one of the key differences is that methods often belong to an object already, whereas functions are customized.

➤ *Conditional statements* enable you to perform different actions based upon a condition. For example, a condition might be whether a variable holding the current time is greater than 12. If the condition is true, code to write "Good Afternoon" might be run. Whereas, if it is less than 12, a different block of code saying "Good Morning" could be shown.

➤ *Loops* can be set up so that a block of code runs a specified number of times or until a condition is met. For example, you can use a loop to get a document to write your name 100 times.

➤ There are also several built-in JavaScript objects that have methods that are of practical use. For example, in the same way that the `document` object of the DOM has methods that enable you to write to the document, the built-in JavaScript `Date` object can tell you the date, time, or day of the week.

The following section looks at these key concepts in more detail.

VARIABLES

Variables store data. To store information in a variable, you can give the variable a name and put an equal sign between it and the value you want it to have. Here is an example:

```
userName = "Bob Stewart";
```

The variable is called `userName` and the value is `Bob Stewart`. If no value is given, its value is *undefined*.

The script can access the value of the variable using its name (in this case `userName`). It can also change the value.

You can create a variable but not store anything with it by using the `var` keyword; this is *declaring* a variable. (Unlike some other languages, you do not *have* to declare a variable before you can use it; although, it is commonly considered good practice to do so.)

```
var userName;
```

Notice the semicolon at the end of the variable declaration. Although they're not strictly required, it is considered good form for statements in JavaScript to end in a semicolon.

There are a few rules you must remember about variables in JavaScript:

➤ They must begin with a letter or the underscore character.

➤ Variable names are case-sensitive.

➤ Avoid giving two variables the same name within the same document because one might override the value of the other, creating an error.

➤ Do not call two variables the same name with different cases to distinguish them (for example, `username` and `UserName`) because this is a common source of confusion later.

➤ Try to use descriptive names for your variables. This makes your code easier to understand. This can help you debug your code later if there is a problem with it and can greatly aid any other developer who tries to figure out what your code does.

Assigning a Value to a Variable

When you want to give a value to a variable, you put the variable name first, then an equal sign, and then on the right the value you want to assign to the variable. You have already seen values assigned to these variables when they were declared a moment ago. So, here is an example of a variable assigned a value and then the value changed:

```
var userName = "Bob Stewart";
userName = "Robert Stewart";
```

`userName` is now the equivalent of `Robert Stewart`.

Lifetime of a Variable

When you declare a variable in a function, it can be accessed only in that function. (You learn about functions shortly.) After the function has run, you cannot call the variable again. Variables in functions are *local variables*.

Because a local variable works only within a function, you can have different functions that contain variables of the same name (because each is recognized by that function only).

> **NOTE** *If you declare a variable using the* var *keyword inside a function, it uses up memory only when the function is run, and after the function finishes it does not take up any memory.*

If you declare a variable outside a function, called a *global variable* because it's available globally to all scripts on the page, all the functions on your page can access it. The lifetime of these variables starts when they are declared and ends when the page is closed.

Local variables take up less memory and fewer resources than page-level variables because they require only the memory during the time that the function runs, rather than having to be created and remembered for the life of the whole page.

Global variables are also dangerous because if you have more than one author of scripts on a page, you can quickly create errors if more than one author relies on a variable of the same name but with quite different purposes.

OPERATORS

The operator is a keyword or symbol that does something to a value when used in an *expression*. For example, the arithmetic operator + adds two values together.

The symbol is used in an expression with either one or two values and performs a calculation on the values to generate a result. For example, here is an expression that uses the multiplication operator:

```
var area = (width * height);
```

An expression is just like a mathematical expression. The values are known as *operands*. Operators that require only one operand (or value) are sometimes referred to as *unary operators*, whereas those that require two values are sometimes called *binary operators*.

The different types of operators you see in this section are

- ➤ Arithmetic
- ➤ Assignment
- ➤ Comparison
- ➤ Logical
- ➤ String

You see lots of examples of the operators in action both later in this chapter and in the next two chapters. First, however, it's time to learn about each type of operator.

Arithmetic Operators

Arithmetic operators perform arithmetic operations upon operands. (Note that in the examples in Table 10-2, $x = 10$.)

TABLE 10-2: JavaScript's Arithmetic Operators

SYMBOL	DESCRIPTION	EXAMPLE (x = 10)	RESULT
+	Addition	x+5	15
–	Subtraction	x–2	8
*	Multiplication	x*3	30
/	Division	x/2	5
%	Modulus (division remainder)	x%3	1
++	Increment (increments the variable by 1—this technique is often used in counters)	x++	11
– –	Decrement (decreases the variable by 1)	x––	9

Assignment Operators

The basic *assignment operator* is the equal sign, but do not take this to mean that it checks whether two values are equal. Rather, it's used to assign a value to the variable on the left of the equal sign, as you saw in the previous section, which introduced variables.

The basic assignment operator can be combined with several other operators to allow you to assign a value to a variable *and* perform an operation in one step. For example, look at the following statement where there is an assignment operator and an arithmetic operator:

```
total = total - profit;
```

This can be reduced to the following statement:

```
total -= profit;
```

Although it might not look like much, this kind of shorthand can save a lot of code if you have many calculations like this to perform (see Table 10-3).

TABLE 10-3: Shorthand Assignment Operators

SYMBOL	EXAMPLE USING SHORTHAND	EQUIVALENT WITHOUT SHORTHAND
+=	x+=y	x=x+y
–=	x–=y	x=x–y
*=	x*=y	x=x*y
/=	x/=y	x=x/y
%=	x%=y	x=x%y

Comparison Operators

Table 10-4 shows that *comparison operators* compare two operands and then return either `true` or `false` based on whether the comparison is true. The comparison for checking whether two operands are equal is two equal signs. (A single equal sign would be an assignment operator.)

TABLE 10-4: Comparison Operators

OPERATOR	DESCRIPTION	EXAMPLE
==	Equal to	1==2 returns `false` 3==3 returns `true`
!=	Not equal to	1!=2 returns `true` 3!=3 returns `false`
>	Greater than	1>2 returns `false` 3>3 returns `false` 3>2 returns `true`
<	Less than	1<2 returns `true` 3<3 returns `false` 3<1 returns `false`
>=	Greater than or equal to	1>=2 returns `false` 3>=2 returns `true` 3>=3 returns `true`
<=	Less than or equal to	1<=2 returns `true` 3<=3 returns `true` 3<=2 returns `false`

There is another way to test equality in JavaScript, the identity comparison operator, `===`. You learn more about that operator later in this chapter after you learn about *types*.

Logical or Boolean Operators

Logical or boolean operators (as shown in Table 10-5) return one of two values: `true` or `false`. They are particularly helpful when you want to evaluate more than one expression at a time.

TABLE 10-5: Boolean Operators

OPERATOR	NAME	DESCRIPTION	EXAMPLE (WHERE *x*=1 AND *y*=2)
&&	And	Enables you to check if both of two conditions are met	(x < 2 && y > 1) Returns true (because both conditions are met)
??	Or	Enables you to check if one of two conditions is met	(x < 2 ?? y < 2) Returns true (because the first condition is met)
!	Not	Enables you to check if something is not the case	! (x > y) Returns true (because *x* is not more than *y*)

The two operands in a logical or boolean operator evaluate to either true or false. For example, if x=1 and y=2, then x<2 is true and y>1 is true. So the following expression returns true because both of the operands evaluate to true. (You can see more examples by referring to the right column in Table 10-4.)

```
(x<2 && y>1);
```

String Operators (Using + with Strings)

You can also add text to strings using the + operator. For example, here the + operator is used to add two variables that are strings together:

```
var firstName = "Bob ";
var lastName = "Stewart";
name = firstName + lastName;
```

The value of the name variable would now be Bob Stewart. The process of adding two strings together is known as *concatenation*.

You can also compare strings using the comparison operators you just met. For example, you could check whether a user has entered a specific value into a textbox. (You see more about this topic when you look at the "Conditional Statements" section.)

FUNCTIONS

A *function* is made up of related code that performs a particular task. For example, a function could be written to calculate the area given the width and height. The function can then be called elsewhere in the script or when an event fires.

How to Define a Function

There are three parts to creating or defining a function:

➤ Define a name for it.

➤ Indicate any values that might be required; these are known as *arguments*.

➤ Add statements to the body of the function.

For example, if you want to create a function to calculate the area of a rectangle, you might name the function calculateArea(). (A function name should be followed by parentheses.) To calculate the area, you need to know the rectangle's width and height, so these would be passed in as *arguments*, which are the information the function needs to do its job. Inside the body of the function (the part between the curly braces) are the *statements*, which indicate that the area is equal to the width multiplied by the height (both of which have been passed into the function). The area is then returned.

```
function calculateArea( width, height ) {
  var area = width * height;
  return area
}
```

If a function has no arguments, it should still have parentheses after its name—for example, you might have a function that runs without any extra information passed as an argument such as logOut().

How to Call a Function

The calculateArea() function does nothing sitting on its own in the head of a document; it must be *called*. In this example, you can call the function from a simple form using the onclick event so that when the user clicks the Submit button, the area will be calculated and shown in an alert box.

Here you can see that the form contains two text inputs for the width and height (ch10_eg03.html):

```
<form name="frmArea">
Enter the width and height of your rectangle to calculate the size:<br>
Width: <input type="text" name="txtWidth" size="5" id="width"><br>
Height: <input type="text" name="txtHeight" size="5" id="height"><br>
<input type="button" value="Calculate area" id="calc">
</form>
```

In the JavaScript file (ch10_eg03.js) you see two blocks of code. The first is the same calculateArea() function you saw before. The second block starts your programming career. For starters it introduces one of the most common methods of the document object, getElementById(). This method enables you to get a reference to an HTML element using the same id attribute you learned about when working with CSS. When you have the reference to the element with the id "calc," you tell the browser that you want to listen for the onclick event and then do something. In this case you ask it to run a function. Unlike calculateArea() this function is without a name and is therefore called an *anonymous function*. Anonymous functions are common in JavaScript, especially when working with jQuery. You learn more about anonymous functions shortly. For now, just focus on the statements inside the curly braces {}. First, there is a call to console.log(). As mentioned, writing program information to the log is common, so it's good to get into the habit of doing so now. The argument to console.log(), which is the text to be logged, is a call to calculateArea(), which is called with two arguments. Both are calls to document.getElementById, reading the value property of the height and width form inputs.

```
function calculateArea( width, height ) {
  var area = width * height;
  return area;
}
```

```
document.getElementById( "calc" ).onclick = function(){
  console.log( calculateArea(
    document.getElementById( "width" ).value,
    document.getElementById( "height" ).value
  ));
}
```

The return Statement

Functions that return a result must use the `return` statement. This statement specifies the value that will be returned to where the function was called. The `calculateArea()` function, for example, returned the area of the rectangle:

```
function calculateArea( width, height ) {
  var area = width * height;
  return area;
}
```

What is returned depends on the code inside the function; for example, your area function returns the area of the rectangle. By contrast, if you have a form where people could enter an e-mail address to sign up for a newsletter, you might use a function to check whether that person entered a valid e-mail address before submitting the form. In that case, the function might just return `true` or `false` values.

What happens when the value is returned depends on how the function was called. With your function to calculate area, you could display the area to the user with some more JavaScript code. If you were checking whether an e-mail address were in a valid format before subscribing that e-mail address to a newsletter, the return value would determine whether the form was submitted.

Function Expressions and Anonymous Functions

As you've seen, there are a couple different ways to define functions in JavaScript. Technically, the format you first learned with the `calculateArea()` function is called a *function declaration*. This is the standard way to define reusable blocks of JavaScript statements. Because you give the function an *identifier*, you can refer to it throughout the life of your application. This is a good thing. Creating reusable code is something you should strive for. This format also uses the `function` keyword. This is a standard function declaration for a function named `name()`.

```
function name(){ /*Code*/}
```

Function declarations can't be nested within other blocks of JavaScript, which means if all you had available to you was a function declaration you would have to define all of your functions in that way before you could use them. Sometimes, as you've already seen, that doesn't need to be the case. If you define a function that will be used as an *event handler* (the code to be run when an event happens) it can be easier to define the function in place without using an identifier.

Doing so uses the second form you've seen, the *function expression*. A function expression is a function that can be defined more flexibly, as part of a larger piece of JavaScript. For example, you can use a function expression as the value of a variable or as an argument to another function. Commonly function expressions used in this way will be defined without using an identifier. Because it doesn't have an identifier, this is an *anonymous function*. A function created in this way works in the same way as a function created with a function declaration. It's still a collection of JavaScript statements. It differs in that it can be created in place. This code shows an example of an anonymous function assigned to a variable anon:

```
var anon = function(){/*code*/}
```

This example shows an anonymous function used as an argument to another function, name():

```
name( function(){
  return "Rob Larsen";
});
```

It may not make complete sense now, but as you continue to program JavaScript, your ability to create anonymous functions will become more apparent.

CONDITIONAL STATEMENTS

Conditional statements enable you to take different actions depending upon different statements. You will learn about three types of conditional statements:

➤ if statements, which are used when you want the script to execute if a condition is true

➤ if...else statements, which are used when you want to execute one set of code if a condition is true and another if it is false

➤ switch statements, which are used when you want to select one block of code from many depending on a situation

if Statements

if statements enable code to be executed when the condition specified is met; if the condition is true then the code in the curly braces is executed. Here is the syntax for an if statement:

```
if ( condition ){
  //code to be executed if condition is true
}
```

For example, you might want to start your homepage with the text "Good Morning" if the time is in the morning. You can achieve this using the following script (ch10_eg04.js):

```
var  date = new Date();
var  time = date.getHours();
  if (time < 12) {
    document.body.innerHTML += '<h1>Good Morning</h1>';
  }
```

This example first creates a Date object (which you learn about later in the chapter) and then calls the getHours() method of the Date object to find the time in hours (using the 24-hour clock). If the time in hours is less than 12, then the script writes an `<h1>` element saying "Good Morning" into the body of the page. (If it is after 12, you see a blank page because nothing is written to it.) This example uses the `innerHTML` property to write the `<h1>` into the page. The `innerHTML` property is a string that represents the HTML markup inside any HTML element. In this case, you add the string `<h1>Good Morning</h1>` to the `body` by using the shorthand `+=` assignment operator on the string.

For clarity this line could be rewritten

```
document.body.innerHTML =
    document.body.innerHTML + '<h1>Good Morning</h1>';
```

if . . . else Statements

When you have two possible situations and you want to react differently for each, you can use an `if...else` statement. This means: "If the conditions specified are met, run the first block of code; otherwise run the second block." The syntax follows:

```
if ( condition ){
  //code to be executed if condition is true
}
else{
  //code to be executed if condition is false
}
```

Returning to the previous example, you can write `Good Morning` if the time is before noon, and `Good Afternoon` if it is after noon (`ch10_eg05.js`).

```
var date = new Date();
var time = date.getHours();

if ( time < 12 ) {
   document.body.innerHTML += '<h1>Good Morning</h1>';
}
else {
   document.body.innerHTML += '<h1>Good Afternoon</h1>';
}
```

As you can imagine there are a lot of possibilities for using conditional statements.

switch Statements

A `switch` statement enables you to deal with several possible results of a condition. You have a single expression, which is usually a variable. This is evaluated immediately. The value of the expression is then compared with the values for each case in the structure. If there is a match, the block of code executes.

Here is the syntax for a `switch` statement:

```
switch ( expression ){
case option1:
  //code to be executed if expression is what is written in option1
  break;
case option2:
  //code to be executed if expression is what is written in option2
```

```
      break;
  case option3:
    //code to be executed if expression is what is written in option3
    break;
  default:
    //code to be executed if expression is different from option1, option2,
    and option3
  }
```

You use the `break` to prevent code from running into the next case automatically. For example, you might check what type of animal a user has entered into a textbox, and you want to write out different things to the screen depending upon what kind of animal is in the text input. Here is a form that appears on the page. When the user enters an animal and clicks the button, the `checkAnimal()` function contained in the head of the document is called (`ch10_eg06.html`) and uses a JavaScript alert box to send a message to the user:

```
<p>Enter the name of your favorite type of animal that stars in a cartoon:</p>
<form name="frmAnimal">
  <input type="text" name="txtAnimal" /><br />
  <input type="button" value="Check animal" onclick="checkAnimal()" />
</form>
```

Here is the function that contains the `switch` statement (`ch10_eg06.js`):

```
function checkAnimal() {
  switch ( document.getElementById( "txtAnimal" ).value.toLowerCase() ){
    case "rabbit":
      alert( "Watch out, it's Elmer Fudd!" );
    break;
    case "coyote":
      alert( "No match for the road runner - meep meep!" );
    break;
    case "mouse":
      alert( "Watch out Jerry, here comes Tom!" );
    break;
    default : alert("Are you sure you picked an animal from a cartoon?");
  }
}
```

The final option—the default—is shown if none of the cases are met. You can see what this would look like when the user has entered "**rabbit**" into the textbox in Figure 10-4.

Note the use of the `toLowerCase()` method in the switch statement. If the user enters text in a different case, it will not match the options in the `switch` statement. Because JavaScript is case-sensitive, if the letter's case does not match the value of the case in the `switch` statement, it will not be a match. This method converts a string to lowercase which solves the issue of matching cases. This is a method of the built-in JavaScript `String` object, which you meet later in the chapter.

FIGURE 10-4

Note the way the `onclick` is set up. See how there is no () after the `checkAnimal`? That means it's a *reference* to the function to use when the user clicks the button. This tells the browser, "I want to run the function with the identifier `checkAnimal` when the user clicks the button." If you did something like the following, with the parentheses, the function would execute as soon as the browser read this line (showing the default case because there would be no time to enter text), and nothing would happen when the user clicked the submit button.

```
document.getElementById( "check" ).onclick =
  checkAnimal;
```

LOOPING

Looping statements are used to execute the same block of code a specified number of times (which is handy because repetitive tasks are something that computers are particularly well suited to):

➤   A `while` loop runs the same block of code while or until a condition is true.

➤   A `do...while` loop runs once before the condition is checked. If the condition is true, it continues to run until the condition is false. (The difference between a `do` and a `do...while` loop is that `do while` runs once whether the condition is met.)

➤   A `for` loop runs the same block of code a specified number of times (for example, five times).

while

In a `while` loop, a code block is executed if a condition is true and for as long as that condition remains true. The syntax is as follows:

```
while ( condition ){
  //code to be executed
}
```

In the following example, you can see a `while` loop that shows the multiplication table for the number 3. This works based on a counter called i. Every time the `while` script loops, the counter increments by one. (This uses the ++ arithmetic operator, as you can see from the line that says i++.) So, the first time the script runs the counter is 1, and the loop writes out the line $1 \times 3 = 3$; the next time it loops around the counter is 2, so the loop writes out $2 \times 3 = 6$. This continues until the condition—that *i* is no longer less than 11—is true (`ch10_eg07.js`):

```
var i = 1;
while ( i < 11 ) {
  document.getElementById( "numbers" ).innerHTML +=
  "<li>" + i + " x 3 = " + (i * 3) +"</li>";
  i ++;
}
```

You can see the result of this example in Figure 10-5.

Before looking at the next type of loop (a `do ... while` loop), it is worth noting that a `while` loop may never run at all because the condition may not be true when it is called.

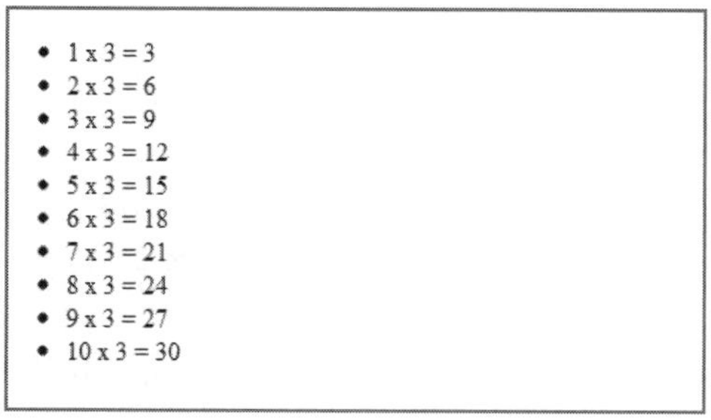

- 1 x 3 = 3
- 2 x 3 = 6
- 3 x 3 = 9
- 4 x 3 = 12
- 5 x 3 = 15
- 6 x 3 = 18
- 7 x 3 = 21
- 8 x 3 = 24
- 9 x 3 = 27
- 10 x 3 = 30

FIGURE 10-5

do . . . while

A do ... while loop executes a block of code once and then checks a condition. For as long as the condition is true, it continues to loop. So, whatever the condition, the loop runs at least once (as you can see the condition is after the instructions). Here is the syntax:

```
do {
  code to be executed
}
while (condition)
```

For example, here is the example with the 3 times table again. The counter is set with an initial value of 12, which is higher than required in the condition, so you see the sum 12 × 3 = 36 once, but nothing after that because when it comes to the condition, it has been met (ch10_eg8.js):

```
var i = 12;
do {
  document.getElementById( "numbers" ).innerHTML +=
  "<li>" + i + " x 3 = " + (i * 3) +"</li>";
  i ++;
}while (i < 11);
```

Now, if you change the value of the initial counter to 1, you see that the script loops through the multiplication table as it did in the last example until it gets to 11.

for

The for statement executes a block of code a specified number of times. You use it when you want to specify how many times you want the code to be executed (rather than running while a particular condition is true/false). It is worth noting here that the number of times that the for loop runs could be specified by some other part of the code. First, here is the syntax (which always takes three arguments):

```
for ( a; b; c ){
  //code to be executed
}
```

Now you need to look at what a, b, and c represent:

➤ a is evaluated before the loop is run and is only evaluated once. It is ideal for assigning a value to a variable; for example, you might use it to set a counter to 0 using i=0.

➤ b should be a condition that indicates whether the loop should be run again; if it returns true the loop runs again. For example, you might use this to check whether the counter is less than 11.

➤ c is evaluated after the loop has run and can contain multiple expressions separated by a comma (for example, i++, j++;). For example, you might use it to increment the counter.

So if you come back to the 3 times table example again, it would be written something like this (ch10_eg09.js):

```
for ( var i=0; i<11; i++ ) {
  document.getElementById( "numbers" ).innerHTML +=
    "<li>" + i + " x 3 = " + (i * 3) +"</li>";
}
```

Now look at the for statement in small chunks:

➤ var i=0 The counter is assigned to have a value of 0.

➤ i<11 The loop should run if the value of the counter is less than 11.

➤ i++ The counter is incremented by 1 every time the loop runs.

The assignment of the counter variable, the condition, and the incrementing of the counter all appear in the parentheses after the keyword for.

You can also assign several variables at once in the part corresponding to the letter a if you separate them with a comma, for example, var i = 0, j = 5;. It is also worth noting that you can count downward, as well as upward, with loops.

Infinite Loops and the break Statement

If you have an expression that always evaluates to true in any loop, you end up with something known as an *infinite loop*. These can tie up system resources and can even crash the computer; although, some browsers try to detect infinite loops and then stop the loop.

You can, however, add a break statement to stop an infinite loop; here it is set to 100 (ch10_eg10.js):

```
for ( var i=0; /* no condition here */ ; i++ ) {
  document.getElementById( "numbers" ).innerHTML +=
    "<li>" + i + " x 3 = " + (i * 3) +"</li>";
  if (i == 100) {
    break;
  }
}
```

When the script gets to a break statement, it simply stops running. This effectively prevents a loop from running too many times.

EVENTS

All browsers are expected to support a set of events known as *intrinsic events* such as the onload event, which happens when a page has finished loading, onclick for when a user clicks on an element, and onsubmit for when a form is submitted. These events can be used to trigger a script.

There are two types of events that can be used to trigger scripts:

➤ Window events, which occur when something happens to a window. For example, a page loads or unloads (is replaced by another page or closed) or focus is moved to or away from a window or frame.

➤ User events, which occur when the user interacts with elements in the page using a mouse (or other pointing device) or a keyboard, such as placing the mouse over an element, clicking an element, or moving the mouse off an element.

Table 10-6 provides a recap of the most common events you are likely to come across.

TABLE 10-6: Intrinsic Events

EVENT	PURPOSE
onload	Document has finished loading. (If used in a frameset, all frames have finished loading.)
onunload	Document is unloaded, or removed, from a window or frameset.
onclick	Button on mouse (or other pointing device) has been clicked over the element.
ondblclick	Button on mouse (or other pointing device) has been double-clicked over the element.
onmousedown	Button on mouse (or other pointing device) has been depressed (but not released) over the element.
onmouseup	Button on mouse (or other pointing device) has been released over the element.
onmouseover	Cursor on mouse (or other pointing device) has been moved onto the element.
onmousemove	Cursor on mouse (or other pointing device) has been moved while over the element.
onmouseout	Cursor on mouse (or other pointing device) has been moved off the element.
onkeypress	A key is pressed and released.
onkeydown	A key is held down.

continues

TABLE 10-6 *(continued)*

EVENT	PURPOSE
onkeyup	A key is released.
onfocus	Element receives focus either by a mouse (or other pointing device) clicking it, tabbing order giving focus to that element, or code giving focus to the element.
onblur	Element loses focus.
onsubmit	A form is submitted.
onreset	A form is reset.
onselect	User selects some text in a text field.
onchange	A control loses input focus and its value has been changed since gaining focus.

You see examples of these events used throughout this and the jQuery chapters.

BUILT-IN OBJECTS

You learned about the document object at the beginning of the chapter, and now it is time to see some of the objects that are built into the JavaScript language. You see the methods that enable you to perform actions upon data and properties that tell you something about the data.

String

The String object enables you to deal with strings of text. Before you can use a built-in object, you need to create an instance of that object. You create an instance of the String object by assigning it to a variable like so:

```
var myString = new String('Here is some text');
```

The String object now contains the words "Here is some text" and this is stored in a variable called myString. After you have this object in a variable, you can write the string to the document or perform actions upon it.

In addition, you can create a string directly using quotes and the wanted text on the right side of the assignment operator.

```
var myString = 'Here is some text';
```

This second pattern is more common in modern JavaScript.

You can check the length of this string like so; the result is the number of characters including spaces and punctuation (in this case 41):

```
var myString = "How many characters are in this sentence?";
console.log( myString.length );
```

Before you can use the `String` object, remember you first must create it and then give it a value.

Properties

The main property for the `String` object is `length` and its purpose is to return the number of characters in a string.

Methods

Table 10-7 lists some common methods for the `String` object and their purposes.

TABLE 10-7: Methods of the String Object

METHOD	PURPOSE
`charAt(index)`	Returns the character at a specified position. (For example, if you have a string that says "banana" and your method reads `charAt(2)`, then you end up with the letter n—remember that indexes start at 0.)
`concat( string2, string3, /*etc…*/ )`	Combines the text of two or more strings and returns a new string.
`indexOf(searchValue, [fromindex])`	Returns the position of the first occurrence of a specified character (or set of characters) inside another string.
	For example, if you have the word "banana" as your string, and you want to find the first occurrence of the letter n within "banana" you use `indexOf('n')`.
	If you supply a value for the `fromIndex` argument, the search begins at that position. For example, you might want to start after the fourth character, in which case you can use `indexOf('n',4)`.
	The method returns -1 if the string searched for never occurs.
`lastIndexOf(searchValue, [fromIndex])`	Same as the `indexOf()` method but runs from right to left.
`slice(beginslice, end-Slice )`	Extracts a piece of a string based on a beginning, zero-based index and optional ending index and returns as a new string. If the second argument is omitted, it extracts to the end of the string.

continues

TABLE 10-7 *(continued)*

METHOD	PURPOSE
split(separator)	Splits a string into an *array* (another built-in object you learn about shortly) of strings by separating the string into substrings based on a separator. A common separator would be " " (to get the words out of a sentence) or "," (to extract the data from a list of Comma Separated Values).
substr(start, [length])	Returns the specified characters. 14,7 returns 7 characters, from the 14th character (starts at 0).
substring(startPosition, endPosition)	Returns the specified characters between the start and end index points. 7,14 returns all characters from the 7th up to but not including the 14th (starts at 0).
toLowerCase()	Converts a string to lowercase.
toUpperCase()	Converts a string to uppercase.
trim()	Trims white space from the beginning and end of the string.

Manipulating Strings with JavaScript

Now that you've learned about strings, it's time to take what you've learned and put it into practice. Manipulating strings is an important part of programming JavaScript, so it's good to practice manipulating them as much as possible.

TRY IT OUT   **Using the String Object**

In this example, you see a subsection of a string collected and turned into all uppercase letters. The full string (at the beginning of the example) holds the words "Learning about Built-in Objects is easy"; then the code just extracts the words "Built-in Objects" from the string, and finally it turns the selected part of the string into uppercase characters.

1. Create a skeleton HTML document, like so:

```
<!DOCTYPE html>
<html>
<head>
<title>String Object</title>
</head>
<body>
</body></html>
```

2. Add the <script> element and link to ch10_eg11.js.

3. Now open a new text file and add the following code

```
var myString = 'Learning about Built-in Objects is easy';
myString = myString.substring( 15, 31 );
```

```
myString = myString.toUpperCase();
document.body.innerHTML += "<h1>" + myString + "</h1>";
```

Now look at this a little closer. First, you need to create an instance of the String object, which is assigned to the variable myString:

```
var myString = 'Learning about Built-in Objects is easy';
```

As it has been created, the String object has been made to hold the words Learning about Built-in Objects is easy. But, the idea of this exercise is just to select the words "Built-in Objects" so that you use the substring() method to extract those words. The syntax follows:

```
substring( startPosition, endPosition )
```

So you select the String object (which is in the variable myString) and make its value the new substring you want (this is reassigning the value of the variable with the substring you want):

```
myString = myString.substring( 15, 32 );
```

This selects the string from the 16th character to the 33rd character—because it starts at position 0.

Next, you must convert the string to uppercase using the toUpperCase() method:

```
myString = myString.toUpperCase();
```

And finally you can write it to the document like so:

```
document.body.innerHTML += "<h1>" + myString + "</h1>";
```

4. Save this file as ch10_eg11.html and when you open it in the browser, you should see the text shown in Figure 10-6.

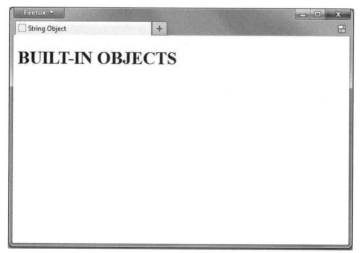

FIGURE 10-6

The result looks quite simple, but when you consider that the original string was `Learning about Built-in Objects is easy`, it now looks substantially different.

How It Works

Strings can be manipulated in several ways using the `index` of characters in the string. Although it might look like a long sentence, it can also be thought of as a collection of individual characters that you can access using their place in the order of the string.

Date

The `Date` object helps you work with dates and times. You create a new `Date` object using the date constructor like so:

```
new Date()
```

You can create a `Date` object set to a specific date or time, in which case you need to pass in one of four parameters:

➤ `milliseconds`: This value should be the number of milliseconds since 01/01/1970.

➤ `dateString`: Can be any date in a format recognized by the `parse()` method.

➤ `yr_num, mo_num, day_num`: Represents year, month, and day.

➤ `yr_num, mo_num, day_num, hr_num, min_num, seconds_num, ms_num`: Represents the years, days, hours, minutes, seconds, and milliseconds.

Here are some examples; the first uses `milliseconds` and reads `Mon Apr 06 1970 21:06:40 GMT-0400 (Eastern Daylight Time)`.

> **NOTE** *If you're working with the* `Date` *object, remember that all the* `Date` *object's workings are performed using Coordinated Universal Time (UTC), even though your computer may display a time consistent with your time zone.*

```
var birthDate = new Date( 8298400000 );
console.log( birthDate );
```

The second uses a `dateString` and reads `Wed Apr 16 1975 00:00:00 GMT-0400 (Eastern Daylight Time)`.

```
var birthDate = new Date("April 16, 1975");
console.log( birthDate );
```

The third uses `yr_num, mo_num,` and `day_num` and reads `Wed May 28 1975 00:00:00 GMT-0400 (Eastern Daylight Time)`.

```
var birthDate = new Date( 1975, 4, 28 );
console.log( birthDate );
```

There are a few things to watch out for:

➤ The first confusing thing you might notice here is that the number 4 corresponds to the month of May! That makes January 0. Similarly, when working with days, Sunday is treated as 0.

➤ You might find that you get different time zones. The author is based in Boston and runs on Eastern Time.

➤ Although you can add or subtract dates, your result ends up in milliseconds. For example, if you want to find out the number of days until the end of the year, you might use something like this:

```
var today = new Date();
var newYear = new Date( 2014,1,1 );
var daysRemaining = ( newYear - today );
console.log( daysRemaining );
```

The problem with this is that you end up with a result that is long. With 86,400,000 milliseconds in each day, you are likely to see a large figure.

So, you need to divide the `daysRemaining` by the number of milliseconds in the day (86400000) to find the number of days (ch10_eg12.html):

```
var today = new Date();
var newyear = new Date( 2014,1,1 );
var remDays = ( newyear - today );
remDays = remDays/86400000;
document.body.innerHTML += "days until the new year: "+
remDays.toLocaleString();
```

When you use the `Date` object, you need to keep in mind that a user's computer click may well be inaccurate and the fact that different users could be in various time zones.

Table 10-8 shows some commonly used methods of the `Date` object.

TABLE 10-8: Common Methods of the Date Object

METHOD	PURPOSE
date()	Returns a Date object.
getDate()	Returns the date of a Date object (from 1 to 31).
getDay()	Returns the day of a Date object (from 0 to 6; 0=Sunday, 1=Monday, and so on).
getMonth()	Returns the month of a Date object (from 0 to 11; 0=January, 1=February, and so on).
getFullYear()	Returns the year of a Date object (four digits).
getYear()	Returns the year of a Date object using only two digits (from 0 to 99).

continues

TABLE 10-8 *(continued)*

METHOD	PURPOSE
getHours()	Returns the hours of a Date object (from 0 to 23).
getMinutes()	Returns the minutes of a Date object (from 0 to 59).
getSeconds()	Returns the seconds of a Date object (from 0 to 59).
getTime()	Returns the number of milliseconds since midnight 1/1/1970.
getTimezoneOffset()	Returns the time difference between the user's computer and GMT.
now()	A shortcut for a common code pattern: var date = new Date(); date.getTime(); Date.now(). Returns the number of milliseconds since midnight 1/1/1970. Only available in modern browsers.
parse()	Returns a string date value that holds the number of milliseconds since January 01 1970 00:00:00.
setDate()	Sets the date of the month in the Date object (from 1 to 31).
setFullYear()	Sets the year in the Date object (four digits).
setHours()	Sets the hours in the Date object (from 0 to 23).
setMinutes()	Sets the minutes in the Date object (from 0 to 59).
setMonth()	Sets the months in the Date object (from 0 to 11; 0=January, 1=February).
setSeconds()	Sets the seconds in the Date object (from 0 to 59).
setTime()	Sets the milliseconds after 1/1/1970.
setYear()	Sets the year in the Date object (00 to 99).
toGMTString()	Converts the Date object to a string, set to GMT time zone.
toLocaleString()	Converts the Date object to a string, set to the current time zone of the user.
toString()	Converts the Date object to a string.

Many of the methods in Table 10-9 were then added offering support for the universal (UTC) time, which takes the format Day Month Date, hh,mm,ss UTC Year.

TABLE 10-9: UTC Methods of the Date Object

METHOD	PURPOSE
getUTCDate()	Returns the date of a Date object in universal (UTC) time.
getUTCDay()	Returns the day of a Date object in universal time.

getUTCMonth()	Returns the month of a Date object in universal time.
getUTCFullYear()	Returns the four-digit year of a Date object in universal time.
getUTCHours()	Returns the hour of a Date object in universal time.
getUTCMinutes()	Returns the minutes of a Date object in universal time.
getUTCSeconds()	Returns the seconds of a Date object in universal time.
getUTCMilliseconds()	Returns the milliseconds of a Date object in universal time.
setUTCDate()	Sets the date in the Date object in universal time (from 1 to 31).
setUTCDay()	Sets the day in the Date object in universal time (from 0 to 6; Sunday=0, Monday=1, and so on).
setUTCMonth()	Sets the month in the Date object in universal time (from 0 to 11; 0=January, 1=February).
setUTCFullYear()	Sets the year in the Date object in universal time (four digits).
setUTCHour()	Sets the hour in the Date object in universal time (from 0 to 23).
setUTCMinutes()	Sets the minutes in the Date object in universal time (from 0 to 59).
setUTCSeconds()	Sets the seconds in the Date object in universal time (from 0 to 59).
setUTCMilliseconds()	Sets the milliseconds in the Date object in universal time (from 0 to 999).

Math

The Math object helps in working with numbers. It has properties for mathematical constants and methods representing mathematical functions such as the tangent and sine functions.

For example, the following sets a variable called numberPI to hold the constant of pi and then write it to the log (ch10_eg13.html):

```
var numberPI = Math.PI;
console.log( numberPI );
```

The following example rounds pi to the nearest whole number (integer) and writes it to the log (also shown in ch10_eg13.html):

```
var numberPI = Math.PI;
numberPI = Math.round( numberPI );
console.log( numberPI );
```

Properties

Table 10-10 lists the properties of the Math object.

TABLE 10-10: Properties of the Math Object

PROPERTY	PURPOSE
E	Returns the base of a natural logarithm
LN2	Returns the natural logarithm of 2
LN10	Returns the natural logarithm of 10
LOG2E	Returns the base-2 logarithm of E
LOG10E	Returns the base-10 logarithm of E
PI	Returns pi
SQRT1_2	Returns 1 divided by the square root of 2
SQRT2	Returns the square root of 2

Methods

Table 10-11 lists the methods for the Math object.

TABLE 10-11: Methods of the Math Object

METHOD	PURPOSE
abs(x)	Returns the absolute value of x
acos(x)	Returns the arccosine of x
asin(x)	Returns the arcsine of x
atan(x)	Returns the arctangent of x
atan2(y,x)	Returns the angle from the x axis to a point
ceil(x)	Returns the nearest integer greater than or equal to x
cos(x)	Returns the cosine of x
exp(x)	Returns the value of E raised to the power of x
floor(x)	Returns the nearest integer less than or equal to x
log(x)	Returns the natural log of x
max(x,y)	Returns the number with the highest value of x and y
min(x,y)	Returns the number with the lowest value of x and y
pow(x,y)	Returns the value of the number x raised to the power of y

`random()`	Returns a random number between 0 and 1
`round(x)`	Rounds *x* to the nearest integer
`sin(x)`	Returns the sine of *x*
`sqrt(x)`	Returns the square root of *x*
`tan(x)`	Returns the tangent of *x*

Array

An *array* is like a special variable. It's special because it can hold more than one value, and these values can be accessed individually. Arrays are particularly helpful when you want to store a group of values in the same variable rather than having separate variables for each value. You may want to do this because all the values correspond to one particular item, or just for the convenience of having several values in the same variable rather than in differently named variables. Or it might be because you do not know how many items of information are going to be stored. (For example, you might store the items that would appear in a shopping basket in an array.) You often see arrays used with loops, where the loop is used to add information into an array or read it from the array.

You can use a *constructor* with an `Array` object, so you can create an array by either specifying the name of the array and how many values it will hold or by adding all the data straight into the array. For example, here is an array created with three items; it holds the names of musical instruments:

```
var instruments = new Array("guitar", "drums", "piano");
```

In addition, you can create an array using an *array literal*, which is a representation of the array on the right side of the assignment operator. For example, creating an empty array called `instruments` would look like this:

```
var instruments = [];
```

Re-creating the earlier example with the same initial values would look like this:

```
var instruments = ["guitar", "drums", "piano"];
```

Whichever version you use, you're still creating arrays, so it's a matter of preference which you use. As was the case with strings, most developers now use the slightly more compact literal syntax.

The items in the array can be referred to by a number that reflects the order in which they are stored in the array. The number is an index, so it begins at 0. For example, you can refer to the guitar as `instruments[0]`, the drums as `instruments[1]`, and so on.

An array does need to know how many items you want to store in it, but you do not need to provide values for each item in the array when it is created. You can just indicate how many items you want to store. (To confuse matters, this value does not start at 0 so it creates three elements, not four.)

```
var instruments = new Array(3);
```

This number is stored in the `length` property of the `Array` object, and the contents are not actually assigned yet. If you want to increase the size of an array, you can just assign a new value to the `length` property that is higher than the current length.

Here is an example that creates an array with five items and then checks how many items are in the array using the `length` property:

```
var fruit = ["apple", "banana", "orange", "mango", "lemon"];
console.log( fruit.length );
```

Here is an example of the `toString()` method, which converts the array to a string:

```
console.log( 'These are ' + fruit.toString() );
```

Keeping the related information in the one variable tends to be easier than having five variables, such as `fruit1`, `fruit2`, `fruit3`, `fruit4`, and `fruit5`. Using one array like this also takes up less memory than storing five separate variables, and in situations when you might have varying numbers of fruit, it allows the variable to grow and shrink in accordance with your requirements (rather than creating ten variables, one-half of which might be empty).

Table 10-12 lists the common methods of an array.

TABLE 10-12: Common Array Methods

METHOD	PURPOSE
`concat()`	Joins (or concatenates) two or more arrays to create one new one.
`join(separator)`	Joins all the elements of an array together separated by the character specified as a separator. (The default is a comma.)
`pop()`	Removes the last element of an array and then returns the element.
`push()`	Adds an element to an array and returns the new array length.
`reverse()`	Returns the array with items in reverse order.
`shift()`	Removes the first element from an array and returns the element.
`slice()`	Returns a selected part of the array (if you do not need it all).
`sort()`	Returns a sorted array, sorted by alphabetical or numerical order.
`splice( index, howMany, [elements])`	Returns a modified array. Modification starts at `index` and removes `howMany` elements from the array, replacing them with the `elements` provided as the third, fourth, fifth, etc. arguments.
`toString()`	Returns a string representing the array and its component elements.
`unshift()`	Adds one or more elements to the beginning of an array; returns the new length of an array.

Table 10-13 lists array methods that are only available in modern browsers such as Internet Explorer 9 and other modern browsers such as Google Chrome and Mozilla Firefox.

TABLE 10-13: New Array Methods

METHOD	PURPOSE
every()	every() accepts a function as an argument. That function tests every element in the array and returns true if all pass.
filter()	filter() accepts a function as an argument. That function tests every element in the array and returns a new array containing every element for which the filtering function returns true.
forEach()	Calls a function for each element in the array.
indexOf()	Returns the first index of an element within the array that matches the specified value. Returns -1 if no match is found.
lastIndexOf()	Returns the last index of an element within the array that matches the specified value. Returns -1 if no match is found.
map()	map() accepts a function as an argument that returns a new array based on the results of calling the function argument on every element in this array.
reduce()	reduce() calls a specified callback function for every element in an array starting with the leftmost element. Every function execution returns the accumulated result as an argument in the next call to the callback function. This allows you to *reduce* the array to a single value.
reduceRight()	reduceRight() calls a specified callback function for every element in an array, starting with the rightmost element. Every function execution returns the accumulated result as an argument in the next call to the callback function. This allows you to *reduce* the array to a single value.
some()	some() accepts a function as an argument. That function tests every element in the array and returns true if at least one element in the array returns true.

Window

Every browser window has a corresponding window object created with every instance of a `<body>` element.

For a simple example (ch10_eg14.html), you can access several pieces of information about the browser window using available properties of the window object. To do this, you need to add a function that is going to be triggered when the page loads, and then use this function to write some information about the innerHeight, innerWidth, and screen.colorDepth:

```
function windowObject(){
   document.body.innerHTML += "<p><b>innerHeight</b>: "+
window.innerHeight + "</p>";
   document.body.innerHTML += "<p><b>innerWidth</b>: "+
window.innerWidth + "</p>";

   document.body.innerHTML+= "<p><b>Color Depth</b>: "+
window.screen.colorDepth + "</p>";
}
```

You then call this function from the <body> element's onload event, like so:

```
document.body.onload = windowObject ;
```

Properties

Table 10-14 lists some common properties of the window object.

TABLE 10-14: Common Properties of the window Object

PROPERTY	PURPOSE
document	The document object contained in that window.
history	A history object that contains details and URLs visited from that window (mainly for use in creating back and forward buttons like those in the browser).
innerHeight	Represents the height of the content area of the browser window including any scrollbars.
innerWidth	Represents the width the content area of the browser including any scrollbars.
location	The location object; the URL of the current window.
name	The window's name.
opener	Contains a reference to the window that opened the current window.
screen	Contains a reference to the screen object. The screen object contains a wealth of information about the page including the height, width, color depth, and pixel depth.
top	A reference for the topmost browser window if several windows are open on the desktop.
window	The current window.

Methods

Table 10-15 lists common methods of the `window` object.

TABLE 10-15: Common Methods of the window Object

METHOD	PURPOSE
`alert()`	Displays an alert box containing a message and an OK button.
`back()`	Same effect as the browser's Back button.
`blur()`	Removes focus from the current window.
`close()`	Closes the current window or another window if a reference to another window is supplied.
`confirm()`	Brings up a dialog box asking users to confirm that they want to perform an action with either OK or Cancel as the options. They return `true` and `false`, respectively.
`focus()`	Gives focus to the specified window and brings it to the top of others.
`forward()`	Equivalent to clicking the browser's Forward button.
`home()`	Takes users to their browser's designated homepage.
`moveBy(horizontalPixels, verticalPixels)`	Moves the window by the specified number of pixels in relation to current coordinates.
`moveTo(Xposition, Yposition)`	Moves the top left of the window to the specified *x-y* coordinates.
`open(URL, name [,features])`	Opens a new browser window (this method is covered in more detail in the Chapter 11, "Working with jQuery").
`print()`	Prints the content of the current window (or brings up the browser's print dialog).
`prompt()`	Creates a dialog box for the user to enter an input.
`stop()`	Same effect as clicking the Stop button in the browser.

WRITING JAVASCRIPT

You need to be aware of a few points when you start writing JavaScript:

> JavaScript is case-sensitive, so a variable called `myVariable` is different from a variable called `MYVARIABLE`, and both are different from a variable called `myvariable`.

➤ When you see symbols such as (, {, [, ", and ' they must have a closing symbol to match: ', ",], }, and). (Note how the first bracket opened is the last one to be closed, which is why the closing symbols are in reverse order here.)

➤ Like HTML, JavaScript ignores extra spaces, so you can add white space to your script to make it more readable. The following two lines are equivalent, even though there are more spaces in the second line:

```
myVariable="some value";
myVariable = "some value";
```

➤ If you have a large string, you can break it up with a backslash, as you can see here:

```
console.log("My first \
  JavaScript example")
```

➤ But you must not break anything other than strings, so this would be wrong:

```
console.log \
  ("My first JavaScript example")
```

➤ You can insert special characters such as ", ', ;, and &, which are otherwise reserved (because they have a special meaning in JavaScript), by using a backslash before them like so:

```
console.log("I want to use a \"quote\" mark \& an ampersand.")
```

This writes out the following line to the log:

```
I want to use a "quote" mark & an ampersand.
```

A Word about Data Types

By now you should get the idea that you can do different things with different types of data. For example, you can add numbers together, but you cannot mathematically add the letter *A* to the letter *B*. Some forms of data require that you deal with numbers that have decimal places (floating point numbers); currency is a common example. Other types of data have inherent limitations; for example, if you deal with dates and time, you want to add hours to certain types of data without getting 25:30 as a time. (Even though you might often wish you could add more hours to a day.)

Different types of data (letters, whole numbers, decimal numbers, and dates) are known to have different *data types*; these allow programs to manage the different types of data in different ways. For example, if you use the + operator with a string, it concatenates two strings, whereas if it is used with numbers, it adds the two numbers together. Some programming languages require that you specifically indicate what type of data a variable is going to hold and require you to convert between types. Although JavaScript supports different data types, as you are about to see, it handles conversion between types, so you don't need to worry about telling JavaScript that a certain type of data is a date or a string (a string being a set of characters that may include letters and numbers).

There are three simple data types in JavaScript:

➤ **Number:** Used to perform arithmetic operations (addition, subtraction, multiplication, and division). Any whole number or decimal number that does not appear between quotation marks is considered a number.

➤ **String:** Used to handle text. It is a set of characters (including numbers, spaces, and punctuation) enclosed by quotation marks.

➤ **Boolean:** A boolean value has only two possible values: `true` and `false`. This data enables you to perform logical operations and check whether something is true or false.

You may also come across two other data types:

➤ **Null:** Indicates that a value does not exist. This is written using the keyword `null`. This is an important value because it explicitly states that no value has been given. This can mean a different thing from a string that just contains a space or a zero.

➤ **Undefined:** Indicates a situation in which the value has not been defined previously in code and uses the JavaScript keyword `undefined`. You might remember that if you declare a variable but do not give it a value, the variable is said to be undefined. (You are particularly likely to see this when something is not right in your code.)

Now that you've learned about types, it's time to look at the two comparison operators mentioned earlier. These two *identity operators* are similar to the `==` and `!=` *equality operators* that you learned about before, except that they test for the same value **and** type when doing a comparison.

Why does this matter? JavaScript is sloppy when it comes to comparisons. When you use the equality operators, the JavaScript engine does what's called a type conversion on the values to convert them to the same type and then does a comparison. So if either value is a number or a boolean, the operands are converted to numbers, and if either value is a string, both are converted to strings if possible. This means that the following would both log `true`:

```
console.log(1 == "1");
console.log(1 == true);
```

As you can see, that might cause problems. To get around this issue you can use the identity operators that test for both type and value and don't do any type conversions. The following now resolve to `false`:

```
console.log(1 === "1");
console.log(1 === true);
```

Keywords

You may have noticed that there are several keywords in JavaScript that perform functions, such as `break`, `for`, `if`, and `while`, all of which have special meaning. Therefore, these words should not be used in variable, function, method, or object names. The following is a list of the keywords that you should avoid using. (Some of these are not actually used yet but are reserved for future use.)

```
abstract boolean break byte case catch char class const
continue default do double else extends false final
finally float for function goto if implements import
in instanceof int interface long native new null
package private protected public return short static
super switch synchronized this throw throws transient
true try var void while with
```

SUMMARY

This chapter introduced you to many new concepts: objects, methods, properties, events, arrays, functions, interfaces, object models, data types, and keywords. Although it's a lot to take in all at once, after you look at some of the examples in the next two chapters, it should be a lot clearer. After reading those chapters and working through jQuery, you can read through this chapter again, and you should understand more examples of what can be achieved with JavaScript.

You started off by looking at how you can access information from a document using the Document Object Model. When you know how to get information from a document, you can use JavaScript to perform calculations upon the data in the document. JavaScript mainly performs calculations using features such as the following:

➤ **Variables:** Store information in memory

➤ **Operators:** Such as arithmetic and comparison operators

➤ **Functions:** Live in the `<head>` of a document and contain code called by an event

➤ **Conditional statements:** Handle choices of actions based on different circumstances

➤ **Loops:** Repeat statements until a condition has been met

As you see in Chapter 11, "Working with JQuery," and Chapter 12, "jQuery: Beyond the Basics," these simple concepts can be brought together to create powerful results. Using jQuery for a variety of tasks, you can see some advanced JavaScript, and you will have a good idea of how basic building blocks can create complex structures.

Finally, you looked at a number of other objects made available through JavaScript; you met the `String`, `Date`, `Math`, `Array`, and `window` objects. Each object contains related functionality; each has properties that tell you about the object (such as the date, time, size of window, or length of string), and methods that allow you to do things with this data stored in the object.

You should be starting to get a grasp of how JavaScript can help you add interactivity to your pages, and you see how it does this in the next chapter when you delve into examples of JavaScript libraries and look at examples that can help you make use of JavaScript.

EXERCISES

1. Create a script to write out the multiplication table for the number 5 from 1 to 20 using a `while` loop.

2. Modify `ch10_eg05.js` so that it can say one of three things:

   ➤ "Good Morning" to visitors coming to the page before 12 p.m. (using an `if` statement).

   ➤ "Good Afternoon" to visitors coming to the page between 12 p.m. and 6 p.m. (again using an `if` statement). (Hint: You might need to use a logical operator.)

   ➤ "Good Evening" to visitors coming to the page after 6 p.m. up until midnight (again using an `if` statement).

The answers to all the exercises are in Appendix A, "Answers to Exercises."

▶ WHAT YOU LEARNED IN THIS CHAPTER

TOPIC	KEY TAKEAWAY
JavaScript	JavaScript is not Java. JavaScript is the programming language that adds interactivity to the web.
DOM	The DOM enables you to access objects, properties, and methods of the HTML document.
Programming basics	Variables hold references to other data. Operators work with variables. Functions contain multiple JavaScript statements to run together. Conditional statements enable you to test your data. Loops enable you to work on collections of data.
Built-in objects	JavaScript has many built-in objects that enable you to work with dates, math, and strings as well as special collections of data in arrays.

11

Working with jQuery

WHAT YOU WILL LEARN IN THIS CHAPTER

➤   What is jQuery and why you should use it

➤   How to get jQuery to use on your pages

➤   How jQuery helps you work with the DOM

➤   Event handling made easy with jQuery

WROX.COM CODE DOWNLOADS FOR THIS CHAPTER

You can find the wrox.com code downloads for this chapter at `www.wrox.com/remtitle .cgi?isbn=9781118340189` on the Download Code tab. The code is in the Chapter 11 download and individually named according to the names throughout the chapter.

There are many collections of JavaScript code available, called libraries or frameworks, to help you make JavaScript applications. These libraries collect utilities and common features together to make you more efficient when coding JavaScript. jQuery is by far the most popular library in the world for working with JavaScript.

jQuery, released in 2006, offers several advantages over writing your own custom JavaScript:

➤   It provides a concise, friendly, human-readable interface to use JavaScript more efficiently.

➤   It smooths over the differences in the implementation of JavaScript in the different web browsers. As you've learned throughout this book, some browsers implement web standards differently. This is *especially* true with older versions of Internet Explorer and the JavaScript programming language.

➤   There is an incredible community full of tutorials, articles, and free code called plug-ins, which can help you get up and running with jQuery.

This chapter and the next chapter focus on introducing the basics of jQuery so that you can start to take advantage of some of these resources in your own web pages. If you can master the basics presented here and can wrap your head around the fundamentals of JavaScript presented in Chapter 10, "Learning JavaScript," the true power of the web can be in your hands.

WHY JQUERY?

As mentioned, jQuery is the most popular JavaScript library on the web. According to BuiltWith.com, a site that tracks technology trends, jQuery is in use on more than 59 percent of the top 10,000 sites on the Internet (http://trends.builtwith.com/javascript). Popularity alone doesn't make something good, however, so the question remains, why should you use jQuery?

For many people, especially those just starting with programming, the most important reason to use jQuery is that jQuery is *fun*. jQuery is powerful and is written in a style that reads like plain English, so it's easier for novice programmers to understand. For example, the following code is valid jQuery:

```
$( "#fluent" ).hide( "slow" ).addClass( "fun" ).show( "fast" );
```

Can you guess what it does? The first part, `$("#fluent")`, might be confusing, but hopefully the rest should make some sense:

➤   The `hide()` method *hides* something.

➤   The `addClass()` method *adds* a CSS *class*.

➤   The `show()` method *shows* something.

You'll learn more about the specifics of how these methods work over the next couple of chapters, but for now just know that as often as possible, jQuery reads just like plain English—at least as much like plain English as a programming language can read.

In addition to being fun, jQuery is also at the center of a vast collection of tutorials, sample code, and plug-ins that make it much easier to make websites. Although some other libraries might be more elegant or more powerful, jQuery's popularity ensures that it is well served in terms of the ecosystem surrounding the library. When you choose jQuery, you're not just choosing a library; you're choosing a vibrant community that's there to help with tutorials, advice, and examples.

Now that you have a taste of *why* you might want to use jQuery, now jump into the *how*. First up is getting jQuery into your pages.

ADDING JQUERY TO YOUR PAGE

The most basic way to get jQuery is to go to www.jquery.com and download the library to your computer. Just accept the default choices in the download form, and click the Download link. Figure 11-1 shows the link on the homepage of the site.

FIGURE 11-1

Save the file to your site. Like you've learned to organize your CSS in a separate folder, it can be helpful to save your JavaScript in a separate folder as well. You can save it to a folder named js. To start using jQuery, all you must do is include it in your page, like any other script (ch11_eg01.html):

```
<script src="js/jquery-1.8.2.min.js"></script>
```

Unless it needs to be in the <head> for some reason (Modernizr is the most common example of a script that needs to be in the <head>), for top performance, JavaScript should be included right before the closing </body> tag. This is as true of jQuery as it is of every other script. The examples throughout this chapter will place jQuery there.

A common alternative to downloading and hosting jQuery is to use a public version served by a Content Delivery Network (CDN). CDNs are fast servers spread around the world and designed to serve files as fast as possible no matter where in the world someone might be. Although the Internet seems immediate and the world seems tightly connected, there is a little bit of a lag when people try to get files from halfway around the world, so using a CDN can sometimes speed up things for your users. This is especially true if you have a global audience. Large companies (such as Google and Microsoft) interested in a fast Internet offer versions of jQuery hosted, for free, on their respective CDNs. This can have a performance benefit for your site. It's also convenient because you can get up and running with jQuery just by linking to the CDN-hosted version—no download required. To do so, simply link to the version on the CDN using the URL provided by the service. To use Google's CDN, for example, simply browse to the Google Hosted Libraries page (https://developers.google.com/speed/libraries/devguide#jquery) and link to the URL provided (ch11_eg02.html):

```
<script
  src="http://ajax.googleapis.com/ajax/libs/jquery/1.8.2/jquery.min.js">
</script>
```

To ensure that you can test your code whether or not you're connected to the Internet, all the remaining jQuery samples in this book link to a local file. You should use the CDN option when you're ready to build out your site and publish it to the web.

JQUERY BASICS

Now that you have a copy of jQuery loaded into your page, it's time to start jQuery programming. This section introduces you to two of the most fundamental parts of the library: the `jQuery` or `$` function and the `$( document ).ready()` event.

Introducing the $ Function

At the heart of every jQuery operation is the `jQuery` object. Everything you do with the library starts there.

You can access this function with two different names: `jQuery` or as the more famous alias `$`. In the context of programming with jQuery, they're equivalent. The rest of the text refers to `$` exclusively.

`$` is used in two different ways. Called as a function, `$()`, it enables you to access, create, and manipulate HTML elements. `$` also enables you to access additional methods and properties of jQuery. You learn more about this second option in Chapter 12, "jQuery: Beyond the Basics," when you learn about `$.ajax()`. For now, focus on the first option.

In its most basic usage, `$()` accepts a string representing a CSS selector and returns the HTML element or elements that match the selector. You can then perform additional operations on the results. Now look at the HTML for this example (`ch11_eg03.html`), which is simple. It's an `<h1>` element with an `id` of "greeting." Notice that there's no actual greeting; it's an empty element.

```
<h1 id="greeting"></h1>
```

Using jQuery (`ch11_eg03.js`) you can quickly add some text to the element. There are two parts to this code. The first is the call to `$()`. Remember the method `document.getElementById()`? This works the same way except the argument includes the same # character that you would use to indicate an `id` in a CSS selector. You learn more about how to use CSS selectors with jQuery in the section "jQuery and the DOM." For now, just understand that you have a reference to the `<h1>` element with the `id` `#greeting`. Because you got that element with `$()`, the reference is empowered with all that jQuery has to offer. In this example you just use the method `$().text()`, which as you might have guessed enables you to set the *text* of an HTML element.

```
$( "#greeting" ).text( "It's time to learn about jQuery" );
```

Chaining

In the first example of jQuery, the one line of code did several different things. This capability to do many things in one line is one of the most powerful features of jQuery. When you get a reference to an element using jQuery, jQuery almost always returns that element when it performs an action. This means you can string multiple commands together on one line. This is an efficient and fun way to code. You'll see many examples of chaining throughout this chapter and the next chapter.

Start Your Scripts the Smart Way with $(document).ready()

When you make web pages, there are times when you want your JavaScript to manipulate the page based on some data you received from the server or because of something interesting about the user's browser or screen. You want this to happen as soon as the browser has read the page's HTML. This means that the DOM is loaded into the browser and there's no chance that you could try to change an element that the browser doesn't know about yet. The W3C DOM offers a method to do this with the DOMContentLoaded event, but, as with many things on the web, older versions of Internet Explorer didn't support it until version 9. Because of that, jQuery offers a method called $(document).ready(), which enables you to run code as soon as the document/DOM is "ready." Rewriting the previous example to use $(document).ready() looks like this (ch11_eg04.js):

```
$( document ).ready( function() {
 $( "#greeting" ).text( "It's time to learn about jQuery" );
});
```

The important difference is that the code you want to run is wrapped in an anonymous function. This means that any statements you want to run are encapsulated in the anonymous function, and they will be executed when the $(document).ready() event fires. If you didn't do that and instead did something like the following, directly placing the jQuery statement inside the $(document).ready() call, the code would execute immediately and wouldn't be saved for when the DOM is loaded.

```
$( document ).ready(
 $( "#greeting" ).text( "It's time to learn about jQuery" )
);
```

Now that you've learned about two of the most fundamental pieces of jQuery, it's time to look in more depth at what it can offer.

JQUERY AND THE DOM

One of jQuery's great strengths is the way it can easily access and manipulate HTML elements. When you have a strong foundation in the way jQuery works, you can easily add dynamic elements to your pages.

Selecting Elements with jQuery

The most common usages of jQuery start with selecting an element or collection of elements using $() and a CSS selector. The following code sample (ch11_eg05.js) shows this in action with three uses of $(), selecting elements by: class name, id/class name/element, and an attribute-equals selector. After the selection is made the $().css() method is used to change some CSS attributes. Notice that multiple elements are changed when using the class-based selector. That's because jQuery automatically changes every element in the matched set.

```
$( document ).ready( function(){
 $( ".item" ).css( "color" , "blue" );
 $( "#menu .item p").css("color" , "red");
 $( "input[type=email]").css( "border" , "10px solid blue" );
});
```

Paired with the following markup (ch11_eg05.html), this code produces the result shown in Figure 11-2:

```html
<ul id="menu">
  <li class="item"><p>This is a paragraph</p></li>
  <li class="item">No paragraph here</li>
  <li class="item">No paragraph here</li>
  <li class="item">No paragraph here</li>
</ul>
<p>
  <label for="email">Email: <input type="email" id="email"></label>
</p>
<p>
  <label for="text">Plain Text: <input type="text" id="text"></label>
</p>
```

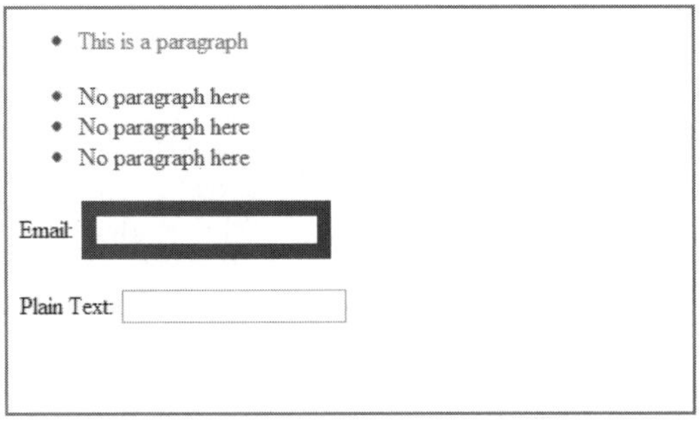

FIGURE 11-2

jQuery supports all the selectors you've learned about so far and several selectors that are new extensions added by jQuery. Table 11-1 lists the jQuery extensions to CSS3.

TABLE 11-1: jQuery Selector Extensions

SELECTOR	DESCRIPTION	EXAMPLE
:animated	Selects all elements in the middle of a jQuery animation	$("p:animated")
Attribute Not Equal Selector	Performs an inverse selection based on the attribute value	$("input[type!='email']")
:eq() Selector	Selects the element at a specific index within the returned collection	$("li:eq(2)")
:even Selector	Selects even elements	$("tr:even")
:first Selector	Selects the first matched element	$("tr:first")
:gt() Selector	Selects all elements greater than a specific index within the returned collection	$("li:gt(2)")

`:has()` Selector	A filter that selects elements, which contain at least one element that matches the specified selector	`$( "div:has(p)" )`
`:header` Selector	Selects all headers	`$( ":header" )`
`:hidden` Selector	Selects all hidden elements	`$( "p:hidden" )`
`:last` Selector	Selects the last matched element	`$( "tr:last" )`
`:lt()` Selector	Selects all elements less than a specific index within the returned collection	`$( "li:lt(2)" )`
`:odd` Selector	Selects all odd elements	`$( "tr:odd" )`
`:parent` Selector	Selects all elements that are the parent of another element	`$( "p:parent" )`
`:selected` Selector	Selects all selected elements	`$( "option:selected" )`
`:visible` Selector	Selects all visible elements	`$( "p:visible" )`

Creating and Adding Elements

In addition to selecting elements, the `$()` function enables you to *create* elements on the fly. This enables you to create elements based on data from a server or user interaction, manipulate them, and then eventually insert them into the DOM. Rewriting the "Good Morning"/"Good Afternoon" example from Chapter 10 illustrates this. The markup, again, is simple—just a single `<div>` element (ch11_eg06.html):

```
<div id="container">
</div>
```

The JavaScript (ch11_eg06.js) is similar to the example from Chapter 10 but does a little bit more because of the power of jQuery. It starts off the same way—by creating a new `Date` object and getting the hours. After that an empty variable `elem` is created. `elem` is then defined depending on the time of day. That's where things get interesting.

First, an `<h1>` element is created by passing the string "`<h1>`" to `$()`. At this point jQuery has reference to a generic `<h1>` element and can perform any of the jQuery methods on it. In this example, the proper greeting is added using `$().text()`. Then, an id attribute added using the method `$.attr()`. `$.attr()` takes two arguments in this form: the `attribute` to set and the attribute's `value`. Finally, the `$.hide()` method is used to hide the text so that you can show it later. You learn even more about using `$().show()`, `$().hide()`, and other effects and animations later in the section "Basic Animations and Effects."

After the element is created, the `elem` variable is added to the container element using the `$().append()` method. `$().append()`, not surprisingly, *appends* a new element to the selected element.

Finally, the `#greeting` element, which is now in the document, is shown with a little animation provided by `$().show()`.

```
$( document ).ready( function(){
  var date = new Date();
  var time = date.getHours();
  var elem;

  if ( time < 12 ) {
    elem = $( "<h1>" )
      .text( "Good Morning" )
      .attr( "id","greeting" )
      .hide();
  }
  else {
    elem = $( "<h1>" )
      .text( "Good Afternoon" )
      .attr( "id","greeting" )
      .hide();
  }
  $( "#container" ).append( elem );
  $( "#greeting").show( "slow" );
});
```

jQuery is flexible. One such example of its flexibility is an alternative method to create the `<h1>` in the previous example. Instead of creating an empty `<h1>` and then using `$().text()` to populate it with text, you can do something like this (ch11_eg07.js), where you pass a string of valid HTML, complete with the text into `$()`:

```
if ( time < 12 ) {
  elem = $( "<h1>Good Morning</h1>" )
    .attr( "id","greeting" ).hide();
}
```

Or you could even do something like this where you embed the `id` directly in the string, skipping both `$().text()` and `$().attr()` (ch11_eg08.js).

```
if ( time < 12 ) {
  elem = $( "<h1 id='greeting'>Good Morning</h1>" ).hide();
}
```

Because you're just starting with jQuery, you should pick one style and stick with it. And because it can teach you the various methods available with jQuery, sticking to the first style can teach you the most about the library. Also, it will probably be clearer to anyone else who might work on your code.

Now that you've learned the basics to select and create elements with jQuery, it's time to learn more about how to manipulate them. You've seen some examples already with methods such as `$().attr()`,

`$().text()`, and `$().css()`. The next section looks at those and some other common methods in a little bit more depth.

Manipulating Elements with jQuery

As you've seen, jQuery makes it easy to select and create HTML elements. You've also had a glimpse at how easy it is to manipulate them using the many powerful methods jQuery offers. This section introduces you to some of these methods.

Manage CSS Classes with $().addClass(), $().removeClass(), $().hasClass(), and $().toggleClass()

Manipulating CSS classes is a common task when building websites or applications. You often need to change the style of an element based on a user interaction (when validating a form, for example,) data from a server or other changes in the application state. Although you can change CSS properties on the HTML element using JavaScript, it's generally better to continue to keep style information in your CSS files. Testing, adding, and removing classes enable you to create dynamic pages while still preserving the ability to manage the look and feel with CSS. Four methods deal with CSS classes provided by jQuery: `$().addClass()`, `$().removeClass()`, `$().hasClass()`, and `$().toggleClass()`. All four methods accept a string representing the class or classes to be targeted by the methods. These can be individual classes or a space-separated list of multiple classes.

`$().addClass()` adds a class or classes to an element or collection of elements. `$().removeClass()` removes a class or classes from an element or collection of elements. `$().hasClass()` tests for the presence of a class or classes on an element. `$().toggleClass()` toggles a class on or off without the program keeping track of its current state.

The following code sample (`ch11_eg09.html`) shows `$().addClass()` in action. The JavaScript (`ch11_eg09.js`) adds a class of "selected" to the "home" menu item. This would be a typical action on the homepage of a website, where a button might need to be *selected*, indicating the place in the site.

```
$( document ).ready( function(){
  $( "#home" ).addClass( "selected" );
});
```

With the following CSS (`ch11_eg09.css`) in place, the end result looks like Figure 11-3:

```
.item {
  list-style-type : none;
  width : 200px;
  height : 25px;
  background : #ccc;
  padding : 2px;
}
.selected {
  background : #666;
  color : #fff;
}
```

FIGURE 11-3

The following code sample (ch11_eg10.js) uses $().hasClass() and $().removeClass() to test for the presence of the "selected" class on an element and removes it if the class is on the element. $().hasClass returns true or false depending on the result of the test, so it's perfect to use with if statements.

```
$( document ).ready( function(){
  if ( $( "#home" ).hasClass( "selected" ) ){
    $( "#home" ).removeClass( "selected" );
  }
});
```

> **NOTE** Because $().hasClass() returns a boolean value, it's one of the jQuery methods that doesn't enable chaining. Several other methods don't allow for chaining. All of them either return a boolean value or return some metric or value (like an element's width, height, or text content) based on the element's properties.

$().toggleClass() is a helpful method that adds logic on top of the functionality provided by $().addClass() and $().removeClass(). With $().toggleClass(), you don't need to test whether a class is present on an element. You just need to tell jQuery to "toggle," and it will take care of everything, turning on or off the element as needed.

The following code sample (ch11_eg11.js) shows a common use of $().toggleClass(), switching menu items from "selected" to the default state. This code sample also briefly introduces event handling in jQuery. You learn more about it in the "Managing Events With jQuery" section. For now just note the similarities to the way you set events in Chapter 10. You have an object reference, and on *click* you run a function.

```
$( document ).ready( function(){
  $( "#home" ).on( "click", function(){
    $( "#home" ).toggleClass( "selected" );
  });
});
```

Get or Set Attributes with $().attr()

You've already seen $().attr() used in an example, setting the id attribute of an element. That's the basic usage, passing in two arguments: The first is the attribute to set, and the second is the value of the attribute. There are two additional features of $().attr() you should know about.

The first is the capability of $() .attr() to *get* values, in addition to set them. The second is the capability to set multiple attributes at once using a plain JavaScript object as a *map* containing a series of attributes and values.

The following code sample (ch11_eg12.js) shows these two uses of $() .attr(), first setting multiple values (id, rel, href, and title) and then getting the value of title to set the text of a newly created element. In the first call to $() .attr(), see how the attribute/value pairs are inside a set of brackets {}, separated by commas and paired using a colon. This is an *object literal*, just like the array literal you learned about in Chapter 10. Because they allow you to set many options at once, they're a common option for arguments in jQuery.

```
$( document ).ready( function(){
  var newLI;
  $( "#contact a" ).attr({
    "href" : "http://htmlcssjavascript.com/",
    "title" : "Visit Rob's blog about web technology",
    "rel" : "me",
    "id" : "htmlcssjavascript"
  });
  newLI = $("<li>").text( $( "#contact a" ).attr("title") );
  $( "ul").append( newLI );
});
```

With the following markup (ch11_eg12.html) the previous jQuery code produces the output shown in Figure 11-4:

```
<ul>
  <li id="contact"><a>Rob Larsen</a></li>
</ul>
```

FIGURE 11-4

Get or Set CSS Properties with $().css()

You've already seen $() .css() in action setting individual elements using two arguments: the name of the property to set and the value of the property. Like $() .attr(), $() .css() also enables you to retrieve values of CSS properties and enables you to set multiple CSS properties using an object literal as a map. The following code sample (ch11_eg13.js) shows both of these in action, setting several CSS properties (font-size, color, height, width, background color, and border) of an <h1> element. Then the script reads back the new border property and writes it into a <span> element.

```
$( document ).ready( function(){
  $( "h1" ).css({
    "font-size" : "200%",
```

```
        "color" : "#ffffff",
        "height" : "100px",
        "width" : "500px",
        "background-color" : "#61b7ff",
        "border" : "10px solid #003366"
    });
    $( "#result" ).text( $( "h1" ).css ( "border" ) );
});
```

> **NOTE** Because of the way that JavaScript interprets the "-" character, any CSS
> property that contains a dash needs to be within quotation marks when using
> the $().css() method along with an object map. The quotation marks for the
> property names are actually not required because JavaScript object labels can
> be unquoted, but because of this quirk, it's better to simply quote them all the
> time. You can also use an alternative written in Camel Case, which uses internal
> capital letters at the word boundaries. For example, font-size would change to
> fontSize. Still, it's nicer and causes less confusion to match the CSS properties
> directly across JavaScript and CSS, so the quoted options are the way to go.

With the following markup (ch11_eg13.html) the page would look like Figure 11-5:

```
<h1>Beginning HTML and CSS</h1>
<p><strong>The border property is:</strong> <span id="result"></span></p>
```

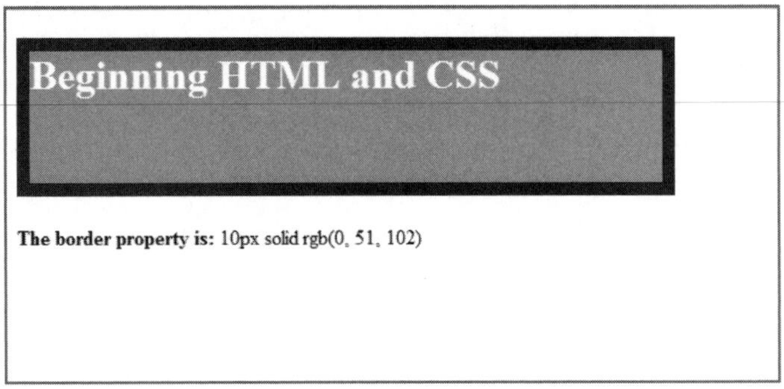

Beginning HTML and CSS

The border property is: 10px solid rgb(0, 51, 102)

FIGURE 11-5

Get or Set the HTML of an Element with $().html()

$().html() is similar to the .innerHTML property you learned about in Chapter 10. This method
enables you to get or set the HTML content of an HTML element. This is a useful method that
enables you to quickly and dynamically create or adjust the contents of an HTML element. The
following code sample (ch11_eg14.js) shows $().html() in action, building up a string that rep-
resents a <ul> element and then inserting it into the document using $().html().

```
$( document ).ready( function(){
    var methods = [ "attr()", "css()", "html()", "addClass()",
        "removeClass()", "hasClass()", "toggleClass()"  ];
```

```
    var list = "";
    for ( var i = 0, len = methods.length; i < len; i++ ){
      list += "<li>" + methods[ i ] +"</li>";
    }
    $( "#methods" ).html( list );
  });
```

Paired with the following markup (ch11_eg14.html) the page looks like Figure 11-6.

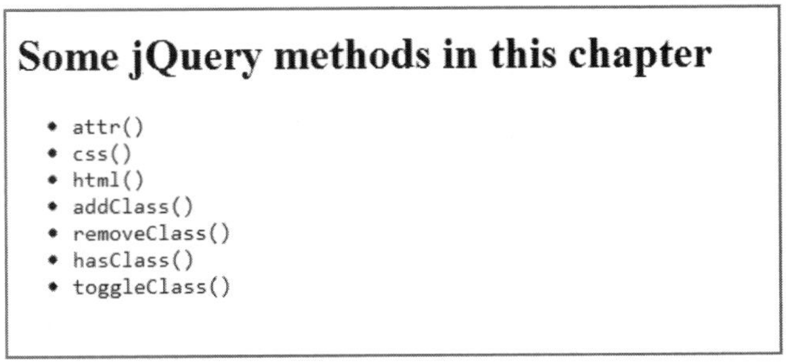

Some jQuery methods in this chapter

- attr()
- css()
- html()
- addClass()
- removeClass()
- hasClass()
- toggleClass()

FIGURE 11-6

You'll often use a pattern like this, looping through a collection and building out HTML, when working with Ajax. You learn more about Ajax in the next chapter.

Basic Animations and Effects

One of the nicest things about jQuery is the easy access it provides to common effects used on web pages. jQuery's animation capabilities are quite deep. This section introduces just a couple of the more common effects and animations so that you can start experimenting with them. If you're excited by the power of jQuery animations and effects, the jQuery documentation is a good place to start learning about all they have to offer (http://api.jquery.com/category/effects/).

Show and Hide Elements with $().show(), $().hide(), and $().toggle()

These methods control the visibility of HTML elements. You've already seen $().show() and $().hide() in action, but there are options available with each method that haven't been covered. You look at those in detail here. You also learn that $().toggle() is a convenience method like $().toggleClass(), which enables you to toggle the visibility of elements without tracking their current state.

In the examples you've seen of $().show() and $().hide(), there's been a keyword argument: "slow." That keyword indicates to jQuery that the element should *slowly* turn on or off, taking 600 ms. There's also a "fast" keyword, which takes 200 ms to perform the animation. There are other options. For example, if $().show() or $().hide() are called without an argument, the element is immediately made visible or invisible. In addition, these methods take a numeric argument, in milliseconds, which is how long the animation should take.

In detail, when "fast" or "slow" or a millisecond argument is used, jQuery animates the width, height, and opacity of the element simultaneously.

The following code illustrates (ch11_eg15.js) all these options in action, with three <div> elements shown using the slow and millisecond arguments. Then a click event is attached to a <button> element, which uses the $().toggle method to show and hide a <div> element.

```
$( document ).ready( function(){
  $( "#slow" ).show( "slow" );
  $( "#fast" ).show( "fast" );
  $( "#ms" ).show( 1500 );
  $( "#toggle" ).on( "click" , function(){
    $( "#toggled" ).toggle();
  });
});
```

Starting with all the <div> elements set to display : none, animation goes through the steps shown in Figure 11-7.

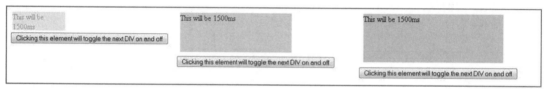

FIGURE 11-7

Animate Opacity with $().fadeIn(), $().fadeOut(), and $().fadeToggle()

Where $().show() and $().hide() in animation mode show several properties at once, this collection of methods operates only on the elements' opacity. These methods also take the "fast" and "slow" keywords and the millisecond arguments. Because these methods *always* animate, there is a default animation timing of 400 ms. Rewriting the previous example to use the fade methods (ch11_eg16.js) looks something like this:

```
$( document ).ready( function(){
  $( "#slow" ).fadeIn( "slow" );
  $( "#fast" ).fadeIn( "fast" );
  $( "#ms" ).fadeIn( 1500 );
  $( "#toggle" ).on( "click" , function(){
    $( "#toggled" ).fadeToggle();
  });
});
```

Starting with all the <div> elements set to visibility : hidden, the animation goes through the steps shown in Figure 11-8.

Create a Sliding Doors Effect with $().slideUp(), $().slideDown(), and $().slideToggle()

This suite of methods animates against the height of an element. $().slideDown() animates from zero height to full element height. $().slideUp() animates from full element height to zero height. $().slideToggle() behaves like all the other toggle methods you've met, toggling the element up and down without you needing to track the current state.

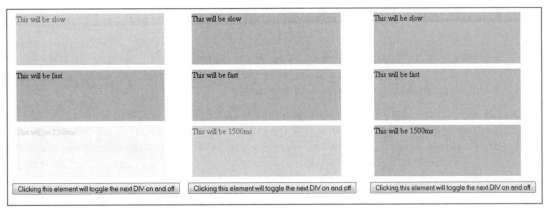

FIGURE 11-8

The following code sample (`ch11_eg17.js`) binds a click event to all the `<dt>` elements in a definition list (`ch11_eg17.html`), which slides down the associated `<dd>` element using the `$().toggle()` method. There are two new wrinkles to the `click` function. The first is the user of the `this` keyword. The `this` keyword can be a complicated subject in JavaScript. For now you should focus on the most basic usage shown here. Inside the body of a function bound to an HTML element, `this` refers to the bound HTML element. So, in this case it would refer to whatever `<dt>` you just clicked. This is a vital feature because it gives you some context to work with when dealing with JavaScript events.

Passing `this` into jQuery loads jQuery with a reference to that element, which means you can use all jQuery's features on the element. You learn more about this in the next section on jQuery events. The second new wrinkle is the method `$().next()`, which returns the next HTML element in the DOM. In this case that works out to be the associated `<dd>`.

```
$( document ).ready( function(){
  $( "dt" ).on( "click" , function(){
    $( this ).next().slideToggle();
  })
});
```

Like the other animation methods, the slide methods also take the "fast" and "slow" keywords and a millisecond argument.

MANAGING EVENTS WITH JQUERY

You learned about basic JavaScript events in Chapter 10 and have seen several examples of binding click events in this chapter. This section expands your knowledge of jQuery's ways of handling events and introduces you to the many events you can use in jQuery. It also points out some old ways that jQuery used to handle events—just in case you see some of these options in legacy code.

As with everything in these sections, this examination of jQuery events is designed to be just enough to get you up and running. As with everything else in the JavaScript chapters in this book, there's always going to be more to explore. The jQuery documentation on events is full of solid examples and paints a complete picture of all of the options available (`http://api.jquery.com/category/events/`).

Bind Events with $().on() and $().off()

jQuery has two main methods to manage events: `$().on()` and `$().off()`. You've already seen `$().on()` in action. In its most basic form, it accepts two arguments: the event to listen for (such as "click" and "submit") and a function to fire when the event occurs. `$().off()`, which you haven't seen, reverses the process, removing events from elements.

The following code sample (`ch11_eg18.js`) shows both of these in action. This example rewrites the slide animation suite example. It adds a `<button>` element that expands all the `<dd>` elements. `$().off()` is then used to make sure the button doesn't try to expand the already expanded elements. The expansion is performed using another new method: `$().trigger()`, which is useful. It manually fires events on elements. It takes a string argument representing the event to be fired.

```
$( document ).ready( function(){
  function toggler(){
    $( this ).next().slideToggle();
  }
  $( "button" ).on( "click" , function(){
    $( "dt" ).trigger( "click" ).off( "click" , toggler );
  });
  $( "dt" ).on( "click" , toggler )
});
```

Table 11-2 lists common events available in jQuery.

TABLE 11-2: Common jQuery Events

EVENT	DESCRIPTION
blur	Fires when an element like an input, select, or anchor loses focus.
change	Fires when the data in a text input or select input changes.
click	Fires when the user clicks the mouse.
dblclick	Fires when the user double-clicks.
focus	Fires when an element such as an input, select, or anchor gains focus.
hover	A shortcut to create "hover" effects. Attaches two event handlers. One is to be executed when the mouse enters an element, and the other is to be fired when the mouse leaves an element.
keydown	Fires when the user presses on a key. This event fires multiple times as long as the user keeps the key depressed.
keypress	Fires when a character is inserted into a text input or text area. This event fires multiple times as long as the user keeps the key depressed.
keyup	Fires when the user releases a key.

mousedown	Fires when a mouse button is pressed.
mouseenter	Fires when the mouse enters an element. This is an enhanced jQuery event that cleans up some issues with the mouseover and mouseout events.
mouseleave	Fires when the mouse enters an element. This is an enhanced jQuery event that cleans some issues with the mouseover and mouseout events.
mousemove	Fires when the mouse moves.
mouseout	Fires when the mouse leaves an element.
mouseover	Fires when the mouse is over an element.
mouseup	Fires when the user releases a mouse button press.
resize	Fires when the window or other element is resized.
scroll	Fires when the window or other element is scrolled.
select	Fires when an element is selected.
submit	Fires when a user clicks a submit button or otherwise submits a form (by pressing Enter, for example).

There's an optional *selector* argument that gives context to your event binding. This enables you to bind events to elements that might not exist when the page is created. This works in two ways. The first is to bind the event in the context of the document and then pass in your target selector as the optional argument. For example, to bind a click event to any <a> element that will exist in your entire document, you would use $().on() like this:

```
$( document ).on( "click", "a", function(){
  //code goes here
});
```

This basically means, "Listen to every click on the whole document, and if it happens on an <a> element, fire this event." The only problem with this is that it forces jQuery to listen for *every* click that happens on the entire document. For certain events or pages this can be slow.

To listen to clicks for <a> elements that might be dynamically created in the future, you can use $().on(), as shown in the following snippet. In it, the event binding starts with an id selector. Because this limits the search to a single element, this means that there will be less overhead when jQuery listens for events:

```
$( "#article" ).on( "click", "a", function(){
  //code goes here
});
```

Legacy jQuery Event Handling

`$().on()` and `$().off()` were introduced in jQuery 1.7. They simplified and replaced several other methods used to bind events. Although these other options exist, you should focus on and use `$().on()` and `$().off()`. If you *do* inherit code written before jQuery 1.7, this section should give you some sense of how these legacy methods work.

These legacy event methods break down into four basic categories:

➤ Event-specific methods such as `$().click()` and `$().submit()` behave similarly to the standard use of `$().on()`, binding a function to an element that already exists in the document. The one exception is that the type of event is encoded in the method name: `$().click( function(){} )` instead of `$().on( "click", function(){} )`.

➤ `$().live()` and `$().die()` behave like the example of binding an event to the `document` and passing in a filtering selector.

➤ `$().delegate()` and `$().undelegate()` behave like the example of binding an event to an element that limits the elements that jQuery must listen to and then passing in a filtering selector.

➤ `$().bind()` and `$().unbind()` behave exactly like the standard usage of `$.on()` and `$().off()`.

If you do run into code that uses these legacy methods, the jQuery API documentation will be your friend to work through any wrinkles. Hopefully, you won't run into too much of this stuff because the new methods are much easier to use.

Using jQuery, CSS, and HTML to Add Interactivity

Now that you've seen the basics of jQuery, it's time to put what you've learned into use. In this example you take a combination of jQuery, CSS, and HTML to create a dynamic interface for the Example Café menu page.

TRY IT OUT Adding Basic Interactivity to a Web Page with jQuery

This example builds on the example you saw when you learned about the `$().slideUp()` and `$().slideDown()` methods to add some interactivity to the Example Café site. The Example Café wants to expand its menu. For you to do that without creating a long scrolling page, each of the menu sections will expand and contract as needed so that only one is visible at a time.

1. Open up the sample application site, and create a folder named `js`.

2. Download a copy of jQuery from `http://www.jQuery.com` to the new `js` folder.

3. Open your text editor and type in the following code:

```
$( document ).ready(function(){
});
```

4. Save the file in the `js` folder as `main.js`.

5. Open the `menu.html` and, before the closing `</body>` tag, add the following code. (Adjust the jQuery reference to match the version you just downloaded.)

```
<script src="js/jquery-1.8.2.min.js"></script>
<script src="js/main.js"></script>
```

6. Continuing in the `menu.html`, adjust the markup so that there is a `<div>` element wrapping every `<ul>` and move the `id` attributes off of the `<a>` elements and onto their parent `<h2>` elements. Finally, add a `class` of "menu" on the `<body>` element. The body of your HTML will look like this:

```
<body class="menu">
<div id="page">

  <a href="index.html" id="top"><img src="images/logo.gif" alt="example cafe"
  width="194" height="80"></a>
  <div id="navigation">
    <a href="index.html">HOME</a>
    <a>MENU</a>
    <a href="recipes.html">RECIPES</a>
    <a href="opening.html">OPENING</a>
    <a href="contact.html">CONTACT</a>
  </div>

  <h1>Menu</h1>
  <h2 id="starters"><a>Starters</a></h2>
  <div>
    <ul>
    <li>Chestnut and Mushroom Goujons (<a href="#vege">v</a>)</li>
    <li>Goat Cheese Salad  (<a href="#vege">v</a>)</li>
    <li>Honey Soy Chicken Kebabs</li>
    <li>Seafood Salad</li>
    </ul>
    <p><small><a href="#top">Back to top</a></small></p>
  </div>
  <h2 id="mains"><a>Main courses</a></h2>
  <div>
    <ul>
    <li>Spinach and Ricotta Roulade (<a href="#vege">v</a>)</li>
    <li>Beef Tournados with Mustard and Dill Sauce</li>
    <li>Roast Chicken Salad</li>
    <li>Icelandic Cod with Parsley Sauce</li>
    <li>Mushroom Wellington (<a href="#vege">v</a>)</li>
    </ul>
    <p><small><a href="#top">Back to top</a></small></p>
  </div>
  <h2 id="desserts"><a>Desserts</a></h2>
  <div>
    <ul>
    <li>Lemon Sorbet (<a href="#vege">v</a>)</li>
    <li>Chocolate Mud Pie (<a href="#vege">v</a>)</li>
    <li>Pecan Pie (<a href="#vege">v</a>)</li>
    <li>Selection of Fine Cheeses from Around the World</li>
    </ul>
    <p><small><a href="#top">Back to top</a></small></p>
```

```
    </div>
  </div>
  <script src="js/jquery-1.8.2.min.js"></script>
  <script src="js/main.js"></script>
```

7. Now go back to your `main.js` file, and type in the following code inside the body of the `$( document ).ready()` function.

```
if ( $( "body" ).hasClass( "menu" ) ) {
  $( "#mains + div, #desserts + div").hide();
  $( "#starters" ).addClass( "expanded" );
  $( "h2" ).on( "click", function(){
    if( !$( this ).hasClass( "expanded" )) {
      $( ".expanded" ).removeClass( "expanded" ).next().slideUp( "fast" );
      $( this ).addClass( "expanded" ).next().slideDown( "slow" );
    }
  });
}
```

8. Open your `interface.css` file, and add the following two lines:

```
h2  {
  padding: 0 0 0 40px;
  background : url(../images/plus-minus.png) no-repeat 0px 0px;
}
h2.expanded  {
  background : url(../images/plus-minus.png) no-repeat 0px -30px;
}
```

9. Open the page in your browser, and you should see something like Figure 11-9.

FIGURE 11-9

How It Works

This example leverages many techniques you've learned about. When the `$( document ).ready()` event fires, the first thing that happens is that the script uses an `if` statement to test whether the body element has a class of "menu" by using the `$().hasClass()` method. This enables you to run this code only if you're on the menu page. This will be important when more interactivity is added to the site in different sections.

After that, you use the adjacent sibling selector to hide two of the three menu `<div>` elements. Take note of the way the two CSS selectors are separated by a comma. jQuery works just like regular CSS selection, so you can use multiple selectors in a single call to jQuery.

Next, the `#starters` element has the class "expanded" added to it using `$().addClass()`. This ensures that it has the "−" next to it in the CSS and ensures that you have easy access to that element in the next section.

Now that the page is initialized properly, it's time to add in the behavior. Using `$().on()`, a function is added to all the `<h2>` elements on the page. This function first tests whether the element being clicked has the "expanded" class. This is accomplished by adding a "!" character in front of the call to `$().hasClass()`. This "!" negates the test, so it now reads, "if this element *doesn't* have the class 'expanded.'" If it doesn't, it continues to run the rest of the function.

The first line inside the conditional block uses jQuery to get a reference to the "expanded" element and then does some housekeeping. First, it removes the "expanded" class because that element will no longer be expanded. Then it gets a reference to the next element using `$().next()` and slides it up with the "fast" keyword as an argument.

Then, the clicked element is referenced using `this`, the expanded class is added to it, and then the next element slides down using the "slow" keyword.

This combination to use CSS classes for both styling elements and then to use them for reference later in scripts is common and, even in this simple example, handy.

SUMMARY

This chapter introduced you to the most popular JavaScript library in the world: jQuery. You learned some reasons to use jQuery, including the remarkable ecosystem that has grown up around the library over the past few years. Then you learned how to obtain and install jQuery in your pages, using either a local copy or a version hosted on a CDN.

Following that you learned about some core library features including using the `$()` function coupled with the same CSS selectors you learned about when working with CSS to access HTML elements quickly and efficiently. You also know several different ways you can manipulate elements using jQuery, including the following:

➤ Adding, removing, and toggling CSS classes

➤ Getting and setting attributes

➤ Setting or getting individual CSS properties

➤ Getting or setting the HTML content of an element

➤ Animating HTML elements in different ways using built-in jQuery methods

Finally, you learned about event handling using jQuery.

With just this simple foundation, you now have the basic building blocks to create rich web pages.

EXERCISES

1. Rewrite the code from the files `ch10_eg03.html` and `ch10_eg03.js` to use jQuery. Instead of a `console.log`, add a `<p>` element to display the results as a child of the `<body>` element. Use the jQuery method `$().val()` to get the value of the form fields.

2. Modify `main.js` in the Example Café site to test the hash of the URL. You can access the hash with the BOM property `window.location.hash`. Use a conditional statement and jQuery to satisfy the following three conditions:

   ➤ If the hash equals "starters," hide the menu items for mains and desserts.

   ➤ If the hash equals "mains," hide the menu items for starters and desserts.

   ➤ If the hash equals "desserts," hide the menu items for starters and mains.

   Test by appending each hash to the file URL (for example: `menu.html"#starters"`).

   ➤ Note that the `window.location.hash` property includes the # character.

The answers to all the exercises are in Appendix A, "Answers to Exercises."

▶ WHAT YOU LEARNED IN THIS CHAPTER

TOPIC	KEY TAKEAWAY
jQuery	jQuery is the most popular JavaScript library in the world. It makes JavaScript easier and more fun to use.
CDN	It's better to use the Google CDN to host your JavaScript on your public web pages. For testing locally it's easier to have a local copy.
$	Everything in jQuery starts with $, a method that (among other features) enables you to access and create HTML elements.
Animations with jQuery	jQuery makes creating animations and effects easy. With just a few basic methods, you can add interactivity to your pages.
jQuery events	Although there are several legacy methods, the only methods you should use for event binding are `$().on()` and `$().off()`.

12

jQuery: Beyond the Basics

WHAT YOU WILL LEARN IN THIS CHAPTER

➤ How to work with Ajax and jQuery

➤ What jQuery UI is and how it can help you make more interactive web pages

WROX.COM CODE DOWNLOADS FOR THIS CHAPTER

You can find the wrox.com code downloads for this chapter at `www.wrox.com/remtitle .cgi?isbn=9781118340189` on the Download Code tab. The code is in the Chapter 12 download and individually named according to the names throughout the chapter.

With the basics of jQuery in hand, it's time to dive a little bit further into what jQuery has to offer. This includes a look at working with a technology called Ajax and the powerful jQuery UI library, which enable you to build rich interactive components with a little bit of code.

AJAX WITH JQUERY

If you had to choose one reason why JavaScript went from an also-ran to being one of the most important programming languages on the planet, a good choice would be a technology pattern called Ajax. The Ajax era in web development, starting in the mid-2000s, has driven enormous interest and development in JavaScript libraries, browsers, and the language itself.

So what is Ajax?

The easiest way to describe it is to first think of the basic web page interaction. As you learned in Chapter 3, "Links and Navigation," links enable users to navigate from page to page. When this happens a new HTML document is requested from the server, and all the JavaScript, CSS, and images that make up the page need to be loaded to render the page. Ajax changes this basic pattern by loading small pieces of data into an already loaded page. Because you're just loading the new or changed data, you can now do things like read an e-mail, view a photo, or post to Twitter without requesting the entire page. This makes for a smoother, more desktop-like experience.

jQuery's Ajax implementation was one of its original killer features and continues to be one of the strongest features in the library.

The foundation of jQuery's Ajax implementation is built on top of the method $.ajax(), which is called from $ directly and doesn't require the context of an HTML element or element fragment.

> **NOTE** *Ajax needs to run on a web server. If you're familiar with existing web servers such as Apache or Microsoft's IIS and have one or the other set up on your machine, you can use one of those to run the code samples in this chapter. If you're not familiar with setting up a web server, you can use the provided web server in the download directory. On Windows, simply click the* mongoose3-3.exe *application, and browse to* http://localhost:8080/ *to see a list of the files in this chapter and work with Ajax applications.*
>
> *If you're on a Mac or Linux, Apache should be installed by default.*

The following code (ch12_eg01.html) sample shows a basic usage of $.ajax(). The script (ch12_eg01.js) has just one call. In it, there is a JavaScript object used as a map for the single argument. This map has two properties: the URL of the file to be requested (data/ch12_eg01 .json) and a callback function to run when the file is successfully retrieved.

In this example, the function uses console.log to log the information that's passed into the callback function. In jQuery's Ajax implementation, there are three arguments passed into callback functions: the data returned from the server, a string representing the status of the request (basically indicating whether things went okay), and the jQuery XMLHttpRequest object (jqXHR), which is an enhanced version of the XMLHttpRequest object that is central to all Ajax applications. This object provides properties and methods that enable JavaScript to communicate with a web server.

The samples in this chapter mostly focus on the data argument, but you must know that those other arguments exist.

```
$( document ).ready( function(){
  $.ajax({
    "url" : "data/ch12_eg01.json",
    "success" : function( data,status,jqxhr ){
        console.log( data,status,jqxhr )
    }
  });
});
```

Figure 12-1 shows the result of this interaction in Google Chrome's console. As you can see, the value of data is a JavaScript object containing one property, title, with a value of "Beginning HTML and CSS." The statusText argument is "success" because this was a successful Ajax request. Finally the jqXHR argument is a JavaScript object that contains several pieces of information about the request, including the server response as a text string.

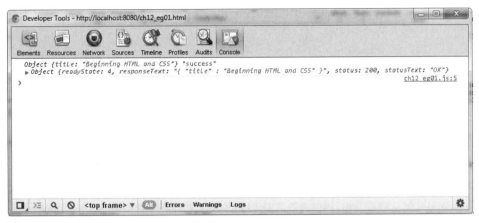

FIGURE 12-1

Because the `data` argument in this case is a JavaScript object, you can access the properties and values the same way you would with any other JavaScript object. The following example (`ch12_eg02.js`) illustrates this ability by accessing the `title` property and writing its value as a new `<h1>` element in a document (`ch12_eg02.html`).

```
$( document ).ready( function(){
  $.ajax({
    "url" : "data/ch12_eg01.json",
    "success" : function( data ){
        $( "#container" ).html( "<h1>"+ data.title +"</h1>" );
      }
  });
});
```

As you can see it is easy to use dot notation to access server data in this way. Because of this ease of use, using JavaScript objects to pass data from a server to a web page is the most popular way to connect a web page to a server. This technology is called *JSON*.

JSON, XML, or Text

Although JSON is by far the most popular way to pass data from a server to the browser, there are two other common methods that you should be aware of: XML and plain text.

Working with XML

When Ajax first burst onto the scene, it used a technology called *Extensible Markup Language* (*XML*) as the format to pass data back and forth from the server. XML looks familiar to you because it shares many conventions with the HTML you've worked with throughout this book.

Rewriting the `data/ch12_eg01.json` file to use XML would look something like the following code sample (`data/ch12_eg03.xml`). As you can see it's similar to the HTML you're familiar with, with a `<books>` element and a child `<title>` element. The one new element that you might be unfamiliar with is the XML declaration at the top, which indicates that this is an XML document, complete with a version and document encoding.

```
<?xml version="1.0" encoding="UTF-8" ?>
<books>
  <title>
    Beginning HTML and CSS
  </title>
</books>
```

Rewriting the previous example to use XML instead (ch12_eg03.js) shows some of the differences between JSON and XML.

In this case, because the data is XML, you need to indicate that in the request with the `dataType` property. You should be aware that, because of its popularity, `json` is the default `dataType`.

In addition, dealing with XML as Ajax data is different from working with JSON. Instead of working with it directly using dot notation like you can with JSON, you must manipulate it a little bit to get your hands on the data.

In this case, you pass the `data` object from the Ajax request into `$()`, which enables you to use all the regular jQuery methods on it. In this case you use a new method `$().find()`, which enables you to filter a collection based on a CSS selector. Normally, you use it to filter a regular collection of DOM elements, but here you use it to filter the XML document passed in as the `data` in the Ajax request. Because you need the value of the `<title>` element, you pass `title` in as the selector. This gets access to the `<title>` element. You can then use the method `$().text()` to get the text needed to fill in the `<h1>` element.

```
$( document ).ready( function(){
  $.ajax({
    "url" : "data/ch12_eg01.xml",
    "dataType" : "xml",
    "success" : function( data ){
      var title = $( data ).find( "title" ).text();
      $( "#container" ).html( "<h1>"+ title +"</h1>" );
    }
  });
});
```

These extra hoops you have to leap through to get the XML data is one of the reasons that people gravitated toward JSON over the past few years.

Working with Text Responses

No matter what format the data is in, it's actually sent over the wire as plain text. It's only in the hands of the browser or in the hands of JavaScript that it converts into the JSON objects or XML fragments that you've seen.

This means you can, at times, short-circuit these data structures and go directly to the text. This doesn't happen often; you more commonly want to get larger blocks of structured data, but sometimes you get server responses that make some sense as plain text. For example, you could have a single piece of information from the server like the availability of a username (which would return true or false) or a block of preformatted HTML. In both of these cases, working directly with the text would be possible and maybe even preferred for reasons of performance or simplicity in server implementation.

The following code sample (ch12_eg04.js) shows both of these in action. The first $().ajax() request uses the same data argument you've been using throughout this chapter. In the first request the URL mimics a server response to a query. The URL data/isAuthor.txt?author=rob%20larsen is standing in for a piece of server code that returns true or false depending on whether the value of the query string author is someone who writes books. Because it's beyond the scope of this book to go into the logic you might see on the server side for this kind of application, it's just a simple text file that contains one word: true. But it's simple to imagine that it would return true or false after looking at a collection of author names and matching against the name in the author query string. In the success function, the data argument, which in this case is just a text string, is used to test whether the provided name is an author. If it is, a second Ajax request is fired, which gets the title of this book as a formatted HTML string. This string is then inserted directly into the DOM.

```
$( document ).ready( function(){
  $.ajax({
    "url" : "data/isAuthor.txt?author=rob%20larsen",
    "dataType" : "text",
    "success" : function( data ){
       if ( data === "true" ){
         $.ajax({
            "url" : "data/ch12_eg04.txt",
            "dataType" : "text",
            "success" : function( data ){
              $( "#container" ).html( data );
            }
         });
       }
    }
  });
});
```

GETting and POSTing

As you learned in Chapter 6, "Forms," there are two ways to make requests to a web server, GET and POST. GET is a simple request for a resource, and POST is used to pass form information to the server. Both GET and POST are used with Ajax.

The default action in jQuery is to use a GET request, so on the basis of the examples you've already seen, you already know how to make a GET request with jQuery.

jQuery offers two ways to specify the HTTP method. The first is to specify the type. Rewriting the earlier JSON example to use an explicit type would look like this (ch12_eg05.js):

```
$( document ).ready( function(){
  $.ajax({
    "type" : "get",
    "url" : "data/ch12_eg01.json",
    "success" : function( data ){
       $( "#container" ).html( "<h1>"+ data.title +"</h1>" );
```

```
      }
    });
  });
```

In addition to setting an explicit `type`, there are two methods that enable you to easily (and mnemonically) set the HTTP method: `$.get()` and `$.post()`. These methods don't offer as many options as `$.ajax()`, but most of the time they're going to offer you all you need—the ability to set the HTTP method, a URL to fetch, an optional `data` object, and a `callback` function to execute on successful completion of the request. Rewriting the previous example to use `$.get()` illustrates usage of the method (`ch12_eg06.js`).

```javascript
$( document ).ready( function(){
  $.get("data/ch12_eg01.json", function( data ){
    $( "#container" ).html( "<h1>"+ data.title +"</h1>" );
  });
});
```

You can send data along with either GET or POST requests, and the jQuery shortcut methods both handle it in the same way. They either accept a JavaScript object containing the name and value pairs representing the data or a formatted string representing the data.

Because POST is more secure and enables more data to be sent over the wire, it's better practice to use the POST method to communicate with a server. The following example shows a simple contact form that uses Ajax to do the form submission using `$.post()`.

First, here's the HTML (`ch12_eg07.html`), which builds up a simple form with three inputs: one e-mail, one URL, and one submit.

```html
<div id="container">
   <form action="ch12_eg07.json" method="post"
        id="frmContact">
    <p><label for="emailFrom">Your email</label>
      <input type="email" name ="emailFrom"
             id="emailFrom" maxLength="250"
             placeholder="rob@example.com">
    </p>
    <p><label for="urlSite">Your Site</label>
      <input type="url" name="urlSite"
             id="urlSite" maxLength="250"
             placeholder="http://htmlcssjavascript.com">
    </p>
    <p><input type="submit" value="Submit"></p>
  </form>
</div>
```

The JavaScript introduces a few new wrinkles, in addition to the use of `$.post()`. For starters the variable `$this` is created, which points to jQuery loaded with reference to the form you just submitted. This makes things slightly faster when you need to access jQuery methods with that `<form>` element as the context. This is because jQuery needs to get loaded with the element only the first time and then every reference to it after that loads from memory. jQuery doesn't need to find that element again.

The second new wrinkle is an argument, event, passed into the callback function for the form submission. This object is automatically passed in as the first argument to any function that is generated by a user interaction. It contains information about the event (for example, what element generated the event) and has several methods available to manage the way the event works its way through the environment. Most of the properties and methods of the event object are a little more advanced and not within the scope of this book, but there is one that you will often use: event.preventDefault(). This method simply prevents the default action of an element. In this case it prevents the form from being submitted in the traditional manner. This enables you to POST it using Ajax. For another common example, calling event.preventDefault() on a link would stop the link from navigating.

Next is the use of $.post(). It's relatively straightforward. First, you access the action attribute of the form to set the url of the Ajax request. Second, a new method, $().serialize(), is used to take the contents of the form, <input> element by <input> element, and concatenates them into a set of name/value pairs that will be passed to the server as a string. Inside the callback function there's a simple test to see if the server accepted the form submission. If it was accepted (and because the data for this example is hard-coded, it will always be) the containing <div> element's contents are replaced with a message sent back by the server.

This replacement is done using the jQuery method $().empty, which empties an HTML element of all content and $().html(), which you're already familiar with (ch12_eg07.js).

```
$( document ).ready( function(){
  $( "#frmContact" ).on( "submit", function( event ){
    var $this = $( this );
    event.preventDefault();
    $.post( $this.attr("action"), $this.serialize(), function( data ){
      if ( data.status === "accepted" ) {
        $( "#frmContact" ).empty().html( "<h1>" + data.message + "</h1>" )
      }
    });
  });
});
The data looks like this


{
  "status" : "accepted",
  "message" : "Thanks! Your message was accepted"
}
```

The two stages of this form submission are illustrated in Figure 12-2.

> **NOTE** $().empty() *is better than simply replacing the HTML or setting the* $().html() *to an empty string because the* $().empty() *method ensures that no stale references to events or other data remain in memory. In certain situations events or data bound to elements can remain even after the element is removed from the DOM. This can cause performance issues. These stale references are referred to as memory leaks, and jQuery makes an effort to avoid them wherever possible. This is another reason why using a library like jQuery is better than coding custom JavaScript—you don't have to pay as much attention to these issues as you would if you were in control of everything.*

FIGURE 12-2

Form Validation

Building on the previous example, the following addresses form validation. This process ensures that the form is filled out properly. This validation process can take two separate approaches: One is to ensure that form fields are filled out, and the other ensures that the right type or format of data is used.

As you learned when you looked at the new form elements and input types, in newer browsers you can use some of the new form tools such as the `required` attribute and polyfills to help with this. But for now if you want the broadest possible support across all types of form elements and validation methods, you should use a little JavaScript. To do this with jQuery, use the core jQuery Validation plug-in, available from `http://bassistance.de/jquery-plugins/jquery-plugin-validation/`.

To start, adjust the markup from the previous example to add a little bit of data to the elements in the form of CSS classes. You also need to ensure that the plug-in is included in the page (ch12_eg08.html).

```
<div id="container">
<form action="data/ch12_eg07.json" method="post" id="frmContact">
  <p><label for="emailFrom" class="required">Your email</label>
    <input type="email" name ="emailFrom"
           id="emailFrom" maxLength="250"
           placeholder="rob@example.com"
           class="email required">
  </p>
  <p><label for="urlSite" class="required">Your Site</label>
    <input type="url" name="urlSite"
           id="urlSite" maxLength="250"
           placeholder="http://htmlcssjavascript.com"
           class="url required">
  </p>
  <p><input type="submit" value="Submit"></p>
</form>
<p class="key">Indicates required field</p>
</div>
<script src="js/jquery-1.8.2.min.js"></script>
```

```
<script src="js/jquery.validate.min.js"></script>
<script src="ch12_eg08.js"></script>
```

The JavaScript is similar to what you've seen before. The biggest change is that the submit event handler is replaced by a call to the Validation plug-in. This call sets up the form to be validated when submitted and creates a `submitHandler` to run when the form is submitted. Inside the handler the reference to the current form is changed from being `$(this)` to being a reference to `$(this.currentForm)`. This is because the context of the function is changed from the direct form submission where `this` refers to the form being submitted to the context of the form validation plug-in where `this` is a reference to the plug-in and contains a reference to the current form as a property (`ch12_eg08.js`).

```
$( document ).ready( function(){
  $( "#frmContact" ).validate(
    {"submitHandler" : function(){
      var $form = $( this.currentForm );
      $.post( $form.attr("action"), $form.serialize(), function( data ){
        if ( data.status === "accepted" ) {
          $( "#frmContact" ).empty().html( "<h1>" + data.message + "</h1>" )
        }
      });
    }
  });
});
```

Finally, some additional styles are added to the CSS to benefit from the plug-in, which adds hints in the form of an error message and CSS classes depending on the status of the form. In this case you add a red border to any form field with an error (`data/ch12_eg08.css`).

```
label {
  display : inline-block;
  width : 200px;
}
#emailFrom, #urlSite {
  width : 300px;
}
.required:after, .key:before {
  content : "*";
  color : #03F;
  font-weight : bold;
  font-size:24px;
}
input.error {
  border : 4px solid red;
}
label.error {
  width : 400px;
}
```

Figure 12-3 shows the initial state, an error state, and the successful submission of a form.

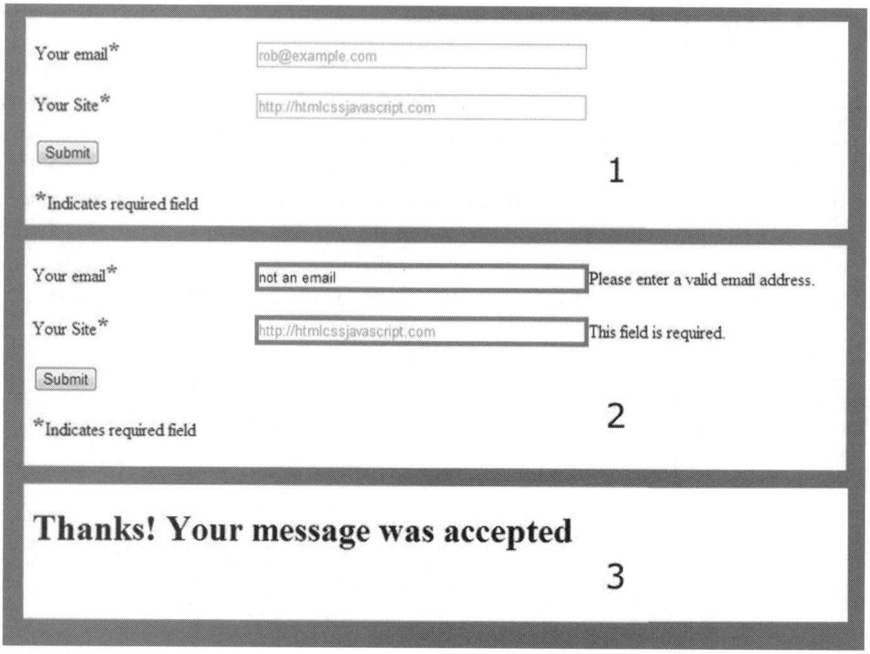

FIGURE 12-3

Using jQuery to Add a Contact Form to a Site

Now that you've had a chance to get your feet wet with using Ajax on a website, put what you've learned into practice on the Example Café site.

TRY IT OUT   Adding a Contact Form to a Site Using jQuery

This example adds a contact form to the Example Café site. This form enables users to save the site's address from being harvested by spammers while still allowing people to write in with their comments.

1. Go to `http://bassistance.de/jquery-plugins/jquery-plugin-validation/` and download the jQuery validation plug-in, saving it in your `js` folder.

2. Open `contact.html` in your text editor. Adjust the markup so that it matches the following output. The biggest changes are to the form, the addition of the `"contact"` class on the `<body>` element, and a `<section>` element to wrap the form up and serve as a placeholder for the server response.

```
<body class="contact">
<div id="page">
  <header>
    <a href="index.html" id="top">
      <img src="images/logo.gif" alt="example cafe logo"
      width="194" height="80" >
    </a>
    <nav id="navigation">
```

```
        <a href="index.html">HOME</a>
        <a href="menu.html">MENU</a>
        <a href="recipes.html">RECIPES</a>
        CONTACT
    </nav>
</header>
<article>
    <h1>Contact</h1>
    <section id="contact">
      <form action="data/response.json"
       method="post" id="frmContact">
        <fieldset>
          <legend>Your Message</legend>
          <p>
            <label for="emailFrom" class="required">Your email
            </label>
            <input type="email" name ="emailFrom"
             id="emailFrom" maxLength="250"
             placeholder="rob@example.com" class="email required"
             tabindex="0">
          </p>
          <p>
            <label for="emailBody" class="required">Your Message
            </label>
            <textarea name="txtBody" id="emailBody"
                    tabindex="2"
                    class="required"></textarea>
          </p>
          <p class="key">Indicates required field</p>
        </fieldset>
        <fieldset>
          <legend>How you found us:</legend>
          <p>
            <label for="selReferrer">How did you hear of us
            </label>
            <select name="selReferrer" tabindex="3">
              <option value="google">Google</option>
              <option value="ad">Local newspaper ad</option>
              <option value="friend">Friend</option>
              <option value="other">Other</option>
            </select>
          </p>
          <p>
            <label for="newsletterSignup">Newsletter</label>
            <input type="checkbox" name="chkBody"
             id="newsletterSignup" checked tabindex="3">
            Ensure this box is checked if you would like to
            receive email updates</p>
        </fieldset>
        <p>
          <input type="submit" value="Submit">
        </p>
      </form>
    </section>
    <p>
```

```
    <address>
    12 Sea View, Newquay, Cornwall, UK
    </address>
    </p>
    <p><a href="http://maps.google.com/maps?q=newquay">Find us on
       Google Maps</a></p>
  </article>
</div>
<script src="js/jquery-1.8.2.min.js"></script>
<script src="js/jquery.validate.min.js"></script>
<script src="js/main.js"></script>
```

3. Open the `interface.css` file, and make sure that the following styles are in place to deal with the new elements and the response from the validation plug-in.

```
label {
  display : inline-block;
  width : 100px;
}
#emailFrom, #emailBody {
  width : 300px;
}
#emailBody {
  height:200px;
}
label[for=emailBody]{
  vertical-align:top;
}
.required:after, .key:before {
  content : "*";
  color : #03F;
  font-weight : bold;
  font-size:24px;
}
input.error {
  border : 4px solid red;
}
label.error {
  width : 400px;
}
```

4. Open your `main.js` file and add the following code:

```
if ( $( "body" ).hasClass( "contact" ) ) {
  $( "#frmContact" ).validate(
    {"submitHandler" : function(){
      var $form = $( this.currentForm );
      $.post( $form.attr("action"), $form.serialize(), function( data ){
        if ( data.status === "accepted" ) {
          $( "#contact" ).empty().html( "<h2>" + data.message + "</h3>" )
        }
      });
    }
  });
}
```

5. Create a `data` folder in your site directory, and create a file named `response.json`. The contents of the file should look like this:

```
{ "status" : "accepted", "message" : "Thanks! Your message was accepted" }
```

6. Open the page in your browser, and you should see something like Figure 12-4.

FIGURE 12-4

How It Works

Nothing here should be all that new to you. However, this example does put together many of the lessons from the book, so the overall package might be a little overwhelming.

To start there's some solid markup in the form, taking advantage of the `<fieldset>` and `<legend>` elements to give some organization to the form. The `tabindex` attribute is used to make sure that the tab order makes sense.

In addition, the new `placeholder` attribute is used to hint at the format for the e-mail address.

Taking the structure and meta data provided by the CSS classes and the form itself, the validator plug-in intercepts the form submission (try it by both clicking on the Submit button and pressing **Enter** on an input) and verifies that the data is in the proper format and is provided for all required fields. The form data is then serialized and passed to `$.post()` to be sent to the server for processing. The Ajax response that comes back is parsed, and a message is shared with end users telling them the submission was successful without them ever needing to leave the page.

JQUERY UI

You've heard a lot about the jQuery ecosystem. One of the most important parts of that ecosystem is jQuery UI. jQuery UI, available from `http://jqueryui.com`, is a curated set of behaviors and widgets designed to make developing rich Internet applications and interactive websites much easier. Developed alongside the core jQuery project with its own dedicated team, jQuery UI greatly enhances core jQuery functionality. This section introduces the components available from the jQuery UI project and illustrates the basics of how jQuery UI works, including downloading the project, getting set up, and implementing some of the available features.

Getting jQuery UI

To get jQuery UI, you just need to go to `http://jqueryui.com` and download the latest stable version. When you have that, extract the files and then, in your HTML file, link to two separate files: the jQuery UI JavaScript and the associated jQuery UI CSS file. Both are required for jQuery UI to work. This code sample (`ch12_eg09.html`) shows the two files linked properly.

```
<!doctype html>
<html>
<head>
<meta charset="utf-8">
<title>jQuery UI Draggable and Droppable</title>
<link href="css/smoothness/jquery-ui-1.9.1.custom.min.css" rel="stylesheet">
<link href="css/ch12_eg09.css" rel="stylesheet">
</head>
<body>
<div id="container">
  <div id="draggable">
    <p>Drag here</p>
  </div>
  <div id="droppable">
    <p>Drop here</p>
  </div>
</div>
<script src="js/jquery-1.8.2.min.js"></script>
```

```
<script src="js/jquery-ui-1.9.1.custom.min.js"></script>
<script src="ch12_eg09.js"></script>
</body>
</html>
```

As you'll see throughout these examples, the CSS file and associated images provide a richly designed interface for jQuery UI widgets. This interface is called a *theme*. If you want to customize a theme for your own site, you should check out the Themeroller, which is a web-based tool that creates custom jQuery UI themes (http://jqueryui.com/themeroller/).

Now that jQuery UI is installed, look at some of the features it offers.

jQuery UI Behaviors

jQuery UI offers as one of its core features, several common interactions as easy-to-implement plug-ins. Unlike the widgets you learn about in the next section, these behaviors don't represent an entire feature but instead enable you to enhance your existing site or application in whatever way that makes sense for your site. Think of them as building blocks.

Draggable and Droppable

Often used in concert with each other, the Draggable (http://jqueryui.com/draggable/) and Droppable (http://jqueryui.com/droppable/) behaviors enable you to click and drag an HTML element and then drop it on a target area.

This example starts with this simple HTML (ch12_eg09.html), which features an element designed to be dragged and a target area for dropping.

```
<div id="container">
  <div id="draggable">
    <p>Drag this</p>
  </div>
  <div id="droppable">
    <p>Drop here</p>
  </div>
</div>
```

To enable the Draggable and Droppable behaviors, all you need to do is call the $().draggable() and $().droppable() methods on the two <div> elements (ch12_eg09.js).

```
$( document ).ready( function(){
  $( "#draggable" ).draggable();
  $( "#droppable" ).droppable( {
  drop: function( event, ui ) {
    $( this )
      .css( "border" , "4px solid hotpink" )
      .html( "<p>Dropped!</p>" );
  }
  });
});
```

This pattern, getting a reference to an element and then calling the associated jQuery UI method, is the basic pattern for all jQuery UI methods.

All jQuery UI methods also accept a JavaScript object as a map representing the different options for the behavior or widget. In this example there is a callback method for the "drop" event, which fires when an element is dropped on a target element. Figure 12-5 shows the finished product.

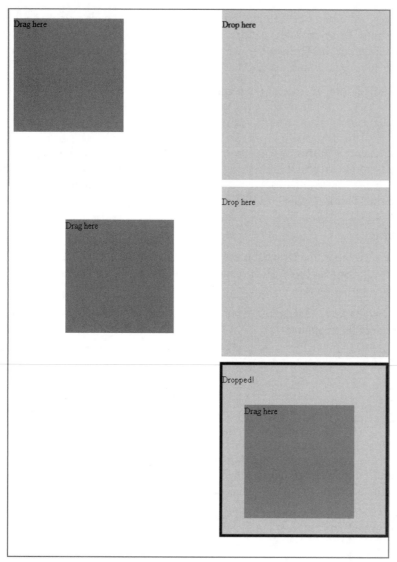

FIGURE 12-5

> **NOTE** This book doesn't go into too much depth in the options available for each feature. Just be aware that there are many options that you can learn about by browsing the excellent jQuery UI documentation at `http://api.jqueryui.com/`.

Resizable

The Resizable (`http://jqueryui.com/resizable/`) behavior adds a small grip to an element and enables that element to be resized by a click-and-drag action.

The HTML for this example is as simple as it gets, just a single `<div>` element with some text (`ch12_eg10.html`).

```
<div id="resizable">
  <p>Resizable Element</p>
</div>
```

And the JavaScript (`ch12_eg10.html`) is also quite simple. Called without arguments `$().resizable()` enhances a div with resize handles and the ability to be resized, as shown in Figure 12-6.

```
$( document ).ready( function(){
  $( "#resizable" ).resizable();
});
```

FIGURE 12-6

Selectable

The Selectable (`http://jqueryui.com/selectable/`) behavior enables HTML elements to become selectable with a mouse click. You can use this to simulate a check box with an arbitrary HTML element. The markup (`ch12_eg11.html`) for this behavior is simple, an `<ol>` element with a series of `<li>` elements representing the selectable elements. While this demo and many of the examples you see on the Internet use lists, this behavior can be called on any wrapper element with child elements.

```
<ol id="selectable">
  <li>These items are selectable</li>
  <li>These items are selectable</li>
  <li>These items are selectable</li>
  <li>These items are selectable</li>
  <li>These items are selectable</li>
</ol>
```

The JavaScript is another simple one-liner (`ch12_eg11.js`); although, it does take advantage of the method `$().disableSelection()`, which disables the ability to select HTML text.

```
$( document ).ready( function(){
  $( "#sortable" ).sortable().disableSelection();
});
```

Figure 12-7 shows a single element in the list selected.

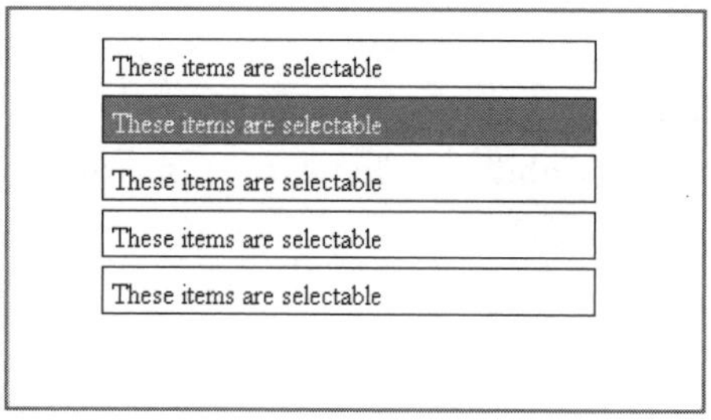

These items are selectable
These items are selectable
These items are selectable
These items are selectable
These items are selectable

FIGURE 12-7

Sortable

The Sortable behavior (`http://jqueryui.com/sortable/`) enables users to rearrange the elements in an ordered collection of elements. This example again uses a list (`ch12_eg12.html`):

```
<ol id="sortable">
  <li>One</li>
  <li>Two</li>
  <li>Three</li>
  <li>Four</li>
  <li>Five</li>
</ol>
```

And again, the most basic example is a one-liner (`ch12_eg12.js`) using `$().disableSelection()`.

```
$( document ).ready( function(){
  $( "#sortable" ).sortable().disableSelection();
});
```

Figure 12-8 shows the list mid-sort.

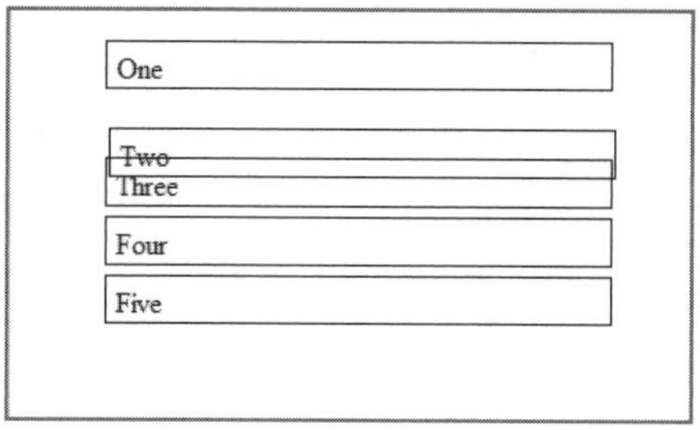

One
Two
Three
Four
Five

FIGURE 12-8

jQuery UI Widgets

Whereas the jQuery UI behaviors represent building blocks to put together your own custom interactions, the jQuery UI widgets are full-blown features you can use simply and easily. This section introduces them with simple examples.

The Accordion Widget

The Accordion widget (`http://jqueryui.com/accordion/`) is similar to the exercise you did with expanding and collapsing content in Chapter 11, "Working with jQuery." It enables you to create an interface that shows or hides blocks of content based on user interaction. The difference here is that it's going to take you one line of code to set up.

The HTML (`ch12_eg13.html`) for this basic example is a `<dl>` element. With this structure the `<dt>` elements act as the toggle switches, and the `<dd>` elements appear as shown and hidden as needed.

```
<dl id="accordion">
  <dt>Expandable</dt>
  <dt>Pickled ethical before they sold out quis, fixie veniam artisan
  cupidatat. Vinyl selvage keffiyeh vero, american apparel sed </dt>
  <dt>Expandable</dt>
  <dt>Pickled ethical before they sold out quis, fixie veniam artisan
  cupidatat. Vinyl selvage keffiyeh vero, american apparel sed </dt>
  <dt>Expandable</dt>
  <dt>Pickled ethical before they sold out quis, fixie veniam artisan
  cupidatat. Vinyl selvage keffiyeh vero, american apparel sed </dt>
  <dt>Expandable</dt>
  <dt>Pickled ethical before they sold out quis, fixie veniam artisan
  cupidatat. Vinyl selvage keffiyeh vero, american apparel sed </dt>
</dl>
```

The JavaScript (`ch12_eg13.js`) is another one-liner, a simple call to `$().accordion()`. The power of jQuery UI widgets, as shown in Figure 12-9, transforms, with a single line of JavaScript, that simple markup into a rich, interactive, professionally styled widget.

```
$( document ).ready( function(){
  $( "#accordion" ).accordion();
});
```

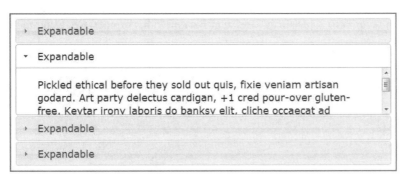

FIGURE 12-9

The Autocomplete Widget

Like the autocomplete functionality provided by the `<datalist>` element you learned about in Chapter 6, the Autocomplete widget (`http://jqueryui.com/autocomplete/`) enables the user to see a list of hints to choose from when trying to complete a form.

The Autocomplete widget uses a data source to feed the hints. This data source can be a hard-coded array or can be a live data source provided by a server. In this case (`ch12_eg14.js`) it's a data source featuring an array. The URL of the resource `"data/ch12_eg14.json"` is passed in as the value of the `source` property and jQuery takes care of the rest, requesting the resource with Ajax.

```
$( document ).ready( function(){
  $( "#widgets" ).autocomplete({
    "source" : "data/ch12_eg14.json"
  });
});
```

The markup is just a familiar text input (`ch12_eg14.html`). The combination of that simple markup and the call to `$().autocomplete()` turns into the cross-browser functionality, as shown in Figure 12-10.

```
<label for="widgets">jQuery UI Widgets: </label>
  <input id="widgets">
```

FIGURE 12-10

The Button Widget

The Button widget (`http://jqueryui.com/button/`) enables you to easily turn `<input>` elements, `<button>` elements, and links into cross-platform consistent buttons. This sample uses a common submit button (`ch12_eg15.html`).

```
<input type="submit" id="button" value="Button">
```

Calling `$().button()` (`ch12_eg15.js`) produces the output shown in Figure 12-11.

```
$( document ).ready( function(){
  $( "input" ).button()
});
```

FIGURE 12-11

The Datepicker Widget

The Datepicker widget (`http://jqueryui.com/datepicker/`) is another jQuery UI widget that maps to functionality provided by the HTML5 specification. Analogous to the new `date` input type, the Datepicker widget provides a themeable, cross-browser, calendar-based date selection utility.

Of all the widgets provided by jQuery UI, this is likely the one that offers the most functionality for the least amount of end user code. With two simple lines (one `<input>` element and one line of jQuery) you can have a fully realized calendar widget that enables your users to easily pick dates.

The markup is a simple input (`ch12_eg16.html`):

```
<input type="text" id="datepicker">
```

And the JavaScript (`ch12_eg16.js`) is a common one-liner. The combination creates the interactive widget, as shown in Figure 12-12.

```
$( document ).ready( function(){
  $( "#datepicker" ).datepicker();
});
```

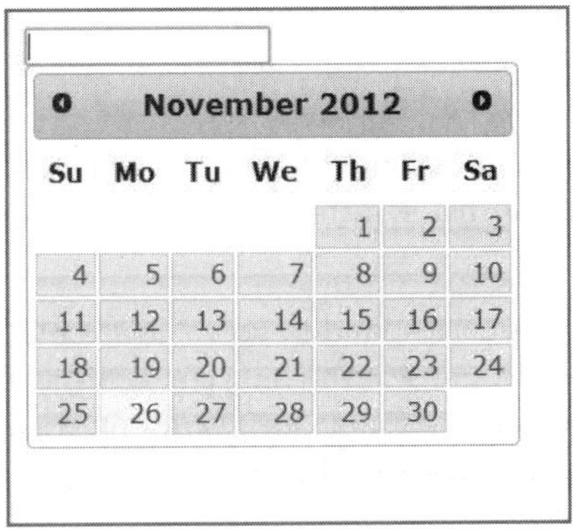

◑	November 2012					◑
Su	Mo	Tu	We	Th	Fr	Sa
				1	2	3
4	5	6	7	8	9	10
11	12	13	14	15	16	17
18	19	20	21	22	23	24
25	26	27	28	29	30	

FIGURE 12-12

The Dialog Widget

The Dialog widget (`http://jqueryui.com/dialog/`) is a themeable, more flexible, more usable replacement for the common JavaScript alert or other application/website dialog.

This widget takes some content and a `title` attribute and creates a neatly designed dialog box. By default the widget is centered vertically and horizontally on the screen.

The markup here is a `<div>` element with a `title` attribute (`ch12_eg17.html`). As the paragraph at the heart of this markup states, the jQuery UI Dialog widget can automatically be resized, moved, and closed. The `title` attribute is moved to the title bar of the dialog.

```
<div id="dialog" title="Dialog Demo">
    <p>This dialog can be moved, resized and closed (with the 'x' icon.)</p>
</div>
```

The pattern of the JavaScript one-liner should be familiar to you by now (`ch12_eg17.js`). It's used here to create the dialog shown in Figure 12-13.

```
$( document ).ready( function(){
  $( "#dialog" ).dialog();
});
```

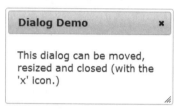

FIGURE 12-13

The resize and move/draggable behavior of the Dialog widget is a clear illustration of the way the jQuery UI behaviors can combine to make new features and functionality.

The Menu Widget

The Menu widget (`http://jqueryui.com/menu/`) takes structured markup like a series of nested `<ul>` elements and transforms it into a themeable cascading menu that can show or hide submenu items based on user interaction.

The markup for this represents a nested list of `<ul>` elements that correspond to topics in the first chapter of this book (`ch12_eg18.html`). Although it's structurally and semantically correct, it can be a bit unwieldy to just spit out such a large block of markup and call it a menu. The Menu widget makes that a more compact structure visually, while still allowing access to the full content.

```
<ul id="menu">
    <li><a href="#">A Web of Structured Documents</a></li>
    <li><a href="#">The Foundations of the Web</a>
      <ul>
        <li><a href="#">The separation of content, style and behavior</a> </li>
      </ul>
    </li>
    <li><a href="#">Introducing HTML5</a></li>
    <li><a href="#">Tags and Elements</a>
      <ul>
        <li><a href="#">Separating Heads from Bodies</a></li>
        <li><a href="#">Attributes Tell Us About Elements</a></li>
```

```html
        <li><a href="#">Learning from Others by Viewing Their Source Code</a></li>
        <li><a href="#">Elements for Marking Up Text</a> </li>
    </ul>
</li>
<li><a href="#">Attribute Groups</a>
    <ul>
        <li><a href="#">Core Attributes</a></li>
        <li><a href="#">Internationalization</a></li>
    </ul>
</li>
<li><a href="#">Core Elements and Attributes</a>
    <ul>
        <li><a href="#">About DOCTYPEs</a></li>
        <li><a href="#">The &lt;html&gt;  Element </a></li>
        <li><a href="#">Character Encodings</a></li>
        <li><a href="#">The &lt;head&gt; Element </a></li>
        <li><a href="#">The &lt;title&gt; Element</a></li>
        <li><a href="#">Links  and Style Sheets</a></li>
        <li><a href="#">Ensuring Backwards Compatibility for HTML5 Tags</a></li>
        <li><a href="#">The &lt;body&gt; Element   </a></li>
        <li><a href="#">Common Content Elements</a></li>
    </ul>
</li>
<li><a href="#">Basic Text Formatting</a>
    <ul>
        <li><a href="#">White Space and Flow </a></li>
        <li><a href="#">Creating Headings Using &lt;hn&gt; Elements</a></li>
        <li><a href="#">Creating Paragraphs Using the &lt;p&gt; Element </a></li>
        <li><a href="#">Creating Line Breaks Using th e&lt;br&gt; Element</a></li>
        <li>
          <a href="#">Creating Preformatted Text Using the
          &lt;pre&gt; Element</a></li>
    </ul>
</li>
<li><a href="#">Understanding Block and Inline Elements</a></li>
<li><a href="#">Grouping Content</a>
    <ul>
        <li><a href="#">Document Outlines in HTML5</a></li>
        <li><a href="#">The &lt;div&gt; element</a></li>
        <li><a href="#">The &lt;header&gt; element</a></li>
        <li><a href="#">The &lt;hgroup&gt; element</a></li>
        <li><a href="#">The &lt;nav&gt; element</a></li>
        <li><a href="#">The &lt;section&gt; element</a></li>
        <li><a href="#">The &lt;article&gt; element</a></li>
        <li><a href="#">The &lt;hr&gt; element</a></li>
        <li><a href="#">The &lt;blockquote&gt; element</a></li>
        <li><a href="#">Using the cite Attribute with the
          &lt;blockquote&gt; Elemen</a></li>
        <li><a href="#">The &lt;aside&gt; element</a></li>
        <li><a href="#">The &lt;footer&gt; element</a></li>
        <li><a href="#">The &lt;address&gt; element</a></li>
    </ul>
</li>
<li><a href="#">Working With Lists</a>
    <ul>
```

```
            <li><a href="#">The &lt;ol&gt; element</a></li>
            <li><a href="#">The &lt;ul&gt; element</a></li>
            <li><a href="#">The &lt;li&gt; element</a></li>
            <li><a href="#">The &lt;dl&gt; element</a></li>
            <li><a href="#">The &lt;dt&gt; element</a></li>
            <li><a href="#">The &lt;dd&gt; element</a></li>
          </ul>
        </li>
      </ul>
```

The JavaScript (ch12_eg18.js) is simple but completely transforms the lists into a compact, interactive menu, as shown in Figure 12-14.

```
$( document ).ready( function(){
  $( "#menu" ).menu();
});
```

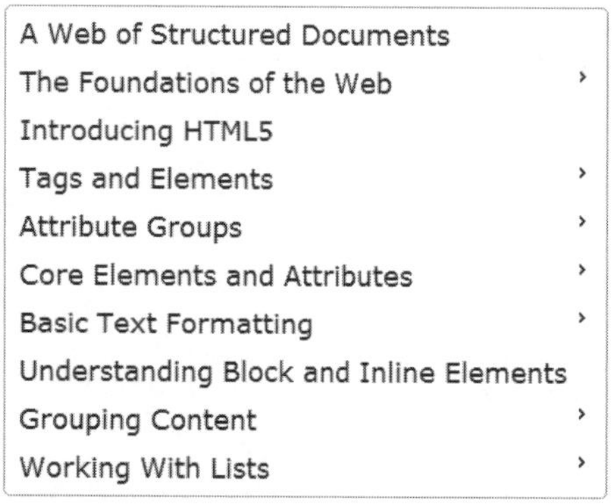

A Web of Structured Documents	
The Foundations of the Web	›
Introducing HTML5	
Tags and Elements	›
Attribute Groups	›
Core Elements and Attributes	›
Basic Text Formatting	›
Understanding Block and Inline Elements	
Grouping Content	›
Working With Lists	›

FIGURE 12-14

The Progressbar Widget

The Progressbar widget (http://jqueryui.com/progressbar/) is similar to the <progress> element you learned about in Chapter 6 but represents a fully cross-browser solution.

The markup starts with a simple <div> element (ch12_eg19.html):

```
<div id="progress"></div>
```

The JavaScript takes a map argument with a single value property, 40, used to set a default value. Unlike the <progress> element that has a value attribute, to access the value of a Progressbar, you need to get the value property of the plug-in instance by passing the string "value" into $().progressbar(). Figure 12-15 shows this widget in action.

```
$( document ).ready( function(){
  $( "#progress" ).progressbar({
    "value" : 40
  });
  console.log( $( "#progress" ).progressbar( "value" ) );
});
```

FIGURE 12-15

The Slider Widget

The Slider widget (`http://jqueryui.com/slider/`) is roughly equivalent to the HTML5 input range input type. Like the Progressbar widget before it, this also starts with a `<div>` element (ch12_eg20.html):

```
<div id="slider"></div>
```

The JavaScript illustrates a couple of things you can do with the slider. The first is to bind an event to the `"sliderchange"` event using `$().on()`. The callback function then illustrates two different ways to access the value of the slider. The first is to access the `value` property of the `ui` argument passed into the callback function by the jQuery UI plug-in. The second is similar to the way you accessed the value of the Progressbar, passing `"value"` in as a string to `$().slider()`.

```
$( document ).ready( function(){
  $( "#slider" ).slider().on( "slidechange", function( e , ui ) {
    console.log( ui.value );
    console.log( $( "#slider" ).slider( "value" ))
  });
});
```

Figure 12-16 shows the widget.

FIGURE 12-16

The Spinner Widget

The Spinner widget (`http://jqueryui.com/spinner/`) enables you to increment and decrement a numerical value using up and down arrows. The markup (ch12_eg21.html) starts with a simple text input.

```
<input id="spinner" type="text">
```

A call to `$().spinner()` transforms it into the element shown in Figure 12-17:

```
$( document ).ready( function(){
  $( "#spinner" ).spinner();
});
```

FIGURE 12-17

The Tabs Widget

The Tabs widget (http://jqueryui.com/tabs/) takes structured content bound together with a hash-based link and creates a series of tabbed elements. The markup (ch12_eg22.html) for this is a little bit more complicated than some of the previous examples. There's a wrapped <div> that can accept the call to $().tabs(). Inside there's a <ul> element that contains several <a> elements with hrefs pointing to several page ids. The ids are then seen in a series of <div> elements that represent the tab "body" content.

```
<div id="tabs">
  <ul>
    <li><a href="#tab1">Tab1</a></li>
    <li><a href="#tab2">Tab2</a></li>
    <li><a href="#tab3">Tab3</a></li>
  </ul>
  <div id="tab1">
    <p>Semiotics aute jean shorts occupy, pour-over raw denim odd
    future organic. Leggings keytar ennui chillwave photo booth</p>
  </div>
  <div id="tab2">
    <p>Semiotics aute jean shorts occupy, pour-over raw denim odd
    future organic. Leggings keytar ennui chillwave photo booth</p>
  </div>
  <div id="tab3">
    <p>Semiotics aute jean shorts occupy, pour-over raw denim odd
    future organic. Leggings keytar ennui chillwave photo booth</p>
  </div>
</div>
```

Calling $().tabs() (ch12_eg22.js) transforms the markup soup above into the component shown in Figure 12-18.

```
$( document ).ready( function(){
  $( "#tabs" ).tabs();
});
```

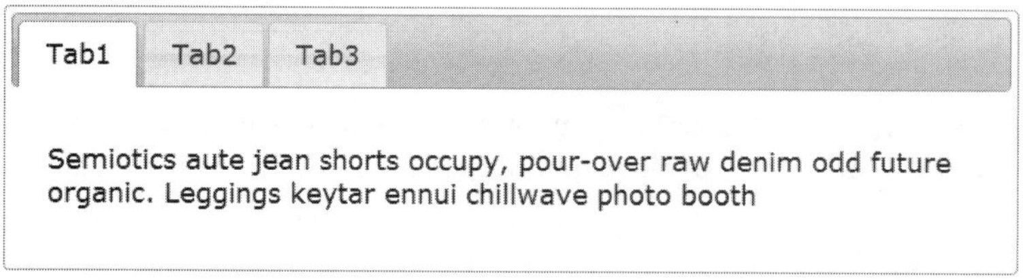

| Tab1 | Tab2 | Tab3 |

Semiotics aute jean shorts occupy, pour-over raw denim odd future
organic. Leggings keytar ennui chillwave photo booth

FIGURE 12-18

The Tooltip Widget

The Tooltip widget (http://jqueryui.com/tooltip/) takes title and alt attributes and transforms them into themeable HTML elements—basically a souped-up version of the standard browser tooltip. The markup (ch12_eg23.html) for this is an <a> element with a title attribute.

```
<p>A <a href="http://htmlcssjavascript.com/" title="Visit Rob's blog:
HTML + CSS + JavaScript">a blog about web technology</a></p>
```

The JavaScript (`ch12_eg23.js`) creates the fancy tooltip shown in Figure 12-19:

```
$( document ).ready( function(){
  $( "#tabs" ).tabs();
});
```

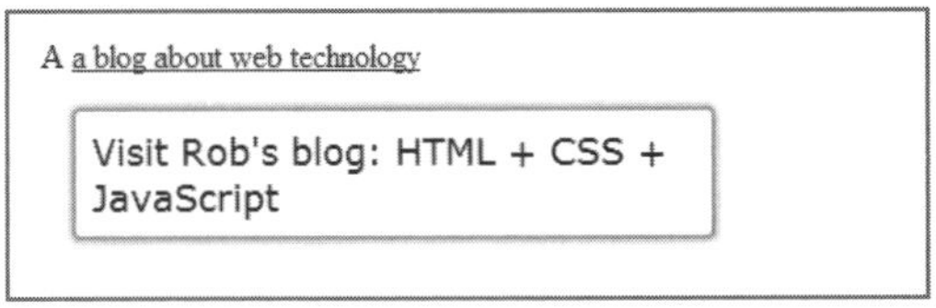

A a blog about web technology

Visit Rob's blog: HTML + CSS +
JavaScript

FIGURE 12-19

SUMMARY

This chapter introduced you to two major components of web development: jQuery Ajax and
jQuery UI.

You learned how to make Ajax requests using jQuery, including how to request JSON, plain text,
and XML. You also learned how to use GET and POST requests.

Using what you learned about POSTing form data, you also learned about the basics of form validation using jQuery Validate.

After that you learned about the different features of the powerful jQuery UI library and saw basic
examples in action.

EXERCISES

1. Use a jQuery GET request to get the file `data/example1.json`. The file contains an array. Every
element in the array is another array full of numbers. Loop through each element in the array and
write every number into the cell of a table with jQuery's DOM manipulation tools. Style the table
so that it has 1-pixel black borders, 3 pixels of padding on all sides, and no space between the
cells. When you finish, the table should look something like Figure 12-20.

6.48	1.83	9.48	8.01	7.22	1.57	3.90	3.20	1.76	1.84
2.20	6.06	4.52	0.79	3.62	5.43	4.35	3.55	6.57	3.60
8.20	1.09	5.29	1.69	6.30	3.90	2.34	6.69	7.42	7.35
9.57	7.43	9.95	9.84	7.02	8.05	4.20	4.35	4.48	8.20
4.39	9.08	3.23	0.86	3.65	3.15	5.84	9.98	4.32	8.54
0.85	2.39	6.43	0.89	4.98	0.49	1.46	7.42	9.72	5.04
5.00	2.04	1.17	9.96	1.66	4.40	1.55	4.73	7.80	1.87
8.27	2.83	2.83	0.67	1.99	9.33	7.92	5.31	7.97	4.08
1.61	3.48	6.20	2.03	5.43	6.81	4.33	6.58	9.21	6.86

FIGURE 12-20

2. Start with the following markup:

```
<div id="container">
  <h1>This book is about <span id="subject"></span></h1>
  <ul id="subjects">
    <li>HTML</li>
    <li>CSS</li>
    <li>JavaScript</li>
    <li>Ajax</li>
    <li>HTML5</li>
    <li>CSS3</li>
    <li>Video</li>
    <li>Audio</li>
  </ul>
  <div id="target">
    <p>Drop subjects here!</p>
  </div>
</div>
```

a. Apply the Draggable behavior to the `<li>` elements. Use the `revert` property (`http://api` `.jqueryui.com/draggable/#option-revert`) to ensure that the `<li>` elements return to their original place after they're dropped.

b. Apply the Droppable behavior to the `<div>` element with the `id` of `target`. If an `<li>` is dropped on it, use the `drop` callback to get the text of the selected `<li>` and insert it into the `<span>` element with the `id` of `subject`.

c. Give the `<li>` elements a single pixel, black border with 3 pixels of padding. Make them 200 pixels wide. The target box should be 300 pixels by 300 pixels, with a background of `#00ccff`, and it should be pinned to the right edge of the page.

d. If everything works, the page should look something like Figure 12-21, and you can update the text of the `<h1>` by dragging subjects over to the target.

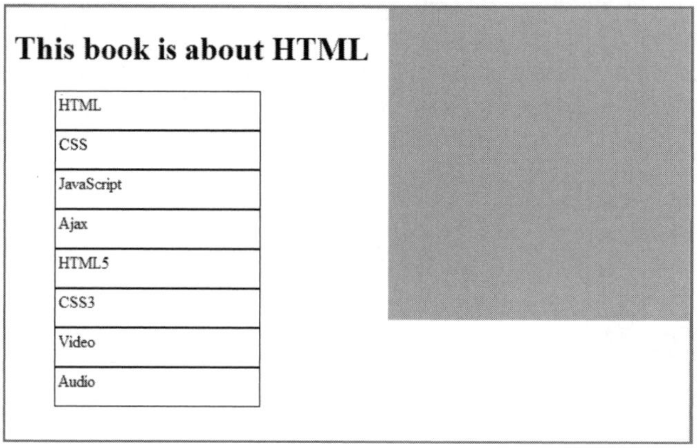

FIGURE 12-21

The answers to all the exercises are in Appendix A, "Answers to Exercises."

▶ **WHAT YOU LEARNED IN THIS CHAPTER**

TOPIC	KEY TAKEAWAY
Ajax	Ajax is a dominant pattern in web application development. It enables you to update a page without hitting the server for a full page request, creating a smoother, more application-like experience.
Ajax and jQuery	jQuery provides rich, cross-browser utilities for handling Ajax interactions.
GET and POST	The two basic methods of requesting information from a server are GET and POST. jQuery makes both of these easy, providing mnemonic convenience methods.
jQuery UI	jQuery UI is a rich collection of JavaScript behaviors and widgets that enable you to create advanced websites and web applications.

13

Checklists

This final chapter contains checklists on some helpful topics. The checklists are not intended to be exhaustive and turn you into an expert on each of these topics (as there are entire books devoted to the subjects of these checklists). Rather, the purpose is to show the key points and bring together some of the things you have learned throughout the book. There are two checklists, covering

- ➤ Search engine optimization
- ➤ Accessibility

SEARCH ENGINE OPTIMIZATION CHECKLIST

On any successful site, a good proportion of traffic comes from search engines. For people to find you on a search engine, you want to be as near the top of their search results as possible.

The techniques you can use to improve your visibility in search engines are known as *search engine optimization*, or *SEO* for short, and can be grouped in two ways:

- ➤ Things you can do on the site (on-page).
- ➤ Things that appear on other people's sites (off-page).

Focus on the former because you have a lot more control over what appears on the pages of your own site. (Although, mentions will be made of off-page techniques.)

On-Page Techniques

Before you can start optimizing your site for search engines, you need to determine what terms users would type into a search engine to find your site; these are known as *keywords* and *key phrases*.

You then need to include these keywords and phrases in the copy for your site. It is important for these words and phrases to appear in four places:

➤ **Title of the page:** This is specified in the `<title>` element, which you met in Chapter 1, "Structuring Documents for the Web." It appears at the top of the browser window (above all the toolbars).

➤ **Description of the page:** This is added using the `<meta>` tag. Although it is not visible on the page, it is often shown on the results pages of search engines.

➤ **Headings:** You met the `<h1>` to `<h6>` tags in Chapter 1, which are used to help structure the page, providing headings that describe what will be found in the subsequent sections.

➤ **Body text:** This is the copy that appears in the `<body>` of the page, for example, in paragraphs, lists, and links.

Search engines rely on text; they cannot see what is in images (other than in the `alt` text that you provide on images and in filenames). Therefore, if you can incorporate the keywords and phrases that you have identified into these four parts of your pages, your site is more likely to get picked up by search engines.

You can further help the search engines by carefully structuring your documents and using semantic markup. A good way to add structure to your pages is to organize the sections of pages using headings that describe what is in the following paragraphs, lists, images, and forms. Furthermore, elements such as the `<address>`, `<cite>`, `<code>`, and `<em>` elements help describe the information found inside those elements.

> **NOTE** *When working with search engines, you should not try to fool them. (For example, do not try to squeeze extra keywords onto your page by writing them in the same color as the background of the page.) Search engines know a lot of ways in which people try to fool them, and they will penalize you for this kind of behavior. You should also avoid free (or paid) tools that promise to submit your site to hundreds of search engines.*

All the preceding information seems straightforward and easy to implement. For many people, the biggest problem about SEO is in identifying the keywords and phrases that they should use in the first place, and that is what this checklist focuses on.

Identifying Keywords and Phrases

When choosing keywords and phrases, in most cases, you must focus not just on attracting volumes of users but also on attracting the right kinds of visitors. For example, if you create a site for a service that is offered locally, such as slate roofing, you probably are not interested in people who

➤ Do not live in the same geographic area you work in

➤ Have a roof made of tiles or shingles

➤ Live in apartment blocks (and do not have roofs to maintain)

Therefore, getting 10,000 people to visit you by searching for "new roof" is not likely to be as valuable to you as getting 100 people who are looking for "slate roof Chicago."

The page people find in the search engine must have a title and description that relate to the keywords people use when they search, because the titles and descriptions are commonly displayed in search engine results. If users do not think the page looks relevant (by looking at the information the search engine returns), they are less likely to click the link to your page.

So, to determine the search terms you should use on your site, use the steps in the following sections.

Brainstorm for Words People Might Search On

List every individual word you think people might search under when looking for your site.

Select Five to Ten Major Keywords

From your brainstorming list, select 5–10 major keywords, most of which will be single words. (Although you may have a couple phrases, such as "slate roof.")

Write these 5–10 major keywords in columns because you are going to create lists underneath them.

List Other Keywords and Phrases That Correspond to Your Major Keywords

Now that you have your list of major keywords, you can go back to your brainstorming session and expand upon the 5–10 major keywords you selected. List keywords and phrases that closely correspond to these major keywords. You might find it helpful to look up synonyms of words in your list and also the root words of terms. (For example, you might add "light" to a list that covers lighting.)

You must also consider more generic terms such as "buy," "download," "free," "info," or "tips," if you think that potential visitors might be hoping for one of these.

You should look for a total of approximately 20–30 popular phrases that you think your target audience will search for.

> **NOTE** *If you have a phrase that contains words such as "the" or "and," do not skip that word in the phrase. For example, "chicken and mushroom pie" should not become "chicken mushroom pie."*

Look Up Related Words (Not Exact Matches)

Sometimes, people search for terms that are not exactly what your site offers, but they are close enough for your site to be relevant to that visitor. For example, thinking back to the café example, you might add "restaurant" and "coffee shop" to the lists.

If there are some terms that are not exact matches but are relevant and related to the content of your site, add them under the major keywords.

Determine the Popularity of Terms

Use one of the following web-based tools to look up the words and phrases on your list.

➤ **Keyword Discovery:** www.keyworddiscovery.com

➤ **Wordtracker:** www.wordtracker.com

These tools both show alternative options for search terms. They also show the number of times people have searched for these words.

When you look at the alternative options for search terms on these sites, you want to look at the top 10 variations to see how many are relevant—if several of the top 10 variations on the term apply to your site, this should be a *core term* and you should list the top 10 variations with it.

Prioritize the Core Terms

To determine the priority of the core terms that you have found, you need to look at the number of searches each core term received, and compare this number with how closely you think that search meets your target audience. At first this will require you to judge which terms you think might be most relevant to your audience, but as your site grows, you can use analytics software to discover how people are finding your site.

If a search term generates 10,000 visitors, but only 10 percent would be interested in the content of your site, that term is not as valuable as a term that attracts just 5,000 viewers of whom 50 percent would be interested in your content.

Location

If the information, service, or product your site offers is location-dependent, the location should be added to your core terms.

The location you choose to include might not just be the name of the town that your business is based in. If you have customers across the state, county, or region that you work in, you might want to use those names, too. (More people might search on the name of the region than on your specific town.)

Mapping Core Terms to Pages

Now you need to take the core terms (and their variations) and map them to the most relevant page.

Most of the core terms will match to internal pages. You might have more than one page focused on one core term, but you should not try to get more than one core term per page (or one core term plus location).

Homepages

The two or three most general (rather than specific) core terms and the most popular core terms should be prime targets for the homepage.

Whenever you look at your on-page techniques for search engine optimization, you must measure the success of your efforts. This involves not only looking at things such as your page rank in Google but also using analytics software like Google Analytics (`http://www.google.com/analytics/`) to see which terms people search on frequently to find your site.

Off-Page Techniques

When search engines calculate where to position your site on a list of search results, the major search engines consider the number of sites that link to you.

The search engines look not just for any site that links to you but rather for sites that contain terms similar to those that people enter into search engines to find your site. For example, a search engine would not consider a link from an acupuncture site to a site about slate roofing as having the importance of a link between a building projects site and a site about slate roofing.

Search engines also look at the words that appear between the opening `<a>` tag and the closing `</a>` tag. If the text in the link contains keywords, the search engines consider that link more relevant than one that just says something like "Click here."

If you use analytics software on your site, you can see which sites link to you. You can then use this information to find more sites that cover similar topics to see if they would like to cover you, too.

ACCESSIBILITY CHECKLIST

Accessibility is about ensuring that as many people as possible can access your web pages. Traditionally, writing on accessibility has focused on people who may have disabilities such as vision impairments (and therefore use screen readers to read the content of websites to them). Others might have poor motor control and find it hard to use a mouse. However, it is increasingly becoming apparent that accessibility techniques apply to people who simply do not use a standard desktop PC to access web pages—for example, those on mobile devices who might not use a mouse or view as many images at the same time.

Entire books have been written on accessible design for the web, but this checklist can help ensure that your site meets basic accessibility requirements, and points you to the relevant part of the book where each of these topics was discussed.

Setting Up Your Document

When creating any new document, you should

➤ Use a DOCTYPE declaration to indicate which version of HTML or XHTML you use.

➤ Specify the language of your document on the `<html>` element. For example:

```
<html lang="en">
```

If the language changes in the middle of the text, specify it with another `lang` attribute indicating the new language on the element.

Structural and Semantic Markup

In Chapter 1, you met many elements used to mark up text. You should always try to use these elements to add structure and semantic information to the words on the page. Where possible

➤ Use the different levels of headings <h1> through <h6> to organize and add structure to your pages.

➤ Use elements for the purpose they were created, not just for visual effects. (Use CSS to control presentation of documents.)

➤ Use any elements available that describe the purpose or meaning of words in your page; for example, use the <abbr> element when you have an acronym or abbreviation on the page, use the <address> element when you have a mail address to write out, and use the <code> element when you write code.

Links and Navigation

As you saw in Chapter 3, "Links and Navigation," links are one of the key things that differentiate the web from other media. Your links need to be as accessible as possible so that people can navigate to your site. When you are creating links

➤ Ensure that your links stand out on the page, so visitors can easily see where they should be clicking and thus can skim the page for links.

➤ Use text or images inside the link that describe what visitors see if they click the link. (Do not just use terms such as "Click here.") If you use images inside a link, ensure that the alt text describes what users see if they click the link.

➤ You can use the title attribute on an <a> element to provide additional information to a visitor.

➤ In Chapter 6, "Forms," you saw how forms can make use of keyboard shortcuts to help visitors navigate the form. Keyboard shortcuts could also be used to link to other parts of pages.

➤ Avoid opening links in new windows because this can often confuse users who either do not see the new window opening or end up with more windows open than they wanted.

➤ Avoid links and interactive elements, such as cascading drop-down menus with many levels, which require a user to have fine control over the mouse (or other pointing device).

Images and Multimedia

Images, audio, and video (as you saw in Chapter 4, "Images, Audio, and Video") can bring a page to life. But assistive technologies used by those who have vision impairments cannot describe the content of an image, audio file, or video. Therefore, there is one key rule for all kinds of multimedia content: Always provide a text description for nontext content. To achieve this

➤ Provide an alt attribute for every image, and ensure that the text you specify as a value of the alt attribute describes the content of that image to a visitor. The only exception to this rule is when the image does not convey any meaning. (Perhaps it is just a decorative element.) In this case you still use the alt attribute, but you do not give it a value.

➤ If the image is complex and the description does not fit nicely into the `alt` attribute (for example, if you have an information graphic), you can use the `longdesc` attribute to specify where a longer description is, or use a letter *D* inside a normal link that points to a longer description.

➤ If you have video or audio track, provide a text-based transcript (on either the same page or a link to it).

➤ If you use an image map, offer a text-based alternative to the image links.

➤ If you provide any animated content, ensure that there is an easy way for the visitor to pause or stop that content.

➤ You should also avoid using animated content that could induce a seizure (for example, strobed content). If you do want to include such content, there should be a clear warning before that content, which the user should be forced to read and agree to.

Color

Color is an important part of any website, but color blindness is far more prevalent than most web designers realize. When you are creating a page, color can help add information and organize the page; however,

➤ No information on the page should be conveyed by color alone.

➤ There must be sufficient contrast between backgrounds and text so that the user can read the content.

Tables

You looked at creating tables in Chapter 5, "Tables." When you create a table, you should

➤ Use `<th>` elements for all headings.

➤ Describe the content of the table using the `<caption>` element.

➤ Use the `scope` and `header`, in complex tables.

➤ Use `scope` attributes to describe which cells each heading corresponds to.

➤ Not use tables as a way to control the layout of entire pages.

Forms

Chapter 6 introduced forms, which you need to use if you want to collect information from visitors to your site. It then discusses them again in the chapters that cover JavaScript. Some instructions for their use follow:

➤ Use the `<label>` element to indicate the label for each individual type of form element.

➤ If a user makes an error, where possible write the error next to the appropriate form field, and give that form element focus, so the user can correct the element.

➤ Make use of the `<fieldset>` and `<legend>` elements to group form controls into related functionality.

➤ Access keys can help users navigate long forms.

Style Sheets

You looked at CSS in Chapters 7 ("Cascading Style Sheets"), 8 ("More Cascading Style Sheets"), and 9 ("Rounded Corners, Animations, Custom Fonts, and More with CSS3"). Using CSS to control the presentation of a document can automatically help improve accessibility of the page because style sheets can be overruled by a user when necessary. But you should still

➤ Organize the page so it can still be read without style sheets.

➤ Ensure that you have provided enough contrast in colors so that any text can easily be read.

➤ Aim to design for device independence, or use CSS to provide alternative style sheets for multiple devices.

JavaScript

JavaScript was covered in Chapters 10 ("Learning JavaScript"), 11 ("Working with jQuery"), and 12 ("jQuery: Beyond the Basics"). Your pages must work even if the user does not have JavaScript enabled. Here are some instructions that help ensure your scripts do not compromise the accessibility of pages:

➤ If you need to use JavaScript on your pages (and they will not work without it), you should use the `<noscript>` element to provide an explanation that the page will not work if the visitor does not have JavaScript enabled.

➤ Do not automatically refresh pages. If you provide this feature, allow visitors the option to turn it off.

➤ Do not use JavaScript to redirect people from one page to another.

➤ Ensure that your scripts can be controlled with accessible/assistive technologies (such as screen readers).

Skip Links

One topic not covered in the main part of this book is the creation of skip links. These are links that enable people who use screen readers (rather than visual browsers) to skip over the common content that appears on every page, such as the header and main navigation. Imagine that you are browsing the web using technology that reads every page to you. You can see that on sites where you viewed many pages, it would not take long to get tired of hearing the same header repeated every time you moved to a new page.

The solution to this problem is a technique generally known as *skip links* or *skip navigation*. It simply involves creating links to specific parts of the page, such as the main content, and then hiding those links from users who browse visually using CSS. For example, look at the following links after the opening body element:

```
<body>
  <div class="skip-links">
    <a href="#content">skip to main content</a>
    <a href="#search">skip to search</a>
    <a href="#footer">skip to footer</a>
  </div>
```

These links correspond to id attributes of <a> elements in the relevant sections of the page. For example, the first <h1> element might look like this:

```
<h1><a id="#content">Introduction to Accessibility</a></h1>
```

The links at the top of the page are hidden using a CSS rule like this so that visitors using a normal visual browser do not see the skip links:

```
.skip-links {display:none;}
```

This makes browsing a site pleasant for those who have the site read to them.

Answers to Exercises

This appendix covers the answers to each of the exercises at the end of each chapter.

CHAPTER 1

Exercise 1

Mark up the following list, with inserted and deleted content:

Ricotta pancake ingredients:

- ➤ 1 ~~1/2~~ <u>3/4</u> cups ricotta
- ➤ 3/4 cup milk
- ➤ 4 eggs
- ➤ 1 cup plain <u>white</u> flour
- ➤ 1 teaspoon baking powder
- ➤ ~~75g~~ <u>50g</u> butter
- ➤ Pinch of salt

Answer

Here is the bulleted list with elements that show which content has been inserted and deleted:

```
<h1>Ricotta pancake ingredients:</h1>
<ul>
  <li>1 <del>1/2</del><ins>3/4</ins> cups ricotta</li>
  <li>3/4 cup milk</li>
  <li>4 eggs</li>
  <li>1 cup plain <ins>white</ins> flour</li>
  <li>1 teaspoon baking powder</li>
```

```
    <li><del>75g</del><ins>50g</ins> butter</li>
    <li>Pinch of salt</li>
</ul>
```

CHAPTER 2

Exercise 1

Mark up the following sentence with the relevant presentational elements.

```
The 1st time the bold man wrote in italics, he emphasized several key words.
```

Answer

The sentence uses superscript, bold, italic, and emphasized elements.

```
<p>The 1<sup>st</sup> time the <b>bold</b> man wrote in
<i>italics</i>, he <em>emphasized</em> several key words.</p>
```

Exercise 2

You have already created the homepage for the Example Café site that you will build throughout the book. You also created a recipes page. Now you need to create three more pages so that you can continue to build the site in upcoming chapters. Each page should start like the homepage, with a level 1 heading titled **Example Café**, followed by this paragraph: **Welcome to Example Café. We will be developing this site throughout the book.** After this

  a. For a menu page, add a level 2 heading titled **Menu**. This should be followed by a paragraph saying **The menu will go here.** Update the content of the `<title>` element to reflect that this page will feature the menus at the café. Save the file with the name `menu.html`.

  b. For an opening times page, add a level 2 heading saying **Opening hours**. This should be followed by a paragraph saying **Details of opening hours and how to find us will go here.** Update the `<title>` element to reflect that the page tells visitors opening hours and where to find the café. Save the file with the name `opening.html`.

  c. For the contact page, add a level 2 heading titled **Contact**. This page should contain this address: **12 Sea View, Newquay, Cornwall, UK.** Update the `<title>` element to reflect that the page tells visitors how to contact the café.

Answer

The markup for `menu.html` should look like this:

```
<!DOCTYPE html>
<html>
<head>
  <meta charset="utf-8">
    <title>Example Cafe - Menu</title>
```

```
    </head>
    <body>
      <h1>Example Café</h1>
      <p>Welcome to Example Café. We will be developing this site
      throughout the book.</p>
      <h2>Menu</h2>
      <p>The menu will go here.</p>
    </body>
  </html>
```

The markup for `opening.html` should look like this:

```
<!DOCTYPE html>
<html>
<head>
  <meta charset="utf-8">
    <title>Example Cafe - Menu</title>
  </head>
  <body>
    <h1>Example Café</h1>
    <p>Welcome to Example Café. We will be developing this site
    throughout the book.</p>
    <h2>Opening Hours</h2>
    <p>Details of opening hours and how to find us will go here. </p>
  </body>
</html>
```

The markup for `contact.html` should look like this:

```
<!DOCTYPE html>
<html>
<head>
  <meta charset="utf-8">
    <title>Example Cafe - Menu</title>
  </head>
  <body>
    <h1>Example Café</h1>
    <p>Welcome to Example Café. We will be developing this site
    throughout the book.</p>
    <h2>Contact</h2>
    <p>12 Sea View, Newquay, Cornwall, UK</p>
  </body>
</html>
```

CHAPTER 3

Exercise 1

Look back at the Try It Out example where you created a menu, and create a new page that links directly to each course on the menu. Then add a link to the main Wrox website (www.wrox.com). The page should look something like Figure A-1.

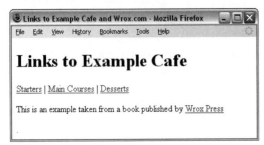

FIGURE A-1

Answer

Here is the page with links to the menu first and then a link to the Wrox Press website:

```
<!DOCTYPE html>
<html>
<head>
  <meta charset="utf-8">
  <title>Links to Example Cafe and Wrox.com</title>
</head>
<body>
  <h1>Links to Example Cafe</h1>
  <p>
    <a href="http://www.examplecafe.com/menu.html#starters">Starters</a> |
    <a href="http://www.examplecafe.com/menu.html#mains">Main Courses</a> |
    <a href="http://www.examplecafe.com/menu.html#desserts">Desserts</a>
  </p>
  <p>This is an example taken from a book published by
    <a href="http://www.wrox.com">Wrox Press</a>
  </p>.
</body>
</html>
```

Exercise 2

Go back to the pages in the sample application and make sure that you have updated the navigation for each page.

Answer

Navigation for the homepage:

```
<nav>
  HOME
  <a href="menu.html">MENU</a>
  <a href="recipes.html">RECIPES</a>
  <a href="contact.html">CONTACT</a>
</nav>
```

Navigation for the menu page:

```
<nav>
  <a href="index.html">HOME</a>
  MENU
  <a href="recipes.html">RECIPES</a>
  <a href="contact.html">CONTACT</a>
</nav>
```

Navigation for the recipes page:

```
<nav>
  <a href="index.html">HOME</a>
  <a href="menu.html">MENU</a>
  RECIPES
  <a href="contact.html">CONTACT</a>
</nav>
```

Navigation for the contact page:

```
<nav>
  <a href="index.html">HOME</a>
  <a href="menu.html">MENU</a>
  <a href="recipes.html">RECIPES</a>
  CONTACT
</nav>
```

CHAPTER 4

Exercise 1

Add the images of icons that represent a diary, a camera, and a newspaper to the following example. All the images are provided in the images folder in the download code for Chapter 4.

```
<h1>Icons</h1>
<p>Here is an icon used to represent a diary.</p>
<img src="images/diary.gif" alt="Diary" width="150" height="120" >

<p>Here is an icon used to represent a picture.</p>
Camera image goes here

<p>Here is an icon used to represent a news item.</p>
Newspaper image goes here
```

Your finished page should resemble Figure A-2.

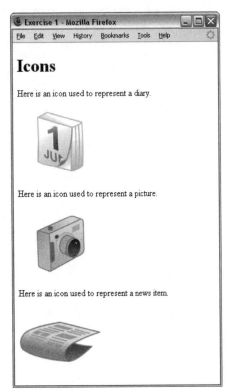

FIGURE A-2

Answer

Here is the code for this page:

```
<!DOCTYPE html>
<html>
<head>
  <meta charset="utf-8">
  <title>Exercise 1</title>
</head>
<body>
  <h1>Icons</h1>
  <p>Here is an icon used to represent a diary.</p>
  <img src="images/diary.gif" alt="Diary" width="150" height="120" >
  <p>Here is an icon used to represent a picture.</p>
  <img src="images/picture.gif" alt="Picture" width="150" height="120" >
  <p>Here is an icon used to represent a news item.</p>
  <img src="images/news.gif" alt="news" width="150" height="120" >
</body>
</html>
```

Exercise 2

Look at the images shown in Figures A-3 and A-4 and decide whether you are more likely to get smaller file sizes and better quality images if you save them as PNGs or JPEGs.

FIGURE A-3

FIGURE A-4

Answer

As discussed in Chapter 3, "Links and Navigation," images with large, flat areas of color, such as Image 1 where you see only the silhouette of the people, compress better as GIFs or PNGs than JPEGs, whereas JPEGs are better for saving photographic images where there is greater variety of colors and more difference in the shades of different colors.

➤   Image 1 (Figure A-3): GIF or PNG

➤   Image 2 (Figure A-4): JPEG

Exercise 3

Go through the files for the sample application and replace the main heading with the logo on each page. On every page except for the homepage, make sure that the image links back to the `index.html` page.

Answer

The new heading should look like this:

```
<a href="index.html" id="top">
  <img src="images/logo.gif" alt="example cafe logo" width="194"
height="80" >
</a>
```

CHAPTER 5

Exercise 1

Where should the `<caption>` element for a table be placed in the document and, by default, where is it displayed?

Answer

The `<caption>` element should appear after the opening `<table>` element but before the first `<tr>` element.

Exercise 2

In what order would the cells in Figure A-5 be read out by a screen reader?

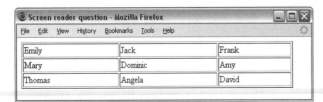

FIGURE A-5

Answer

The names would be read in the following order: Emily, Jack, Frank, Mary, Dominic, Amy, Thomas, Angela, and David.

CHAPTER 6

Exercise 1

Create an e-mail feedback form that looks like the one shown in Figure A-6.

Reply to ad

Use the following form to respond to the ad:

To
[Star Seller]

To
[ ]

Subject
[ ]

Body
[ ]

[Send email]

FIGURE A-6

The first textbox is a `readonly` textbox so that the user cannot alter the name of the person the e-mail is sent to.

Answer

Here is the code for the feedback form:

```
<!DOCTYPE html>
<html>
<head>
  <meta charset="utf-8">
  <title>Reply to ad</title>
</head>
```

```
<body>
<h1>Reply to ad</h1>
<p>Use the following form to respond to the ad:</p>
<form action="http://www.example.com/ads/respond.aspx" method="post"
      name="frmRespondToAd">
<table>
  <tr>
    <td><label for="emailTo">To</label></td>
    <td><input type="text" name="txtTo" readonly="readonly" id="emailTo"
        size="20" value="Star Seller" /></td>
  </tr>
  <tr>
    <td><label for="emailFrom">To</label></td>
    <td><input type="text" name="txtFrom" id="emailFrom" size="20" /></td>
  </tr>
  <tr>
    <td><label for="emailSubject">Subject</label></td>
    <td><input type="text" name="txtSubject" id="emailSubject"
        size="50" /></td>
  </tr>
  <tr>
    <td><label for="emailBody">Body</label></td>
    <td><textarea name="txtBody" id="emailBody" cols="50" rows="10">
        </textarea></td>
  </tr>
</table>
  <input type="submit" value="Send email" >
</form>
</body>
</html>
```

Exercise 2

Create a voting or ranking form that looks like the one shown in Figure A-7.

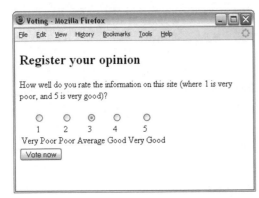

FIGURE A-7

The following `<style>` element was added to the `<head>` of the document to make each column of the table the same fixed width, with text aligned in the center.

```
<head>
  <title>Voting</title>
  <style type="text/css">td {width:100px; text-align:center;}</style>
</head>
```

Answer

Here is the code for the voting form. The checked attribute is used on the middle value for this form so that it loads with an average score (in case the form is submitted without a value selected):

```
<!DOCTYPE html>
<html>
<head>
  <meta charset="utf-8">
  <title>Voting</title>
  <style type="text/css">td {width:100px; text-align:center;}</style>
</head>
<body>
<h2>Register your opinion</h2>
<p>How well do you rate the information on this site (where 1 is
    very poor and 5 is very good)?</p>
<form action="http://www.example.com/ads/respond.aspx" method="get"
      name="frmRespondToAd">
  <table>
    <tr>
      <td><input type="radio" name="radVote" value="1" id="vpoor" /></td>
      <td><input type="radio" name="radVote" value="2" id="poor" /></td>
      <td><input type="radio" name="radVote" value="3" id="average"
         checked="checked" /></td>
      <td><input type="radio" name="radVote" value="4" id="good" /></td>
      <td><input type="radio" name="radVote" value="5" id="vgood" /></td>
    </tr>
    <tr>
      <td><label for="vpoor">1 <br />Very Poor</label></td>
      <td><label for="poor">2 <br />Poor</label></td>
      <td><label for="average">3 <br />Average</label></td>
      <td><label for="good">4 <br />Good</label></td>
      <td><label for="vgood">5 <br />Very Good</label></td>
    </tr>
  </table>
  <input type="submit" value="Vote now" />
</form>
</body>
</html>
```

CHAPTER 7

Exercise 1

In this exercise (and the next), you continue to work on the Example Café website. Open the `index .html` page, and add a `<div>` element just inside the opening `<body>` tag and the closing `</body>` tag. Give the element an `id` attribute whose value is `page`. Repeat this for each page of the site.

a. In the style sheet add a rule that gives this element a margin, border, and padding so that it looks like the border in Figure A-8.

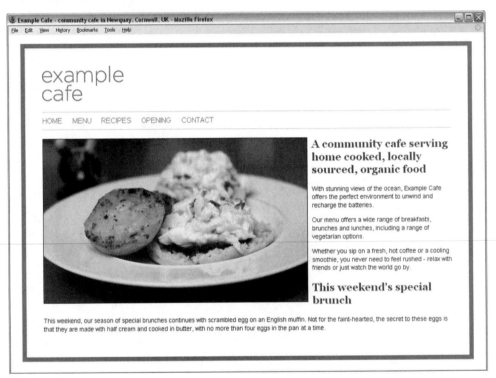

FIGURE A-8

Answer

Here is the HTML for the homepage; you can see the new `<div>` element has been highlighted:

```
<!DOCTYPE html>
<html>
<head>
  <meta charset="utf-8">
  <title>Example Cafe - community cafe in Newquay, Cornwall, UK</title>
  <link rel="stylesheet" href="css/interface.css">
</head>
```

```
<body>
  <div id="page">
    <header>
      <a id="top"><img src="images/logo.gif" alt="example cafe logo"
        width="194" height="80" >
      <nav id="navigation">
        HOME
        <a href="menu.html">MENU</a>
        <a href="recipes.html">RECIPES</a>
        <a href="contact.html">CONTACT</a>
      </nav>
    </header>
    <article>
      <h1>Home</h1>
      <img src="images/scrambled_eggs.jpg" width="622" height="370"
        alt="Photo of scrambled eggs on an English muffin" align="left" >
      <h2>A community cafe serving home cooked, locally sourced, organic
food</h2>
      <p>With stunning views of the ocean, Example Cafe offers the
perfect environment to unwind and recharge the batteries.</p>
      <p>Our menu offers a wide range of breakfasts, brunches and
lunches,
 including a range of vegetarian options.</p>
      <p>Whether you sip on a fresh, hot coffee or a cooling smoothie,
you
 never need to feel rushed. Relax with friends or just watch the world go
 by.</p>
      <h2>This weekend's special brunch</h2>
      <p>This weekend, our season of special brunches continues with
scrambled
 egg on an English muffin. Not for the faint-hearted, the secret to these
eggs
 is that they are made with half cream and cooked in butter, with no more
than four eggs in the pan at a time.</p>      </article>
    </div>
  </body>
</html>
```

Now here is the CSS rule that creates the blue border:

```
#page {
  width:960px;
  border:10px solid #3399cc;
  padding:40px;
  margin:20px;
}
```

b. Create a CSS rule that makes the following changes to the navigation:

i. Add a single-pixel gray border on the top and bottom.

ii. Give it 20 pixels of margin above and below the gray lines.

iii. Give it 10 pixels of padding on the top and bottom in the box.

iv. Add a margin to the right of each link in the navigation.

Answer

The first three changes (for points a, b, and c) can be handled using one CSS rule. The rule must control four properties:

➤ The `border-top` and `border-bottom` properties add a single-pixel gray line above and below the navigation.

➤ The `padding` property adds space between the lines and the items in the navigation.

➤ The `margin` property adds a bit of space above and below the gray lines.

➤ The `margin-right` property can be used to add space to the right of each individual link.

```
#navigation {
  border-top:1px solid #d6d6d6;
  border-bottom:1px solid #d6d6d6;
  padding:10px 0px 10px 0px;
  margin:20px 0px 20px 0px;
}
#navigation a {
  color:#3399cc;
  text-decoration:none;
  margin-right:20px;
}
```

c. Give the main image on the homepage a `class` attribute whose value is `main_image`. Then create a rule that gives the image a single-pixel black border, and also give the image a 10-pixel margin on the right and bottom sides of the image.

Answer

Here is the new CSS rule that controls the appearance of the image:

```
.main_image {
  border:1px solid #000000;
  margin:0px 10px 10px 0px;}
```

d. Increase the gaps between each line of text within paragraphs to 1.3 em.

Answer

You can add the `line-height` property to the rule that controls the `<p>` elements to change the gap between the text, which typesetters refer to as leading.

```
p {
  color:#333333;
  font-size:90%;
  line-height:1.3em;
}
```

Exercise 2

Take a look at the following HTML:

```
<!DOCTYPE html>
<html>
<head>
  <title>Font test</title>
  <link rel="stylesheet" href="tableStyles.css" />
</head>
<body>
<table>
  <tr>
    <th>Quantity</th>
    <th>Ingredient</th>
  </tr>
  <tr class="odd">
    <td>3</td>
    <td>Eggs</td>
  </tr>
  <tr>
    <td>100ml</td>
    <td>Milk</td>
  </tr>
  <tr class="odd">
    <td>200g</td>
    <td>Spinach</td>
  </tr>
  <tr>
    <td>1 pinch</td>
    <td>Cinnamon</td>
  </tr>
</table>
</body>
</html>
```

Now create the `tableStyles.css` style sheet, which makes this example look like Figure A-9.

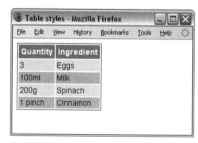

FIGURE A-9

Don't worry about getting the sizes exactly the same as the screen shot, but do make sure you have padding in the cells and a border around the outside. The white border is created by default in IE; you find out how to remove this in Chapter 8.

Answer

First, you need to add a style rule for either the `<body>` element or all elements using the universal selector *, which indicates that the rule applies to all elements. As mentioned in the chapter, set the `background-color` property of the `<body>` element on a site in case the user has set it to another value. You can also set the `font-family` and `font-size` properties to control how the text appears.

```
body {
  background-color:#ffffff;
  font-family:arial, verdana, sans-serif;
  font-size:14px;
}
```

To give the entire table a single-pixel, dark gray border, you can use the following style rules, or you could just use the `border` property shorthand:

```
table {
  border-style:solid;
  border-width:1px;
  border-color:#666666;
}
```

The table headings have a dark background with light writing; the font is also bold. In addition, there is no border to the headings. Note how the shorthand `border` property is used this time and the cells have padding:

```
th {
  color:#ffffff;
  background-color:#999999;
  font-weight:bold;
  border:0;
  padding:4px;
}
```

By default, the table rows will have a light background color:

```
tr {background-color:#cccccc;}
```

To alternate the colors of the rows, the `<tr>` elements that have a `class` attribute whose value is `odd` will have a different background color:

```
tr.odd {background-color:#efefef;}
```

Finally, you should give two pixels of padding to each table cell, and ensure that the color of the text in the cells is black.

```
td {
  color:#000000;
  padding:2px;
}
```

CHAPTER 8

Exercise 1

In this exercise, you create a linked table of contents that sits at the top of a long document in an ordered list and links to the headings in the main part of the document.

The HTML file `exercise1.html` is provided with the download code for this book, ready for you to create the style sheet. Your style sheet should do the following:

➤ Set the styles of all links including active and visited links.

➤ Make the contents of the list bold.

➤ Make the background of the list light gray and use padding to ensure the bullet points show.

➤ Make the width of the links box 250 pixels wide.

➤ Change the style of heading bullet points to empty circles.

➤ Change the style of link bullet points to squares.

Your page should look something like Figure A-10.

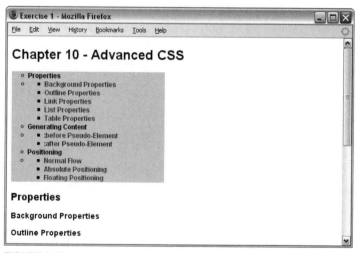

FIGURE A-10

Answer

You can create a rule that applies to the `<body>` element to control the background color of the page and the font used.

```
body {
    background-color:#ffffff;
    font-family:arial, verdana, sans-serif;
    font-size:12px;}
```

There were several tasks that related to the list of bullet points that make up the contents. If you look at the following rule, you can see it starts by setting the background color of the list to a light gray. This is followed by a property that sets the default style of bullet points to empty circles. Then all the text is made bold. The fourth property sets the padding to the left of the list. Finally, the width of the lists is set to 250 pixels wide.

```
ul {
    background-color:#d6d6d6;
    list-style:circle;
    font-weight:bold;
    padding-left:30px;
    width:250px;}
```

The links to the sections are in nested unordered lists, and there are a couple of properties you need to set for these lists. First, you must set the bullet points to squares. Second, because all unordered lists have a gray background and are 250 pixels wide, the nested lists would poke out to the right side if you did not make them less wide.

```
ul ul {
    list-style:square;
    width:220px;}
```

The final item on the list was to set the styles of all links including active and visited links, which requires another four rules:

```
a:link {
    color:#0033ff;;
    text-decoration:none;}
a:visited {
    color:#0066ff;
    text-decoration:none;}
a:active {
    text-decoration:underline;}
a:link:hover {
    color:#003399;
    background-color:#e9e9e9;
    text-decoration:underline;}
```

Exercise 2

In this exercise, you test your CSS positioning skills. You should create a page that represents the links to the different sections of the chapter in a different way. Each of the sections must be shown in a different block, and each block must be absolutely positioned in a diagonal top-left to bottom-right direction. The middle box should appear on top, as shown in the Figure A-11.

You can find the source HTML file (exercise2.html) with the download code for this chapter.

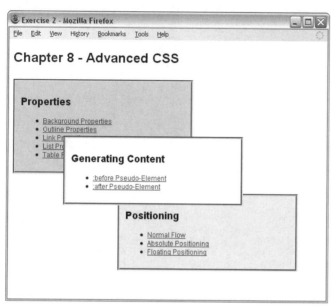

FIGURE A-11

Answer

To begin, set the background color for the entire page and default font in a rule that applies to the `<body>` element.

```
body {
    background-color:#ffffff;
    font-family:arial, verdana, sans-serif;
    font-size:12px;}
```

Next, set a rule that applies to all the `<div>` elements. Even though you will change the background color of two of the boxes, whenever boxes are taken out of normal flow, there is a risk that they will overlap, so you should give them a background color (because by default boxes have no background).

You can also set some common properties, adding padding to each box, as well as a border and the width of the boxes.

```
div {
    background-color:#ffffff;
    padding:10px;
    border-style:groove; border-width:4px; border-color:#999999;
    width:300px;}
```

Finally, you simply position each of the boxes. Because the containing element is the `<body>` element, you position each box from the top-left corner of the browser window.

```
div.page1 {
    position:absolute;
    top:70px;
```

```
        z-index:2;
        background-color:#d6d6d6;}

div.page2 {
    position:absolute;
    top:170px; left:100px;
    z-index:3;}

div.page3 {
    position:absolute;
    top:270px; left:200px;
    z-index:1;
    background-color:#efefef;}
```

CHAPTER 9

Exercise 1

In this exercise, you create a linked table of contents that sits at the top of a long document in an ordered list and links to the headings in the main part of the document.

The HTML file `exercise1.html` is provided with the download code for this book, ready for you to create the style sheet. Your style sheet should do the following:

➤ Round the corners of the `#contents` `<div>` element with a 12-pixel corner radius.

➤ Make the background color of the `#contents` element 70 percent opaque, leaving the text black.

➤ Change the font to be Inconsolata using `http://www.fontsquirrel.com/fonts/Inconsolata`.

Your page should look something like Figure A-12.

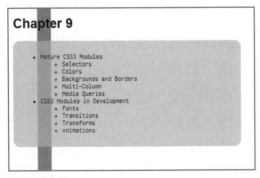

FIGURE A-12

Answer

Your CSS should look something like the following:

```
@font-face {
    font-family: 'InconsolataMedium';
    src: url('fonts/Inconsolata-webfont.eot');
    src: url('fonts/Inconsolata-webfont.eot?#iefix')
    format('embedded-opentype'),
        url('fonts/Inconsolata-webfont.woff') format('woff'),
        url('fonts/Inconsolata-webfont.ttf') format('truetype'),
        url('fonts/Inconsolata-webfont.svg#InconsolataMedium')
        format('svg');
    font-weight: normal;
    font-style: normal;

}
#contents {
  padding : 10px;
  font-family : InconsolataMedium;
  background-color : hsla( 0,0%,80%,.7 );
  width : 400px;
  -webkit-border-radius: 12px;
  border-radius: 12px;
}
```

Exercise 2

In this exercise, you test your understanding of `border-radius` and the Transitions module to make a neat hover effect. Your style sheet should do the following:

➤ Set 1 second transitions for both the `:hover` and standard state. Transition the `border-radius` and `background-color` properties.

➤ In the `#hover:hover` definition, change the background color to `#00ccff` and change the `border-radius` to 100 pixels, which makes the box a circle.

The hover state of your page should look like Figure A-13.

You can find the source HTML file (`exercise2.html`) with the download code for this chapter.

Hover Me

FIGURE A-13

Answer

Your style sheet should look like the following. It may look different depending on the number of prefixed browser variations you use:

```
#hover {
  width : 200px;
  height : 200px;
  background-color : #ffcc00;
  -webkit-transition-property : background-color,
    -webkit-border-radius;
  -moz-transition-property : background-color,
    -moz-border-radius;
  -o-transition-property :  background-color,
    -o-border-radius;
  transition-property :  background-color,
     border-radius;
  -webkit-transition-duration: 1s;
  -moz-transition-duration: 1s;
  -o-transition-duration: background-color 1s;
  transition-duration: background-color 1s;
  text-align: center;
  line-height:200px;
}
#hover:hover {
  width : 200px;
  background-color : #00ccff;
  -webkit-transition-property : background-color,
    -webkit-border-radius;
  -moz-transition-property : background-color,
    -moz-border-radius;
  -o-transition-property :  background-color,
    -o-border-radius;
  transition-property :  background-color,
    border-radius;
 -webkit-transition-duration: 1s;
  -moz-transition-duration: 1s;
  -o-transition-duration: background-color 1s;
  transition-duration: background-color 1s;
 -webkit-border-radius : 100px;
  border-radius : 100px;
}
```

CHAPTER 10

Exercise 1

Create a script to write out the multiplication table for the number 5 from 1 to 20 using a while loop.

Answer

The exercise is based around a counter (to work out where you are in your tables); each time the code is run, the counter increments by 1. So, you need to make sure the counter can go up to 20, rather than 10. This goes in the condition of the `while` loop:

```
while (i < 21) {
```

Then you need to change the multiplier, which is both written out and used in the calculation:

```
document.body.innerHTML+= "<p>" + i + " x 5 = " + (i * 5) + "</p>";
```

Depending on how you write out the results, your answer should look something like this:

```
var i = 1;
while ( i < 21 ) {
  document.body.innerHTML+= "<p>" + i + " x 5 = " + (i * 5) + "</p>";
  i++;
}
```

Exercise 2

Modify `ch10_eg05.js` so that it can say one of three things:

➤ "Good Morning" to visitors coming to the page before 12 p.m. (using an `if` statement).

➤ "Good Afternoon" to visitors coming to the page between 12 p.m. and 6 p.m. (again using an `if` statement). (Hint: You might need to use a logical operator.)

➤ "Good Evening" to visitors coming to the page after 6 p.m. up until midnight (again using an `if` statement).

Answer

This script needs to use the `getHours()` method of the date object to determine the time and then uses `if` statements to check the appropriate time for each statement presented to the user.

The afternoon uses a logical operator to check that it is after 12 p.m. but before 6 p.m.

```
var date = new Date();
var time = date.getHours();

if ( time < 12 ) {
  document.body.innerHTML += '<h1>Good Morning</h1>';
}
if ( time >= 12 && time < 18 ) {
  document.body.innerHTML += '<h1>Good Afternoon</h1>';
}
if ( time >= 18 ) {
    document.body.innerHTML += '<h1>Good Evening</h1>';
}
```

CHAPTER 11

Exercise 1

Rewrite the code from the files `ch10_eg03.html` and `ch10_eg03.js` to use jQuery. Instead of a `console.log`, add a `<p>` element to display the results as a child of the `<body>` element. Use the jQuery method `$().val()` to get the value of the form fields.

Answer

First, you need to add jQuery and add the `<p>` element to hold the results.

```
<!DOCTYPE html>
<html>
<head>
<title>Area calculator</title>
</head>
<body>
<form name="frmArea">
Enter the width and height of your rectangle to calculate the size:<br>
Width: <input type="text" name="txtWidth" size="5" id="width"><br>
Height: <input type="text" name="txtHeight" size="5" id="height"><br>
<input type="button" value="Calculate area" id="calc">
</form>
<p id="results">
</p>
<script src="js/jquery-1.8.2.min.js"></script>
<script src="exercise1.js"></script>
</body>
</html>
```

Then you need to adjust the script. Most of it is similar to the core JavaScript example; you just use the jQuery convenience methods. The biggest difference is getting a reference to the `#results` `<p>` element and using `$().html()` to write out the results of the calculation:

```
function calculateArea( width, height ) {
  var area = width * height;
  return area
}

$( "#calc" ).on( "click" , function(){
  $( "#results" ).html( calculateArea(
    $( "#width" ).val(),
    $( "#height" ).val()
  ));
});
```

Exercise 2

Modify `main.js` in the Example Café site to test the hash of the URL. You can access the hash with the BOM property `window.location.hash`. Use a conditional statement and jQuery to satisfy the following three conditions:

➤ If the hash equals "starters," hide the menu items for mains and desserts.

➤ If the hash equals "mains," hide the menu items for starters and desserts.

➤ If the hash equals "desserts," hide the menu items for starters and mains.

Test it by appending each hash to the file URL (for example, `menu.html"#starters"`).

➤ Note that the `window.location.hash` property includes the # character.

Answer

All the pieces for this script, with the exception of testing `window.location.hash`, are already in place from the earlier Try It Out. The differences are as follows:

➤ You need to hide all the menu items instead of just the desserts and mains.

➤ You need to test the `window.location.hash` against the options and then show the correct menu using a conditional statement.

➤ If there's not a hash set at all or the hash doesn't match any of the predefined options, you need to show the default.

```
$( document ).ready(function(){
  if ( $( "body" ).hasClass( "menu" ) ) {
    $( "#starters + div, #mains + div, #desserts + div").hide();
    if ( document.location.hash === "#starters" ) {
      $( "#starters" ).addClass( "expanded" ).next().show();
    } else if ( document.location.hash === "#mains" ) {
      $( "#mains" ).addClass( "expanded" ).next().show();
    } else if ( document.location.hash === "#desserts" ) {
      $( "#desserts" ).addClass( "expanded" ).next().show();
    } else {
      $( "#starters" ).addClass( "expanded" ).next().show();
    }
    $( "h2" ).on( "click", function(){
      if( !$( this ).hasClass( "expanded" )) {
        $( ".expanded" ).removeClass( "expanded" ).next().slideUp( "fast" );
        $( this ).addClass( "expanded" ).next().slideDown( "slow" );
      }
    });
  }
});
```

CHAPTER 12

Exercise 1

Use a jQuery GET request to get the file `data/example1.json`. The file contains an array. Every element in the array is another array full of numbers. Loop through each element in the array and write every number into the cell of a table with jQuery's DOM manipulation tools. Style the table so that it has 1-pixel black borders, 3 pixels of padding on all sides, and no space between the cells.

When you finish, the table should look something like Figure A-14.

6.48	1.83	9.48	8.01	7.22	1.57	3.90	3.20	1.76	1.84
2.20	6.06	4.52	0.79	3.62	5.43	4.35	3.55	6.57	3.60
8.20	1.09	5.29	1.69	6.30	3.90	2.34	6.69	7.42	7.35
9.57	7.43	9.95	9.84	7.02	8.05	4.20	4.35	4.48	8.20
4.39	9.08	3.23	0.86	3.65	3.15	5.84	9.98	4.32	8.54
0.85	2.39	6.43	0.89	4.98	0.49	1.46	7.42	9.72	5.04
5.00	2.04	1.17	9.96	1.66	4.40	1.55	4.73	7.80	1.87
8.27	2.83	2.83	0.67	1.99	9.33	7.92	5.31	7.97	4.08
1.61	3.48	6.20	2.03	5.43	6.81	4.33	6.58	9.21	6.86

FIGURE A-14

Answer

Using the `$.get()` convenience method, you need to get a reference to the cells from the `data.cells` array. Then you build up a string of HTML in a `for` loop, using simple concatenation. There are different ways to build up HTML. This example simply uses a string that will eventually be passed into `$().html()` to insert it into the DOM.

```
$( document ).ready( function(){
  $.get( 'data/example1.json' , function( data ){
    var cells = data.cells,
        html = "<table>";
    for (var i = 0, len = cells.length; i < len; i++ ) {
      html += "<tr>";
      for (var j = 0; j < cells[i].length; j++){
        html += "<td>" + cells[i][j] +"</td.>";
      }
      html += "<tr>";
    }
    html+="</table>";
    $( "#container" ).html( html );
  });
});
```

Exercise 2

Start with the following markup:

```
<div id="container">
  <h1>This book is about <span id="subject"></span></h1>
  <ul id="subjects">
    <li>HTML</li>
    <li>CSS</li>
    <li>JavaScript</li>
    <li>Ajax</li>
    <li>HTML5</li>
    <li>CSS3</li>
    <li>Video</li>
    <li>Audio</li>
  </ul>
  <div id="target">
    <p>Drop subjects here!</p>
  </div>
</div>
```

a. Apply the Draggable behavior to the `<li>` elements. Use the `revert` property (http://api .jqueryui.com/draggable/#option-revert) to ensure that the `<li>` elements return to their original place after they're dropped.

b. Apply the Droppable behavior to the `<div>` element with the `id` of `target`. If an `<li>` is dropped on it, use the `drop` callback to get the text of the selected `<li>` and insert it into the `<span>` element with the `id` of `subjects`.

c. Give the `<li>` elements a single-pixel, black border with 3 pixels of padding. Make them 200 pixels wide. The target box should be 300 pixels by 300 pixels, with a background of `#00ccff`, and it should be pinned to the right edge of the page.

d. If everything works, the page should look something like Figure A-15, and you can update the text of the `<h1>` by dragging subjects over to the target.

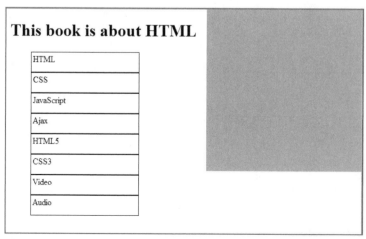

FIGURE A-15

Answer

This is another example of how powerful jQuery UI can be after you get the hang of it.

First, you instantiate the Draggable behavior on the `<li>` elements, setting the `revert` property to `true` so that the elements return to their original place after being dropped:

```
$( document ).ready( function(){
  $( "#subjects li" ).draggable({
     "revert" : true
  });
```

Then you need to set up the Droppable behavior with a callback function that reads the text of the dropped `<li>` and writes it into the `subject` element.

```
  $( "#target" ).droppable({
     "drop" : function( e, ui ){
       $( "#subject" ).text( $( ui.draggable ).text() );
     }
  });
});
```

CHAPTER 13

There are no exercises in Chapter 13.

B

HTML Element Reference

This appendix is a quick reference to the elements in the W3C HTML5 Candidate Recommendation. They are listed with the attributes each element can carry and a brief description of their purpose.

Note that if an attribute can be "empty," that means it can be set without a value. For instance,

```
<span contenteditable> ... </span>
```

Also, obsolete attributes are not included here. They are listed in Appendix I, "Changes between HTML4 and HTML5," for your reference.

Core Attributes

Unless otherwise stated, the core attributes can be used with all the elements in this appendix.

accesskey = list_of_key_labels	Defines a space-separated list of hotkeys/keyboard shortcuts for the current element.
class = list_of_class_names	Specifies a space-separated list of CSS classes for the current element.
contenteditable = true | false | "" | empty	Indicates whether the element is editable by the user.
contextmenu = id	Specifies the id of an HTML element to serve as a context menu for the current element.
dir = ltr | rtl | auto	Defines a unique identification value for that element within the document.
draggable = true | false	Specifies whether the element should be draggable.
dropzone = copy | move | link	Specifies which kind of content can be dropped on an element.

continues

(continued)

`hidden = hidden	""	empty`	The `boolean` attribute indicates whether the element is hidden.
`id = id`	Specifies a unique identifier for an element.
`lang = language_tag`	Specifies the (human) language for the content of the element.
`spellcheck = true	false	""	empty`	Indicates whether the current element should be checked for spelling errors.
`style = CSS_rule`	Specifies an inline CSS style rule for the element.
`tabindex = integer`	Defines this element's position in the tabbing order.
`title = title`	Defines explanatory text for the element, which can be displayed as a tooltip.
`translate = yes	no`	Specifies whether the element's attributes and contents should be translated when the page is localized.

\<a\>

Defines a hyperlink.

`href = url`	Specifies the URL of the hyperlink target.
`hreflang = language_tag`	Specifies the language of the link's destination.
`media = media_query`	Specifies, using a media query, the media the linked resource applies to.
`rel = relationship (same | next | parent | previous | string)`	Indicates the relationship of the current document to the target document.
`target = <window_name>	_parent	_blank	_top	_self`	Defines the name of the frame or window that should load the linked document.
`type = mime_type`	Defines the MIME type of the target.

\<abbr\>

Indicates that the content of the element is an abbreviation or an acronym. Use the `title` attribute to provide the expansion of the abbreviation or acronym.

\<address\>

Indicates that the content of the element is an address.

<area>

Used to specify coordinates for a clickable area or hotspot in an image map. This element must have an ancestor <map> element.

alt = text	Specifies alternative text for the area if the image cannot be loaded.
coords = string	Specifies a list of coordinates for the area.
href = url	Specifies the URL of the hyperlink target.
hreflang = language_code	Specifies the language encoding for the target of the link.
media = media_query	Specifies, using a media query, the media the linked resource applies to.
rel = relationship (same | next | parent | previous | string)	Indicates the relationship of the current area to the target document.
shape = circ | circle | poly | polygon | rect | rectangle	Defines the shape of a region.
target = <window_name> | _parent | _blank | _top| _self	Defines the name of the frame or window that should load the linked document.
type = mime_type	Defines the MIME type of the target.

<article>

Indicates standalone content that can live outside the context of the page. Must not be written as a child of an <address> element.

<aside>

Defines content that is tangentially related to the content of the page. Must not be written as a child of an <address> element.

<audio>

Embeds audio within a document.

autoplay = autoplay | "" | empty	Specifies whether the audio should automatically begin playing.
controls = controls | "" | empty	Specifies whether the audio should have playback controls.

continues

(continued)

`loop = loop | "" | empty`	Specifies whether the audio should play on a loop.
`mediagroup = keystring`	Sets the browser to link together audio and video streams with the same keystring.
`muted = muted | "" | empty`	Specifies whether the audio should be muted initially.
`preload = none | metadata | auto | "" | empty`	Provides a hint to the browser as to how to handle preloading the video content.
`src = url`	Specifies the URL of the video.

\<b\>

The content of the element should be displayed in a bold font.

\<base\>

Specifies a base URL for the links in a document. You must set at least one of the `href` and `target` attributes.

`href = url`	Specifies the URL of the base for the links in this document.
`target = <window_name> | _parent | _blank | _top | _self`	Defines the name of the frame or window that should load the linked document.

\<bdi\>

Isolates text from its context for the purposes of bidirectional text formatting.

\<bdo\>

Turns off the bidirectional rendering algorithm for selected fragments of text.

A `bdo` element must have a `dir` attribute.

\<blockquote\>

The content of the element is a quotation. Usually used for a paragraph quote or longer. Otherwise use the \<q\> element.

`cite = url`	Specifies a URL for the source of the quote.

<body>

Specifies the start and end of the body section of a page. All nonglobal attributes enable you to set functions to run at a particular point in the document's life cycle.

`onafterprint = functionbody`	After the user has printed the current document.
`onbeforeprint = functionbody`	Before the user has printed the current document but after the print has been requested.
`onbeforeunload = functionbody`	When the document is about to be unloaded.
`onblur = functionbody`	When the document has lost focus. For example, the cursor has moved out of the frame containing the document.
`onerror = functionbody`	When the document has failed to load properly.
`onfocus = functionbody`	When the document has received focus.
`onhashchange = functionbody`	When part of the document's current address has changed.
`onload = functionbody`	When the document has finished loading.
`onmessage = functionbody`	When the document has received a message.
`onoffline = functionbody`	When network connections have failed.
`ononline = functionbody`	When network connections have returned.
`onpagehide = functionbody`	When the user has selected a page to view from session history.
`onpageshow = functionbody`	When the user has arrived at a page to view from session history.
`onpopstate = functionbody`	User navigated session history.
`onresize = functionbody`	When the document viewing area has been resized.
`onstorage = functionbody`	When a web storage area has changed.
`onunload = functionbody`	When the document is being unloaded.

Inserts a line break.

\<button\>

Creates an HTML button. Any enclosed markup is used as the button's caption.

`autofocus = autofocus	""	empty`	Specifies that the button should have focus when the page loads.
`disabled = disabled	""	empty`	Specifies the button is disabled, preventing user intervention.
`form = formID`	Indicates the associated `<form>` element for the `<button>` element. Value should be the `id` of the associated `<form>`.
`formaction = URL`	Specifies the URL of the processing application that will handle the form. If set on the button, it overrides the `action` attribute of the form itself.
`formenctype = "application/x-www-form-urlencoded"	"multipart/form-data"	"text/plain"`	Specifies the encoding method for form values. If set on the button, it overrides the `enctype` attribute of the form itself.
`formmethod = get	post`	Specifies how the data gets sent from the browser to the processing application. If set on the button, it overrides the `method` attribute of the form itself.
`formnovalidate = formnovalidate	""	empty`	Specifies whether the form should be validated when submitted. If set on the button, it overrides the `novalidate` attribute of the form itself.
`formtarget = <window_name>	_parent	_blank	_top	_self`	Defines the name of the frame or window that should load the results of the form. If set on the button, it overrides the `target` attribute of the form itself.
`name = name`	Specifies a name for the form control passed to the forms processing application as part of the name/value pair.
`type = button	submit	reset`	Specifies the type of button.
`value = string`	Specifies the value of the parameter sent to the processing application as part of the name/value pair (required).

\<canvas\>

Defines a scriptable bitmap image canvas in the document.

`height = number`	Specifies the height of the canvas in pixels.
`width = number`	Specifies the width of the canvas in pixels.

<caption>

The content of this element specifies a caption to be placed next to a table. It must be the child of a `<table>` element.

<cite>

The content of the element is the title of a cited work.

<code>

The content of the element is code and should be rendered in a fixed-width font.

<col>

Represents one or more columns in its `<colgroup>` parent.

`span = number`	Number of columns spanned by the `<col>` tag.

<colgroup>

Used to contain a group of columns in its `<table>` parent.

`span = number`	Number of columns affected by the `<colgroup>` tag.

<command type="checkbox">

Represents a command that can be toggled.

`checked = checked | "" | empty`	Specifies the command is selected.
`disabled = disabled | "" | empty`	Specifies the command is not currently available.
`icon = url`	A URL for the image that represents the command.
`label = string`	The name of the command.

<command type="command">

Represents a command that a user can invoke; for example, a keyboard shortcut or menu option.

`disabled = disabled | "" | empty`	Specifies the command is not currently available.
`icon = url`	A URL for the image that represents the command.
`label = string`	The name of the command.

<command type="radio">

Represents a selection of one command from a list.

checked = checked | "" | empty	Specifies the command is selected.
disabled = disabled | "" | empty	Specifies the command is not currently available.
icon = url	A URL for the image that represents the command.
label = string	The name of the command.
radiogroup = string	The name of the group of commands that will be toggled when the command is toggled.

<datalist>

Specifies a list of predefined options for use in other form controls.

<dd>

Represents a description or value of an item in a definition list. This is usually indented from other text.

<del>

The content of the element has been marked as having been deleted from an earlier version of the document.

cite = url	Specifies a URL for justification of deletion.
datetime = date	Specifies the date and time it was deleted.

<details>

With the summary element, creates an interactive widget, which can show/hide information.

open = open | "" | empty	Specifies the <details> element should initially be visible on the page.

<dfn>

Defines an instance of a term.

<div>

A containing element to hold other elements, defining a generic section of a page. This is a block-level container.

<dl>

Denotes a definition list. Contains one or more <dt> elements, followed by one or more <dd> elements.

<dt>

Denotes a term or a name within a definition list.

<em>

Represents a span of text to be emphasized, usually by rendering it in an italic font.

<embed>

Embeds files in a page that requires a plug-in.

height = number	Specifies the height of the embedded object in pixels.
src = url	Specifies the URL of the data to be used by the object.
type = mime_type	Specifies the MIME type of the data used by the object.
width = number	Specifies the width of the embedded object in pixels.

<fieldset>

Creates a box around the contained elements indicating that they are related items in a form.

disabled	The boolean attribute disables the button, preventing user intervention.
form = formID	Indicates the associated <form> element for the <button> element. Value should be the id of the associated <form>.
name = string	The name of this element for use in form submission.

<figcaption>

The caption for a <figure> element.

<figure>

Defines content that illustrates or otherwise gives additional context to the main content.

<footer>

Defines a footer of a document or section of a document.

<form>

Containing element for form controls and elements.

`accept-charset = list_of_encoding_names`	Specifies a list of accepted character sets the processing application can handle.
`action = url`	Specifies the URL of the processing application that will handle the form.
`autocomplete = on	off`	Indicates whether the browser can automatically complete values for elements in this form.
`enctype = application/x-www-form-urlencoded	multipart/form-data	text/plain`	Specifies the encoding method for form values.
`method = get	post`	Specifies how the data gets sent from the browser to the processing application.
`name = string`	The name of the form.
`novalidate = novalidate	""	empty`	The `boolean` attribute indicates whether the form should be validated when submitted.
`target = <window_name>	_parent	_blank	_top	_self`	Defines the name of the frame or window that should load the results of the form.

<head>

Container element for heading information *about* the document; its content will not be displayed in the browser.

<header>

Defines the header of a document or section of a document.

<hgroup>

Groups a set of <hn> headers.

<hn>

Headings from <h1> (largest) through <h6> (smallest).

<hr>

Creates a horizontal rule across the page (or containing element) representing a thematic break in a section of a document.

<html>

Containing element for an HTML or XHTML page.

`manifest = url`	Specifies a resource manifest for files that should be cached.

<i>

The content of this element should be rendered in an italic font.

<iframe>

Embeds an HTML document within a page.

`height = number`	Specifies the height of the iframe in pixels.
`name = string`	Specifies the name for the iframe for use as the target of hyperlinks.
`sandbox = allow-same-origin | allow-top-navigation | allow-forms | allow-scripts | empty`	Enables security restrictions on the content contained in the iframe.
`seamless = seamless | "" | empty`	Specifies whether the browser should render the iframe as if it were part of the containing document.
`src = url`	Specifies the URL of the file to be displayed in the iframe.
`srcdoc = markup`	A string representing the content the iframe should contain.
`width = number`	Specifies the width of the iframe in pixels.

<img>

Embeds an image within a document. The `src` attribute is mandatory.

`alt = text`	Specifies alternative text if the application cannot load the image (required); also used in accessibility devices.
`height = number`	Specifies the height of the image in pixels.
`ismap = ismap | "" | empty`	Specifies whether the image is a server-side image map.

continues

(continued)

`src = url`	Specifies the URL of the image.
`usemap = url`	Specifies the map containing coordinates and links that define the links for the image (server-side image map).
`width = name`	Specifies the width of the image in pixels.

\<input type="button"\>

Creates a form input control that is a button a user can click.

`autofocus = autofocus | "" | empty`	Indicates this element should receive focus when the document is loaded.
`disabled = disabled | "" | empty`	Disables the button, preventing user intervention.
`form = formID`	Indicates the associated \<form\> element for the button. The value should be the id of the associated \<form\>.
`name = name`	Specifies a name for the form control passed to the form's processing application as part of the name/value pair.
`value = string`	Specifies the value of the control sent to the processing application as part of the name/value pair.

\<input type="checkbox"\>

Creates a form input control that is a check box a user can check.

`autofocus = autofocus | "" | empty`	Indicates this element should receive focus when the document is loaded.
`checked = checked | "" | empty`	Specifies that the check box is checked. (This can be used to make the check box selected by default.)
`disabled = disabled | "" | empty`	Disables the check box, preventing user intervention.
`form = formID`	Indicates the associated \<form\> element for the check box. The value should be the id of the associated \<form\>.
`name = name`	Specifies a name for the form control passed to the form's processing application as part of the name/value pair.

`required = required | "" | empty`	Specifies whether the check box is a required element.
`value = string`	Specifies the value of the control sent to the processing application as part of the name/value pair.

<input type="color">

Creates a form input control that enables a user to select a color using a color picker.

`autocomplete = on | off`	Indicates whether the browser can automatically complete values for elements in this form.
`autofocus = autofocus | "" | empty`	Indicates this element should receive focus when the document is loaded.
`disabled = disabled | "" | empty`	Disables the control, preventing user intervention.
`form = formID`	Indicates the associated `<form>` element for the `<input>` element. The value should be the `id` of the associated `<form>`.
`list = id`	Specifies the id of a `<datalist>` element containing a list of predefined options for the control.
`name = name`	Specifies a name for the form control passed to the form's processing application as part of the name/value pair.
`value = string`	Specifies the value of the control sent to the processing application as part of the name/value pair.

<input type="date">

Creates a form input control that enables a user to select a date.

`autocomplete = on | off`	Indicates whether the browser can automatically complete values for elements in this form.
`autofocus = autofocus | "" | empty`	Indicates this element should receive focus when the document is loaded.
`disabled = disabled | "" | empty`	Disables the control.
`form = formID`	Indicates the associated `<form>` element for the control. The value should be the `id` of the associated `<form>`.

continues

(continued)

`list = id`	Specifies the `id` of a `<datalist>` element containing a list of predefined options for the control.
`max = date`	Sets the maximum date value for the input.
`min = date`	Sets the minimum date value for the input.
`name = name`	Specifies a name for the form control passed to the form's processing application as part of the name/value pair.
`readonly = readonly | "" | empty`	Specifies whether the user can modify content.
`required = required | "" | empty`	Specifies whether the input is a required element.
`step = any | number`	Specifies the granularity of the input.
`value = date`	Specifies the value of the control sent to the processing application as part of the name/value pair.

\<input type="datetime">

Creates a form input control that enables a user to select a date and time.

`autocomplete = on | off`	Indicates whether the browser can automatically complete values for elements in this form.
`autofocus = autofocus | "" | empty`	Indicates this element should receive focus when the document is loaded.
`disabled = disabled | "" | empty`	Disables the control.
`form = formID`	Indicates the associated `<form>` element for the control. The value should be the `id` of the associated `<form>`.
`list = id`	Specifies the `id` of a `<datalist>` element containing a list of predefined options for the control.
`max = datetime`	Sets the maximum `datetime` value for the input.
`min = datetime`	Sets the minimum `datetime` value for the input.
`name = name`	Specifies a name for the form control passed to the form's processing application as part of the name/value pair.

`readonly = readonly | "" | empty`	Specifies whether the user can modify content.
`required = required | "" | empty`	Specifies whether the input is a required element.
`step = number`	Specifies the granularity of the input.
`value = datetime`	Specifies the value of the control sent to the processing application as part of the name/value pair.

<input type="datetime-local">

Creates a form input control that enables a user to select a date and time without a time zone.

`autocomplete = on | off`	Indicates whether the browser can automatically complete values for elements in this form.
`autofocus = autofocus | "" | empty`	Indicates this element should receive focus when the document is loaded.
`disabled = disabled | "" | empty`	Disables the control.
`form = formID`	Indicates the associated <form> element for the control. The value should be the id of the associated <form>.
`list = id`	Specifies the id of a <datalist> element containing a list of predefined options for the control.
`max = local_datetime`	Sets the maximum datetime value for the input.
`min = local_datetime`	Sets the minimum datetime value for the input.
`name = name`	Specifies a name for the form control passed to the form's processing application as part of the name/value pair.
`readonly = readonly | "" | empty`	Specifies whether the user can modify content.
`required = required | "" | empty`	Specifies whether the input is a required element.
`step = any | number`	Specifies the granularity of the input.
`value = local_datetime`	Specifies the value of the control sent to the processing application as part of the name/value pair.

<input type="email">

Creates a form input control that enables a user to enter an e-mail address.

`autocomplete = on	off`	Indicates whether the browser can automatically complete values for elements in this form.
`autofocus = autofocus	""	empty`	Indicates this element should receive focus when the document is loaded.
`disabled = disabled	""	empty`	Disables the textbox, preventing user intervention.
`form = formID`	Indicates the associated `<form>` element for the `<input>` element. The value should be the `id` of the associated `<form>`.
`list = id`	Specifies the `id` of a `<datalist>` element containing a list of predefined options for the control.
`maxlength = number`	Maximum number of characters the user can enter.
`multiple = multiple	""	empty`	Indicates whether more than one value is valid. (And multiple e-mails can be written as a comma-separated list.)
`name = name`	Specifies a name for the form control passed to the form's processing application as part of the name/value pair.
`pattern = pattern`	Specifies a regular expression to test the input's value against.
`placeholder = placeholder_text`	Specifies a sample value to show to users as a hint.
`readonly = readonly	""	empty`	Specifies whether the user can modify content.
`required = required	""	empty`	Specifies whether the input is a required element.
`size = number`	Specifies the width of the input in numbers of characters.
`value = string`	Specifies the value of the control sent to the processing application as part of the name/value pair.

<input type="file">

Creates a form input control that enables a user to select a file.

`accept = list_of_MIME_Types`	Indicates what file types the server may upload. Uses a comma-separated list of MIME types.
`autofocus = autofocus	""	empty`	Indicates this element should receive focus when the document is loaded.

`disabled = disabled	""	empty`	Disables the file control, preventing user intervention.
`form = formID`	Indicates the associated `<form>` element for the file control. The value should be the `id` of the associated `<form>`.
`multiple = multiple	""	empty`	Indicates whether more than one value is valid (and multiple files can be uploaded).
`name = name`	Specifies a name for the file control passed to the form's processing application as part of the name/value pair.
`readonly = readonly	""	empty`	Specifies whether the user can modify content.

<input type="hidden">

Creates a form input control, similar to a text input, but is hidden from the user's view. (Although, the value can still be seen if the user views the source for the page.)

`disabled = disabled	""	empty`	Disables the control.
`form = formID`	Indicates the associated `<form>` element for the control. Value should be the `id` of the associated `<form>`.
`name = name`	Specifies a name for the form control passed to the form's processing application as part of the name/value pair.
`value = string`	Specifies the value of the control sent to the processing application as part of the name/value pair.

<input type="image">

Creates a form input control that is like a button or submit control, but uses an image instead of a button.

`alt = string`	Provides alternative text for the image.
`autofocus = autofocus	""	empty`	Indicates this element should receive focus when the document is loaded.
`disabled = disabled	""	empty`	Disables the control, preventing user intervention.
`form = formID`	Indicates the associated `<form>` element for the control. The value should be the `id` of the associated `<form>`.

continues

(continued)

`formaction = URL`	Specifies the URL of the processing application that will handle the form. If set on the button, this overrides the `action` attribute of the form itself.
`formenctype = "application/x-www-form-urlencoded" | "multipart/form-data" | "text/plain"`	Specifies the encoding method for form values. If set on the button, this overrides the `enctype` attribute of the form itself.
`formmethod = get | post`	Specifies how the data gets sent from the browser to the processing application. If set on the button, this overrides the `method` attribute of the form itself.
`formnovalidate = formnovalidate | "" | empty`	Specifies whether the form should be validated when submitted. If set on the button, this overrides the `novalidate` attribute of the form itself.
`formtarget = <window_name> | _parent | _blank | _top | _self`	Defines the name of the frame or window that should load the results of the form. If set on the button, this overrides the `target` attribute of the form itself.
`height = number`	Specifies the height of the input in pixels.
`src = url`	Specifies the URL of the image.

\<input type="month"\>

Creates a form input control that enables a user to select a month.

`autocomplete = on | off`	Indicates whether the browser can automatically complete values for elements in this form.
`autofocus = autofocus | "" | empty`	Indicates this element should receive focus when the document is loaded.
`disabled = disabled | "" | empty`	Disables the control.
`form = formID`	Indicates the associated `<form>` element for the control. Value should be the `id` of the associated `<form>`.
`list = id`	Specifies the `id` of a `<datalist>` element containing a list of predefined options for the control.
`max = month`	Sets the maximum month value ($yyyy-mm$) for the input.
`min = month`	Sets the minimum month value ($yyyy-mm$) for the input.

`name = name`	Specifies a name for the form control passed to the form's processing application as part of the name/value pair.
`readonly = readonly |  "" | empty`	Specifies whether the user can modify content.
`required = required | "" | empty`	Specifies whether the input is a required element.
`step = number`	Specifies the granularity of the input.
`value = month`	Specifies the value of the control sent to the processing application as part of the name/value pair.

<input type="number">

Creates a form input control that enables a user to select a number.

`autocomplete = on | off`	Indicates whether the browser can automatically complete values for elements in this form.
`autofocus = autofocus | "" | empty`	Indicates this element should receive focus when the document is loaded.
`disabled = disabled | "" | empty`	Disables the control.
`form = formID`	Indicates the associated <form> element for the control. Value should be the id of the associated <form>.
`list = id`	Specifies the id of a <datalist> element containing a list of predefined options for the control.
`max = number`	Sets the maximum value for the input.
`min = number`	Sets the minimum value for the input.
`name = name`	Specifies a name for the form control passed to the form's processing application as part of the name/value pair.
`placeholder = placeholder_text`	Specifies a sample value to show to users as a hint.
`readonly = readonly | "" | empty`	Specifies whether the user can modify content.
`required = required | "" | empty`	Specifies whether the input is a required element.
`step = any | number`	Specifies the granularity of the input.
`value = number`	Specifies the value of the control sent to the processing application as part of the name/value pair.

<input type="password">

Creates a form input control that is like a single-line text input control but shows asterisks or bullet marks rather than the characters to prevent an onlooker from seeing the values a user has entered. This should be used for sensitive information; although, the values get passed to the servers as plain text. (If you have sensitive information, you should still consider making submissions safe using a technique such as SSL.)

`autocomplete = on | off`	Indicates whether the browser can automatically complete values for elements in this form.
`autofocus = autofocus | "" | empty`	Indicates this element should receive focus when the document is loaded.
`disabled = disabled | "" | empty`	Disables the box, preventing user intervention.
`form = formID`	Indicates the associated `<form>` element for the `<input>` element. The value should be the `id` of the associated `<form>`.
`maxlength = number`	Maximum number of characters the user can enter.
`name = name`	Specifies a name for the form control passed to the form's processing application as part of the name/value pair.
`pattern = pattern`	Specifies a regular expression to test the input's value against.
`placeholder = placeholder text`	Specifies a sample value to show to users as a hint.
`readonly = readonly | "" | empty`	Specifies whether the user can modify content.
`required = required | "" | empty`	Specifies whether the input is a required element.
`size = number`	Specifies the width of the input in numbers of characters.
`value = string`	Specifies the value of the control sent to the processing application as part of the name/value pair.

<input type="radio">

Creates a form input control that is a radio button. These appear in groups that share the same value for the `name` attribute and create mutually exclusive groups of values. (Only one of the radio buttons in the group can be selected.)

`autofocus = autofocus | "" | empty`	Indicates this element should receive focus when the document is loaded.
`checked = checked | "" | empty`	Specifies that the radio button is checked.

`disabled = disabled | "" | empty`	Disables the radio button, preventing user intervention.
`form = formID`	Indicates the associated `<form>` element for the check box. Value should be the `id` of the associated `<form>`.
`name = name`	Specifies a name for the form control passed to the form's processing application as part of the name/value pair.
`required = required | "" | empty`	Specifies whether the radio button is a required element.
`value = string`	Specifies the value of the radio button sent to the processing application as part of the name/value pair.

<input type="range">

Creates a form input control that represents a range of values.

`autocomplete = on | off`	Indicates whether the browser can automatically complete values for elements in this form.
`autofocus = autofocus | "" | empty`	Indicates this element should receive focus when the document is loaded.
`disabled = disabled | "" | empty`	Disables the control.
`form = formID`	Indicates the associated `<form>` element for the control. The value should be the `id` of the associated `<form>`.
`list = id`	Specifies the `id` of a `<datalist>` element containing a list of predefined options for the control.
`max = number`	Sets the maximum value for the input.
`min = number`	Sets the minimum value for the input.
`name = name`	Specifies a name for the form control passed to the form's processing application as part of the name/value pair.
`step = any | number`	Specifies the granularity of the input.
`value = number`	Specifies the value of the control sent to the processing application as part of the name/value pair.

`<input type="reset">`

Creates a form input control that is a button to reset the values of the form to the same values present when the page loaded.

`autofocus = autofocus | "" | empty`	Indicates this element should receive focus when the document is loaded.
`disabled = disabled | "" | empty`	Disables the button, preventing user intervention.
`form = formID`	Indicates the associated `<form>` element for the button. The value should be the `id` of the associated `<form>`.
`name = name`	Specifies a name for the form control passed to the form's processing application as part of the name/value pair.
`value = string`	Specifies the value of the control sent to the processing application as part of the name/value pair.

`<input type="search">`

Creates a form input control that is optimized for search keywords.

`autocomplete = on | off`	Indicates whether the browser can automatically complete values for elements in this `<form>`.
`autofocus = autofocus | "" | empty`	Indicates this element should receive focus when the document is loaded.
`dirname = formElementName`	Specifies the name of a `<form>` element containing the direction of the text in the element.
`disabled = disabled | "" | empty`	Disables the textbox, preventing user intervention.
`form = formID`	Indicates the associated `<form>` element for the `<input>` element. The value should be the `id` of the associated `<form>`.
`list = id`	Specifies the `id` of a `<datalist>` element containing a list of predefined options for the control.
`maxlength = number`	Maximum number of characters the user can enter.
`name = name`	Specifies a name for the form control passed to the form's processing application as part of the name/value pair.
`pattern = pattern`	Specifies a regular expression to test the input's value against.

placeholder = placeholder_text	Specifies a sample value to show to users as a hint.
readonly = readonly | "" | empty	Specifies whether the user can modify content.
required = required | "" | empty	Specifies whether the input is a required element.
size = number	Specifies the width of the input in numbers of characters.
value = string	Specifies the value of the control sent to the processing application as part of the name/value pair.

<input type="submit">

Creates a form input control that is a Submit button to send the form values to the server.

autofocus = autofocus | "" | empty	Indicates this element should receive focus when the document is loaded.
disabled = disabled | "" | empty	Disables the button, preventing user intervention.
form = formID	Indicates the associated <form> element for the button. The value should be the id of the associated <form>.
formaction = URL	Specifies the URL of the processing application that will handle the form. If set on the button, this overrides the action attribute of the form itself.
formenctype = "application/x-www-form-urlencoded" | "multipart/form-data" | "text/plain"	Specifies the encoding method for form values. If set on the button, this overrides the enctype attribute of the form itself.
formmethod = get | post	Specifies how the data gets sent from the browser to the processing application. If set on the button, this overrides the method attribute of the form itself.
formnovalidate = formnovalidate | "" | empty	Specifies whether the form should be validated when submitted. If set on the button, this overrides the novalidate attribute of the form itself.
formtarget = <window_name> | _parent | _blank | _top | _self	Defines the name of the frame or window that should load the results of the form. If set on the button, this overrides the target attribute of the form itself.
name = name	Specifies a name for the form control passed to the form's processing application as part of the name/value pair.
value = string	Specifies the value of the control sent to the processing application as part of the name/value pair.

<input type="tel">

Creates a form input control that is optimized for telephone numbers.

`autocomplete = on	off`	Indicates whether the browser can automatically complete values for elements in this form.
`autofocus = autofocus	""	empty`	Indicates this element should receive focus when the document is loaded.
`disabled = disabled	""	empty`	Disables the textbox, preventing user intervention.
`form = formID`	Indicates the associated <form> element for the <input> element. The value should be the id of the associated <form>.
`list = id`	Specifies the id of a <datalist> element containing a list of predefined options for the control.
`maxlength = number`	Maximum number of characters the user can enter.
`name = name`	Specifies a name for the form control passed to the form's processing application as part of the name/value pair.
`pattern = pattern`	Specifies a regular expression to test the input's value against.
`placeholder = placeholder_text`	Specifies a sample value to show to users as a hint.
`readonly = readonly	""	empty`	Specifies whether the user can modify content.
`required = required	""	empty`	Specifies whether the input is a required element.
`size = number`	Specifies the width of the input in numbers of characters.
`value = string`	Specifies the value of the control sent to the processing application as part of the name/value pair.

<input type="text">

Creates a form input control that is a single-line text input.

`autocomplete = on	off`	Indicates whether the browser can automatically complete values for elements in this form.
`autofocus = autofocus	""	empty`	Indicates this element should receive focus when the document is loaded.

`dirname = formElementName`	Specifies the name of a `<form>` element containing the direction of the text in the element.
`disabled = disabled	""	empty`	Disables the textbox, preventing user intervention.
`form = formID`	Indicates the associated `<form>` element for the `<input>` element. The value should be the `id` of the associated `<form>`.
`list = id`	Specifies the `id` of a `<datalist>` element containing a list of predefined options for the control.
`maxlength = number`	Maximum number of characters the user can enter.
`name = name`	Specifies a name for the form control passed to the form's processing application as part of the name/value pair.
`pattern = pattern`	Specifies a regular expression to test the input's value against.
`placeholder = placeholder_text`	Specifies a sample value to show to users as a hint.
`readonly = readonly	""	empty`	Specifies whether the user can modify content.
`required = required	""	empty`	Specifies whether the input is a required element.
`size = number`	Specifies the width of the input in numbers of characters.
`value = string`	Specifies the value of the control sent to the processing application as part of the name/value pair.

<input type="time">

Creates a form input control that enables a user to select a time.

`autocomplete = on	off`	Indicates whether the browser can automatically complete values for elements in this form.
`autofocus = autofocus	""	empty`	Indicates this element should receive focus when the document is loaded.
`disabled = disabled	""	empty`	Disables the control.
`form = formID`	Indicates the associated `<form>` element for the control. The value should be the `id` of the associated `<form>`.

continues

(continued)

`list = id`	Specifies the `id` of a `<datalist>` element containing a list of predefined options for the control.
`max = time`	Sets the maximum time value (`hh:mm:ss`) for the input.
`min = time`	Sets the minimum time value (`hh:mm:ss`) for the input.
`name = name`	Specifies a name for the form control passed to the form's processing application as part of the name/value pair.
`readonly = readonly | "" | empty`	Specifies whether the user can modify content.
`required = required | "" | empty`	Specifies whether the input is a required element.
`step = number`	Specifies the granularity of the input.
`value = time`	Specifies the value of the control sent to the processing application as part of the name/value pair.

\<input type="url"\>

Creates a form input control that enables a user to input a URL.

`autocomplete = on | off`	Indicates whether the browser can automatically complete values for elements in this form.
`autofocus = autofocus | "" | empty`	Indicates this element should receive focus when the document is loaded.
`disabled = disabled | "" | empty`	Disables the textbox, preventing user intervention.
`form = formID`	Indicates the associated `<form>` element for the `<input>` element. The value should be the `id` of the associated `<form>`.
`list = id`	Specifies the `id` of a `<datalist>` element containing a list of predefined options for the control.
`maxlength = number`	Maximum number of characters the user can enter.
`name = name`	Specifies a name for the form control passed to the form's processing application as part of the name/value pair.
`pattern = pattern`	Specifies a regular expression to test the input's value against.

`placeholder = placeholder_text`	Specifies a sample value to show to users as a hint.
`readonly = readonly | "" | empty`	Specifies whether the user can modify content.
`required = required | "" | empty`	Specifies whether the input is a required element.
`size = number`	Specifies the width of the input in numbers of characters.
`value = string`	Specifies the value of the control sent to the processing application as part of the name/value pair.

<input type="week">

Creates a form input control that enables a user to select a week.

`autocomplete = on | off`	Indicates whether the browser can automatically complete values for elements in this form.
`autofocus = autofocus | "" | empty`	Indicates this element should receive focus when the document is loaded.
`disabled = disabled | "" | empty`	Disables the control.
`form = formID`	Indicates the associated `<form>` element for the control. Value should be the `id` of the associated `<form>`.
`list = id`	Specifies the `id` of a `<datalist>` element containing a list of predefined options for the control.
`max = week`	Sets the maximum week value (`yyyy-Wnn`) for the input.
`min = week`	Sets the minimum week value (`yyyy-Wnn`) for the input.
`name = name`	Specifies a name for the form control passed to the form's processing application as part of the name/value pair.
`readonly = readonly | "" | empty`	Specifies whether the user can modify content.
`required = required | "" | empty`	Specifies whether the input is a required element.
`step = number`	Specifies the granularity of the input.
`value = week`	Specifies the value of the control sent to the processing application as part of the name/value pair.

<ins>

The content of the element has been added since an earlier version of the document.

`cite = url`	Specifies a URL indicating why the content was added.
`datetime = date	datetime`	Specifies a date and time for the addition of content.

<kbd>

The content of the element is something that should be entered on a keyboard and is rendered in a fixed-width font.

<keygen>

This element enables users to generate a key pair used in encryption.

`autofocus = autofocus	""	empty`	Indicates this element should receive focus when the document is loaded.
`challenge = string`	A challenges strip submitted along with the public key.
`disabled = disabled	""	empty`	Disables the control.
`form = formID`	Indicates the associated `<form>` element for the `<keygen>` element. The value should be the `id` of the associated `<form>`.
`keytype = rsa`	The type of key generated.
`name = name`	Specifies a name for the form control passed to the form's processing application as part of the name/value pair (required).

<label>

The content of the element is used as a label for a form element.

`for = controlID`	Specifies the `id` of the form element it is a label for.
`form = formID`	Indicates the associated `<form>` element for the `<label>` element. The value should be the `id` of the associated `<form>`.

<legend>

The content of this element is the title text to place in a <fieldset>. It must be the first child element of that <fieldset>.

<li>

The content of this element is an item in a list. The element is referred to as a line item. For appropriate attributes, see the parent element for that kind of list (<ul>, <ol>, and <menu>).

`value = number`	Specifies the number of the item in the list (when in an <ol> list).

<link>

Defines a link between the document and another resource. Often used to include style sheets in documents. This element has two mandatory attributes: `href` and `rel`.

`href = url`	Specifies the URL of the linked document.
`hreflang = language_code`	Specifies the language encoding for the target of the link.
`media = list`	Comma-separated list of media types the document is intended for, for example, screen, print, braille, and so on.
`rel = list`	Space-separated list of relationships between document and target document. You can find a list of potential values at `http://microformats.org/wiki/existing-rel-values`.
`sizes = any	list_of_sizes`	If the `rel` attribute is set to icon, use sizes to specify a space-separated list of dimensions of the icons provided by the resource.
`type = type`	Specifies the MIME type of the document being linked to.

<map>

Creates a client-side image map and specifies a collection of clickable areas or hotspots. The `name` attribute is mandatory.

`name = string`	Name of the map.

\<mark\>

Defines highlighted content.

\<menu\>

Creates a list of commands.

`type = context	toolbar`	Indicates the type of menu.
`label = string`	Provides a label for the menu.

\<meta charset\>

Specifies the document's character encoding, for example, UTF-8.

`charset = character_set`	Specifies the character set used to encode the document.

\<meta http-equiv=content-type\>

Specifies the document's character encoding. Equivalent to `<meta charset>`.

`content= text/html;charset= character_set`	Specifies the character set used to encode the document.
`http-equiv = content-type`	Specifies that the `<meta>` tag defines the document's content-type.

\<meta http-equiv=default-style\>

Enables the user to nominate a style sheet already `<link>`ed to as the preferred one. Both attributes are mandatory.

`content = style-title`	Specifies the title for either the `<link>` or the `<style>` element containing the document's preferred style sheet.
`http-equiv = default-style`	Specifies the document's preferred style sheet.

<meta http-equiv=refresh>

Enables the user to tell the browser when to refresh the page or go to a different page if content is set to a URL. Both attributes are mandatory.

`content= number[;url=URL]`	Specifies the number of seconds before the page is reloaded and optionally the URL of the new page to load.
`http-equiv = refresh`	Indicates either the number of seconds after which to reload the current page or the number of seconds after which to load a different page and the URL for the new page.

<meta name>

Represents meta data about the document. Both attributes are mandatory.

`content= meta_content`	Specifies the value for the meta information.
`name = application-name	author	description	generator	keywords`	Specifies the name of the meta information. Further valid, non-HTML5 values can be found at `http://wiki.whatwg.org/wiki/MetaExtensions`.

<meter>

This form control illustrates a scalar value within a known range.

`high = number`	Specifies the low end of the "high" range.
`low = number`	Specifies the high end of the "low" range.
`max = number`	Sets the maximum range for the meter.
`min = number`	Sets the minimum range for the meter.
`optimum = number`	The optimal numeric value.
`value = string`	The current value of the control.

<nav>

Defines a navigation section in a document.

<noscript>

The content of the element is displayed for browsers that do not support the script. Most browsers also display this content if scripting is disabled.

\<object\>

Adds an embedded object or non-HTML control to the page. At least one of the data and type attributes must be set for this element.

`data = url`	Specifies the data URL for the object.
`form = formID`	Indicates the association `<form>` element for the `<button>` element. The value should be the `id` of the associated `<form>`.
`height = number`	Specifies the height of the object in pixels.
`name = name`	Specifies a name for the object.
`type = mime_type`	Specifies the MIME type for the object's data.
`usemap = url`	Defines an image map for use with the object.
`width = number`	Specifies the object's width in pixels.

\<ol\>

Creates an ordered or numbered list.

`reversed = reversed | "" | empty`	Specifies whether the list should run in reverse order.
`start = integer`	Specifies the number with which the list should start.
`type = 1 | a | A | i`	Specifies the marker type for the list.

\<optgroup\>

Used to group `<option>` elements with a common label inside a `<select>` element. The `label` attribute is mandatory.

`disabled = disabled | "" | empty`	Disables the entire group of options.
`label = string`	Specifies a label for the option group.

\<option\>

Represents one choice in a `<select>` drop-down list or select box, an `<optgroup>`, or a `<datalist>` of options for use in other form elements.

`disabled = disabled | "" | empty`	Disables the option.
`label = string`	Specifies a label for the option.

`selected = selected | "" | empty`	Indicates that the option should be selected by default when the page loads.
`value = string`	Specifies the value of this option.

<output>

Displays the output of a calculation.

`for = list_of_IDs`	A space-separated list of element IDs associated with the output's calculation.
`form = formID`	Indicates the associated `<form>` element for the `<output>` element. The value should be the `id` of the associated `<form>`.
`name = string`	Specifies a name for the form control passed to the form's processing application as part of the name/value pair.

<p>

The content of this element is a paragraph.

<param>

Used as a child of an `<object>` element to set properties of the object.

`name = name`	Specifies the name of the parameter.
`value = value`	The value of the parameter.

<pre>

The content of this element is rendered in a fixed-width type that retains the formatting (such as spaces and line breaks) in the code.

<progress>

This form control illustrates the completeness of a task.

`max = number`	Sets the total amount of work required in the task.
`value = number`	Specifies how much of the task has been completed.

<q>

The content of the element is a short quotation from another source.

`cite = url`	Specifies the URL for the content of the quote in question.

<rp>

Defines a set of parentheses around a ruby annotation for nonsupporting browsers.

<rt>

Defines the text of a ruby annotation.

<ruby>

Defines a set of ruby annotations. Ruby annotations show pronunciation information for East Asian characters.

<s>

Indicates the content of the element is no longer accurate and has been "struck" from the document.

<samp>

The content of the element is sample output from a program.

<script>

The content of the element is script code that the browser should execute.

`async = async | "" | empty`	Indicates whether the script should be executed asynchronously or as soon as it is loaded.
`charset = character_set`	Specifies the character set used to encode the script.
`defer = defer | "" | empty`	Indicates whether the execution of the script should be deferred until after the document has been parsed.
`src = url`	URL for the location of the script file.
`type = MIME_Type`	Specifies the MIME type of the script.

<section>

Defines a thematic section in a document.

<select>

Creates a select or drop-down list box.

`autofocus = autofocus | "" | empty`	Indicates this element should receive focus when the document is loaded.
`disabled = disabled | "" | empty`	Disables the select box, preventing user intervention.
`form = formID`	Indicates the associated <form> element for the <select> element. The value should be the id of the associated <form>.
`multiple = multiple | "" | empty`	Indicates whether more than one value can be selected from the list at a time.
`name = name`	Specifies a name for the form control passed to the form's processing application as part of the name/ value pair (required).
`required = required | "" | empty`	Specifies whether the input is a required element.
`size = number`	Specifies the number of items that may appear at once.

<small>

Indicates the content of this element is "small print" such as disclaimers or terms and conditions.

<source>

As a child element of <video> or <audio>, this enables the specification of multiple media sources. The src attribute is mandatory.

`src = url`	Specifies the URL of the resource.
`type = MIME_Type`	Indicates the MIME type of the resource.
`media = list`	Comma-separated list of media types the resource is intended for, for example, screen, print, braille, and so on.

<span>

Used as a generic wrapper for inline elements (as opposed to block-level elements).

<strong>

The content of this element has strong importance.

\<style\>

Contains CSS style rules that apply to that page.

`type = MIME_Type`	Indicates the MIME type of the style section.
`media = list`	Comma-separated list of media types the styles are intended for, for example, screen, print, braille, and so on.
`scoped = scoped | "" | empty`	If used, indicates that the styles should apply to just the parent element and all that element's children.

\<sub\>

The content of this element is subscript.

\<summary\>

Specifies the hidden information for its parent `<details>` element.

\<sup\>

The content of this element is superscript.

\<table\>

Creates a table.

`border = 1 | ""`	Indicates that its table element is not being used for layout purposes.

\<tbody\>

Denotes the body section of a table.

\<td\>

Creates a cell of a table.

`colspan = number`	Specifies the number of columns this cell spans.
`headers = list_of_IDs`	A space-separated list of IDs for the `<th>` header elements associated with this cell.
`rowspan = number`	Specifies the number of rows the cell spans.

<textarea>

Creates a multiple-line text input control in a form.

`autofocus = autofocus | ""` `| empty`	Indicates this element should receive focus when the document is loaded.
`cols = number`	Specifies the number of columns of characters the text area should be (the width in characters).
`dirname = formElementName`	Specifies the name of a form element containing the direction of the text in the element.
`disabled = disabled | "" |` `empty`	Disables the control, preventing user intervention.
`form = formID`	Indicates the associated `<form>` element for the `<textarea>` element. The value should be the `id` of the associated `<form>`.
`maxlength = number`	Maximum number of characters the user can enter.
`name = string`	Specifies a name for the form control passed to the form's processing application as part of the name/value pair (required).
`placeholder =` `placeholder_text`	Specifies a sample value to show users as a hint.
`readonly = readonly | "" |` `empty`	Specifies whether the user can modify content.
`required = required | "" |` `empty`	Specifies whether the input is a required element.
`rows = number`	Specifies the number of rows of text that should appear in the text area without the scrollbar appearing.
`wrap = hard | soft`	Specifies whether the text in a text area should be forced to wrap at the value of the `cols` attribute.

<tfoot>

Denotes the row or rows of a table to be used as a footer for the table.

\<th>

Denotes the header cell of a table. By default, content is often shown in bold font.

`colspan = number`	Specifies the number of columns this cell spans.
`headers = list_of_IDs`	A space-separated list of IDs for the `<th>` header elements associated with this `<th>` element.
`rowspan = number`	Specifies the number of rows the cell spans.
`scope = row | col | rowgroup | colgroup`	Specifies the scope of a header cell.

\<thead>

Denotes the row or rows of a table to be used as a header for the table.

\<time>

Represents a date or time.

`datetime = date | datetime`	Specifies a valid date or date/time stamp for the element.

\<title>

The content of this element is the title of the document. It must be a child of the page's `<head>` element.

\<tr>

Denotes a row of a table.

\<track>

Specifies timed text track for an `<audio>` or `<video>` element. The `src` attribute is mandatory.

`default = default | "" | empty`	Indicates this is the default track for the parent `<audio>` or `<video>` file.
`kind = subtitles | captions | descriptions | chapters | metadata`	Defines the usage of the track element.
`label = label`	The label for the track.
`src = url`	The URL of the track.
`srclang = language code`	A language code indicating the language of the track.

`<u>`

The convoluted language of the specification at `http://www.w3.org/TR/2011/WD-html5-author-20110809/the-u-element.html`. Defines this element as "Represents a span of text offset from its surrounding content without conveying any extra emphasis or importance, and for which the conventional typographic presentation is underlining; for example, a span of text in Chinese that is a proper name (a Chinese proper name mark), or span of text that is known to be misspelled."

For the rest of us, the content of this element is rendered with underlined text.

`<ul>`

Creates an unordered list.

`<var>`

The content of this element is a programming variable.

`<video>`

Embeds a video within a document.

`autoplay = autoplay	""	empty`	Indicates whether the video should play automatically.
`controls = controls	""	empty`	Indicates whether the video should have playback controls.
`height = number`	Specifies the height of the video in pixels.
`loop = loop	""	empty`	Indicates whether the video should play on a loop.
`mediagroup = keystring`	Sets the browser to link together audio and video streams with the same keystring.
`muted = muted	""	empty`	Indicates whether the video should initially be muted.
`preload = none	metadata	auto	""	empty`	Provides a hint to the browser as to how to handle preloading the video content.
`src = url`	Specifies the URL of the video.
`poster = url`	Specifies the URL of a frame to show until the user interacts with the video; defaults to the first frame if no poster is specified.
`width = number`	Specifies the width of the video in pixels.

<wbr>

Indicates a point in a text where a suggested line break should occur.

`alt = string`	Provides alternative text for the image.
`autofocus = autofocus | "" | empty`	Indicates this element should receive focus when the document is loaded.
`disabled = disabled | "" | empty`	Disables the control, preventing user intervention.
`form = formID`	Indicates the associated `<form>` element for the control. The value should be the `id` of the associated `<form>`.
`formaction = URL`	Specifies the URL of the processing application that will handle the form. If set on the button, this overrides the `action` attribute of the form itself.
`formenctype = "application/ x-www-form-urlencoded" | "multipart/form-data" | "text/plain"`	Specifies the encoding method for form values. If set on the button, this overrides the `enctype` attribute of the form itself.
`formmethod = get | post`	Specifies how the data gets sent from the browser to the processing application. If set on the button, this overrides the `method` attribute of the form itself.
`formnovalidate = formnovalidate | "" | empty`	Specifies whether the form should be validated when submitted. If set on the button, this overrides the `novalidate` attribute of the form itself.
`formtarget = <window_name> | _parent | _blank | _top | _self`	Defines the name of the frame or window that should load the results of the form. If set on the button, this overrides the `target` attribute of the form itself.
`height = number`	Specifies the height of the input in pixels.
`src = url`	Specifies the source of the image.
`width = number`	Specifies the width of the input in pixels.

CSS Properties

This appendix is a reference to the main CSS properties that you can use to control the appearance of your documents.

The majority of the properties covered here are from CSS2. Because the full universe of CSS3 properties is large and still changing, only the CSS3 properties covered in this book are included here, which can be found in the section "Selected CSS3 Properties."

For each property covered, you first see a brief description of the property and then an example of its usage. This is followed by a table that shows the possible values the property can take, along with the first versions of Internet Explorer to support these values, whether the property can be inherited, what the default value for the property is, and which elements it applies to.

These tables focus on Internet Explorer support because, with a few rare exceptions, *any* version of Google Chrome, Safari, Firefox, or Opera that you encounter in the wild can support the full complement of CSS2 properties.

The CSS3 section contains a full set of compatibility tables.

Although browsers may support the `inherit` value of many properties, if the browser cannot set the property to some other value in the first place (perhaps because that value is not supported), then the `inherit` value is of little use.

At the end of the appendix are units of measurement.

FONT PROPERTIES

The font properties enable you to change the appearance of a typeface.

font

This enables you to set several font properties at the same time, separated by spaces. You can specify `font-size`, `line-height`, `font-family`, `font-style`, `font-variant`, and `font-weight` in this one property.

```
font {color:#ff0000; arial, verdana, sans-serif; 12pt;}
```

font-family

This enables you to specify the typefaces you want to use. It can take multiple values separated by commas, starting with your first preference, then moving to your second choice, and ending with a generic font-family (`serif`, `sans-serif`, `cursive`, `fantasy`, or `monospace`).

```
p {font-family:arial, verdana, sans-serif;}
```

font-size

This enables you to specify the size of a font. The `font-size` property has its own specific values:

➤ **Absolute sizes:** `xx-small`, `x-small`, `small`, `medium`, `large`, `x-large`, and `xx-large`

➤ **Relative sizes:** `larger` or `smaller`

➤ **Percentage:** Percentage of the parent font

➤ **Length:** A unit of measurement (as described at the end of the appendix)

font-size-adjust

This enables you to adjust the aspect value of a font, which is the ratio between the height of a lowercase letter x in the font and the height of the font.

```
{font-size-adjust:0.5;}
```

VALUE	IE	INHERITED	YES
[number]	-	Default	Specific to font
none	-	Applies to	All elements
inherit	-		

font-stretch

This enables you to specify the width of the letters in a font (not the space between them).

➤ **Relative values:** `normal`, `wider`, or `narrower`

➤ **Fixed values:** `ultra-condensed`, `extra-condensed`, `condensed`, `semi-condensed`, `semi-expanded`, `expanded`, `extra-expanded`, or `ultra-expanded`

```
p {font-family:courier; font-stretch:semi-condensed;}
```

VALUE	IE	INHERITED	YES
[relative]	-	Default	Specific to font
[fixed]	-	Applies to	All elements
inherit	-		

font-style

This applies styling to a font. If the specified version of the font is available, it can be used; otherwise, the browser renders it.

```
p {font-style:italic;}
```

VALUE	IE	INHERITED	YES
normal	3	Default	normal
italic	3	Applies to	All elements
oblique	4		
inherit	8		

font-variant

This creates capital letters that are the same size as normal lowercase letters.

VALUE	IE	INHERITED	YES
normal	4	Default	normal
small-caps	4	Applies to	All elements
inherit	8		

font-weight

This specifies the thickness of the text—its "boldness."

- ➤ **Absolute values:** normal or bold
- ➤ **Relative values:** bolder or lighter
- ➤ **Numeric value:** Between 0 and 100

```
p {font-weight:bold;}
```

VALUE	IE	INHERITED	YES
[absolute]	3	Default	normal
[relative]	4	Applies to	All elements
[number 1–100]	4		
inherit	8		

TEXT PROPERTIES

Text properties change the appearance and layout of text in general (as opposed to the font).

letter-spacing

This specifies the distance between letters as a unit of length.

```
p {letter-spacing:1em;}
```

VALUE	IE	INHERITED	YES
[length]	4	Default	normal
normal	4	Applies to	All elements
inherit	8		

text-align

This specifies whether text is aligned `left`, `right`, `center`, or `justified`.

```
p {text-align:center}
```

VALUE	IE	INHERITED	YES
left	3	Default	Depends on user agent and element (usually left except for <th> elements, which are center)
right	3	Applies to	All elements
center	3		
justify	4		
inherit	8		

text-decoration

This specifies whether text should have an `underline`, `overline`, `line-through`, or `blink` appearance.

```
p {text-decoration:underline;}
```

VALUE	IE	INHERITED	NO
none	3	Default	none
underline	3	Applies to	All elements

overline	4		
line-through	3		
blink	-		
inherit	8		

text-indent

This specifies the indentation in length or as a percentage of the parent element's width.

```
p {text-indent:3em;}
```

VALUE	IE	INHERITED	YES
[length]	4	Default	0
[percentage]	4	Applies to	Block elements
inherit	8		

text-shadow

This creates a drop shadow for the text. It should take three lengths; the first two specify X and Y coordinates for the offset of the drop shadow, whereas the third specifies a blur effect. This is then followed by a color, which can be any valid color value.

```
.dropShadow {text-shadow: 0.3em 0.3em 0.5em black}
```

VALUE	INHERITED	NO
[shadow effects]	Default	none
none	Applies to	All elements
inherit		

Browser Support is as follows:

IE	FF	SAFARI	CHROME	OPERA
10	3.5	4	1	9.6

text-transform

This specifies capitalization of text in an element:

➤ **none:** Removes inherited settings.

➤ **uppercase:** All characters are uppercase.

➤ **lowercase:** All characters are lowercase.

➤ **capitalize:** First letter of each word is capitalized.

```
p {text-transform:uppercase;}
```

VALUE	IE	INHERITED	YES
none	4	Default	none
uppercase	4	Applies to	All elements
lowercase	4		
capitalize	4		
inherit	8		

white-space

This indicates how white space should be dealt with:

➤ **normal:** White space should be collapsed.

➤ **pre:** White space should be preserved.

➤ **nowrap:** Text should not be broken to a new line except with the `<br>` element.

```
p {white-space:pre;}
```

VALUE	IE	INHERITED	YES
normal	5.5	Default	normal
pre	5.5	Applies to	Block elements
nowrap	5.5		
inherit	8		

word-spacing

This specifies the gap between words.

```
p {word-spacing:2em;}
```

VALUE	IE	INHERITED	YES
normal	6	Default	normal
[length]	6	Applies to	All elements
inherit	8		

COLOR AND BACKGROUND PROPERTIES

The following properties enable you to change the colors and backgrounds of both the page and other boxes.

background

This is shorthand for specifying background properties for color, url, repeat, scroll, and position; separated by a space. By default, the background is transparent.

```
body {background: #efefef url("images/background.gif"); }
```

VALUE	IE	INHERITED	NO
[background-attachment]	4	Default	Not defined (by default background is transparent)
[background-color]	3	Applies to	All elements
[background-image]	3		
[background-position]	4		
[background-repeat]	3		
inherit	-		

background-attachment

This specifies whether a background image should be fixed in one position or scroll along the page.

```
body {background-attachment:fixed;
      background-image: url("images/background.gif");}
```

VALUE	IE	INHERITED	NO
fixed	4	Default	scroll
scroll	4	Applies to	All elements
inherit	8		

background-color

This sets the color of the background. This can be a single color or two colors blended together. Colors can be specified with any valid color value. By default the box will be transparent.

```
body {background-color:#efefef;}
```

VALUE	IE	INHERITED	NO
[color]	4	Default	transparent
transparent	4	Applies to	All elements
inherit	8		

background-image

This specifies an image to be used as a background, which by default will be tiled. Value is a URL for the image.

```
body {background-image: url("images/background.gif");}
```

VALUE	IE	INHERITED	NO
[url]	4	Default	none
none	4	Applies to	All elements
inherit	8		

background-position

This specifies where a background image should be placed in the page, from the top-left corner. Values can be an absolute distance, a percentage, or one of the keywords. If only one value is given, it is assumed to be horizontal.

➤ The keywords available are top, bottom, left, right, and center.

```
body {background-position:center;
      background-image: url("images/background.gif");}
```

VALUE	IE	INHERITED	NO
[length - x y]	4	Default	top, left
[percentage - x% y%]	4	Applies to	Block-level elements
top	4		
left	4		

bottom	4		
right	4		
center	4		
inherit	8		

background-positionX

The position of a background image runs horizontally across the page. Values are the same as for background-position (default: top).

background-positionY

The position of a background image runs vertically down the page. Values are the same as for background-position (default: left).

background-repeat

This specifies if a background image should be repeated and if so in which directions. Values are repeat to repeat horizontally and vertically, repeat-x to just repeat horizontally, repeat-y to just repeat vertically, and no-repeat to prevent it from repeating.

VALUE	IE	INHERITED	NO
repeat	4	Default	none
repeat-x	4	Applies to	All elements
repeat-y	4		
no-repeat	4		
inherit	8		

BORDER PROPERTIES

The border properties enable you to control the appearance and size of a border around any box.

border (border-bottom, border-left, border-top, border-right)

This is shorthand for specifying border-style, border-width, and border-color properties.

VALUE	IE	INHERITED	NO
[border-style]	4	Default	none, medium, none
[border-width]	4	Applies to	All elements
[border-color]	4		
inherit	8		

border-color (border-bottom-color, border-left-color, border-top-color, border-right-color)

This specifies the color of a border; values can be any valid color value.

```
table {border-color:#000000;}
```

VALUE	IE	INHERITED	NO
[color value]	4	Default	none
inherit	8	Applies to	All elements

border-style (border-bottom-style, border-left-style, border-top-style, border-right-style)

This specifies the style of line that should surround a block box.

```
div.page {border-style:solid;}
```

VALUE	IE	INHERITED	NO
none	4	Default	none
dotted	5.5	Applies to	All elements
dashed	5.5		
solid	4		
double	4		
groove	4		
ridge	4		
inset	4		

outset	4
hidden	-
inherit	8

border-width (border-bottom-width, border-left-width, border-top-width, border-right-width)

This specifies the width of a border line; it can be a width or a keyword.

```
div.page {border-width:2px;}
```

VALUE	IE	INHERITED	NO
[length]	4	Default	medium
thin	4	Applies to	All elements
medium	4		
thick	4		
inherit	8		

DIMENSIONS

The dimensions properties enable you to specify the size that boxes should be.

height

This specifies the vertical height of a block element.

```
table {height:400px;}
```

VALUE	IE	INHERITED	NO
auto	4	Default	auto
[length]	4	Applies to	Block-level elements
[percentage]	4		
inherit	8		

line-height

This specifies the height of a line of text. It is a way of controlling leading (space between multiple lines of text) because the line height may be more or less than the size of the font.

```
p {line-height:18px;}
```

VALUE	IE	INHERITED	YES
normal	3	Default	Depends on browser
[number]	4	Applies to	All elements
[length]	3		
[percentage]	3		
inherit	8		

max-height

This specifies the maximum height of a block-level element (same values as for `height`).

```
td {max-height:200px;}
```

VALUE	IE	INHERITED	NO
auto	7	Default	auto
[length]	7	Applies to	Block-level elements
[percentage]	7		
inherit	8		

max-width

This specifies the maximum width of a block-level element (same values as for `width`).

```
td {max-width:400px;}
```

VALUE	IE	INHERITED	NO
auto	7	Default	auto
[length]	7	Applies to	Block elements
[percentage]	7		
inherit	8		

min-height

This specifies the minimum height of a block-level element (same values as for `height`).

```
td {min-height:100px;}
```

VALUE	IE	INHERITED	NO
auto	7	Default	auto
[length]	7	Applies to	Block-level elements
[percentage]	7		
inherit	8		

min-width

This specifies the minimum width of a block-level element (same values as for `width`).

```
td {min-width:200px;}
```

VALUE	IE	INHERITED	NO
auto	7	Default	auto
[length]	7	Applies to	Block elements
[percentage]	7		
inherit	8		

width

This specifies the horizontal width of an element.

```
td {width:150px;}
```

VALUE	IE	INHERITED	NO
auto	4	Default	auto
[length]	4	Applies to	Block-level elements
[percentage]	4		
inherit	8		

MARGIN PROPERTIES

Margin properties enable you to specify a margin around a box and therefore create a gap between elements' borders.

margin (margin-bottom, margin-left, margin-top, margin-right)

This specifies the width of a margin around a box.

```
p {margin:15px;}
```

VALUE	IE	INHERITED	NO
auto	3	Default	0
[length]	3	Applies to	All elements
[percentage — relative to parent element]	3		
inherit	8		

PADDING PROPERTIES

Padding properties set the distance between the border of an element and its content. They are important for adding white space to documents (in particular table cells).

padding (padding-bottom, padding-left, padding-right, padding-top)

This specifies the distance between an element's border and its content.

```
td {padding:20px;}
```

VALUE	IE	INHERITED	NO
auto	4	Default	0
[length]	4	Applies to	All elements
[percentage—relative to parent element]	4		
inherit	8		

LIST PROPERTIES

List properties affect the presentation of bulleted, numbered, and definition lists.

list-style

This is shorthand allowing you to specify `list-style-position` and `list-style-type`.

```
ul {list-style: inside disc}
```

VALUE	IE	INHERITED	YES
<position>	4	Default	Depends on browser
<type>	4	Applies to	List elements
<image>	4		
inherit	8		

list-style-position

This specifies whether the marker should be placed inside each item of a list or to the left of them.

```
ul {list-style-position:inside;}
```

VALUE	IE	INHERITED	YES
inside	4	Default	outside
outside	4	Applies to	List elements
inherit	8		

list-style-type

This indicates the type of bullet or numbering that a bullet should use.

```
ul {list-style-type:circle;}
```

VALUE	IE	INHERITED	YES
none	4	Default	disc
disc ·(default)	4	Applies to	List elements
circle	4		
square	4		
decimal	4		

continues

(continued)

VALUE	IE	INHERITED	YES
decimal-leading-zero	-		
lower-alpha	4		
upper-alpha	4		
lower-roman	4		
upper-roman	4		

Additional numbered list styles are available in CSS, but unfortunately they are not supported in any versions of Internet Explorer. Support exists in Chrome 1+, Firefox 1+, Opera 7+, and Safari 1+.

Hebrew	Traditional Hebrew numbering
Georgian	Traditional Georgian numbering (an, ban, gan, . . . , he, tan, in, in-an, . . .)
Armenian	Traditional Armenian numbering
cjk-ideographic	Plain ideographic numbers
Hiragana	(a, i, u, e, o, ka, ki, . . .)
Katakana	(A, I, U, E, O, KA, KI, . . .)
hiragana-iroha	(i, ro, ha, ni, ho, he, to, . . .)
katakana-iroha	(I, RO, HA, NI, HO, HE, TO, . . .)

marker-offset

This specifies the space between a list item and its marker.

    ol {marker-offset:2em;}

VALUE	IE	INHERITED	NO
[length]	7	Default	auto
auto	7	Applies to	Marker elements
inherit	8		

POSITIONING PROPERTIES

Positioning properties allow you to use CSS for positioning boxes on the page.

bottom

This sets the vertical position of an element from the bottom of the window or containing element.

VALUE	IE	INHERITED	NO
auto	5	Default	auto
[length]	5	Applies to	Positioned elements
[percentage—relative to parent's height]	5		
inherit	8		

clip

This controls which part of an element is visible. Parts outside the clip are not visible. If value is `rect()`, it takes the following form:

➤ `rect([top] [right] [bottom] [left])`

`rect(25 100 100 25)`

VALUE	IE	INHERITED	NO
auto	4	Default	auto
rect	4	Applies to	Block elements
inherit	8		

left

This sets the horizontal position of an element from the left of the window or containing element.

VALUE	IE	INHERITED	NO
auto	4	Default	auto
[length]	4	Applies to	Positioned elements
[percentage—relative to parent's width]	4		
inherit	8		

overflow

This specifies how a container element will display content that is too large for its containing element.

```
p {width:200px; height:200px; overflow:scroll;}
```

VALUE	IE	INHERITED	NO
auto	4	Default	visible
hidden	4	Applies to	Block elements
visible	4		
scroll	4		
inherit	8		

overflow-x

This is the same as `overflow` but only for the horizontal *x* axis. This was first supported in IE5.

overflow-y

This is the same as `overflow` but only for the vertical *y* axis. This was first supported in IE5.

position

This specifies the positioning schema that should be used for an element. When an element is positioned, you also need to use the box-offset properties covered next (`top`, `left`, `bottom`, and `right`). Note that you should not use `top` and `bottom` or `left` and `right` together (if you do, `top` and `left` take priority).

➤ `absolute` can be fixed on the canvas in a specific position from its containing element (which is another absolutely positioned element); it will also move when the user scrolls the page.

➤ `static` will fix it on the page in the same place and keep it there even when the user scrolls.

➤ `relative` will be placed offset in relation to its normal position.

➤ `fixed` will fix it on the background of the page and not move when the user scrolls.

```
p.article{position:absolute; top:10px; left:20px;
```

VALUE	IE	INHERITED	NO
absolute	4	Default	static
relative	4	Applies to	All elements

static	4		
fixed	7		
inherit	8		

right

This sets the horizontal position of an element from the right of the window or containing element.

VALUE	IE	INHERITED	NO
auto	5	Default	auto
[length]	5	Applies to	Positioned elements
[percentage—relative to parent's width]	5		
inherit	8		

top

This sets the vertical position of an element from the top of the window or containing element.

VALUE	IE	INHERITED	NO
auto	4	Default	auto
[length]	4	Applies to	Positioned elements
[percentage—relative to parent's height]	4		
inherit	8		

vertical-align

This sets the vertical positioning of an inline element:

➤ baseline aligns element with base of parent.

➤ middle aligns midpoint of element with half the height of parent.

➤ sub makes element subscript.

➤ super makes element superscript.

➤ text-top aligns element with the top of parent element's font.

➤ `text-bottom` aligns element with the bottom of parent element's font.

➤ `top` aligns top of element with the top of tallest element on current line.

➤ `bottom` aligns element with the bottom of lowest element on the current line.

`span.superscript {vertical-align:super;}`

VALUE	IE	INHERITED	NO
baseline	4	Default	baseline
middle	4	Applies to	Inline elements
sub	4		
super	4		
text-top	4		
text-bottom	4		
top	4		
bottom	4		
[percentage—relative to line height]	8		
[length]	-		
inherit	8		

z-index

This controls which overlapping element appears to be on top. Positive and negative numbers are permitted.

`p {position:absolute; top:10px; left:20px; z-index:3;}`

VALUE	IE	INHERITED	NO
auto	4	Default	Depends on position of element in XHTML source document
[number]	4		
inherit	8	Applies to	Positioned elements

OUTLINE PROPERTIES

Outlines act like borders, but do not take up any space—they sit on top of the canvas.

outline (outline-color, outline-style, outline-width)

This is a shortcut for the `outline-color`, `outline-style`, and `outline-width` properties:

```
outline {solid #ff0000 2px}
```

Note that `outline-color`, `outline-style`, and `outline-width` take the same values as `border-color`, `border-style`, and `border-width`.

VALUE	IE	INHERITED	NO
outline-color	8	Default	none
outline-style	8	Applies to	All elements
outline-width	8		
outline	8		

TABLE PROPERTIES

Table properties enable you to affect the style of tables, rows, and cells.

border-collapse

This specifies the border model that the table should use (whether adjacent borders should be collapsed into one value or kept separate).

```
table {border-collapse:separate;}
```

VALUE	IE	INHERITED	YES
collapse	5	Default	collapse
separate	5	Applies to	Table and inline elements
inherit	8		

border-spacing

This specifies the distance between adjacent cells' borders.

```
table {border-spacing:2px;}
```

VALUE	IE	INHERITED	YES
[length]	8	Default	0
inherit	8	Applies to	Table and inline elements

caption-side

This indicates which side of a table a caption should be placed on.

```
caption {caption-side:bottom;}
```

VALUE	IE	INHERITED	YES
top	8	Default	top
left	8	Applies to	<caption> elements in <table> elements
bottom	8		
right	8		
inherit	8		

empty-cells

This specifies whether borders should be displayed if a cell is empty.

```
td, th {empty-cells:hide;}
```

VALUE	IE	INHERITED	YES
show	5	Default	show
hide	5	Applies to	Table cell elements
inherit	8		

table-layout

This specifies how the browser should calculate the layout of a table; it can affect the speed of rendering a large or graphics-intensive table.

VALUE	IE	INHERITED	NO
auto	5	Default	auto
fixed	5	Applies to	Table and inline elements
inherit	8		

CLASSIFICATION PROPERTIES

Classification properties affect how the boxes in the box model are rendered.

clear

This forces elements, which would normally wrap around an aligned element, to display below it. Value indicates which side may not touch an aligned element.

```
p {clear:left;}
```

VALUE	IE	INHERITED	NO
none	4	Default	none
both	4	Applies to	All elements
left	4		
right	4		
inherit	8		

display

This specifies how an element is rendered, if at all. If set to none the element is not rendered, and it does not take up any space. This property can also force an inline element to display as a block or vice versa.

```
span.important {display:block;}
```

VALUE	IE	INHERITED	YES
none	4	Default	inline
inline	5	Applies to	All elements
block	5		
list-item	5		
inherit	8		

Although the default value of this property is inline, browsers tend to treat the element depending on its inherent display type. Block-level elements, such as headings and paragraphs, get treated as if the default were block, whereas inline elements such as <i>, <b>, or <span> get treated as inline.

float

Subsequent elements should be wrapped to the left or right of the element, rather than below.

```
img.featuredItem {float:left;}
```

VALUE	IE	INHERITED	NO
none	4	Default	none
left	4	Applies to	All elements
right	4		
inherit	8		

visibility

This specifies whether an element should be displayed or hidden. Even if hidden, elements take up space on the page but are transparent.

VALUE	IE	INHERITED	NO
visible	4	Default	inherit
show	8	Applies to	All elements
hidden	4		
hide	8		
collapse	8		
inherit	8		

INTERNATIONALIZATION PROPERTIES

Internationalization properties affect how text is rendered in different languages.

direction

This specifies the direction of text from left to right or right to left. This should be used in association with the unicode-bidi property.

```
td.word{direction:rtl; unicode-bidi:bidi-override;}
```

VALUE	IE	INHERITED	YES
ltr	5	Default	ltr
rtl	5	Applies to	All elements
inherit	8		

unicode-bidi

The `unicode-bidi` property enables you to override Unicode's built-in directionality settings for languages.

```
td.word{unicode-bidi:bidi-override; direction:rtl; }
```

VALUE	IE	INHERITED	NO
normal	5	Default	normal
embed	5	Applies to	All elements
bidi-override	5		
inherit	8		

SELECTED CSS3 PROPERTIES

This section covers a subset of CSS3 properties, focused on the ones covered in this book. Unlike the earlier tables, a full support matrix showing Chrome, Firefox, Safari, and Opera support is included in addition to information about support in Internet Explorer.

For full support tables of all CSS3 modules, the interactive tool at `http://caniuse.com/` can't be beat.

Color

The CSS3 Color module offers the ability to specify colors using the Hue Saturation and Lightness (HSL) scheme, as well as the ability to set an alpha channel to define transparency using both RGBA and HSLA notation.

```
.hsl {
  background-color : hsl( 333,50%,50% );
}
.hsla {
  background-color : hsla( 0, 100%, 50%, 0.5 );
}
.rgba {
  background-color : rgba( 255, 0, 0, 0.5);
}
```

VALUE	IE	FF	SAFARI	CHROME	OPERA
hsl	9	1	3.1	1	9.5
hsla	9	3	3.1	1	10
rgba	9	3	3.1	1	10

Backgrounds and Borders

The Backgrounds and Borders module extends the border and background properties introduced in earlier versions of CSS to include rounded corners and drop shadows.

border-radius (border-top-left-radius, border-top-right-radius, border-bottom-right-radius, border-bottom-left-radius)

```
.rounded-corners {
  -webkit-border-radius : 12px;
  border-radius : 12px;
}
```

VALUE	INHERITED	NO
auto	Default	auto
[length]	Applies to	All elements
[percentage]		
inherit		

box-shadow

The possible values for this property are

```
inset offset-x offset-y blur-radius spread-radius color
.drop-shadow {
  // inset offset-x offset-y blur-radius spread-radius color
  -webkit-box-shadow : 0px 0px 4px 0px #000000;
  box-shadow : 0px 0px 4px 0px #000000;
}
```

VALUE	INHERITED	NO
none	Default	auto
[inset]	Applies to	All elements
[offset-x] [offset-y]		
[blur-radius]		
[spread-radius]		
[color]		

Browser support is as follows:

VALUE	IE	FF	SAFARI	CHROME	OPERA
box-shadow	9	3.5*/4.0	3*/5.1	1*/10	10.5
border-radius	9	1*/2.0	3*/5	.2*/4	10.5

*Indicates support with browser prefix.

Multi-Column

The CSS Multi-Column layout module enables the definition of multiple columns of text.

```
.fixed-width {
  width:500px;
  height:200px;
  -webkit-column-count: 3;
  -webkit-column-gap: 15px;
  -moz-column-count: 3;
  -moz-column-gap: 15px;
  column-count: 3;
  column-gap: 15px;
}
.percentage-width {
  width:100%;
  height:200px;
  -webkit-column-width: 100px;
  -webkit-column-gap: 15px;
  -moz-column-width: 100px;
  -moz-column-gap: 15px;
  column-width: 100px;
  column-gap: 15px;
}
```

column-count

This defines the number of columns in an element.

VALUE	INHERITED	NO
auto	Default	auto
[integer]	Applies to	Block-level elements, table cells, and inline-block elements

column-gap

This defines the gutter between the columns of a multi-column element.

VALUE	INHERITED	NO
normal	Default	1em
[length]	Applies to	Multi-column elements

column-width

This defines the width of the columns of a multi-column element.

VALUE	INHERITED	NO
auto	Default	auto
[length]	Applies to	Multi-column elements

Browser support is as follows:

PROPERTY	IE	FF	SAFARI	CHROME	OPERA
column-count	10	1.5*	3*	1*	11.1
column-gap	10	1.5*	3*	1*	11.1
column-width	10	1.5*	3*	1*	11.1

*Indicates support with browser prefix.

Media Queries

The CSS Media Queries module enables the definition of styles based on device and browser characteristics.

```
#container {
  width : 940px;
}
@media screen and (max-width:999px) {
  #container {
    width : 740px;
  }
}

@media screen and (max-width:480px)
{
```

```
    #container {
      width : 400px;
    }
  }
```

The module supports the following properties:

PROPERTIES	DESCRIPTION
width	Tests the width of the display area of the device in a browser. This is equal to the width of the browser window.
height	Tests the height of the display area of the device. In a browser this is equal to the height of the browser window.
device-width	Tests the width of the rendering surface of the device. In a browser this is equal to the full screen width.
device-height	Tests the height of the rendering surface of the device. In a browser this is equal to the full screen height.
orientation	Tests the orientation of a device.
aspect-ratio	Tests the aspect-ratio as measured by the width and height properties.
device-aspect-ratio	Tests the aspect-ratio as measured by the device-width and device-height properties.
color	Tests the color depth of the device.
color-index	Tests the number of entries in the lookup table of the device.
monochrome	Tests the number of bits per pixel in a monochrome frame buffer.
resolution	Tests the pixel density of the target device.
scan	Tests the scanning process of "tv" devices.
grid	Tests whether the device is a grid or bitmap. An example of a grid would be a text browser such as Lynx run from the terminal.

Basic support is as follows:

	IE	FF	SAFARI	CHROME	OPERA
@media (basic support)	9	3.5	4	1	9.5

@font-face

The CSS Fonts Modules enable the use of custom fonts.

```
@font-face {
  font-family: 'InconsolataMedium';
  src: url('Inconsolata-webfont.eot');
  src: url('Inconsolata-webfont.eot?#iefix') format('embedded-opentype'),
   url('Inconsolata-webfont.woff') format('woff'),
   url('Inconsolata-webfont.ttf') format('truetype'),
   url('Inconsolata-webfont.svg#InconsolataMedium') format('svg');
  font-weight: normal;
  font-style: normal;
}
```

Basic support is as follows:

	IE	FF	SAFARI	CHROME	OPERA
@font-face	4	3.5	3.1	4	10

2D Transforms

The 2D Transforms module introduces a new property that enables the rotation, translation, and scaling of a box, without changing its place in the flow of the document.

```
#rotate {
  -webkit-transform : rotate(20deg);
  -moz-transform : rotate(20deg);
  -ms-transform : rotate(20deg);
  -o-transform : rotate(20deg);
  transform : rotate(20deg);
  background : #00ffcc;
  top : 100px;
  left : 50px;
}
#scale {
  -webkit-transform : scale(0.5);
  -moz-transform : scale(0.5);
  -ms-transform : scale(0.5);
  -o-transform : scale(0.5);
  transform : scale(0.5);
  background : #ccff00;
  top : 400px;
  left : 50px;
}
```

The following table lists the common functions of the transform property and gives a small example of each.

VALUE	DESCRIPTION	EXAMPLE
translate	Moves an element up/down or left/right without changing the element's place in the flow of the document.	transform : translate(10px, 10px);
translateX	Moves an element left or right without changing the element's place in the flow of the document.	transformX : translate(10px);
translateY	Moves an element up or down without changing the element's place in the flow of the document.	transformY : translate(10px);
rotate	Rotates an element around an axis. The rotation can be specified in degrees or using other values like the turn keyword.	transform : rotate(180deg)
scale	Scales an element without changing the element's place in the document. Scale is set as a multiple of 1, so scale(2) tells the browser to make the element twice as big.	transform : scale(2)
scaleX	Scales an element on its x axis without changing the element's place in the document.	transform : scale(2)
scaleY	Scales an element on its y axis without changing the element's place in the document.	transform : scale(2)

Basic support is as follows:

VALUE	IE	FF	SAFARI	CHROME	OPERA
transform	9*/10	3.5*/16	3.1*	1*	10.5*/12.1

*Indicates support with browser prefix.

3D Transforms

The 3D Transforms module extends 2D Transforms with a perspective transform function.

```
#perspective {
  top : 200px;
  left : 200px;
  position : absolute;
  -webkit-transform : perspective(500px) rotateY(75deg);
  -moz-transform : perspective(500px) rotateY(75deg);
  -ie-transform : perspective(500px) rotateY(75deg);
  transform : perspective(500px) rotateY(75deg);
```

```
    width : 500px;
    height : 100px;
    background : #ccff00;
}
```

Basic support is as follows:

VALUE	IE	FF	SAFARI	CHROME	OPERA
transform	10	10*/16	4*	12*	none

*Indicates support with browser prefix.

Animations

The Animations module enables you to assign an animation to an element. You do this by specifying the properties to animate, the timing, and the units to change during the animation.

```
#animated {
    position : absolute;
    width : 100px;
    height : 100px;
    left:0px;
    top:100px;
    background: #ffcc00;
    animation-name: scroll;
    animation-duration: 5s;
    animation-iteration-count: infinite;
    animation-timing-function: ease-in-out;
    animation-direction: alternate;

}
@keyframes scroll {
    to {
        left:100%;
        transform: rotate(180deg);
    }
}
```

The @keyframes directive defines named states that define standard CSS properties to use as animation keyframes.

The following table lists the subproperties of the animation property.

PROPERTY	DESCRIPTION
animation-name	Defines the name of the @keyframes rule that defines the animation's keyframes.
animation-duration	Defines the length of time the animation should take to run once.

`animation-timing-function`	Defines the transition of animations through keyframes using keyword-based functions.
`animation-iteration-count`	Defines the number of times the animation should run.
`animation-direction`	Defines whether the animation should reverse direction during each iteration.
`animation-play-state`	Defines the play/pause state of the animation.
`animation-delay'`	Defines the animation delay.
`animation-fill-mode`	Defines how an animation should apply target styles.

Basic support is as follows:

	IE	FF	SAFARI	CHROME	OPERA
Basic Support	10	5*/16	4*	1*	12*/12.1

*Indicates support with browser prefix.

Transitions

The Transitions module defines a property to animate the transitions between pseudo-classes, for example, when an element enters or leaves the `:hover` state.

```
#transition li{
  font:16px arial, helvetica, sans-serif;
  color:#fff;
  padding:2px 10px;
  width :  200px;
  list-style-type : none;
  height : 50px;
  background-color : #06F;
  -webkit-transition-property: background-color,width,height;
  -moz-transition-property: background-color,width,height;
  -o-transition-property:  background-color,width,height;
  transition-property:  background-color,width,height;

  -webkit-transition-duration: 1s;
  -moz-transition-duration: 1s;
  -o-transition-duration: background-color 1s;
  transition-duration: background-color 1s;

}
#transition li:hover {
  background-color: #036;
  width:225px;
  height:60px;
```

```
    -webkit-transition-duration: 1s;
    -moz-transition-duration: 1s;
    -o-transition-duration: 1s;
    transition-duration: 1s;
}
```

The following table lists the transition properties.

VALUE	DESCRIPTION
transition-property	Defines the property or properties to transition through.
transition-duration	Defines the length of time the transition should take to run once.
transition-timing-function	Defines a keyword-based function used to shape the transition.
transition-delay	Defines the transition delay.

Basic support is as follows:

	IE	FF	SAFARI	CHROME	OPERA
Basic Support	10	4*/16	3*	1*	11.6*/12.1

*Indicates support with browser prefix.

LENGTHS

Following are the unit measurements for lengths that can be used in CSS.

Absolute Lengths

UNIT	IE
cm	3
in	3
mm	3
pc	3
pt	3

Relative Lengths

UNIT	IE
em	4
ex	4
px	3

CSS3 Relative Length Properties

	IE	FF	SAFARI	CHROME	OPERA
rem	9	3.6	5	6.0	11.6
vw	10	19	6	20	12.5
vh	10	19	6	20	12.5

Color Names and Values

The first thing you need to learn about color is how to specify exactly the color you want; after all, there are a lot of different hues, tones, and shades and you must choose the right ones.

In HTML you can specify a color in four key ways:

➤ **Hex codes:** These are six-digit codes representing the amount of red, green, and blue that make up the color, preceded by a pound or hash sign # (for example, #333333).

➤ **Color names:** A set of names that represent more than 200 colors, such as red, lightslategray, and fuchsia.

➤ **RGB color values:** Here, numbers between 0 and 255 represent the amount of red, green, and blue that makes up each color.

➤ **HSL color values:** HSL is an alternative to RGB and closely mirrors the way that people actually think about color. Instead of mixing three RGB values together to create the target color, HSL enables you to set the hue with one number between 0 and 360, where, for example, 0 is red, 120 is green, and 240 is blue. Then, you adjust the saturation of the color using 0 percent as gray and 100 percent as full saturation. Finally you adjust lightness/darkness of the color where 0-percent lightness is black, 100-percent lightness is white, and 50-percent lightness is "normal."

USING HEX CODES TO SPECIFY COLORS

When you start using *hexadecimal codes* (or *hex codes* for short), they can be daunting because they use a mix of numbers and letters to represent colors. Although you are used to numbers represented with 10 digits (0–9), hexadecimal codes are represented with 16 digits (0–9 and A–F). Table D-1 provides some examples of colors and their hex values; you will understand hex codes shortly (in the "Understanding Hex Codes" section), after you see what they represent.

TABLE D-1: Common Hex Codes

COLOR	HEXADECIMAL CODE
Black	#000000
White	#FFFFFF
Red	#FF0000
Green	#00FF00
Blue	#0000FF
Purple	#800080

The idea that colors are represented by a mix of numbers and letters might seem a little strange, but what follows the # sign is actually the amount of red, green, and blue that makes up the color. The format for hex codes is as follows:

    #rrggbb

As you might already know, the screens on computer monitors consist of thousands of tiny squares called *pixels*. (If you look closely at your monitor, you can see them.) When it is not turned on, the screen is black because it does not emit any light. When it is turned on, a picture is created because each pixel can be a different color. Every one of these colors is expressed in terms of a mix of red, green, and blue (just like a television screen).

It's hardly surprising, therefore, that you specify colors in the amounts of red, green, and blue required to make a given color. The values of red, green, and blue required to make a color are specified using numbers between 0 and 255, so when red, green, and blue all have a value of 0, you get black, whereas if each has a value of 255, you get white. If red is given a value of 255 and green and blue have a value of 0, you get red. You can make other colors by mixing the amounts of red, green, and blue as well—for example, if red and blue are given values of 255 and blue a value of 0, you get pink.

You may have seen that some software represents colors using three sets of numbers between 0 and 255. Figure D-1 shows the color window in Adobe Photoshop.

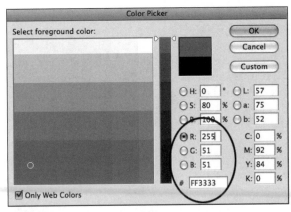

FIGURE D-1

The hexadecimal codes used on the web for color are a direct translation of these values between 0 and 255, except they use two characters, not three, to represent the numbers between 0 and 255. For example, FF represents 255 and 00 represents 0.

When designing a site, you can use a tool such as Photoshop or a number of free resources on the web to find hex codes for colors:

➤ www.colorschemer.com

➤ www.colourlovers.com/colors/add

However, if you want to understand how hex codes work, you need to understand how computers store information, so read the following section.

UNDERSTANDING HEX CODES

You may have heard people say that computers store all their information in 0s and 1s, and although it may sound hard to believe, it's true! The smallest unit of information a computer stores in is known as a *bit*, and a bit can have only one of two values:

➤ 0, which means off (or false)

➤ 1, which means on (or true)

These two values on their own do not store much information, but if you combine 4 bits together, you can get 16 different values. For example, using combinations of four 0s and 1s, you can represent the digits 0 through 9 (and still have values to spare):

```
0000 0001 0010 0011 0100 0101 0110 0111 1000 1001 1010 1011 1100 1101 1110 1111
  0    1    2    3    4    5    6    7    8    9    -    -    -    -    -    -
```

Four bits can be replaced by a single hexadecimal digit. There are 16 digits in hexadecimal numbers to represent the 16 possible values of four 0s and 1s:

```
0000 0001 0010 0011 0100 0101 0110 0111 1000 1001 1010 1011 1100 1101 1110 1111
  0    1    2    3    4    5    6    7    8    9    A    B    C    D    E    F
```

0 is the smallest; F is the largest.

Still, computers need to work with more than 16 possible values, so they tend to store information in even larger segments. A group of 8 bits is known as a *byte*. A byte can therefore be represented using just two hexadecimal digits, for example:

```
Binary        0100    1111
Hexadecimal     4       F
```

This gives 256 possible combinations of 0s and 1s (16 × 16), plenty for the characters of the English language, which is why colors are represented in numbers between 0 and 255.

So, although hexadecimal codes for web colors may appear a little complicated, #4F4F4F is a lot easier to read than 010011110100111101001111. Table D-2 shows some more hexadecimal codes and their corresponding decimal numbers.

TABLE D-2: Select Hex Codes and Their Corresponding Decimal Values

HEXADECIMAL	DECIMAL
00	0
33	51
66	102
99	153
AA	170
BB	187
CC	204
DD	221
EE	238
FF	255

USING COLOR NAMES TO SPECIFY COLORS

Rather than using hex values to specify colors, you can also use the names of many colors such as red, green, and white to specify the color you want. There are more than 200 different color names supported by IE, Firefox, and Safari, all of which are listed at the end of this appendix.

Although names might sound a lot easier to understand than hex codes, some of the colors are easier to remember than others, and remembering which color corresponds to each of the 200 names is very difficult. Here is a sample of some of the color names:

```
aqua black blue fuchsia gray green lime maroon navy olive purple red silver
   teal white yellow
```

Furthermore, if you do jobs for larger companies, such companies often want to specify exact colors that represent their brand, and their color might not have an HTML name. Indeed, when clients specify the color they want, they usually specify a hex code.

Because hex codes give you many more choices of shades, tints, and hues of colors than color names, and because a lot of companies ask for specific colors to represent their company, hex codes tend to be the choice of web professionals.

COLOR NAME AND NUMBER REFERENCE

Table D-3 shows the color names supported by the main browsers and their corresponding hex values. It is worth noting, however, that these are browser extensions, not part of the HTML recommendation.

TABLE D-3: Color Names

COLOR NAME	HEX VALUE
Aliceblue	#f0f8ff
Antiquewhite	#faebd7
Aqua	#00ffff
Aquamarine	#7fffd4
Azure	#f0ffff
Beige	#f5f5dc
Bisque	#ffe4c4
Black	#000000
Blanchedalmond	#ffebcd
Blue	#0000ff
Blueviolet	#8a2be2
Brown	#a52a2a
Burlywood	#deb887
Cadetblue	#5f9ea0
Chartreuse	#7fff00
Chocolate	#d2691e
Coral	#ff7f50
Cornflowerblue	#6495ed
Cornsilk	#fff8dc
Crimson	#dc143c
Cyan	#00ffff
Darkblue	#00008b

continues

TABLE D-3 *(continued)*

COLOR NAME	HEX VALUE
Darkcyan	#008b8b
Darkgoldenrod	#b8860b
Darkgray	#a9a9a9
Darkgreen	#006400
Darkkhaki	#bdb76b
Darkmagenta	#8b008b
Darkolivegreen	#556b2f
Darkorange	#ff8b04
Darkorchid	#9932cc
Darkred	#8b0000
Darksalmon	#e9967a
Darkseagreen	#8fbc8f
Darkslateblue	#483d8b
Darkslategray	#2f4f4f
Darkturquoise	#00ced1
Darkviolet	#9400d3
Deeppink	#ff1493
Deepskyblue	#00bfff
Dimgray	#696969
Dodgerblue	#1e90ff
Firebrick	#b22222
Floralwhite	#fffaf0
Forestgreen	#228b22
Fuchsia	#ff00ff
Gainsboro	#dcdcdc
Ghostwhite	#f8f8ff

Gold	#ffd700
Goldenrod	#daa520
Gray	#808080
Green	#008000
Greenyellow	#adff2f
Honeydew	#f0fff0
Hotpink	#ff69b4
Indianred	#cd5c5c
Indigo	#4b0082
Ivory	#fffff0
Khaki	#f0e68c
Lavender	#e6e6fa
Lavenderblush	#fff0f5
Lawngreen	#7cfb04
Lemonchiffon	#fffacd
Lightblue	#add8e6
Lightcoral	#f08080
Lightcyan	#e0ffff
Lightgoldenrodyellow	#fafad2
Lightgreen	#90ee90
Lightgrey	#d3d3d3
Lightpink	#ffb6c1
Lightsalmon	#ffa07a
Lightseagreen	#20b2aa
Lightskyblue	#87cefa
Lightslategray	#778899
Lightsteelblue	#b0c4de

continues

TABLE D-3 *(continued)*

COLOR NAME	HEX VALUE
Lightyellow	#ffffe0
Lime	#00ff00
Limegreen	#32cd32
Linen	#faf0e6
Magenta	#ff00ff
Maroon	#800000
Mediumaquamarine	#66cdaa
Mediumblue	#0000cd
Mediumorchid	#ba55d3
Mediumpurple	#9370db
Mediumseagreen	#3cb371
Mediumslateblue	#7b68ee
Mediumspringgreen	#00fa9a
Mediumturquoise	#48d1cc
Mediumvioletred	#c71585
Midnightblue	#191970
Mintcream	#f5fffa
Mistyrose	#ffe4e1
Moccasin	#ffe4b5
Navajowhite	#ffdead
Navy	#000080
Oldlace	#fdf5e6
Olive	#808000
Olivedrab	#6b8e23
Orange	#ffa500
Orangered	#ff4500

Orchid	#da70d6
Palegoldenrod	#eee8aa
Palegreen	#98fb98
Paleturquoise	#afeeee
Palevioletred	#db7093
Papayawhip	#ffefd5
Peachpuff	#ffdab9
Peru	#cd853f
Pink	#ffc0cb
Plum	#dda0dd
Powderblue	#b0e0e6
Purple	#800080
Red	#ff0000
Rosybrown	#bc8f8f
Royalblue	#4169e1
Saddlebrown	#8b4513
Salmon	#fa8072
Sandybrown	#f4a460
Seagreen	#2e8b57
Seashell	#fff5ee
Sienna	#a0522d
Silver	#c0c0c0
Skyblue	#87ceeb
Slateblue	#6a5acd
Slategray	#708090
Snow	#fffafa
Springgreen	#00ff7f

continues

TABLE D-3 *(continued)*

COLOR NAME	HEX VALUE
Steelblue	#4682b4
Tan	#d2b48c
Teal	#008080
Thistle	#d8bfd8
Tomato	#ff6347
Turquoise	#40e0d0
Violet	#ee82ee
Wheat	#f5deb3
White	#ffffff
Whitesmoke	#f5f5f5
Yellow	#ffff00
Yellowgreen	#9acd32

Character Encodings

Appendix D, "Color Names and Values," discusses how computers store information, how a character-encoding scheme is a table that translates between characters, and how they are stored in the computer.

The most common character set (or character encoding) in use on computers is The American Standard Code for Information Interchange (ASCII), which is probably the most widely used character set for encoding text electronically. You can expect all computers browsing the web to understand ASCII.

The problem with ASCII is that it supports only the uppercase and lowercase Latin alphabet, the numbers 0–9, and some extra characters: a total of 128 characters. Table E-1 lists the printable characters of ASCII. (The other characters are things such as line feeds and carriage-return characters.)

TABLE E-1: Printable Characters of ASCII

	!	"	#	$	%	&	`	(	)	*	+	,	-	.	/
0	1	2	3	4	5	6	7	8	9	:	;	<	=	>	?
@	A	B	C	D	E	F	G	H	I	J	K	L	M	N	O
P	Q	R	S	T	U	V	W	X	Y	Z	[	\	]	^	_
`	a	b	c	d	e	f	g	h	i	j	k	l	m	n	o
p	q	r	s	t	u	v	w	x	y	z	{			}	~	

However, many languages use either accented Latin characters or completely different alphabets. ASCII does not address these characters, so you need to learn about character encodings if you want to use any non-ASCII characters.

Character encodings are also important if you want to use symbols because these cannot be guaranteed to transfer properly between different encodings (from some dashes to some quotation mark characters). If you do not indicate the character encoding the document is written in, some of the special characters might not display.

The International Standards Organization created a range of character sets to deal with different national characters. ISO-8859-1 is commonly used in Western versions of authoring tools such as Adobe Dreamweaver, as well as applications such as Windows Notepad, as shown in Table E-2.

TABLE E-2: ISO Character Sets

CHARACTER SET	DESCRIPTION
ISO-8859-1	Latin alphabet part 1 Covering North America, Western Europe, Latin America, the Caribbean, Canada, and Africa
ISO-8859-2	Latin alphabet part 2 Covering Eastern Europe including Bosnian, Croatian, Czech, Hungarian, Polish, Romanian, Serbian (in Latin transcription), Serbo-Croatian, Slovak, Slovenian, Upper Sorbian, and Lower Sorbian
ISO-8859-3	Latin alphabet part 3 Covering SE Europe, Esperanto, Maltese, Turkish, and miscellaneous others
ISO-8859-4	Latin alphabet part 4 Covering Scandinavia/Baltics (and others not in ISO-8859-1)
ISO-8859-5	Latin/Cyrillic alphabet part 5
ISO-8859-6	Latin/Arabic alphabet part 6
ISO-8859-7	Latin/Greek alphabet part 7
ISO-8859-8	Latin/Hebrew alphabet part 8
ISO-8859-9	Latin 5 alphabet part 9 (same as ISO-8859-1 except Turkish characters replace Icelandic ones)
ISO-8859-10	Latin 6 Lappish, Nordic, and Eskimo
ISO-8859-15	The same as ISO-8859-1 but with more characters added
ISO-8859-16	Latin 10 Covering SE Europe, Albanian, Croatian, Hungarian, Polish, Romanian and Slovenian, plus can be used in French, German, Italian, and Irish Gaelic
ISO-2022-JP	Latin/Japanese alphabet part 1
ISO-2022-JP-2	Latin/Japanese alphabet part 2
ISO-2022-KR	Latin/Korean alphabet part 1

It is helpful to note that the first 128 characters of ISO-8859-1 match those of ASCII, so you can safely use those characters as you would in ASCII.

The *Unicode Consortium* was then set up to devise a way to show *all* characters of different languages, rather than have these different, incompatible character codes for different languages.

Therefore, if you want to create documents that use characters from multiple character sets, you can do so using the single Unicode character encodings. Furthermore, users can view documents written in different character sets, providing their processor (and fonts) supports the Unicode standards, no matter what platform they are on or which country they are in. By having the single-character encoding, you can reduce software development costs because the programs do not need to be designed to support multiple character encodings.

One problem with Unicode is that a lot of older programs were written to support only 8-bit character sets (limiting them to 256 characters), which is nowhere near the number required for all languages.

Unicode therefore specifies encodings that can deal with a string in special ways to make enough space for the huge character set it encompasses. These are known as UTF-8, UTF-16, and UTF-32, as shown in Table E-3.

TABLE E-3: Unicode Character Sets

CHARACTER SET	DESCRIPTION
UTF-8	A Unicode Translation Format that comes in 8-bit units. That is, it comes in *bytes*. A character in UTF-8 can be from 1 to 4 bytes, making UTF-8 a variable width.
UTF-16	A Unicode Translation Format that comes in 16-bit units. That is, it comes in *shorts*. It can be 1 or 2 shorts, making UTF-16 a variable width.
UTF-32	A Unicode Translation Format that comes in 32-bit units. That is, it comes in *longs*. It is a fixed-width format and is always 1 "long" in length.

The first 256 characters of Unicode character sets correspond to the 256 characters of ISO-8859-1.

By default, HTML 4 processors should support UTF-8, and XML processors are supposed to support UTF-8 and UTF-16; therefore, all XHTML-compliant processors should also support UTF-16 (because XHTML is an application of XML). The HTML5 specification is strongly biased toward UTF-8.

In practice you almost always want to use UTF-8.

For more information on internationalization and different character sets and encodings, see www.i18nguy.com and the article "The Absolute Minimum Every Software Developer Absolutely, Positively Must Know about Unicode and Character Sets (No Excuses!)" at www.joelonsoftware .com/articles/Unicode.html.

Special Characters

Some characters are reserved in HTML; for example, you cannot use the greater-than and less-than signs or angle brackets within your text because the browser could mistake them for markup. HTML processors must support the five special characters listed in Table F-1.

TABLE F-1: Special Characters

SYMBOL	DESCRIPTION	ENTITY NAME	NUMBER CODE
&	Ampersand	&amp;	&#38;
<	Less than	&lt;	&#60;
>	Greater than	&gt;	&#62;
"	Double quote	&quot;	&#34;
	Non-breaking space		

To write an element and attribute into your page so that the code is shown to the user rather than being processed by the browser (for example, as `<div id="character">`), you would write

```
&lt;div id=&quot;character&quot;&gt;
```

There is also a long list of special characters that HTML 4.0–aware processors should support. For these to appear in your document, you can use either the numerical code or the entity name. For example, to insert a copyright symbol, you can use either of the following:

```
&copy; 2008
&#169; 2013
```

The special characters have been split into the following sections:

➤ Character Entity References for ISO 8859-1 Characters

➤ Character Entity References for Symbols, Mathematical Symbols, and Greek Letters

➤ Character Entity References for Markup-Significant and Internationalization Characters

They are taken from the W3C website at `www.w3.org/TR/REC-html40/sgml/entities.html`.

CHARACTER ENTITY REFERENCES FOR ISO 8859-1 CHARACTERS

SYMBOL	DESCRIPTION	ENTITY NAME	NUMBER CODE
	No-break space = non-breaking space		
¡	Inverted exclamation mark	&iexcl;	&#161;
¢	Cent sign	&cent;	&#162;
£	Pound sign	&pound;	&#163;
¤	Currency sign	&curren;	&#164;
¥	Yen sign = yuan sign	&yen;	&#165;
¦	Broken bar = broken vertical bar	&brvbar;	&#166;
§	Section sign	&sect;	&#167;
¨	Diaeresis = spacing diaeresis	&uml;	&#168;
©	Copyright sign	&copy;	&#169;
a_	Feminine ordinal indicator	&ordf;	&#170;
«	Left-pointing double angle quotation mark = left-pointing guillemet	&laquo;	&#171;
¬	Not sign	&not;	&#172;
SHY	Soft hyphen = discretionary hyphen	&shy;	&#173;
®	Registered sign = registered trademark sign	&reg;	&#174;
¯	Macron = spacing macron = overline = APL overbar	&macr;	&#175;
°	Degree sign	&deg;	&#176;
±	Plus-minus sign = plus-or-minus sign	&plusmn;	&#177;

²	Superscript two = superscript digit two = squared	`&sup2;`	`&#178;`
³	Superscript three = superscript digit three = cubed	`&sup3;`	`&#179;`
´	Acute accent = spacing acute	`&acute;`	`&#180;`
µ	Micro sign	`&micro;`	`&#181;`
¶	Pilcrow sign = paragraph sign	`&para;`	`&#182;`
·	Middle dot = Georgian comma = Greek middle dot	`&middot;`	`&#183;`
¸	Cedilla = spacing cedilla	`&cedil;`	`&#184;`
¹	Superscript one = superscript digit one	`&sup1;`	`&#185;`
º	Masculine ordinal indicator	`&ordm;`	`&#186;`
»	Right-pointing double angle quotation mark = right-pointing guillemet	`&raquo;`	`&#187;`
¼	Vulgar fraction one-quarter = fraction one-quarter	`&frac14;`	`&#188;`
½	Vulgar fraction one-half = fraction one-half	`&frac12;`	`&#189;`
¾	Vulgar fraction three-quarters = fraction three-quarters	`&frac34;`	`&#190;`
¿	Inverted question mark = turned question mark	`&iquest;`	`&#191;`
À	Latin capital letter A with grave = Latin capital letter A grave	`&Agrave;`	`&#192;`
Á	Latin capital letter A with acute	`&Aacute;`	`&#193;`
Â	Latin capital letter A with circumflex	`&Acirc;`	`&#194;`
Ã	Latin capital letter A with tilde	`&Atilde;`	`&#195;`
Ä	Latin capital letter A with diaeresis	`&Auml;`	`&#196;`
Å	Latin capital letter A with ring above = Latin capital letter A ring	`&Aring;`	`&#197;`
Æ	Latin capital letter AE = Latin capital ligature AE	`&AElig;`	`&#198;`

continues

(continued)

SYMBOL	DESCRIPTION	ENTITY NAME	NUMBER CODE
Ç	Latin capital letter C with cedilla	&Ccedil;	&#199;
È	Latin capital letter E with grave	&Egrave;	&#200;
É	Latin capital letter E with acute	&Eacute;	&#201;
Ê	Latin capital letter E with circumflex	&Ecirc;	&#202;
Ë	Latin capital letter E with diaeresis	&Euml;	&#203;
Ì	Latin capital letter I with grave	&Igrave;	&#204;
Í	Latin capital letter I with acute	&Iacute;	&#205;
Î	Latin capital letter I with circumflex	&Icirc;	&#206;
Ï	Latin capital letter I with diaeresis	&Iuml;	&#207;
Ð	Latin capital letter ETH	&ETH;	&#208;
Ñ	Latin capital letter N with tilde	&Ntilde;	&#209;
Ò	Latin capital letter O with grave	&Ograve;	&#210;
Ó	Latin capital letter O with acute	&Oacute;	&#211;
Ô	Latin capital letter O with circumflex	&Ocirc;	&#212;
Õ	Latin capital letter O with tilde	&Otilde;	&#213;
Ö	Latin capital letter O with diaeresis	&Ouml;	&#214;
×	Multiplication sign	&times;	&#215;
Ø	Latin capital letter O with stroke = Latin capital letter O slash	&Oslash;	&#216;
Ù	Latin capital letter U with grave	&Ugrave;	&#217;
Ú	Latin capital letter U with acute	&Uacute;	&#218;
Û	Latin capital letter U with circumflex	&Ucirc;	&#219;
Ü	Latin capital letter U with diaeresis	&Uuml;	&#220;
Ý	Latin capital letter Y with acute	&Yacute;	&#221;
Þ	Latin capital letter THORN	&THORN;	&#222;
ß	Latin small letter sharp s = ess-zed	&szlig;	&#223;
à	Latin small letter a with grave = Latin small letter a grave	&agrave;	&#224;

á	Latin small letter a with acute	&aacute;	&#225;
â	Latin small letter a with circumflex	&acirc;	&#226;
ã	Latin small letter a with tilde	&atilde;	&#227;
ä	Latin small letter a with diaeresis	&auml;	&#228;
å	Latin small letter a with ring above = Latin small letter a ring	&aring;	&#229;
æ	Latin small letter ae = Latin small ligature ae	&aelig;	&#230;
ç	Latin small letter c with cedilla	&ccedil;	&#231;
è	Latin small letter e with grave	&egrave;	&#232;
é	Latin small letter e with acute	&eacute;	&#233;
ê	Latin small letter e with circumflex	&ecirc;	&#234;
ë	Latin small letter e with diaeresis	&euml;	&#235;
ì	Latin small letter i with grave	&igrave;	&#236;
í	Latin small letter i with acute	&iacute;	&#237;
î	Latin small letter i with circumflex	&icirc;	&#238;
ï	Latin small letter i with diaeresis	&iuml;	&#239;
đ	Latin small letter eth	&eth;	&#240;
ñ	Latin small letter n with tilde	&ntilde;	&#241;
ò	Latin small letter o with grave	&ograve;	&#242;
ó	Latin small letter o with acute	&oacute;	&#243;
ô	Latin small letter o with circumflex	&ocirc;	&#244;
õ	Latin small letter o with tilde	&otilde;	&#245;
ö	Latin small letter o with diaeresis	&ouml;	&#246;
÷	Division sign	&divide;	&#247;
ø	Latin small letter o with stroke = Latin small letter o slash	&oslash;	&#248;
ù	Latin small letter u with grave	&ugrave;	&#249;
ú	Latin small letter u with acute	&uacute;	&#250;
û	Latin small letter u with circumflex	&ucirc;	&#251;

continues

(continued)

SYMBOL	DESCRIPTION	ENTITY NAME	NUMBER CODE
ü	Latin small letter u with diaeresis	&uuml;	&#252;
ý	Latin small letter y with acute	&yacute;	&#253;
þ	Latin small letter thorn	&thorn;	&#254;
ÿ	Latin small letter y with diaeresis	&yuml;	&#255;

CHARACTER ENTITY REFERENCES FOR SYMBOLS, MATHEMATICAL SYMBOLS, AND GREEK LETTERS

SYMBOL	DESCRIPTION	ENTITY NAME	NUMBER CODE
LATIN EXTENDED-B			
f	Latin small f with hook = function = florin	&fnof;	&#402;
GREEK			
A	Greek capital letter alpha	&Alpha;	&#913;
B	Greek capital letter beta	&Beta;	&#914;
Γ	Greek capital letter gamma	&Gamma;	&#915;
Δ	Greek capital letter delta	&Delta;	&#916;
E	Greek capital letter epsilon	&Epsilon;	&#917;
Z	Greek capital letter zeta	&Zeta;	&#918;
H	Greek capital letter eta	&Eta;	&#919;
Θ	Greek capital letter theta	&Theta;	&#920;
I	Greek capital letter iota	&Iota;	&#921;
K	Greek capital letter kappa	&Kappa;	&#922;
Λ	Greek capital letter lambda	&Lambda;	&#923;
M	Greek capital letter mu	&Mu	&#924;
N	Greek capital letter nu	&Nu;	&#925;
Ξ	Greek capital letter xi	&Xi;	&#926;

O	Greek capital letter omicron	`&Omicron;`	`&#927;`
Π	Greek capital letter pi	`&Pi;`	`&#928;`
P	Greek capital letter rho	`&Rho;`	`&#929;`
Σ	Greek capital letter sigma	`&Sigma;`	`&#931;`
T	Greek capital letter tau	`&Tau;`	`&#932;`
Υ	Greek capital letter upsilon	`&Upsilon;`	`&#933;`
Φ	Greek capital letter phi	`&Phi;`	`&#934;`
X	Greek capital letter chi	`&Chi;`	`&#935;`
Ψ	Greek capital letter psi	`&Psi;`	`&#936;`
Ω	Greek capital letter omega	`&Omega;`	`&#937;`
α	Greek small letter alpha	`&alpha;`	`&#945;`
β	Greek small letter beta	`&beta;`	`&#946;`
γ	Greek small letter gamma	`&gamma;`	`&#947;`
δ	Greek small letter delta	`&delta;`	`&#948;`
ε	Greek small letter epsilon	`&epsilon;`	`&#949;`
ζ	Greek small letter zeta	`&zeta;`	`&#950;`
η	Greek small letter eta	`&eta;`	`&#951;`
θ	Greek small letter theta	`&theta;`	`&#952;`
ι	Greek small letter iota	`&iota;`	`&#953;`
κ	Greek small letter kappa	`&kappa;`	`&#954;`
λ	Greek small letter lambda	`&lambda;`	`&#955;`
μ	Greek small letter mu	`&mu;`	`&#956;`
ν	Greek small letter nu	`&nu;`	`&#957;`
ξ	Greek small letter xi	`&xi;`	`&#958;`
o	Greek small letter omicron	`&omicron;`	`&#959;`
π	Greek small letter pi	`&pi;`	`&#960;`
ρ	Greek small letter rho	`&rho;`	`&#961;`
ς	Greek small letter final sigma	`&sigmaf;`	`&#962;`

continues

(continued)

SYMBOL	DESCRIPTION	ENTITY NAME	NUMBER CODE
σ	Greek small letter sigma	&sigma;	&#963;
τ	Greek small letter tau	&tau;	&#964;
υ	Greek small letter upsilon	&upsilon;	&#965;
φ	Greek small letter phi	&phi;	&#966;
χ	Greek small letter chi	&chi;	&#967;
ψ	Greek small letter psi	&psi;	&#968;
ω	Greek small letter omega	&omega;	&#969;
θ	Greek small letter theta symbol	&thetasym;	&#977;
ϒ	Greek upsilon with hook symbol	&upsih;	&#978;
ϖ	Greek pi symbol	&piv;	&#982;
GENERAL PUNCTUATION			
•	Bullet = black small circle	&bull;	&#8226;
…	Horizontal ellipsis = three dot leader	&hellip;	&#8230;
′	Prime = minutes = feet	&prime;	&#8242;
″	Double prime = seconds = inches	&Prime;	&#8243;
‾	Overline = spacing overscore	&oline;	&#8254;
⁄	Fraction slash	&frasl;	&#8260;
LETTERLIKE SYMBOLS			
℘	Script capital P = power set = Weierstrass p	&weierp;	&#8472;
ℑ	Blackletter capital I = imaginary part	&image;	&#8465;
ℜ	Blackletter capital R = real part symbol	&real;	&#8476;
™	Trademark sign	&trade;	&#8482;
ℵ	Alef symbol = first transfinite cardinal	&alefsym;	&#8501;
ARROWS			
←	Left arrow	&larr;	&#8592;
↑	Up arrow	&uarr;	&#8593;
→	Right arrow	&rarr;	&#8594;

↓	Down arrow	`&darr;`	`&#8595;`
↔	Left-right arrow	`&harr;`	`&#8596;`
↵	Down arrow with corner leftward = carriage return	`&crarr;`	`&#8629;`
⇐	Left double arrow	`&lArr;`	`&#8656;`
⇑	Up double arrow	`&uArr;`	`&#8657;`
⇒	Right double arrow	`&rArr;`	`&#8658;`
⇓	Down double arrow	`&dArr;`	`&#8659;`
⇔	Left-right double arrow	`&hArr;`	`&#8660;`

MATHEMATICAL OPERATORS

∀	For all	`&forall;`	`&#8704;`
∂	Partial differential	`&part ;`	`&#8706;`
∃	There exists	`&exist;`	`&#8707;`
∅	Empty set = null set = diameter	`&empty;`	`&#8709;`
∇	Nabla = backward difference	`&nabla;`	`&#8711;`
∈	Element of	`&isin;`	`&#8712;`
∉	Not an element of	`&notin;`	`&#8713;`
∋	Contains as member	`&ni;`	`&#8715;`
∏	n-ary product = product sign	`&prod;`	`&#8719;`
∑	n-ary summation	`&sum;`	`&#8721;`
−	Minus sign	`&minus;`	`&#8722;`
∗	Asterisk operator	`&lowast;`	`&#8727;`
√	Square root = radical sign	`&radic;`	`&#8730;`
∝	Proportional to	`&prop;`	`&#8733;`
∞	Infinity	`&infin;`	`&#8734;`
∠	Angle	`&ang;`	`&#8736;`
∧	Logical and = wedge	`&and;`	`&#8743;`
∨	Logical or = vee	`&or ;`	`&#8744;`
∩	Intersection = cap	`&cap;`	`&#8745;`

continues

(continued)

SYMBOL	DESCRIPTION	ENTITY NAME	NUMBER CODE
∪	Union = cup	&cup;	&#8746;
∫	Integral	&int;	&#8747;
∴	Therefore	&there4;	&#8756;
~	Tilde operator = varies with = similar to	&sim;	&#8764;
≅	Approximately equal to	&cong;	&#8773;
≈	Almost equal to = asymptotic to	&asymp;	&#8776;
≠	Not equal to	&ne;	&#8800;
≡	Identical to	&equiv;	&#8801;
≤	Less than or equal to	&le;	&#8804;
≥	Greater than or equal to	&ge;	&#8805;
⊂	Subset of	&sub;	&#8834;
⊃	Superset of	&sup;	&#8835;
⊄	Not a subset of	&nsub;	&#8836;
⊆	Subset of or equal to	&sube;	&#8838;
⊇	Superset of or equal to	&supe;	&#8839;
⊕	Circled plus = direct sum	&oplus;	&#8853;
⊗	Circled times = vector product	&otimes;	&#8855;
⊥	Up tack = orthogonal to = perpendicular	&perp;	&#8869;
·	Dot operator	&sdot;	&#8901;

MISCELLANEOUS TECHNICAL

SYMBOL	DESCRIPTION	ENTITY NAME	NUMBER CODE
⌈	Left ceiling = apl upstile	&lceil;	&#8968;
⌉	Right ceiling	&rceil;	&#8969;
⌊	Left floor = apl downstile	&lfloor;	&#8970;
⌋	Right floor	&rfloor;	&#8971;
⟨	Left-pointing angle bracket = bra	&lang;	&#9001;
⟩	Right-pointing angle bracket = ket	&rang;	&#9002;

GEOMETRIC SHAPE			
◊	Lozenge	`&loz;`	`&#9674;`
MISCELLANEOUS SYMBOLS			
♠	Black spade suit	`&spades;`	`&#9824;`
♣	Black club suit = shamrock	`&clubs;`	`&#9827;`
♥	Black heart suit = valentine	`&hearts;`	`&#9829;`
♦	Black diamond suit	`&diams;`	`&#9830;`

CHARACTER ENTITY REFERENCES FOR MARKUP-SIGNIFICANT AND INTERNATIONALIZATION CHARACTERS

SYMBOL	DESCRIPTION	ENTITY NAME	NUMBER CODE
"	Quotation mark = APL quote	`&quot;`	`&#34;`
&	Ampersand	`&amp;`	`&#38;`
<	Less-than sign	`&lt;`	`&#60;`
>	Greater-than sign	`&gt;`	`&#62;`
Œ	Latin capital ligature OE	`&OElig;`	`&#338;`
œ	Latin small ligature oe	`&oelig;`	`&#339;`
Š	Latin capital letter S with caron	`&Scaron;`	`&#352;`
š	Latin small letter s with caron	`&scaron;`	`&#353;`
Ÿ	Latin capital letter Y with diaeresis	`&Yuml;`	`&#376;`
SPACING MODIFIERS			
ˆ	Modifier letter circumflex accent	`&circ;`	`&#710;`
˜	Small tilde	`&tilde;`	`&#732;`
GENERAL PUNCTUATION			
	En space	` `	` `
	Em space	` `	` `
	Thin space	` `	` `

continues

(continued)

SYMBOL	DESCRIPTION	ENTITY NAME	NUMBER CODE
ZW NJ	Zero width non-joiner	&zwnj;	&#8204;
ZW J	Zero width joiner	&zwj;	&#8205;
LRM	Left-to-right mark	&lrm;	&#8206;
RLM	Right-to-left mark	&rlm;	&#8207;
–	En dash	&ndash;	&#8211;
—	Em dash	&mdash;	&#8212;
'	Left single quotation mark	&lsquo;	&#8216;
'	Right single quotation mark	&rsquo;	&#8217;
‚	Single low-9 quotation mark	&sbquo;	&#8218;
"	Left double quotation mark	&ldquo;	&#8220;
"	Right double quotation mark	&rdquo;	&#8221;
„	Double low-9 quotation mark	&bdquo;	&#8222;
†	Dagger	&dagger;	&#8224;
‡	Double dagger	&Dagger;	&#8225;
‰	Per mille sign	&permil;	&#8240;
‹	Single left-pointing angle quotation mark (proposed, but not yet standardized)	&lsaquo;	&#8249;
›	Single right-pointing angle quotation mark (proposed, but not yet standardized)	&rsaquo;	&#8250;
€	Euro sign	&euro;	&#8364;

Language Codes

Table G-1 shows the two-letter ISO 639 language codes that you can use to declare the language of a document in the `lang` attribute. It covers many of the world's major languages.

TABLE G-1: ISO 639 Language Codes

LANGUAGE	ISO CODE
Abkhazian	AB
Afan (Oromo)	OM
Afar	AA
Afrikaans	AF
Albanian	SQ
Amharic	AM
Arabic	AR
Armenian	HY
Assamese	AS
Aymara	AY
Azerbaijani	AZ
Bashkir	BA
Basque	EU
Bengali; Bangla	BN

continues

TABLE G-1 *(continued)*

LANGUAGE	ISO CODE
Bhutani	DZ
Bihari	BH
Bislama	BI
Breton	BR
Bulgarian	BG
Burmese	MY
Byelorussian	BE
Cambodian	KM
Catalan	CA
Chinese	ZH
Corsican	CO
Croatian	HR
Czech	CS
Danish	DA
Dutch	NL
English	EN
Esperanto	EO
Estonian	ET
Faroese	FO
Fiji	FJ
Finnish	FI
French	FR
Frisian	FY
Galician	GL
Georgian	KA
German	DE

Greek	EL
Greenlandic	KL
Guarani	GN
Gujarati	GU
Hausa	HA
Hebrew	HE
Hindi	HI
Hungarian	HU
Icelandic	IS
Indonesian	ID
Interlingua	IA
Interlingue	IE
Inuktitut	IU
Inupiak	IK
Irish	GA
Italian	IT
Japanese	JA
Javanese	JV
Kannada	KN
Kashmiri	KS
Kazakh	KK
Kinyarwanda	RW
Kirghiz	KY
Korean	KO
Kurdish	KU
Kurundi	RN
Laothian	LO

continues

TABLE G-1 *(continued)*

LANGUAGE	ISO CODE
Latin	LA
Latvian; Lettish	LV
Lingala	LN
Lithuanian	LT
Macedonian	MK
Malagasy	MG
Malay	MS
Malayalam	ML
Maltese	MT
Maori	MI
Marathi	MR
Moldavian	MO
Mongolian	MN
Nauru	NA
Nepali	NE
Norwegian	NO
Occitan	OC
Oriya	OR
Pashto; Pushto	PS
Persian (Farsi)	FA
Polish	PL
Portuguese	PT
Punjabi	PA
Quechua	QU
Rhaeto-Romance	RM
Romanian	RO

Russian	RU
Samoan	SM
Sangho	SG
Sanskrit	SA
Scots Gaelic	GD
Serbian	SR
Serbo-Croatian	SH
Sesotho	ST
Setswana	TN
Shona	SN
Sindhi	SD
Singhalese	SI
Siswati	SS
Slovak	SK
Slovenian	SL
Somali	SO
Spanish	ES
Sudanese	SU
Swahili	SW
Swedish	SV
Tagalog	TL
Tajik	TG
Tamil	TA
Tatar	TT
Telugu	TE
Thai	TH
Tibetan	BO

continues

TABLE G-1 *(continued)*

LANGUAGE	ISO CODE
Tigrinya	TI
Tonga	TO
Tsonga	TS
Turkish	TR
Turkmen	TK
Twi	TW
Uigur	UG
Ukrainian	UK
Urdu	UR
Uzbek	UZ
Vietnamese	VI
Volapuk	VO
Welsh	CY
Wolof	WO
Xhosa	XH
Yiddish	YI
Yoruba	YO
Zhuang	ZA
Zulu	ZU

MIME Media Types

You have seen the `type` attribute used throughout this book on a number of elements, the value of which is a MIME media type.

Multipurpose Internet Mail Extension (MIME) media types were originally devised so that e-mail could include information other than plain text. MIME media types indicate the following things:

➤ How the parts of a message, such as text and attachments, are combined into the message

➤ The way in which each part of the message is specified

➤ The way the items are encoded for transmission so that even software that was designed to work only with ASCII text can process the message

As you have seen, however, MIME types are not just for use with e-mail; they were adopted by web servers as a way to tell web browsers what type of material was being sent to them so that they could cope with that kind of file correctly.

MIME content types consist of two parts:

➤ A main type

➤ A subtype

The main type is separated from the subtype by a forward slash character—for example, `text/html` for HTML.

This appendix is organized by the main types:

➤ `text`

➤ `image`

➤ `multipart`

➤ `audio`

- ➤ `video`
- ➤ `message`
- ➤ `model`
- ➤ `application`

For example, the `text` main type contains types of plain text files, such as

- ➤ `text/plain` for plain text files
- ➤ `text/html` for HTML files
- ➤ `text/rtf` for text files using rich text formatting

MIME types are officially supposed to be assigned and listed by the Internet Assigned Numbers Authority (IANA).

Many of the popular MIME types in this list (all those that begin with x-) are not assigned by the IANA and do not have official status. (Some of these are popular and browsers support them, such as `audio/x-mp3`. You can see the list of official MIME types at `www.iana.org/assignments/media-types/`.)

Those preceded with `vnd.` are vendor-specific.

The most popular MIME types are listed in this appendix in a bold typeface to help you find them.

TEXT

When specifying the MIME type of a content-type field (for example, in a `<meta>` element), you can also indicate the character set for the text being used, for example:

```
content-type:text/plain; charset=iso-8859-1
```

If you do not specify a character set, the default is US-ASCII.

calendar	richtext
css	**rtf**
directory	**sgml**
enriched	t140
html	tab-separated-values
parityfec	uri-list
plain	vnd.abc
prs.fallenstein.rst	vnd.curl
prs.lines.tag	vnd.DMClientScript
rfc822-headers	vnd.fly

vnd.fmi.flexstor

vnd.in3d.3dml

vnd.in3d.spot

vnd.IPTC.NewsML

vnd.IPTC.NITF

vnd.latex-z

vnd.motorola.reflex

vnd.ms-mediapackage

vnd.net2phone.commcenter.command

vnd.sun.j2me.app-descriptor

vnd.wap.si

vnd.wap.sl

vnd.wap.wml

vnd.wap.wmlscript

xml

xml-external-parsed-entity

IMAGE

bmp

cgm

g3fax

gif

jpeg

Ief

naplps

png

prs.btif

prs.pti

t38

tiff

tiff-fx

vnd.cns.inf2

vnd.djvu

vnd.dwg

vnd.dxf

vnd.fastbidsheet

vnd.fpx

vnd.fst

vnd.fujixerox.edmics-mmr

vnd.fujixerox.edmics-rlc

vnd.globalgraphics.pgb

vnd.microsoft.icon

vnd.mix

vnd.ms-modi

vnd.net-fpx

vnd.sealed.png

vnd.sealedmedia.softseal.gif

vnd.sealedmedia.softseal.jpg

vnd.svf

vnd.wap.wbmp

vnd.xiff

x-portable-pixmap

x-xbitmap

MULTIPART

alternative	mixed
appledouble	parallel
byteranges	related
digest	report
encrypted	signed
form-data	voice-message
header-set	

AUDIO

1d-interleaved-parityfec	dsr-es202050
32kadpcm	dsr-es202211
3gpp	dsr-es202212
3gpp2	DV
ac3	DVI4
AMR	eac3
AMR-WB	EVRC
amr-wb+	EVRC0
asc	EVRC1
ATRAC-ADVANCED-LOSSLESS	EVRCB
ATRAC-X	EVRCB0
ATRAC3	EVRCB1
audio/qcelp	EVRC-QCP
basic	EVRCWB
BV16	EVRCWB0
BV32	EVRCWB1
clearmode	example
CN	fwdred
DAT12	G719
dls	G722
dsr-es201108	G7221

G723	PCMU-WB
G726-16	prs.sid
G726-24	QCELP
G726-32	raptorfec
G726-40	RED
G728	rtp-enc-aescm128
G729	rtp-midi
G7291	rtx
G729D	SMV
G729E	SMV-QCP
GSM	SMV0
GSM-EFR	sp-midi
GSM-HR-08	speex
iLBC	t140c
ip-mr_v2.5	t38
L8	telephone-event
L16	tone
L20	UEMCLIP
L24	ulpfec
LPC	VDVI
mobile-xmf	VMR-WB
MPA	vnd.3gpp.iufp
mp4	vnd.4SB
MP4A-LATM	vnd.audiokoz
mpa-robust	vnd.CELP
mpeg	vnd.cisco.nse
mpeg4-generic	vnd.cmles.radio-events
ogg	vnd.cns.anp1
parityfec	vnd.cns.inf1
PCMA	vnd.dece.audio
PCMA-WB	vnd.digital-winds
PCMU	vnd.dlna.adts

vnd.dolby.heaac.1

vnd.dolby.heaac.2

vnd.dolby.mlp

vnd.dolby.mps

vnd.dolby.pl2

vnd.dolby.pl2x

vnd.dolby.pl2z

vnd.dolby.pulse.1

vnd.dra

vnd.dts

vnd.dts.hd

vnd.dvb.file

vnd.everad.plj

vnd.hns.audio

vnd.lucent.voice

vnd.ms-playready.media.pya

vnd.nokia.mobile-xmf

vnd.nortel.vbk

vnd.nuera.ecelp4800

vnd.nuera.ecelp7470

vnd.nuera.ecelp9600

vnd.octel.sbc

vnd.rhetorex.32kadpcm

vnd.rip

vnd.sealedmedia.softseal.mpeg

vnd.vmx.cvsd

vorbis

vorbis-config

x-aiff

x-midi

x-mod

x-mp3

x-wav

VIDEO

3gpp

3gpp-tt

3gpp2

BMPEG

BT656

CelB

DV

example

H261

H263

H263-1998

H263-2000

H264

H264-RCDO

H264-SVC

JPEG

jpeg2000

MJ2

MP1S

MP2P

MP2T

mp4

MP4V-ES

MPV

mpeg

mpeg4-generic

Nv

ogg

parityfec

pointer

quicktime

raptorfec

raw

rtp-enc-aescm128

rtx

SMPTE292M

ulpfec

vc1

vnd.CCTV

vnd.dece.hd

vnd.dece.mobile

vnd.dece.mp4

vnd.dece.pd

vnd.dece.sd

vnd.dece.video

vnd.directv.mpeg

vnd.directv.mpeg-tts

vnd.dlna.mpeg-tts

vnd.dvb.file

vnd.fvt

vnd.hns.video

vnd.iptvforum.1dparityfec-1010

vnd.iptvforum.1dparityfec-2005

vnd.iptvforum.2dparityfec-1010

vnd.iptvforum.2dparityfec-2005

vnd.iptvforum.ttsavc

vnd.iptvforum.ttsmpeg2

vnd.motorola.video

vnd.motorola.videop

vnd.mpegurl

vnd.ms-playready.media.pyv

vnd.nokia.interleaved-multimedia

vnd.nokia.videovoip

vnd.objectvideo

vnd.sealed.mpeg1

vnd.sealed.mpeg4

vnd.sealed.swf

vnd.sealedmedia.softseal.mov

vnd.uvvu.mp4

x-msvideo

x-sgi-movie

MESSAGE

CPIM

delivery-status

disposition-notification

external-body

http

news

partial

rfc822

s-http

sip

sipfrag

MODEL

iges	vnd.gtw
mesh	vnd.mts
vnd.dwf	vnd.parasolid.transmit.binary
vnd.flatland.3dml	vnd.parasolid.transmit.text
vnd.gdl	vnd.vtu
vnd.gs-gdl	**vrml**

APPLICATION

activemessage	iges
andrew-inset	index
applefile	index.cmd
atomicmail	index.obj
batch-SMTP	index.response
beep+xml	index.vnd
cals-1840	iotp
cnrp+xml	ipp
commonground	isup
cpl+xml	mac-binhex40
cybercash	macwriteii
dca-rft	marc
dec-dx	mathematica
dicom	mpeg4-generic
dvcs	msword
EDI-Consent	news-message-id
EDI-X12	news-transmission
EDIFACT	ocsp-request
eshop	ocsp-response
font-tdpfr	octet-stream
http	oda
hyperstudio	ogg

parityfec	timestamp-query
pdf	timestamp-reply
pgp-encrypted	tve-trigger
pgp-keys	vemmi
pgp-signature	vnd.3gpp.pic-bw-large
pidf+xml	vnd.3gpp.pic-bw-small
pkcs10	vnd.3gpp.pic-bw-var
pkcs7-mime	vnd.3gpp.sms
pkcs7-signature	vnd.3M.Post-it-Notes
pkix-cert	vnd.accpac.simply.aso
pkix-crl	vnd.accpac.simply.imp
pkix-pkipath	vnd.acucobol
pkixcmp	vnd.acucorp
postscript	vnd.adobe.xfdf
prs.alvestrand.titrax-sheet	vnd.aether.imp
prs.cww	vnd.amiga.ami
prs.nprend	vnd.anser-web-certificate-issue-initiation
prs.plucker	vnd.anser-web-funds-transfer-initiation
qsig	vnd.audiograph
reginfo+xml	vnd.blueice.multipass
remote-printing	vnd.bmi
riscos	vnd.businessobjects
rtf	vnd.canon-cpdl
sdp	vnd.canon-lips
set-payment	vnd.cinderella
set-payment-initiation	vnd.claymore
set-registration	vnd.commerce-battelle
set-registration-initiation	vnd.commonspace
sgml	vnd.contact.cmsg
sgml-open-catalog	vnd.cosmocaller
sieve	vnd.criticaltools.wbs+xml
slate	vnd.ctc-posml

vnd.cups-postscript

vnd.cups-raster

vnd.cups-raw

vnd.curl

vnd.cybank

vnd.data-vision.rdz

vnd.dna

vnd.dpgraph

vnd.dreamfactory

vnd.dxr

vnd.ecdis-update

vnd.ecowin.chart

vnd.ecowin.filerequest

vnd.ecowin.fileupdate

vnd.ecowin.series

vnd.ecowin.seriesrequest

vnd.ecowin.seriesupdate

vnd.enliven

vnd.epson.esf

vnd.epson.msf

vnd.epson.quickanime

vnd.epson.salt

vnd.epson.ssf

vnd.ericsson.quickcall

vnd.eudora.data

vnd.fdf

vnd.ffsns

vnd.fints

vnd.FloGraphIt

vnd.framemaker

vnd.fsc.weblaunch

vnd.fujitsu.oasys

vnd.fujitsu.oasys2

vnd.fujitsu.oasys3

vnd.fujitsu.oasysgp

vnd.fujitsu.oasysprs

vnd.fujixerox.ddd

vnd.fujixerox.docuworks

vnd.fujixerox.docuworks.binder

vnd.fut-misnet

vnd.genomatix.tuxedo

vnd.grafeq

vnd.groove-account

vnd.groove-help

vnd.groove-identity-message

vnd.groove-injector

vnd.groove-tool-message

vnd.groove-tool-template

vnd.groove-vcard

vnd.hbci

vnd.hhe.lesson-player

vnd.hp-HPGL

vnd.hp-hpid

vnd.hp-hps

vnd.hp-PCL

vnd.hp-PCLXL

vnd.httphone

vnd.hzn-3d-crossword

vnd.ibm.afplinedata

vnd.ibm.electronic-media

vnd.ibm.MiniPay

vnd.ibm.modcap

vnd.ibm.rights-management

vnd.ibm.secure-container

vnd.informix-visionary

vnd.intercon.formnet

vnd.intertrust.digibox

vnd.intertrust.nncp

vnd.intu.qbo

vnd.intu.qfx

vnd.ipunplugged.rcprofile

vnd.irepository.package+xml

vnd.is-xpr

vnd.japannet-directory-service

vnd.japannet-jpnstore-wakeup

vnd.japannet-payment-wakeup

vnd.japannet-registration

vnd.japannet-registration-wakeup

vnd.japannet-setstore-wakeup

vnd.japannet-verification

vnd.japannet-verification-wakeup

vnd.jisp

vnd.kde.karbon

vnd.kde.kchart

vnd.kde.kformula

vnd.kde.kivio

vnd.kde.kontour

vnd.kde.kpresenter

vnd.kde.kspread

vnd.kde.kword

vnd.kenameaapp

vnd.kidspiration

vnd.koan

vnd.liberty-request+xml

vnd.llamagraphics.life-balance.desktop

vnd.llamagraphics.life-balance.exchange+xml

vnd.lotus-1-2-3

vnd.lotus-approach

vnd.lotus-freelance

vnd.lotus-notes

vnd.lotus-organizer

vnd.lotus-screencam

vnd.lotus-wordpro

vnd.mcd

vnd.mediastation.cdkey

vnd.meridian-slingshot

vnd.micrografx.flo

vnd.micrografx.igx

vnd.mif

vnd.minisoft-hp3000-save

vnd.mitsubishi.misty-guard.trustweb

vnd.Mobius.DAF

vnd.Mobius.DIS

vnd.Mobius.MBK

vnd.Mobius.MQY

vnd.Mobius.MSL

vnd.Mobius.PLC

vnd.Mobius.TXF

vnd.mophun.application

vnd.mophun.certificate

vnd.sss-ntf

vnd.street-stream

vnd.svd

vnd.swiftview-ics

vnd.triscape.mxs

vnd.trueapp

vnd.truedoc

vnd.ufdl

vnd.uiq.theme

vnd.uplanet.alert

vnd.uplanet.alert-wbxml

vnd.uplanet.bearer-choice

vnd.uplanet.bearer-choice-wbxml

vnd.uplanet.cacheop

vnd.uplanet.cacheop-wbxml

vnd.uplanet.channel

vnd.uplanet.channel-wbxml

vnd.uplanet.list

vnd.uplanet.list-wbxml

vnd.uplanet.listcmd

vnd.uplanet.listcmd-wbxml

vnd.uplanet.signal

vnd.vcx

vnd.vectorworks

vnd.vidsoft.vidconference

vnd.visio

vnd.visionary

vnd.vividence.scriptfile

vnd.vsf

vnd.wap.sic

vnd.wap.slc

vnd.wap.wbxml

vnd.wap.wmlc

vnd.wap.wmlscriptc

vnd.webturbo

vnd.wqd

vnd.wrq-hp3000-labelled

vnd.wt.stf

vnd.wv.csp+wbxml

vnd.wv.csp+xml

vnd.wv.ssp+xml

vnd.xara

vnd.xfdl

vnd.yamaha.hv-dic

vnd.yamaha.hv-script

vnd.yamaha.hv-voice

vnd.yamaha.smaf-audio

vnd.yamaha.smaf-phrase

vnd.yellowriver-custom-menu

watcherinfo+xml

whoispp-query

whoispp-response

wita

wordperfect5.1

x-debian-package

x-gzip

x-java

x-javascript

x-msaccess

x-msexcel

x-mspowerpoint

x-rpm

x-zip

x400-bp

xhtml+xml

xml

xml-dtd

xml-external-parsed-entity

zip

I

Changes between HTML4 and HTML5

This document outlines the major element differences between HTML4 and HTML5. For a full view of all the changes, see the W3C's document "HTML5 Differences from HTML4" at www.w3.org/TR/html5-diff/.

NEW ELEMENTS

The following list represents all the new elements introduced in HTML5. For descriptions of these elements, see Appendix B, "HTML Element Reference":

- ➤ section
- ➤ article
- ➤ aside
- ➤ hgroup
- ➤ header
- ➤ footer
- ➤ nav
- ➤ figure
- ➤ figcaption
- ➤ video
- ➤ audio
- ➤ track
- ➤ embed

- mark
- progress
- meter
- time
- ruby
- rt
- rp
- bdi
- wbr
- canvas
- command
- cetails
- catalist
- keygen
- output

NEW <INPUT> ELEMENT TYPES

The input element's type attribute now has the following new values. For descriptions of these elements, see Appendix B, "HTML Element Reference":

- tel
- search
- url
- email
- datetime
- date
- month
- week
- time
- datetime-local
- number
- range
- color

NEW ATTRIBUTES

Many new attributes have been added to existing elements. These new attributes either are existing attributes added to new elements or are completely new attributes. These are also covered in depth alongside their elements in Appendix B, "HTML Element Reference":

ELEMENT	ATTRIBUTES
`<a>`	media
`<area>`	hreflang, media, rel, type
`<base>`	target
`<button>`	autofocus, form, formaction, formenctype, formmethod, formnovalidate, formtarget
`<fieldset>`	disabled, form, name
`<form>`	novalidate
`<html>`	manifest
`<iframe>`	sandbox, seamless, srcdoc
`<img>`	crossorigin
`<input>`	autocomplete, autofocus, dirname, form, formaction, formenctype, formmethod, formnovalidate, formtarget list, max, min, multiple, pattern, placeholder, required, step, height, width
`<label>`	form
`<link>`	sizes
`<menu>`	label, type
`<meta>`	charset
`<object>`	form, typemustmatch
`<ol>`	reversed
`<output>`	form
`<script>`	async
`<select>`	autofocus, form, required
`<style>`	scoped
`<textarea>`	autofocus, form, maxlength, placeholder, required, wrap, dirname

GLOBAL ATTRIBUTES

HTML5 greatly expands on the number of global attributes. The following list includes all the new global attributes and the global attributes present in previous versions of HTML:

➤ accesskey

➤ class

➤ contenteditable

➤ contextmenu

➤ dir

➤ draggable

➤ dropzone

➤ hidden

➤ id

➤ lang

➤ spellcheck

➤ style

➤ tabindex

➤ title

➤ translate

CHANGED ATTRIBUTES

Several existing attributes have had their meanings changed:

ATTRIBUTE	ELEMENT	CHANGE
accept	`<input>`	`audio/*`, `video/*`, and `image/*` are now valid values.
accesskey	global	Now allows multiple characters to be specified.
action	`<form>`	No longer allowed to have an empty URL.
colspan	`<td><th>`	Now has to be greater than zero.
coords	`<area>`	No longer allows a percentage value of the radius when the element is a circle.

data	`<object>`	No longer relative to the `codebase`.
defer	`<script>`	Explicitly executes the script when the page has finished parsing.
dir	global	Now allows the value `auto`.
enctype	`<form>`	Now supports the value `text/plain`.
width/height	`<img>`, `<iframe>`, `<object>`	No longer allowed to contain percentages. No longer allowed to stretch the image to a different aspect ratio than its intrinsic aspect ratio.
href	`<link>`	No longer allowed to have an empty URL.
href	`<base>`	Allowed to contain a relative URL.
Attributes that accept URLs	global	Now support IRIs if the document's encoding is UTF-8 or UTF-16.
http-equiv	`<meta>`	No longer said to be used by HTTP servers to create HTTP headers in the HTTP response. Instead, it is said to be a pragma directive to be used by the user agent.
id	global	Now allowed to have any unique value, as long as it is not an empty string and does not contain spaces.
lang	global	Takes the empty string in addition to a valid language identifier.
media	`<link>`	Now accepts a media query. Defaults to "all."
Event handlers	global	Defaults to JavaScript as the scripting language.
value	`<li>`	No longer deprecated.
start/type	`<ol>`	No longer deprecated.
style	global	Always uses CSS as the style language.
tabindex	global	Allows negative values, which indicates that the element can receive focus but cannot be tabbed to.
target	`<a><area>`	No longer deprecated.

continues

(continued)

ATTRIBUTE	ELEMENT	CHANGE
`type`	`<script>` `<style>`	No longer required if the scripting language is JavaScript and the styling language is CSS, respectively.
`usemap`	`img`	No longer takes a URL, but instead takes a valid hash-name reference to a map element.

OBSOLETE ELEMENTS

The elements in this section are no longer part of the HTML specification:

➤ `basefont`

➤ `big`

➤ `center`

➤ `font`

➤ `strike`

➤ `tt`

➤ `frame`

➤ `frameset`

➤ `noframes`

➤ `acronym`

➤ `applet`

➤ `isindex`

➤ `dir`

OBSOLETE ATTRIBUTES

Some attributes from HTML4 are no longer allowed in HTML5:

ELEMENT	ATTRIBUTES
`<a>`	`charset, coords, rev, shape`
`<area>`	`nohref`

`<body>`	`alink, background, bgcolor, link, text, vlink`
` `	`clear`
`<caption>`	`align`
`<col>`	`align, char, charoff, valign, width`
`<colgroup>`	`align, char, charoff, valign, width`
`<div>`	`align`
`<dl>`	`Compact`
`<head>`	`profile`
`<hn>`	`align`
`<hr>`	`align, noshade, size, width`
`<html>`	`version`
`<iframe>`	`align, frameborder, longdesc, marginheight, marginwidth, scrolling`
`<img>`	`align, hspace, longdesc, name, vspace`
`<input>`	`align`
`<legend>`	`align`
`<li>`	`type`
`<link>`	`charset, rev, target`
`<menu>`	`compact`
`<meta>`	`scheme`
`<object>`	`align, archive, border, classid, codebase, codetype, declare, space, standby, vspace, hspace`
`<ol>`	`compact`
`<p>`	`align`
`<param>`	`type, valuetype`
`<pre>`	`width`
`<table>`	`align, bgcolor, cellpadding, cellspacing, rules, summary, width, frame`
`<tbody>`	`align, char, charoff, valign`

continues

(continued)

ELEMENT	ATTRIBUTES
`<td>`	`abbr, align, axis, bgcolor char, charoff, height, nowrap, scope, valign, width`
`<tfoot>`	`align char, charoff, valign`
`<th>`	`abbr, align, axis, bgcolor char, charoff, height, nowrap, valign, width`
`<thead>`	`align, char, charoff, valign`
`<tfoot>`	`align, char, charoff, valign`
`<tr>`	`align, bgcolor, char, charoff, valign`
`<ul>`	`compact, type`

AT-RISK ELEMENTS

The following elements and attribute types are at risk of being removed from the specification:

➤ `<hgroup>`

➤ `<command>`

➤ `<menu>`

➤ `<dialog>`

➤ `<details>`

➤ `<summary>`

➤ `<input type=color>`

➤ `<input type=datetime>`

➤ `<input type=month>`

➤ `<input type=week>`

➤ `<input type=time>`

➤ `<input type=datetime-local>`

➤ `<output>`

➤ `<style scoped>`

➤ `<iframe seamless>`

INDEX

G

I

J

W

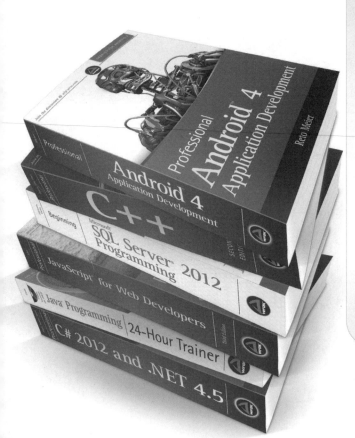